THE WORLD'S MAJOR
AIRLINES

THE WORLD'S MAJOR
AIRLINES
AND THEIR AIRCRAFT

DAVID WRAGG

PSL

Patrick Stephens Limited

AN IMPRINT OF HAYNES PUBLISHING

First published in 1998

British Library Cataloguing-in-Publication Data
A catalogue record for this book is
available from the British Library

ISBN 1 85260 587 1

Library of Congress catalog card no. 98-72314

Patrick Stephens Limited is an imprint of Haynes Publishing,
Sparkford, Nr Yeovil, Somerset, BA22 7JJ.

Tel: 01963 440635 Fax: 01963 440001
Int. tel: +44 1963 440635 Int. fax: +44 1963 440001

E-mail: sales@haynes-manuals.co.uk
Web site: http:/www.haynes.com

Haynes North America, Inc., 861 Lawrence Drive,
Newbury Park, California 91320 USA.

Designed by G&M, Raunds, Northamptonshire.
Typeset by J. H. Haynes & Co. Ltd., Sparkford, Nr Yeovil, Somerset.
Printed and bound by J. H. Haynes & Co. Ltd., England.

Contents

Preface

Researching and obtaining material for a book such as this is a demanding task, and I am especially grateful to those who have made it much easier. Airlines which have stood out as being particularly helpful include Aéroméxico, Air Canada, Air Foyle, Air Malta, Air One, Air Pacific, Air 2000, Ansett Australia, Aurigny, Braathens SAFE, Brit Air, British International, Cathay Pacific, Continental, Continental Express, Gronlandsfly, Hawaiian, Hazelton, Lufthansa and Lufthansa City Line, Malév, Manx/British Regional, Miami Air, Skywest, Southwest, Singapore Airlines, THY Turkish Airlines, and Volga-Dnepr. All the photographs have been provided by the operators whose aircraft are depicted, to whom I extend my thanks for their generosity in granting me permission to reproduce them.

David Wragg

Introduction

Some maintain that the glamorous days of air travel have gone, but for many of us the fascination is still there. Nor have the pioneering days gone for good. New routes are still created, but today greater emphasis is being placed on how air transport can develop. There is a world of variety in the activities of the airlines in this book. Bangkok Air, for example, has gone back to basics in actually building airports for itself at tourist destinations, while Channel Express developed its market in flying flowers from the Channel Islands to the British mainland by using plant to cool the flowers before loading onto the aircraft, preserving their freshness. At the other end of the scale there is the movement of exceptionally heavy loads by air, with airlines such as Volga-Dnepr, Air Foyle, and now the Antonov Design Bureau itself; the railways played a part in developing air transport in a number of countries, but now even railway locomotives can be carried by air.

Traditionally air travel has been expensive, but over the years moves have been made to bring down costs. In Europe, inclusive tour, or package holiday, charter airlines have reduced the expense of air travel. Their role is often overlooked in comparisons of air fares between North America and Europe, but they account for more than 40 per cent of all air travel in Europe, as opposed to some ten per cent in the United States, and once they are taken into account the difference in the average price of a ticket in the United States and Europe is not as vast as it might appear from a glance at the tariffs of the scheduled airlines.

Now, too, there are many 'low fare, no frills' scheduled airlines. These are also playing a part in cutting the cost of air travel, but their history has not been an altogether happy one, some having proved to be under-financed and unable to face competition from the established operators. Some observers believe that such operations may one day extend from purely short-haul services to intercontinental services, by cutting out inflight entertainment and reducing the meal service.

Not that the established airlines have had everything their own way. De-regulation on both sides of the Atlantic has seen many famous names disappear, notably Braniff and Pan American in the United States. In Europe, the European Commission has also been forced by the single market rules to look closely at the subsidies given to many bloated and inefficient state-owned airlines. One means of reducing costs in both Europe and America has been for the major airlines to move away from attempting to operate every kind of route, saving themselves for the domestic trunk routes and the busier international services, but retaining a strong presence by franchising smaller airlines, with lower costs and aircraft better-suited to less busy and shorter routes.

In preparing any work of reference, there has to be a compromise between coverage and convenience. There is no point in covering every airline if the resulting tome is so heavy that it is difficult to use and has to be left at home or in the office. There is another point as well. The failure rate of new businesses, or 'start ups' to use the modern management jargon, is high in any sector, but in transport it is higher than most. Airlines with one or two aircraft are vulnerable, not least because if, for any reason, one aircraft is grounded, the impact on their income is crippling. For this reason the airlines covered in this book have been restricted to those with five or more aircraft with more than 18 passenger seats, or the freight equivalent. Helicopter charter operators have also been excluded. However, recognition of the fact that limiting the scope of the book could be frustrating for readers who will, in the main, be living in North America or the British Isles has meant that a few exceptions to this rule have crept in.

The contents are presented alphabetically by country and then, within each country, by airline. Registration prefixes have been given for major countries, and two and three letter flight designators have been given whenever possible in the case of individual airlines, along with radio callsigns. Each entry includes some background to the airline, which in the case of many of the major airlines, and even some of the smaller ones, amounts to a sometimes substantial history. Details of senior officers within airlines, and their route structure, have also been given where available.

Whenever possible statistical information has been given, allowing comparisons to be made regarding airline employee numbers, traffic figures, and revenue, in which case both US dollar and pound sterling figures have been used, at an exchange rate of US $1.65 to the pound. Comparisons can never be exact, and readers should be cautious in drawing any. The practice in some airlines of devolving most, if not all, of their maintenance and engineering activities into a separate subsidiary can often mean that they look decidedly short of engineering staff. The ratio of flight-deck crew – mainly pilots but in some instances engineers as well – to cabin crew will often depend on the type of aircraft which predominate in a fleet. If larger aircraft are operated, there will be many more cabin crew than pilots, but the reverse happens on smaller aircraft with two pilots and one cabin attendant.

Obviously, air freight operators don't have cabin crew as such, although they may have a loadmaster. It is also important to remember that charter operators will have far fewer ground staff than scheduled airlines, not needing to sell their own tickets but leaving that to the tour operators who have block-booked space. Another factor in airline staffing levels depends on whether or not they leave ground-handling and passenger-processing arrangements to other airlines or specialised contractors, such as Servisair in the UK.

Finally, the book looks at the main aircraft currently in service which fit within the aircraft size definitions outlined above. Here, too, there is currently a state of flux. What will happen to the McDonnell Douglas line now that the company is owned by Boeing? Will the next generation of regional jet airliner be built in China, or will airlines prefer to buy equipment from the traditional manufacturing companies? Will Aero International, or AI(R), be absorbed into Airbus? Can manufacturers such as Bombardier and AI(R) continue to compete with the new manufacturers in low-cost economies, such as Embraer and IPTN, or will they follow Saab in withdrawing from civil airliner production altogether or, even worse, follow the sad example of Fokker, and collapse? Only time will tell.

PART ONE

THE WORLD'S MAJOR AIRLINES

Afghanistan – YA

ARIANA

Ariana Afghan Airlines Co Ltd

Incorporated: 1955

HISTORY

During the early 1950s, Indamer – at the time the largest Indian charter airline – enjoyed a successful business carrying pilgrims on special charters from Kabul to Jeddah. Aware of the commercial opportunities that the then untapped Afghan market offered, in 1955 Indamer approached the Afghan Government with a proposal to establish a national airline, and Ariana was established that year as a direct result, with Indamer having a 49 per cent interest in the new airline and the Afghan Government holding the rest. Indamer had to supply the equipment. Operations began the following year, initially using a single Douglas DC-3 on internal routes within Afghanistan, but services to India and some of the Gulf states followed later the same year.

Indamer's interest was bought out in 1957 by Pan American World Airways, and Douglas DC-4s were introduced, and the DC-3s refurbished. Using the DC-4s, services reached Beirut in 1958, and were extended to Frankfurt in 1959 using a Douglas DC-6B, but cut back again to Beirut in 1961. It was not until 1967 that Frankfurt was again served, and the service was extended to London. Later, Boeing 727s joined the fleet.

The emphasis moved away from American equipment after the Soviet invasion in 1979, with Antonov An-24 and An-26, and Yakovlev Yak-40 and Tupolev Tu-154 aircraft joining the fleet, while the emphasis of the route network shifted as well, away from London and Frankfurt, to Prague, Tashkent, and Moscow. Services to the Indian sub-continent and to Dubai in the Gulf continued.

The collapse of the Soviet Union has led to a return to western equipment, although some old Soviet aircraft remain in the fleet. Civil war within Afghanistan, and the poor shape of the economy, is nevertheless limiting domestic operations and also making re-equipment difficult for the foreseeable future.

Executive Directors & Officers: Rohullah Aman, President; G.H. Jelani, Vice-President, Commercial.

HQ Airport & Main Base: Kabul

Radio callsign: ARIANA

Designator: FG/AFG

Employees: 1,584

Main destinations served: Domestic services when possible, plus international services to Amritsar, Delhi, Dubai, Moscow, Prague, Tashkent.

FLEET
2 Boeing 727-200
2 Boeing 727-100C
1 Tupolev Tu-154M
2 Antonov An-24RV
2 Antonov An-26B
2 Yakovlev Yak-40

Algeria – 7T

AIR ALGERIE

Société Nationale des Transports Aériens

Incorporated: 1953

HISTORY

Air Algérie's history pre-dates Algerian independence, going back to the time when the country was still a French colony. Two airlines had been formed, one of which was Air Algérie, which dated from 1949, while the other was the Compagnie Générale de Transports Aériens. The two airlines were merged to form Air Algérie in 1953, a mixed state and private enterprise undertaking, with Air France (qv) at one stage having a 28 per cent interest. The airline became completely state-owned in 1972.

Today, Air Algérie operates both scheduled and charter air services within Algeria and to destinations in Africa and Europe, although services to France were suspended for a period in 1997. Unusually for a modern airline, air taxi work and agricultural aviation are both features of the airline's operations, although the aircraft used in these activities are excluded from the fleet list below.

Executive Directors & Officers: Chakib Belleili, Director-General; Mahfoud Benkhelil, Secretary General; Ali Bey Soukhane, Finance Director; D. Ilali Temoulgui, Operations Director; Mustapha Benaissa, Commercial Director; Rachid Akrour, Technical Director; Ali Djeraba, Marketing Director; Farid R. Cuilkhi, Training Director.

HQ Airport & Main Base: Algiers

Radio callsign: AIR ALGERIE

Designator: AH/DAH

Employees: 9,000 (including air taxi and agricultural)

Main destinations served: Algiers to Amman, Amsterdam, Athens, Bamato, Barcelona, Beirut, Berlin, Brussels, Cairo, Casablanca, Dakar, Damascus, Frankfurt, Geneva, Istanbul, Lille, Lyons, London Heathrow, Madrid, Marseilles, Moscow, Niamey, Nice, Novakchett, Ougadougou, Prague, Rome, Sharjah, Toulouse, Tunis.

LINKS WITH OTHER AIRLINES
Code-share with Royal Air Maroc (qv).

FLEET
2 Airbus A310-203
3 Boeing 767-300
11 Boeing 727-200
13 Boeing 737-200
2 Boeing 737-200C
7 Fokker F-27-400M
2 Lockheed L-100-300 Hercules

Angola – D2

AAC ANGOLA AIR CHARTER

Angola Air Charter, SARL

HISTORY

A wholly-owned subsidiary of TAAG (qv), Angola Air Charter handles international and domestic, cargo and passenger charters.

HQ Airport & Main Base: Luanda

Radio callsign: ANGOLA CHARTER

Designator: C3/AGO

LINKS WITH OTHER AIRLINES
The charter subsidiary of TAAG (qv).

FLEET
2 Lockheed L-100-30 Hercules
4 Boeing 707-320C
1 Boeing 727-100C
1 Boeing 737-200

TAAG-ANGOLA AIRLINES

TAAG-Angola Airlines (Linhas Aéreas de Angola)

Incorporated: 1939

HISTORY

Originally founded in 1939 as Direçcuo de Exploraçao do Transportes Aéreos, development of services was inhibited at first by shortages of fuel and equipment during World War Two, despite Angola being a colony of neutral Portugal. Post-war, a network of internal services was developed and cargo and passenger charters operated as well, while most international services remained with TAP (qv). On Angola achieving independence in 1973 the current title was adopted and a network of international services has been steadily developed.

The company is entirely state-owned, and the international route network reflects Angola's post-independence alliances. A subsidiary is Angola Air Charter (qv).

Executive Directors & Officers: Julio Sampaio Almeida, Chairman; Abel Antonio Lopes, General Director; Jose Machado Jorge, Flight Operations Director; Brito Teixeira, Engineering Director; Alberto Espírito Santo, Marketing Director; Antonio Fernandes, Commercial Director; Fernanda Viera, Human Resources Director.

HQ Airport & Main Base: Luanda

Radio callsign: DTA

Designator: DT/DTA

Employees: 5,770

Main destinations served: 18 domestic airports, plus international services from Luanda to Brazzaville, Harare, Havana, Kinshasa, Lisbon, Lusaka, Moscow, Rio de Janeiro, Rome, São Tome, Windhoek.

FLEET
1 Boeing 747-300
1 Lockheed L-1011 TriStar 500
2 Ilyushin Il-62M
1 Boeing 707-320B
4 Boeing 737-200
1 Boeing 737-200C
3 Fokker F-27-600
1 Fokker F-27-500
1 Fokker F-27-400
1 Fokker F-27-100

TRANSAFRIK

Transafrik International, SARL

Incorporated: 1984

HISTORY
Formed by Erich Koch, Renato Hermino, and Joao Rodrigues, Transafrik is a cargo specialist, operating ad hoc and contract charters mainly in Africa from its bases at Luanda and São Tome. Medical evacuation flights can be undertaken, while the com-

pany is able to handle difficult loads and relatively primitive airports.

Executive Directors & Officers: Erich F. Koch, Managing Director; João Rodrigues, Finance Director; Henrique Setas, Operations & Commercial Director; A. Collins-Orford, Maintenance Director.

HQ Airport & Main Base: Luanda

Employees: 205

FLEET
2 Lockheed L-100-30 Hercules
1 Lockheed L-100-20 Hercules
4 Boeing 727-100F

Antigua – V2

LIAT

Liat (1974)

Incorporated: 1956

HISTORY
The present Liat was formed in 1974 as the successor to LIAT (Leeward Islands Air Transport), which was established in 1956 as a subsidiary of British West Indian Airways, itself in turn controlled by BOAC, the British Overseas Airways Corporation. From its formation, the main purpose of the airline was to establish and operate scheduled air services within the Caribbean. In 1971, the airline was sold to a UK-based inclusive tour charter operator, Court Line, and when this airline and its parent group collapsed in 1974, Liat was rescued and re-established with ownership in the hands of 11 Caribbean governments – Antigua/Barbuda, Barbados, Dominica, Grenada, Guyana, Jamaica, St Kitts/Nevis, St Lucia, St Vincent/the Grenadines, Montserrat, and Trinidad and Tobago – who purchased the airline from the liquidators. It was privatised in 1995, although the Caribbean governments still retain a substantial minority interest of 30.8 per cent, and BWIA (qv) also has a 29.2 per cent stake.

The fleet has changed in recent years, with the disappearance of the Hawker Siddeley 748s which at one time were the backbone of the fleet, and the emergence of a completely de Havilland fleet.

Executive Directors & Officers: Azid Hadeed, Chairman; Fred Jarvis, Chief Executive Officer; Heralal Nandial, Chief Financial Officer.

HQ Airport & Main Base: V.C. Bird International Airport, Antigua

Radio callsign: LIAT

Designator: LI/LIA

Employees: 990

Main destinations served: Anguilla, Antigua, Barbados, Barbuda, Caracas, Carnacou, Grenada, Guadeloupe, Guyana, Martinique, Montserrat, Nevis, San Juan, Santiago, St Croix, St Kitts, St Maarten, St Thomas, St Vincent, Tobago, Tortola, Trinidad, Union Island.

LINKS WITH OTHER AIRLINES
BWIA has a 29.2 per cent interest.

FLEET
3 de Havilland Dash 8-300
9 de Havilland Dash 8-100
6 de Havilland DHC-6 Twin Otter

SEAGREEN

Seagreen Air Transport

Incorporated: 1964

HISTORY
Seagreen has operated charter cargo operations in the Caribbean since 1964, and after a period of inactivity operations restarted in 1987. The airline now operates charters from its base at Antigua and from Ostend in Belgium.

Executive Directors & Officers: David Tolloph, President; Gary Tolloph, Vice-President.

HQ Airport & Main Base: V.C. Bird International Airport, Antigua, and Ostend, Belgium

Radio callsign: SEAGREEN

Designator: ES/ESA

Main destinations served: Caribbean, African, and world-wide cargo charters.

FLEET
4 Boeing 707-320C
2 Boeing 727-100
1 de Havilland DHC-6 Twin Otter

Argentina – LV

AEROLINEAS ARGENTINAS

Aérolineas Argentinas, Empresa del Estado

Incorporated: 1949

HISTORY
The main Argentine airline, Aérolineas

Argentinas was formed in 1949 on the nationalisation of all Argentine airlines other than the Air Force-operated LADE.

Of the four airlines brought together to form Aérolineas Argentinas, the most significant was Aéroposta Argentina, which had commenced operations in 1927 using French Latecoere 25s. A subsidiary of the French Cie. Générale Aéropostale, Aéroposta's first route had been to Asunçion in Paraguay, but on nationalisation several other nearby capitals were being served, and a network of domestic services within Argentina had been created. Another airline was ALFA (Aviacion del Litoral Fleuva Argentina), which operated Short Sandringham flying-boats on services along the Parana River, a tributary of the River Plate. The third airline was ZONDA (Zonas Oeste y Norte de Aérolineas Argentinas), which had only taken over the internal operations of PANAGRA in 1947, using a fleet of Douglas DC-3s. Prior to nationalisation the Argentine Government already had a 20 per cent stake in both ALFA and ZONDA, as well as a one-third interest in the fourth airline, FAMA (Flota Aéro Mercante Argentina), which had been formed in 1946 to operate international services.

Bringing together four such disparate airlines in this way meant that Aérolineas Argentinas started life with a very mixed fleet, including Douglas DC-3s, DC-4s and DC-6s, Convair 240s, Vickers Vikings, Avro Yorks, and three old Junkers Ju.52/3M tri-motors, as well as a small Avro Anson and Avro Lancastrians, converted from ex-wartime Lancaster bombers. Inevitably, this resulted in many operational difficulties during the early years. Nevertheless, a major step forward came in 1959, when Argentina became just the fourth nation in the world to operate jet airliners, introducing six de Havilland Comet 4 aircraft, and following these in 1962 with three Sud Aviation Caravelle 6Rs for shorter routes. The first of what was to become a fleet of 12 Hawker Siddeley HS 748 turbo-prop airliners followed, replacing the last of the DC-3s and Convair 240s, although the DC-4s soldiered on for some time afterwards.

No doubt much of the pressure for modernisation came from the fact that, from 1955 onwards, privately-owned airlines were once again permitted in Argentina, and by the mid-1960s almost all of the domestic network enjoyed competition.

Boeing 707-320s were placed in service in 1966, and the following year a non-stop Buenos Aires–Madrid service was inaugurated using these aircraft, giving the airline what was then the longest non-stop scheduled air service in the world, covering a distance of 6,275 miles.

Denationalisation of Aérolineas Argentinas has seen the state's shareholding fall to just 7 per cent, with 10 per cent for employees, while Iberia (qv) has taken a 20 per cent interest. The remaining shares belong to investing institutions. In addition to a marketing alliance and combined frequent flyer programme with Iberia, Aérolineas Argentinas also has marketing alliances with another Argentine airline, Austral (qv), which operates domestic scheduled services and is now a subsidiary of Aérolineas, and with Malaysian Airlines (qv).

Executive Directors & Officers: Manuel Moran, President & Chief Executive Officer; Jaime Castillo, Operations Director & Chief Pilot; Fernando del Valle, Vice-President, Commercial; Fernando Sternfeld, Vice-President, Maintenance; J.M. Gallego, Director, Commercial; Eugenio Negre, Director, Planning; R. Lehmacher, Director, Marketing; J. Cubero, Director, Personnel.

HQ Airport & Main Base: Buenos Aires

Radio callsign: ARGENTINA

Designator: AR/ARG

Employees: 7,000

Main destinations served: International destinations from Buenos Aires are Asunçion, Auckland, Bogotá, Cape Town, Caracas, Frankfurt, Guayaquil, Johannesburg, La Paz, Lima, London, Los Angeles, Madrid, Mexico City, Miami, Montreal, Montevideo, New York JFK, Panama, Paris, Pôrto Alegre, Rio de Janeiro, Rome, Santa Cruz, São Paulo, Toronto, Zürich.

Annual turnover: US $947 million (£573.9 million)

LINKS WITH OTHER AIRLINES
Iberia (qv) has a 20 per cent shareholding, with a marketing alliance and code-sharing.

Austral (qv) is a subsidiary, and there is a marketing alliance with Austral and Malaysia Airlines (qv).

Ground-handling joint ventures with Varig (qv) and PLUNA (Primeras Lineas Uruguayas de Navegacion Area).

FLEET
7 Boeing 747-200B
1 Boeing 747-100F
2 Airbus A310-324
1 McDonnell Douglas MD-83
8 Boeing 727-200
17 Boeing 737-200Adv
6 McDonnell Douglas MD-88

AUSTRAL

Austral Lineas Aéreas

Incorporated: 1971

HISTORY
Austral was formed in 1971 on the merger of Austral Compania Argentina de Transportes Aéros and ALA (Aérotransportes Litoral Argentino), although both airlines had effectively been operating an integrated route network for five years prior to this, after Austral CATA had taken a 30 per cent shareholding in ALA in 1966. ALA had been formed as an air taxi company in 1957, and had moved into scheduled domestic services in 1958. In 1990 the newly privatised Aérolineas Argentinas took a shareholding in Austral, later acquiring the airline outright.

HQ Airport & Main Base: Buenos Aires

Radio callsign: AUSTRAL

Designator: AU/AUT

Employees: 1,900

Main destinations served: Almost 30 domestic destinations.

LINKS WITH OTHER AIRLINES
A subsidiary of Aérolineas Argentinas, with which it has a marketing alliance.

FLEET
3 McDonnell Douglas MD-83
2 McDonnell Douglas MD-81
7 McDonnell Douglas DC-9-32
2 BAC One-Eleven 500
2 CASA/IPTN C-235

LAPA

Lineas Aéreas Privadas Argentinas SA

Incorporated: 1976

HISTORY
Originally established as a charter airline, LAPA commenced operations in 1978 and started scheduled operations the following year. The route network is primarily domestic, but a scheduled service is operated to Uruguay, and charters continue to be operated.

Executive Directors & Officers: Gustavo Andres Deutsch, President; Jorge Daniel Vuletich, Commercial Director.

HQ Airport & Main Base: Buenos Aires

Radio callsign: LAPA

Designator: MJ/LPR

Employees: 460

Main destinations served: Buenos Aires to Bahia Blanca, Bariloche, Catamaroa, Colonia, Comodoro Rivadavia, Córdoba, Formosa, Gral Roca, Iguazu, Lorrientes, Mar del Plata, Marcedas, Mendoza, Neocochea, Neuquen, Posadas, Rio Gallegos, Rio Grande, Salia, San Luis, Tandil.

LINKS WITH OTHER AIRLINES
Marketing alliances with United Airlines (qv) and British Airways (qv).

FLEET
2 Boeing 757-200
6 Boeing 737-200
2 Saab 340
1 Beech King Air 300
1 Cessna Citation
plus 2 Boeing 737-700 (leased) for delivery January 1999

Armenia – EK

ARMENIAN INTERNATIONAL AIRLINES

Armenian International Airlines

Incorporated: 1990

HISTORY
Known until recently as Armenian Airlines, this is one of the many airlines which were suddenly cast into existence by the break-up of the Soviet Union and of the Soviet airline Aeroflot (qv). It is completely state-owned and is reported to be having difficulties in the aftermath of the war between Armenia and Azerbaijan, and as a consequence of the severe economic climate.

Executive Directors & Officers:
J.J. Dekker, Managing Director;
G. Voskanian, Finance Director;
E.M. Grigorian, Operations Director;
R. Grigorian, Commercial Director;
A.K.H. Martirossian, Maintenance Director.

HQ Airport & Main Base: Yerevan

Radio callsign: ARMENIAN

Designator: R3/RME

Employees: 2,180

Main destinations served: Adler, Amsterdam, Ashkabad, Athens, Beirut, Burgas, Fusayzah, Moscow, Novosilizsk, Paris, Rostov, Sverdlovsk, Tehran.

LINKS WITH OTHER AIRLINES
Marketing alliances with Air France (qv) and KLM (qv).

FLEET
6 Tupolev Tu-204-120
8 Tupolev Tu-154B
7 Tupolev Tu-134
2 Ilyushin Il-86
9 Yakovlev Yak-40

Aruba – P4

AIR ARUBA

Air Aruba

Incorporated: 1986

HISTORY
Originally founded in 1986 by the Aruban Government as a ground-handling agent, in 1988 the business was privatised and started to operate scheduled air services to other Caribbean destinations using a NAMC YS-11 turboprop airliner. Services were inaugurated to Miami in 1990, and to Amsterdam and Frankfurt in 1991 using a wet-leased Boeing 767 of Air Holland, although these latter routes were subsequently discontinued.

The airline has since passed back into state-ownership after an evaluation of its role and fleet following the unsuccessful attempt at introducing European services. It has a marketing alliance with US Airways (qv).

Executive Directors & Officers: E.R. Arends, Chairman; P. Look-Hong, President & Chief Executive Officer.

HQ Airport & Main Base: Queen Beatrix International Airport, Aruba

Radio callsign: ARUBA

Designator: FQ/ARU

Employees: approx 300

Main destinations served: Aruba to Baltimore, Bogotá, Bonaire, Caracas, Curaçao, Houston, Medellin, Miami, New York Newark, São Paulo, Tampa/St Petersburg.

LINKS WITH OTHER AIRLINES
Marketing alliances with US Airways (qv), Avianca (qv), and KLM (qv).

FLEET
2 McDonnell Douglas MD-88 (leased)
1 McDonnell Douglas MD-83 (leased)
1 McDonnell Douglas DC-9-31 (leased)

Australia – VH

ANSETT AUSTRALIA

Ansett Australia Ltd

Incorporated: 1936

HISTORY
Ansett is the largest airline in the world to retain the name of its founder. It is also the second largest Australian airline and the third largest in the southern hemisphere. Nevertheless, Reginald Ansett's first venture in transport was much more mundane – he started a taxi service in 1931. He learnt to fly in 1932, and in 1936, with his brother Jack and a radial-engined Porterfield aircraft, he won an air race from Brisbane to Adelaide, for which the prize was £500 (equivalent to US $2,000 at the time). A six-passenger Fokker Universal was acquired, and an airline, Ansett Airways Pty Ltd, was established, making its first flight between Hamilton and Melbourne, both in Victoria, on 17 February 1936. The following year the new airline became a publicly-quoted company, and the base moved to Melbourne.

Early expansion was rapid, with the vast distances and low population density of much of Australia lending itself to air transport. Three Lockheed L10B Electras were obtained in 1937, and services introduced from Melbourne to Adelaide, Broken Hill, and Sydney. A serious fire at the airline's hangar destroyed four aircraft, and the advent of World War Two brought an end to most commercial air services. Ansett moved into servicing Allied military aircraft, while its aircraft were used to carry Allied service personnel around Australia, and to evacuate civilians from Darwin and Broome after Japanese air raids on these towns.

Airline services were resumed post-war, with Reginald Ansett obtaining three ex-USAAF Douglas C-47 Dakotas, which were converted to 28-seat airliners. In 1946 the name was changed to Ansett Transport Industries Ltd, or ATI, reflecting the growing diversification of the business, which by this time included coaches and hotels. The Australian Government now decided on a 'two airline' policy, which effectively reserved the trunk routes for the state-owned Trans Australia Airways and its private enterprise competitor, ANA (Australian National Airways). This left Ansett to make the best of the non-trunk routes. This situation did not last for long, and when ANA ran into severe financial difficulties in 1957 ATI purchased the company, creating a new airline, Ansett-ANA. In these dramatically changed circumstances the newly merged airline benefited when the two airline policy was enshrined in the Airlines Agreement Act 1957, giving TAA and Ansett-ANA the sole rights to the domestic trunk routes.

Given such a strong operational base, Ansett-ANA was able to expand further. In 1958 it bought New South Wales-based Butler Air Transport and Queensland Airlines. Expansion and acquisition meant that a varied fleet was created, with six Douglas DC-6s and DC-6Bs, two DC-4s, 20 DC-3s, two Vickers Viscount 700s, eight Convair Metropolitans, a Bristol 170 Freighter, and two Short Sandringham flying-boats, as well as two helicopters. Expansion was kept in check to some extent by the Airline Equipment Act 1958, which sought to maintain a balance on the capacity and frequencies offered by the two main airlines on the trunk routes. This meant that many innovations had to be synchronised, as with the first jet aircraft for the two airlines, Boeing 727s in 1964, and the introduction of Douglas DC-9s three years later.

A further name change followed in 1969, with Ansett-ANA becoming Ansett Airlines of Australia. One of the oldest Australian airlines, McRobertson Miller Aviation, dating from 1927, was purchased the same year, making Ansett Australia's largest domestic airline. Ansett's diversifications were to be its undoing, however, and after the collapse of a finance company in which Ansett had invested the airline was taken over by another transport operator, TNT (originally founded as Thomas Nationwide Transport), working in partnership with the newspaper publisher, News Corporation.

The first steps in expansion outside Australia came in 1987, with the formation of Ansett New Zealand (qv). The present title was adopted in 1990, coinciding with deregulation of Australian domestic air services, and the present livery dates from 1994. Meanwhile, Ansett Australia had gained permission to introduce international services, starting with operations to Denpasar in Bali from Perth, Darwin, Sydney, and Melbourne in September 1993. Boeing 747s were acquired, and services to Osaka, Hong Kong, Kuala Lumpur, Taipei, Jakarta, Auckland, and Seoul followed.

Ansett Australia has a substantial fleet of Airbus A320-200s, used primarily on domestic services.

In 1996 Air New Zealand acquired TNT's half-share in Ansett Australia, while, to prevent a monopoly arising on New Zealand's domestic services, News Corporation became the sole owner of Ansett New Zealand (qv). Ansett was then restructured so that 51 per cent of the Group belongs to Australian institutional investors, with the balance split equally between Air New Zealand and News Corporation.

Executive Directors & Officers: Rob Eddington, Chairman; David Irvine, Chief Financial Officer; Rob Turner, Corporate Counsel; Captain Fred Bloomsma, Director Flight Operations; Keith Herdman, Director of Regional Airlines; Paul Harvalias, Revenue Management & Pricing Director; Alice Williams, Director Strategy & Planning; Jim Tully, Director Operational Policy Development; John Benson, Schedules Director; Garry

Spreading its wings on to intercontinental services, Ansett Australia is now operating Boeing 747-300s.

Themed colour schemes have become fashionable, although not with the purists – this is Ansett's celebration of being chosen as the official airline for the Sydney Olympic Games in the year 2000.

Kingshott, Director Marketing; Michael Reed, Director of Sales Operations; Ron Rosalky, Director Airport Services; Pamela Catty, Director Corporate Affairs; Geoff Young, Director of Employee Relations.

HQ Airport & Main Base: Melbourne, with additional hubs at Brisbane, Perth and Sydney.

Radio callsign: ANSETT

Designator: AN/AAA

Employees: Flight-crew: 957; Cabin staff: 2,122; Engineering: 2,112; Ground staff: 7,767; Total: 12,958.

Main destinations served: Adelaide, Albury, Alice Springs, Ayers Rock, Auckland, Ballina, Blenheim, Brisbane, Broken Hill, Broome, Bundaberg, Burnie (Wynyard), Cairns, Canberra, Christchurch, Christmas Island, Cocos Island, Coffs Harbour, Coolangatta, Darwin, Denpasar (Bali), Devonport, Exmouth, Gold Coast, Gove, Hamilton

Island, Hobart, Hong Kong, Jakarta, Kalgoorlie, Kuala Lumpur, Launceston, Mackay, Melbourne, Mount Isa, Mount Gambier, Newcastle, Norfolk Island, Osaka, Perth, Portland, Proserpine, Rockhampton, Seoul, Sydney, Taipei, Townsville, Wagga Wagga.

Annual turnover: US $2,505 million (£1,518 million)

Revenue passenger km pa: 15,469 million

Passengers pa: 12,160,000

LINKS WITH OTHER AIRLINES
Marketing alliances with Air Facilities, Air New Zealand (qv), All Nippon (qv), Augusta, Austrian (qv), Cathay Pacific (qv), EVA*, Flightwest, Hazelton (qv), Impulse, Kendell, KLM (qv), Lufthansa (qv), Malaysia (qv), Sabair, Singapore (qv), Skywest (qv), Swissair (qv), Tamair, and United (qv).
* code-share

FLEET
3 Boeing 747-300
3 Airbus A300B4
1 Boeing 767-300ER
9 Boeing 767-200
4 Boeing 727-200LR
1 Boeing 727F
22 Boeing 737-300
18 Airbus A320-200
4 British Aerospace 146-300
7 British Aerospace 146-200
2 British Aerospace 146-200F
4 Fokker F-28-4000

Mainstay of Ansett's longer-haul operations are Boeing 767s.

EASTERN AUSTRALIA

Eastern Australia Airlines Ltd

HISTORY
Formed during the late-1980s with the support of Australian Regional Airlines, a subsidiary of Australian Airlines, which held a 42 per cent stake in the new airline, Eastern Australia started to establish a network of regional air services within New South Wales. Today, the airline is a wholly-owned subsidiary of Qantas (qv).

Executive Directors & Officers: Neil Shea, General Manager; Paul Glaser, Commercial Manager.

HQ Airport & Main Base: Kingsford-Smith Airport, Sydney

Designator: QF/ECO

Employees: 300

Main destinations served: Sydney to Armidale, Coffs Harbour, Dubbo, Grafton, Kempsey, Lord Howe Island, Moree, Narrabri, Port Macquarie, Tamworth, Taree.

Annual turnover: Included in the Qantas Group total

LINKS WITH OTHER AIRLINES
A subsidiary of Qantas (qv).

FLEET
8 de Havilland Dash 8-100
1 de Havilland Dash 8-200 (plus 3 on option)
4 British Aerospace Jetstream 31

HAZELTON

Hazelton Airlines Ltd

Incorporated: 1953

HISTORY
Formed in 1953 by Max Hazelton as an air taxi operator, Hazelton expanded into air charter and agricultural operations before starting its first scheduled air service in 1975, with a service from Orange to Canberra, the Federal capital. The airline operations continued to expand, mainly in New South Wales, in family ownership under the name of Hazelton Air Services Pty Ltd, until it was acquired in October 1993 by a newly-formed company, Hazelton Airlines, which was listed on the Australian Stock Exchange in December.

Though the original Orange–Canberra route has been dropped, a network of services is operated out of Sydney and there is a marketing alliance with Ansett Australia (qv). The founder remains as Deputy Chairman.

A subsidiary is Hazelton Air Charter Pty Ltd, and, while the two fleets are generally kept separate, one of the Air Charter Piper Navajo Chieftains is used on some scheduled services. The current fleet for scheduled operations is based on Saab 340Bs and Fairchild Metro 23s, while two Short 360s have been withdrawn from airline operations.

Executive Directors & Officers: Sir Brian Massey-Greene, Chairman; Max Hazelton, Deputy Chairman; Raymond Fung, Financial Controller; Rod Nelson, General Manager; Captain Alan Terrell, Operations Manager.

HQ Airport & Main Base: HQ airport is at Cudal, New South Wales, but the main base and hub is at Kingsford-Smith Airport, Sydney.

Radio callsign: HAZELTON

Designator: ZL/HZL

Employees: Flight-crew: 87; Cabin staff: 28; Engineering: 54; Ground staff: 78; Total: 247.

Main destinations served: Sydney Kingsford-Smith to Albury-Wodonga, Armidale, Bathurst, Broken Hill, Casino, Cudal, Dubbo, Griffith, Lismore, Merimbula, Moruya, Mudgee, Narrandera,

Orange, Parkes, Traralgon/Morwell, Wagga Wagga.

Annual turnover: US $42.5 million (£25.7 million)

Passengers pa: 390,000

LINKS WITH OTHER AIRLINES
Marketing alliance with Ansett Australia (qv), including shared frequent flyer plan.
Marketing alliance with Airlink and Air Facilities.

FLEET
6 Saab 340B (leased)
4 Fairchild Metro 23
1 Shorts 360*
3 Piper Navajo Chieftain*
2 Cessna 310*
* aircraft operated by Hazelton Air Charter Pty Ltd, although one Chieftain is used for certain scheduled services.

KENDELL

Kendell Airlines Ltd

Incorporated: 1967

HISTORY
Originally founded in 1967 as Premiair Aviation, for the first four years the airline concentrated on charter services and moved into regional scheduled services in 1971. The current title was adopted in 1982. Although based at Wagga Wagga, an extensive network of scheduled services has been built up operating out of two hubs, Adelaide and Melbourne, with services now reaching as far afield as Canberra in 1996, with further expansion taking place into airports in New South Wales.

The airline is now a wholly-owned subsidiary of Ansett Australia (qv).

Executive Directors & Officers: D.M. Kendell, Chairman & Managing Director; Ben Ryan, Chief Financial Officer; Captain Max Langshaw, Director of Operations; C.J. Breust, General Manager; R.J. Godwin, Chief Engineer.

HQ Airport & Main Base: Wagga Wagga, with the main base and hub at Adelaide and further hubs at Melbourne and Sydney.

Designator: KD/KDA

Employees: 360

Main destinations served: Albury, Ayers Rock, Ballina, Broken Hill, Burnie, Canberra, Ceduna, Coffs Harbour, Coober Pedy, Devonport, King Island, Kingscote,

Operating throughout eastern Australia, Saab 340B turboprops now form the backbone of the Hazelton fleet.

Merimbula, Mildura, Mount Gambier, Olympic Dam, Port Lincoln, Portland, Wagga Wagga, Whyalla, Woomera.

Annual turnover: AUS $73.5 million (included in the figures for Ansett Australia (qv)).

LINKS WITH OTHER AIRLINES
Subsidiary of Ansett Australia.

FLEET
8 Saab 340A
8 Saab 340B
7 Fairchild Metro 23

NATIONAL JET SYSTEMS

National Jet Systems Pty Ltd

Incorporated: 1989

HISTORY
National Jet Systems was established in 1989 and commenced operations the following year, initially offering charter flights. The airline soon took on the Australian Airlink network for Australian Airlines, initially providing the major carrier with a regional feeder service in eastern Australia, which was later extended to cover much of the country. The connection survived Australian's absorption into Qantas (qv), so that today National Jet operates services for Qantas. Charter services are still operated.

Executive Directors & Officers: Warren Seymour, Managing Director & Chief Executive Officer; Greg Bourne, Chief Operating Officer; Bruce Wales, Chief Financial Officer; Daniella Marsilli, Financial Director; Jorge Washington, Operations Director; David Edward, Commercial Director; Barry Lodge, Technical Director; Kevin Bain, Engineering Director; Geoff Lauder, Marketing Director.

HQ Airport & Main Base: Adelaide

Radio callsign: NATIONAL JET

Designator: NC/NJS

Employees: 800

Main destinations served: Adelaide, Alice Springs, Ayers Rock, Broome, Brisbane, Cairns, Canberra, Darwin, Kalgoorlie, Karratha, Geraldton, Mackay, MacArthur River, Mount Isa, Perth, Rockhampton, Townsville.

LINKS WITH OTHER AIRLINES
Operates scheduled services on behalf of Qantas (qv).

FLEET
4 British Aerospace 146-300
5 British Aerospace 146-200
8 British Aerospace 146-100
3 Avro RJ70
5 de Havilland Dash 8
1 Embraer EMP-110 Bandeirante
1 IAI 1124A Westwind

QANTAS

Qantas Airways Ltd

Incorporated: 1920

HISTORY
It was as the Queensland and Northern Territory Aerial Service, or QANTAS, that the history of Qantas started in 1920, after other names, such as the Western Queensland Auto Aerial Service and the Australian Transcontinental Aerial Services Co, had been tried and rejected. None of these would have done justice to the resultant airline.

Operations began in 1921, flying charters throughout Queensland with an Avro 504K and a Royal Aircraft Factory BE.2, while the directors pressed the Australian Government to grant a subsidy for scheduled services. Eventually the Government agreed, although the airline still had to compete, producing the best tender to operate the services. The first service was between Charleville and Cloncurry, and began in November 1922.

The early days of the airline saw struggles with the limitations of the aircraft then available, and it was not unknown for aircraft to be cancelled when it became apparent that they could not meet the severe operating conditions of the Queensland summer. Nevertheless, the airline survived, and even held a licence to manufacture aircraft such as the de Havilland DH.50, which proved to be a considerable improvement over earlier types. With commercial aviation still in its infancy there were opportunities to diversify and innovate, and in 1926 two flying schools were established, while in 1928 a significant advance was made in the use of aviation by the creation of a flying doctor service using a DH.50 modified as an ambulance, although a Queensland doctor had chartered Qantas aircraft before this time for what were literally flying visits to his patients. Qantas held the contract for the flying doctor service for four years, laying the foundations for the Royal Australian Flying Doctor Service.

The route network had expanded meanwhile, with the airline moving to a new head office in Brisbane and widening

its horizons. In 1934 it became Qantas Empire Airways Ltd, and the following year its aircraft – four-engined de Havilland DH.86s – took over the Darwin-Singapore section of the Imperial Airways' route to London, which had been extended to Australia the previous year. Over the next five years several new types of aircraft were introduced, of which the most famous was probably the Short Empire 'C' class flying-boat, six of which entered service in 1938, enabling Qantas to operate the Sydney–Karachi section of the Empire Airmail service to London, although the aircraft landed at Southampton. In practice aircraft operated the entire route with their passengers and mail, with Qantas crews operating the southern section and those of Imperial Airways operating from the UK to Karachi. It was also in 1938 that Qantas moved its headquarters from Brisbane to Sydney.

While the outbreak of World War Two, in Europe from 1939 and then in the Pacific from 1941, meant that further expansion was limited, during the war years Qantas and the newly-created British Overseas Airways Corporation – one of the predecessors of British Airways (qv) – operated a joint non-stop Perth–Colombo service after the fall of Singapore. The airline also helped evacuate casualties from New Guinea and maintained some essential Australian domestic air services. The Empire flying-boats, meanwhile, had formed the nucleus of a Royal Australian Air Force flying-boat squadron.

Post-war, ownership of Qantas passed to the Australian Government. Qantas embarked on a programme of expansion. Initially some of the aircraft pressed into service were converted wartime types, including modified Consolidated Liberator and Avro Lancaster (Lancastrian) bombers and Catalina flying-boats, but there were also Short Sandringham flying-boats, and the Douglas DC-3 for services to New Guinea and within both New Guinea and Queensland, as well as new Douglas DC-4s and Lockheed Constellations. Lockheed Super Constellations were introduced in 1954, and four years later one of these aircraft inaugurated the airline's round-the-world service. The following year the Lockheed Electra turboprop was introduced and Qantas became the first non-American airline to introduce Boeing 707s, initially using a longer-range variant unique to the airline, the 707-138B, before these were eventually replaced by Boeing 707-338Cs.

Meanwhile, post-war Australian civil aviation policy had not only seen Qantas become a state-owned airline, it had also meant that the airline concentrated exclusively on international services, with domestic operations being given to another state enterprise, Trans Australia Airlines, or TAA, which commenced operations in 1946 with a fleet of Douglas DC-3s. TAA also took over the Flying Doctor service in 1949, and internal services in New Guinea in 1960. A nationwide network of services was developed, with many routes operating in competition with private enterprise airlines, of which the largest was Ansett Australia (qv). Equipment operated included Vickers Viscounts and, later, Boeing 737s and Fokker F-27s. In 1986 Trans Australia was renamed Australian Airlines.

It was eventually decided that the state-owned airlines would be privatised, but before this happened Qantas purchased Australian Airlines in 1992, creating a new large airline carrying the Qantas name. By this time Australian Airlines had 36 aircraft in its own fleet, including Airbus A300s, and another 37 in subsidiary airlines operating regional services.

Today, Qantas has grown from its small beginnings to be the fourteenth largest airline in the world, and the largest airline in the southern hemisphere by a substantial margin. The old link with Imperial Airways has been resurrected with British Airways (qv) having successfully bid for a 25 per cent shareholding on privatisation of Qantas, while marketing links exist with a substantial number of major airlines (see below). Qantas is also the parent of a large number of subsidiaries, and has investments in a large number of companies. Many of these are in support or travel and tourism services, but one subsidiary – Qantas Ltd – was originally Australia-Asia Airlines, formed to inaugurate services to Taipei in 1990.

Executive Directors & Officers: Gary Pemberton, Chairman; James Strong, Chief Executive; Gary Toomey, Finance Director; Geoff Dixon, Group Executive General Manager, Commercial; Doug Gillies, Group Executive General Manager, Associated Business; David Burden, Group Executive General Manager, Information Technology.

HQ Airport & Main Base: Sydney, but there are also major hub operations at Adelaide, Brisbane, Melbourne, and Perth.

Radio callsign: QANTAS

Designator: QF/QFA

Employees: 29,600

Main destinations served: Adelaide, Alice Springs, Armidale, Auckland, Ayers Rock, Bamaga, Bangkok, Beijing, Blackwater, Brampton Island, Brisbane, Broken Hill, Broome, Bundaberg, Burnie, Cairns, Canberra, Christchurch, Coffs Harbour, Coolangatta, Darwin, Denpasar, Devonport, Dubbo, Dunk Island, Emerald, Frankfurt, Fukuoka, Gladstone, Gove, Grafton, Great Keppel Island, Harare, Hervey Bay, Ho Chi Minh City, Hobart, Hong Kong, Honolulu, Jakarta, Johannesburg, Kalgoorlie, Karratha, Kuala Lumpur, Launceston, Lizard Island, London Heathrow, Lord Howe Island, Los Angeles, Mackay, Manila, Maroochydore, Maryborough, Melbourne, Mildura, Moree, Mumbai (Bombay), Nadi, Nagoya, Narrabri, Newcastle (New South Wales), Noumee, Osaka, Papeete, Parabúrdoo, Perth, Port Hedland, Port Macquarie, Port Moresby, Proserpine, Renmark, Rockhampton, Rome, Sapporo, Seoul, Shanghai, Singapore, Sydney, Taipei, Tamworth, Taree, Tuesday Island, Tokyo, Townsville, Wellington. International services are from Brisbane, Melbourne, Perth, and Sydney.

Annual turnover: US $5,766 million (£3,495 million)

Revenue passenger km pa: 54,627 million

Passengers pa: 17,486,000

LINKS WITH OTHER AIRLINES
British Airways (qv) has a 25 per cent shareholding in Qantas, supported by a marketing alliance which may be extended into operations.
Qantas has four subsidiary airlines: Airlink, Eastern Australia Airlines (qv), Southern Australia Airlines (qv), and Sunstate Airlines (qv).
Marketing alliances, and in some cases code-shares too, exist with Canadian Airlines (qv), American Airlines (qv), US Airways (qv), Deutsche BA (qv), TAT (qv), Air Pacific (qv), Air New Zealand (qv), SAS Scandinavian Airlines (qv), Air Zimbabwe (qv), Solomon Airlines, Air Vanuatu, Air Nuigini (qv), Japan Airlines (qv), and Asiana Airlines (qv).

FLEET
18 Boeing 747-400 (plus 14 options)
6 Boeing 747-300
4 Boeing 747-200
2 Boeing 747SP
19 Boeing 767-300ER (plus 2 options)
7 Boeing 767-200ER
4 Airbus A300B4
22 Boeing 737-400
16 Boeing 737-300
These exclude aircraft operated by the subsidiary airlines.

SKYWEST

Skywest Airlines

Incorporated: 1963

HISTORY
Skywest Airlines is the regional operator within Western Australia, and since its formation in 1963 has developed a network of scheduled passenger and freight services out of Perth. It became a member of the Ansett Group, and is now a subsidiary of Ansett Australia (qv), with which it has a marketing alliance. During 1996 Skywest took over a number of destinations previously served by Ansett Australia.

Executive Directors & Officers: Bob Mason, General Manager; Ian Drennan, Financial Director; Trevor Douglas, Operations Director; David Thomas, Engineering Director.

HQ Airport & Main Base: Perth Domestic Airport

Designator: YT

Employees: 165

Main destinations served: Perth to Albany, Broome, Carnarvon, Cue, Derby, Esperance, Exmouth, Geraldton, Kalgoorlie, Karratha, Laverton, Leinster, Leonora, Meekathharra, Mount Keith, Mount Magnet, Port Hedland, Shark Bay, Wiluna.

Annual turnover: Included in the figures for Ansett Australia (qv).

LINKS WITH OTHER AIRLINES
A subsidiary of Ansett Australia (qv).

FLEET
5 Fokker 50
3 British Aerospace Jetstream 31

SOUTHERN AUSTRALIA

Southern Australia Airlines

Incorporated: 1981

HISTORY
Founded in 1981 as the regional carrier for Victoria, Southern Australia soon became a subsidiary of Australian Airlines, and ownership passed to Qantas (qv) in 1990.

Executive Directors & Officers: Tony Mathews, General Manager; Lionel Rose, Maintenance Manager; Keith Dunham, Marketing Manager.

HQ Airport & Main Base: Melbourne

Designator: QF

Employees: 155

Main destinations served: Melbourne to Burnie, Devonport, Launceston, Mildura, Sydney.

Annual turnover: Included in the figures for the Qantas Group (qv).

LINKS WITH OTHER AIRLINES
A wholly-owned subsidiary of Qantas (qv).

FLEET
2 British Aerospace 146-200
3 de Havilland Dash 8-100
2 Cessna 404 Titan

SUNSTATE AIRLINES

Sunstate Airlines Ltd

Incorporated: 1982

HISTORY
Established as a regional operator within Queensland, Sunstate Airlines was formed in 1982, and had early support from Australian Regional Airlines, a subsidiary of Australian Airlines, which held a 33 per cent interest before finally buying the airline outright in 1990. From the beginning, Sunstate has been a de Havilland Twin Otter operator, expanding to larger aircraft as demand grew. It is now a wholly-owned subsidiary of Qantas (qv).

Executive Directors & Officers: Ashley Kilroy, General Manager; Geoff Clem, Airline Operations Manager; Roger Barnes, Flight Operations Manager & Chief Pilot; Ian Lander, Commercial Manager; Dave Delahaye, Maintenance Manager; Gerry Hudson, Planning & Performance Manager.

HQ Airport & Main Base: Brisbane

Designator: OF

Employees: 220

Main destinations served: Brisbane to Barnega, Blackwater, Brampton Island, Bundaberg, Cairns, Dunk Island, Emerald, Gladstone, Great Keppel Island, Hervey Bay, Lizard Island, Lord Howe Island, Mackay, Maroochydore, Maryborough, Rockhampton, Thursday Island, Townsville.

Annual turnover: Included in the figures for the Qantas Group (qv).

LINKS WITH OTHER AIRLINES
A wholly owned subsidiary of Qantas (qv).

FLEET
4 de Havilland Dash 8-100
6 Short 360-200
2 Short 360-300
5 de Havilland DHC-6-300 Twin Otter

Austria – OE

AUSTRIAN AIRLINES

Österreichische Luftverkehrs AG

Incorporated: 1957

HISTORY
Olag Österreichische Luftverkehrs (founded in 1923) had ceased operating after Germany's occupation of Austria in 1938, by which time it had established a network of services from Vienna to many of the major cities of central Europe. It was only in 1957 that the new Austrian Airlines was formed, commencing operations with a service between Vienna and London Heathrow in 1958 using one of four chartered Vickers Viscount 700 aircraft, which were later replaced by four of the later Viscount 800s. Domestic services did not restart until 1963, initially using a Douglas DC-3, by which time the international services had seen the Viscounts joined by Sud Aviation Caravelle 6Rs. Two Hawker Siddeley HS 748s were also operated at this time.

Transatlantic services were introduced in 1969 using a Boeing 707 chartered from Sabena (qv), and flying from Vienna to New York via Brussels. This service was withdrawn after two years. Development of European services continued, nevertheless, with nine Douglas DC-9-32 aircraft joining the fleet in 1971, these being followed in 1980 by the first MD-80s. The decision to concentrate on European services must have been correct, since the airline declared its first profit in 1972. Throughout this period the airline remained in state ownership, but in 1988 24.2 per cent of its shares were offered to the public, and Swissair (qv) took a 3 per cent interest, which was later raised to 8 per cent, while All Nippon Airways (qv) acquired 3.5 per cent. Closer collaboration with other European airlines was considered in 1993, with KLM (qv), SAS (qv), and Swissair considering whether a form of strategic co-operation, code-named Alcazar, would be beneficial,. However, in the end the four participants decided not to proceed.

In 1994 Austrian acquired 42.85 per cent of the shares of Tyrolean Airways (qv), a regional operator. A marketing alliance and code-share was instigated with Delta Air Lines (qv) on the Vienna–New York route the same year.

When first formed more than 40 years ago, Austrian Airlines concentrated on developing a European network, but aircraft such as this Airbus A330-200 have established the airline on long-haul services as well.

2 Airbus A340-200
4 Airbus A330-200 (1 leased)
4 Airbus A310-300
3 Airbus A321 (plus 3 on order)
7 Airbus A320 on order
3 McDonnell Douglas MD-81
6 McDonnell Douglas MD-82
2 McDonnell Douglas MD-83
5 McDonnell Douglas MD-87
6 Fokker 70

LAUDA AIR

Lauda Air Luftfahrt

Incorporated: 1979

HISTORY

Founded in 1979 by former racing driver Niki Lauda, the eponymous Lauda Air did not begin operations until 1985, when it used two Fokker F-27 Friendships and BAC One-Elevens, leased from Tarom (qv), on charter flights, including inclusive tour operations to Mediterranean destinations using the One-Elevens. Licences for domestic scheduled services were granted in 1987, and in 1990 approval was given for international scheduled services, which had previously been the sole monopoly of Austrian Airlines (qv). An early supporter of the airline was Lufthansa (qv), which took an initial 26.4 per cent interest, increased to 39.7 per cent in 1994, though three years later Lufthansa agreed to sell part of its holding to Austrian Airlines, which has since built up a 36 per cent share. Today, Lufthansa has a 20 per cent interest in the airline.

Lauda Air was the first European operator of the Canadair Regional Jet, which appeared on services operated under the Lufthansa Express banner. An Italian subsidiary is Lauda Air S.p.A.

Executive Directors & Officers: Niki Lauda, Chairman; Peter H. Thöle, Financial Affairs; Derek Scherer, Flight Operations & Chief Pilot; Ing Otmar Lenz, Commercial Affairs; Walter Hechenberger, Technical Director; Martin Wiesinger, Marketing.

HQ Airport & Main Base: Vienna, with an additional base at Salzburg.

Radio callsign: LAUDA AIR

Designator: NG/LDA

Employees: Flight-crew: 155; Cabin staff: 417; Engineering: 201; Ground staff: 427; Total: 1,300.

Main destinations served: Bangkok, Budapest, Hong Kong, London Gatwick, Los Angeles, Manchester, Melbourne,

The most long-legged aircraft of Austrian's fleet, however, is the Airbus A340-300.

The arrangement with Delta later led to a Vienna–Atlanta service. Austrian acquired a 36 per cent interest in Lauda Air (qv) in 1997. The investments in Tyrolean and Lauda reflect Austrian's policy of creating a single Austrian airline grouping, and in 1997 Austrian doubled its stake in Tyrolean to 85.7 per cent. Today, the Austrian Government remains the single largest shareholder, with 51.9 per cent of the airline's shares. Many of the McDonnell Douglas MD-80 series aircraft are likely to be replaced by new Airbus A320/321s currently on order.

Executive Directors & Officers: Rudolf Streicher, Chairman; Mario Rehulka, President; Dr Herbert Bammer, President; Wolfgang Prock Schaver, Director General; Dr Walter Bock, Chief Operating Officer & Chief Pilot; Dr Hans Lob, Personnel Director; Michael Murwald, Vice-President Operations; Fritz Simunek, Vice-President Technical; Gunther Matschnighg, Vice-President, Maintenance.

HQ Airport & Main Base: Vienna

Radio callsign: AUSTRIAN

Designator: OS/AUA

Employees: Flight-crew: 388; Cabin staff: 985; Engineering: 626; Ground staff: 1,483; Total: 4,061.

Main destinations served: Aleppo, Almaty, Amman, Amsterdam, Ankara, Athens, Beijing, Beirut, Belgrade, Berlin Tegel, Brussels, Bucharest, Budapest, Cairo, Copenhagen, Damascus, Djerba, Dnepropetrovsk, Dubai, Düsseldorf, Frankfurt, Geneva, Istanbul, Johannesburg, Kiev, Larnaca, London Heathrow, Male, Milan, Minsk, Moscow, Munich, New York JFK, Odessa, Osaka, Paris CDG, Riga, Rome, Sarajevo, Shanghai, Skopje, Sofia, St Petersburg, Stockholm, Teheran, Tel Aviv, Thessaloniki, Tirana, Tokyo, Vilnius, Warsaw, Washington, Zürich. There are also charter flights to more than 80 destinations.

Annual turnover: US $1,240 million (£751.2 million)

Revenue passenger km pa: 5,438.3 million

Cargo tonne km pa: 128 million

Passengers pa: 3,520,300 (of which 2,924,900 scheduled)

LINKS WITH OTHER AIRLINES
Swissair (qv) has a 10 per cent interest, All Nippon (qv) 9 per cent, and Air France (qv) 1.5 per cent.
Austrian has 85.7 per cent of Tyrolean Airways (qv) and 36 per cent of Lauda Air (qv).
There are marketing alliances and code-shares with ARIA (qv), British Midland (qv), CSA (qv), Delta (qv), Iberia (qv), KLM (qv), LOT (qv), Lufthansa (qv), SAS (qv), Swissair (qv), TAROM (qv), and Ukraine International (qv), as well as joint agreements with Air China (qv), Air France, All Nippon, Finnair (qv), and Malev (qv).

FLEET
2 Airbus A340-300

Miami, Phuket, Sydney, plus more than 20 charter destinations world-wide.

Annual turnover: US $273.7 million (£165.9 million)

Aircraft km pa: 26,252 million (scheduled), 11,478 million (charter)

Revenue passenger km pa: 2,638,565,000 (scheduled)

Cargo tonne km pa: 317,557 million

Passengers pa: 710,992 (scheduled), 513,592 (charter)

LINKS WITH OTHER AIRLINES
Austrian Airlines has a 36 per cent interest. Lufthansa has a 20 per cent interest. There are marketing alliances with both airlines.

FLEET
1 Boeing 777-200IGW (plus 3 on order)
5 Boeing 767-300ER (1 assigned to Lauda Air S.p.A.)
2 Boeing 737-400
2 Boeing 737-300
7 Canadair Regional Jet 100ER (leased)
1 Dassault Falcon 20 (leased)
1 Cessna Citation II
1 Learjet 36A
plus 2 Boeing 737-800 on order

TYROLEAN AIRWAYS

Tiroler Luftfahrt AG

Incorporated: 1958

HISTORY
Originally founded in 1958 as Aircraft Innsbruck, Tyrolean Airways adopted its present title in 1980. The first scheduled services were domestic, but international services from Innsbruck followed, initially to destinations in Switzerland and what was then West Germany, and then more recently to destinations as far afield as Amsterdam. Because of the often steep approaches and departure routes from many of the airports served within Austria, the airline has a long tradition of employing aircraft with good short take-off characteristics.

Austrian Airlines (qv) acquired an interest in the airline, initially 42.85 per cent, doubled to 85.7 per cent in 1997, while a major shareholder is Leipnik-Lundenburger Industrie, with 14.3 per cent.

Tyrolean now has hubs at Graz, Linz, and Salzburg as well as at Innsbruck, and operates many short haul services on behalf of Austrian.

Executive Directors & Officers: Fritz A. Feitl, President & Chief Executive Officer.

HQ Airport & Main Base: Innsbruck, with additional bases/hubs at Graz, Linz, and Salzburg.

Radio callsign: TYROLEAN

Designator: VO/TYR

Employees: 810

Main destinations served: Tyrolean operates to six destinations in Austria and more than 25 in Europe, as well as operating charter flights.

LINKS WITH OTHER AIRLINES
Austrian owns 85.7 per cent of Tyrolean, as well as having a marketing alliance. There are also marketing alliances with KLM (qv), Sabena (qv), and Swissair (qv).

FLEET
16 de Havilland Dash 8-300
5 de Havilland Dash 8-100
1 de Havilland Dash 7
8 Canadair Regional Jet Series 200
4 Fokker 70
plus 5 de Havilland Dash 8-400 on order for 1999-2001

Azerbaijan – 4K

AZALAVIA – AZERBAIJAN AIRLINES

Azerbaijan Hava Yollari

Incorporated: 1992

HISTORY
Split off from Aeroflot (qv) on the break-up of the former Soviet Union, Azerbaijan Airlines is suffering from the severe economic climate as well as the aftermath of the war with Armenia, but is slowly re-equipping with western aircraft. In 1997 it acquired the sole remaining Canadair CL-44 Conroy for air cargo charters involving outsize loads. It is completely state-owned.

Executive Directors & Officers: Aliev Adaeat, General Director; Sabir Ilyasov, Deputy General Director; Nazim Szhavadov, Chief Engineer.

HQ Airport & Main Base: Baku

Radio callsign: AZAL

Designator: J2/AHY

Main destinations served: Adler/Sochi, Aleppo, Ankara, Athens, Bishkek, Chelyabinsk, Dubai, Ekaterinburg, Frankfurt, Gaziantep, Gomel, Istanbul, Kazan, Kharkov, Krasnodar, London Gatwick, Moscow, Nizhniy Novgorod, Orenburg, Perm, Samara, St Petersburg, Tbilisi, Tehran, Tel Aviv, Trabzon, Ufa, Volgograd, Zaporozhye.

FLEET
12 Tupolev Tu-154B
3 Tupolev Tu-154M
1 Canadair CL-44 Conroy
2 Boeing 757-200
1 Boeing 707-320C
3 Boeing 727-200
8 Tupolev Tu-134
3 Antonov An-26
6 Antonov An-32
14 Yakovlev Yak-40

Bahamas – C6

BAHAMASAIR

Bahamasair Ltd

Incorporated: 1973

HISTORY
The operational subsidiary of Bahamas Government-owned Bahamasair Holdings, Bahamasair was founded in 1973 to improve communications between the many small islands in the Bahamas chain. Operations soon reached some 20 islands both in the Bahamas and in neighbouring groups, while international services are operated to New York, Miami, and Orlando in the United States.

Executive Directors & Officers: Lester Turncuest, Chairman; Basil Ineraham, Financial Director; Aeusestin Roberts, Operations Director; Glen Pickard, Director of Privatisation; Arthur Barnett, Engineering Director; Oliver Hutchinson, Customer Services Director; Jesse Hinsey, Personnel Director; William Curtiss, General Manager.

HQ Airport & Main Base: Nassau, Bahamas

Radio callsign: BAHAMAS

Designator: UP/BHS

Employees: 650

Main destinations served: Fort Lauderdale, Freeport, Miami, New York JFK, Orlando, West Palm Beach, plus inter-island operations.

FLEET
3 Boeing 737-200

5 de Havilland Dash 8-300
1 BAe 748-2A
3 Short 360

Bahrain – A9C

GULF AIR

Gulf Air

Incorporated: 1950

HISTORY

Although based in Bahrain, Gulf Air is the airline for four small states in the Gulf – Abu Dhabi, Bahrain, Oman, and Qatar. Interest in establishing an airline for these territories came about after an Englishman, Freddie Bosworth, started operating a war-surplus Avro Anson in 1949, offering sight-seeing trips and air charters. The following year Bosworth and several local businessmen founded the Gulf Aviation Company, obtaining a de Havilland Dove and a small Auster. The early operations were largely charter work on behalf of the major oil companies.

In 1951 BOAC became a major share-holder, and in addition to providing oper-ating capital also provided technical assis-tance, adding Gulf Air to the network of locally-based airlines throughout the world whose operations fed into those of the British airline. New aircraft – de Havilland Herons – were added to the fleet, and ser-vices operated from Bahrain to Abu Dhabi, Al Ain, Kuwait, Muscat, and Sharjah. Douglas DC-3s were later added to the fleet, followed by Fokker F-27s and then a BAC One-Eleven jet. A Vickers VC-10 wet-leased from BOAC marked the commence-ment of services to London in 1970.

In 1973 the airline was effectively nationalised, with the four governments buying out the BOAC shareholding, and a treaty the following year officially changed Gulf Aviation into Gulf Air, formally recog-nising the airline as the flag carrier for the four states. Investment in the airline saw Lockheed L-1011 TriStars and Boeing 737s join the fleet, displacing the older types and providing the equipment suitable for

Top: *Mainstay of Gulf Air's long-haul fleet is the Boeing 767-300ER (extended range).*

Middle: *Gulf Air also has a number of Airbus A340-300s. This one is coming in to land at Bahrain.*

Bottom: *For shorter routes Gulf uses its Airbus A320-200 fleet.*

expansion, with a network which stretched from London and Amsterdam in Europe to Hong Kong. Later, in 1992, Gulf Air became the first Arab airline to operate to Melbourne and Johannesburg.

Today, Gulf Air is the second-largest Arab airline, and by sales is 51st in size world-wide. It has one of the youngest fleets in the industry, with an average age per aircraft of around three years.

Executive Directors & Officers: Sheik Ahmed Bin Nasser Al Thani, Chairman; Sheik Ahmed Bin Saif Al Nehyan, President & Chief Executive; Walter Van West, Vice-President Finance, Strategy & Information Technology; Ray Slayer, Vice-President Commercial; Ahmed Abdulghani, Vice-President Technical Affairs; Abdulrahman Al Busaidi, Vice-President PCE Office.

HQ Airport & Main Base: Bahrain International (Muharraq), with additional hubs at Abu Dhabi, Doha (Qatar), and Muscat (Oman). Maintenance base is at Abu Dhabi International.

Radio callsign: GULF AIR

Designator: GF/GFA

Employees: Flight-crew: 480; Cabin staff: 1,449; Engineering: 528; Ground staff: 3,115; Total: 5,572.

Main destinations served: Bahrain to Abu Dhabi, Al Ain, Amman, Amsterdam, Athens, Bahrain, Bangkok, Beirut, Bombay, Cairo, Casablanca, Colombo, Damascus, Dar-es-Salaam, Dhahran, Dhaka, Doha, Dubai, Entebbe, Frankfurt, Fujeirah, Hong Kong, Istanbul, Jakarta, Jeddah, Karachi, Khartoum, Kuala Lumpur, Kuwait, Larnaca, London Heathrow, Madras, Manila, Melbourne, Muscat, Nairobi, Paris CDG, Ras Al Khaimah, Riyadh, Rome, Sanaa, Sharjah, Shiraz, Singapore, Sydney, Tehran, Trivandrum, Zanzibar.

Annual turnover: US $1,048 million (£635 million)

Aircraft km pa: 87.6 million

Revenue passenger km pa: 11,034,788

Cargo tonne km pa: 423 million

Passengers pa: 5 million plus

LINKS WITH OTHER AIRLINES
Code-sharing with Alitalia (qv), American Airlines (qv), and British Midland (qv). Joint maintenance venture – GAMCO (Gulf Maintenance Company) – with government of Abu Dhabi.

FLEET
5 Airbus A340-300

11 Boeing 767-300ER
13 Airbus A320
plus 6 Airbus A330-300 on order

Bangladesh – S2

BIMAN BANGLADESH AIRLINES

Bangladesh Airlines Corporation

Incorporated: 1972

HISTORY
Biman dates from 1972, when it was formed by the Bangladesh Government shortly after secession from Pakistan late the previous year. Prior to this, services to and from what had been East Pakistan had been operated by PIA (qv). Scheduled operations began in February 1972, a month after the airline was founded. The initial services were domestic, with routes into India, and London Heathrow as an early long-haul destination using Boeing 707s.

Executive Directors & Officers: Al-Almeen Chaudhury, Managing Director; Anwar Hossain, Director Finance; Captain Kamal Mahmud, Director Flight Operations; Group Captain K. Iftekhar Ahmad, Director of Engineering; Lieutenant-Colonel M. Mahmoodur Rahman, Director Project Planning; Squadron-Leader Ahsan Quadir, Director Administration; Captain S.A.N. Oqba, Director Marketing & Sales; Captain Mahbubar Rahman, Director Customer Services; Major M.A. Salam, Director Stores & Purchasing.

HQ Airport & Main Base: Dhaka

Radio callsign: BANGLADESH

Designator: BG/BBC

Employees: 6,013

Main destinations served: Domestic destinations plus Abu Dhabi, Bangkok, Bombay, Brussels, Calcutta, Delhi, Dubai, Doha, Frankfurt, Hong Kong, Jeddah, Karachi, Kathmandu, Kuala Lumpur, Kuwait, London Heathrow, Muscat, New York JFK, Paris CDG, Rome, Riyadh, Singapore, Tokyo.

FLEET
4 McDonnell Douglas DC-10-30
2 Airbus A310-300

2 Fokker F-28-4000 Fellowship
2 British Aerospace ATP

Belarus – EW

BELAIR

Belair-Belarussian Airlines

Incorporated: 1991

HISTORY
Established as an offshoot of Aeroflot's division in the former Soviet Republic of Belarus, Belair is exclusively a charter airline.

HQ Airport & Main Base: Minsk

Radio callsign: AIR BELARUS

Designator: BL/BLI

Main destinations served: Charters within Belarus and the CIS.

FLEET
3 Ilyushin Il-76TD
2 Tupolev Tu-134
1 Yakovlev Yak-40

BELAVIA

Belavia-Belarussian Airlines

Incorporated: 1993

HISTORY
One of the many airlines created out of the shattering of Aeroflot (qv), Belavia is essentially the former Aeroflot Division within what was the Soviet Republic of Belarus.

Executive Directors & Officers: Valisly Ermakov, Director General.

HQ Airport & Main Base: Minsk

Radio callsign: BELARUS AVIA

Designator: B2/BRU

Main destinations served: Many CIS cities, plus Minsk to Anapa, Berlin, Frankfurt, Moscow, Shannon, St Petersburg, Tel Aviv, Vienna, Warsaw, Zürich.

FLEET
21 Tupolev Tu-154M
19 Tupolev Tu-134
18 Antonov An-24
7 Antonov An-26
8 Yakovlev Yak-40

Belgium – OO

DAT DELTA AIR TRANSPORT

DAT Walloonie

Incorporated: 1966

HISTORY

A Belgian regional scheduled and charter airline, DAT is a wholly-owned subsidiary of Sabena (qv), and has developed from services out of its Antwerp base to operating some of the thinner or less frequent services from Brussels for its parent airline. Most of the fleet now carries Sabena colours and most flights use the Sabena designator. For many years an operator of Fokker F-28 Fellowship jet airliners, these aircraft have now been replaced by further deliveries of AI(R) RJ series aircraft.

Executive Directors & Officers: Willy Buysse, General Manager; Nicolas d'Otreape, Director, Operations; Bert Desiron, Director, Personnel; Jean Louis Herremans, Director, Finance.

HQ Airport & Main Base: HQ is at Antwerp, with the main base of operations is Brussels Zaventem.

Radio callsign: DELTAIR

Designator: DL/DAT, but most flights carry Sabena SN

Employees: 420

Main destinations served: Usually the thinner, short-haul Sabena routes, including Brussels to Edinburgh, Glasgow, Leeds/Bradford, Newcastle.

Annual turnover: Included in Sabena total.

LINKS WITH OTHER AIRLINES
Wholly-owned by Sabena.

FLEET
14 AI(R) RJ85 (1 owned)
9 AI(R) RJ100
6 British Aerospace 146-200 (all owned)
1 de Havilland Dash 8-300
9 Embraer EMB-120 Brasilia
(All these aircraft are also included in the Sabena list)

EAT EUROPEAN AIR TRANSPORT

European Air Transport NV/SA

Incorporated: 1971

HISTORY

Originally started with a Beech Queen Air for light charters, EAT soon progressed to a Rockwell 685. In 1975 additional aircraft were purchased to meet growing demand for an air taxi service. In 1976 EAT was awarded a contract to operate feeder services to Brussels from Cologne, Düsseldorf, Eindhoven, and Luxembourg for Sabena (qv), for which it became the first European operator of the Swearingen Metro. In 1981 the company was acquired by DHL Worldwide Express (qv), whose colours its aircraft now carry. The main business is regular scheduled air cargo operations as part of the DHL network, but ad hoc charters, including livestock-transport, are also available.

Executive Directors & Officers: Gordon Olafson, Managing Director; Captain Iwein van Caelenberg, Director of Operations; Desmond Fitzgerald, Finance Manager; Stan Wilski, Manager of Charter & Contract Services; Jan Simon, MIS Manager.

HQ Airport & Main Base: Brussels Zaventem

Radio callsign: EUROTRANS

Designator: QY/BCS

Employees: Flight-crew:104; Engineering: 80; Ground staff: 76; Total: 260.

Main destinations served: Athens, Barcelona, Basle, Budapest, Cologne, Copenhagen, Dublin, East Midlands,

EAT's fleet operates in DHL livery on cargo services throughout Europe. Pictured here are a Boeing 727, the workhorse of many air freight airlines on both side of the Atlantic, and one of the veteran Convair 580 turboprop conversions of the Convair Metropolitan series.

Frankfurt, Geneva, Gothenburg, Hamburg, Helsinki, Istanbul, Lisbon, London Heathrow, Lyons, Madrid, Marseilles, Milan, Nuremberg, Oslo, Paris, Rome, Stockholm, Tampere, Toulouse, Valencia, Vienna, Warsaw.

Cargo tonne km pa: 485,349,000

LINKS WITH OTHER AIRLINES
A subsidiary of DHL Worldwide Express (qv).

FLEET
5 McDonnell Douglas DC-8
1 Boeing 757
10 Boeing 727-200
4 Boeing 727-100F
9 Convair 580 (3 leased to Swift Air)
7 Lockheed L-188 Electra
3 Let L-410
4 Antonov An-26
1 Fokker F-27

SABENA

Société Anonyme Belge d'Exploitation de la Navigation Aérienne

Incorporated: 1923

HISTORY
Belgium's national flag carrier, Sabena was founded in May 1923 as the successor to SNETA, Société Nationale pour l'Etude de Transports Aériens, which itself dated from 1919, when it had been founded to operate services from Brussels to Amsterdam, London, and Paris, using ex-World War One aircraft. Sabena's first service was far less ambitious, flying newspapers from Brussels to Lympne on the south coast of England, via Ostend. It was in 1924 that a passenger service first started, from Brussels to Basle via Strasbourg with a three-engined Handley Page W.8. Nevertheless, the airline, in common with many other European carriers of the day, had its ambitions set on flights to colonial destinations, and in 1925 a Handley Page W.8 flew to the Belgian Congo, the 75-hour journey being spread over 51 days.

Given the capabilities of the aircraft of the day, the priority had to be the creation of a European network, and by 1938 Sabena had one which extended to Stockholm in the north and as far south as Vienna, which was reached that year. Services to the Belgian Congo were inaugurated in 1935, initially using a Fokker F.VII, which took five-and-a-half days. The following year this was reduced to three days using a Savoia-Marchetti S-73, and in 1938 was further reduced to 24 hours with a Savoia-Marchetti S-83, reputed to be the

fastest aircraft in commercial service at the time.

In 1939, on the eve of war in Europe, Sabena took delivery of its first Douglas DC-3, but the invasion and occupation of Belgium in 1940 meant that all air services were suspended, and aircraft which could be evacuated were placed at the disposal of the Allied powers for the duration of the war.

When commercial services were eventually resumed in 1946, the first aircraft were Douglas DC-3s and DC-4s, with the larger aircraft being used to start services to the United States and reintroduce services to the Belgian Congo. In 1947 Sabena became the first European airline to operate the pressurised Douglas DC-6. Yet another European 'first' for Sabena followed in 1949, when helicopter services were introduced. Sabena went on to introduce the world's first international helicopter services in 1953, initially using Sikorsky S-55s and then later Sikorsky S-58s, until the services were abandoned in 1966 with the realisation that these could never be made to meet their costs.

These innovations apart, there was steady progress elsewhere, with Convair 440 Metropolitans introduced onto European services in 1956, and the following year Douglas DC-7Cs were placed on intercontinental services. The first jet aircraft for the airline were Boeing 707s in 1960, while in 1961 Sabena introduced Sud Aviation Caravelles to its European

routes. The Caravelles were later supplemented by Boeing 727s. Collaboration with Austrian Airlines (qv) on transatlantic services from Vienna via Brussels during the late-1960s proved unsuccessful.

In recent years Sabena has been pressing for its main base at Brussels Zaventem airport to become a major European hub, but, in common with many of the older European airlines, has had to struggle to reduce costs. A regional airline, DTA or Delta Air Transport (qv), was acquired in 1986, and this airline's aircraft have been used in Sabena colours to operate new routes at a lower cost than the parent airline could manage. Sabena also has a charter subsidiary, Sobelair (qv), in which Sabena has a 72 per cent controlling interest. State ownership of the airline has been reduced, with Swissair (qv) acquiring 49.5 per cent, leaving the Belgian Government with 33.8 per cent and private investors with the remainder.

Previous plans for alliances with other European airlines did not come to fruition, but the Swissair connection provides a strong strategic alliance, while there are also marketing alliances with Austrian Airlines Maintenance (qv), Delta Air Lines (qv), and TAP Air Portugal (qv). A number of services, including Rome, London Gatwick, and most London Heathrow flights, are operated by Virgin Express (qv), while DTA operates many other less heavily-used short-haul routes using aircraft in Sabena colours. Future plans

Look closely and you can just see the Swissair logo on the fuselage of this Sabena Airbus A340-200, while the Belgian and European Union flags are on the starboard engine nacelles.

Another recent addition to the Sabena fleet is this Airbus A330-200.

centre on replacing the Boeing 737-200 fleet with a mixture of AI(R) RJ100s and Airbus A-319s by 2000.

Executive Directors & Officers: Valere Cross, Chairman; Philippe Suinen, Vice-Chairman; Paul Reutlinger, President & Chief Executive Officer; Pedter Ramel, Executive Vice-President Finance; Jacques Drappier, Executive Vice-President Flight Operations; Patrick du Bois, Executive Vice-President Secretary General; Claude Palmero, Executive Vice-President

Services; Hilde Burie, Executive Vice-President Human Resources; Alain Bertrand, Vice-President Cargo.

HQ Airport & Main Base: Brussels Zaventem

Radio callsign: SABENA

Designator: SN/SAB

Employees: Flight-crew: approx 500; Cabin staff: approx 1,100; Ground staff (including engineering): approx 6,900; Total: 9,766.

Main destinations served: Abidjan, Amsterdam, Athens, Bamako, Banjul, Berlin Templehof, Brazzaville, Bilbao, Bologna, Bordeaux, Boston, Bristol, Budapest, Casablanca, Chicago, Cincinnati, Conakry, Copenhagen, Cotonou, Dakar, Douala, Dublin, Düsseldorf, Edinburgh, Entebbe/Kampala, Florence, Frankfurt, Freetown, Geneva, Glasgow, Gothenburg, Hamburg, Hanover, Helsinki, Istanbul, Johannesburg, Kigali, Kinshasa, Lagos, Leeds/Bradford, Lisbon, Lome, London City, London Heathrow, Luanda, Luxembourg, Lyon, Madrid, Malaga, Manchester, Marseille, Milan, Moscow, Munich, Nairobi, Nantes, Naples, Newcastle, New York JFK, Nice, Nouakchott, Oporto, Oslo, Ougadougou, Paris CDG, Prague, Stockholm, Strasbourg, Stuttgart, Tel Aviv, Tokyo, Turin, Venice, Vienna, Warsaw.
A number of these services are operated by Delta Air Transport (qv) aircraft in Sabena colours.

Annual turnover: US $1,995 million (£1,209 million)

Revenue passenger km pa: 9,011 million

Cargo tonnes pa: 113.028

Passengers pa: 5,173,568

LINKS WITH OTHER AIRLINES
Strategic alliance with Swissair (qv) which has a 49.5 per cent interest. DTA Delta Air Transport (qv) is a wholly-owned subsidiary, while a 72 per cent controlling interest is held in Sobelair (qv). Operating agreements with Virgin Express (qv).
Alliances with Austrian Airlines (qv), Delta Air Lines (qv), and TAP Air Portugal (qv).

FLEET
2 Boeing 747-349
4 Airbus A340-200 (leased)
3 Airbus A330-300
4 Airbus A330-200
2 McDonnell Douglas MD-11
2 Airbus A310-200
1 Airbus A310-300
3 Boeing 737-400
6 Boeing 737-300
13 Boeing 737-200 (leased)
6 Boeing 737-500
14 Avro RJ85 (operated by DAT) (1 owned)
9 Avro RJ100 (operated by DAT)
6 British Aerospace 146-200 (operated by DAT) (all owned)
1 de Havilland Dash 8-300 (operated by DAT)
9 Embraer EMB-120 Brasilia (operated by DAT)

Despite the large numbers of Airbus aircraft produced in recent years, the Boeing 737 is set to remain a common site at European airports. This is one of Sabena's older 737-200s.

SOBELAIR

Société Belge de Transports par Air

Incorporated: 1946

HISTORY
Sobelair was established in 1946 to operate passenger and freight charters, mainly to the former Belgian Congo (now Zaire), but this business was much reduced after the Congo attained independence in 1960. The airline has since become effectively a subsidiary of Sabena (qv), which has a 72 per cent interest, and the emphasis on operations has switched to inclusive tour charters, mainly within Europe but with a growing business in services across the Atlantic and to the Far East.

Executive Directors & Officers: Paul Reutlinger, Chairman; Luc Cloetens; Chief Executive Officer & General Manager; Pascale Minet, Financial Director; Captain Ivon Delplancke, Operations Director & Chief Pilot; Monique Lebersorg, Commercial Director; Reaoud Willame, Personnel Director; Andre Muller, Technical Manager.

HQ Airport & Main Base: Brussels Zaventem

Radio callsign: SOBELAIR

Designator: S3/SLR

Employees: 251

Main destinations served: Charters, mainly inclusive tour, within Europe and North Africa, the Caribbean, North America, and the Far East.

LINKS WITH OTHER AIRLINES
Sabena (qv) has a 72 per cent interest.

FLEET
2 Boeing 767-300ER
3 Boeing 737-400
2 Boeing 737-300

VIRGIN EXPRESS

Virgin Express

Incorporated: 1991

HISTORY
Originally founded in 1991 as a 'low cost, no frills' scheduled airline under the name of EuroBelgium Airlines, backed by the City Hotels Group, the company was acquired by the Virgin Group in 1996 and the name changed to Virgin Express. The airline has remained at Brussels since the acquisition, although the high cost of employing staff in Belgium has prompted speculation that the main base might be moved, and meanwhile a further hub is being developed at Paris Charles de Gaulle, where it has a subsidiary, Air Provence Charter. In addition to flying its own services, Virgin Express is also operating a number of services on behalf of Sabena (qv). City Hotels retains a 10 per cent stake in the airline, with 51 per cent of the shares held by Virgin Group.

Executive Directors & Officers:
Jonathan Ormstein, Managing Director; James Swigart, Finance Director; Luc Tack, Operations Director.

HQ Airport & Main Base: HQ at Melsbroek Airport, with hubs at Brussels Zaventem and Paris CDG.

Radio callsign: BELSTAR

Designator: BQ/EBA

Employees: 350

Main destinations served: Barcelona, Copenhagen, London Heathrow, London Gatwick, Madrid, Milan, Nice, Rome, Vienna, plus charters.

LINKS WITH OTHER AIRLINES
Owned by Virgin Group, parent company for Virgin Atlantic (qv).
Operates certain Sabena (qv) services.

FLEET
10 Boeing 737-300
1 Boeing 737-400

VLM

Vlaamse Luchttransportmaatschappij

Incorporated: 1992

HISTORY
Founded in 1992, VLM commenced operations between Antwerp and London City Airport the following year using a Fokker 50 airliner. A service from London City to Liverpool was operated for a short period before the airline started to concentrate on services to and from London City and European destinations. Charter flights are also operated.

Executive Directors & Officers: Jaap Rosen Jacobson, Chairman; Frederick Van Gaever, Managing Director; Rolf Stenberg, Chief Operating Officer; Eugene Reyniers, Chief Financial Officer.

HQ Airport & Main Base: Luchthaven Gebouw, with the main centre of operations being London City Airport.

Radio callsign: RUBENS

Designator: VG/VLM

Employees: 105

Main destinations served: London City to Antwerp, Düsselfdorf Express, Monchengladbach, Rotterdam.

LINKS WITH OTHER AIRLINES
Code-sharing with Air UK (qv) on services from Rotterdam to London City Airport.

FLEET
6 Fokker 50

Bolivia – CP

LAB – LLOYD AERO BOLIVIA

Lloyd Aéro Boliviano

Incorporated: 1925

HISTORY
Lloyd Aéro Bolivia was founded in 1925, during a period which saw many South American airlines established. Operations were within Bolivia initially, but international services followed, although these were not operated in any substantial way until well after World War Two. The Bolivian Government eventually took control of the airline, but in 1995 the major Brazilian carrier VASP (qv) acquired a 49 per cent stake, while there are also some small private interests, leaving just 48.27 per cent in state hands.

Executive Directors & Officers: Ulisses Canhedo Azevedo, President; Antonio Spagnuolo Sanchez, Executive President Advisor; Wagner Ferreira, Commercial Director; Julio Cezar Tavares Neto, Finance Manager; Captain Hans Beckmann, Operations Manager; Jose Rodriguez Calvo, Commercial Manager; Eng Carlos Cardozo, Technical Manager; Gonzalo Ferrufino, Traffic Manager; Marcio Magno Rodrigues, Administrative Manager; Elysabeth Montano, Freight Manager; Mauro Cesar Cherruli, Supplies Manager.

HQ Airport & Main Base: HQ at Aéropuerto Jorge Wilstermann, Cochabamba, with operations based on La Paz.

Radio callsign: LLOYDAERO

Designator: LB/LAB

Employees: 1,546

Main destinations served: La Paz to Arica, Asunçion, Belo Horizonte, Buenos Aires, Caracas, Cobija, Cochabamba, Guayaramerin, Iquique, Lima, Magdalena, Manaus, Mexico City, Miami, Montevideo, Panama City, Puerto Suárez, Quito, Riberalta, Rio de Janeiro, Salta, San Joaquin, Santa Ana, Santa Cruz, Santiago de Chile, São Paulo, Sucre, Tarija, Trinidad.

LINKS WITH OTHER AIRLINES
VASP (qv) holds 49 per cent stake.

FLEET
2 Airbus A310-300
1 Boeing 707-320C
3 Boeing 727-200Adv
2 Boeing 727-100
1 Boeing 737-300
2 Fokker F-27-200

Brazil – PP

ITA – ITAPEMIRIM

Itapemirim Transportes Aéreos SA

Incorporated: 1989

HISTORY
Brazil's main scheduled and charter cargo operator, ITA was founded in 1989 as a subsidiary of Transportadora Itapemirim, the transport division of the Itapemirim Corporation. Operations did not commence until 1991. The airline operates within Brazil and throughout the Americas, including operations for FedEx (qv).

The current shareholders are Transportadora Itapemirim and Camilo Cola, the airline's Chairman and President.

Executive Directors & Officers: Camilo Cola, Chairman & President; Girceu Machado, Senior Vice-President & Chief Operating Officer; Jose Mauricio Gazola, Financial Officer; Jose Luis Santolin, Commercial Director; Ruy Lotz, Engineering & Maintenance Director.

HQ Airport & Main Base: HQ at Rio de Janeiro and main base at Campinas Viracopos.

Designator: IT/ITM

Employees: 2,000

Main destinations served: Charters plus scheduled flights to Belem, Brasilia, Fortaleza, Manaus, Pôrto Alegre, Recife, Rio de Janeiro, Salvador.

LINKS WITH OTHER AIRLINES
Operations on behalf of FedEx (qv). Marketing alliances with KLM (qv) and Lufthansa (qv).

FLEET
4 Boeing 727-100C/F
2 Boeing 727-200
2 Cessna 208B Grand Caravan

NORDESTE

SA Nordeste Linhas Aéreos Regionais

Incorporated: 1976

HISTORY
Founded in 1976, Nordeste is the main regional passenger and cargo airline in north-east Brazil, and is a subsidiary of Rio-Sul (qv), itself in turn a subsidiary of Varig (qv).

Executive Directors & Officers: Roberto Coelho, President; Fausto Pontes, Administration Director; Francisco Guge, Technical Director.

HQ Airport & Main Base: Salvador, with an additional hub at Belo-Horizonte.

Radio callsign: NORDESTE

Designator: JH/NES

Employees: 300

Main destinations served: Almost 30 airports, most of which are in north-eastern Brazil.

Annual turnover: Included in the figures for Varig (qv).

LINKS WITH OTHER AIRLINES
A subsidiary of Rio-Sul (qv).

FLEET
2 Boeing 737-500
2 Fokker 50
4 Embraer EMB-120 Brasilia
9 Embraer EMB-110

RIO-SUL

SA Rio-Sul Serviços Aéreos Regionais

Incorporated: 1976

HISTORY
Rio-Sul was founded in 1976 as a regional airline operating in the south of Brazil, taking over the feeder services which had been operated by Cruzeiro do Sol after ownership of that airline passed to Varig (qv). Another driving force behind the airline's creation was a government-inspired initiative to rationalise and invigorate

Brazil's regional air services, known as SITAR, or the Integrated System of Regional Air Transport. Under SITAR, the country was divided into five regions for air transport purposes, and Rio-Sul was allocated the southern region. Varig has 95 per cent of Rio-Sul's shares, effectively making it a subsidiary of the former. Nordeste Linhas Aéreos (qv) is officially a subsidiary of Rio-Sul.

Executive Directors & Officers: Paulo Enrique Moraes Coco, President & Chief Executive Officer; Percy Rodrigues, Financial & Administration Director; Nilson Alberto Guilhem, Commercial Director; Jose Segundo, Controller; Ilson Oliviera, Finance General Manager; Helio Miciel, Operations General Manager; Alfredo Mavalli, Traffic General Manager; Evandro Braga de Oliveira, Engineering & Maintenance General Manager; Marcos Telore, Sales General Manager; Carlos Mateus, Reliability & Services Quality General Manager; Paulo Mota, Administration General Manager; Marcelo Faria, Human Resources General Manager; Glenda Romano, Legal Counsel.

HQ Airport & Main Base: HQ at Rio de Janeiro, but the main base/hub is São Paulo Congonhas Airport.

Radio callsign: RIOSSUL

Designator: SL/RSL

Employees: 1,150

Main destinations served: More than 50 domestic destinations, including Belem, Belo Horizonte, Brasilia, Recife, Rio de Janeiro, Rio Grande, São Paolo.

Annual turnover: Included in the figures for Varig (qv).

LINKS WITH OTHER AIRLINES
A subsidiary of Varig, and owner of Nordeste.

FLEET
12 Boeing 737-500
10 Fokker 50
12 Embraer EMB-120 Brasilia
(All these aircraft are also included in the Varig list)

TABA

Transportes Aéreos Regionais da Bacia Amazonica

Incorporated: 1976

HISTORY
TABA was one of a number of Brazilian airlines whose birth was accelerated and

development encouraged by a government-inspired initiative to rationalise and invigorate Brazil's regional air services, known as SITAR, or the Integrated System of Regional Air Transport. Under SITAR, Brazil was divided into five regions for air transport purposes. TABA was allocated the vast Amazonian Basin, giving the airline operations into the states of Amazonas, Para, Amapa, Acre, Rondonia, and Mato Grosso, offering scheduled services for passengers and cargo, and air taxi services as well.

The major shareholder is the current chairman.

Executive Directors & Officers: Marcelio Gibson Jacques, Chairman; Bruno Gibson, Executive Vice-President; Alexandre Gibson, Planning Vice-President.

HQ Airport & Main Base: Belem

Radio callsign: TABA

Designator: T2/TAB

Employees: 750

Main destinations served: More than 50 regional destinations, including Belo Horizonte, Belem, Brasilia, and Rio de Janeiro.

FLEET
2 Fokker 100
4 Fairchild FH-227B
4 de Havilland Dash 8-300
3 Embraer EMB-110C Bandeirante
5 Embraer EMB-110P Bandeirante

TAM

TAM Transportes Aéreos Regionais SA

Incorporated: 1976

HISTORY
TAM was founded in 1976 with the support of VASP (qv), which took just under a quarter of its shares, and a holding company, TAM (Taxi Aéro Marilia). The driving force behind the move into airline operations by what was essentially an air taxi operator was a government-inspired initiative to rationalise and invigorate Brazil's regional air services, known as SITAR, or the Integrated System of Regional Air Transport. Under SITAR, TAM was allocated the mid-west region of the country.

TAM moved quickly to establish itself as a significant scheduled carrier within its allocated area, using a variety of aircraft including Fokker F-27 Friendships and Embraer EMB-110 Bandeirantes, while Fokker 100 jets were introduced in 1992. The VASP stake in the airline is now much reduced, at 3.35 per cent.

Executive Directors & Officers: Rolim Adolfo Amaro, Chairman & President; Ivo Alcaldi Soares, Chief Executive Officer; Wagner Milani, Chief Financial Officer; Armando Lucente Fiho, Planning Director; Umberto L. de Angelis, Commercial Director; Ruy A.M. Amparo, Engineering, Technical & Maintenance Director; Maria L.P.T. Candelaria, Marketing Director; Dr Ramiro E.A.G. Tojal, Senior Vice-President Planning Strategies; Eng Luiz E. Falco P. Correa, Vice-President, Commercial & Technical, Marketing, Operations; Daniel Mandelli Martin, Vice-President Administration, Financial & Planning Strategies.

HQ Airport & Main Base: HQ at Jardim Aéroporto, São Paulo

Radio callsign: TAM

Designator: KK/TAM

Employees: 2,144

Main destinations served: São Paulo to almost 40 destinations in the states of São Paulo, Mato Grosso, Rio Grande Sul. Shuttle service from São Paulo Congonhas and Rio de Janeiro Santos Dumont to connect with the Air Bridge Shuttle operated jointly by Varig (qv), VASP (qv), and Transbrasil (qv).

LINKS WITH OTHER AIRLINES
Links with other Brazilian airlines as shown above.
VASP has a 3.35 per cent interest in the airline.

FLEET
28 Fokker 100
7 Fokker 50
3 Fokker F-27-600
4 Fokker F-27-500
15 Cessna 208B Grand Caravan

TRANSBRASIL

Transbrasil Linhas Aéreos SA

Incorporated: 1955

HISTORY
Originally founded in 1955 as an offshoot of the Sadia Organisation, to carry meat, the airline was known as Sadia SA Transportes Aéreos until 1972. Passenger flights started in 1956. Transportes Aéreos Salvador was acquired in 1962, and its operations absorbed into those of Transbrasil. Later the regional airline Interbrasil Star was acquired, and while this has a small fleet of just four aircraft at present, substantial investment is being made in a major expansion programme which may see Embraer EMB-145 regional jets introduced.

Today, Transbrasil operates international and domestic scheduled and charter flights for passengers and cargo with an all-Boeing fleet. Ownership has passed to the Fontana family. In conjunction with Varig (qv) and VASP (qv). Transbrasil (qv) is a participant in the Air Bridge Shuttle between Rio de Janeiro and São Paulo. The airline plans to double the number of aircraft in its fleet by 2010.

Executive Directors & Officers: Dr Omar Fontana, Chairman & President; Norival de Barros, Director Accounting & Finance; Adilson Hijano, Director Flight & Ground Operations; Sergio Kuczynski, Director Route & Fleet Planning; Carlos Adalberto Ferreira, Director Administration & Control; Carlos Eduardo Bonato, Director Information Services; Valeria Pereira Fontana, Director Planning of Inflight Services; Francisco Eustaquio Mendes, Director Maintenance & Engineering; Gianfranco Zioni Beting, Director Marketing & Advertising; Carlos Augstroze, Director International Sales; Mario Jorge Bento, Director National Sales; Flavio Marcio B. Carvalho, Director Cargo; Gabriel Athayde, Senior Vice-President Administration & Finance; Francisco Carlos Fonseca, Advisor, Legal Affairs.

HQ Airport & Main Base: São Paulo, with an additional hub at Brasilia

Radio callsign: TRANSBRASIL

Designator: TR/TBA

Employees: 5,288

Main destinations served: More than 20 destinations are served in eastern Brazil, as well as international operations to Amsterdam, Buenos Aires, Miami, New York, Orlando, Vienna.

LINKS WITH OTHER AIRLINES
Owns Interbrasil Star.

FLEET
3 Boeing 767-300ER
5 Boeing 767-200ER
3 Boeing 767-200
4 Boeing 737-400
8 Boeing 737-300

Varig is Latin America's largest airline.

VARIG

SA Empresa de Viçao Aérea Rio Grandense

Incorporated: 1927

HISTORY

The largest airline in Latin America and second-largest in the southern hemisphere, Varig was founded by a German immigrant, Otto Ernst Meyer. The new airline started operations in 1927 with technical assistance from the German Condor syndicate, which had itself been formed by Lufthansa (qv) to operate the South American section of the German airline's trans-South Atlantic air-sea mail service. Varig's role was to operate the Brazilian routes, which it did using a Dornier Wal flying-boat, ideal for operations from the many rivers which provided the best landing places in dense jungle.

Although Varig expanded its operations throughout the 1930s and 1940s – despite the shortages of equipment and spares from North America and Europe during World War Two – it remained a domestic carrier. In 1951 the airline's operations, which had been concentrated on the southern part of Brazil, were expanded by the acquisition of Aéro Geral. Two years later, in 1953, the first international service came, with a route to the United States. More significant international expansion did not follow until 1961, when Varig acquired the REAL consortium, including Aérovias Brasilia, Nacionale, and Aéronorte, which at a stroke quadrupled Varig's international network and doubled

its domestic network as well. Transatlantic services eventually came in 1965 when Panair do Brasil collapsed, forcing the Brazilian Government to offer the route rights to Varig, which also took over the defunct airline's equipment, including the lease on a Douglas DC-8.

Another major addition to Varig's operations were the routes and equipment of another airline with a mixture of domestic and some international routes within South America, Cruzeiro do Sol, which also dated from 1926 but which had been nationalised in 1943. Varig's owners, the Ruben Berta Foundation, acquired Cruzeiro do Sol in 1975 and integrated its operations with those of Varig to prevent duplication, especially on the international routes. Many of Cruzeiro do Sol's regional services passed to a new airline, Rio-Sul (qv), founded in 1976 with a major route network throughout southern Brazil; this is a subsidiary of Varig, which owns 95 per cent of its shares. A wholly-owned subsidiary of Rio-Sul is Nordeste Linhas Aéreas Regionais (qv).

Today, Varig remains Brazil's leading airline, with a world-wide route network and, in contrast to many airlines in the region, an outstanding safety record. In conjunction with VASP (qv) and Transbrasil (qv) it is a participant in the Air Bridge Shuttle between Rio de Janeiro and São Paulo, and in 1997 it joined the 'Star Alliance', which brings together frequent flyer programmes and other services for Air Canada (qv), Lufthansa (qv), SAS (qv), Thai International (qv), and United Airlines (qv), as well as Varig.

Executive Directors & Officers:
Fernando Abs da Cruz de Souza Pinto, Chairman, President & Chief Executive Officer; Carlos Ebner Neto, Finance Director; Eldy Jorge Binder, Flight Operations Director; Luis C. Gama Mons, Operational Logistics Director; Gilson Gomes Novo, Commercial Director; Claudio Afonso Junqueira, Engineering Director; Manoel Jose F. Torres, Planning Director; Odilon Junqueira, Administration & Human Resources Director.

HQ Airport & Main Base: Rio de Janeiro

Radio callsign: VARIG

Designator: RG/VRG

Employees: 18,203

Main destinations served: Almost 40 domestic destinations are served, including Belem, Brasilia, Natal, Recife, and São Paulo, with a number of international flights routed through or having connections from Belem, Brasilia, Recife, or São Paulo. Main international destinations from Rio de Janeiro are Amsterdam, Asunçion, Bogotá, Buenos Aires, Cancun, Caracas, Frankfurt, Hong Kong, Johannesburg, Lima, Lisbon, London Heathrow, Los Angeles, Madrid, Mexico City, Miami, Montevideo, New York JFK, Panama, Paris, Rome, Santiago, Tokyo, Zürich.

Annual turnover: US $2,963 million (£1,795.8 million).

LINKS WITH OTHER AIRLINES

Rio-Sul (qv) and Nordeste (qv) are subsidiaries.

Star Alliance member with Air Canada (qv), Lufthansa (qv), SAS (qv), Thai International (qv), and United Airlines (qv). Marketing alliances exist with Delta Air Lines (qv), Ecuatoriana (qv), Japan Air Lines (qv), LACSA (qv), and TAP Air Portugal (qv).

FLEET

5 Boeing 747-300
9 McDonnell Douglas MD-11
7 McDonnell Douglas DC-10-30
2 McDonnell Douglas DC-10-30F
6 Boeing 767-300ER
6 Boeing 767-200ER
5 Boeing 727-100F
17 Boeing 737-200Adv
30 Boeing 737-300 (5 leased)
12 Boeing 737-500 (operated by Rio-Sul)
10 Fokker 50 (operated by Rio-Sul)
12 Embraer EMB-120 Brasilia (operated by Rio-Sul)

VASP

SA Viaçao Aérea de São Paulo

Incorporated: 1933

HISTORY

Originally founded by the state government of São Paulo in Brazil in 1933, VASP has grown to become Brazil's second-largest airline, with an extensive domestic network serving all of the major airports in Brazil as well as regional routes within São Paulo, and with a growing international network. In 1991 the airline was privatised, when a majority stake was acquired by the VOE/Canhedo Group. VASP itself has extensive stakes in three other airlines – Ecuatoriana, LAB (Lloyd Aéro Boliviano) (qv), and TAN in Argentina. The most important of the airlines in which VASP has an investment, however, is TAM (qv), a major Brazilian regional carrier which moved out of air taxi operations and into airline work with the support of VASP in 1976. Although VASP has just 3.35 per cent of TAM today, when the airline was formed VASP held almost a quarter of the shares. There has been speculation that VASP might buy the stake in Aérolineas Argentinas (qv) held by Iberia (qv) should the Spanish airline need to sell it to meet European Union constraints on state aid.

In conjunction with Varig (qv) and Transbrasil (qv), VASP is a participant in the Air Bridge Shuttle between Rio de Janeiro and São Paulo.

Executive Directors & Officers: Wagner Canhedo Azevedo, President & Chief Executive Officer; Wagner de Goes, Marketing Director; Cesar Antonio Canhedo Azevedo, Vice-President Financial & Administration; A.H. Browne, Vice-President Operations & Planning; Wagner Ferreira, Vice-President Marketing & Sales; Luiz Sergio Chiessi, Vice-President Industry Affairs & Commercial Planning; Rodoefo Canhedo, Vice-President USA/Canada/Europe; Jose Fernando Martins Ribeiro, Vice-President Legal Affairs.

HQ Airport & Main Base: Aéroport de Congonhas, São Paolo

Radio callsign: VASP

Designator: VP/VSP

Employees: 6,400

Main destinations served: Almost 30 destinations within Brazil, as well as international services from São Paolo to Aruba, Barcelona, Brussels, Buenos Aires, Frankfurt, Guayaquil, Quito, Los Angeles, Miami, New York JFK, Osaka, Seoul, Toronto, Zürich.

Annual turnover: US $1,165 million (£706 million)

LINKS WITH OTHER AIRLINES

Has shareholdings in TAM (qv) (3.35 per cent), Ecuatoriana (50.1 per cent), LAB (qv) (51 per cent), and TAN (82 per cent).
Marketing alliances with Olympic (qv) and LAB (qv).

FLEET

9 McDonnell Douglas MD-11
3 Airbus A300B2
3 Boeing 727-200F

20 Boeing 737-200
2 Boeing 737-200C/F
2 Boeing 737-300

Brunei – V8

ROYAL BRUNEI

Royal Brunei Airlines Sendirian Berhad

Incorporated: 1974

HISTORY

Owned by the government of Negara Brunei Darussalam, Royal Brunei Airlines was founded in 1974, initially having a fleet of two Boeing 737s, one of which operated the first scheduled flight from Banar Seri Begawan to Singapore on 14 May. Before the year was out services had also been introduced to Hong Kong, Kota Kinabalu, and Kuching. Further routes were added in the succeeding years and an additional 737 was acquired in 1980. Longer range aircraft followed in 1986 with three Boeing 757-200s, which enabled new services to Taipei, Dubai, and Frankfurt to be introduced, with London Gatwick following after the delivery of Boeing 767s in 1990. Services to London switched to Heathrow the following year.

While international air services were being established the potential for domestic air services was not neglected, with the delivery of Fokker 50 turboprops in 1994, since replaced by Fokker 100s. A joint marketing agreement and code-sharing has been introduced with United Airlines (qv), while there is also a code-sharing agreement with British Midland. The airline intends in the near future to sell its Boeing 757s and 767-300ERs as well as the

This Royal Brunei Boeing 767-300ER is one of the airline's largest aircraft.

Fokker 100s and concentrate on creating a more standardised fleet of aircraft powered by Pratt & Whitney engines.

Executive Directors & Officers:
Pengiran Laila Kanun Diraja Pengiran Haji Bahrin, Chairman; Haji Brahim bin Haji Ismail, Managing Director & Chief Executive Officer; Nelson Chong, Finance Director; Captain Mike Fox, Flight Operations Director; Arthur Austin, Engineering Director; Susie Wong, Administration Services Director; Brian Johnson, Management Information Services Director; George Tan, Sales & Services Director; Haji Yahya Cheman, Human Resources & Services Director.

HQ Airport & Main Base: Bandar Seri Begawan

Radio callsign: BRUNEI

Designator: BI/RBA

Employees: Flight-crew: 147; Cabin staff: 475; Engineering: 441; Administration: 268; Ground staff: 188; Total: 1,519.

Main destinations served: Bandar Seri Begawan to Abu Dhabi, Bali, Balikpapan, Bangkok, Beijing, Bintulu, Brisbane, Calcutta, Darwin, Dubai, Frankfurt, Hong Kong, Jakarta, Jeddah, Kota Kinabalu, Kuala Lumpur, Kuching, Labuan, London Heathrow, Manila, Miri, Osaka, Perth, Singapore, Taipei, Yangon.

Aircraft km pa: 24,385,097

Revenue passenger km pa: 2,712,406,133

Cargo tonne km pa: 108,079,081

LINKS WITH OTHER AIRLINES
Marketing and code-sharing link with United Airlines (qv).
Code-sharing with British Midland (qv).

FLEET
9 Boeing 767-300ER
2 Boeing 757-200ER
2 Fokker 100

Bulgaria - LZ

BALKAN BULGARIAN

Balkan Bulgarian Airlines

Incorporated: 1947

HISTORY
The national airline of Bulgaria, Balkan was founded by the Bulgarian Government in 1947 as BVS, and operations on domestic routes started the following year. The new airline had but a short existence, however, for in 1949 its services were taken over by TABSO, owned jointly by the Bulgarian Government and the Soviet Union. The emphasis remained on domestic operations until 1954, when control of TABSO finally passed to the Bulgarian Government and a start was made on developing an international network. The first services were to Warsaw, Copenhagen, Frankfurt, Paris, Athens, Moscow, and Beirut, using Lisunov Li-2s (Russian-built DC-3s) and Ilyushin Il-14s. Turbine equipment did not appear until 1962, when Ilyushin Il-18 turboprops were introduced and new services were started to Tunisia and Algeria. The potential of the Black Sea resorts for holidaymakers began to be appreciated at this time, and charter flights were operated from the rest of Europe from 1963 onwards.

Other aircraft followed the Il-18s, including Antonov An-12s and An-24s, and the first jets, Tupolev Tu-134s, introduced in 1968. Later the larger Tupolev Tu-154 also entered service with TABSO.

Throughout most of its existence TABSO was more than simply an airline, being also responsible for many other aspects of civil aviation. This changed in 1986, when the non-airline functions were removed and the current title was adopted. The breaking up of the old Soviet empire also paved the way for Balkan to obtain modern western equipment, more economical and efficient than the aircraft available from the former Soviet Union. While the fleet is currently a mixture of Russian and American aircraft, it seems likely that, as funding permits, new equipment will be of Boeing manufacture. Meanwhile considerable route expansion has taken place across the Atlantic and into Africa and the Middle East.

Executive Directors & Officers: Valeri Doganov, President & Chief Executive Officer; Plamen Nakev, Vice-President Finance; Rashko Rashkov, Vice-President Operations; Vassil Barnev, Vice-President Maintenance; Kostadin Vatev, Vice-President Marketing; Anguel Antonov, Vice-President External Relations; Yordan Bobev, Personnel Director.

HQ Airport & Main Base: Sofia

Radio callsign: BALKAN

Designator: LZ/LAZ

Employees: 3,900

Main destinations served: A small domestic network is operated, plus inter-national flights from Sofia to Abu Dhabi, Algiers, Amsterdam, Athens, Bangkok, Barcelona, Cairo, Calcutta, Casablanca, Colombo, Copenhagen, Delhi, Dresden, Frankfurt, Harare, Helsinki, Istanbul, Jakarta, Johannesburg, Khartoum, Kiev, Kuala Lumpur, Lagos, Lisbon, London Heathrow, Madrid, Malta, Moscow, Munich, Nairobi, New York JFK*, Nicosia, Paris, Prague, Rome, Singapore, St Petersburg, Stockholm, Tunis, Vienna, Warsaw, Zürich.
* via Malta

LINKS WITH OTHER AIRLINES
Marketing alliances with Air Malta (qv), Iberia (qv) (plus a code-share), and a joint venture with Air France (qv).

FLEET
2 Boeing 767-200ER
7 Tupolev Tu-154M
7 Tupolev Tu-154B-2
6 Antonov An-24
4 Antonov An-12
2 Ilyushin Il-18
3 Boeing 737-500

Burma

See Myanmar

Cambodia – XU

ROYAL AIR CAMBODGE

Royal Air Cambodge

Incorporated: 1994

HISTORY
Originally founded in 1994 by the Cambodian Government and Malaysian Airlines (qv), Royal Air Cambodge commenced operations the following year. A fleet of three ATR 72s was acquired for domestic routes, while two Boeing 737-400 were wet-leased from Malaysian Airlines for international services. After a military coup, a wholly state-owned airline, Kampuchea Airlines, was formed to take over Royal Air Cambodge's routes, but further changes have meant that this possibility has now receded and that Royal Air Cambodge will continue to operate, although it seems that just one Boeing 737 will be used for the time-being.

Executive Directors & Officers: Vichit

Ith, Chairman & Chief Executive Officer;
David Chew, Chief Operating Officer;
George Tam, Chief Financial Officer;
Morris Ong, Vice-President, Commercial;
Rosly Kassim, Vice-President, Engineering
& Flight Operations.

HQ Airport & Main Base: Phnom Penh

Radio callsign: CAMBODGE

Designator: VJ/RCU

Main destinations served: Some seven
domestic destinations are served from
Phnom Penh, plus Guangzhou, Ho Chi
Minh City, Hong Kong, Kuala Lumpur,
Singapore.

FLEET
1 Boeing 737-400
3 ATR 72

Cameroon – TJ

CAM-AIR

Cameroon Airlines

Incorporated: 1971

HISTORY
Cameroon Airlines was formed in 1971
after the Cameroon Government decided
to cease support of the Air Afrique (qv)
consortium, and initially the airline was
owned 75 per cent by the government and
25 per cent by Air France (qv), although
the latter is now reduced to a nominal
shareholding.

Executive Directors & Officers: Joseph
Belibi, Chairman; Jean-Gabriel Ceccareli,
Director General & Chief Executive
Officer; A. Oumarou, Financial Director;
Bernard Nsang, Commercial Director;
Ignatius Sama Juma, Technical Director;
L.P. Mota, Development & Audit Director.

HQ Airport & Main Base: Douala

Radio callsign: CAM-AIR

Designator: UY/UYC

Employees: 1,400

Main destinations served: Abidjan,
Accra, Bamako, Bangui, Bata, Brazzaville,
Brussels, Bujumbura, Cotonou, Garoua,
Harare, Jeddah, Johannesburg, Khartoum,
Kinshasa, Lagos, Libreville, Lome, London
Gatwick, Malabo, Maroua, Nairobi,
Ndjamena, Ngaoundere, Paris CDG,
Principe, São Tome, Yaounde.

LINKS WITH OTHER AIRLINES
Marketing alliances with Air France (qv),
Air Gabon (qv), Air Zaire (qv), Nigeria
Airways (qv), and Oman Air (qv).

FLEET
1 Boeing 747-200B Combi
1 Boeing 737-300
2 Boeing 737-200C
1 British Aerospace 748 Super 2B

Canada – C

AIR ALLIANCE

Air Alliance

Incorporated: 1988

HISTORY
Established as an Air Canada Connector in
1988 with the Deluce family holding 25
per cent of the shares and Air Canada (qv)
the remainder, Air Alliance is now completely owned by Air Canada. Operations
are centred upon the province of Quebec,
but there are services from Montreal to the
United States.

Executive Directors & Officers: Paul
Letourneau, Chairman; Robert Perrault,
President & Chief Executive Officer;
Mario Lemay, Financial Director; Christian
Leger, Maintenance & Operations
Director; Lucie Francoeur, Director,
Commercial.

HQ Airport & Main Base: Aéroport
International Jean Lesage, Saint Foy,
Quebec, with a further hub at Montreal.

Radio callsign: LIAISON

Designator: 3J/AAQ (or Air Canada AC)

Employees: 300

Main destinations served: Montreal to
Boston, New York Newark, Philadelphia.
Domestic destinations include Bagotville,
Baie Comeau, Gaspe, Hartford, Iles de la
Madeleine, Mont Joli, Montreal, Ottawa,
Quebec City, Rouyn-Noranda, Sept Iles,
Val d'Or, Wabush.

Annual turnover: Included in Air
Canada figures.

LINKS WITH OTHER AIRLINES
Subsidiary of Air Canada (qv). An Air
Canada Connector operator.

FLEET
7 de Havilland Dash 8-100
5 Beech 1900D

AIR ATLANTIC

Air Atlantic Ltd

Incorporated: 1986

HISTORY
Formed in 1986, Air Atlantic operates as a
Canadian Partner (qv), and, under a
restructuring plan designed to rationalise
operations and reduce costs, has now
been given responsibility for all Canadian
(qv) operations into and out of St John's in
Newfoundland. The airline was acquired
by the Halifax, Nova Scotia, based IMP
Group early in 1995.

Executive Directors & Officers:
Stephen Wetmore, Executive Vice-
President & Chief Executive Officer;
Angus Marks, Vice-President, Finance;
Robert J. Gosse, Vice-President,
Operations; Captain Robert Lierschaft,
Director of Flight Operations; James
Penwell, Director of Maintenance; Kirk
Rowe, Director of Marketing & Sales.

HQ Airport & Main Base: St John's,
Newfoundland

Radio callsign: AIR ATLANTIC

Designator: 9A/ATL

Employees: 520

Main destinations served: St John's to
Boston, Charlo, Charlottetown, Chatham,
Deer Lake, Fredericton, Gander, Halifax,
Moncton, Montreal, Ottawa, Prince
Edward Island, St John (New Brunswick),
Stephenville, Sydney (Nova Scotia).

LINKS WITH OTHER AIRLINES
A Canadian Partner (qv).

FLEET
3 British Aerospace 146-200
6 de Havilland Dash 8-100
5 British Aerospace Jetstream 41

AIR BC

Air BC

Incorporated: 1980

HISTORY
Air BC was formed in 1980 on the merger
of several small airlines in the west of
Canada. From 1983 to 1986 it operated as
a Canadian Pacific Commuter, but this
alliance with the predecessor of Canada's
other major airline, Canadian International
(qv), ended when Air Canada (qv)
acquired an 85 per cent shareholding in
November 1986, later increasing this to

100 per cent. The fleet has included Jetstream 31 and Twin Otter aircraft, but has now standardised on British Aerospace 146s and de Havilland Dash 8s. The policy of major airlines handing shorter and less heavily used routes to smaller airlines who can operate them more economically means that, in this case, Air BC has the distinction of operating Air Canada's original route between Vancouver and Seattle.

Executive Directors & Officers: Mel Cooper, Chairman; H. Alan Thompson, President & Chief Executive Officer; Darrel G. Smith, Senior Vice-President, Operations; Robert Payne, Vice-President, Finance & Chief Financial Officer; Laureen Davies, Vice-President, Commercial; Bill Rattle, Vice-President, Maintenance; Scott Tapson, Vice-President, Customer Service; Sheila Mayo, Personnel Director.

HQ Airport & Main Base: HG at Richmond, British Columbia; hubs at Calgary and Vancouver.

Radio callsign: AIRCOACH

Designator: ZX/ABL (and Air Canada AC)

Employees: 1,200

Main destinations served: Air Canada Connector services throughout Alberta, British Columbia, and Saskatchewan, as well as Air Canada services from Vancouver to Portland and Seattle.

Annual turnover: Included in Air Canada figures.

LINKS WITH OTHER AIRLINES
Subsidiary of Air Canada (qv). An Air Canada Connector operator.

FLEET
5 British Aerospace 146-200
6 de Havilland Dash 8-300
12 de Havilland Dash 8-100

AIR CANADA

Air Canada

Incorporated: 1937

HISTORY
Air Canada dates from the formation of Trans-Canada Air Lines in 1937, brought into being by the Trans-Canada Air Lines Act of that year. The new airline was owned 100 per cent by Canadian National Railways, a Crown corporation, which meant that from the outset the airline was nationalised. An earlier plan for a mixed state and private enterprise operation with Canadian Pacific Railways as the other partner failed to materialise.

The new airline started operations by purchasing the Canadian Airways Company and its equipment, giving it an initial fleet of two twin-engined Lockheed 10A Electras and a single-engined Stearman biplane. With this equipment, a Vancouver–Seattle service was inaugurated. In 1938 additional services were introduced, with TCA flying from Winnipeg to Vancouver, Montreal, and Toronto, and to Edmonton and Lethbridge, so that by the end of the year the fleet had grown to five Lockheed 10A Electras and nine of the larger Lockheed 14Hs. Expansion continued eastwards, even after the outbreak of war in Europe, so that by 1940 operations had reached the Maritime Provinces, and Canada had its first transcontinental air services.

Development of domestic and cross-border services continued until 1943, when the airline obtained what was later to be an invaluable experience of transatlantic operation when it started the Canadian Government Trans-Atlantic Air Service, using Avro Lancastrians (converted Lancaster bombers) between Montreal and Prestwick in Scotland. The service carried important passengers and Canadian forces' mail between Canada and Europe.

The return of peace in 1945 saw TCA introduce a fleet of 30 Douglas DC-3s, and further expansion of both its domestic and cross-border services. In 1947 the Canadair DC-4M North Star (a licence-built Douglas DC-4 with Rolls-Royce Merlin engines) was placed in service, and TCA returned to transatlantic services, this time operating them in its own right. The DC-4 also operated a service to Mexico City. This expansion continued throughout the decade that followed, including, in 1957, a non-stop Toronto–London service operated by Lockheed Super Constellations, which had first been introduced in 1954. In 1955 TCA became the first North American operator of the Vickers Viscount turboprop airliner. Not all of the expansion was straightforward. In 1955 TCA traded its service to Mexico City in exchange for Canadian Pacific's network of services within Ontario and Quebec.

TCA's first jet airliners were Douglas DC-8-40s, introduced to the transatlantic services in 1960, while on domestic routes the Vickers Vanguard, another turboprop, entered service in 1961. Trans-Canada was one of just two airlines to operate this aircraft (the other was BEA), which was too slow and too late for passengers enchanted with the idea of jet air travel.

In 1964 the name was changed to Air Canada, finally reflecting the fact that the airline was no longer primarily a domestic operator, and that year the first short-haul jets, Douglas DC-9s, were ordered to begin Viscount replacement.

In common with many larger airlines, Air Canada has created a network of feeder services through the Air Canada Connector operation. The first Air Canada

Air Canada's growing fleet of Canadair Regional Jets has brought jet speeds and greater comfort to the less busy routes, and has improved frequencies on others.

Connector was Air Nova (qv) in 1986, followed soon afterwards by Air BC (qv). In Air Canada's case the feeder airlines are all subsidiaries, and now include Air Alliance (qv), Air Ontario (qv), and NWT Air, as well as Air Nova and Air BC.

The airline was privatised in 1989, and the greater flexibility this offered was exercised in 1992, when Air Canada decided to collaborate with Texas-based Air Partners and jointly invest $450 million in the restructuring programme for Continental Airlines (qv), enabling the American airline to emerge from Chapter 11 Protection in 1993. Today, Air Canada has a 19.6 per stake in Continental. In addition to code-sharing with Continental, the airline is a founder-member of the 'Star Alliance', which brings together frequent flyer programmes and other services for Lufthansa (qv), SAS (qv), Thai International (qv) and, in 1997, United Airlines (qv) and Varig (qv) as well as Air Canada. There is a further strategic alliance with Lufthansa.

Including the Air Canada Connector destinations, Air Canada today serves more than 120 destinations world-wide. An innovation has been the introduction of high frequency 'Rapidair' services between Montreal, Toronto, and Ottawa, with flights at half-hourly intervals at peak periods, and every quarter-hour on Montreal–Toronto in the early morning peak! A slightly less frequent 'Rapidair' network operates between Calgary and Edmonton International, and Calgary and Vancouver.

Executive Directors & Officers: John F. Fraser, Chairman; R. Lamar Durrett, President & Chief Executive Officer; Jean-Jacques Bourgeault, Senior Executive Vice-President; Robert A. Milton, Executive Vice-President & Chief Operating Officer; M. Robert Preston, Senior Vice-President, Finance & Chief Financial Officer; Douglas D. Port, Senior Vice-President, Europe; Geoffrey Elliot, Senior Vice-President, Corporate Affairs & Government Relations; John M. Baker, Vice-President & General Counsel; Paul E. Brotto, Vice-President, Finance & Treasurer; B. Wayne MacLellan, Vice-President, Flight Operations; Chris W. Nassenstein, Vice-President, Technical Operations; Lise Fournel, Vice-President, Information Technology & Chief Information Officer; Paul R. Garratt, Vice-President, Human Resources; G. Ross MacCormack, Vice-President, Corporate Strategy; Eileen McCoy, Vice-President, Airports; Rupert Duchesne, Vice-President, Marketing; Marc Rosenberg, Vice-President, Sales & Product

Distribution; H. Alan Thompson, President & Chief Executive Officer, Air BC; Paul Letourneau, Secretary of the Company.

HQ Airport & Main Base: Montreal Dorval International, with further hubs at Calgary, Halifax, Toronto, and Vancouver.

Radio callsign: AIR CANADA

Designator: AC/ACA

Employees: Flight-crew: 1,700; Cabin staff: 3,400; Engineering: 8,000; Ground staff: 3,300; Total: 21,000.

Main destinations served: More than 60 destinations within Canada and more than 30 in the United States and the Caribbean, plus Amman, Athens, Brussels, Delhi, Düsseldorf, Geneva, Glasgow, Helsinki, Hong Kong, Honolulu, London Heathrow, Manchester, Osaka, Paris CDG, Seoul, Tel Aviv, Zurich.

Annual turnover: US $3,578 million (£2,168 million)

Revenue passenger km pa: 19,199,000

Cargo tonne km pa: 1,252.8 million

Passengers pa: 12.6 million

LINKS WITH OTHER AIRLINES
Owns Air Alliance (qv), Air BC (qv), Air Nova (qv), Air Ontario (qv), and NWT Air, which operate as Air Canada Connector (qv).
Has a 19.6 per cent stake in Continental Airlines (qv).
A strategic alliance exists with British Midland (qv) and Lufthansa (qv).
Star Alliance member with Lufthansa (qv), SAS (qv), Thai International (qv), United Airlines (qv), and Varig (qv).
Code-sharing with Continental (qv), Korean Air (qv), and Royal Jordanian (qv).

FLEET
3 Boeing 747-400 Combi
3 Boeing 747-200 Combi
3 Boeing 747-100
8 Airbus A340-300 (leased) (plus 3 options)
6 Boeing 767-300ER
2 Boeing 767-300
23 Boeing 767-200
34 Airbus A320 (plus 6 on order)
35 Airbus A319 (leased) (1 painted in TCA livery to celebrate 60th anniversary)
35 McDonnell Douglas DC-9-30 (being replaced as A319s delivered)
24 Canadair CL-65 Regional Jet (leased) (plus 24 options)
Of the above four Boeing 747s, 18 767s, and 11 A320s are leased.

AIR CANADA CONNECTOR

Air Canada Connector first started in 1986, and embraces the operations of five Air Canada subsidiaries, namely Air Alliance (qv), Air BC (qv), Air Nova (qv), Air Ontario (qv), and NWT Air (Northwest Territorial Airways).

Air Canada Connector fleets are listed under the individual airline, although NWT Air has 3 Boeing 737 Combis and a Lockheed Hercules.

AIR CLUB INTERNATIONAL

Air Club International, Inc

Incorporated: 1993

HISTORY
Air Club International was founded in 1993 and commenced operations the following year, undertaking inclusive tour air charter services. During the summer months domestic charters and flights to Europe are undertaken, while during the winter months charters are operated to Hawaii and destinations in and around the Caribbean.

Executive Directors & Officers: Guy Dulude, Chairman; Claud Levesque, President & Chief Executive Officer; Sabin Chasse, Financial Controller; Denis Carbonneau, Operations Director; Michel Trepanier, Maintenance Director; Johanne Comte, Marketing Director; Gisele Trepanier, Personnel Director.

HQ Airport & Main Base: Montreal International Airport

Radio callsign: AIR CLUB

Designator: HB/CLI

Employees: 350

Main destinations served: Inclusive tour charters within North America, to Europe and the Caribbean.

FLEET
2 Boeing 747-200
5 Airbus A310-300

AIR CREEBEC

Air Creebec, Inc

Incorporated: 1982

HISTORY
The unusual name reflects ownership of Air Creebec by the Cree Indians' Creeco Corporation. The airline was founded in 1982 to operate regional services from Val d'Or in Quebec, and in 1989 it acquired the northern routes of Air Ontario (qv).

Executive Directors & Officers: Albert Diamond, President; David Bertrand, General Manager; Alain Laplante, Controller; Denis Prevost, Operations Manager; Joel Virtanen, Maintenance Manager.

HQ Airport & Main Base: Val d'Or, Quebec

Radio callsign: CREE

Designator: YN/CRQ

Employees: 166

Main destinations served: 18 destinations from Val d'Or, including Quebec City and Montreal.

LINKS WITH OTHER AIRLINES
Marketing alliances with Air Alliance (qv), Air Canada (qv), and Air Ontario (qv).

FLEET
5 British Aerospace 748
1 de Havilland Dash 8-100
2 Beech 1900D
2 Embraer EMB-110 Bandeirante

AIR INUIT

Air Inuit, Inc

Incorporated: 1977

HISTORY
Taking its name from its Inuit, or Eskimo, owners, Air Inuit was founded in 1977 as a regional scheduled and charter airline, operating mainly in northern Quebec. A subsidiary is Johnny May Air Charters. The airline is owned by Makivik, which also own First Air (qv).

Executive Directors & Officers: Mark T. Gordon, President; Robert J. Davis, Chief Executive Officer; Bill Thompson, Chief Operating Officer; Mike Voland, Chief Financial Officer; Peter Horsman, Chief Inspector; Tony Martin, Maintenance Director.

HQ Airport & Main Base: Montreal Dorval

Radio callsign: AIR INUIT

Designator: 3H/AIE

Employees: 200

Main destinations served: Destinations in northern Quebec.

LINKS WITH OTHER AIRLINES
Marketing alliances with First Air (qv).

FLEET
4 British Aerospace 748
4 Convair 580
1 de Havilland Dash 8-100 (leased)
4 de Havilland DHC-6 Twin Otter
1 de Havilland DHC-3 Otter

AIR LABRADOR

Labrador Airways Ltd
Incorporated: 1948

HISTORY
A small regional airline providing scheduled and charter services throughout Labrador, Air Labrador operates independently of the two main Canadian airline groups.

HQ Airport & Main Base: Goose Bay, Labrador

Radio callsign: LAB AIR

Designator: WJ/LAL

Employees: 75

Main destinations served: 13 destinations throughout Labrador.

FLEET
2 Short 360
3 Short 330
2 de Havilland Dash 8
4 de Havilland DHC-6 Twin Otter

AIR MANITOBA

Air Manitoba Ltd

Incorporated: 1963

HISTORY
Originally founded as Ilford Riverton Airways, the name of this regional airline was changed to Northlands Air Manitoba in 1983, and then again to Air Manitoba in 1990 when the Deluce family took a 50 per cent stake, with the remainder being held by Ilford Riverton Holdings.

Executive Directors & Officers: Terry Deluce, President & Chief Executive Officer; Todd Lamb, Vice-President, Finance; Abe Heibert, Flight Operations Director; Colin Carswell, Maintenance Director; Scott Edgar, Commercial Services Director.

HQ Airport & Main Base: HQ at Winnipeg International Airport, with an additional hub at Churchill.

Radio callsign: MANITOBA

Designator: 7N/NAM

Employees: 100

Main destinations served: Services within the province of Manitoba and the Northwest Territories.

FLEET
5 British Aerospace 748
3 Curtiss C-46 Commando
1 de Havilland Dash 8-100
1 Douglas DC-3

AIR NOVA

Air Nova

Incorporated: 1986

HISTORY
Air Nova was the first airline to became an Air Canada Connector when it was founded in 1986, to feed into Air Canada's (qv) route network at Halifax. Originally the airline was owned 49 per cent by Air Canada, with the remaining shares held by Atlantis Investments, although these were sold to a merchant bank, Shieldings, in 1989. Today Air Nova is a wholly-owned subsidiary of Air Canada. It has an extensive network in the Maritime Provinces, and also operates from Halifax to Boston and other airports in the north-east of the United States.

Executive Directors & Officers: Dr Angus Bruneau, Chairman; Joseph Randell, President & Chief Executive Officer; Lynn Loewen, Vice-President, Finance; Captain Grant Warner, Vice-President, Flight Operations; Keith Jones, Vice-President, Maintenance; Rick Flynn, Vice-President, Marketing; Laurel Clark, Vice-President, Customer Advocacy & Organisational Development; Winston Clarke, Director, Human Resources; Norm Richard, General Manager, Passenger Safety.

HQ Airport & Main Base: Halifax International Airport

Radio callsign: NOVA

Designator: QK/ARN (or Air Canada AC)

Employees: 600

Main destinations served: Halifax to Bathurst, Boston, Charlottetown, Deer Lake, Fredericton, Gander, Goose Bay, Moncton, Montreal, Ottawa, Quebec City, Saint Anthony, Saint Leonard, Saint John (New Brunswick), St John's (Newfoundland), Sydney, Yarmouth, Wabush.

Annual turnover: Included in Air Canada figures.

LINKS WITH OTHER AIRLINES
Subsidiary of Air Canada (qv). An Air Canada Connector operator.

FLEET
5 British Aerospace 146-20 (leased)
14 de Havilland Dash 8-100

AIR ONTARIO

Air Ontario

Incorporated: 1961

HISTORY
Originally founded in 1961 as an air taxi company, Air Ontario moved into scheduled services in 1967 under the name of Great Lakes Airlines, not adopting the present title until 1981. In 1987 it merged with Austin Airways, which dated from 1934 and which had acquired the scheduled services of Toronto Airways the previous year.

Air Ontario became an Air Canada Connector during the late-1980s, feeding into Air Canada (qv) services from smaller communities in central Canada and the northern United States. Air Canada acquired 75 per cent of the shares initially, leaving the remainder in the hands of the Deluce family, but the airline is now completely owned by Air Canada. The fleet consists entirely of de Havilland Dash 8s.

Executive Directors & Officers: David R. McCamus, Chairman; Stephen C. Smith, President & Chief Operating Officer; Judy Maxwell, Director of Finance; Brian Morris, Director Flight Operations & Inflight Service; John Aguiar, Director Maintenance; Bruce Maxim, Director System Operations Control; Anne Wilson, Director Marketing; Roy Colangelo, Director, Sales & Service, Central Canada & USA; Franco Gimapa, Director, Sales & Service, Intra-Ontario.

HQ Airport & Main Base: HQ at London, Ontario, main hub at Toronto.

Radio callsign: ONTARIO

Designator: GX/ONT (or Air Canada AC)

Employees: 744

Main destinations served: Baltimore, Cleveland, Hartford, London (Ontario), Montreal, New York La Guardia, New York Newark, North Bay, Ottawa, Sarnia, Sault St Marie, Sudbury, Thunder Bay, Timmins, Toronto City Centre, Washington National, Windsor, Winnipeg.

Annual turnover: Included in Air Canada figures.

LINKS WITH OTHER AIRLINES
Subsidiary of Air Canada (qv). An Air Canada Connector operator.

FLEET
6 de Havilland Dash 8-300
20 de Havilland Dash 8-100

AIR TRANSAT

Air Transat Ltd

Incorporated: 1986

HISTORY
Primarily a passenger charter carrier, Air Transat was founded in 1986, and has created a fleet of Lockheed L-1011 TriStars, to which it has recently added Boeing 757-200ERs.

Executive Directors & Officers:
François Legault, President; Philippe Sureau, Executive Vice-President; Alfred Ouimet, Senior Vice-President, Maintenance & Engineering; Pierre Menaud, Vice-President, Operations; Denis Petrin, Vice-President, Fleet Planning; Denis Jacob, Vice-President, Marketing & Sales.

HQ Airport & Main Base: Montreal International

Radio callsign: TRANSAT

Designator: TS/TSC

Employees: 900

Main destinations served: Charter operations throughout the Americas and to Europe.

Passengers pa: 1.75 million

FLEET
5 Lockheed L-1011-50 TriStar
1 Lockheed L-1011-100 TriStar
1 Lockheed L-1011-1 TriStar
2 Lockheed L-1011-500 TriStar
2 Airbus A330-200
5 Boeing 757-200ER
2 Boeing 737-400

CALM AIR

Calm Air Ltd

Incorporated: 1962

HISTORY
Founded in 1962 by Arnold Morberg, now President of the airline, and his wife, Calm Air initially operated charters in northern Saskatchewan. Expansion was boosted by the airline's 1976 acquisition of services operated by Transair in the Northwest Territories, while in 1987 Pacific Western acquired a 45 per cent shareholding, which has now passed to Canadian Regional Airlines (qv). Operating as a Canadian Partner (qv), Calm Air feeds into the Canadian network at Thompson and Winnipeg.

Executive Directors & Officers: C. Arnold Morberg, President; Steve Cymbalisty, Chief Financial Officer; Gary Beaurivage, Vice-President, Operations; R. Reeve, Director of Flight Operations; S. Abele, Chief of Maintenance.

HQ Airport & Main Base: Thompson, Manitoba

Radio callsign: CALM AIR

Designator: MO/CAV

Employees: 230

Main destinations served: Some 30 destinations in Northern Manitoba, the Northwest Territories, and Ontario.

LINKS WITH OTHER AIRLINES
Canadian Regional Airlines (qv) has a 45 per cent interest.
A Canadian Partner.

FLEET
5 British Aerospace 748
3 Saab 2000
2 de Havilland DHC-6 Twin Otter
1 Piper PA-31 Navajo Chieftain

CANADA 3000

Canada 3000 Airlines Ltd

Incorporated: 1988

HISTORY
Originally founded as Air 2000 in 1988, the name was changed the following year to avoid confusion with another airline. The first aircraft were Boeing 757-200ERs for long-haul passenger charter operations, and while this fleet has grown to nine aircraft they have also been augmented by Airbus A320s and A330s.

Executive Directors & Officers: John M.S. Lecky, Chairman; Nagus J. Kinner, President; D.P. Kennedy, Vice-President, Finance; D.V. Thompson, Vice-President, Flight Operations; Ike Rahemtulla, Vice-President, Engineering & Marketing; Brad C. Rawson, Vice-President, Sales & Marketing.

HQ Airport & Main Base: HQ at Toronto, but charters are also flown from Calgary, Edmonton, Halifax, Montreal, Vancouver, and Winnipeg.

Radio callsign: ELITE

Designator: 2T/CMM

Employees: 1,406

Main destinations served: Charters throughout North America, to Hawaii, the Caribbean, and Europe.

FLEET
2 Airbus A330-200 (leased)
9 Boeing 757-200ER
6 Airbus A320-200

CANADIAN

Canadian Airlines Ltd

Incorporated: 1988

HISTORY
Canadian is the main operating subsidiary of Canadian Airlines International and the result of a merger between four airlines which took effect in 1988. The largest two of these were Canadian Pacific, which had been Canada's second-largest airline for many years, and Pacific Western Airlines, which was one of Canada's largest regional carriers at the time. The other two were Eastern Provincial Airways and Nordair, which had already been acquired by CP Air in 1984 and 1985 respectively, along with Eastern Provincial's subsidiary, Air Maritime.

Canadian Pacific Airlines, more usually known in its latter days as CP Air, was the airline subsidiary of a major group, Canadian Pacific, which had been formed in the 19th century to build and operate a transcontinental railway, and whose operations had spread to include, at one time, transatlantic ocean liner operation. By the 1960s the group was involved in container shipping and ferries, hotels, road transport, oil, gas, and timber production, mining, and property development, in addition to the airline.

Canadian Pacific had rejected Canadian Government proposals for a joint venture airline during the late-1930s, leaving the Government to form Trans Canada

Airlines, the predecessor of today's Air Canada (qv). Instead, Canadian Pacific Airlines was eventually formed in 1942 on the merger of ten small airlines, most of which were bush operators. The largest of these was Canadian Airways, a Winnipeg-based operator in which the Canadian Pacific Railway had held the controlling interest since 1930. The others comprised Ginger Coote Airways of Vancouver; Yukon Southern Air Transport of Vancouver and Edmonton; Wings of Winnipeg; Prairie Airways of Moose Jaw; Mackenzie Air Services of Edmonton; Arrow Airways of Manitoba; Starratt Airways of Hudson; Quebec Airways; and Montreal and Dominion Skyways. The CPR had in fact held a permit to operate aircraft commercially since 1919. The decision to press ahead with the formation of Canadian Pacific Airlines had been taken in 1939, realising that many of the small airlines were in poor financial shape and operating aircraft ill-suited to their services. Before the new airline was born, the CPR had already been involved directly in aviation, helping to establish the North Atlantic Ferry Service for the delivery of bombers to the Royal Air Force in 1940, and during the war years it was to operate six flying schools.

CP Air's initial priorities were to continue and consolidate the bush services of its predecessor companies, doing this in the midst of wartime demands which made re-equipment difficult. Post-war, the airline had its strategy firmly set on transpacific operations, and in 1949 services to Sydney and Hong Kong were inaugurated. The Korean War also saw the airline undertake some 700 military charter flights between Vancouver and Tokyo. The airline was one of the select band to operate the unfortunate de Havilland Comet I jet airliner before this was withdrawn during the early-1950s. In exchange for its services in Ontario and Quebec, in 1955 CP Air obtained Air Canada's Mexico City route, which it was able to extend to Buenos Aires. That same year a polar route between Vancouver and Amsterdam was established, using Douglas DC-6Bs. The transformation from bush airline to long-haul operator was completed in 1959, when CP Air introduced its first transcontinental service, using Bristol Britannias. The Canadian Government then granted the airline authority to expand its transcontinental operations so that by 1970 it could operate 25 per cent of the long-haul domestic market. Jet equipment followed, with Douglas DC-8s for the longer routes, and, later, Boeing 737-100s for the shorter domestic and cross-border services.

Pacific Western (PWA) dated from 1946, when it was founded as Central British Columbia Airlines, but adopted the title Pacific Western in 1953. In 1955 PWA acquired Queen Charlotte Airlines and Associated Airways. The third level operations were sold in 1966 to Northward Aviation. During this period a very mixed fleet was operated, including a Douglas DC-3, two DC-4s, two DC-6Bs, two DC-7Cs, four Convair 640s, a Lockheed Hercules, and a Boeing 707-138B, while disposal of the third level operations had meant that an Otter and two Beavers left the fleet, along with three Grumman Goose amphibians! PWA took over BC Airlines in 1970, and a further acquisition occurred in 1979 with the merging of PWA and Winnipeg-based Transair, in which PWA had acquired a 72 per cent stake in 1977.

On its formation, Canadian Airlines found itself with a mixed fleet of Airbus, Boeing, and McDonnell Douglas manufacture, but it also had a route network which was well spread across Canada, rather than, as previously, heavily slanted towards the western provinces. In addition it had interests in other airlines, while it also inherited the 'Canadian Pacific Commuter' network of feeder services. Some standardisation of the fleet occurred, so that it no longer operated both Airbus A310s and Boeing 767s, for example. Between 1991 and 1994 the organisation itself was streamlined, and AMR Corporation, the parent company for American Airlines, took a 31 per cent share in Canadian Airlines International, the parent for both Canadian and Canadian Regional Airlines (qv), with the remainder being held by a holding company, Canadian Airlines Corporation.

Today, Canadian operates transatlantic and transpacific flights, services to Mexico, Brazil, and Argentina, and a major transcontinental and trunk route network in Canada itself, augmented by the feeder operations of its Canadian Partner (qv) network, which includes airlines owned by Canadian's sister company, Canadian Regional Airlines. Shuttle services are run under the 'Canadian Shuttle' branding, linking Toronto and Montreal, and Ottawa and Toronto in the east, and in the west Calgary and Vancouver, Edmonton and Vancouver, and Calgary and Edmonton. In addition to close co-operation with American Airlines, marketing alliances exist with many other major international airlines.

Executive Directors & Officers: H.R. Steele, Chairman; K.E. Benson, President & Chief Executive Officer; D.A. Carty,

Senior Vice-President & Chief Financial Officer; S.P. Sibold, Senior Vice-President, General Counsel & Corporate Secretary; D.G. Bell, Vice-President & Treasurer.

HQ Airport & Main Base: Calgary, with additional major bases/hubs at Edmonton, Montreal, Toronto, Vancouver, and Winnipeg.

Radio callsign: CANADIAN

Designator: CP/CDN

Employees: Flight-crew: 1,133; Cabin staff: 2,568; Engineering: 4,234; Ground staff: 5,293; Total: 13,228.

Main destinations served: More than 125 destinations in Canada and the United States, as well as Auckland, Bangkok, Beijing, Buenos Aires, Frankfurt, Hong Kong, Honolulu, Kuala Lumpur, London Heathrow, Melbourne, Nadi, Nagoya, Mexico City, Monterrey, Paris CDG, Rio de Janeiro, Rome, Santiago de Chile, São Paulo, Shanghai, Sydney, Tokyo.

Annual turnover: US $2,271 million (£1,376 million)

Revenue passenger km pa: 25,832 million

Passengers pa: 8,578 million

LINKS WITH OTHER AIRLINES
Sister company of Canadian Regional Airlines (qv), and feeder services are provided by Canadian Partner (qv). American Airlines has a 31 per cent stake, and a strategic alliance includes marketing co-operation and code-sharing. Marketing alliances with Air New Zealand (qv), Alitalia (qv), Japan Airlines (qv), Lufthansa (qv), Malaysian Airlines (qv), Mandarin Airlines (qv), Philippine Airlines (qv), Qantas (qv), and Varig (qv).

FLEET
4 Boeing 747-400
10 McDonnell Douglas DC-10-30
11 Boeing 767-300ER
14 Airbus A320-200
43 Boeing 737-200

CANADIAN PARTNER

The Canadian Airlines (qv) network of regional feeder services is marketed as Canadian Partner, or Partnaire Canadien. The participating airlines are Air Alma, Air Atlantic (qv), Aklak Air, Calm Air International (qv), Canadian Regional Airlines (qv), Canadian's sister airline with-

in Canadian Airlines International, and Inter Canadien (qv). Details are recorded in the entries for the individual airlines.

CANADIAN REGIONAL AIRLINES

Canadian Regional Airlines Ltd

Incorporated: 1991

HISTORY
Canadian Regional Airlines is a wholly-owned subsidiary of Canadian Airlines International and the sister company of Canadian Airlines (qv). It was established in 1991, three years after the merger which created Canadian Airlines, to take over the shareholdings in smaller regional airlines inherited mainly from PWA (Pacific Western Airlines). The merged operations of two 100 per cent-owned subsidiaries, Time Air and Ontario Express, provided the basis for the fleet and network of Canadian Regional Airlines, but it was also given responsibility for the investments in other airlines, including Inter-Canadien (qv) (70 per cent) and Calm Air (qv) (45 per cent).

Time Air operated both scheduled and charter flights in the west of Canada, as well as the Yukon and Northwest Territories, and across the border into the United States. Formed in 1966, at the time of its merger into Canadian Regional it was operating a fleet consisting mainly of de Havilland Dash 8s, of which there were 18, including both 8-10 and 8-300 versions, as well as three older Convair 580s, three Short 360s, and its first jet equipment, six Fokker F-28 Fellowships. Pacific Western's involvement dated from 1984, when it had acquired a 40 per cent shareholding, and the airline was bought out in 1991.

Ontario Express dated from 1987 and operated in Ontario and Quebec. PWA had a 49 per cent shareholding in the airline, and again this was increased to 100 per cent in 1991. At the time of the merger, Ontario Express was operating 14 British Aerospace Jetstream 31s, nine EMB-120 Brasilias, and six ATR42-300s.

Since the merger Canadian Regional Airlines has been through a programme of consolidation and rationalisation, with far fewer aircraft types in the fleet following the recent retirement of the ATR-42 and Short 360 aircraft. The route network is based on central and western Canada, with no involvement in the east, which

remains the preserve of other Canadian Partners. The stake in Inter-Canadien has been increased to 100 per cent. As part of a restructuring and rationalisation plan, all services into St John's in Newfoundland are now being operated by Air Atlantic (qv), a Canadian Partner.

Executive Directors & Officers: Mary B. Jordan, President; Ted Sheldon, Director, Corporate Accounting & Business Planning; Peter Scheiwiller, Director Flight Operations; Wally Beck, Director Maintenance; Sue Dabrensky, Director, In-Flight Services; Steve Bullock, Director, Customer Service & Corporate Quality; Mike Miller, Director, People & Information Systems.

HQ Airport & Main Base: Calgary International Airport, with further hubs at Toronto and Vancouver.

Radio callsign: CANADIAN REGIONAL

Designator: KI/CDR (or Canadian CP)

Employees: 2,000

Main destinations served: Calgary, Campbell River, Castelgar, Comox, Cranbrook, Edmonton, Fort McMurray, Fort Nelson, Fort Smith, Fort St John, Grande Prairie, Hay River, High Level, Kamloops, Kelowna, Kingston, Lethbridge, London (Ontario), Medicine Hat, Nanaimo, Peace River, Penticton, Port Hardy, Prince George, Rainbow Lake, Regina, Sandspit, Sarnia, Saskatoon, Sault Ste Marie, Smithers, Sudbury, The Pas, Thompson, Thunder Bay, Toronto, Vancouver, Victoria.

Annual turnover: Included in figure for Canadian Airlines.

LINKS WITH OTHER AIRLINES
Subsidiary of Canadian Airlines International.
Inter-Canadien (qv) is a wholly-owned subsidiary.
A 45 per cent stake is held in Calm Air (qv).
A Canadian Partner (qv).
Marketing agreements with American Airways (qv) and British Airways (qv).

FLEET
18 Fokker F-28-1000
14 de Havilland Dash 8-300
10 de Havilland Dash 8-100
10 ATR 42

CANAIR

Taken over by Royal Airlines (qv) in August 1997.

CONIFAIR

Conifair Aviation, Inc

Incorporated: 1979

HISTORY
Conifair started operations as a charter specialist and operator of tanker aircraft for forest fire-fighting duties. Restructuring and reorganisation in 1992 after the creation of a passenger charter airline, Royal Airlines (qv), led to Conifair becoming one of the operating divisions of what had become Groupe Royal Aviation.

Executive Directors & Officers:
Victor M. Rivas, Chairman & Chief Executive Officer; John R. Walters, President & Chief Operating Officer; Charles Horn, Chief Financial Officer; Ken Skinner, Director Operations; James Crowder, Maintenance Director.

HQ Airport & Main Base: Aéroport de Quebec, Sainte-Foy

Designator: QN/ROY

Main destinations served: Ad hoc cargo charter flights and fire-fighting.

LINKS WITH OTHER AIRLINES
A subsidiary of Groupe Royal Aviation.

FLEET
1 Lockheed Constellation
5 Douglas DC-6
4 Douglas DC-4
1 Convair 580

FIRST AIR

First Air Ltd

Incorporated: 1946

HISTORY
First Air dates from 1946, when it was formed as Bradley Flying School before later moving into scheduled and charter air services as Bradley Air Services. it operates throughout Canada, but is best known as a specialist in Arctic air services. In 1971 the company opened what was then the world's most northerly air service, to Eureka on Ellesmere Island, although this is no longer operated. First Air is a wholly-owned subsidiary of Makivik, Air Inuit (qv) is a sister company, and a subsidiary is Ptarmigan Airways.

Executive Directors & Officers: Kamal B. Hanna, President; Donald K. Orr, Senior Director, Flight Operations; Rene Creton, Director, Engineering; Stephen Nourse, Director, Planning & Projects;

Steven R. Rourke, Vice-President, Finance; Andrew G. Campbell, Vice-President, Sales & Commercial Operations.

HQ Airport & Main Base: Carp Airport, Ontario, with additional bases at Hall Beach, Iqaluit, Resolute Bay, and Yellowknife.

Designator: 7F/FAB

Employees: 700

Main destinations served: Some 20 destinations in and around the province of Ontario, including Montreal.

LINKS WITH OTHER AIRLINES
Marketing alliances with Air Inuit (qv) and Greenlandair (qv).

FLEET
3 Boeing 727-200F
1 Boeing 727-200C
3 Boeing 727-100C
1 Boeing 737-200
1 British Aerospace 748-2B
7 British Aerospace 748-2A
12 de Havilland DHC-6 Twin Otter
1 Grumman Gulfstream 1
1 Beech 99
1 Beech King Air 100
1 Beech Super King Air 200
2 de Havilland DHC-2 Beaver

FLIGHTCRAFT

Kelowna Flightcraft Air Charter Ltd

Incorporated: 1974

HISTORY
Kelowna Flightcraft was formed in 1970 as an aircraft engineering organisation, specialising in the conversion of Convair 240/340/440 Metropolitan airliners. Its air charter subsidiary dates from 1974, and undertakes cargo charters, usually on a long-term contract basis for couriers such as Purlator and FedEx (qv). Passenger operations take anglers to fishing lodges in British Columbia. A recent joint venture has been the provision of scheduled low fare passenger services with Greyhound Air, but these services, which used seven Boeing 727s, were abandoned in September 1997.

Executive Directors & Officers: Barry Lapointe, President; Ralph Wagner, Chief Financial Officer; Greg Carter, Chief Operating Officer; Jim Rogers, General Manager; Dave Rowlands, Vice-President, Maintenance.

HQ Airport & Main Base: Kelowna Airport, British Columbia

Radio callsign: FLIGHTCRAFT

Designator: KF/KFA

Employees: 60

Main destinations served: Charter freight and ad hoc passenger services to remote areas.

FLEET
7 Boeing 727-200Adv
2 Boeing 727-200C
9 Boeing 727-100C
16 Convair 580
1 Douglas DC-3
1 Gulfstream I
2 Cessna 402B
1 Beech 60 Duke
1 Cessna 340

INTER-CANADIEN

Inter-Canadien Ltd

Incorporated: 1991

HISTORY
Although the Inter-Canadien airline dates officially from 1991, it can trace its history back to the founding of Air Rimouski in 1946, the name of which changed to Quebecair in 1952. In 1983 the Quebec Provincial Government acquired the airline, but in 1986 announced that Quebecair was to be returned to the private sector. The following year was a remarkable one for a small airline, not only returning to the private sector with the support of a 35 per cent shareholding by CP Air, a predecessor of Canadian Airlines (qv), but also operations and equipment were merged with two other airlines, Nordair Metro and Quebec Aviation, and the name was changed to Inter-Canadien. The merged airline operated as a Canadian Pacific Commuter operator initially, but in 1989, after the creation of Canadian Airlines, the main body of shareholders based in Quebec terminated their agreement with Canadian Airlines, and changed the company name to Intair. For its short life, Intair operated seven Fokker 100 jet airliners and seven ATR-42s.

Intair was in need of restructuring and refinancing by 1991, and at one time operations ceased. Canadian Regional Airlines (qv), a sister company of Canadian Airlines, took a 70 per cent majority shareholding to restart the airline as a regional turboprop operation, and revived the Inter-Canadien title dropped so abruptly some two years earlier. From the start the revived airline operated as a Canadian Partner. In 1994 the remaining shares were also purchased by Canadian Regional.

Canada's leading passenger charter airline, Royal has two Lockheed L-1011 TriStars for use on its longer routes.

Executive Directors & Officers:
Duncan Fischer, President; Ted Sheldon, Financial Director; Laurent Marcoux, Operations Director; Wally Beck, Maintenance Director; Mike Miller, Personnel Director; Michael Gagne, General Manager.

HQ Airport & Main Base: Montreal Dorval International

Radio callsign: INTER-CANADIEN

Designator: QB/ICN

Employees: 450

Main destinations served: Some 30 destinations in Quebec Province and the surrounding provinces.

Annual turnover: US $53 million (£31 million)

LINKS WITH OTHER AIRLINES
A wholly-owned subsidiary of Canadian Regional Airlines (qv).
A Canadian Partner (qv).

FLEET
3 Fokker F28
7 ATR 42-300

MILLARDAIR

Millardair Ltd

Incorporated: 1954

HISTORY
Founded by the eponymous Carl Millard in 1954, the airline operated as Carl Millard Ltd until 1962, when the present title was adopted. Today it is owned and managed by the founder's son. Operations are charter, both passengers and cargo, mainly within North America and the Caribbean.

Executive Directors & Officers: Wayne Millard, President; Carl Millard, Senior Vice-President & Operations Director.

HQ Airport & Main Base: Mississauga, Ontario

Radio callsign: MILLARDAIR

Designator: MAB
Main destinations served: Charters within North America and the Caribbean.

FLEET
4 Douglas DC-4

4 Douglas DC-3
4 Piper PA-31 Navajo

ROYAL

Royal Airlines, Inc

Incorporated: 1992

HISTORY
Royal Airlines is the operating division of Groupe Royal Aviation, which was founded as Conifair Aviation in 1979, and today Conifair (qv) continues to operate as a sister company to Royal. The airline was formed in 1992 as a passenger charter specialist, operating its first flight on 29 April 1992 when a Boeing 727-200 flew from Toronto to Vancouver. A second 727 was added before the end of the first year. Wide-bodied equipment for transatlantic charter flights entered service in 1993 with the arrival of a Lockheed L-1011 TriStar. Rapid growth followed, although, faced with fierce competition, the airline had to reduce its capacity in 1996.

Today, Royal is Canada's leading charter

The Boeing 727-200 is another popular charter aircraft, ideal over medium ranges of around 2,000 miles.

airline, operating services for inclusive tour operators throughout North America and across the Atlantic, reinforcing its position in August 1997 by the acquisition of CanAir Cargo. CanAir Cargo dated from 1989, and operated international and domestic cargo services from its base at Toronto International Airport. Royal is continuing CanAir's trans-Canada cargo service and has absorbed its employees and aircraft. For the immediate future, Royal plans to find a replacement for its Boeing 727s.

Royal Vacations Inc is a subsidiary.

Executive Directors & Officers: Michel Leblanc, President & Chief Executive Officer; Louis McGuire, Vice-President, Finance & Chief Financial Officer.

HQ Airport & Main Base: Montreal Dorval International, with maintenance base at Quebec City.

Designator: QN/ROY

Employees: Aircrew: 555; Engineering: 90; Ground staff: 105; Total: 750.

Main destinations served: North America and the Caribbean, Europe including France and the UK, Ireland, the Netherlands, Sweden, Germany, Austria, and Greece, plus a scheduled trans-Canada freight service.

Annual turnover: US $195.2 million (£118.3 million)

Revenue passenger km pa: 3,195.7 million

Cargo tonnes pa: 25,000

LINKS WITH OTHER AIRLINES
Subsidiary of Groupe Royal Aviation.

FLEET
3 Lockheed L-1011 TriStar
4 Airbus A310-300 (2 leased)
1 Boeing 757
2 Boeing 727-200
2 Boeing 737-200F

WESTJET

Westjet Ltd

Incorporated: 1996

HISTORY
A 'low fare, no frills' carrier, Westjet was formed in 1996 to pioneer this type of operation in the deregulated Canadian market, concentrating principally on the main centres in the western provinces.

Executive Directors & Officers: Clive Beddoe, Chairman & Chief Executive Officer; Don Clark, Chief Financial Officer

& Chief Operating Officer; Tim Morgan, Director, Flight Operations; Mark Hill, Director, Corporate Planning; George Cazamier, Director, Maintenance & Engineering; Gareth Davies, Director, Technical Services; Marlene Egeland, Director, Inflight Services; Dan Gallaher, Director, Customer Services; Bill Lamberton, Director, Marketing; Don Bell, Director, Reservations & Information Systems.

HQ Airport & Main Base: Calgary

Designator: M3/NLF

Employees: 340

Main destinations served: Calgary, Edmonton, Kelowna, Vancouver, Victoria, Winnipeg.

FLEET
2 Boeing 737-200
3 Boeing 737-200A

Cape Verde – D4

TACV CABO VERDE AIRLINES

Transportes Aéreos de Cabo Verde

Incorporated: 1958

HISTORY
Originally formed in 1958 to fly scheduled and charter flights within the Cape Verde Islands, operations were suspended in 1967 pending a reorganisation. After independence in 1975 the airline was designated the national carrier, and was nationalised in 1983. For a time long-haul operations to Amsterdam, Lisbon, and Paris were attempted, using a McDonnell Douglas DC-10-30 of Linhas Aéreas de Mocambique (qv), but these have since been abandoned. Today services within the islands continue, with regional services to the African mainland.

HQ Airport & Main Base: Praia, Santiago, Cape Verde

Radio callsign: TRANSVERDE

Designator: VR/TCV

Employees: 580

Main destinations served: Praia to Banjul, Bissau, Boa Vista, Brava, Dakar, Maio, Mosteiros, Sal, San Antonao, São Nicolau, São Vicente.

FLEET
1 Boeing 757
4 ATR 42-300
2 de Havilland DHC-6 Twin Otter

Chile – CC

LADECO

Ladeco Chilean Airlines – Línea Aérea del Cobre SA

Incorporated: 1958

HISTORY
Originally founded as a domestic airline, Ladeco has since expanded into international services. All of the main cities in Chile are on the route network. In recent years the airline has replaced its Boeing 707s, four British Aerospace One-Elevens, and a McDonnell Douglas DC-8F. A marketing alliance exists with Carnival Air Lines, which has been taken over by PanAm (qv).

Ladeco is owned by Boris Hirmas and the Cueto family.

Executive Directors & Officers: Jose Luis Ibanez, President; Alfonso Laval, Vice-President, Finance & Administration; Jorge Goles, Vice-President, Commercial.

HQ Airport & Main Base: Santiago de Chile

Radio callsign: LADECO

Designator: UC/LCO

Employees: 1,800

Main destinations served: Santiago to Antofagasta, Arica, Balmaceda, Calama, Concepción, Guatemala City, Havana, Iquique, La Serena, Mendoza, Miami, Montego Bay, Montevideo, Neuquin, New York JFK, Panama City, Puerto Montt, Punta Arenas, Rio de Janeiro, San Jose, San Juan, Santo Domingo, São Paulo, Temuco, Ushaja, Valdivia, Vina del Mar, Washington Dulles.

LINKS WITH OTHER AIRLINES
Marketing alliance with PanAm (qv).

FLEET
2 Boeing 757-200ER
2 Boeing 727-100
1 Boeing 737-300
11 Boeing 737-200

LAN-CHILE

Línea Aérea Nacional de Chile

Incorporated: 1929

HISTORY
The story of LAN-Chile dates from 1929, when the Chilean Government formed

Línea Aérospostal Santiago-Arica, which was managed by the air force. A fleet of eight de Havilland Gipsy Moths operated the service. Growth was rapid, and during its first three years the airline acquired a varied fleet, including Ford Trimotors, Curtiss Condors, and Potez 56s. It passed into civilian control in 1932, and the present title dates from that time.

The first international service was not started until 1946, when a service to Buenos Aires was introduced using Douglas DC-3s to fly over the Andes. Martin 202s soon augmented the DC-3 fleet and the airline did not acquire its first four-engined equipment – pressurised Douglas DC-6Bs – until 1955. These were used to establish new services, first to Lima and Guayaquil, and then, in 1958, to Panama City. The first jet aircraft were Caravelles, introduced in 1962.

A change of government in 1964 led to a serious attempt to stem the airline's losses and cut the government subsidy, which was reduced substantially over the next two years. In 1966 a modernisation programme started, with Hawker Siddeley (later BAe) 748 turboprops introduced to replace the DC-3s. Long-haul jet equipment followed, although the first Boeing 707-330 was obtained second-hand from Lufthansa (qv), and services were introduced to Miami and New York. In 1974 the airline was the first to link Australia with South America via the South Pole. Another innovation some years later, in 1986, was the use of a Boeing 767 for the first twin-jet scheduled service across the Atlantic, operating from Santiago de Chile to Madrid via Rio de Janeiro. Three years later the airline was privatised, and today ownership is in the hands of four major shareholders.

The airline plans to replace its Boeing 737-200s in the near future.

Executive Directors & Officers: Enrique Cueto, President; Luis Ernesto Videla, General Manager.

HQ Airport & Main Base: Santiago de Chile

Radio callsign: LAN

Designator: LA/LAN

Employees: 2,700

Main destinations served: Antofagasta, Arica, Balmaceda, Buenos Aires, Calama, Caracas, Concepción, Copiapo, Coyhaique, Easter Island, El Salavdor (Chile), Frankfurt, Iquique, Isla de Pascua, La Paz, La Serena, Lima, Madrid, Mexico City, Montevideo, New York JFK, Osorno, Papeete, Puerto Montt, Punta Arenas, Rio de Janeiro, Santa Cruz de la Sierra, São Paulo, Temuco, Valdivia.

LINKS WITH OTHER AIRLINES
A marketing alliances exists with Air New Zealand (qv).

FLEET
7 Boeing 767-300ER
2 Boeing 767-200
9 Boeing 737-200
2 British Aerospace 146-200

China – B

AIR CHINA

Air China

Incorporated: 1988

HISTORY
Air China dates from 1988, when the Chinese Government decided to reorganise and break up the former CAAC (Civil Aviation Administration of China), which had run the Chinese national airline of that name and almost everything else connected with civil aviation. Today, CAAC is purely an administrative body with responsibility for controlling Chinese civil aviation.

CAAC itself had dated from 1964, when it took over the merged operations of Skoga – a joint Soviet Union–Communist Chinese airline dating from 1950 – and the China Civil Aviation Corporation, a wholly Chinese-owned domestic airline. The Soviet interest in Skoga was lost in the take-over, which had followed years of increasing tension between the two countries. This led to the new CAAC operating not only a very mixed fleet, but also a very elderly one. While utility aircraft were built in China to Soviet designs, China looked to the West for new equipment, buying Hawker Siddeley Tridents and Boeing 707-320s, which augmented an earlier purchase of Vickers Viscounts.

After 1988 Air China became the main domestic trunk and international carrier, while other parts of the former CAAC were spun off into regional carriers, many of which soon began to operate international services and even to appear on certain domestic trunk routes. The need to modernise soon saw more American and European aircraft appear in service, not simply because of continuing tensions with the former Soviet Union and its successors, but because of the superior operating economics of these aircraft. Route expansion also followed, so that today Air China serves 30 cities in 23 countries. Reflecting a more liberal economic out-look, the airline expects a stock exchange listing during 1998, but meanwhile ownership remains with the Chinese Government. In a direct challenge to the Hong Kong-based airlines, a Beijing–Hong Kong–London route has been introduced.

Executive Directors & Officers: Yin Wenlong, President & Chief Executive Officer; Wang Jiewu, Vice-President, Commercial & Deputy Chief Executive Officer; Zhang Fu Gui, Vice-President, Operations; Fu Baoxin, Vice-President, Technical.

HQ Airport & Main Base: Beijing

Radio callsign: AIR CHINA

Designator: CA/CCA

Employees: 14,000

Main destinations served: Beijing to Addis Ababa, Amsterdam, Ankara, Anqing, Bangkok, Beihai, Belgrade, Berlin, Bucharest, Cairo, Changchun, Changzhou, Chengdu, Copenhagen, Dalian, Datonge, Dubai, Frankfurt, Fukuoka, Fuzhou, Guangzhou, Guilin, Haikoou, Hailar, Hangzhou, Harbin, Helsinki, Hohhot, Hong Kong, Huanghua, Istanbul, Jakarta, Karachi, Kunming, Kuwait, London Heathrow, Melbourne, Milan, Moscow, Nanchang, Nanjing, Nanning, Nantong, New York JFK, Ningbo, Osaka, Paris CDG, Qingdao, Rome, San Francisco, Sendai, Seoul, Shanghai, Sharjah, Shenyang, Singapore, Stockholm, Sydney, Taiyuan, Tanjing, Tel Aviv, Tokyo, Tunxi, Ulan Bator, Vancouver, Vienna, Wuhan, Xiamen, X'an, Xiungfan, Yangon, Yantai.

Annual turnover: US $1,299 million (£787.3 million)

LINKS WITH OTHER AIRLINES
Revenue-sharing with Asiana (qv) and Korean Airlines (qv).
Marketing alliances with Austrian (qv), Finnair (qv), and Lufthansa (qv).

FLEET
8 Boeing 747-400
1 Boeing 747-200F
3 Boeing 747-200 Combi
4 Boeing 747SP
8 Airbus A340-300
7 Boeing 777-200 (deliveries start late-1998)
4 Boeing 767-300
6 Boeing 767-200ER
5 Boeing 737-700/880
19 Boeing 737-300
4 British Aerospace 146-100
2 Antonov An-12
2 Antonov An-24

AIR GREAT WALL

Air Great Wall

Incorporated: 1992

HISTORY
Air Great Wall was formed in 1992 by the Civil Aviation Flying Institute of China, and operates regional services mainly in Sichuan province.

Executive Directors & Officers: Huang Mingshun, President.

HQ Airport & Main Base: Jiangbei Airport, Chongqing, Sichuan

Radio callsign: CHANGCHENG

Designator: G8/CGW

Employees: 150

Main destinations served: Chongqing to Shanghai and other domestic and regional destinations.

FLEET
2 Tupolev Tu-154M
1 Boeing 727-200
3 Boeing 737-200
3 XAC Y-7-100

AIR WUHAN

Wuhan Airlines

Incorporated: 1986

HISTORY
A comparatively small scheduled service airline operating from its base at Wuhan in Hubei Province, mainly on domestic services and also to Ho Chi Minh City and Hanoi in Vietnam.

Executive Directors & Officers: Cheng Yaokin, Chief Executive Officer.

HQ Airport & Main Base: Wuhan, Hubei

Designator: WU/CWU

Employees: 400

Main destinations served: Beijing, Chengdu, Chongqing, Dalian, Enshi, Fuzhour, Guangzhou, Guiyang, Haikou, Hanoi, Hangzhou, Ho Chi Minh City, Huangyan, Kunming, Nanjing, Ningbo, Shanghai, Shantou, Shenyang, Shenzhen, Tianjin, Wenzhou, Xian, Xiamen, Yiwu.

FLEET
6 Boeing 737-300 (leased)
2 SAP Y-5
4 XAC Y-7-100

CHINA EASTERN

China Eastern Airlines

Incorporated: 1988

HISTORY
One of the remnants of the former CAAC, China Eastern was formed in 1988 and ownership remains with the Chinese Government. Shanghai-based, the airline has undergone considerable expansion, especially on international services, reflecting a more relaxed economic regime in Shanghai and the surrounding area, where foreign investment in industry has been encouraged. In 1997 the airline floated on both the New York and Hong Kong stock exchanges, the first mainland Chinese airline to do so, selling 32 per cent of its stock to private investors and making the raising of funds for future expansion easier.

Executive Directors & Officers: Wang Lian, President; Hu Ding Zhou, Vice-President.

HQ Airport & Main Base: Hongqiao International Airport, Shanghai

Radio callsign: CHINA EASTERN

Designator: MU/CES

Employees: 6,290

Main destinations served: Some 50 domestic destinations from Shanghai, plus Bangkok, Brussels, Chicago O'Hare, Fukuoka, Hong Kong, Los Angeles, Madrid, Nagasaki, Nagoya, Osaka, Seattle, Seoul, Singapore, Tokyo.

LINKS WITH OTHER AIRLINES
Revenue-sharing agreement with Asiana (qv).

FLEET
1 McDonnell Douglas MD-11F
5 McDonnell Douglas MD-11
7 Airbus A340-300
10 Airbus A300-600
9 McDonnell Douglas MD-90-30
13 McDonnell Douglas MD-82
10 Fokker 100
3 Antonov An-24
7 XAC Y-7

CHINA FLYING DRAGON

Feilong Airlines

Incorporated: 1981

HISTORY
One of the few airlines to precede the break up of CAAC in 1988, China Flying Dragon, or Feilong Airlines, was established in 1981 by the Harbin Aircraft Manufacturing Corporation and the Ministry of Geological Mineral Resources to operate short-haul passenger and cargo flights. Initially operations were linked into the founders' business activities, but the airline now operates on a more commercial basis. Maritime surveillance, forestry protection, and aerial photographic duties are also undertaken.

Executive Directors & Officers: Wu Caibao, President.

HQ Airport & Main Base: Harbin

Radio callsign: FEILONG

Designator: CFA

Employees: 600

Main destinations served: Primarily local operations.

FLEET
14 HAMC Y-11
8 HAMC Y-12
4 de Havilland DHC-6 Twin Otter
8 Eurocopter Ecureil

CHINA GENERAL AVIATION

China General Aviation Corporation

Incorporated: 1989

HISTORY
Another operator which has emerged from the former CAAC, China General Aviation Corporation is sometimes described as the only substantial general aviation concern in China, reflecting the broad diversity of CAAC's operations. While the company reflects western ideas of 'general aviation' in some respects, with a fleet which includes Bell 212 and Eurocopter Bo-105 helicopters, as well as Beech Super King Airs, some aircraft in the fleet are larger, including the Antonov An-30s and Yakovlev Yak-42Ds. Again in contrast to western ideas of general aviation, there is a scheduled network.

Executive Directors & Officers: Zhang Changjing, President.

HQ Airport & Main Base: Wu-SU Airport, Taiyuan, Shanxi

Radio callsign: TONGHANG

Designator: GP/CTH

Employees: 3,800

Main destinations served: Domestic charter plus a scheduled network covering some 30 destinations.

FLEET
3 Antonov An-30
7 Yakovlev Yak-42D
5 HAMC Y-12
8 SAP Y-5
3 XAC Y-7-100
10 Mil Mi-8
5 de Havilland DHC-6 Twin Otter
9 Bell 212
2 Beech Super King Air 200
2 Eurocopter Bo-105

CHINA NORTHERN

China Northern Airlines

Incorporated: 1990

HISTORY
One of the largest airlines in China, China Northern is a descendent of a division of CAAC. It has recently taken over the operations of Swan Airlines, based at Harbin. Most of the fleet is of western origin, if Chinese-assembled MD-82s are included. In addition to serving the main internal destinations, charter flights are operated to Japan and Korea, as well as to other points in South-East Asia, and it has been designated as the major Chinese carrier to Macau, the Portuguese enclave which will be reverting to Chinese rule in the near future.

Executive Directors & Officers: Wang Kaiyuan, President; Wang Guqun, Deputy General Manager Commercial; Wang Xuanwen, Flight Operations.

HQ Airport & Main Base: Shenyang, with additional hubs at Shenzhen and Harbin.

Radio callsign: CHINA NORTHERN

Designator: CJ/CBF

Employees: 4,800

Main destinations served: Beijing, Changchun, Changsha, Chengdu, Chongqing, Dalian, Dandong, Fuzhou, Guangzhou, Haikou, Hangzhou, Harbin, Hefei, Jilin, Jinan, Kunming, Macau, Nanjing, Nanning, Ningbo, Qingdao, Qinhuangdao, Shanghai.

FLEET
6 Airbus A300-600R
11 McDonnell Douglas MD-90-30
18 SAIC/McDonnell Douglas MD-82
7 McDonnell Douglas MD-82
25 SAP Y-5
11 XAC Y-7
9 Mil Mi-8

CHINA NORTHWEST

China Northwest Airlines

Incorporated: 1990

HISTORY
A fairly substantial airline with its origins in CAAC, China Northwest operates from Xian and has more than 70 routes, including international services to Macau, Nagoya, and Singapore, and services to Hong Kong, now an autonomous region within China. The airline is believed to have applied for authority to operate to Bangkok. The fleet is becoming orientated towards European aircraft, although a number of Russian and Chinese types are also operated. Charter flights are also undertaken.

Executive Directors & Officers: Gao Junqui, President; Wang Wancai, Vice-President; Wang Fu Tang, Vice-President.

HQ Airport & Main Base: Xian, Shanxi Province

Radio callsign: CHINA NORTHWEST

Designator: WH/CNW

Employees: 2,000

Main destinations served: More than 70 routes within China, as well as to Hong Kong, Macau, Nagoya, and Singapore.

FLEET
5 Airbus A300-600R
3 Airbus A310-200
9 Tupolev Tu-154M
10 Airbus A320
7 British Aerospace 146-300
3 British Aerospace 146-100
11 SAP Y-5
7 XAC Y-7

CHINA SOUTHERN

China Southern Airlines

Incorporated: 1989

HISTORY
One of the largest Chinese airlines, but with its origins in the old CAAC, China Southern has an extensive route network which includes a number of international destinations. An alliance with United Airlines is being considered, while the fleet shows Boeing aircraft to be heavily represented. China Southern has a 60 per cent stake in Xiamen Airlines (qv).

Executive Directors & Officers: Captain Yu Yanen, President & General Manager; Liue Wen Bo, Financial Director; Yu Zhong Can, Commercial Director; Shen Tai Ran, Engineering Director; Chen Ren De, Maintenance Director; Huang Yan Tang, Marketing Director; Hu Zhi Qun, Personnel Director; Li Zhong Mina, Vice-President, Operations; Hu Yun Qi, Vice-President, Maintenance; Zhang Rui Ai, Vice-President, Commercial.

HQ Airport & Main Base: Baiyun Airport, Guangzhou

Radio callsign: CHINA SOUTHERN

Designator: CZ/CSN

Employees: 7,820

Main destinations served: Bangkok, Beijing, Changsha, Changchun, Chengdhu, Chongqing, Dalian, Guangzhou, Fuzhou, Hangzhou, Harbin, Haikou, Hanoi, Hefei, Hong Kong, Jakarta, Kuala Lumpur, Kunming, Manila, Nanning, Nantong, Ningbo, Osaka, Penang, Quilin, Shantou, Shanghai, Shashi, Shenzhen, Surabaya, Vientiane, Wenzhou, Wuhan, Wulumqi, Yantai, Yichang, Zhanjiang, Zhuhai, Xiamen, Xian.

LINKS WITH OTHER AIRLINES
Holds a 60 per cent stake in Xiamen Airlines (qv).

FLEET
5 Boeing 777-200IGW
6 Boeing 767-300
23 Boeing 737-300
19 Boeing 737-200
19 Boeing 737-500
20 Airbus A320-200
5 Antonov An-24V
4 Saab 340B
21 SAP Y-5
5 XAC Y-7
4 Sikorsky S-76
2 Eurocopter S-76A

CHINA SOUTHWEST

China Southwest Airlines

Incorporated: 1989

HISTORY
A medium-sized airline by Chinese standards, China Southwest – another offshoot of CAAC – is based at Chengdu in Sichuan. Scheduled and charter operations are undertaken, usually internally, but also to Lhasa in Tibet, an autonomous region, and Kathmandu in Nepal.

Executive Directors & Officers: Zhou Zhengquan, President; Song Xian Jie, Vice-President.

HQ Airport & Main Base: Shuangliu Airport, Chengdu, Sichuan Province

Radio callsign: CHINA SOUTHWEST

Designator: SZ/CXN

Employees: 4,000

Main destinations served: More than 70 domestic routes from Chengdu, as well as Lhasa and Kathmandu.

FLEET
1 Boeing 707-320
5 Tupolev Tu-154M
13 Boeing 757-200
20 Boeing 737-300
4 HAMC Y-12
3 XAC Y-7

CHINA UNITED

China United Airlines

Incorporated: 1986

HISTORY
Unusually, China United is not a product of the break-up of CAAC, but instead is a unit of the Chinese Air Force, or Air Force of the People's Liberation Army, which operates commercial air services in co-operation with local enterprises. Although most of the aircraft are of Soviet origin, some western types are operated.

Executive Directors & Officers: Yang Kang-Qi, President; Nie Sheng Li, General Manager.

HQ Airport & Main Base: Beijing

Radio callsign: LIANHANG

Designator: HR/CUA

Main destinations served: Entirely domestic, to around 50 destinations.

FLEET
16 Tupolev Tu-154M
5 Ilyushin Il-76
5 Canadair CRJ-100
6 Boeing 737-300
9 Antonov An-24RV
8 Antonov An-26

CHINA XINJIANG AIRLINES

Xinjiang Airlines

Incorporated: 1985

HISTORY
A joint venture between the province of Xinjiang and CAAC, each of which holds 50 per cent of the shares, Xinjiang Airlines dates from 1985, and was originally a division within the old CAAC.

Executive Directors & Officers: Zhang Ruifu, President; Yang Yan Pingo, Director General; Zhang Rei Pu, Vice-President.

HQ Airport & Main Base: Diwopu International Airport, Urumqi, Xinjiang

Radio callsign: XINJIANG

Designator: XO/CXJ

Employees: 4,600

Main destinations served: Urumqi to some 30 domestic destinations, including Beijing, Harbin, and Shanghai, as well as to Aimaty, Hong Kong, and Islamabad.

FLEET
8 Tupolev Tu-154M
2 Ilyushin Il-86
4 Boeing 757-200
2 Boeing 737-300
2 Antonov An-24
5 ATR 72
7 SAP Y-5
2 de Havilland DHC-6 Twin Otter

CHINA YUNNAN

China Yunnan Airlines

Incorporated: 1992

HISTORY
A subsidiary of CAAC, China Yunnan operates from Kunming in Yunnan Province with a Boeing fleet. Services are predominantly domestic, despite the capabilities of its Boeing 767-300ERs.

Executive Directors & Officers: Xue Xiaoming, President; Zhao Zong Bao, Vice-President, Maintenance.

HQ Airport & Main Base: Wujaba Airport, Kunming, Yunnan Province

Radio callsign: YUNNAN

Designator: 3Q/CYH

Employees: 2,200

Main destinations served: Domestic scheduled.

FLEET
3 Boeing 767-300ER
12 Boeing 737-300

HAINAN AIRLINES

Hainan Airlines

Incorporated: 1989

HISTORY
One of the few truly private enterprise airlines in China, with some ten shareholders including American investors, Hainan Airlines was formed in 1989, though operations did not start until 1993. While scheduled services are operated, the airline also undertakes charters, including executive jet charters. It was the first domestic Chinese airline to seek a stock market listing, in this case on the Shanghai Stock Exchange.

Executive Directors & Officers: Cheng Feng, Chairman & President; Wang Jian, Executive Vice-President; Li Qing, Vice-President; Chen Wen Li, General Manager, Flight Operations.

HQ Airport & Main Base: HQ at Haikou, with a secondary base at Ningbo.

Radio callsign: HAINAN

Designator: H4/CHH

Employees: approx 1,100

Main destinations served: Beijing, Beihai, Changsha, Chengdu, Chongqing, Dalian, Fuzhou, Guiyang, Guangzhou, Hangzhou, Kunming, Nanchang, Nanjing, Sanya, Shanghai, Shenzhen, Urumqi, Wenzhou, Wuhan, Xiamen, Xian, Zhanjiang, Zhuhai.

FLEET
3 Boeing 737-800 (due late 1998)
4 Boeing 737-400 (plus 4 on order)
5 Boeing 737-300
9 Fairchild Metro 23
1 Learjet 55
2 Learjet 60

SHANGHAI AIRLINES

Shanghai Airlines

Incorporated: 1985

HISTORY
Claiming to be the first airline in China independent of any CAAC origins, Shanghai Airlines is a mixed venture airline, owned 75 per cent by the provincial government of Shanghai and 25 per cent by private interests. Services are entirely domestic, and are almost all scheduled.

Executive Directors & Officers: Sun Zhongli, President; Sun Zong Li, General Manager; Li Sheng Qin, Manager, Finance; Xu Bao Fang, Manager, Flight Operations; Ruan Zhu Rui, Manager, Maintenance.

HQ Airport & Main Base: Shanghai Hongqiao International

Radio callsign: SHANGHAI AIR

Designator: SF/CSH

Employees: 1,300

Main destinations served: Beijing, Chengidu, Fuzhou, Guangtzhou, Guilin, Harbin, Kunming, Lanzhou, Nanning, Shantou, Shenzhen, Wenzhou, Xiamen, Xian, Zhubai.

FLEET
4 Boeing 767-300 (plus 1 on order)
11 Boeing 757-200
3 Boeing 737-700 (deliveries start late-1998)

SHENZHEN AIRLINES

Shenzhen Airlines

Incorporated: 1993

HISTORY
A small scheduled domestic airline, Shenzhen is owned by a group of investors, including the state-owned Bank of China and China Travel Services.

Executive Directors & Officers: Duan Dayang, President & General Manager.

HQ Airport & Main Base: Shenzhen Airport, Shenzhen

Radio callsign: SHENZHEN AIR

Designator: 4G/CSZ

Employees: 385

Main destinations served: Beijing, Chengdu, Haikou, Hangzhou, Meixian, Nanjing, Shanghai, Wenzhou, Xiamen, Yantai, Zhengzhou.

FLEET
5 Boeing 737-300

SICHUAN AIRLINES

Sichuan Airlines

Incorporated: 1986

HISTORY
Founded in 1986, with operations starting in 1988.

Executive Directors & Officers: Lan

Xinglio, President; Xu Feng, Chief Executive Officer; Wu Qimm, Finance Director; Liu Changxia, Senior Vice-President; He Zhimin, Vice-President, Operations; Wang Tinghui, Vice-President, Technical.

HQ Airport & Main Base: Chengdu, Sichuan

Radio callsign: CHUANHANG

Designator: 3U/CSC

Employees: 1,100

Main destinations served: Some 24 destinations within China.

FLEET
4 Tupolev Tu-154M
4 Airbus A321
6 Airbus A320 (leased)
5 XAC Y-7-100

XIAMEN AIRLINES

Xiamen Airlines

Incorporated: 1992

HISTORY
Founded in 1992 and operating scheduled and charter flights from Xiamen in Fuijan Province, Xiamen Airlines has China Southern Airlines (qv) as its main shareholder, holding a 60 per cent stake.

Executive Directors & Officers: Wu Rongnan, President.

HQ Airport & Main Base: Gaoqi International Airport, Xiamen, Fuijan

Radio callsign: XIAMEN AIR

Designator: MF/CXA

Employees: 2,000

Main destinations served: Beijing, Changchun, Changsha, Changzhou, Chengdu, Chongqing, Dalian, Fuzhou, Guangzhou, Guilin, Guiyang, Haikou, Hangzhou, Harbin, Hefei, Jinan, Kunming, Luoyang, Nanchang, Nanjing, Nantong, Ningbo, Qindao, Shanghai, Shenzhen, Tianjin, Wenzhou, Wuhan, Wuyishan, Xian, Zhengzhou.

LINKS WITH OTHER AIRLINES
China Southern (qv) has a 60 per cent shareholding.

FLEET
5 Boeing 757-200
4 Boeing 737-200
5 Boeing 737-500

AIR HONG KONG

Air Hong Kong Ltd

Incorporated: 1988

HISTORY
Originally formed as a cargo charter operator, Air Hong Kong started scheduled cargo operations in 1989, initially operating to Manchester and Nagoya. Cathay Pacific (qv) now has a 75 per cent interest in the airline and has a management contract, while Air Hong Kong operates certain services for Cathay.

Executive Directors & Officers: Dr Stanley Ho, Chairman; Kenny Tang, Chief Operating Officer; Japhet Wai, Chief Financial Officer; Gerry Clemmow, Director of Operations & Engineering.

HQ Airport & Main Base: Chek Lap Kok, Hong Kong

Designator: LD/AHK

Employees: 178

Main destinations served: Brussels, Chicago, Dubai, Manchester.

LINKS WITH OTHER AIRLINES
Cathay Pacific (qv) has a 75 per shareholding and a management contract.

FLEET
3 Boeing 747-200 (leased from Cathay Pacific)

CATHAY PACIFIC

Cathay Pacific Airways Ltd

Incorporated: 1947

HISTORY
Although incorporated in 1947, Cathay Pacific's history started two years earlier, in October 1945, when an American, Roy Farrell – who during World War Two had flown supplies over the 'hump' between India and China – bought a war surplus Douglas C-47, which he had converted to DC-3 airliner standard. After arriving in Shanghai with the aircraft's first cargo from the United States, Farrell met a former wartime China National Aviation Company colleague, an Australian, Sydney de

Possibly repainted by now, this Cathay Pacific Boeing 747-200 was rendered in its special colour scheme in 1997 to mark the transfer of sovereignty to China.

Krantzow, and the two formed a partnership, flying woollen goods from Australia to China. The business was sufficiently successful for a second DC-3 to be obtained in 1946. Nevertheless, local rivalry led the partners to move to Hong Kong, where Cathay Pacific was founded in 1947.

Initially the airline operated charter passenger and freight flights from its new base, mainly to Manila, Macau, Bangkok, and Singapore, although on occasion the aircraft ranged as far afield as the United Kingdom. Five more DC-3s were pressed into service before the year was out, along with two Consolidated Catalina flying-boats, although flying-boat operations were abandoned after an aircraft was hijacked, all but one of the occupants and the aircraft being lost in the accident which followed.

By 1948 the airline was facing competition from Hong Kong Airways, formed by the local trading house of Jardine Matheson and BOAC (British Overseas Airways Corporation), with both airlines fighting to obtain licences for scheduled services. Another of Hong Kong's trading companies came to the rescue, investing in Cathay Pacific, and there was support from Australian National Airways (ANA). The new Cathay Pacific was owned 45 per cent by Butterfield and Swire, predeces-

sors of today's Swire Group, and 35 per cent by ANA, one of the predecessors of Ansett (qv), with the founders having 10 per cent each. The battle for route licences was resolved by the Hong Kong Government's proposal that the available licences be divided amongst the two companies, with Hong Kong Airways taking those to China and Japan, and Cathay Pacific taking Bangkok, Manila, and Singapore. Given the political upheavals taking place in mainland China, the choice was fortunate for Cathay.

With the security of strong backing and lucrative routes, Cathay started a programme of steady expansion. In 1949 Douglas DC-4s were introduced, and in 1950 a maintenance subsidiary, Hong Kong Aircraft Engineering Company, or HAECO, was established. P&O, the major British shipping group, bought a shareholding in 1954. Four years later the airline bought its first new aircraft, Douglas DC-6Bs, introducing pressurised comfort and the safety of radar to its services. By this time the route network had reached Calcutta in India. In 1959 Cathay purchased its rival, Hong Kong Airways, and introduced its first turboprop aircraft, two Lockheed L-188A Electras.

Faced with strong competition from jet aircraft, including Qantas (qv) Boeing 707-120s which forced Cathay off the Sydney

service, Convair 880 Coronado jet airliners were introduced in 1961. Nevertheless, having faced competition from a major state-owned airline, for the next decade Cathay became predominantly a regional carrier, ranging as far afield as Calcutta, Kuala Lumpur, and Singapore to the west, Seoul and Tokyo to the east, and Manila to the south. Between 1962 and 1967 the airline enjoyed growth of 20 per cent per annum, operating a fleet which consisted of just five Convair 880s, although three more were soon added.

Cathay started to break out of the region in 1970, when Perth was added to the route network. Boeing 707-320s were introduced to complement and then replace the Convairs, and flights to Sydney were subsequently resumed. Ten 707s were eventually operated, before being replaced by Lockheed L-1011 TriStars, and then in 1979 the airline obtained its first Boeing 747, a 747-200. The next few years saw Cathay move into the intercontinental market, with services to London introduced in 1980, Brisbane in 1982, Frankfurt and Vancouver in 1984, Amsterdam, Rome, and San Francisco in 1986, Paris in 1987, Zürich in 1988, and Manchester in 1989. The frequency of services to its traditional Asian destinations also increased sharply.

More recently Cathay has become a

Always maintaining a modern fleet, Cathay also operates the Boeing 747-400, which has the -300's fuselage but can be recognised by the winglets on its wing-tips.

major operator of Airbus A330s and A340s and the Boeing 777 and Boeing 747-400, and during 1997–98 has been equipping its fleet with the Future Air Navigation Systems (FANS). P&O and ANA involvement with the airline are both long past, but the Swire Group remains the largest single shareholder at 43.9 per cent, with the Chinese-Government backed CITIC having a 25 per cent stake. Cathay has interests in other airlines: Air Hong Kong (qv), in which Cathay has a 75 per cent stake, and Dragonair (qv), in which 18 per cent is held by Cathay, but in which the China National Aviation Corporation has taken a 35.9 per cent interest. Today, Cathay is one of the top 20 airlines in the world.

The transfer of Hong Kong's sovereignty to China in 1997 has introduced a degree of uncertainty for the future. Despite assurances that the existing politi-cal and economic structures will remain in place for 50 years, the initial result post-transfer has been a 40 per cent drop in air traffic to and from Hong Kong. Cathay itself has reported a fall in traffic of around 12–13 per cent.

Executive Directors & Officers: Peter Sutch, Chairman; David Turnbull, Managing Director; Philip Chen, Deputy Managing Director; Simon Heale, Deputy Managing Director; Victor Hughes, Financial Director; Tony Tyler, Director, Corporate Development; Ken Barley, Director, Flight Operations; Robert Cutler, Director, Service Delivery; Roland Fairfield, Engineering Director.

HQ Airport & Main Base: Chek Lap Kok, Hong Kong

Radio callsign: CATHAY

Designator: CX/CPA

Employees: Flight-crew: 1,379; Cabin staff: 5,525; Ground staff: 8,853; Total: 15,757.

Main destinations served: Adelaide, Amsterdam, Auckland, Bahrain, Bangkok, Brisbane, Cairns, Cebu, Colombo, Denpasar, Dubai, Frankfurt, Fukuoka, Hanoi, Ho Chi Minh City, Jakarta, Johannesburg, Kuala Lumpur, London Heathrow, Los Angeles, Manchester, Manila, Mauritius, Melbourne, Mumbai (Bombay), Nagoya, New York JFK, Osaka, Paris CDG, Penang, Perth, Rome, Sapporo, Seoul, Singapore, Surabaya, Sydney, Taipei, Tokyo, Toronto, Vancouver, Zürich,

Annual turnover: US $4,187 million (£2,538 million)

Aircraft km pa: 182 million

Revenue passenger km pa: 40,185 million

Cargo tonne km pa: 7,072 million

Passengers pa: 10,985, 000

LINKS WITH OTHER AIRLINES
Cathay has a 75 per cent interest in Air Hong Kong (qv), and 18 per cent in Dragonair (qv).
25 per cent interest in Hong Kong Aircraft Engineering Company (HAECO) Ltd.
10 per cent stake in TAECO Engineering with Singapore Airlines (qv) and Japan Airlines (qv).
Alliances with Air Canada (qv), Air Mauritius (qv), Lufthansa (qv), and Singapore Airlines (qv).
Code-sharing with Ansett New Zealand (qv), British Midland (qv), and Vietnam Airlines (qv).

Cathay is one of a number of airlines to operate both the Boeing 777 and Airbus A330 large twins – this is an A330-300.

FLEET
19 Boeing 747-400 (2 leased)
2 Boeing 747-400F
6 Boeing 747-300
7 Boeing 747-200
7 Boeing 747-200F (3 leased to Air Hong Kong)
4 Boeing 777-200
4 Boeing 777-300
13 Airbus A330-300
11 Airbus A340-300

DRAGONAIR

Hong Kong Dragon Airlines Ltd

Incorporated: 1985

HISTORY
Originally founded in 1985 as a regional carrier, initially concentrating on services between Hong Kong and China, a number of changes in the shareholders eventually led to Cathay Pacific (qv) and Swire Pacific taking a 30 per cent holding, while major shareholdings were also taken by China International Trust and Investment of China (CITIC) and the China National Aviation Corporation. Cathay now has just 18 per cent of Dragonair, with CNAC having 35.9 per cent.

In addition to services to China, the airline also operates a number of services to destinations in South-East Asia for Cathay Pacific.

Executive Directors & Officers: Kuang Piu Chao, Chairman; Philip Chen, Chief Operating Officer; Francis Wai, Chief Financial Officer; Felix Hart, General Manager, Operations; Ian Shiu, General Manager, Marketing & Sales.

HQ Airport & Main Base: Chek Lap Kok, Hong Kong

Radio callsign: DRAGONAIR

Designator: KA/HDA

Employees: 1,207

Main destinations served: Bandar Seri Begawan, Beijing, Changsha, Chengdu, Dhaka, Dalian, Guilin, Haikou, Hangzhou, Hiroshima, Kaohsiung, Kota Kinbalu, Kuching, Kunming, Nanjing, Ningbo, Phnom Penh, Phuket, Qindao, Sendai, Shanghai, Tianjin, Xiamen, Xian.

LINKS WITH OTHER AIRLINES
Cathay Pacific (qv) has an 18 per cent interest and provides commercial support.

FLEET
6 Airbus A330-300 (at least 1 leased)
9 Airbus A320-200 (plus 5 options)

ACES COLOMBIA

Aérolineas Centrales de Colombia

Incorporated: 1971

HISTORY
Operations by ACES began in February 1972, some six months after the airline was formed, with de Havilland Twin Otter aircraft playing a prominent role during the early days. The airline's first jet aircraft, Boeing 727s, were introduced in 1981, and were followed by Fairchild FH-227s in 1986, since replaced by ATR 42s. At first the airline concentrated on developing internal scheduled services, often to smaller communities, but international charter flights were introduced in 1986, and more recently international scheduled operations have been operated to Panama. Airbus A320 aircraft are being introduced, and, options being held for others, time may see these replace the Boeing 727s.

Executive Directors & Officers: Mario Gomez, Chairman; Juan E. Posada, President; Alvaro Martinez, Deputy President & Vice-President, Finance; Eduardo Lombana, Vice-President, Operations; Miguel Montoya, Vice-President, Maintenance; Alberto Gallego, Vice-President, Marketing; Dario Betancur, Financial Director; Lucia C. Ardila, Marketing Director; Juan B. Palacio, Personnel Director.

HQ Airport & Main Base: Medellin, plus additional hubs at Bogotá and Manizales.

Radio callsign: ACES

Designator: VX/AES

Employees: 1,650

Main destinations served: Some 40 domestic destinations, plus Miami, Panama City, and San Juan.

LINKS WITH OTHER AIRLINES
Member of the LatinPass frequent flyer programme.

FLEET
4 Airbus A320 (leased)
5 Boeing 727-200 (leased)
6 ATR 42-300 (leased)
10 de Havilland DHC-6 Twin Otter (leased)

AEROREPUBLICA

AéroRepublica SA

Incorporated: 1992

HISTORY
Founded in late-1992, AéroRepublica commenced operations the following June, operating on internal scheduled and charter passenger and cargo flights. The airline has a mixed fleet of Boeing 727s and McDonnell Douglas DC-9s.

Executive Directors & Officers: Alfonso Avila, President; Alberto Acero Barbosa, Vice-President, Finance; Juan Manuel Pulido, Vice-President, Operations; Juan Pablo Tranky, Vice-President, Commercial; Jorge Parra, Vice-President, Technical & Maintenance; Ernesto Sanchez, Engineering Director; Guillermo Bernal Alonso, Personnel Director.

HQ Airport & Main Base: Bogotá, with a second hub at Cali

Radio callsign: AEROREPUBLICA

Designator: 5P/RPB

Employees: 196

Main destinations served: Aruba, Barranquilla, Cartegena, La Habana, Leticia, Medellin, Monteria, San Andres, Santa Marta.

LINKS WITH OTHER AIRLINES
Marketing alliances with ACES (qv), Aires (qv), Avensa (qv), and Varig (qv).

FLEET
2 Boeing 727-100
9 McDonnell Douglas DC-9-30

AEROSUCRE

Aérosucre SA

Incorporated: 1969

HISTORY
Originally founded in 1969, Aérosucre started operations the following year as a small third level operator on regional feeder services in the north of the country. It subsequently moved into scheduled and charter cargo services, initially with two Handley Page Heralds, which were later joined by two Sud Caravelle jets. The fleet still includes the Caravelles, as well as Boeing 727s.

Executive Directors & Officers: Captain Jorge Solano Recio, President.

HQ Airport & Main Base: Barranquilla, with a base also at Bogotá

Radio callsign: AEROSUCRE

Designator: 6N/KRE

Main destinations served: Scheduled and charter operations within Colombia.

FLEET
3 Boeing 727-100

AIRES COLOMBIA

Aérovias de Integracion Regional SA

Incorporated: 1980

HISTORY
Founded in late-1980, AIRES Colombia started operations the following February, and has since developed a network of regional passenger services from its base at Bogotá.

Executive Directors & Officers:
Guiomar Pinto Echeverri, President; Ricardo Calderon, Director, Operations; Julio Nova, Engineering Director.

HQ Airport & Main Base: Bogotá

Radio callsign: AIRES

Designator: 4C/ARE

Employees: 390

Main destinations served: Cali, Ibaque, Leguizamo, Medellin, Neiva, Pereira, Puerto Assis, Tame, Villavcencio, Yopal.

FLEET
4 de Havilland Dash 8-300 (leased)
2 de Havilland Dash 8-100 (leased)
3 Fairchild FH-227
2 Embraer EMB-110 Bandeirante

ARCA COLOMBIA

Aérovias Colombianas SA

Incorporated: 1959

HISTORY
An air charter cargo operator, ARCA operates a mixed DC-10 and DC-8 fleet from its base at Bogotá on internal and international flights.

Executive Directors & Officers:
Hernando Gutierrez, General Manager.

HQ Airport & Main Base: Bogotá, with a further base at Cali

Radio callsign: ARCA

Designator: ZU/AKC

Main destinations served: Charters, including international operations.

FLEET
1 McDonnell Douglas DC-10-10F
3 McDonnell Douglas DC-8-50F

AVIANCA

Aérovias Nacionales de Colombia SA

Incorporated: 1940

HISTORY
Avianca can trace its history back to 1919, when SCADTA – the first airline in the Americas and the second in the world – started operations using a Junkers seaplane on a service between Barranquilla and Giradot. SCADTA's founders were three Germans and five Colombians. The many natural difficulties in surface travel in Colombia enabled the new airline to expand rapidly.

SCADTA also managed a number of 'firsts' during its operations over two decades. One of the airline's Fokker aircraft won a prize offered by a newspaper for the first aircraft to land at Colombia's capital, Bogotá, which is nearly 9,000 feet (2,700 metres) up in the Andes. This was followed in 1925 by the first air service between North and South America when a SCADTA flying-boat flew from Barranquilla to Florida. In 1931 Pan American, still in its own infancy, acquired an 80 per cent interest in SCADTA.

Avianca was formed in 1940 when SCADTA merged with another Colombian airline, Servicio Aéreo Colombiano. During its first few years attention was paid to consolidation, and new equipment was almost impossible to obtain because of the demands of World War Two on the aircraft manufacturing industry world-wide. Nevertheless, once the war ended Avianca was the first South American airline to fly into Miami (1947), and the first to reach New York the following year. In 1954 Avianca took over another Colombian airline, SAETA. In 1960 it introduced the first non-stop jet airliner service between Miami and Bogotá, and in 1964 the first between New York and Bogotá.

The Pan American interest was gradually reduced over the years, first to 38 per cent and then to 13 per cent, at which stage, in 1978, Avianca finally bought out the Pan Am shareholding. This was clearly a wise move as it pre-empted any difficulties which might have arisen if Pan Am had still been heavily involved with Avianca at the time of the American airline's final collapse. Before this, Avianca acquired SAM Sociedad Aéronautica de Medellin Consolidada (qv).

Although services to the United States have developed over the years, the airline has been a comparatively recent arrival in Europe, with London being served from 1997, following Madrid and Paris, which had joined Avianca's network somewhat earlier.

Throughout its history Avianca has been a private enterprise operation.

Executive Directors & Officers:
Augusto Lopez, Chairman; Gustavo A. Lenis, President; Julio E. Amador, Treasurer; Fernando Cruz, Operations Director; Maria Cristina Canizares, Commercial Director; Jamie Aguirre, Maintenance Director; Austin Arango, Engineering Director; Pablo Arango, Marketing Director; Marco A. Tamayo, Personnel Directo; Jaime Baena, Vice-President, Finance; Julian Adiv, Vice-President, Flight Operations; Francisco Mendez, Vice-President, Technical & Operations; Neil Warren, Vice-President, Maintenance & Engineering; Juan M. Beltran, Vice-President, Commercial; Roberto Herz, Vice-President, Sales & Marketing.

HQ Airport & Main Base: Bogotá

Radio callsign: AVIANCA

Designator: AV/AVA

Employees: 3,400

Main destinations served: Aruba, Buenos Aires, Caracas, Curaçao, Guatemala City, Lima, London Heathrow, Los Angeles, Madrid, Manaus, Miami, Montego Bay, New York JFK, Panama City, Quito, Paris CDG, Rio de Janeiro, Santiago de Chile, São Paulo, San Jose.

LINKS WITH OTHER AIRLINES
SAM Sociedad Aéronautica de Medellin Consolidada (qv) is a subsidiary. Marketing alliances with SAir Aruba (qv) and Saeta Air Ecuador (qv). Member of the LatinPass frequent flyer programme.

FLEET
1 Boeing 767-300
4 Boeing 767-200
4 Boeing 757-200 (leased)
2 Boeing 727-200Adv
11 McDonnell Douglas MD-83
10 Fokker 50 (leased)

INTER

Intercontinental de Aviacion SA

Incorporated: 1965

HISTORY
Originally founded as Aéropesca Colombia, the current title was adopted in 1983 to mark plans to move into international services. The airline is still predominantly a domestic carrier, operating charter and passenger, charter and scheduled services, but there are a few international services to destinations in and around the Caribbean. Some regional destinations

have been dropped in recent years, marking the end of the airline's Twin Otter operations, while two Vickers Viscount 700s have also been replaced.

Executive Directors & Officers:
Captain Luis Hernandez Zia, President; Luis Alfredo Gallego, Managing Director; Hilda Merchan, Financial Director; Eduardo Paz, Operations Director; Jairo Torrente, Commercial Director; Milton Jimenez, Engineering Director; Gilberto Aleman, Maintenance Director; Maria Victoria Rodriguez, Marketing Director; Manuel Jose Ruiz, Personnel Director; William Velez, General Manager.

HQ Airport & Main Base: Bogotá, with a further base/hub at Cali

Radio callsign: CONTAVIA

Designator: RS/ICT

Employees: 650

Main destinations served: Some 20 domestic destinations, plus Havana and Panama City.

FLEET
11 McDonnell Douglas DC-9-15
5 McDonnell Douglas DC-9-10
2 de Havilland Dash 8-300

LINEAS AEREAS SURAMERICANAS

Líneas Aéreas Suramericanas Colombia SA

HISTORY
A cargo charter operator, handling domestic and international flights from Bogotá.

Executive Directors & Officers: Luis Enrique Prieto, President.

HQ Airport & Main Base: Bogotá

Radio callsign: SURAMERICANO

Designator: LAU

Main destinations served: Domestic and international cargo charter.

FLEET
2 Boeing 727-100C
1 Boeing 727-100F
3 Sud Aviation Caravelle 10

SAM COLOMBIA

Sociedad Aéronautica de Medellin Consolidada

Incorporated: 1945

HISTORY
SAM was founded in 1945 and charter operations started a year later, with the first scheduled operations following in 1947. The airline was initially known as Sociedad Aéronautica de Medellin, and the present title was adopted in 1962. The airline became a subsidiary of Avianca (qv) and today operates a largely domestic route network, but with international flights to Havana and Panama City. AI(R) RJ100s have replaced a fleet which at one stage was comprised entirely of Boeing 727s.

Executive Directors & Officers:
Gustavo Lenis, President; Victor Machado, Chief Executive Officer; Francisco Mendez, Chief Operating Officer; Jaime Baena, Chief Financial Officer; Luis Restrepo, Commercial Director; Eduardo Dueri, Personnel Director; Camilo Villegas, Vice-President, General; Juan M. Beltran, Vice-President, Marketing.

HQ Airport & Main Base: Bogotá

Radio callsign: SAM

Designator: MM/SAM

Employees: 430

Main destinations served: Aruba, Barranquilla, Cali, Cartagena, Cucuta, Havana, Panama City, Pereira, San Andres, Santa Marta, San Jose.

LINKS WITH OTHER AIRLINES
A subsidiary of Avianca (qv).
Member of the LatinPass frequent flyer programme.

FLEET
9 AI(R) RJ100

SATENA

Servicio de Aéreonavegacion a Territorios Nacionales

Incorporated: 1962

HISTORY
The only Colombian state-owned airline, Satena was established to aid development of the Amazon and Orinoco regions of the country, and is operated as a special unit of the Colombian Air Force. Satena provides charter and scheduled operations for passengers and cargo within the two regions, and also provides services for mail.

Executive Directors & Officers:
Brigadier-General Alfredo Garcia Rojas, Chief Executive Officer & General Manager; Colonel Juan Gabriel Varela, Deputy General Manager; Colonel Hugo Beltron, Operations Manager; Colonel Hernando Alvarado, Marketing Manager.

HQ Airport & Main Base: Bogotá, with a further base at Medellin

Radio callsign: SATENA

Designator: ZT/NSE

Employees: 300

Main destinations served: Serves 112 points from its two bases.

FLEET
1 Fokker F-28-3000 Fellowship
2 British Aerospace 748
4 CASA 212-300
3 CASA 212-200
2 Cessna 208 Caravan 1
2 Pilatus PC-6 Turbo Porter

TAMPA

Transportes Aéreos Mercantiles Panamericanos

Incorporated: 1973

HISTORY
Tampa Airlines dates from 1973 and operates international scheduled cargo services as well as cargo charters from its base at Medellin and from Bogotá. Marketing alliances exist with Martin Air (qv) and Million Air (qv).

Executive Directors & Officers: Fabio Echeverry, Chairman; Jorge Coulson Rodriguez, President; Antonio Campillo, Deputy President; Alvaro Jaramillo, Vice-President, Finance; Juan Carlos de Grieff, Vice-President, Operations; Alvaro Londono, Vice-President, Commercial; Jorge Correa, Commercial Director; Marco Bravo, Maintenance Director; Diego Restrepo, Personnel Director.

HQ Airport & Main Base: Bogotá, with a further base at Medellin

Radio callsign: TAMPA

Designator: QT/TPA

Employees: 750

Main destinations served: Barranquilla, Cali, Caracas, Lima, Miami, Panama City, Pereira, Quito, San Juan.

LINKS WITH OTHER AIRLINES
Marketing alliances with Martin Air (qv) and Million Air (qv).

FLEET
2 McDonnell Douglas DC-8-71F
4 Boeing 707-320C

Costa Rica – TI

LACSA

Líneas Aéreas Costarricenses SA

Incorporated: 1946

HISTORY
Originally formed in 1946 as a joint venture between the Costa Rican Government, Pan American World Airways, and private interests based in Costa Rica, in 1952 the company acquired Taca de Costa Rica, which dated from 1939. An extensive Caribbean network has been created, with services further afield to New York and Rio de Janeiro. A subsidiary is SANSA, Servicios Aéreos Nacionales, which operates a small domestic network with a fleet of four Cessna Caravans.

The government shareholding today is small, and share ownership is highly fragmented.

Executive Directors & Officers: Alonso Lara, Chairman; Jose G. Rojas, General Manager; Indra Rivera, Finance Director; Raul Campos, Commercial Director; Carlos Carvajal, Maintenance Director; Enrique Odio, Technical Director; Carlos Lizama, Marketing Director.

HQ Airport & Main Base: San Jose, Costa Rica

Radio callsign: LACSA

Designator: LR/LRC

Employees: 1,150

Main destinations served: Barranquilla, Cancun, Caracas, El Salvador, Guatemala, Guayaquil, Havana, Lima, Los Angeles, Managua, Mexico City, Miami, New Orleans, New York JFK, Orlando, Panama City, Quito, Rio de Janeiro, San Juan, San Pedro Suala, Santiago, Tegucigalpa.

FLEET
3 Boeing 727-200
5 McDonnell Douglas MD-83
2 McDonnell Douglas DC-9-15

Croatia – 9A

CROATIA AIRLINES

Croatia Airlines

Incorporated: 1990

HISTORY
Originally formed in 1990 as the national airline of the newly-independent Croatian Republic after the break-up of the former Yugoslavia, operations started in 1991. Being some distance away from the conflict in Bosnia, the new airline has been able to develop an international route network, although tourist traffic is still far below pre-independence levels. The airline's shares are split amongst six shareholders, including Zagreb Airport.

Executive Directors & Officers: Antun Vrdojiak, Chairman; Matija Katcic, President & Chief Executive Officer; Anita Pavicic, Director, Finance & Accounting; Dubravka Turkaji, Director, Planning & Development; Mirko Tatalovic, Director, Traffic; Ivon Nola, Director, Security; Mirna Hecimovic, Director, Legal Affairs, Personnel & Administration; Natasa Mijacika, Director, Marketing; Kristijana Kelava, Director, Purchase & Supply; Ranko Ilej, Vice-President, Flight Operations; Roman Gebauer, Vice-President, Maintenance & Engineering.

HQ Airport & Main Base: Zagreb, with some services from Split

Radio callsign: CROATIA

Designator: OU/CTN

Employees: 675

Main destinations served: Zagreb to Amsterdam, Berlin, Brussels, Copenhagen, Dublin, Düsseldorf, Frankfurt, Istanbul, London Heathrow, Moscow, Munich, Paris CDG, Prague, Rome, Skopje, Stuttgart, Tirana, Vienna, Zürich.

LINKS WITH OTHER AIRLINES
Agreement with Air France (qv).

FLEET
5 Boeing 737-200Adv
5 Airbus A319
3 ATR 42

Cuba – CU

AERO CARIBBEAN

Aéro Caribbean

Incorporated: 1982

HISTORY
The Cuban charter operator, handling passengers and cargo internationally and to internal destinations as well. It is state-owned.

Executive Directors & Officers: Alberto Sanchez, President; Idiana Letian, Vice-President, Financial; Arturo Mirabel, Vice-President, Operations; Pedro Manduley, Vice-President, Commercial; Mauricio Isaac, Vice-President, Technical.

HQ Airport & Main Base: Havana

Designator: CRN

Main destinations served: International and domestic charter flights.

FLEET
4 Antonov An-26
3 Ilyushin Il-18
3 Yakovlev Yak-40
3 Douglas DC-3

CUBANA

Empresa Consolidada Cubana de Aviacion

Incorporated: 1929

HISTORY
Originally formed in 1929 as the Compania Cubana de Aviacion SA, with operations beginning the following year, Cubana initially operated services to nearby Florida from its base in Havana. The airline was nationalised and the current title adopted in 1959 after the Cuban revolution saw Fidel Castro sweep into power. At the time, Cubana was operating a fleet of Douglas DC-3s and modern Bristol Britannia airliners to destinations throughout the Caribbean. The Britannias remained in service for more than 15 years after the revolution, but increasingly equipment procurement switched to aircraft of Soviet manufacture, including Antonov An-24s and Ilyushin Il-14s and Il-18s. The only western aircraft in the fleet today are Fokker F-27 Friendships.

Since the collapse of the Soviet Union, the scope of the international network has increased, largely in an attempt to boost tourist revenues, although American sanctions and the lack of Soviet sponsorship has effectively cut the country off from what were historically its main trading partners.

Executive Directors & Officers: Heriberto Priego, Director General; Luis Capo, Deputy Director; Fausto Canet, Director Finance; E. Mator, Director Operations; Lazaro Banguela, Director Commercial.

HQ Airport & Main Base: Havana

Radio callsign: CUBANA

Designator: CU/CUB

Employees: 1,100

Main destinations served: 13 domestic

destinations, plus Barcelona, Berlin, Brussels, Buenos Aires, Cancun, Frankfurt, Kingston, Lima, London Stansted, Madrid, Mexico City, Milan, Montreal, Moscow, Panama City, Paris CDG, Rome, Santiago de Chile, Vienna.

FLEET
12 Ilyushin Il-62M
2 Ilyushin Il-76MD
4 Tupolev Tu-154M
4 Tupolev Tu-154B2
10 Antonov An-24
20 Antonov An-26
3 Yakovlev Yak-42D
6 Yakovlev Yak-40
8 Fokker F-27-600 Friendship

Cyprus – 5B

CYPRUS AIRWAYS

Cyprus Airways Ltd

Incorporated: 1947

HISTORY
Cyprus Airways celebrated its 50th anniversary in 1997. Originally the airline had been formed as a joint venture between British European Airways – predecessor of today's British Airways (qv) – and the government of Cyprus, both of which held 40 per cent of the shares, leaving 20 per cent for private interests. In the beginning it operated services from Nicosia to Athens and destinations in the Middle East, using aircraft leased from BEA, but in 1948 it acquired three Douglas DC-3s. Additional DC-3s followed in 1950, when Rome and destinations in Arabia were added to the route network. Increases in the airline's capital to cater for this expansion meant that by 1950 the shareholdings were: BEA, 23 per cent; BOAC (British Overseas Airways Corporation), 23 per cent; the Cypriot Government, 31 per cent; and private interests, 23 per cent.

The rapid expansion of the airline went into a decline during 1955 and 1956, when terrorist activity on Cyprus led to a sharp drop in traffic and heavy financial losses. This came at a time when the airline had been planning to replace its DC-3s with its own fleet of Vickers Viscounts, but in order that the airline itself should survive the route network was pruned dramatically, the DC-3s were sold, and instead of buying Viscounts the airline opted to lease two aircraft from BEA.

The revival of the old relationship with BEA was to last more than 20 years, taking Cyprus Airways into the jet age with

five Hawker Siddeley Tridents leased from BEA, while the Cypriot Government acquired BOAC's interest. A further setback occurred when the island was invaded by Turkey in 1973, resulting in the partitioning of Cyprus and the eventual closure of Nicosia Airport.

Over the last 20 years Cyprus Airways has recovered strongly, buying its own aircraft and building up a fleet of Airbus airliners, some of which replaced an interim fleet of British Aerospace One-Elevens, which had augmented the Tridents. A charter subsidiary, Eurocypria, has been established, recognising the potential to carry more of the many visitors to Cyprus, many of whom arrive on inclusive tour charter flights on the airline's own aircraft. Cyprus Airways now flies from the new airports at Larnaca and Paphos, and is owned 80 per cent by the Cypriot Government and 20 per cent by private shareholders.

Executive Directors & Officers: Takis G. Kyriakides, Chairman; Achilles S. Kyprianou, Vice Chairman; Demetris M. Pantazis, Group Chief Executive; Christos Kyriakides, General Manager; Eleni Kaloyirou, Financial Controller; John Kythreotis, Head of Flight Operations; Olga Ellades, Head of Airline Planning & International Affairs; Marios Michael, Chief Engineer; Andreas Georgiou, Head of Human Resources & Administration; Marios Pefkaros, Head of Sales.

HQ Airport & Main Base: HQ is at Nicosia, but the main base/hub is Larnaca, with operations also from Paphos.

Radio callsign: CYPRUS

Designator: CY/CYP

Employees: Flight-crew: 108; Cabin staff: 304; Engineering: 236; Ground staff: 938; Total: 1,587.

Main destinations served: Larnaca to Amman, Amsterdam*, Athens*, Bahrain, Beirut, Berlin*, Birmingham (UK), Brussels*, Cairo, Corfu, Damascus, Dresden*, Dubai, Frankfurt*, Geneva, Hamburg*, Heraklion, Jeddah, London Gatwick*, London Heathrow*, London Stansted, Lyon, Manchester*, Moscow, Paris CDG*, Rhodes, Riyadh, Rome, Strasbourg, Tel Aviv, Thessaloniki, Vienna, Zürich*.
* also served from Paphos.

Annual turnover: US $67.4 million (£111.2 million)

Aircraft km pa: 19.2 million

Revenue passenger km pa: 2,631.2 million

Cargo tonne km pa: 35.3 million

Passengers pa: 1,226,000

LINKS WITH OTHER AIRLINES
Code-sharing with Alitalia (qv), Gulf Air (qv), and KLM (qv).
Marketing alliances with ARIA-Aeroflot (qv), Austrian Airlines (qv), Kuwait Airways (qv), and Syrian Arab Airlines (qv).
Owns 100 per cent of Eurocypria.

FLEET
1 Airbus A310-203
3 Airbus A310-204
8 Airbus A320-200 (3 of which leased to Eurocypria)

Northern Cyprus

KIBRIS TURKISH AIRLINES

Kibris Turk Hava Yolari

Incorporated: 1974

HISTORY
The airline of Turkish Northern Cyprus, Kibris was founded in December 1974 after the Turkish invasion of Cyprus led to partition of the island. The first services were operated early the following year, using aircraft and crews loaned by THY Turkish Airlines (qv). An airfield was put into service at Ercan, some eight miles east of Nicosia, and the first services were to Ankara in Turkey. Ownership of the airline is divided between THY and the Turkish Cypriot Government.

Development of the airline is difficult, given that Northern Cyprus is only recognised by Turkey.

Executive Directors & Officers: Umit Utku, President; Captain Ferda Ones, General Manager.

HQ Airport & Main Base: Ercan, near Nicosia

Radio callsign: AIRKIBRIS

Designator: YK/KYV

Employees: 279

Main destinations served: Adana, Ankara, Antalya, Istanbul, Izmir.

LINKS WITH OTHER AIRLINES
Closely allied with THY (qv), which has a 50 per cent stake.

FLEET
1 Airbus 310-200
4 Boeing 727-200

Czech Republic – OK

AIR OSTRAVA

Air Ostrava

Incorporated: 1977

HISTORY
A regional operator of feeder services, Air Ostrava was founded in 1977 as Air Vitkovice.

Executive Directors & Officers: Pavel Hradec, Managing Director.

HQ Airport & Main Base: HQ at Ostrava International Airport, Mosnov, but main base is Prague.

Radio callsign: VITEK

Designator: 8K/VTR

Employees: approx 180

Main destinations served: Prague to Brno, Braunschweig, Nuremberg, Ostrava, Vienna.

FLEET
3 Let L-410
4 Saab 340A
2 British Aerospace Jetstream 31
1 Cessna Citation III

CZECH AIRLINES

CSA Czech Airlines

Incorporated: 1923

HISTORY
Originally Ceskoslovenské Aerolinie, the present title was adopted in 1995 after the division of Czechoslovakia into the Czech Republic and Slovakia.

The history of CSA dates from 1923, when a state air transport group was formed, carrying the title Czechoslovak State Airlines, which used military Brandenburg A-14s and military personnel. The new airline conducted trial flights on a route between Prague and Bratislava (now in the Slovak Republic), and scheduled services along this route followed in 1924. In the same year the first Czech-built and designed aircraft, the Aero 10, entered service between Prague and Kosicé. The Aero aircraft factory also operated a route between Prague and Mariánské Lázne between 1925 and 1927, when the state-owned airline took over the service.

During the next few years the state airline expanded rapidly, and civil airports were opened at Brno, Mariánské Lázne,

and Bratislava, reducing the dependence on military aerodromes, while a succession of ever more modern aircraft brought advances in comfort, reliability, and speed. These aircraft included the de Havilland 50, the Farman Goliath (eventually manufactured under licence in Czechoslovakia), and the country's own Aero 23s and 38s. While CSA concentrated on internal services international routes were being developed by CLS (Ceskoslovenská Letecká Spolecnost), a privately-owned airline which, founded in 1927, commenced services to Berlin, Rotterdam, and Vienna in 1928. In 1930 CLS inaugurated services from Prague to Basle, Munich, and Zürich. It was not until 1930 that CSA started an international service, to Zagreb.

It was CSA which had the distinction of becoming the first western airline to offer an air service to the Soviet Union in 1936, using Airspeed Envoys. The aircraft became known as the 'Russian Express' – it still took ten hours, but this was highly competitive when compared with the 45 hours taken by a fast train! Another innovation for CSA in 1936 was the airline's first stewardesses, introduced on Douglas DC-2s first delivered that year. The DC-2s were soon followed by their larger development, the famous DC-3. Both CSA and CLS had extensive networks by 1938, when operations abruptly ceased on the German occupation of Czechoslovakia.

A new airline was established after the end of World War Two. Ceskoslovenské Aerolinie started operations in 1945, initially using three salvaged ex-Luftwaffe Junkers Ju52/3ms and some lighter aircraft. Ex-military Douglas C-47s – the military variant of the DC-3 – were soon purchased and modified for airline operations, so that services from Prague to Bratislava and Brno could begin early in 1946. The old routes were re-established rapidly, urged on by the war-battered state of the European railway network, so that by the end of 1946 many pre-war European destinations were being served once more. Meanwhile Czechoslovakia was being dragged into the post-war Soviet Bloc, and in 1948 the airline was nationalised.

Equipment purchases soon began to reflect the new regime, with Ilyushin Il-12s being the next new aircraft, followed by Il-14s. The route network also began to become more concerned with links to East European capitals than those in the west. The first jets, Tupolev Tu-104s, were introduced in 1957, and remained prominent in the fleet for more than a decade. Ilyushin Il-18 turboprop airliners were also acquired. Tupolev Tu-134s and the long-

range Ilyushin Il-62 appeared during the 1960s. For a short period during the late-1960s a turboprop Bristol Britannia 318 was leased. In common with many Soviet Bloc airlines, CSA's operations were all-embracing, including air taxi services and aerial crop-spraying.

The break-up of the Soviet Union and the dismantling of the Warsaw Pact, which was an economic as well as a military entity, saw western equipment placed in service, so that today just a few Tupolev aircraft are to be found in a fleet dominated by western types. The route network also now extends to every European capital with the exception of Oslo. On the debit side, the division of Czechoslovakia has meant that the airline has lost its secondary hub at Bratislava, although Slovak Air Services is a subsidiary. The airline has transferred its four remaining Tupolev Tu-154M aircraft into a new charter division.

Marketing alliances exist with several European airlines, as well as code-sharing with Continental Airlines (qv).

Executive Directors & Officers:
Antonin Jakubse, President; Frantisek Slaby, Vice-President, Finance & Economics; Miroslav Belovsky, Vice-President, Operations; Ivan Trhlik, Vice-President, Flight Operations; Miroslav Kula, Vice-President, Technical.

HQ Airport & Main Base: Prague

Radio callsign: CSA LINES

Designator: OK/CSA

Employees: 3,900

Main destinations served: All European capitals other than Oslo, including London Heathrow and Stansted, plus Abu Dhabi, Bahrain, Bangkok, Beirut, Cairo, Damascus, Dubai, Istanbul, Kiev, Kuwait, Larnaca, Lvov, Manchester, Montreal, Ostrava, Riga, Sharjah, Singapore, Toronto.

LINKS WITH OTHER AIRLINES
Code-sharing with Luxair (qv) and Continental Airlines (qv).
Joint services with Air France (qv), Iberia (qv), and THY Turkish (qv).
Block space arrangements with KLM (qv), LOT Polish (qv), and Lufthansa (qv).

FLEET
2 Airbus A310-304
4 Tupolev Tu-154M (operated by charter division)
2 Boeing 737-400
10 Boeing 737-500
4 ATR 72-200
2 ATR 42-400

Denmark – OY

See also Scandinavia

CIMBER

Cimber Air A/S

Incorporated: 1950

HISTORY

Cimber Air was formed in 1950 by Captain Ingolf Lorenz Nielson, who took over Sonderjyllands Flyveselskab. Initially the airline operated charter flights and the early fleet included a de Havilland Heron as well as Piper Apache and Beech King Air C90 aircraft. In 1964 it was granted a licence for a scheduled service between its base at Sonderborg and Copenhagen, operating a feeder into the international services of SAS (qv). This route was later, in 1967, to see the introduction of the Nord 262 turboprop feeder-liner. In November 1971 Cimber's scheduled services were merged into those of Danair, a consortium between SAS, Maersk (qv), and Cimber, in which the latter held a 5 per cent stake.

The airline received its first jet equipment in 1975, as launch customer for the German VFW 614 airliner, although these were replaced three years later by two Fokker F-28 Fellowships. Given the small size of the Danish market, Cimber had to look for other business opportunities, and in 1980 its aircraft started to operate feeder services in Saudi Arabia for Saudi Arabian Airlines (qv). While services from Sonderborg grew, and the airline started operations from Aarhus, in 1987 a further development was the provision of feeder services from Kiel, just over the border in Germany, on sub-charter to DLT – now Lufthansa CityLine (qv) – for which a German subsidiary, Cimber Air GmbH, had to be established. By this time Cimber had introduced three AI(R) ATR 42 regional airliners.

Services to Montpellier in southern France were introduced in 1989. The following year Cimber negotiated an alliance with Lufthansa (qv) for operation of further feeder services in Germany, for which an additional three ATR 42s were acquired, with a seventh joining the fleet in 1992, the same year that the two F-28s were sold.

Danair ceased operations in 1995, being largely replaced by SAS Commuter (qv). Today, Cimber Air remains in the hands of the Nielsen family, with a third generation running the business. It has a fleet of 12 ATR 42s and a Cessna Citation, and while Sonderborg remains the airline's home base it continues to develop services from other bases, including Kiel and Berlin.

Executive Directors & Officers: Captain Jorgen Nielsen, President & Chief Executive Officer; Alex Dyregard, Chief Financial Officer.

HQ Airport & Main Base: Sonderborg, but with additional bases at Copenhagen, Berlin, and Kiel.

Radio callsign: CIMBER

Designator: QI/CIM

Employees: Flight-crew: 100; Cabin staff: 50; Engineering: 35; Ground staff: 65; Total: 250.

Main destinations served: Copenhagen to Aalborg, Aarhus, Karup, Sonderborg. Other services are operated on behalf of Lufthansa CityLine (qv).

Annual turnover: US $44.36 million (£26.9 million)

Revenue passenger km pa: 162,654,944

LINKS WITH OTHER AIRLINES
Alliances with both Lufthansa (qv) and SAS (qv).

FLEET
9 ATR 42-300 (2 leased)
3 ATR 42-500 (leased)
1 Cessna Citation

Greenlandair, or Grönlandsfly, serves many isolated communities where good take-off and landing characteristics are important, hence the presence of de Havilland Dash 7s in the fleet.

GREENLANDAIR

Grönlandsfly A/S

Incorporated: 1960

HISTORY

Greenlandair was formed in 1960 and is owned equally by the Danish Government, the Greenland Home Rule Government, and SAS (qv). The airline was formed to provide air transport to the many small and remote settlements in Greenland, where air transport is the best option due to sparse population and rugged terrain, and this has led to a varied fleet, including small helicopters, and operations which include air taxi, special lift, offshore supply, and ice reconnaissance in addition to internal passenger and freight, scheduled and charter operations. Many smaller communities receive air transport on what amounts to a scheduled air taxi basis, and a number of destinations can only be reached by helicopter. Services to Canada, Denmark, and Iceland are operated through arrangements with SAS, First Air (qv), and Icelandair (qv).

Executive Directors & Officers: Peter Fich, President; Ove Nielsen, Financial Director; Kristen Grodem, Director of Flight Operations; Bjarne Jorgensen, Technical Director; Michael Hojgaard, Director of Sales & Marketing.

HQ Airport & Main Base: Nuuk

Radio callsign: GREENLANDAIR

Designator: GL/GRL

Employees: Flight-crew: 83; Cabin staff: 20; Engineering: 108; Ground staff: 231; Total: 442.

Main destinations served: Aasiaat, Ilulissat, Iqaluit, Ittoqqortoormiit, Kangerlussuaq, Kangilinnguit, Kulusuk, Maniitsoq, Nanortalik, Narsaq, Narsarsuaq, Nerlerit Inlet, Nuuk, Paamiut, Pituffik, Qaanaaq, Qaqortoq, Qasigiannguit, Qeqertarsuaq, Sisimiut, Tasiilaq, Upernavik, Uummannaq.

Annual turnover: US $67.23 million (£40.75 million)

Revenue passenger km pa: 117 million (excluding figures for charter flights)

Cargo tonne km pa: 14.4 million (excluding figures for charter flights)

Passengers pa: 237,000

LINKS WITH OTHER AIRLINES
SAS (qv) has a 33.3 per cent shareholding. Alliances with SAS (qv), First Air (qv), and Icelandair (qv).

FLEET
4 de Havilland Dash 7
4 Sikorsky S-61
2 de Havilland DHC-6 Twin Otter
4 Bell 212
1 Beech Super King Air 200
6 Eurocopter AS 350 Ecureil
4 McDonnell Douglas MD 500D

MAERSK

Maersk Air A/S

Incorporated: 1970

HISTORY

Maersk Air started operations in 1970, initially operating charter flights but rapidly developing a network of scheduled flights within Denmark. During the early 1990s a network of international scheduled services was also started, initially with a route from Billund to Southend, on the Thames Estuary, but this has since developed to serve a number of major destinations within Europe, operating from both Billund and Copenhagen. Maersk had a 38 per cent stake in Danair, as one of three partners, and had aircraft and routes operating under the Danair brand until operations ceased in 1995.

Expanding outside Denmark, Maersk was a shareholder in the Plimsoll Line, which at one time was the holding company for both Brymon Airways (qv) and Birmingham European Airways, now Maersk Air UK. More recently the airline acquired a 49 per cent stake in Estonian

Air (qv) when the latter was privatised by the Estonian Government. Another subsidiary is the Danish air cargo operator, Star Air (qv). At one time Maersk operated some of the airline's feeder services under the name of Maersk Commuter, but this operation ceased in 1990 and the services have now been taken over by Maersk itself. In addition to scheduled and charter services, Maersk has for many years also specialised in wet-leasing operations to help new airlines or those with a temporary shortage of capacity.

Maersk is a subsidiary of the A.P. Moller Group, whose other major interests are in shipping.

Executive Directors & Officers: Bjarne Hansen, President; Ole Dietz, Executive Vice-President; Jorn Eriksen, Senior Vice-President.

HQ Airport & Main Base: Copenhagen

Radio callsign: MAERSK

Designator: DM/DAN

Employees: Flight-crew: 300; Cabin staff: 300; Engineering: 200; Ground staff: 300; Total: 1,300.

Main destinations served: Copenhagen to Billund, Bornholm, Esbjerg, Faroe Islands, Kristiansand, London Gatwick, Odense, Stockholm, Tallinn, Vojens. Billund to Aalborg, Aarhus, Amsterdam, Brussels, Faroe Islands, Frankfurt, London Gatwick, Nice, Odense, Paris CDG.

Annual turnover: US $300 million (£181.8 million)

Passengers pa: 2 million

LINKS WITH OTHER AIRLINES
Maersk Air Cargo has marketing alliances with a large number of airlines, in addition to selling space for Maersk Air. Maersk Air Limited (qv) and Star Air (qv) are subsidiaries.
Maersk has a 49 per cent stake in Estonian Air (qv).

FLEET
3 Boeing 737-700 (plus 9 on order)
16 Boeing 737-300
1 Boeing 737-500
13 Boeing 737-500SP
6 Fokker 50
1 British Aerospace 125-800
3 Eurocopter AS 332L Super Puma
2 Eurocopter AS 365 Dauphin

PREMIAIR

Premiair A./S

Incorporated: 1994

HISTORY

Premiair was formed in 1994 on the merger of two airlines, Scanair of Sweden and Conair of Denmark. Scanair had been originally founded as a Danish charter carrier in 1961, specialising in the inclusive tour market, but in 1965 had been reorganised as a Scandinavian charter airline by the three parent airlines of SAS (qv), and operated as an independent charter airline within the SAS Group, with the main base moving to Stockholm. Conair, or Consolidated Aircraft Corporation, was also an inclusive tour charter operator, founded in 1964 and beginning operations in 1965. From the outset it was owned by the Simon Spies travel organisation, and operated exclusively for them.

The merged airline, Premiair, was itself owned by Simon Spies, until that company in turn was acquired in 1996 by Airtours, the British tour operator and

The McDonnell Douglas DC-10 provides the long-haul element in Danish air charter operator Premiair's fleet.

travel agency group, as a result of which Premiair is now controlled by the holiday charter airline Airtours (qv).

Executive Directors & Officers: Tom Clausen, Managing Director; Torben Ostergaard, Director, Accounts; Hugo Bak Jensen, Director, Flight Operations; Niels Selling, Director, Technical; Lennart Holmgren, Director, In-Flight.

HQ Airport & Main Base: Copenhagen, with additional bases at Stockholm and Oslo.

Radio callsign: VIKING

Designator: DK/VKG

Employees: 1,150

Main destinations served: Charter flights from the main Scandinavian cities to holiday destinations world-wide.

LINKS WITH OTHER AIRLINES
A subsidiary of Airtours (qv).

FLEET
4 McDonnell Douglas DC-10-10
1 McDonnell Douglas DC-10-30
3 Airbus A300
6 Airbus A320

STAR AIR

Star Air A/S

Incorporated: 1987

HISTORY
A subsidiary of Maersk Air (qv), Star Air operates charter and contract freight services, including several scheduled routes on behalf of UPS (qv), which requires all seven of the airline's Boeing 727s.

Executive Directors & Officers: Bjarne Hansen, President.

HQ Airport & Main Base: Copenhagen

Radio callsign: WHITESTAR

Designator: SRR

Employees: 70

Main destinations served: Operates from the UPS European cargo hub at Copenhagen.

LINKS WITH OTHER AIRLINES
A wholly-owned subsidiary of Maersk Air (qv).
Operates UPS (qv) scheduled freight services from Copenhagen.

FLEET
7 Boeing 727-100QF

STERLING

Sterling European Airlines A/S

Incorporated: 1993

HISTORY
Sterling European Airways was founded at the end of 1993, just a few months after the bankruptcy of Sterling Airways in September. The original airline had been founded in 1962 by the Tjaereborg Rejser travel group to operate inclusive tour charters from points throughout Scandinavia, initially using Douglas DC-6s, which were later joined by Sud Caravelle jets. At the time of the airline's collapse, a fleet of Caravelles and Boeing 727-200s was being operated. The current fleet of Boeing 727s might be reduced as Boeing 737-800 deliveries are received.

The new airline's shareholders include the management team plus two companies, Ganger Rolf and Bonheur.

Executive Directors & Officers: F. Hirsch, Chairman; Lars O. Svenheim, President; Anita Simonsen, Chief Financial Officer; Captain Per Volstrup Petersen, Chief Operating Officer; Knud K. Pedersen, Maintenance Director.

HQ Airport & Main Base: Copenhagen

Radio callsign: STERLING

Designator: NB/SNB

Employees: 250

Main destinations served: Inclusive tour passenger charters within Europe, and to North Africa and the Canary Islands, plus ad hoc cargo charters.

FLEET
5 Boeing 727-200
1 Boeing 727-200F
2 Boeing 737-800 (plus 2 on order)

Djibouti – J2

DAALLO AIRLINES

Airline of Horn of Africa

Incorporated: 1992

HISTORY
Founded in 1992 as a privately-owned charter cargo and passenger operator with a fleet of Cessna Caravans, Daallo has since acquired a fleet of aircraft of Eastern European origin. Scheduled and charter flights are operated to a number of destinations in East Africa and the Middle East.

Executive Directors & Officers: Mohamed I. Yassin, Managing Director; Koshy Philip, Financial Director.

HQ Airport & Main Base: Djibouti

Radio callsign: DAALLO AIRLINES

Designator: D3/DAO

Main destinations served: Berbera, Dubai, Jeddah, Mogadishu, Sharjah.

LINKS WITH OTHER AIRLINES
Marketing alliances with Alitalia (qv), Emirates (qv), and Saudi Arabian Airlines (qv).

FLEET
1 Tupolev Tu-154M
4 Antonov An-24
1 Ilyushin Il-18
3 Let L-410

Dominican Republic – HI

DOMINICANA

Companía Dominicana de Aviación SA
Incorporated: 1944

HISTORY
The state-owned carrier of the Dominican Republic, Dominicana operates scheduled and charter passenger services as far afield as New York.

Executive Directors & Officers: Dr Ridolfo Rincon, Chairman; Marina Ginebra de Bonnelly, Chief Executive Officer; Captain Eddy A. Tineo, Operations Director; Angel Christopher, Technical Director.

HQ Airport & Main Base: Santo Domingo

Radio callsign: DOMINICANA

Designator: DO/DOA

Employees: 600

Main destinations served: Aruba, Caracas, Curaçao, Miami, New York JFK, Port-au-Prince, San Juan, plus some domestic services.

LINKS WITH OTHER AIRLINES
Code-share with Iberia (qv).

FLEET
1 Boeing 707-320
2 Boeing 727-200
2 Boeing 727-100

Ecuador – HC

SAETA – AIR ECUADOR

Sociedad Ecuatoriana de Transportes Aéreos

Incorporated: 1967

HISTORY
Formed in 1967, this privately-owned airline operates a mixture of domestic and international services as far afield as New York.

Executive Directors & Officers:
Roberto Dunn Barreirro, President, Patricio Suárez, Director.

HQ Airport & Main Base: Quito

Radio callsign: SAETA

Designator: EH/SET

Employees: 600

Main destinations served: Bogotá, Buenos Aires, Caracas, Guayaquil, Lima, Los Angeles, Mexico City, Miami, New York JFK, Santiago de Chile, plus cargo charters throughout the Americas.

LINKS WITH OTHER AIRLINES
Owns 80 per cent of LAPSA Air Paraguay (qv).

FLEET
2 Airbus A310
3 Airbus A320-200
1 Boeing 727-200Adv
1 Boeing 727-100
1 Boeing 737-200

SAN

SAN Servicios Aéreos Nacionales
Incorporated: 1964

HISTORY
The second-largest airline in Ecuador, SAN has been operating since 1964, mainly between its base at Guayaquil and Quito, the capital, and the Galapagos Islands.

Executive Directors & Officers:
Patricio Suárez, President; Carlos Degado, Managing Director; Mauro Entreadun, Director, Financial & Administration; Captain Lugiebre Jepez, Director, Operations.

HQ Airport & Main Base: Guayaquil

Radio callsign: AEREOS

Designator: WB/SAN

Employees: 150

Main destinations served: Galapagos Islands, Quito, plus charters.

FLEET
1 Boeing 727-100
1 Douglas DC-3
2 CASA 212-200 Aviocar

TAME

Transportes Aéreos Militares Ecuatorianos CA

Incorporated: 1962

HISTORY
Ecuador's largest airline, TAME was founded in 1962 as a domestic carrier and is operated as a unit of the Fuerza Aérea Ecuatoriana, or air force. Today it has a limited number of international routes.

Executive Directors & Officers:
General Luis Iturralde, President; Colonel Nelson Altamirano, Operations Manager; Lieutenant-Colonel Ernesto Armas, Finance Manager; Lieutenant-Colonel Luis Acosta, Maintenance Manager.

HQ Airport & Main Base: Quito

Radio callsign: TAME

Designator: EQ/TAE

Employees: 750

Main destinations served: Bahia, Cali, Coca, Cuenca, Esmeraldas, Galapagos Islands, Guayaquil, Havana, Loja, Macas Lago Agrio, Machala, Manta, Panama City, Portoviejo, Salinas, Santiago de Chile, Tulcan.

FLEET
4 Boeing 727-200
3 Boeing 727-100
1 Fokker F-28-4000

Egypt – SU

EGYPTAIR

Egyptair

Incorporated: 1932

HISTORY
By African standards Egyptair has a long history, dating from 1932 and the formation of Misr Airwork with a single de Havilland DH60 trainer. The new operator was being supported by a British company, Airwork, a predecessor of British United Airways and, eventually, British Airways (qv). The first scheduled service appeared the following year, linking Cairo, Alexandria, and Mersa Matruh with de Havilland Dragon Rapide aircraft. By 1936 the fleet consisted of nine aircraft, all of de Havilland manufacture, including two Dragon Rapides, five Rapides, and two Dragon Expresses. Progress with these aircraft continued, so that in addition to destinations within Egypt, by 1939 the airline also served many important points in the Middle East.

While World War Two saw many restrictions placed on airline operations, with such activity as existed confined to the movement of Allied officers, post-war the airline was able to introduce Vickers Vikings. In 1949 the name was changed to Misrair, and during the period under this title the airline introduced Vickers Viscount turboprop airliners and then became the first Middle East airline to operate jet aircraft when it introduced de Havilland Comet 4Cs in 1960.

At this time Egypt and Syria declared that they were to become a United Arab Republic, and although this concept had practical limitations, Egypt immediately declared itself as the 'United Arab Republic', and in 1960 the state-owned Misrair became United Arab Airlines, incorporating the privately-owned Syrian Airways, the Misrair title being retained for a new domestic airline. Even after Syria decided to operate its own airline in 1961, the United Arab Airlines title was retained by the Egyptian airline until October 1971, when the present title was adopted.

While the Comet fleet eventually reached seven aircraft, in 1968 the airline introduced three Boeing 707-366 aircraft, while Egypt's alignment with the Soviet Union at the time also meant that Antonov An-24s entered the fleet on loan from both the air force and Misrair.

The airline has now absorbed its domestic subsidiary and operates a strong fleet of Airbus and Boeing origin. Ownership remains with the Egyptian Government.

Executive Directors & Officers: Eng Mohamed Fahim Rayan, Chairman & President; Abel H. Esmat, Senior Vice-President, Europe; Said Refaat, Vice-President, Finance; Captain H. Mesharafa, Vice-President, Operations; Abdel Fatah Hanafi, Vice-President, Commercial; Eng M. Elmasry, Vice-President, Technical.

HQ Airport & Main Base: Cairo

Radio callsign: EGYPTAIR

Designator: MS/MSR

Employees: 14,000

Main destinations served: Abu Dhabi, Abu Simbel, Accra, Addis Ababa, Aden, Al Ain, Aleppo, Alexandria, Algiers, Amman, Amsterdam, Asmara, Aswan, Athens, Bahrain, Barcelona, Beirut, Berlin, Bombay, Brussels, Budapest, Cape Town, Copenhagen, Damascus, Dar-es-Salaam, Dhahran, Doha, Dubai, Durban, Düsseldorf, Entebbe, Frankfurt, Geneva, Harare, Hurghada, Istanbul, Jeddah, Jerusalem, Johannesburg, Kano, Khartoum, Kiev, Kuwait, Lagos, Larnaca, London Heathrow, Luxor, Madrid, Malta, Mersa Matruh, Milan, Mogadishu, Moscow, Munich, Muscat, Nairobi, New Valley, Paris, Port Said, Prague, Ras al Khaimah, Riyadh, Rome, Sanaa, Sharjah, Sharm el Sheikh, Stockholm, Taba, Tunis, Vienna, Zürich.

LINKS WITH OTHER AIRLINES
Marketing alliance with Air Sinai.

FLEET
3 Boeing 777-200
1 Airbus A340-300 (leased)
4 Airbus A340-200 (1 leased)
2 Boeing 767-300ER
3 Boeing 767-200
9 Airbus A300-600R
3 Airbus A300B4
4 Airbus A321-100
7 Airbus A320-200
5 Boeing 737-500

PETROLEUM AIR SERVICES

Petroleum Air Services

Incorporated: 1982

HISTORY
An operator of charter services mainly for passengers, Petroleum Air Services operates a fleet of light helicopters and de Havilland Dash 7 aircraft in the Western Desert and the Gulf of Suez. Ownership rests with the state-owned Egyptian General Petroleum Corporation (75 per cent) and Air Logistics International (25 per cent).

Executive Directors & Officers: Amir A. Riad, Chairman & Managing Director; Tameen Fahmy, Deputy Managing Director.

HQ Airport & Main Base: Cairo

Designator: PAS

Employees: 500

FLEET
5 de Havilland Dash 7
3 Bell 412HP
10 Bell 212
6 Bell 206-L LongRanger
2 Bell 206B JetRanger

El Salvador – YS

TACA

TACA International Airlines

Incorporated: 1931

HISTORY
Originally formed in 1931, TACA developed a scheduled service network initially in Central America, but in 1990 the network reached New York and Washington. The airline acquired a 30 per cent stake in Aviateca (qv) of Guatemala in 1989 when that airline was privatised, and also has a 10 per cent interest in LACSA (qv) of Costa Rica and 49 per cent of Nica of Nicaragua.

Executive Directors & Officers:
Federico Bloch, President & Chief Executive Officer; William J. Handal, Chief Operating Officer & General Manager; Milton Solano, Financial Director; Mauricio Sol, Commercial Director; Jaime Gonzalez, Operations Director; Ernesto Ruiz, Maintenance Director; Edwardo Corona, Personnel Director.

HQ Airport & Main Base: San Salvador

Radio callsign: TACA

Designator: TA/TAI

Employees: 2,100

Main destinations served: Belize, Guatemala City, Houston, Los Angeles, Managua, Mexico City, Miami, New Orleans, New York JFK, Panama City, San Francisco, San Jose, San Pedro Sula, Tegucigalpa, Washington.

LINKS WITH OTHER AIRLINES
Has interests in Aviateca (qv), 30 per cent; Nica, 49 per cent; and LACSA (qv), 10 per cent.

FLEET
1 Boeing 767-300ER
1 Boeing 767-200ER
2 Airbus A320-200 (plus orders for 5)
5 Boeing 737-300
5 Boeing 737-200

Estonia – ES

ELK AIRWAYS

Elk Estonian Aviation Company Ltd
Incorporated: 1991

HISTORY
Founded in 1991, Elk operates a small network of services from Tallin to destinations in the Baltic region with a fleet of five aircraft. It is owned by Tivik and Aviacor, and has Baltic Express Line as a subsidiary. Marketing alliances exist with several airlines.

Executive Directors & Officers:
Alexander Beloussov, President; Rita Lillipuu, Vice-President; Vladimir Slonchevsky, Deputy General Director; Vello Sild, Financial Director; Alphons Raubichko, Commercial Director; Vladimir Shkolnik, Technical Director.

HQ Airport & Main Base: Tallin

Radio callsign: ELKA

Designator: S8/520

Employees: Flight-crew: 17; Cabin staff: 9; Engineering: 12; Ground staff: 61; Total: 105.

Main destinations served: Helsinki, Moscow, Riga, St Petersburg, Turku.

Revenue passenger km pa: 7,786,983

Cargo tonne km pa: 790,840

LINKS WITH OTHER AIRLINES
Alliances with Air Baltic (qv), British Airways (qv), Estonian Air (qv), and Finnair (qv).

FLEET
3 Tupolev Tu-154M
2 Let L-410

ESTONIAN AIR

Estonian Air
Incorporated: 1991

HISTORY
Originally the local division of ARIA-Aeroflot (qv), Estonian Air assumed its independence in 1991 as a state-owned concern. In 1995 the Estonian Government offered 66 per cent of the shares for sale, and Maersk Air (qv) obtained a 49 per cent stake in the airline, with an Estonian investment organisation, the Baltic Cresco Investment Group, obtaining the remaining 17 per cent.

The Boeing 737-500 is a big improvement over the former Soviet types which Estonian Air operated before the Baltic States regained their independence.

The fleet has seen the rapid disappearance of Tu-134 and Yak-40 equipment of Aeroflot origin, but Maersk has provided more up-to-date western equipment.

Executive Directors & Officers: Boerge Thornbech, President; Kaja Kirillova, Financial Director; Toomas Leis, Vice-President, Commercial; Aarne Tork, Vice-President, Technical.

HQ Airport & Main Base: Tallinn

Radio callsign: ESTONIAN

Designator: OV/ELL

Employees: Flight-crew: 34; Cabin staff: 53; Engineering: 79; Ground staff: 189; Total: 380.

Main destinations served: Amsterdam, Copenhagen, Hamburg, Helsinki, Kiev, London Gatwick, Minsk, Moscow, Stockholm, Vilnius.

Aircraft km pa: 3,994,871

Revenue passenger km pa: 147.4 million

Cargo tonne km pa: 740,187

LINKS WITH OTHER AIRLINES
Maersk Air has a 49 per cent interest. Code-sharing with Finnair (qv) on Tallin–Helsinki service.

FLEET
2 Boeing 737-500 (leased)
2 Fokker 50 (leased from Maersk)

Ethiopia – ET

ETHIOPIAN AIRLINES

Ethiopian Airlines

Incorporated: 1945

HISTORY
Founded in 1945, Ethiopian Airlines commenced scheduled services the following year, receiving technical and operational assistance from TWA (qv). The airline now operates both internal and international services. It is wholly-owned by the Ethiopian Government.

Executive Directors & Officers: Ato Seeye Abraha, Chairman; Dr Ahmed Kellow, Chief Executive Officer; Wzo Anchinalu Tamer, Executive Officer, Corporate Finance; Ato Sultan Mohammed, Executive Officer, Operations & Technical; Ato Gebrehiwet G. Egziabher, Executive Officer, Marketing; Wzo Frehiwot Worku, Executive Officer, Human Resources Management.

HQ Airport & Main Base: Addis Ababa

Radio callsign: ETHIOPIAN

Designator: ET/ETH

Employees: 3,370

Main destinations served: Some 50 domestic destinations plus Abidjan, Abu Dhabi, Accra, Asmara, Athens, Bamako, Beijing, Bombay, Brazzaville, Bujumbura, Cairo, Dakar, Dar-es-Salaam, Delhi, Djibouti, Dubai, Durban, Entebbe, Frankfurt, Harare, Johannesburg, Karachi, Kilimanjaro, Kigali, Kinshasa, Jeddah, Lagos, Lilongwe, Lome, London Heathrow, Luanda, Muscat, Nairobi, Ndjamena, Niamey, Riyadh, Rome, Sanaa.

LINKS WITH OTHER AIRLINES
Marketing alliances with Air India (qv) and Nigeria Airways (qv).

FLEET
1 Boeing 767-300ER
2 Boeing 767-200ER
1 Boeing 757-200ER
4 Boeing 757-200
1 Boeing 707-320C
1 Boeing 737-200
2 Lockheed L-100-30 Hercules
5 Fokker 50
2 ATR 42
1 de Havilland DHC-5A Buffalo
5 de Havilland DHC-6-300 Twin Otter

Fiji – DO

AIR PACIFIC

Air Pacific Limited

Incorporated: 1947

HISTORY
Formed in 1947 by an Australian, Harold Gatty, Air Pacific was initially known as Katafaga Estates, but the name of Fiji Airways was adopted in 1951 when the airline started regular air services to the islands within the Fiji group. The early aircraft were of de Havilland manufacture, with first Dragon Rapides, then Herons and the relatively rare trimotor Drovers manufactured in Australia. These were later replaced by de Havilland Canada Turbo Beavers and Douglas DC-3s, as well as Hawker Siddeley 748s.

The current title was adopted in 1972, reflecting the airline's move into longer-haul services, and the first jet aircraft – three British Aerospace One-Elevens – were acquired the same year. Today the route network extends as far as Japan, the west coast of the United States, Australia, and New Zealand, while domestic services are operated by smaller feeder airlines. The airline is controlled by the Fiji Government with 79.55 per cent of the shares, while Qantas (qv) holds 10 per cent.

Executive Directors & Officers:
Gerrald Barrack, Chairman; T.A.
Drysdale, Managing Director & Chief
Executive Officer; A. Wong, General
Manager, Operations; J. Yee-Joy, General
Manager, Commercial; R. Narayan,
General Manager, Corporate Affairs;
Kamikamica, Director of Finance; B.
Geddes, Director of Engineering; E.
Dutta, Director of Marketing; M. Taukave,
Director, Customer Services; I.
Komailevuka, Director, Human
Resources.

HQ Airport & Main Base: Nadi

Radio callsign: PACIFIC NADI

Designator: FJ/FJI

Employees: Flight-crew: 76; Cabin staff:
282; Engineering: 118; Ground staff: 305;
Total: 781.

Main destinations served: Apia,
Auckland, Brisbane, Christchurch, Los
Angles, Melbourne, Osaka, Papeete, Port
Vila, Sydney, Tokyo, Tonga, Wellington.

Annual turnover: Fiji $211 million

Top: *A line up on Fiji of the main types in
Air Pacific service with, in the foreground,
a Boeing 737-500, then a Boeing 767-
300ER, and in the background a Boeing
747-200.*

Middle: *This Air Pacific Boeing 737-300 is
operated jointly with Royal Tongan
Airlines.*

Bottom: *Pride of the Air Pacific fleet is this
Boeing 767-300ER for the airline's long-
haul operations.*

Revenue passenger km pa: 1,242 million

Cargo tonne km pa: 71.065 million

LINKS WITH OTHER AIRLINES
Qantas (qv) owns 10 per cent of Air Pacific shares.
Code-sharing with Air Calin, Air Vanuatu, Polynesian Airlines, Qantas (qv), Royal Tongan Airlines, and Solomon Airlines (qv).

FLEET
1 Boeing 747-200 (leased)
2 Boeing 767-300ER (leased)
1 Boeing 737-300 (leased jointly with Royal Tongan)
1 Boeing 737-500 (leased)
plus 3 Boeing 737-700 on order

Finland – OH

FINNAIR

Finnair O/Y
Incorporated: 1923

HISTORY
Finnair was founded in 1923 under the title of 'Aero' by Bruno Lucander, who commenced operations the following March using a single Junkers F-13 mono-plane seaplane. During the summer months this aircraft served Tallin and Stockholm from Helsinki, and during the winter months services were operated within Finland. For the summer of 1925 the Helsinki–Tallin service was extended to Berlin. During the severe winter which followed, when the ferry services between Helsinki and Tallin were cancelled and those between Helsinki and Stockholm were severely curtailed, the Finnish Parliament became convinced of the potential offered by air transport. This led to the Finnish Government providing the new airline with a loan to purchase a Junkers G-24, and a subsidy for the Stockholm route, as well as a contract to provide air mail services.

By 1928 the fleet consisted of four Junkers F-13s and a single G-24. An ambitious new route was introduced that year when the 'Scandinavian Air Express' was inaugurated linking Tallin and Helsinki to London and Paris via Stockholm, Malmö, Copenhagen, and Amsterdam, taking 24 hours end to end. Several new routes were added to the airline's network over the next few years, and Finnair played a significant role in the development of overnight air mail services, which were helped significantly during the early 1930s by the introduction of a Junkers Ju.52/3m, which was able to establish its position using signals from a ground-based radio station. Yet another advance was the opening of airports at Turku and Helsinki in 1935 and 1936 respectively, enabling the airline to convert to an all landplane fleet. In the years immediately before the outbreak of World War Two a domestic route network was built up using two de Havilland Dragon Rapide biplanes.

Although not initially involved with the war in Europe, Finland was dragged in after being attacked by the Soviet Union, which wished to annex it. Most civil operations had to stop during the war, although the service from Helsinki to Stockholm was maintained until the winter of 1944–45. The position of Finland during the closing months of the war was made more difficult after Finland had allied herself with Germany, facing a common enemy in the Soviet Union. Nevertheless, an early resumption of domestic services was possible once the war ended, using Douglas DC-3s, although international services did not resume until 1947, when the Helsinki–Stockholm service was reintroduced.

The expansion of both domestic and international services continued throughout the 1950s, and in 1956 Finnair became the first western airline to be allowed to operate services to Moscow, although this concession was probably allowed because Finland had neutrality forced upon her post-war. While the DC-3s remained in service throughout this period they were increasingly confined to domestic duties,

A Father Christmas theme for one of Finnair's McDonnell Douglas MD-11s.

In a more conventional colour scheme, a Finnair McDonnell Douglas MD-87 touches down.

while international routes were taken over by the Convair 340 and 440 Metropolitan.

Finnair entered the 1960s with the introduction of its first jet airliners, Sud Aviation Caravelles, which by the mid-1960s were used on all of its main international routes. In 1969 the airline introduced two Douglas DC-8-62s for its first transatlantic services. By this time another change had occurred: after using the name 'Finnair' for some years, but officially remaining Aero O/Y, the legal title had also been changed to Finnair.

Finnair's broader horizons did not mean that domestic services were neglected, and one of the most intensive domestic networks anywhere, relative to population, was developed.

In 1996 a major reorganisation of Finnish civil aviation led to Finnair absorbing the operations of two other airlines, Finnaviation and Karair. Karair dated from 1950, when it had been formed as Karhumaki Airways, the operating offshoot of the Karhumaki Group, which dated from the 1920s and had been founded by three brothers with an interest in aircraft manufacturing and operations. At first the new airline had operated de Havilland Dragon Rapides on a service between Helsinki and Joensuu, but these were soon joined by two Lockheed Lodestars, and the route was extended to Sundsvall in Sweden via two other domestic route points, although the Swedish section soon had to be dropped. A service to Tampere was later introduced, and Douglas DC-3s were added to the fleet.

Karhumaki Airways' name was changed to Karair in 1957, the same year as a Convair 440 Metropolitan was introduced to the fleet, soon followed by a second aircraft. In addition to a small network of domestic services, Karair was by this time expanding into the air charter business, and Douglas DC-6B Cloudmasters soon joined the fleet, including a swing-tail variant for cargo. Finnair acquired a 29.8 per cent stake in Karair in 1963, and an operating agreement between the two airlines effectively left Karair to operate charters, apart from two scheduled domestic routes and Finnair scheduled services. This arrangement continued for some time, although eventually Karair became a domestic scheduled airline operating ATR 72s and a twin Otter, serving 16 destinations as well as undertaking some international operations on behalf of Finnair, so that charter operations became much less significant. It also became a subsidiary of Finnair.

Finnaviation also dated from 1950, when it had been formed as Lentohuolto, later changing to Wihuri Finnwings and finally to Finnaviation in 1979 when Oy Nordair, which dated from 1970, was acquired. Finnair eventually acquired a 90 per cent shareholding. Finnaviation operated a domestic network, night mail, and air taxi operations, as well as undertaking a number of services on behalf of Finnair. By the 1990s the fleet included six Saab 340s, one of which was configured for executive use and flown on charters for business and government customers.

Finnair today is owned 60.69 per cent by the state, with the remaining shares belonging to banks and insurance companies, nominees, and individuals. While Finnaviation's operations are integrated with those of Finnair the name is still used operationally. Finnair serves more than 20 domestic destinations in addition to a comprehensive European network and transatlantic and Asian services. The airline has been a staunch supporter of Douglas and then McDonnell Douglas aircraft types for most of its history, and it will be interesting to see what the future shape of the fleet will be now that Boeing has acquired McDonnell Douglas. Four Boeing 757s have meanwhile been introduced to the fleet for charter traffic.

In 1997 a marketing alliance was signed with Lufthansa (qv).

Executive Directors & Officers: Antti Potila, President & Chief Executive Officer; Mauri Annala, Executive Vice-President, Accounting, Subsidiaries, Catering; Henrik Arle, Executive Vice-President, Financing, International Relations, Information Management; Jorma Eloranta, Executive Vice-President, Operations; Jouko Malen, Executive Vice-President, Technical; Leif Lundstrom, Executive Vice-President, Marketing; Juhani Suomela, Executive Vice-President, Human Resources & Service; Erkki Lehtinen, Vice-President, Internal Auditing.

HQ Airport & Main Base: Helsinki

Radio callsign: FINNAIR

Designator: AY/FIN

Employees: 8,319

Main destinations served:
Finnair/Finnaviation serve 26 domestic destinations, plus Amsterdam, Athens, Bangkok, Barcelona, Beijing, Bergen, Berlin, Brussels, Budapest, Copenhagen, Delhi, Dubai, Dublin, Düsseldorf, Frankfurt, Geneva, Gothenburg, Hamburg, Istanbul, Larnaca, Lisbon, London Gatwick, London Heathrow, London Stansted, Madrid, Malaga, Manchester, Miami, Milan, Murmansk, New York, Osaka, Oslo, Paris, Petrozavodsk, Prague, Riga, Rome, San Francisco, Singapore, St Petersburg, Stockholm, Tallin, Tokyo, Toronto, Vienna, Vilnius, Warsaw, Zürich.

Annual turnover: US $1,577 million (£955.75 million)

Revenue passenger km pa: 10,998 million

Cargo tonne km pa: 66,668,000

Passengers pa: 6,280,000

LINKS WITH OTHER AIRLINES

Marketing alliance and code-sharing with Lufthansa (qv). Code-sharing with Air Canada (qv), Air China (qv), Alitalia (qv), Aer Lingus (qv), Austrian Airlines (qv), Braathens SAFE (qv), Delta Air Lines (qv), El Al (qv), Estonian Air (qv), Lithuanian Airways (qv), Maersk Air (qv), Sabena (qv), Swissair (qv), and Transwede (qv).

FLEET

4 McDonnell Douglas MD-11
4 Boeing 757-200
22 McDonnell Douglas MD-82/83 (13 leased)
3 McDonnell Douglas MD-87
12 McDonnell Douglas DC-9-51
6 ATR 72 (1 leased)
6 Saab 340 (4 leased)
plus 12 Airbus A320 on order

France – F

AEROPOSTALE

Société d'Exploitation Aéropostale

Incorporated: 1991

HISTORY

Previously known as Intercargo Service, which operated two Boeing 737-200Cs and a Vickers Merchantman on cargo flights for Air France (qv) and night mail services from Orly to Montpellier and Toulouse, Aéropostale was established by Air France and La Poste in 1991. Since that time the fleet has grown considerably, and while ownership remains 50:50 Groupe Air France and Groupe La Poste, the airline also undertakes day passenger flights for Air France using quick change (QC) aircraft.

Executive Directors & Officers: Marten Vial, President; Gilbert Rovetto, Director General; Maurice Serinet, Vice-President, Finance; Patrick Fourticq, Vice-President, Operations; Jean-François Dominiak, Vice-President, Commercial; Jean-Claude Billot, Vice-President, Maintenance.

HQ Airport & Main Base: Paris CDG

Radio callsign: AEROPOSTE

Designator: ARP

Employees: 395

Main destinations served: Day passenger and cargo flights on Air France network, night flights from Paris to major French cities on behalf of La Poste.

LINKS WITH OTHER AIRLINES

Air France has a 50 per cent interest.

FLEET

2 Boeing 727-200F
15 Boeing 737-300QC
2 Boeing 737-200F
2 Boeing 737-200QC

AIR CHARTER

Société Aérienne Française d'Affrètement SA

Incorporated: 1966

HISTORY

Air Charter was formed in 1966 by Air France (qv) as the Société Aérienne Française d'Affrètement, eventually assuming the current title for everyday use. Originally a wholly-owned subsidiary of Air France, in 1977 Air Inter – now Air France Europe (qv) – was granted 20 per cent of the shares in return for an agreement to abandon the charter market. Today both airlines are owned by Groupe Air France, which also owns 100 per cent of Air France and has a 72.3 per cent interest in Air France Europe. The fleet is leased in from Air France and Air France Europe.

An unusual feature is that the average load factor for the airline is just 69.9 per cent, below that for Air France at 72.8 per cent. Charter airlines normally expect load factors of 90 per cent or more, while 70 per cent is reasonable for a scheduled operator.

HQ Airport & Main Base: Paris CDG, but operates from airports throughout France.

Radio callsign: AIR CHARTER

Designator: SF/ACF

Employees: 95

Main destinations served: Primarily air charters in Europe, North Africa, and the Canaries, for inclusive tour holiday operators.

Annual turnover: Included in figures for Air France.

Revenue passenger km pa: 2,323 million

Passengers pa: 1,343 million

LINKS WITH OTHER AIRLINES

Owned 80 per cent by Air France, 20 per cent by Air France Europe.

FLEET

2 Airbus A300
4 Airbus A320
3 Boeing 737

AIR FRANCE

Compagnie Nationale Air France

Incorporated: 1933

HISTORY

Although Air France itself dates from 1933, it resulted from the merger of five earlier airlines, the oldest of which, Farman Airlines, dated from 1919. The other four were CIDNA (Cie International de Navigation Aérienne), Air Union, Air Orient, and Aéropostale.

Farman Airlines, owned by the aircraft manufacturer of that name, had been amongst the first generation of airlines when it was formed in 1919, and amongst the first to operate on the Paris–London service, soon followed by a service from Paris to Brussels. On both these services the airline used Farman Goliath 13-seat converted bombers. Steady expansion ensured that the airline was serving most western European capitals by 1930.

Air Union concentrated on services to the Mediterranean area of France, while Air Orient, as the name implies, operated from France to the Far East. The latter operated its first service in 1931, from Marseilles in the south of France to Saigon in what was then French Indo-China, flying via Damascus. The journey took ten days, and involved two aircraft, with a Liore-et-Olivier 242 on the Mediterranean section, and a Brequet 280 for the remainder.

Aéropostale was already owned by the French Government, which had rescued it after it became bankrupt, restarting its postal operations. The airline had been started in the early 1920s, and had also played a part in the development of an ancestor airline to Aérolineas Argentinas (qv).

The French Government had a 25 per cent interest in Air France. The new airline expanded rapidly after its formation, so that by 1939 it had a fleet of 90 aircraft, of which 15 were seaplanes. On the outbreak of World War Two the airline's operations were diverted entirely to the war effort, with the needs of the diplomats and the military being met by an hourly frequency on the Paris to London route in 1939. The fall of France in 1940 led to operations being abandoned until 1942, when the airline was reassembled in North Africa, where it operated a small network of services based on Algiers and Dakar, with Damascus being added later after the Allies had occupied Vichy French territory in North Africa. When the war ended the airline was nationalised, although provision was later made for 30

The end of a transatlantic flight for one of Air France's BAC/Aérospatiale Concorde supersonic transports.

per cent of the shares to be held by private individuals or organisations.

Normal services were not resumed until 1946, when Air France restarted services to the French colonies and inaugurated its first transatlantic services, using a fleet of Douglas DC-4s, with DC-3s for the shorter routes. More modern aircraft were to follow, including Lockheed Super Constellations for inter-continental services, and, for routes in Europe and to North Africa, Vickers Viscounts. The airline was the first in the west to introduce jet aircraft to short-haul services as the launch airline for the Sud Aviation Caravelle in May 1959, and this subsequently went on to become the first, and only, French airliner to enjoy commercial success. In January 1976 Air France became one of just two western airlines to operate supersonic air services when it and British Airways (qv) launched the world's first supersonic air services simultaneously.

Throughout this period Air France also became heavily involved in the formation of airlines in French colonies as these approached independence. Amongst these were Air Vietnam, in which Air France had a 25 per cent interest; Royal Air Cambodge (30 per cent); Tunis Air (49 per cent); Air Madagascar (qv) (30 per cent); Royal Air Maroc (qv) (21 per cent); and Middle East Airlines (qv) (30 per cent). Air France also took an interest in Air Afrique (qv), the airline created to provide services to the former colonies. When French domestic airline Air Inter – now Air

France Europe (qv) – was established, Air France took a 25 per cent shareholding. A charter subsidiary, Société Aérienne Français d'Affrètement, was formed in 1966, the predecessor of today's Air Charter (qv), Air France having an 80 per cent interest in this and a 20 per cent holding in its sister company, Air France Europe.

In 1991 Air France acquired a majority 84.95 per cent stake in UTA (Union de Transportes Aériens), which had been formed in 1963 following a merger between UAT (Union Aéromaritime de Transport) and TAI (Transport Aériens Intercontinentaux), which both dated from the early post-war period and both had strong shipping connections. UAT had been one of the few airlines to operate the ill-starred de Havilland Comet I airliner and had concentrated on services to Africa, while TAI had operated as a charter airline until starting services to the Pacific, including Tahiti, in 1956. At the time of acquisition by Air France, UTA was operating a fleet of three Boeing 747-300s and six McDonnell Douglas DC-10-30s. The acquisition meant that Air France gained a well-established route network in Africa and the Pacific which complemented its own.

In 1994 a major restructuring of French air transport took place to cut costs and state support, made necessary both by pressure from the European Union to end massive state subsidies to state-controlled airlines, and by growing competition both on domestic routes by the independent

French airlines, and on international routes by strong competition encouraged by the free market. A new holding company, Groupe Air France SA, was established to take over both Air France and Air Inter, which became Air France Europe and now operates a number of international services. As a transitional stage, Air France Europe (qv) operated as Air Inter Europe.

As Europe's third-largest airline, Air France operates an extensive route network and with the other group companies has more than 200 aircraft. Almost 200 destinations are served, including 14 which are served by both Air France and Air France Europe. Co-operation agreements exist with some 30 airlines.

Executive Directors & Officers: Jean-Cyril Spinetta, President & Chief Executive Officer; Marc Veron, Chief Operating Officer; Pierre-Alain Jeanneney, Director General, Finance & Administration; Marc Lamidey, Director General, Development.

HQ Airport & Main Base: Paris CDG

Radio callsign: AIRFRANS

Designator: AF/AFR

Employees: Flight-crew: 2,745; Cabin staff: 6,438; Ground staff: 27,346; Total: 36,529.

Main destinations served: Abidjan, Abu Dhabi, Agadir, Amman, Amsterdam, Antanarivo, Antigua, Athens, Basle, Barnako, Bangkok, Bangui, Barcelona, Beijing, Belgrade, Berlin, Beyrouth, Bogotá, Brazzaville, Brussels, Bucharest, Budapest, Buenos Aires, Cancun, Caracas, Cayenne, Chicago, Cologne, Conakry, Copenhagen, Cotonou, Dakar, Damascus, Delhi, Douala, Dubai, Düsseldorf, Edinburgh, Florence, Frankfurt, Geneva, Gothenburg, Hamburg, Hanoi, Hanover, Harare, Ho Chi Minh City, Hong Kong, Houston, Istanbul, Jakarta, Jeddah, Johannesburg, Kiev, Kinshasa, Kuwait, Cairo, Cape Town, Lagos, Leipzig, Libreville, Lisbon, Ljubljana, Lome, London, Los Angeles, Luanda, Lugano, Luxembourg, Lyons, Madrid, Malaga, Manchester, Manilla, Maputo, Marrakech, Mauritius, Mexico City, Miami, Milan, Montevideo, Montreal, Moscow, Mumbai, Munich, Nairobi, Naples, N'djamana, New York JFK, Niamey, Nice, Nouakchott, Noumea, Nuremberg, Oporto, Osaka, Oslo, Ougadougou, Oujda, Papeete, Pointe Noire, Point-a-Pitre, Port-au-Prince, Port Harcourt, Prague, Quito, Rio de Janeiro, Riyadh, Rome, Saint Dominque, Saint Martin, San Francisco, Santiago, São

Air France has been a strong supporter of Airbus, of which this A340-200 is one of the more recent examples . . .

Paulo, Seoul, Seville, Seychelles, Sfax, Singapore, Sofia, Southampton, Split, St Lucia, St Petersburg, Stockholm, Stuttgart, Tehran, Tel Aviv, Tokyo, Toronto, Turin, Venice, Vienna, Warsaw, Washington, Yaounda, Zagreb, Zürich.

Annual turnover: US $10,631 million (£6,443 million) – Group Air France figure

Revenue passenger km pa: 51,712 million

Cargo tonne km pa: 4,766 million

Passengers pa: 15 million

LINKS WITH OTHER AIRLINES
Owns 80 per cent of Air Charter (qv). Air France Europe (qv) is a sister company within the same group. Alliances with Continental Airlines (qv), Delta Air Lines (qv), and Japan Airlines (qv).
Co-operation with Adria (qv), Aeroflot (qv), Aéromexico (qv), Aéropostale (qv), Air Afrique (qv), Air Austral of Reunion Island, Air Canada (qv), Air Gabon (qv), Air Madagascar (qv), Air Mauritius (qv), Air Seychelles, Austrian (qv), Balkan (qv), Cameroon (qv), Croatia (qv), CSA (qv), Japan Airlines (qv), Korean (qv), LOT (qv), Lufthansa (qv), Malev (qv), Sabena (qv), Tarom (qv), Tunis Air (qv), Ukraine

International (qv), and Vietnam Airlines (qv).

FLEET
32 Boeing 747
11 Boeing 747 Freighter
5 BAe/Aerospatiale Concorde

11 Airbus A340 (plus 12 A340-300 on order)
4 Airbus A330
5 Boeing 767
13 Airbus A300 (6 Air France Europe, 2 Air Charter)
9 Airbus A310

. . . but still needs to operate the Boeing 747-400 on the busier long-haul routes.

5 Airbus A321 (all Air Charter)
62 Airbus A320 (35 Air France Europe, 4 Air Charter)
9 Airbus A319
43 Boeing 737 (3 Air Charter)
5 Fokker 100 (all Air France Europe)
plus 10 Boeing 777-200 IGW on order

AIR FRANCE EUROPE

Compagnie Nationale Air France Europe

Incorporated: 1954

HISTORY

Known until 1996 as Air Inter, and then as Air Inter Europe until April 1997, Air France Europe was originally founded in 1954 as a domestic airline for France. The founders were Air France (qv), SNCF (the French railway company), and the Compagnie de Transports Aériens, with banks, regional groups, and some private companies also providing capital, with the latter including the airline TAI. Services were started in 1958 using chartered aircraft, but suspended after a few months, so that it was not until June 1960 that a more determined effort was made, this time successfully. The first route was Paris to Toulouse, and before the end of the first year Paris–Pau and Lille–Lyon–Nice were also introduced, with services to Dinard, Quimper, La Baule, Tarbes, and Biarritz following shortly afterwards. The early routes were co-ordinated with the services of both Air France and SNCF, with some of the routes intended either to fill in gaps in existing air and railway services, or to by-pass Paris, as in the case of Lille–Lyon–Nice.

Once the operation was established ex-Air France Vickers Viscount 700 series aircraft were acquired, the first five being introduced in 1962, when the airline established its maintenance base at Paris Orly, to this day the main hub for French domestic air services. In 1963 TAI became part of UTA, the leading French independent airline, and UTA thereby became a shareholder in Air Inter, so that Air France and SNCF each held a 25 per cent stake in the airline, with UTA having a further 15 per cent. The Viscount fleet continued to grow during the early-1960s, while in 1964 Air Inter also received four small 26-seat Nord 262 airliners for the quieter routes.

Air Inter's first jet aircraft were Sud Aviation Caravelle IIIs, with the first two leased from Air France. These were later augmented and then replaced during the early-1970s by 11 Dassault Mercure jet airliners, of which Air Inter was the sole operator in a market dominated by the similarly-sized Boeing 737. Meanwhile Fokker F-27 Friendships were introduced to fill the size gap between the Nord 262s and the Caravelles.

For the first three decades of its existence the airline was forbidden by law to operate scheduled services outside France, but it developed charter services. In 1977 Air Inter agreed with Air France to cease competing in the charter market, and in return received 20 per cent of Air Charter (qv). Slightly more than a decade later Air Inter was able to operate scheduled services to Ibiza and Madrid, using an Air France designator, while in return Air France was able to operate from Paris Charles de Gaulle to Marseilles. In 1987 a night cargo airline, Intercargo Service, was established in conjunction with Europe Air Service and Banque Paribas. By this time Air Inter was owned 37 per cent by Air France and 35.8 per cent by UTA, and Air France's acquisition of almost 90 per cent of UTA's shares in 1991 effectively made Air Inter a subsidiary of Air France.

In 1990 a major restructuring of Air France led to both Air France and Air Inter, along with Air Charter, becoming subsidiaries of Groupe Air France, with Air Inter becoming Air France Europe in April 1997 after first being marketed as Air Inter Europe for an interim period of a year. Today, Air France Europe still retains a 20 per cent interest in Air Charter, while the airline is operating a number of routes on behalf of Air France. The long term aim is to integrate the operations of Air France Europe with the short-haul operations of Air France. Air Inter is owned 72.3 per cent by Groupe Air France, while SNCF still retains a 12.3 per cent shareholding.

The fleet includes aircraft of Airbus manufacture for the most part, although delivery of six out of an order for ten of the large Airbus A330-300 has been deferred, and three have been sold to Sabena (qv), reflecting not only the need to improve the financial performance of Groupe Air France, but growing competition both from the newly deregulated independent airlines and from SNCF's expanding TGV high-speed railway network.

Executive Directors & Officers:
Christian Blanc, President-Director General; Jean-Pierre Courcol, Director General; Pierre-Alain Jeanneney, Director General, Finance & Administration; Marc Lamidy, Director General, Development; Gilbert Jehl, Director General, Maintenance.

HQ Airport & Main Base: Paris Orly

Radio callsign: AIR INTER

Designator: IT/ITF (or Air France AF)

Employees: Flight-crew: 700; Cabin staff: 1,489; Ground staff: 7,836; Total: 10,025.

Main destinations served: Ajaccio,

This Air France Europe Airbus A320 is still in Air Inter Europe colours, the interim arrangement between Air Inter and Air France Europe.

Basle/Mulhouse, Bastia, Biarritz, Beziers, Bordeaux, Brest, Calvi, Clermont Ferrand, Frejus, Lille, Limoges, Lorient, Lourdes/Tarbes, Lyon, Marseilles, Montpellier, Nantes, Nice, Nîmes, Pau, Perpignan, Quimper, Rennes, Strasbourg, St Etienne, Toulon, Toulouse.
Most flights are from Paris, but there are also a considerable number of cross-country routes, and some 15 international services (12 Europe, 3 North Africa) are operated under Air France designators.

Annual turnover: Included in figure for Air France

Revenue passenger km pa: 9,214 million

Cargo tonne km pa: 39 million

Passengers pa: 15.8 million

LINKS WITH OTHER AIRLINES
Owned 72.7 per cent by Groupe Air France.
Owns 20 per cent of Air Charter (qv).
Jersey European (qv) is a franchisee.

FLEET
1 Airbus A330
5 Airbus A300
5 Airbus A321
35 Airbus A320
5 Fokker 100

AIR LIBERTE

Air Liberté SA

Incorporated: 1987

HISTORY
Air Liberté was founded in 1987 and began charter operations the following year, initially operating to Mediterranean holiday resorts for inclusive tour operators, but in 1990 scheduled services were begun from Paris to Bangkok, Montreal, New York, and Saint Denis, on Reunion Island in the Indian Ocean. The initial fleet of McDonnell Douglas MD-83s had grown by this time to include two Airbus A300s and an Airbus A310.

Growing liberalisation of air transport in France enabled the airline to develop its own scheduled domestic services. Early in 1997 British Airways (qv), who already owned TAT (qv), acquired 70 per cent of Air Liberté's shares, and has approval to acquire the remaining 30 per cent shareholding held by Banque Rivaud. It is likely that both Air Liberté and TAT will be operated through a BA-owned holding company.

Executive Directors & Officers: Marc Robert, Chairman; André Lopez, Chief Operating Officer; Marc Hayoun, Chief Financial Officer; Marie-Thérése Murcoceroi; Commercial Director; Thierry Dutertre, Marketing Director; Mourad Majoul, Operations Manager.

HQ Airport & Main Base: Paris CDG

Radio callsign: AIR LIBERTE

Designator: VD/LIB

Employees: 1,550

Main destinations served: Fort-de-France, Montreal, Point-a-Pitre, Saint Denis (Reunion Island), Salzburg, Toulouse, plus holiday charter flights world-wide.

LINKS WITH OTHER AIRLINES
Controlled by British Airways (qv), and a sister company of TAT (qv).

FLEET
3 McDonnell Douglas DC-10-30 (leased from Finnair (qv))
2 Airbus A300-600
2 Airbus A310-300
1 Airbus A310-200
3 Boeing 737
8 McDonnell Douglas MD-83

AIR LITTORAL

Groupe Air Littoral SA

Incorporated: 1972

HISTORY
Founded in 1972, Air Littoral has developed a network of services based on Montpellier, Nice, and destinations in the south-west of France, including international services and operations on behalf of both Air France (qv) and Air France Europe (qv). In 1988 it acquired the routes and assets of another Montpellier-based airline, Compagnie Aérienne du Languedoc. At one stage Euralair (qv) had a 35 per cent stake which it acquired from KLM (qv), but Air Littoral is now the operating subsidiary of Groupe Air Littorial, and has a number of subsidiaries including Air Littoral Riviera and Air Littoral Express. In 1997 it became a Lufthansa (qv) partner.

Executive Directors & Officers: Marc Dufour, President & Chairman; Jean-Marie Vignes, Managing Director; Pascal Fulla, General Manager; Christian Clavel, Chief Financial Officer; Jean Durand, Financial Director; Eric Dufour, Commercial Director; Jacqueline Delport, Operations Director; Jean Lorenzi, Maintenance & Technical Director; Jacques Vernette, Personnel Director.

HQ Airport & Main Base: Montpellier, with a further base at Nice

Radio callsign: AIR LITTORAL

Designator: FU/LIT (or Lufthansa LH)

Employees: 1,100

Main destinations served: Agen, Ajaccio, Barcelona, Bastia, Bergerac, Biarritz, Bologne, Bordeaux, Clermont Ferrand, Epinal, Florence, Geneva, Lille, Lyons, Manchester, Marseilles, Milan, Nantes, Naples, Palermo, Paris Orly, Pau, Perigueaux, Perpignan, Rome, Sarrebruck, Toulouse.

LINKS WITH OTHER AIRLINES
A Lufthansa (qv) partner.

FLEET
1 Fokker 100
5 Fokker 70
7 Canadair Regional Jet 100 (plus 5 options)
10 ATR 42-500 (plus 5 options)
6 Beechcraft 1900C

AIR TOULOUSE

Air Toulouse International SA

Incorporated: 1990

HISTORY
An air charter operator, Air Toulouse started operations in late 1990, and today has a fleet of Boeing 737s and Embraer Bandeirantes.

Executive Directors & Officers: Philippe Aubry, President & Director General; Antoine Ferretti, Managing Director.

HQ Airport & Main Base: Toulouse Blagnac

Radio callsign: AIR TOULOUSE

Designator: SH/TLE

Employees: 130

Main destinations served: Charters within Europe and to North Africa.

FLEET
4 Boeing 737-200
2 Embraer EMB-110 Banderante

AOM

AOM French Airlines

Incorporated: 1992

HISTORY
Although AOM dates from January 1992, it

was formed from the merger of two older airlines, Air Outre Mer and Minerve. Air Outre Mer had been formed almost five years earlier and had been operating scheduled services with three McDonnell Douglas DC-10s between Paris and Reunion in the Indian Ocean. Minerve (Compagnie Française de Transports Aériens) had been founded in 1975 by René Meyer and had been operating charter and scheduled services, with the former including ad hoc world-wide cargo operations as well as inclusive tour passenger charters. The Minerve fleet included a Boeing 747 and a McDonnell Douglas DC-10, as well as several DC-8s and MD-83s.

The new airline now operates a much rationalised fleet, with McDonnell Douglas DC-10s and MD-83s. Inclusive tour charters are operated world-wide, while scheduled services are operated within France and to destinations in the Indian and Pacific Oceans.

HQ Airport & Main Base: Paris Orly

Radio callsign: FRENCH LINES

Designator: IW/AOM

Employees: 1,020

Main destinations served: Bangkok, French Polynesia, French West Indies, Ho Chi Minh City, Los Angeles, Marseilles, Nice, Reunion, Sydney, Tokyo, Toulouse.

FLEET
8 McDonnell Douglas DC-10-30
13 McDonnell Douglas MD-83

BRIT AIR

Brit Air SA

Incorporated: 1973

HISTORY
Founded in 1973, Brit Air commenced operations in 1975 to provide direct air services from Western France to the rest of the country and to other European destinations. A service to London Gatwick was introduced in 1979. The fleet at one time included six Saab 340s, but these have been replaced by Canadair Regional Jets. The airline is the launch customer for the stretched Canadair CRJ-700 regional jet. In 1995 it became an Air France (qv) franchisee, and in 1997 reached an agreement with Air France that all services will be flown as franchises, with Air France preparing to transfer 12 routes to Brit Air.

Executive Directors & Officers: Xavia Leclercq, President; Jacques Pellerin, Director General; Jacques Albert,

Financial Director; Jacques Enjalbert, Director, Operations.

HQ Airport & Main Base: HQ is at Morlaix, but services operate from Brest, Caen, Deauville, Le Havre, Nantes, Rennes, and Toulouse.

Radio callsign: BRITTANY

Designator: DB/BZH (or Air France AF)

Employees: 559

Main destinations served: Brest, Caen, Deauville, Le Havre, Limoges, London Gatwick, Lyons, Marseilles, Montpellier, Nice, Paris CDG, Paris Orly, Quimper, Rennes, Southampton, Toulouse.

Annual turnover: US $121 million (£73.4 million)

LINKS WITH OTHER AIRLINES
Air France franchisee.

FLEET
10 Canadair Regional Jet 100
2 ATR-72
10 ATR-42
plus 4 Canadair CRJ-700 on order

CORSAIR

Corse Air International SA

Incorporated: 1981

HISTORY
Corse Air International was founded in 1981 as a charter airline specialising in services to destinations in the Mediterranean, maintaining bases at Paris Orly and Ajaccio. Operations soon expanded to include North America, while the tour operator Nouvelles Frontiers acquired a 30 per cent interest in the airline.

Executive Directors & Officers: Jacques Maillot, Chairman; P. Chesnau, Chief Executive Officer; J.J. Kerhoas, Chief Operating Officer; F. Kotelnikoff, Chief Financial Officer.

HQ Airport & Main Base: Paris Orly

Radio callsign: CORSAIR

Designator: SS/CRL

Employees: 850

Main destinations served: Charters to destinations in the Mediterranean, North America, the Caribbean, South-East Asia, and the Pacific.

FLEET
1 Boeing 747-300
2 Boeing 747-200

2 Boeing 747-100
1 Boeing 747SP
1 McDonnell Douglas DC-10-30
2 Boeing 737-400
1 Boeing 737-200

CORSE MEDITERRANEE

Compagnie Corse Mediterranée

Incorporated: 1990

HISTORY
Founded in 1990, Corse Mediterranée is a regional airline operating passenger scheduled and charter services from its base at Ajaccio in Corsica. It specialises in providing direct services from the island to important destinations in southern Europe, but in 1997 two Boeing 747-300s were acquired from Singapore Airlines for long distance charters. Maintenance is carried out by a subsidiary, Compagnie Aérienne Corse Mediterranée.

Executive Directors & Officers: Pierre Philippe Ceccaldi, Chairman & Chief Executive Officer.

HQ Airport & Main Base: Ajaccio, with operations also from Bastia and Calvi.

Radio callsign: CORSICA

Designator: XK/CCM

Employees: Flight-crew: 60; Cabin staff: 90; Total: 400.

Main destinations served: Geneva, Marseilles, Milan, Nice, Rome, Zürich.

Annual turnover: US $79.27 million (£48 million)

Aircraft km pa: 9 million

Revenue passenger km pa: 700 million

Cargo tonne km pa: 27 million

FLEET
2 Boeing 747-300
3 Fokker 100 (2 leased)
5 ATR-72

EURALAIR

Euralair International SA

Incorporated: 1964

HISTORY
Originally founded in 1964 as an air taxi and executive air charter operation, Euralair has since developed into an air charter operator, in addition to the execu-

tive charter operations which have continued. At one stage the airline operated two British Aerospace 146-200QTs on behalf of TNT (qv). Currently operations include passenger and cargo charters, and some executive charters.

Executive Directors & Officers: Antoine de Sizemont, President.

HQ Airport & Main Base: HQ is at Paris Le Bourget, plus additional bases at Paris Orly and Paris CDG.

Radio callsign: EURALAIR

Designator: RN/EUL

Employees: 250
Main destinations served: Charters within Europe and to North Africa.

FLEET
5 Boeing 737-500
2 Boeing 737-200
1 Cessna Citation I
2 Cessna Citation II

FLANDRE AIR

Flandre Air Service SA

Incorporated: 1976

HISTORY
Not to be confused with a former Belgian airline with a similar name, Flandre Air was founded in 1976 and began air taxi and executive air charter operations the following year, not moving into scheduled services until 1985. Today, a number of domestic scheduled routes are operated, mainly from the airline's base at Lille, sometimes on behalf of other airlines.

Executive Directors & Officers: Luc Delesalle, President & Chief Executive Officer; Jean Philippe Durand, Director General; Yves Le De, Operations Director.

HQ Airport & Main Base: Aéroport de Lille Lesquin

Radio callsign: FLANDRAIR

Designator: IX/FRS

Employees: 160

Main destinations served: Aurillac, Basle/Mulhouse, Bergerac, Brest, Clermont Ferrand, Epinal, Lyons, Metz, Montpellier, Nancy, Nantes, Paris Orly, Reims, Rennes, Roanne, Strasbourg.

FLEET
5 Embraer EMB-120 Brasilia
4 Beech 1900D
6 Beech 1900C

2 Beech Super King Air 200
plus up to 20 Embraer EMB-135

REGIONAL AIRLINES

Regional Airlines SA

Incorporated: 1992

HISTORY
Regional Airlines was founded in 1992 on the acquisition of Airlec and Air Vendée, two regional airlines. Air Vendée, by far the larger of the two, dated from 1975, and operated from Nantes, Rouen, and Rennes to a dozen destinations within France and neighbouring countries with a fleet which included Dornier Do.228s, Fairchild Metros, and a Beech King Air 200.

Today, Regional Airlines operates more than 200 flights daily, and has alliances with several leading European carriers.

Executive Directors & Officers: Jean-Paul Dubreuil, President & Chief Executive Officer; Michel Dubreuil, Vice-President, Operations; Philippe Chevalier, Vice-President, Commercial; Patrick Ceretti, Technical Director.

HQ Airport & Main Base: Nantes Atlantique Aéroport, with additional bases at Rouen and Rennes.

Radio callsign: REGIONAL AIRLINES

Designator: VM/RGI

Employees: 420

Main destinations served: Amsterdam, Angoulême, Basle/Mulhouse, Brussels, Bordeaux, Clermont Ferrand, Dijon, Le Havre, Limoges, Lyons, Marseilles, Paris Orly, Pau, Poitiers, San-Brieuc, Strasbourg, Toulouse.

LINKS WITH OTHER AIRLINES
Marketing alliances with Crossair (qv), Iberia (qv), KLM (qv), SAS (qv), and Swissair (qv).

FLEET
10 Saab 2000
8 Saab 340B
2 ATR 42-300
9 British Aerospace Jetstream 31
5 Embraer EMB-145

TAT

TAT European Airlines

Incorporated: 1968

HISTORY
Originally formed by Michel Marchais in 1968 as an air taxi company, at a time when French air transport was tightly regulated leaving Air Inter with a virtual monopoly of internal air services. Initially known as Touraine Air Transport, the airline moved into scheduled services in 1968, and in 1973 became a subsidiary of Société Auxiliaire de Services et de Matériel Aéronautiques. An extensive network of domestic services was gradually developed centred on Paris Orly and Lyons, with services from Poitiers and Tours to London Gatwick during the summer months.

The airline's expansion was accelerated by the acquisition of other airlines, including Air Alpes, Air Paris, Air Alsace, Air Rouerque, Taxi Avia France and, one of the largest, Rousseau Aviation. The wider base of its activities led to a name change to Transport Aérien Transregional. Meanwhile the fleet had grown to include a wide variety of aircraft, ranging from Beech King Air 90, through de Havilland Twin Otters, to Fairchild FH-227s and Boeing 737-200s. The international route network was further expanded through operating services on behalf of Air France (qv), usually with new ATR-72s.

In 1993 British Airways (qv) acquired a 49.9 per cent share, the maximum permitted to a non-French airline at the time, and this was later increased to 100 per cent in 1996. By this time it had become the largest independent carrier in France, a position which will have been strengthened by BA's purchase of 70 per cent of Air Liberté (qv), which may eventually be acquired outright, with both the French airlines operated through a BA-owned holding company.

Executive Directors & Officers: Marc Rochet, Chairman; Rodolphe Marchais, President & Director General; Alain Corbel, Deputy President; Claude Jeanteur, Deputy Director General; John Hanlon, Deputy Managing Director; M. Wittenburg, Financial Director; Pascal Sainson, Director, Operations; M. de Villeneuve, Director, Commercial; M. Durand, Director, Programmes; M. Leclerg, Director, Technical.

HQ Airport & Main Base: HQ is at Tours, with hubs at Paris Orly, Paris CDG, Lyons, and Marseilles.

Radio callsign: TAT

Designator: IJ/TAT

Employees: 1,200

Main destinations served: Athens, Berlin, Bordeaux, Brive-la-Gaillarde,

Calvi, Copenhagen, Figari, Frankfurt, Geneva, Helsinki, London Gatwick, London Heathrow, London Stansted, Marseilles, Milan Gergamo, Munich, Nice, Poitiers, Stockholm, Toulouse, Tours, Vienna.

LINKS WITH OTHER AIRLINES
A subsidiary of British Airways (qv). Operates services on behalf of Air France (qv).
A sister company of Air Liberté (qv).

FLEET
2 Boeing 737-300
5 Boeing 737-200
12 Fokker 100
3 Fokker F-28-4000
4 Fokker F-28-2000
4 Fokker F-28-1000
7 ATR 72-200
7 ATR 42-300
2 Beech 99

French Polynesia – F

AIR TAHITI

Air Tahiti

Incorporated: 1953

HISTORY
Air Tahiti dates from the formation of Réseau Aérien Interinsulaire in 1953, when the colonial authorities in French Oceania nationalised the operations of the original Air Tahiti, which had been founded in 1950. The airline's operations consisted entirely of inter-island services, and in 1958 it was acquired by TAI (Transportes Aériens Intercontinentaux), the predecessor of UTA (Union Transportes Aériens), which has since been acquired by Air France (qv).

The title Air Polynesie was taken in 1970, before the present title was adopted in 1987. The French Polynesian Government owns 19 per cent of Air Tahiti, with Air France being another significant shareholder with 7.5 per cent.

Executive Directors & Officers: Christian Vernaudon, President; Marcel Galenon, Director General; Augusta Yu, Director, Finance; Patrick Martineau, Director, Commercial; Maurice Laversin, Director, Technical.

HQ Airport & Main Base: Papeete, Tahiti

Radio callsign: AIR TAHITI

Designator: VT/VTA

Employees: 540

Main destinations served: Operates to more than 30 islands in French Polynesia.

LINKS WITH OTHER AIRLINES
Marketing alliance with Air France (qv), which has a 7.5 per cent stake in the airline.

FLEET
3 ATR 72-200
3 ATR 42-500
2 ATR 42-300
2 Fairchild Dornier 228

Gabon – TR

AIR GABON

Compagnie Nationale Air Gabon

Incorporated: 1951

HISTORY
The national carrier of the African state of Gabon, Air Gabon was founded in 1951 under French colonial rule as Compagnie Aérienne Gabonaise. Later the name Société Nationale Transgabon was adopted, and the present title was not taken until 1974. For the first quarter-century of its existence the airline concentrated on domestic services, leaving international routes to Air Afrique (qv), but since withdrawing from the Air Afrique consortium in 1977 Air Gabon has been steadily developing its own international route network.

The airline is 80 per cent owned by the state.

Executive Directors & Officers: Martin Bongo, Chairman; René Morvan, Director General; Martin Louri, Deputy Director General, Administration & Commerce; G. Bertomeu, Finance Director; R. Oyogou, Operations Director; Jacob Cabina, Commercial Director.

HQ Airport & Main Base: Libreville

Designator: GN/AGN

Employees: approx 1,400

Main destinations served: Domestic services to more than 20 destinations, plus Abidjan, Bamako, Bangui, Cotonou, Dakar, Douala, Johannesburg, Kinshasa, Lagos, Lome, Luanda, Point Noire.

LINKS WITH OTHER AIRLINES
Marketing alliances with Air France (qv), Cameroon Airlines (qv), Lina Congo, and Swissair (qv).

FLEET
1 Boeing 747-200B Combi
1 Boeing 767-200
1 Boeing 727-200Adv
1 Boeing 737-200C
1 Fokker 100
1 Fokker F-28-2000 Fellowship

Georgia – 4L

ORBI

Orbi Georgian Airlines

Incorporated: 1992
HISTORY
As with so many airlines in the former Soviet Union, Orbi's origins and history lie with Aeroflot (qv), being the Georgian division of that airline until the break up of the Soviet Union. Operations include scheduled services to internal destinations, to major points in the Commonwealth of Independent States, and to points in the Middle East.

Executive Directors & Officers: Vasili S. Jambazishvili, General Director.

HQ Airport & Main Base: Tbilisi

Radio callsign: ZENA

Designator: NQ/DVU

Main destinations served: Domestic and CIS destinations, plus Cairo and Tel Aviv.

FLEET
9 Tupolev Tu-154B
8 Tupolev Tu-134
10 Yakovlev Yak-40
12 Mil Mi-8

TAIFUN

Adjal Avia/Sukhomi United Air Detachment

Incorporated: 1992

HISTORY
A quasi-military operation based on Sukhumi in Georgia, Taifun is believed to operate mainly charters as well as a scheduled service to Tbilisi.

Executive Directors & Officers: Zaur K. Khaindrava, Commander.

HQ Airport & Main Base: Sukhumi

Radio callsign: GIGLA

Designator: GIG

Main destinations served: Charters plus
Sukhumi–Tbilisi.

FLEET
7 Tupolev Tu-134

Germany – G

AERO LLOYD

Aero Lloyd Flugreisen GmbH

Incorporated: 1980

HISTORY
Formed in December 1980 by brokers Air
Charter Market and by Reinhold Braumer
and Jan Klimitz, Aero Lloyd started operations the following March with a fleet of
three Sud Caravelles. The initial business
was the operation of inclusive tour charters, but starting in October 1988 the airline developed an international scheduled
network aiming to undercut Lufthansa
fares. However, this was abandoned in
April 1992 when it was decided to concentrate on IT charters once again.

Executive Directors & Officers:
Reinhard B. Kipke, Managing Director;
Dr Walter Schneider, Managing Director;
Wolfgang John, Managing Director.

HQ Airport & Main Base: HQ at
Oberursel, with operational bases at
Berlin, Düsseldorf, Frankfurt, and
Hamburg.

Radio callsign: AERO LLOYD

Designator: YP/AEF

Employees: 850

Main destinations served: Charters to
holiday resorts in the Mediterranean and
North Africa, Portugal, and the Atlantic
Islands.

FLEET
6 Airbus A320
2 McDonnell Douglas MD-82
14 McDonnell Douglas MD-83
4 McDonnell Douglas MD-87
plus up to 11 Airbus A321-200s on order,
which may replace part of the MD series
fleet

AIR BERLIN

Air Berlin GmbH

Incorporated: 1992

HISTORY
A charter operator based in Berlin, Air

Berlin offers executive charters as well as
inclusive tour charters to the
Mediterranean and the Canary Islands.

Executive Directors & Officers:
Joachim Hunold, Managing Director;
Hans Söhnchen, Operations Director;
Siegfried Olivio, Maintenance Director.

HQ Airport & Main Base: Berlin Tegel

Radio callsign: AIR BERLIN

Designator: AB/BER

Employees: 300

Main destinations served:
Mediterranean and Canary Islands.

FLEET
10 Boeing 737-400
4 British Aerospace Jestream 31
1 Embraer EMB-110 Bandeirante
plus 6 Boeing 737-800 on order

AUGSBURG
AIRWAYS

Augsburg Airways GmbH

Incorporated: 1980

HISTORY
Originally founded as an air charter operator
under the name of Interot Airways, scheduled services began in 1986 with a Beech
King Air 200 operating between Augsburg
and Düsseldorf. A year later the original aircraft was replaced by a Beech 1900 on this
route, offering more than twice as many

seats. The airline then started to expand the
route network, first to Hamburg, then to
Berlin Templehof and Cologne/Bonn, while
from 1992 onwards expansion took place to
destinations in what had been East
Germany. This expansion was helped by
the introduction of larger aircraft, starting
with the delivery of the airline's first de
Havilland Dash 8 in late-1993.

The first international service was introduced in 1994, to Florence, and was followed by a service to Birmingham in 1995,
and then from Cologne/Bonn to London
City Airport later that year (although this
service is no longer operated). In 1996 the
airline adopted its present title.

Augsburg Airways is a subsidiary of a
freight forwarding agency, Interot
Speditions. Many of its services are operated under the Lufthansa designator as
'Team Lufthansa'.

Executive Directors & Officers: Olaf
Dlugi, Managing Director.

HQ Airport & Main Base: Augsburg,
with a further hub at Munich

Radio callsign: AUGSBURG AIR

Designator: 1Q/AUB

Employees: Aircrew: approx 100;
Engineering: approx 50; Ground staff:
approx 50; Total: 200.

Main destinations served: Augsburg to
Berlin Templehof, Dresden, Düsseldorf,
Frankfurt*, Cologne/Bonn, Neapel.
Munich to Dortmund*, Elba*, Erfurt*,
Leipzig*, Paderborn*, St Tropez*, Turin*.
* Team Lufthansa service.

*Augsburg Airways is one of many operators of the popular de Havilland Dash 8 series,
some of which are in Team Lufthansa colours.*

Annual turnover: US $16.8 million
(£10.2 million)

Passengers pa: 135,100

LINKS WITH OTHER AIRLINES
Team Lufthansa member.

FLEET
6 de Havilland Dash 8-300
5 de Havilland Dash 8-100

CONDOR

Condor Flugdienst GmbH

Incorporated: 1961

HISTORY
Condor takes its name from one of the great pioneering airlines, the Condor Syndicate, which helped to develop air transport in South America, and particularly in Brazil, to support the transatlantic ambitions of Lufthansa (qv) during the inter-war years. The present airline was formed in 1961 on the acquisition of Condor Luftreederei by Deutsche Flugdienst, a subsidiary of Lufthansa. Condor Luftreederei had been formed by the Hamburg-based Oetker Group and dated from 1957, when it began operations with two Convair 440 Metropolitans.

Deutsche Flugdienst dated from 1955, and had been acquired by Lufthansa in 1959.

The new airline commenced operations with the Metropolitans and two Vickers Vikings, although the latter were relegated to cargo charters when Vickers Viscounts 800s joined the airline in its first year, these aircraft also gradually displacing the Metropolitans as a fleet of four was eventually created. Inclusive tour holiday charters were seen as Condor's main business, and in 1965 – by which time it was carrying 40 per cent of German package holidaymakers – the airline introduced its first Boeing 727. Long-haul flights to destinations as far afield as Bangkok and Kenya were introduced in 1966, although the first long-haul jet, a Boeing 707, was not introduced until 1967. By 1969 the fleet included six Boeing 727s, three Boeing 737s, and a Boeing 707, although a Douglas DC-8 was also operated on short lease. Transatlantic charters to the United States did not begin until 1972, by which time the airline had become the first package holiday charter airline to operate the Boeing 747.

In 1979 the Boeing 747s in the fleet were replaced by the McDonnell Douglas DC-10, which although smaller was more flexible. The need for this measure had been shown by recession in Germany, and by crisis in the oil industry. The airline

has always attempted to maintain a modern fleet, being one of the first in its category to operate the Airbus A310. During the 1990s a fleet of Boeing 757s and 767s was introduced, as well as later marks of the Boeing 737.

After an attempt in 1964 to operate scheduled services from Düsseldorf to Bremen, Hanover, and Munster had been abandoned in 1966, Condor returned to scheduled services in 1991, with flights to the Seychelles and Mauritius. Other changes by this time had included the transfer of operations to a subsidiary, Condor Sudflug, which provided flights for the parent company under contract (although this arrangement was terminated in 1992), and the transfer of operations at Berlin to Schonefeld. By this time too, Condor was not simply chartering flights to tour operators, but was also selling seat-only tickets through more than 2,000 travel agents.

More recently Condor has assumed Lufthansa's 40 per cent stake in the Turkish airline, Sun Express (qv).

Executive Directors & Officers: Dr Franz Schoiber, Chairman; Dr Dietmar Kirchner, Managing Director; Rudolf von Oertzen, Managing Director; Dieter Born, Director, Operations; Fritz Lubke, Director, Operations; Thomas Decher, Technical Director; Rainer Kropke,

Originally purely a charter airline, Condor now operates a number of scheduled flights to major holiday destinations, using McDonnell Douglas DC-10-30s on the longer routes.

In common with many charter and leisure market operators, Condor finds the Boeing 757 an economical workhorse.

Director, Marketing; Wilfried Meyer, Flight Operations Director; Herbert Euler, Director, Public Relations.

HQ Airport & Main Base: HQ at Frankfurt, with an additional base at Munich.

Radio callsign: CONDOR

Designator: DE/CFG

Employees: Flight-crew: 450; Cabin staff: 1,300; Engineering: 500; Ground staff: 750; Total: 3,000.

Main destinations served: Acapulco, Agadir, Alicante, Almeria, Anchorage, Antalya, Antigua, Arrecife, Athens, Bahamas, Bangkok, Barbados, Cancun, Cania, Catania, Colombo, Corfu, Crete, Dakar, Dalaman, Djerba, Faro, Fort Lauderdale, Fuerteventura, Havana, Ibiza, Jamaica, Jerez, Kos, Larnaca, Las Palmas, Las Vegas, Madeira, Malaga, Maldives, Malta, Mauritius, Menorca, Mombasa, Monastir, Naples, Palermo, Palma de Mallorca, Paphos, Porlamar, Puerto Plata, Puerto Vallarta, Rhodes, Rimini, Samos, San José, San Juan, Santo Domingo, Seychelles, Shannon, Sharjah, St Lucia, Tampa/St Petersburg, Teneriffe, Thessaloniki, Tobago. Flights are from most major German cities.

Annual turnover: US $1.173 million (£710.9 million)

Aircraft km pa: 65.8 million

Revenue passenger km pa: 11, 938 million

LINKS WITH OTHER AIRLINES
A subsidiary of Lufthansa (qv). Owns 40 per cent of Sun Express (qv). Cargo space sold through Lufthansa Cargo (qv).

FLEET
5 McDonnell Douglas DC-10-30
9 Boeing 767-300
18 Boeing 757-200
4 Boeing 737-300 (leased)

CONTACT AIR

Contact Air Flugdienst GmbH

Incorporated: 1974

HISTORY
Formed in 1974, Contact Air started operations as a charter carrier based at Stuttgart. Scheduled domestic services were introduced operating for DLT, the predecessor of Lufthansa CityLine (qv), and when this airline decided to maintain an all-jet fleet its Fokker 50s were transferred to Contact Air, also replacing a small fleet of de Havilland Dash 8s operated by the airline.

Contact Air is owned by its president, Gunther Eheim.

Executive Directors & Officers: Gunther Eheim, President.

HQ Airport & Main Base: Stuttgart

Radio callsign: CONTACTAIR

Designator: 3T/KIS (or Lufthansa LH)

Employees: 253

Main destinations served: Charters, plus scheduled services under the Lufthansa CityLine banner.

LINKS WITH OTHER AIRLINES
Operates on behalf of Lufthansa CityLine.

FLEET
11 Fokker 50
2 Beech King Air 200
1 Cessna Citation II

DEUTSCHE BA

Deutsche BA Luftfahrtgesellschaft GmbH

Incorporated: 1978

HISTORY
The German subsidiary of British Airways (qv), Deutsche BA was originally founded in 1978 by an industrialist, Alfred Scholpp, as Delta Air Regionalflugverkehr, and based at Friedrichshafen on Lake

For longer-haul operations, the Boeing 767 is more economical to operate than the DC-10, and is favoured by Condor and many other European charter operators.

Constance. The airline had been formed to fill a gap in the air transport network, and to begin with operations were from Friedrichshafen to Stuttgart and Zürich using de Havilland Twin Otters. In 1982 the Swiss airline Crossair (qv) acquired a 25 per cent stake, and the industrialist Justus Dornier also acquired an interest. A Metroliner was put into service that year, and a service opened between Zürich and Bremen.

In 1986 Saab 340As were introduced. Co-operation with Lufthansa (qv) started in 1988, with Delta operating a Friedrichshafen–Frankfurt service for the national airline. Crossair increased its stake in Delta to 40 per cent. Additional Saabs were acquired, and the airline also took over more Lufthansa services during the late-1980s and early-1990s.

In March 1992 British Airways and three German banks acquired the airline, with BA taking 49 per cent, the maximum permitted to a non-German airline at that time. The current title was adopted in May 1992, and the fleet was repainted into British Airways livery. At the time of BA's involvement the airline was operating six Saab 340s and a single Dornier Do.228, but under BA it has moved rapidly to an all-jet fleet, with Boeing 737s and Fokker 100s. Scheduled services for business travellers are operated on weekdays, with

schedules and charter flights for holiday-makers at weekends. It is no longer a regional feeder, but a domestic trunk airline with international services. Although supposedly a 'low cost' airline, inflight service is provided and seats are upholstered in leather. The headquarters has been moved to Munich, but Berlin is also a major base.

Executive Directors & Officers: Carl Michel, Chief Executive Officer; Adrian Hunt, Chief Operating Officer.

HQ Airport & Main Base: Munich, with an additional base at Berlin

Radio callsign: SPEEDWAY

Designator: DI/DBA

Employees: Flight-crew: 319; Cabin staff: 177; Engineering: 152; Ground staff: 152; Total: 800.

Main destinations served: Munich to Berlin, Cologne/Bonn, Düsseldorf, Hamburg, London Gatwick.
Berlin to Cologne/Bonn, Düsseldorf, London Gatwick, Stuttgart.
Hamburg to London Gatwick.

Annual turnover: US $274.9 million (£166.1 million)

Revenue passenger km pa: 1,482 million

LINKS WITH OTHER AIRLINES
Owned by British Airways (qv).
Code-share with US Airways (possibly subject to review if BA/AA alliance is permitted).

FLEET
18 Boeing 737-300 (plus 5 on order) (leased)

EUROWINGS

Eurowings Luftverkehrs AG

Incorporated: 1994

HISTORY
Eurowings was formed by the merger of NFD Luftverkehrs and RFG Regionalflug on 1 January 1994. NFD, based at Nuremberg, dated from 1974, and had developed an extensive domestic and international passenger operation, including flights undertaken for Lufthansa, as well as inclusive tour and cargo charters, including operation of a British Aerospace 146-200QT for TNT. RFG operated feeder services from Dortmund to destinations in Germany and to London Gatwick, as well as a Stuttgart–Lyon service. While both fleets had a variety of aircraft they also

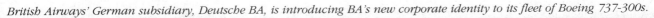

British Airways' German subsidiary, Deutsche BA, is introducing BA's new corporate identity to its fleet of Boeing 737-300s.

included ATR 42s, and these provide the backbone of the merged airline.

Unusually, in 1995 the new airline was able to swap its NS IATA designator with the EW code previously used by East-West Airlines of Australia. Eurowings claims to be Europe's largest independently-owned regional carrier.

Executive Directors & Officers: Reinhard Santner, Chairman & Chief Executive Officer; Ulrich Sigman, Director, Finance, Sales & Marketing; Karl-Heinz Krüger, Director, Personnel & Maintenance.

HQ Airport & Main Base: Nuremberg, with further bases at Berlin and Dortmund.

Radio callsign: EUROWINGS

Designator: EW/EWG

Employees: 1,634

Main destinations served: Amsterdam, Bayreuth, Cologne/Bonn, Dresden, Düsseldorf, Frankfurt, Guernsey, Hamburg, Hanover, Jersey, Katowice, Krakow, Leipzig, London Gatwick, Lyons, Munich, Munster, Newcastle, Nice, Olbia, Paderborn, Poznan, Prague, Stuttgart, Sylt, Vienna, Warsaw, Wroclaw, Zürich.

LINKS WITH OTHER AIRLINES
Alliances with Air France (qv), KLM (qv), and Northwest Airlines (qv).

FLEET
4 Airbus A319
4 British Aerospace 146-300
2 British Aerospace 146-200
2 British Aerospace 146-200QT
10 ATR 72-200
17 ATR 42-300/500

GERMANIA

Germania Fluggesellschaft GmbH

Incorporated: 1978

HISTORY
Known until 1986 as SAT (Special Air Transport) Fluggesellschaft, Germania is an inclusive tour charter operator, whose flights mainly serve the Mediterranean, the Canaries, and the Near East.

Executive Directors & Officers: Dr Heinrich Bischoff, Chairman & Managing Director; Thomas Scheel, Operations Director & Chief Pilot; P. Kiesling, Director, Maintenance & Engineering.

HQ Airport & Main Base: Berlin Tegel

Radio callsign: GERMANIA

Designator: GM/GMI

Employees: 335

Main destinations served: Holiday destinations in the Mediterranean, the Canaries, and the Near East.

FLEET
12 Boeing 737-300
plus 7 Boeing 737-700 and 4 Boeing 737-800 on order, which may replace most of the above

HAMBURG AIRLINES

Hamburg Fluggesellschaft GmbH

Incorporated: 1988

HISTORY
A regional airline operating scheduled and charter passenger operations, Hamburg Airways has operating agreements with Lufthansa (qv), with whose services it interlines.

Executive Directors & Officers: Udo Kien, Managing Director.

HQ Airport & Main Base: Hamburg

Radio callsign: HAMBURG AIR

Designator: HX/HAS

Employees: 330

Main destinations served: Berlin Templehof, Dresden, Leipzig, Riga, Saarbrucken, Salzburg, plus charter destinations.

LINKS WITH OTHER AIRLINES
Operates on behalf of Lufthansa (qv), and inter-lines with Aer Lingus (qv) and Lufthansa.

FLEET
2 British Aerospace 146-300
2 British Aerospace 146-200
2 de Havilland Dash 8-300
3 de Havilland Dash 8-200

HAPAG-LLOYD

Hapag-Lloyd Fluggesellschaft GmbH

Incorporated: 1973

HISTORY
A major German charter airline, Hapag-Lloyd is a subsidiary of the German shipping line of the same name. The airline was founded in 1973, and in 1979 acquired Bavaria Flug, another charter air-

line dating from 1957, when it had been formed as an air taxi operator, moving into air charter operations in 1964 with Handley Page Heralds.

Executive Directors & Officers: Wolfgang Kurth, Managing Director; Dieter Schenk, Director; Diethart Muhge, Director, Finance; Dietrich Stuwe, Director, Controlling; Friedrich Keppler, Director, Flight Operations; Benno Beck, Director, Maintenance; Thomas Wolff, Director, EDP; Ermelinde Sye, Director, Customer Services; Juergen Oehlmann, Director, Personnel.

HQ Airport & Main Base: Hanover

Radio callsign: HAPAG-LLOYD

Designator: HF/HLF

Employees: Flight-crew: 290; Cabin staff: 680; Engineering: 326; Ground staff: 389; Total: 1,685.

Main destinations served: Charters to the Mediterranean, especially Spain, Greece, and Turkey, and to the Dominican Republic.

Annual turnover: US $669.16 million (£405.6 million)

Revenue passenger km pa: 11,032 million

FLEET
4 Airbus A310-300 (1 leased)
4 Airbus A310-200
12 Boeing 737-400 (1 leased)
5 Boeing 737-500
plus up to 16 Boeing 737-800 on order

LTU

LTU International Airways/Lufttransport-Unternehmen GmbH & Co

Incorporated: 1955

HISTORY
Originally founded as Lufttransport Union, this airline was established to operate inclusive tour and freight charters. The present title was adopted in 1958. Feeder services were operated from Düsseldorf to a number of destinations on behalf of Lufthansa, usually using Fokker F-27 Friendships and Nord 262s, while Caravelles were used for the IT charter work. The airline has acquired tour operating subsidiaries of its own, and owns a Munich-based operation, LTU Sud International Airways, as well as having a 25 per cent stake in the Spanish charter carrier, LTE International Airways, which operates three Boeing 757-200s from its base at Palma de Mallorca.

Executive Directors & Officers: Hans-Joachim Driessen, General Manager.

HQ Airport & Main Base: Düsseldorf

Radio callsign: LTU

Designator: LT/LTU

Main destinations served: World-wide inclusive tour charters.

LINKS WITH OTHER AIRLINES
Owns LTU Sud and has a 25 per cent stake in LTE International.

FLEET
5 Boeing 767-300ER
13 Boeing 757-200

LUFTHANSA

Deutsche Lufthansa AG

Incorporated: 1926

HISTORY
Although the present airline was established in 1955, after a prolonged period without commercial aviation in Germany following World War Two, the history of Lufthansa goes back much further, to the formation of an airline of the same name in 1926. The original Lufthansa was formed by a merger of Deutsche Aero-Lloyd – ownership of which was divided between the Deutsche Bank and the Hamburg-Amerika Line and North German Lloyd shipping companies – with Junkers Luftverkehr, the operating subsidiary of the famous aircraft manufacturer. These two airlines in turn had been formed from the rationalisation of several smaller companies which had been engaged in unprofitable competition, and the eventual Aero-Lloyd merger with Junkers was the result of a similar situation which had arisen as the two airlines had grown and their route networks had overlapped. The message was clear at this early stage that there was little scope for effective and prolonged competition.

The new airline's capital was held by the founding airlines (27.5 per cent), the German Government (26 per cent), the German state governments (19 per cent), and various private interests (25 per cent). Lufthansa must have been one of the largest airlines in the world at the time, with a combined fleet of 120 aircraft, although some 80 of these were single-engined types. In addition to an extensive domestic route network, the new airline inherited international services which stretched as far as London in the west and Stockholm in the north.

The new airline immediately set about expanding its network further, both in Germany and elsewhere, with ambitious plans for services across the Atlantic and to the Far East. In Germany itself beacons were established along its routes for night flying, building on Junkers' experience of night flying, and a chain of 73 radio stations was created along its routes as additional navigation aids.

On the Atlantic, an associate, the Condor syndicate, had been paving the way for South American services with Dornier Wal flying-boats, and a number of today's airlines in South America owe their origins to these German pioneers, having been formed to provide connecting services. The aircraft of the day lacked the range and reliability for true transoceanic flight, but it was possible to accelerate the mail service by catapulting a small seaplane from a liner as the ship approached the coast. On the South Atlantic, further acceleration of the mail was also possible on the South American service by flying it to Las Palmas in the Canary Islands. The huge Dornier X 12-engined flying-boat made a flight to South America in 1932, and occasionally Zeppelin airships would be used instead of a steamer.

By 1934 on the South Atlantic route and 1936 on the North Atlantic, flying-boats could be used for the crossing, using three ships converted as floating bases. The aircraft would land close to one of the ships, where it was hoisted aboard for servicing and refuelling, and then launched again to continue the flight. Even so, the service was confined to mail, and the North Atlantic service had to be routed southwards via the Azores and the Bahamas rather than by the more direct northerly route because of the shorter over-water stages and better sea conditions. Aircraft used included the Wal and a larger development, the 'Ten Ton Wal', these being followed later by the diesel-engined Dornier Do.18 and Blohm und Voss Ha.139 flying-boats. Overland sections of route in Europe were often flown by the Junkers Ju.52/3m trimotor, of which Lufthansa eventually operated 79, while in South America the Dornier Wal proved ideal for operating up-country from the many waterways.

By the outbreak of World War Two in Europe, Lufthansa had a route network which extended to Santiago de Chile in the west, and to Bangkok in the east. Obviously, flights were conducted in many stages, and westwards in particular also entailed many changes of aircraft. The start of hostilities saw most services suspended, except for a few operated to neutral countries such as Sweden and Switzerland, and even these were restricted to those on urgent government business, especially as shortages of fuel and aircrew began to take effect. All services were officially suspended in 1945, and eventually Lufthansa was liquidated in 1951. An associate company, Eurasia, in which Lufthansa held a one-third interest and the Chinese Transport Ministry the remainder, became China Air Transport, predecessor of CAAC's airline operations after the Chinese Communists swept to power.

Lufthansa operates the Boeing 747-400 in both all-passenger and mixed passenger-cargo Combi versions.

In 1952 the Allied Powers agreed to the formation of a new German airline by the German Government. Known initially as Luftag, the old title of Lufthansa was adopted in 1954, and operations began the following year with eight Lockheed Super Constellations, four Convair 340 Metropolitans and three Douglas DC-3s. Such an impressive start was made possible by the support of airlines from Western European countries, with TWA (Trans World Airlines) (qv) and Eastern Airlines providing captains for the Super Constellations, while BEA did the same for the other aircraft. The more important European destinations saw services introduced during 1955, as did New York. By 1958 the South American route once again reached Santiago de Chile, and in 1964 a polar route was opened to Tokyo.

A small number of Vickers Viscount turboprop airliners entered service in 1958, followed by Boeing 707 jet airliners in 1960, marking the start of a programme to virtually standardise on Boeing aircraft, with the exception of a fleet of McDonnell Douglas DC-10s for which there was no Boeing equivalent, which lasted until the introduction of the Airbus range some 15 years later. Lufthansa was the first airline to operate the Boeing 737-100, which it dubbed the 'City Jet', as well as operating a large fleet of Boeing 727s and, of course, the Boeing 747 from 1970 onwards.

One of the world's largest airlines, Lufthansa has reorganised in recent years. It has for many years operated its charter subsidiary, Condor (qv), as a separate entity, and more recently has hived off its cargo operation, Lufthansa Cargo (qv), as a separate entity, although retaining ownership. A feeder operation created around the network of another subsidiary, DLT, has become known as Lufthansa CityLine (qv). Establishing a strong base for itself in Europe's strongest economy and largest country has also led Lufthansa to take an interest in other airlines, buying a 20 per cent stake in Lauda Air (qv), which also operates services on its behalf, while interests are also held in Luxair (qv), Sun Express (qv), and DHL International (qv), the parcels and courier service. Services to the former East Germany started in 1989.

For many years the German – or, at the time, West German – Government held 65 per cent of Lufthansa's shares, but this holding was dramatically reduced after a 1994 share issue in which the government did not participate, leaving control of the airline with private investors, so that the state now owns just 36 per cent. Lufthansa has code-sharing and marketing alliances with a number of airlines, but the most significant of these is the 'Star Alliance', announced in May 1997, which includes Lufthansa, Air Canada (qv), SAS (qv), Thai Airways (qv), and United Airlines (qv), and has since been joined by Varig (qv).

The post-war development of Germany, and its division for four decades, means that airline operations have been from many more German cities than might otherwise have been the case. The most important hub for Lufthansa is Frankfurt, and it remains to be seen whether the airline will continue to be based at Cologne once the federal capital moves to Berlin. For the future, it is understood to be considering the creation of a 'low cost, no frills' division.

Executive Directors & Officers: Juergen Weber, Chairman; Dr Klaus G. Schlede, Vice-Chairman & Chief Financial Officer; Dr Klaus Nittinger, Chief Executive, Operations; Hemio Klein, Chief Executive, Marketing; Dr Heiko Lange, Chief Executive, Personnel.

HQ Airport & Main Base: HQ at Cologne/Bonn, with additional bases/hubs at Berlin Templehof, Bremen, Düsseldorf, Frankfurt, Hamburg, Hanover, Munich, and Stuttgart.

Radio callsign: LUFTHANSA

Designator: LH/DLH

Employees: Flight-crew: 3,174; Cabin staff: 8,898; Engineering: 10,205 (Lufthansa Technik AG); Ground staff: 16.052; Total: 28,124 (excluding Lufthansa Technik personnel).

Main destinations served: Abu Dhabi, Accra, Addis Ababa, Alexandria, Almaty, Amsterdam, Ankara, Ashkhabad, Asmara, Athens, Atlanta, Bahrain, Baku, Bangkok, Barcelona, Basle, Bastia, Beijing, Beirut, Belgrade, Bergen, Bilbao, Birmingham, Bogotá, Bologna, Bombay, Bornholm, Boston, Brussels, Bucharest, Budapest, Buenos Aires, Cagliari, Cairo, Cape Town, Caracas, Casablanca, Catania, Chicago, Copenhagen, Dallas/Fort Worth, Damascus, Delhi, Denpasar, Dresden, Dubai, Dublin, Edinburgh, Faro, Florence, Freidrichshafen, Geneva, Glasgow, Gothenburg, Graz, Guernsey, Harare, Helsinki, Heraklion, Ho Chi Minh City, Hong Kong, Houston, Innsbruck, Istanbul, Izmir, Jakarta, Jeddah, Jersey, Johannesburg, Karachi, Karlstad, Katowice, Khartoum, Kiel, Kiev, Klagenfurt, Kuala Lumpur, Lagos, Larnaca, Las Palmas, Leipzig-Halle, Lima, Linz, Lisbon, London City, London Gatwick, London Heathrow, Los Angeles, Ljubljana, Luxembourg, Lyon, Madras, Madrid, Malaga, Malmö, Malta, Manchester, Manila, Marseilles, Mexico City, Miami, Milan, Minsk, Moscow, Munich, Munster/Osnabruck, Nagoya, Nairobi, Naples, New York JFK, Newcastle, Nice, Nizhniy Novgorod, Novozibirsk, Nuremberg, Odessa, Olbia, Oporto, Osaka, Oslo, Palma de Mallorca, Paris, Pisa, Prague, Quito, Reykjavik, Riga, Rio de Janeiro, Riyadh, Rome, Salzburg, Samara, San Francisco, Sanaa, Santiago de Chile, São Paulo, Seoul, Shanghai, Singapore, Sofia, St Petersburg, Stavanger, Stockholm, Strasbourg, Stuttgart, Tallin, Tashkent, Teheran, Tel Aviv, Tenerife,

Lufthansa was one of the first major operators of the Airbus A340-300.

Thessaloniki, Tirana, Tokyo, Toronto,
Toulouse, Trieste, Tunis, Turin, Turku,
Valencia, Venice, Verona, Vienna, Vilnius,
Visby, Warsaw, Washington, Westerland,
Windhoek, Yekaterinburg, Zagreb, Zürich.
Destinations of Lufthansa CityLine (qv) are
included in this list.

Annual turnover: US $13,865 million
(£8,403 million)

Aircraft km pa: 720.5 million

Revenue passenger km pa: 81,716.3
million

Cargo tonne km pa: 6,234.7 million
(includes Lufthansa Cargo (qv))

Passengers pa: 41.4 million

LINKS WITH OTHER AIRLINES
'Star Alliance' with Air Canada (qv), SAS
(qv), Thai Airways (qv), United Airlines
(qv), and Varig (qv).
Alliances also with Adria (qv), Air
Dolomiti (qv), Ansett (qv), Canadian
Airlines (qv), South African Airways (qv),
Finnair (qv), Lauda Air (qv), and Luxair
(qv).
Has shareholdings in Luxair (13 per cent)
and Lauda Air (20 per cent).
Owns Lufthansa CityLine (qv), Lufthansa
Cargo (qv), and Lufthansa Technik.

FLEET
15 Boeing 747-400
7 Boeing 747-400 Combi
7 Boeing 747-200
1 Boeing 747-200 Combi
10 Airbus A340-300
6 Airbus A340-200
13 Airbus A300-600
12 Airbus A310-300
20 Airbus A321
33 Airbus A320
20 Airbus A319
6 Boeing 737-400
39 Boeing 737-300
7 Boeing 737-300QC
30 Boeing 737-500

LUFTHANSA CARGO

Lufthansa Cargo AG

Incorporated: 1996

HISTORY
On 1 January 1996 Lufthansa (qv) sepa-
rated its cargo operations from the main-
stream airline to operate as an
autonomous business. In addition to
maintaining its separate cargo network
and selling cargo space on Lufthansa
flights, Lufthansa Cargo also operates
freight charters. The airline has a 40 per
cent shareholding in an Indian joint venture, airline Hinduja Cargo Services (qv),
which uses a fleet of Boeing 727 freighters
to feed freight into a hub and spoke operation at Sharjah, in the Gulf. Lufthansa
Cargo has pioneered the use of rail freight
to feed cargo into its Frankfurt hub.

Executive Directors & Officers:
Wilhelm Althen, Chairman.

HQ Airport & Main Base: Frankfurt,
with an additional hub at Sharjah

Radio callsign: LUFTHANSA CARGO

Designator: GEC

Employees: 5,041

Main destinations served: Serves
directly more than 60 destinations world-
wide.

Annual turnover: Included in the figure
for Lufthansa (qv).

LINKS WITH OTHER AIRLINES
A subsidiary of Lufthansa.
Has a 40 per cent shareholding in
Hinduja Cargo Services (qv).
Alliances with SAS (qv), Singapore
Airlines (qv), South African Airways (qv),
Thai Airways (qv), and United Airlines
(qv).

FLEET
12 Boeing 747-200F
5 McDonnell Douglas MD-11F
1 Boeing 737-300F

LUFTHANSA CITYLINE

Lufthansa CityLine GmbH

Incorporated: 1958

HISTORY
Lufthansa CityLine's history dates back to

Lufthansa CityLine has a large fleet of the new Canadair Regional Jet.

1958 when Jan Janssen and Martin Decker established Ostfriesïsche Lufttaxi or OLT (the name means East Friesian Air Taxi Service) in Emden, backed by a shipping line, Fisser & van Dornum. In 1970 an industrial group, AGIV, also became a shareholder, before acquiring the company outright in 1973, by which time the fleet included a de Havilland Canada DHC-6 Twin Otter. The following year restructuring occurred, accompanied by the adoption of the new title DLT (Deutsche Luftverkehrsgesellschaft).

The new airline began to develop a network of regional services, acquired larger aircraft, including a fleet of Short 330s, and started to operate services on behalf of Lufthansa (qv). In 1978 it took over a couple of short international services, Bremen–Copenhagen and Hanover–Amsterdam, and operated these under the Lufthansa name. In return Lufthansa subscribed to new share capital, leaving the national carrier with a 26 per cent shareholding in DLT. By 1984 most of DLT's operations were operating under the Lufthansa designator. Meanwhile Hawker Siddeley 748 turboprops had been introduced, marking a further increase in the size of aircraft being operated. These were soon joined by Embraer EMB-120 Brasilias, and in 1987 DLT became the first operator of the new Fokker 50.

Lufthansa acquired a controlling interest in 1989, before finally acquiring the airline outright in 1993. Meanwhile, in 1992 the name was changed from DLT to Lufthansa CityLine, and the new Canadair Regional Jet was added to the fleet. Under Lufthansa ownership planning and marketing tasks were transferred to the parent airline, and the decision was taken to move the fleet away from turboprop operation to jet operation as far as possible, with Avro RJ85s being added to the fleet. Lufthansa livery was adopted, and onboard facilities were modelled on those offered on Lufthansa's domestic and European services. Canadair CRJ-700 regional jets are due to be introduced shortly. The remaining turboprop operation has been transferred to Contact Air (qv).

Lufthansa CityLine also includes a number of other airlines operating as partners, and apart from Contact Air these also include Lauda Air (qv) and Air Littoral (qv). A number of training subsidiaries are owned, including simulator facilities.

Executive Directors & Officers: Karl-Heinz Kopfle, Managing Director; Georg Steinbacher, Managing Director, Personnel; Udo Ulbig, General Manager, Flight Operations; Wolf-Eckard Herholz,

General Manager, Technical; Manfred Garner, General Manager, Administration.

HQ Airport & Main Base:
Cologne/Bonn

Radio callsign: HANSALINE

Designator: CLH

Employees: Flight-crew: 485; Cabin staff: 596; Engineering: 161; Ground staff: 287; Total: 1,529.

Main destinations served: Domestic and short-haul European destinations from the Lufthansa timetable.

Annual turnover: US $614.5 million (£372.4 million)

LINKS WITH OTHER AIRLINES
A subsidiary of Lufthansa (qv). Partner airlines include Air Littoral (qv), Contact Air (qv), and Lauda Air (qv).

FLEET
18 Avro RJ85
29 Canadair Regional Jets
plus an unspecified number of Canadair CRJ-700s

WDL AVIATION

WDL Flugdienst GmbH

Incorporated: 1955

HISTORY
WDL offers passenger and freight charter services, and has in the past also offered aerial survey work and undertaken passenger schedules for DLT, predecessor of Lufthansa CityLine (qv). Originally based at Essen, the airline is now based at Cologne/Bonn.

Executive Directors & Officers: Walter Bohnke, President.

HQ Airport & Main Base:
Cologne/Bonn

Radio callsign: WDL

Designator: WDL

FLEET
9 Fokker F-27-600 Friendship
1 Fokker F-27-400 Friendship
4 Fokker F-27-200 Friendship
1 Fokker F-27-100 Friendship

Greece – SX

OLYMPIC

Olympic Airways SA

Incorporated: 1957

HISTORY
Olympic Airways started operations in 1957 as the successor to TAE National Greek Airlines, which had been formed in 1951 by the merger of Hellos, serving several destinations in Europe and the Middle East; TAE, concentrating mainly on domestic routes; and Aero Metaforai Ellados. All three airlines had been formed shortly after the end of World War Two. TAE had been acquired by the Greek Government in 1955 after experiencing financial difficulties, but the other two were privately owned.

The new airline was owned by shipping magnate Aristotle Onassis, who had been given a 50 year concession by the Greek Government, and with his backing Olympic Airways was able to expand

The Greek national airline, Olympic, uses Airbus A300-600s on its busiest routes.

Olympic's shorter and less busy routes are served by Boeing 737s, of which this 737-400 is one of the more recent. The airline plans to replace its Boeing 727/737 fleet with 737-800s.

quickly. The initial fleet of aircraft included a Fairchild Argus, a Douglas DC-4, and 14 Douglas DC-3s, all of which had belonged to TAE. Douglas DC-6Bs were acquired urgently, and new de Havilland Comet 4Bs were ordered. The Comets were introduced in 1960, and immediately produced a London–Athens record of 3 hours 13 minutes. Re-equipped, the airline was able to add new routes to its network, so that it was soon serving the major destinations in Europe, the Middle East, and around the Mediterranean. In 1966 the arrival of Boeing 707s saw the airline inaugurate an Athens–New York service. At this time it also had a single Sud Aviation Super Frelon helicopter for summer services to some of the Greek islands.

The Boeing 707s were soon joined by Boeing 720s and 727s, which replaced the Comets. Construction of airports on the Greek islands led to the development of conventional air services to many of these, and Japanese-built NAMC YS-11 turboprop airliners and small Short Skyvan aircraft were introduced on these routes. Olympic also conducted trials with two Yakovlev Yak-40 airliners, the first airline outside of the Soviet Bloc to test these small regional jets. The route network meanwhile reached Sydney in 1972, and the following year Olympic received its first Boeing 747.

This optimistic picture changed during the early-1970s. Continuing heavy losses forcing Onassis to withdraw in 1974, and operations were suspended. After reaching a settlement with him the following year, the government nationalised the airline and operations started again in January 1976. Olympic quickly re-established itself, helped by the growing popularity of Greece as a holiday destination. One of the early moves was to acquire

Boeing 737s, and in 1979 the first Airbus A300s were introduced.

Today, Olympic remains in state ownership, and continues to operate domestic, international, and intercontinental services from its main base at Athens. Two subsidiaries are Macedonian Airlines, which operates four aircraft from Skopje in Macedonia, and Olympic Aviation (qv).

Executive Directors & Officers:
Nicholas Blesseos, Chairman; Jordan Karatzas, Chief Executive Officer; Miltiadis Tsangarakis, Director General; Stavros Daliakas, Assistant Chief Executive Officer, Commercial; George Stamatis, Assistant Chief Executive Officer, Support Services; Thedoros Kombolis, Assistant Director General, Ground Services; Ekaterini Tsangaraka, Director, Financial Services; Spyros Lambropoulos, Director, Flight Operations; Apostolos Kagias, Director, Technical Services; Konstantinos Mandroukas, Director, Marketing.

HQ Airport & Main Base: Athens

Radio callsign: OLYMPIC/OLYMPAIR

Designator: OA/OAL

Employees: Flight-crew: 1,800; Cabin staff: 1,250; Ground staff: 6,774; Total: 9,824.

Main destinations served: More than 30 domestic destinations, including Heraklion, Thessaloniki, Corfu, and Rhodes, plus Alexandria, Amman, Amsterdam, Bangkok, Barcelona, Beirut, Belgrade, Boston, Brussels, Bucharest, Budapest, Cairo, Cologne/Bonn, Copenhagen, Dubai, Düsseldorf, Frankfurt, Geneva, Istanbul, Jeddah, Johannesburg, Kiev, Kuwait, Larnaca,

London Heathrow, Madrid, Marseilles, Melbourne, Montreal, Moscow, Munich, Nairobi, Naples, New York JFK, Paris CDG, Riyadh, São Paulo, Sofia, Stuttgart, Sydney, Tel Aviv, Tirana, Toronto, Vienna, Zürich.

Annual turnover: US $992 million (£601.2 million)

LINKS WITH OTHER AIRLINES
Code-sharing with Saudi Arabian Airlines (qv) and VASP (qv).
Subsidiaries include Macedonian Airlines and Olympic Aviation.

FLEET
6 Airbus A340-300 (plus 4 options)
6 Airbus A300B4
2 Airbus A300-600
4 Boeing 727-200
7 Boeing 737-400
11 Boeing 737-200
7 ATR 72 (operated by Olympic Aviation)
4 ATR 42 (operated by Olympic Aviation)
5 Short 330-200 (operated by Olympic Aviation)
7 Dornier Do.228-201 (operated by Olympic Aviation)
1 Agusta A109 (operated by Olympic Aviation)
2 Eurocopter AS355 Ecureuil (operated by Olympic Aviation)
plus plans to replace 737/727 fleet with up to 25 Boeing 737-800s

OLYMPIC AVIATION

Olympic Aviation SA

Incorporated: 1971

HISTORY
Originally formed as a private airline, Olympic Aviation was taken over by the Greek Government in 1974 and today operates feeder services for Olympic Airways (qv), of which it is a wholly-owned subsidiary. Management is also in the hands of Olympic. Charter operations are also flown, including the use of small helicopters.

Executive Directors & Officers: As for Olympic Airways.

HQ Airport & Main Base: Athens, with further bases at Rhodes and Thessaloniki.

Radio callsign: OLAVIA

Designator: 7U/OLY

Employees: See Olympic

Main destinations served: Destinations on the Olympic domestic network.

Annual turnover: Included in the figures for Olympic Airways (qv)

LINKS WITH OTHER AIRLINES
Subsidiary of Olympic Airways.

FLEET
7 ATR 72
4 ATR 42
5 Short 330-200
7 Dornier Do.228-201
1 Agusta A109
2 Eurocopter AS355 Ecureuil

VENUS

Venus Airlines SA

Incorporated: 1993

HISTORY
A Greek charter airline flying inclusive tour passengers to resorts in Greece from Western Europe.

Executive Directors & Officers:
Theodore Karabatis, President; K. Giakonstidis, Deputy President; Ser Papassis, General Manager; A. Piatus, Financial Director; T. Sideris, Operations Director; N. Andreou, Commercial Director; J. Raptakis, Technical Director; P. Margoudis, Personnel Director.

HQ Airport & Main Base: Athens, with a further base at Heraklion (Crete)

Radio callsign: SUMMER EXPRESS

Designator: V4/EUH

Employees: 450

FLEET
2 Boeing 757-200
2 Boeing 727-200
2 McDonnell Douglas MD-83

Guadeloupe

AIR GUADELOUPE

Compagnie Nationale Air Guadeloupe

Incorporated: 1970

HISTORY
Established in 1970 by the Guadeloupe Government and Air France (qv), Air Guadeloupe operates scheduled services to the Leeward Islands and also provides passenger charters. It is owned 45 per cent by the government and 45 per cent by Air France.

Executive Directors & Officers:
Françoise Paneole, President; Jocelyne Hatchi, Finance Director; M. Gabali, Commercial Director; Gerard Ballonad, Operations Director; M. Arnassalon, Technical Director; Raymond Dupont, General Manager.

HQ Airport & Main Base: Aéroport du Raizet, Guadeloupe

Designator: TX/AGU

Main destinations served: About 12 island destinations, as well as San Juan and St Maarten.

LINKS WITH OTHER AIRLINES
Air France has a 45 per cent interest.

FLEET
2 ATR 42-300
4 Fairchild Dornier 228-200
2 de Havilland DHC-6 Twin Otter

Guatemala – TG

AVIATECA

Aérolineas de Guatemala

Incorporated: 1945

HISTORY
Aviateca was established in 1945 by the government of Guatemala to acquire the services and equipment of Aérovias de Guatemala, which had been founded in 1939. A network of services to neighbouring capitals was established. The airline was privatised in 1989, when TACA (qv) of El Salvador acquired a 30 per cent interest.

Executive Directors & Officers: Ing Julio Obols Gomes, President; Jorge Palacios, Finance Director; Claudi Arenas, Commercial Director; Rene Debroy, Maintenance Director; Enrique Beltrona, General Manager.

HQ Airport & Main Base: Guatemala City

Designator: GU/GUG

Employees: 400

Main destinations served: Cancun, Flores, Houston, Los Angeles, Managua, Merida, Mexico City, Panama City, San Salvador, San José.

LINKS WITH OTHER AIRLINES
TACA (qv) has a 30 per cent interest.

FLEET
5 Boeing 737-200

Guinea – 3X

AIR GUINEE

Compagnie Nationale Air Guinee

Incorporated: 1960

HISTORY
The national airline of the former French African colony of Guinee, Air Guinee was formed after independence in 1960 with assistance from the Soviet Union and Czechoslovakia. Not surprisingly, Antonov aircraft types predominated initially.

The airline remains state-owned and concentrates on domestic and regional services to neighbouring countries.

Executive Directors & Officers:
Mamadou Aliou Sanch, President.

HQ Airport & Main Base: Conakry

Radio callsign: AIR GUINEE

Designator: G1/GIB

Employees: approx 400

Main destinations served: About eight domestic destinations, plus Abidjan, Bamako, Dakar, Freetown, Lagos, Monrovia.

FLEET
2 Tupolev Tu-154M
1 Boeing 727-200
3 Boeing 737-200
6 Antonov An-24
3 XAC Y-7

Hungary – HA

MALEV

Malév – Magyar Legikozlekedesi Vallalat

Incorporated: 1946

HISTORY
Hungary's national airline, Malév was formed in March 1946 as Maszovlet, the Hungarian-Soviet Airlines Company, and operations started later that year. At first it was confined to domestic services, operating Ilyushin Il-12 aircraft, but by 1950 international services were being operated to Prague, Bucharest, Belgrade, and Warsaw, and there was also a short-lived service to Venice.

The present title was adopted in 1954, when control of the airline passed into Hungarian hands. Expansion gained pace at this time, and services began to be

Freed from the constraints of the past, Malév has quickly assembled a fleet of modern western aircraft, including this Fokker 70.

introduced to major centres in Western Europe, starting with Vienna. A service to Cairo was started in 1963, followed by Damascus in 1965 and Beirut in 1966. The fleet by this time included Ilyushin Il-18s and Il-14s, Malév having been the first Warsaw Pact country to put the Il-18 into service. Starting in 1968 the Il-14s were withdrawn when the first jets – Tupolev Tu-134s – were introduced.

While expansion of the international network continued, heavy losses on domestic routes meant that the 1960s saw these services steadily reduced, and then abandoned altogether. Fares, which were low, could not cover costs, and repairs to the war-damaged infrastructure had also meant that road and rail travel had become feasible once more.

Larger aircraft in the form of the Tupolev Tu-154 were introduced in 1973, and later these were to introduce first-class service on Malév flights. The airline remained committed to purchasing Soviet aircraft until 1988, when Malév leased the first of three Boeing 737-200s and was also selected to operate British Aerospace 146-200QT aircraft for TNT (qv). The move to more productive western equipment marked the beginning of the end for the old Tupolev aircraft, which started to be replaced. Malév was operating a dozen Boeing 737s when, in 1993, Boeing 767-200ER aircraft were introduced on long-haul services. No less significant a sign of changing times in Eastern Europe, in 1992 Malév had been privatised, with Alitalia (qv) taking a 30 per cent stake, and shares being offered to financial institutions and the airline's own employees.

Today, Malév operates a modern fleet which is mainly of western manufacture, and its services extend throughout Europe, and to the Middle East, Africa, and North America. The remaining Tupolev Tu-154Ms are confined to charter operations.

Executive Directors & Officers: Andras Derzsi, Chairman; Sandor Szathmary, Chief Executive Officer; Peter Kis, Financial Director; Vilmos Bencsik, Operations Director; Ferenc Turi, Commercial Director; Janos Szabo, Maintenance Director; Mihaly Hideg, Engineering Director; Dr Geza Kovacs, Personnel Director; Andras Zboray, Marketing Manager.

HQ Airport & Main Base: Budapest

Radio callsign: MALEV

Designator: MA/MAH

Employees: 3,600

Main destinations served: Amsterdam, Athens, Barcelona, Beirut, Berlin, Brussels, Bucharest, Cairo, Cologne, Copenhagen, Damascus, Dresden, Dubai, Düsseldorf, Frankfurt, Hamburg, Helsinki, Istanbul, Kiev, Larnaca, Leipzig, London Heathrow, Madrid, Milan, Moscow, Munich, New York JFK, Paris CDG, Prague, Rome, St Petersburg, Sofia, Stockholm, Stuttgart, Tel Aviv, Thessaloniki, Tirana, Trieste, Varna, Venice, Vienna, Vilnius, Warsaw, Zürich.

Revenue passenger km pa: 2,396 million

Cargo tonne km pa: 29.6 million

Passengers pa: 1.6 million

LINKS WITH OTHER AIRLINES
Alitalia (qv) has a 30 per cent interest. Code-share with Delta Airlines (qv).

Boeing 767-200s now handle Malév's longer-distance routes.

Malév still has a small number of Tupolev Tu-154Ms, but these are now relegated to charter operations.

FLEET
2 Boeing 767-200ER
5 Tupolev Tu-154M (charters only)
2 Boeing 737-400
4 Boeing 737-300
6 Boeing 737-200
5 Fokker 70 (leased)

Iceland – TF

AIR ATLANTA ICELANDIC

Air Atlanta Icelandic

Incorporated: 1986

HISTORY
Originally founded to offer wet-leasing services to international scheduled carriers, Air Atlanta moved into charter operations in 1993, although wet-leasing to airlines such as Iberia (qv) remains the major element of its business since the airline's capacity is well beyond that of a country with a population of only about 250,000. The airline is owned by Captain Arngrimur Johannsson and his family.

Executive Directors & Officers:
Captain Arngrimur Johannsson, President; Thora Gudmundsdottir, Chairman; Magnus Fridjonsson, Finance Director; Hafthor Hafsteinsson, Operations

Director; Finnbogi Oskarsson, Engineering Director; Gudmundur Hafsteinsson, Personnel Director.

HQ Airport & Main Base: HQ at Mosfellsbaer, main base at Reykjavik.

Designator: CC/ABD (on wet-leasing, the client airline's designator is used)

Employees: 560

Main destinations served: Wet-leasing operations include work for Lufthansa (qv) and Tunis Air (qv).
Charter flights to mainland Europe.

FLEET
1 Boeing 747-200B (wet-leased to Iberia)
4 Boeing 747-100
1 Lockheed L-1011-1 TriStar
4 Lockheed L-1011-100 TriStar
1 Boeing 737-300
3 Boeing 737-200

ICELANDAIR

Flugleidir hf

Incorporated: 1973

HISTORY
Icelandair was formed by the merger of two much older airlines, one trading as Icelandair and the other as Loftleidir, in 1973. The original Icelandair had been founded in 1937 as Flugfelag Akureyrar, or Flugfelag Islands, operating a seaplane

service. The first international service came in 1945, when a Consolidated Catalina flying-boat was used for a route to Glasgow. A second service, to Copenhagen, soon followed. Landplane services were introduced the following year, using converted Liberator bombers leased from Scottish Aviation for services to Prestwick, near Glasgow, and Copenhagen. Douglas DC-4s were purchased in 1948. The title of Icelandair was introduced in 1950, when the Icelandic Government acquired a 13.2 per cent shareholding. In 1957 the airline bought two Vickers Viscounts and these were followed by DC-6s.

Reflecting the considerable distances and sparse population which makes road-building uneconomic, a 13-point domestic network was established post-war, especially after rival Loftleidir decided to concentrate on international services. Initially DC-3s were used, but these were eventually replaced by Fokker F-27 Friendships.

Although originally formed as a domestic carrier in 1944, with just one Stinson seaplane, Loftleidir developed post-war into a pioneer of low cost transatlantic air services, utilising a legal loophole which allowed non-IATA scheduled international services across the Atlantic so long as passengers changed planes in Iceland! (At the time frequency of flights, capacity, and fares were all strictly controlled between IATA members by means of bilateral service agreements.) The domestic operations were withdrawn in 1952, by which time the airline had been operating to Copenhagen since 1947 and New York since 1948 using Douglas DC-4s. In 1960 it was given a government-guaranteed loan to buy Douglas DC-6Bs, later augmenting and then replacing these with Canadair CL-44s – stretched Bristol Britannias with Rolls-Royce Tyne engines, enabling the airline to market the aircraft as the Rolls-Royce 400! Douglas DC-8 jet airliners were later acquired.

After the merger in 1973 Icelandair initially acted as a holding company for the two airlines, but operations were also merged in 1979. The route network still offers transatlantic opportunities for the traveller, but liberalisation of air services has meant that passengers no longer need to fly via Iceland for a cheap fare across the Atlantic. The domestic route network has been trimmed back to ten points, aided by the emergence of a third level carrier, Islandsflug, with a fleet of small aircraft well suited to services to the smaller communities. The main shareholder is an Icelandic shipping company, Eimskip, with 34 per cent. The airline is one of the country's largest employers.

Executive Directors & Officers:
Sigurdur Helgason, President & Chief Executive Officer; Valur Asgeirsson, Financial Director; Gudmundur Magnusson, Operations Director; Kristinn Halldorsson, Engineering & Maintenance Director.

HQ Airport & Main Base: Reykjavik

Radio callsign: ICEAIR

Designator: FI/ICE

Employees: 1,400

Main destinations served: Ten domestic destinations, plus Amsterdam, Baltimore, Barcelona, Berlin, Boston, Cologne/Bonn, Copenhagen, Faroe Islands, Fort Lauderdale, Frankfurt, Glasgow, Halifax, Hamburg, London Heathrow, Luxembourg, Milan, Nasarsuaq, New York JFK, Orlando, Oslo, Paris CDG, Salzburg, Stockholm, Vienna, Zürich.

FLEET
4 Boeing 757-200
4 Boeing 737-400 (2 leased)
4 Fokker 50

India – VT

AIR-INDIA

Air India Ltd

Incorporated: 1932

HISTORY
Air India's history dates from 1932, when J.R.D. Tata formed an airline known initially as Tata & Sons, but which became Tata Airlines in 1938. It had been formed to operate airmail services, and for the first few years mail used almost the entire payload, and it was not until 1938 that passenger services started with the introduction of de Havilland Rapide biplanes.

The start of World War Two ended the airmail services, and such flying as was permitted was confined to operations on behalf of the government and armed forces. Progress nevertheless continued, and during the war Tata Airlines had experience of operating larger and more modern aircraft. Post-war it was able to expand rapidly using war surplus aircraft, becoming a public company and changing

its name to Air-India in 1946. TWA (qv) provided assistance in training cabin crew for the Douglas C-47s and C-54s converted to airline DC-3 and DC-4 standard, and in return Air-India became a sales agent for the American airline in India.

Two months after Indian independence in 1948 the airline changed its name again, to Air-India International, while the Indian Government took a 49 per cent share, with an option on another 2 per cent. International operations started later the same year with a service from Bombay to London. The frequency of this service was soon increased, and it was not until 1950 that the next international service could be introduced, from Bombay to Nairobi. This steady progress continued until 1953, when all Indian airlines were nationalised and the aircraft and routes of Air-India and six other airlines were merged into two corporations, Indian National Airlines Corporation for domestic routes, and Air-India International Corporation for international services. The new airline continued to expand its network of services, helped by the introduction of Lockheed Super Constellations in 1954. A further name change occurred in 1962,

Air India is another operator of the Boeing 747-300, in this case in mixed passenger-cargo Combi form.

Airbus A310-300s are ideal for the less busy routes.

when the airline became simply Air-India, the hyphen being subsequently dropped.

Traditionally the airline's route structure favoured services to the United Kingdom, both as the former colonial power and because of immigration, while East Africa was also important because of the substantial Indian communities there. The growth of the oil economies of the Middle East, often in countries with small populations, also created new traffic patterns as expatriate Indian workers moved to these areas.

The early-1960s saw the introduction of Boeing 707 jet airliners, developing what was for the day a small, but modern fleet of nine aircraft, with routes from Bombay and Delhi ranging as far afield as New York, Moscow, Tokyo, and Sydney. These were subsequently replaced with Boeing 747s and augmented with Airbus A300s and A310s. Occasionally aircraft such as Ilyushin Il-62s and Il-76s were chartered in for a short period, the latter being used on freight duties.

In 1981 Air India and Indian Airlines (qv), as Indian National Airlines had become, established a third airline in which both had equal shares, Vayadoot, to operate feeder services with aircraft which included Indian-built Hawker Siddeley 748s, Fokker F-27 Friendships, and Dornier Do.228s.

Today, Air India is still in state control, although privatisation has been considered. It has a number of subsidiaries, mainly involved in hotels but including Air India Charters, which operates with aircraft provided by the parent airline. Future plans are to introduce what Air India describes as 'medium capacity long range' aircraft for medium density long-haul routes, offering more non-stop flights and also accelerating the withdrawal of the older Boeing 747-200s by the turn of the century.

Executive Directors & Officers: P.C. Sen, Chairman; M.P. Mascerenhas, Deputy Managing Director; N.C. Padhi, Deputy Managing Director; T.G. Sundararajan, Director, Finance; H.S. Uberoi, Commercial Director; Captain K. Mohan, Director, Operations; J.N. Gogoi, Director, Engineering; Mrs A. Mascarenhas, Director, Planning & International Relations; Dr P. Sen, Director, IT; S. Mukherjee, Director, Inflight Service & Business Development; R. Satish, Director, Airport Services; V. Vishwanathan, Director, Stores & Purchase; Deepak Samal, Director, Internal Audit; N.S. Rajam, Director, Human Resources.

HQ Airport & Main Base: Sahar Airport, Mumbai (Bombay), but Calcutta, Delhi, Chennai, Trivandrum, Goa, Bangalore, Hyderabad and Ahmedabad are also points for international services.

Radio callsign: AIRINDIA

Designator: AI/AIC

Employees: Flight-crew: 426; Cabin staff:

Essentially a long-haul airline, Air India also has the latest Boeing 747-400 in service.

1,991; Engineering: 3,062; Ground staff: 12,771; Total: 18,250.

Main destinations served: Abu Dhabi, Amsterdam, Bahrain, Bangkok, Chicago, Dar-es-Salaam, Dhahran, Doha, Dubai, Frankfurt, Geneva, Hong Kong, Jakarta, Jeddah, Kuala Lumpur, Kuwait, London Heathrow, Manchester, Moscow, Muscat, Nairobi, New York JFK, Osaka, Paris CDG, Riyadh, Rome, Seoul, Singapore, Tel Aviv, Tokyo, Toronto.

Annual turnover: US $1,024 million (£620.6 million)

Revenue passenger km pa: 9,501.2 million

Cargo tonne km pa: 546 million

Passengers pa: 2,274,939

LINKS WITH OTHER AIRLINES
Global alliance with Air France (qv), including code-sharing on services beyond Paris CDG.
Code-sharing and marketing agreements with Air Mauritius, Kuwait Airways (qv), SAS (qv), Singapore Airlines (qv), and United Airlines (qv).
Hubs and spoke operations at Mumbai (Bombay) and Delhi operated jointly with Indian Airlines (qv), as are operations from Calcutta to the Gulf.

FLEET
6 Boeing 747-400
2 Boeing 747-300
9 Boeing 747-200
3 Airbus A300B4
10 Airbus A310 (2 leased)

ALLIANCE AIR

Alliance Air Ltd

Incorporated: 1996

HISTORY
Alliance Air was formed by Indian Airlines (qv) in 1996 as a regional subsidiary serving destinations in the west of the country, initially operating four of the parent airline's Boeing 737s. The transfer of a further 12 aircraft is planned.

HQ Airport & Main Base: Delhi Safdarjung

Designator: CD/AAS

Main destinations served: Currently a dozen destinations, mainly in the west of India, including Bombay and Goa.

LINKS WITH OTHER AIRLINES
A subsidiary of Indian Airlines (qv).

FLEET
4 Boeing 737-200 (plus 12 due to be transferred)

HINDUJA

Hinduja Cargo Services Ltd

Incorporated: 1996

HISTORY
A new airline, Hinduja Cargo Services is a joint venture with Lufthansa (qv) operating feeder services to the German airline's hub at Sharjah in the Gulf.

Executive Directors & Officers: Robert Strodel, Managing Director & Chief Executive Officer.

HQ Airport & Main Base: Delhi, although the main hub is Sharjah

Designator: LH (Lufthansa)

Main destinations served: Sharjah to Bangalore, Bombay, Calcutta, Delhi, Hyderabad, Madras.

LINKS WITH OTHER AIRLINES
Feeder services are operated on behalf of Lufthansa (qv), which has a 40 per cent stake.

FLEET
5 Boeing 727-200F

INDIAN AIRLINES

Indian Airlines Ltd

Incorporated: 1953

HISTORY
This was formed in 1953 as the Indian National Airlines Corporation on the nationalisation of all Indian airlines, and was allocated the domestic services hitherto operated by Air-India International and six other airlines. Initially its fleet included a large number of Douglas DC-3s, but these were later replaced by Indian-built Hawker Siddeley 748 turboprop airliners. As air travel developed in India, the airline became one of the world's largest domestic carriers, with larger aircraft needed for the trunk routes. This led in 1981 to the formation of a third level airline, Vayudoot, as a 50:50 joint venture with Air India (qv). Vayudoot had Indian Airlines' fleet of HS 748s transferred to it, and also operated Fokker F-27 Friendships and Dornier Do.228s. Its operations were re-absorbed by Indian Airlines in 1995, following concerns over safety.

In recent years Indian Airlines has moved beyond purely domestic services and now operates to neighbouring countries as well as to South-East Asia and the Gulf, the latter in co-operation with Air India. These changes have been made possible by the types of aircraft now operated, which have the range and capacity to relieve Air India of some of its shorter routes.

A subsidiary, Alliance Air (qv), was established in 1996 as a regional subsidiary. Indian Airlines' Boeing 737 fleet is gradually being transferred to the new airline.

Although Indian Airlines is still nationalised and under the control of the Ministry of Tourism and Civil Aviation, it is no longer operated as a state corporation, but as a limited company.

Executive Directors & Officers: Russi Mody, Chairman; P.C. Sen, Managing Director; P.J. Crasta, Deputy Managing Director, Commercial; Dr G.K. Agrawal, Director, Planning; B.K. Sinha, Director, Engineering.

HQ Airport & Main Base: New Delhi, with additional hubs and bases at Calcutta, Mumbai (Bombay), and Madras.

Radio callsign: INDAIR

Designator: IC/IAC

Employees: 22,112

Main destinations served: More than 70 domestic destinations, plus Bangkok, Chittagong, Colombo, Dhaka, Fujairah, Karachi, Kathmandu, Kuala Lumpur, Male, Muscat, Ras-al-Khaimah, Singapore.

Annual turnover: US $737 million (£466.6 million)

LINKS WITH OTHER AIRLINES
Hub and spoke operation with Air India (qv) and co-operation on services from Calcutta to the Gulf.

FLEET
8 Airbus A300B2
2 Airbus A300B4
30 Airbus A320-200
20 Boeing 737-200 (12 being transferred to Alliance Air)

JET

Jet Airways (India) Ltd

Incorporated: 1992

HISTORY
One of the largest independent airlines in India, Jet Airways was founded in April 1992 and commenced operations a little

over a year later in May 1993. Support was provided by Gulf Air (qv) and Kuwait Airways (qv), each with a 20 per cent stake in the new airline, although the largest shareholder is Tailwinds, an Indian company owned by Naresh Goyal, the airline's chairman. This support and a co-operation agreement with KLM (qv), including a common frequent flyer programme, has ensured rapid growth, but a new Indian Government in 1997 has demanded that Gulf Air and Kuwait Airways dispose of their shareholdings and that all airlines must be completely Indian-owned.

Executive Directors & Officers: Naresh Goyal, Chairman & Managing Director; Nikos Kardassis, Chief Executive Officer; B.P. Baliga, Executive Director; Saroj K. Datta, Senior Vice-President, Maintenance & Engineering; Ananth Iyer, Vice-President, Finance; David Exekiel, Vice-President, Operations; Anita Goyal, Vice-President, Marketing.

HQ Airport & Main Base: Mumbai (Bombay), with additional hubs at Calcutta and Delhi.

Radio callsign: JET AIRWAYS

Designator: 9W/JAI

Employees: 1,860

Main destinations served: Some 20 destinations throughout India, including Bangalore, Calicut, Cochin, Goa, and Madras.

LINKS WITH OTHER AIRLINES
Gulf Air (qv) and Kuwait Airways (qv) each have a 20 per cent shareholding. A co-operation agreement exists with KLM (qv).

FLEET
13 Boeing 737-400 (at least 4 leased)
4 Boeing 737-300 (leased from Ansett (qv))

MODILUFT

Modiluft Ltd

Incorporated: 1993

HISTORY
Originally established by Lufthansa (qv) and Satish Kumar Modi, owner of the Indian-based Modi Group, Modiluft commenced operations in 1993 and now flies to more than 20 destinations across India. In addition to its scheduled network, charter services are also provided.
    There have been signs of strain in the

relationship with Lufthansa recently.

Executive Directors & Officers: Satish Kumar Modi, Chairman & President; Captain P. Kling, Senior Vice-President, Operations; H. Mittenddorfer, Senior Vice-President, Technical.

HQ Airport & Main Base: Delhi

Radio callsign: MODILUFT

Designator: M9/MOD

Employees: 944

Main destinations served: More than 20 destinations, including Bangalore, Calcutta, Calicut, Cochin, Goa, Madras, and Mumbai (Bombay).

LINKS WITH OTHER AIRLINES
Marketing and training alliance with Lufthansa (qv).

FLEET
4 Boeing 737-400
4 Boeing 737-200 (leased from Lufthansa)

NEPC

NEPC Airlines Ltd

Incorporated: 1993

HISTORY
Although NEPC was the first Indian private airline to apply for a licence, operations did not start until March 1994, initially in the state of Tamil Nadu in southern India. In contrast with many of the other new privately-owned Indian airlines, NEPC is primarily a regional operator, operating turboprop rather than jet aircraft.

HQ Airport & Main base: Madras

Radio callsign: NEPCAIR

Designator: D5/NEP

Main destinations served: More than 30 destinations, mainly in southern India.

FLEET
9 Fokker F-27-500 (leased)
1 Beech King Air C90

SAHARA INDIA AIRLINES

Sahara India Airlines Ltd

Incorporated: 1991

HISTORY
Founded in 1991 as the operating division of the Sahara Group, Sahara India Airlines

did not commence operations until 1993, when two Boeing 737-200s were introduced, joined the following year by two 737-400s. The airline has developed a network of scheduled passenger and cargo services from Delhi and Mumbai (Bombay), and has recently added ATR-42s for its shorter routes.

Executive Directors & Officers: Subrata Roy Sahara, Chairman; Uttam Kumar Bose, Chief Executive.

HQ Airport & Main Base: Delhi, with a further base at Mumbai.

Designator: S2/SIAL

Employees: 450

Main destinations served: Upwards of 12 domestic destinations from Delhi, including Goa and Mumbai, but fewer from Mumbai.

FLEET
4 Boeing 737-400 (leased)
5 ATR-42 (leased)

Indonesia – PK

AIRFAST

Airfast Indonesia

Incorporated: 1971

HISTORY
Originally founded to provide air services for the oil industry in Indonesia, Airfast has expanded its operations to include contract and ad hoc passenger and freight charters, with a very wide variety of aircraft ranging from small Piper and Beech air taxis and Bell helicopters to Boeing 737s.

Executive Directors & Officers: Frank D. Reuneker, President; Garry Hunt, General Manager; E. Surydarma, Operations Director.

HQ Airport & Main Base: Jakarta

Radio callsign: AIRFAST

Designator: AFE

Employees: 450

FLEET
3 Boeing 737-200
4 British Aerospace 748 (leased)
3 de Havilland DHC-6 Twin Otter
1 CASA/IPTN 212-200 Aviocar
3 Sikorsky S-58ET
2 Bell 412
1 Bell 212

1 Beech Queen Air B80
2 Bell 204
2 Bell 206B JetRanger
1 Piper Apache

BOURAQ

Bouraq Indonesia Airlines

Incorporated: 1970

HISTORY

Bouraq operates throughout the eastern part of the Indonesian archipelago, including Bali and Java, and to parts of Malaysia.

Executive Directors & Officers: J.A. Sumendap, President; H.A. Hucunan, Director, Finance; G.B. Rung Kat, Technical Director; Subardi Ruslanhandi, Director, Maintenance.

HQ Airport & Main Base: Jakarta

Radio callsign: BOURAQ

Designator: BO/BOU

Employees: 731

Main destinations served: Scheduled services throughout eastern Indonesia.

FLEET

8 Boeing 737-200
2 British Aerospace 748-2B
3 British Aerospace 748-2A
5 IPTN-N-250

GARUDA

PT Garuda Indonesia Airways

Incorporated: 1950

HISTORY

Air services in Indonesia were originally started by KLM (qv) in the 1930s, which operated an Inter Island Division in Indonesia before establishing a subsidiary airline, KNILM, or Royal Dutch East Indies Airlines, before the outbreak of World War Two. Post-war operations were slow to start as Indonesia pressed hard for independence.

Garuda was founded as Garuda Indonesian Airways in 1950, by the government of the newly-independent Indonesia and KLM. KLM's interest was taken over by the Indonesian Government in 1954, and during the next decade it acquired many of the smaller airlines operating within Indonesia. While the initial objective was to create a viable air transport operation within Indonesia – a large country, with tropical rain forests and mountains, spread over a large number of islands – intercontinental services

were also subsequently introduced. Having originally commenced operations with Douglas DC-3s, Garuda acquired Convair 340 and 440 Metropolitans and then Fokker F-27s and Lockheed Electras, some of which were ex-KLM, before moving into the jet age with Convair 990s and Douglas DC-8s, followed by DC-9s.

In 1962 Garuda acquired the domestic services operated by a KLM subsidiary, de Kronduif, but after two years these were passed to a new airline formed by the Indonesian Government to operate domestic services, Merpati (qv). Merpati, which operates an intensive network of domestic air services, was acquired in 1978, but has been left as a separate operational entity.

In terms of annual turnover, Garuda is today well up the list of the world's top 50 airlines, having risen from 34th in 1996 to 31st in 1997. Its route network extends throughout Asia and the Pacific, and to primarily European destinations beyond, as well as to Los Angeles. A major domestic route network is also operated. The airline is likely to be denationalised shortly to reduce its dependence on the government, possibly by an offering of shares to raise capital for future expansion. Meanwhile, some of the aircraft due for delivery in 1998 may be delayed while financial packages are arranged.

HQ Airport & Main Base: Jakarta, with a further hub at Denpasar (Bali).

Radio callsign: INDONESIA

Designator: GA/GIA

Employees: 13,272

Main destinations served: More than 30 domestic destinations, plus Abu Dhabi, Adelaide, Amsterdam, Auckland, Bangkok, Beijing, Bombay, Brisbane, Cairns, Darwin, Dhahran, Frankfurt, Fukuoka, Guangzhou, Ho Chi Minh City, Hong Kong, Honolulu, Jeddah, Kuala Lumpur, London Gatwick, Los Angeles, Manila, Nagoya, Osaka, Paris CDG, Perth, Riyadh, Rome, Seoul, Singapore, Sydney, Tokyo, Vienna, Zürich.

Annual turnover: US $2,070 million (£1,254.5 million)

LINKS WITH OTHER AIRLINES

Owns Merpati (qv).
Code-sharing with China Airlines (qv), Iberia (qv), and KLM (qv). Joint flights with Aeroflot (qv). Pooled operations with EVA (qv) and Japan Airlines (qv).

FLEET

10 Boeing 747-400
6 Boeing 747-200B

9 McDonnell Douglas MD-11
9 Airbus A330-300
9 Airbus A300-600
8 Airbus A300B4
7 Boeing 737-400
12 Boeing 737-300
plus 6 Boeing 777-200 on order for delivery in 2000

MANDALA AIRLINES

PT Mandala Airlines

Incorporated: 1969

HISTORY

Amongst the first privately-owned airlines in Indonesia after nationalisation of air transport in the 1950s, Mandala initially operated charters before establishing a network of scheduled services.

Executive Directors & Officers: V. Subageo, President; S.E. Subagiyo, Chief Executive Officer; Veronica H. Subarkah, Commercial & Finance Director; Captain Gunadi Sugoto, Director of Operations; R.J. Tumenggung, Technical Director.

HQ Airport & Main Base: Jakarta

Radio callsign: MANDALA

Designator: RI/MDL

Main destinations served: Some 20 destinations throughout Indonesia, including Bali.

FLEET

5 Lockheed L-188 Electra
10 Boeing 737-200
2 Fokker F-28 Fellowship

MERPATI

Merpati Nusantara Airlines

Incorporated: 1962

HISTORY

Merpati is Indonesia's main domestic airline, operating scheduled passenger and cargo services throughout the Indonesian archipelago, as well as charter flights. It was founded by the Indonesian Government in 1962, as a domestic partner to Garuda (qv), and although that airline continued to operate an extensive domestic trunk network, the services previously operated by de Kroonduif – a subsidiary of KLM (qv) – which Garuda had been operating were transferred to Merpati in 1964. The core of Merpati's operations at first were routes which had been flown by the Indonesian Air Force, which had been developing services to isolated communities from 1958 onwards.

In 1978 ownership of Merpati was transferred to Garuda, but the airline has maintained its own identity and management team since that time. Today, in terms of airports used, Merpati has one of the world's largest domestic networks, reaching more than 130 destinations all within Indonesia.

Executive Directors & Officers: Captain Frans H. Sumolang, President.

HQ Airport & Main Base: Jakarta, with additional hubs at Denpasar (Bali) and Padang.

Radio callsign: MERPATI

Designator: MZ/MNA

Employees: 2,150

Main destinations served: More than 130 domestic destinations.

LINKS WITH OTHER AIRLINES
Owned 100 per cent by Garuda (qv).

FLEET
3 Boeing 737-200
6 Fokker 100
25 Fokker F-28-4000 Fellowship
5 British Aerospace ATP
13 Fokker F-27-500 Friendship
5 Fokker F-27-300 Friendship
14 CASA/IPTN CN-235
11 CASA/IPTN CN-212
8 de Havilland DHC-6 Twin Otter

PELITA

Pelita Air Service

Incorporated: 1970

HISTORY
Another state-owned airline, Pelita is a subsidiary of the state-owned oil company, Pertamina, and operates executive air services as well as passenger and freight charter and contract operations.

Executive Directors & Officers: Captain Oedyono, Director.

HQ Airport & Main Base: Jakarta

Radio callsign: PELITA

Designator: EP/PAS

Employees: 1,850

FLEET
4 Lockheed L-100-30 Hercules
1 Avro RJ85

1 British Aerospace 146-200
1 Fokker 100
1 Fokker 70
4 Fokker F-28-4000 Fellowship
1 Fokker F-28-1000 Fellowship
5 de Havilland Dash 7
1 Grumman Gulfstream III
1 Grumman Gulfstream II
12 CASA/IPTN 212
15 Aérospatiale SA330 Puma
4 Sikorsky S-76A
25 MBB Bo.105C

SABANG

Sabang Merauke Raya Air Charter

Incorporated: 1969

HISTORY
Originally founded as a joint venture with a Malaysian company and known as Malaysian Air Charter, in 1972 the airline split from its Malaysian partner and adopted its current title. Although its operations are predominantly charter, some scheduled services are now operated in and around Sumatra.

Executive Directors & Officers: Toto Iman Dewanto, President; Lawrence Natamiharja, Finance Director; Captain Syamsir Kinan, Operations Director; Moch Sunarjo, Personnel Director.

HQ Airport & Main Base: Medan, Sumatra

Radio callsign: SAMER

Designator: SMC

Main destinations served: Charter flights plus scheduled flights to destinations in and around Sumatra.

FLEET
2 Fokker F-27-200 Friendship
4 CASA/IPTN 212
2 Piper Navajo/Navajo Chieftain
2 Pilatus Britten-Norman BN-2A Islander

SEMPATI

PT Sempati Air

Incorporated: 1969

HISTORY
Formed in the first wave of enthusiasm to start privately-owned airlines after nationalisation of air transport in Indonesia during the 1950s, for the first 20 years after it was founded in 1969 Sempati concen-

trated on charter services. Restructuring in 1989 paved the way for the start of scheduled services in 1990. More recently it has started to operate to Singapore and Taipei.

Executive Directors & Officers: Hasan M. Soedjono, President; Cenik Ardana, Senior Vice-President, Finance; Captain Boedi Rahardjo, Senior Vice-President, Operations; Eddy Playitno, Senior Vice-President, Maintenance & Engineering; Suroso Wening, Senior Vice-President, General Affairs.

HQ Airport & Main Base: Jakarta

Radio callsign: SPIROW

Designator: SG/SSR

Employees: 3,400

Main destinations served: Almost 30 domestic destinations, plus Singapore and Taipei.

FLEET
3 Airbus A300B4
7 Boeing 737-200
7 Fokker 100
2 Fokker 70
2 Fokker F-27-600
2 Fokker F-27-200

Iran – EP

IRAN AIR

Iran Air/Homa

Incorporated: 1944

HISTORY
Iranian Airways, The predecessor of Iran Air, was founded in 1944 as a private company with TWA (qv) holding 10 per cent of the shares. Operations did not begin until the following year, when charter flights were operated, the first scheduled flights starting in 1946 with services from Tehran to Baghdad, Beirut, and Cairo, mainly using Douglas DC-3 aircraft, soon joined by DC-4s. A domestic route network was developed during this time, and international expansion continued, with services to Athens, Paris, and Rome being introduced in 1947.

Convair 240 Metropolitans and Douglas DC-6s, including DC-6Bs, were introduced later, and in 1959 the airline received two Vickers Viscount 700s. Two years later, at the request of the government, the airline absorbed Persian Air Services, which was in serious financial difficulties. Persian Air Services dated from 1954, and had had the benefit of assistance from both Sabena (qv) and KLM (qv). The merger resulted in an extensive reorganisation of Iranian Airways, and it was nationalised in 1962 to become the Iran National Airlines Corporation, or Iranair. After nationalisation, a three-year technical assistance agreement was reached with Pan American in 1964.

The airline's first jets – Boeing 727s – were introduced in 1966, and enabled it to inaugurate a service to London. Both Boeing 707s and 737s soon followed.

Revolution in Iran and the creation of an Islamic republic saw a slight change to the name, which became Iran Air, but it is now otherwise known as HOMA, based on the acronym of the airline's name in Farsi. Operations were disrupted after the revolution and then again during the lengthy war with Iraq. Despite frequent diplomatic difficulties with the west, the airline has developed a substantial fleet of European and American aircraft. However, many of these are now elderly, and Iran Air has been planning to modernise its fleet with Airbus A321 and A330 aircraft, although at the time of writing no orders have been announced.

A subsidiary is Iran Air Tours (qv), operating a charter fleet of Russian origin.

Executive Directors & Officers: Eng S.H. Shafti, Chairman & Managing Director; Sanei Ghalibaf, Finance Director; A. Oghation, Operations Director; A. Mohammadirad, Engineering Director; R. Rezaein, Supply Services Director; N. Hasheiman, In-Flight Services Director; H. Sharestani, Personnel Director.

HQ Airport & Main Base: Tehran

Radio callsign: IRANAIR

Designator: IR/IRA

Employees: 11,855

Main destinations served: Some 20 domestic destinations, including Bandar Abbas, plus international services to Abu Dhabi, Almaty, Amsterdam, Ashkabad, Athens, Bahrain, Baku, Beijing, Bombay, Damascus, Doha, Dubai, Frankfurt, Geneva, Hamburg, Istanbul, Jeddah, Karachi, Kuala Lumpur, Kuwait, Larnaca, London Heathrow, Madrid, Moscow, Muscat, Paris CDG, Rome, Sharjah, Tashkent, Tokyo, Vienna.

LINKS WITH OTHER AIRLINES
Owns Iran Air Tours (qv).

FLEET
2 Boeing 747-200B
1 Boeing 747-200F
1 Boeing 747-100
4 Boeing 747SP
2 Airbus A300-600
5 Airbus A300B2
4 Boeing 707-320
5 Boeing 727-200
2 Boeing 727-100
3 Boeing 737-200

IRAN AIR TOURS

Iran Air Tours

Incorporated: 1973

HISTORY
Although formed as a subsidiary of Iran Air (qv) in 1973, Iran Air Tours did not start operating aircraft until 1990, and while today most of its business is air charter, including pilgrimage flights, it has also developed a network of domestic services.

Executive Directors & Officers: A.M. Khalili, Chairman; S.M. Ghaffar, President & Managing Director; H. Taghdissi, Commercial Director; S. Mirmirani, Maintenance Director; N. Rassouli, Marketing Director; A. Amjadi, Personnel Director.

HQ Airport & Main Base: Tehran, with a further base at Mashad.

Designator: IRB

Employees: 600

Main destinations served: Charter flights, plus flights to more than a dozen domestic destinations.

LINKS WITH OTHER AIRLINES
A subsidiary of Iran Air (qv).

FLEET
11 Tupolev Tu-154M
4 Yakovlev Yak-42D

IRAN ASSEMAN

Iran Asseman Airlines

Incorporated: 1980

HISTORY
Iran Asseman Airlines was founded after the Iranian revolution in 1980, on the nationalisation and merger of four operators: Air Taxi, dating from 1958; Air Service, formed 1962; Paris Air, formed 1969; and Hoor Asseman. The aircraft included a number of types suitable for air taxi and feeder services.

Today, the airline remains in state ownership but independent of and distinct from Iran Air (qv). A high frequency domestic network is operated, as well as domestic and international charters.

Executive Directors & Officers: Ali Abedzadeh, Managing Director; Hamid Reza Fekri, Deputy Managing Director; A. Khalili, Chief Financial Officer; Iraj Ronaghi, Technical Director.

HQ Airport & Main Base: Tehran

Designator: Y7/IRC

Employees: 1,100

Main destinations served: More than 20 domestic destinations, plus charters.

FLEET
4 Boeing 727-200Adv
6 Fokker F-28 Fellowship
4 ATR 72
1 ATR 42
4 Dassault Falcon 20
2 Pilatus Britten-Norman BN-2A Islander
3 Piper Navajo Chieftain

KISH AIR

Kish Airlines

Incorporated: 1991

HISTORY
Kish Airlines was founded in 1991 and started operations the following year from its base on Kish Island, off the coast of Iran. The airline is owned by the Kish Free Zone organisation, and operates scheduled services and passenger charters.

Executive Directors & Officers: M. Dadpay, President; Y. Khalili, Vice-President.

HQ Airport & Main Base: Kish

Radio callsign: KISHAIR

Designator: KN/IRK

Employees: Flight-crew: 73; Cabin staff: 78; Ground staff: 45; Total: 206.

Main destinations served: Dubai, Isfahan, Kermanshah, Mashad, Shiraz, Tabriz, Tehran.

Annual turnover: US $24 million (£15.6 million)

Aircraft km pa: 2,254,933

Revenue passenger km pa: 1,332 million

FLEET
6 Tupolev Tu-154M (leased)

An unusual view of a Kish Air Tupolev Tu-154M.

Iraq – YI

IRAQI AIRWAYS

Iraqi Airways

Incorporated: 1945

HISTORY

The status of Iraqi Airways is uncertain at the moment due to United Nations sanctions and shortages of spares and other equipment following the Gulf War.

Originally founded in 1945 as a branch of the state-owned railways, Iraqi Airways commenced operations the following year with a service between Baghdad and Basra, using de Havilland Rapide biplanes. Douglas DC-3s followed soon after, and by the end of the first year the airline had services operating from Baghdad to Beirut, Damascus, Lydda, and Cairo. Assistance was then received from BOAC (British Overseas Airways Corporation), and this arrangement lasted until 1960.

Early expansion was steady, with Tehran and Kuwait added to the network in 1947, and in 1948 services were introduced to Athens, Bahrain, and Cyprus. The Rapides and DC-3s were replaced by de Havilland Doves and Vickers Vikings, and it was not until 1957 that the airline received its first four-engined aircraft, Vickers Viscount 735s. The Viscounts enabled the airline to start a service from Baghdad to London via Istanbul and Vienna in 1957. The first jet equipment, Hawker Siddeley Trident 1Es, joined the fleet in 1965.

While Boeings were added in subsequent years, increasingly the fleet reflected Iraq's close collaboration with the Soviet Union, Antonov and Ilyushin aircraft being acquired. Operations were affected by the long war between Iraq and Iran, and the Gulf War of 1991 saw a complete ban on fixed wing flights as part of the cease-fire terms. Nevertheless, the United Nations Security Council eventually agreed to a resumption of civil internal flights, and a service between Baghdad and Basra using Antonov An-24s was restarted in January 1992. Since then, operations are believed to have been suspended.

Executive Directors & Officers: Rabie M.S. Abdulbaki, Chairman & Director General; Iyad A. Haman, Deputy Director General, Commercial; Mahdi Al-Allak, Deputy Director General, Technical; Abdul Sattar Jabbar, Deputy Director General, Administration; Abdulla Al Jobouri, Deputy Director, Flight Operations.

HQ Airport & Main Base: Baghdad

Radio callsign: IRAQI

Designator: IA/IAW

Employees: 2,770

FLEET
3 Boeing 747-200C
1 Boeing 747SP
2 Boeing 707-320C
6 Boeing 727-200
2 Boeing 737-200
5 Antonov An-24

AER LINGUS

Aer Lingus Ltd

Incorporated: 1936

HISTORY

Aer Lingus operates as a single airline but is in fact two airlines as a result of a 1993 reorganisation: Aer Lingus, which operates European services; and Aer Lingus Shannon, which operates transatlantic services. Although this is the result of legislation passed in 1993, it also reflects the history of the airline, Aer Lingus being formed in 1936 while Aerlinte Eireann was formed in 1947 to operate a transatlantic service.

Operations began in May 1936 with a flight by a de Havilland Dragon Rapide biplane from Dublin to Bristol, although by the end of the year the service had been extended to London. Steady expansion took place up to the outbreak of World War Two in 1939, when, despite Irish neutrality, operations were limited to a Dublin–Liverpool service.

Aerlinte Eireann's first routes linked Dublin and Shannon with New York and Boston, using Lockheed Super Constellation airliners. The Constellations were later replaced by three Boeing 707s, which in turn were replaced by Boeing 747-100s before these too were replaced by Airbus A330s. The airline's transatlantic operations were restricted for many years by an enforced call at Shannon in the west of Ireland for political reasons, largely to protect the local economy after transatlantic flights began to bypass the airport. A compromise has now been reached, with the A330s starting their transatlantic flights by flying eastwards from Shannon to Dublin, before beginning their 'nonstop' transatlantic flights – a measure considered important to tap into the potential market offered from airports in England and Scotland.

Aer Lingus also operates services to most of the major centres in Europe, as well as providing charter flights for package holidays and for pilgrims to Lourdes. A wholly-owned subsidiary, Aer Lingus Commuter (qv), operates feeder services within Ireland and from Great Britain. A number of services to Europe are routed through airports in England, especially Manchester, because of the limited market offered by Ireland's small population. A major overhaul facility at Shannon, TEAM Aer Lingus, is used by a large number of airlines.

Executive Directors & Officers: Bernie Cahill, Executive Chairman; Garry Cullen, Chief Operating Officer; Gary McGann, Group Chief Executive Officer; Tom McInerney, General Manager, Aer Lingus Shannon; Donal Foley, General Manager, Flight Operations; Louis Harkin, General Manager, Customer Delivery; Victor Garland, General Manager, International Marketing.

HQ Airport & Main Base: Dublin, with transatlantic services located on Shannon. The main maintenance base is at Shannon.

Radio callsign: SHAMROCK

Designator: EI/EIN

Employees: 5,620

Main destinations served: (includes Aer Lingus Commuter) Dublin to Amsterdam, Birmingham, Boston*, Bristol, Brussels, Connaught, Copenhagen, Cork, Düsseldorf, East Midlands, Edinburgh, Frankfurt, Galway, Glasgow, Jersey, Kerry, Leeds/Bradford, London Heathrow, Madrid, Manchester, Milan, Newcastle, New York JFK*, Paris, Rome, Salzburg, Shannon, Sligo, Zürich.
* also from Shannon.

Annual turnover: US $1,225 million (£742.4 million)

LINKS WITH OTHER AIRLINES
Marketing alliance with British Airways (qv).
Code-share with Delta Air Lines (qv).
Owns Aer Lingus Commuter (qv).

FLEET
5 Airbus A330-300
6 Boeing 737-400
10 Boeing 737-500 (leased)
7 British Aerospace 146-300 (leased) (used by Aer Lingus Commuter)
6 Fokker 50 (used by Aer Lingus Commuter)

AER LINGUS COMMUTER

Aer Lingus Commuter Ltd

Incorporated: 1984

HISTORY
Aer Lingus Commuter was formed by its parent company, Aer Lingus (qv), to take over its services to Great Britain, with the exception of London and Manchester, and also to develop a network of feeder services within Ireland. The initial fleet was largely composed of Short 360 feeder liners. More recently Fokker 50s and British Aerospace 146s have been introduced in a bid to attract travellers from provincial cities in Britain to the parent airline's transatlantic services. At peak periods some services are operated by Aer Lingus Boeing 737-500s.

Executive Directors & Officers: Garry Cullen, Chairman; Seamus Kearney, Chief Executive Officer.

HQ Airport & Main Base: Dublin

Radio callsign: SHAMROCK

Designator: EI/EIN

Employees: 300

Main destinations served: With the exception of London and Manchester, Aer Lingus services to Great Britain and within Ireland.

Annual turnover: Included in figure for Aer Lingus

LINKS WITH OTHER AIRLINES
Subsidiary of Aer Lingus.

FLEET
7 British Aerospace 146-300 (leased)
6 Fokker 50

IRELAND AIRWAYS

Ireland Airways Ltd

Incorporated: 1991

HISTORY
A small scheduled and charter airline. Future expansion plans centre on routes from Dublin to Galway and Kerry.

Executive Directors & Officers: Ruadhan Neeson, Chief Executive Officer.

HQ Airport & Main Base: Dublin

Designator: EIX

Main destinations served: Donegal and Sligo, plus charters.

FLEET
3 British Aerospace ATP
1 Fokker F-27
1 Fairchild FH-227
1 Short 360
1 Short 330
1 Piper Navajo Chieftain

RYANAIR

Ryanair

Incorporated: 1985

HISTORY
The pioneer in 'low fares, no frills' service within the British Isles, Ryanair was formed in 1985, and initially operated Rombac One-Elevens on services between Ireland and England, with its main UK base at London Luton. Now Europe's largest low fare airline, Ryanair has since moved its main UK hub to London Stansted. It has introduced a low fare service between that airport and Glasgow Prestwick, and undertakes charter services from Dublin to Europe. A fleet of Boeing 737-200s has replaced the One-Elevens.

Executive Directors & Officers: David Bondermann, Chairman; Cathal Ryan, Deputy Chairman; Declan Ryan, Managing Director; Michael O'Leary, Chief Executive; Howard Millar, Finance Director; Conor McCarthy, Operations Director; Brian Taylor, Engineering Director.

HQ Airport & Main Base: Dublin, but with a further base at London Stansted, for which different callsigns and designators are used.

Radio callsign: RYANAIR (Ireland), BUDGET JET (UK)

Designator: FR/RYR (Ireland), CYR (UK)

Employees: 700

Main destinations served: Birmingham, Cardiff, Cork, Glasgow Prestwick, Knock, Leeds/Bradford, Liverpool, London Gatwick, London Luton, London Stansted, Manchester.

LINKS WITH OTHER AIRLINES
Marketing links with Air UK (qv)

FLEET
20 Boeing 737-200

TRANSAER

TransAer Ltd

Incorporated: 1991

HISTORY
Formed in 1991 as Translift Airways, this airline started operations in 1992, adopting the current title of TransAer in 1996. It is the operating subsidiary of Translift Holdings, the main shareholder being All Leisure Travel Holdings, with 49 per cent. The main business is inclusive tour charter operations from the British Isles.

Executive Directors & Officers: J. McGoldrick, Chairman and Chief Executive.

Israel's domestic airline, Arkia, uses de Havilland Dash 7s on its scheduled network.

Israel – 4X

ARKIA

Arkia Israeli Airlines Ltd

Incorporated: 1949

HISTORY
Israel's domestic airline, Arkia was formed in 1949 and commenced operations in 1950 as Arkia Inland Airlines, with El Al (qv) owning half of its shares. In addition to operating domestic services, the airline also moved into the air charter market, initially with equipment leased from El Al, although the latter sold its shares in Arkia in 1980.

Executive Directors & Officers: Prof Israel Borovich, President & Chief Executive Officer; David Borovitz, Executive Vice-President; Shlomo Hanael, Executive Vice-President, Operations & Maintenance; Uri Miller, Vice-President, Finance; Dori Soshan, Vice-President, Commercial; Dan Yaari, Vice-President, Corporate Secretary & Legal.

HQ Airport & Main Base: Dov Airport, Tel Aviv

Radio callsign: ARKIA

Designator: IZ/AIZ

HQ Airport & Main Base: Dublin, with aircraft also based at Shannon and Manchester.

Radio callsign: TRANSAER

Designator: T8/TLA

Employees: 700

Main destinations served: Inclusive tour charter flights from Dublin, Shannon, and Manchester to European and North African holiday resorts.

FLEET
6 Airbus A300B4
8 Airbus A320-200

Arkia's important international charter operations, bringing visitors to Israel, are handled by Boeing 737-200s such as this, as well as by the larger Boeing 757.

Employees: Flight-crew: 130; Cabin staff: 100; Engineering: 210; Ground staff: 780; Total: 1,220.

Main destinations served: Dead Sea, Eilat, Gush Katif, Haifa, Jerusalem, Lod, Masada, Rosh Pina.

LINKS WITH OTHER AIRLINES
Charter marketing alliance with El Al (qv).

FLEET
2 Boeing 757-200
4 Boeing 737-200
12 de Havilland Dash 7-100
1 de Havilland DHC-6 Twin Otter
plus a number of light aircraft

EL AL

El Al Israel Airlines Ltd

Incorporated: 1948

HISTORY
Israel's national airline, El Al (from the Hebrew for 'to the skies', or 'onward and upward') was founded in November 1948, and commenced operations in July 1949 with services from Tel Aviv to Rome and Paris using Douglas DC-4 Skymasters. Early development of the route network was rapid, with Athens, Vienna, Zürich, London, Nairobi, Johannesburg, and New York soon being added, Lockheed Super Constellations flying the transatlantic services. Before long El Al was flying to every capital city in western Europe.

Turboprop airliners were introduced in 1957, with Bristol Britannias operating the transatlantic flights via London. Four years later Boeing 707s were introduced on these services, and within months of their introduction were operating Tel Aviv to New York non-stop. Fluctuating traffic and restrictions which prevent the airline from operating on the Sabbath have meant that the airline has encountered financial difficulties in the past, and this is delaying its privatisation.

El Al operates international services only, with domestic operations handled by Arkia (qv).

Executive Directors & Officers: Joseph Ciechanover, Chairman; J. Feldschuh, President; E. Magid, Operations Director & Chief Pilot; D. Goralnik, Engineering Director; S. Danor, Marketing Director; D. Saadon, Personnel Director.

HQ Airport & Main Base: Ben Gurion International, Tel Aviv

Radio callsign: ELAL

Designator: LY/ELY

Employees: 3,400

Main destinations served: Amsterdam, Antalya, Athens, Baltimore, Bangkok, Barcelona, Beijing, Berlin, Bombay, Boston, Brussels, Bucharest, Budapest, Cairo, Chicago, Cologne/Bonn, Copenhagen, Delhi, Frankfurt, Geneva, Helsinki, Hong Kong, Istanbul, Larnaca, Leipzig, Lisbon, Los Angeles, London Heathrow, Luxembourg, Madrid, Manchester, Marseilles, Miami, Milan, Montreal, Moscow, Munich, New York JFK, New York Newark, Orlando, Paris CDG, Prague, Rome, Sofia, Stockholm, St Petersburg, Tashkent, Vienna, Warsaw, Washington Dulles, Zürich.

Annual turnover: US $1,195 million (£724.2 million)

FLEET
3 Boeing 747-400
1 Boeing 747-200F
3 Boeing 747-200B Combi
4 Boeing 747-200B
1 Boeing 747-100F
2 Boeing 767-200ER
2 Boeing 767-200
7 Boeing 757-200
2 Boeing 737-200
plus 5 Boeing 737-700/800 on order

Italy – I

AIR DOLOMITI

Air Dolomiti SpA

Incorporated: 1989

HISTORY
After being founded in 1989, Air Dolomiti started operations in May 1991 using a single de Havilland Dash 8 on a service between Trieste and Geneva. Today the fleet consists entirely of aircraft of manufacture.

Executive Directors & Officers: Alcide Leali, President & Chief Executive Officer; Gianmarco Solari, Vice-President, Accounting; Marco Cesa, Vice-President, Commercial; Giacomo Manzon, Vice-President, Operations; Valerio Dell'Angela, Vice-President, Technical.

HQ Airport & Main Base: Trieste

Radio callsign: DOLOMITI

Designator: EN/DLA

Employees: Flight-crew: 65; Cabin staff: 70; Engineering: 30; Ground staff: 65; Total: 230.

Main destinations served: Barcelona, Frankfurt, Genoa, Munich, Paris CDG, Pisa, Turin, Venice, Verona.

Annual turnover: US $51.4 million (£31.2 million)

FLEET
4 ATR 42-500 (leased)
5 ATR 42-300 (leased)

AIR EUROPE

Air Europe Italy SpA

Incorporated: 1988

HISTORY
Established in 1988 as part of the Airlines of Europe Group, which collapsed in 1991 with the parent International Leisure Group, Air Europe Italy has since passed into wholly-Italian ownership. Operations originally began in 1989 with a single Boeing 757, but the fleet is now completely standardised on the larger Boeing 767. The airline flies long-distance inclusive tour charters. Alitalia (qv) has a 24.6 per cent stake.

Executive Directors & Officers: Lupo Rattazzi, Chairman; Antonello Isabella, Managing Director; Flavio Granaglia, Financial Director; Giancarlo Tedeschi, Operations Director; Francesco Banal, Engineering Director; Maurizio Trombetta, Commercial Director; Antonello Bonolis, Marketing Director; Franco Sebasti, Personnel Director.

HQ Airport & Main Base: HQ at Varese, with departures from major Italian cities.

Radio callsign: AIR EUROPE

Designator: PE/AEL

Employees: 500

Main destinations served: Destinations in the Caribbean, Indian Ocean, East Africa, and Red Sea.

LINKS WITH OTHER AIRLINES
Alitalia (qv) owns 24.6 per cent of the airline's shares.

FLEET
7 Boeing 767-300ER

AIR ONE

Air One SpA

Incorporated: 1983

HISTORY
Originally founded in 1983 as Aliadriatica,

Fast-growing Italian independent airline Air One has based its fleet mainly on the Boeing 737, with a -200 nearest the camera and a -400 next to it.

a flying school, in 1988 the company was taken over by the Toto Group, a major Italian civil engineering contractor. A Boeing 737 was acquired in 1994, initially for charter operations, but in April 1995, the airline started scheduled operations between Milan and Brindisi and Reggio Calabria. That November a new corporate identity was unveiled to coincide with Air One's move onto the Rome Fiumicino to Milan Linate trunk route, Italy's busiest domestic route and the fifth busiest in Europe, offering competition on this route for the first time with up to 13 flights in each direction daily.

In 1996 Air One took over the operations of another Italian airline, Noman, on a three-year lease; this had originally been called Fortune Aviation before taking its new name in 1994.

Air One has grown rapidly and now operates international services to Athens and London Stansted, as well as domestic scheduled services and international charters, although the latter account for around just 5 per cent of traffic. It is in the Swissair (qv) Qualiflyer frequent flyer programme.

Executive Directors & Officers:
Giovanni Sebastiani, Chairman; Carlo Toto, President; Franco Giudice, General Manager; Gianni Rossi, Finance & Administration Director; Paulo Rubino, Commercial Director; Nicola Ruccia, Operations Director; Maurizio Munno, Technical Director.

HQ Airport & Main Base: Rome Fiumicino

Radio callsign: HERON

Designator: AP/ADH

Employees: Flight-crew: 70; Cabin staff: 130; Engineering: 70; Ground staff: 210; Total: 480.

Main destinations served: Rome to Athens, Bari, Crotone, Milan, Olbia, Reggio Calabria, Torino.
Milan to Athens, Bari, Lamezia, London Stansted, Naples, Olbia.

Annual turnover: US $68.5 million (£41.53 million)

Passengers pa: 713,000 (scheduled)

LINKS WITH OTHER AIRLINES
Marketing alliances with Air UK (qv) and Swissair (qv).

FLEET
3 Boeing 737-400
4 Boeing 737-300
2 Boeing 737-230
2 McDonnell Douglas DC-9-15

ALITALIA

Linee Aeree Italiane SpA

Incorporated: 1946

HISTORY
Alitalia was formed in September 1946 as one of two airlines supported by the Italian Government through the Istituto per la Ricostruzione Industrial (IRI), with the technical and operational assistance of BEA (British European Airways). The other airline was Linee Aeree Italiane (LAI), which received assistance from TWA (qv). Under its agreement, BEA owned a 30 per cent shareholding in Alitalia.

Alitalia operations began in May 1947, and for the next ten years both airlines developed separately, and absorbed all other Italian airlines. Both operated on domestic and European routes, while Alitalia also operated to the Middle East, Africa, and South America, while LAI operated to Egypt and North America. In 1957 the two airlines were merged at IRI's behest, largely to eliminate the overlap on many domestic and European routes, but also to provide a single strong airline rather than dividing the available resources. The fleet name Alitalia was chosen for the merged airline, which immediately started a major rationalisation programme. The combined fleet in 1958 included six Douglas DC-7Cs for the North Atlantic services, eight Douglas DC-6Bs, three DC-6s, 12 DC-3s, six Vickers Viscounts, and six Convair 440 Metropolitans. The Viscount fleet was enlarged, so that eventually 15 series 785s were operated.

Alitalia's first jet equipment entered service in 1960, with Douglas DC-8s for the longer-haul routes and Sud Aviation Caravelles for the European and Middle Eastern services. The route network continued to grow, and soon reached Australia.

During the late-1960s the airline replaced its Viscounts with a fleet of Douglas DC-9s, also taking later versions of the DC-8 and its successor, the DC-10. Prior to this, in 1963 most of the domestic services were hived off into a new airline, ATI (Aero Transporti Italiani), which was a wholly-owned subsidiary of Alitalia. ATI also took over services which had been operated by SAM (Societal Aerea Mediterranea), which became Alitalia's charter subsidiary. ATI continued the relationship with Douglas, acquiring a fleet of DC-9s and then adding McDonnell Douglas MD-82s to this, as well as a fleet of ATR 42s. The route network included mainland Italy, Sicily, and Sardinia.

The operations of SAM were incorporated into those of ATI in 1985, and in 1994 – in a complete reversal of the decision taken more than 30 years earlier – ATI was absorbed into Alitalia. Further integration came in 1996, when the operations of Avianova, which operated services from Olbia and had been formed by Alitalia and Alisarda (now Meridiana (qv)) in 1986, were also taken over by Alitalia. Alitalia is today owned 89.31 per cent by IRI, although there are plans for employees to eventually take a 30 per cent interest, despite the most recent capital injection having come from IRI. Alitalia has shareholdings in several other airlines, including Malév (qv) (30 per cent), Eurofly (qv) (45 per cent), and Air Europe Italy (qv) (24.6 per cent), while it is establishing a low cost subsidiary, Alitalia Team, whose initial services are likely to be based on the former Avianova network. A feeder operation, Alitalia Express, is also under development.

Executive Directors & Officers: Fausto Cereti, Chairman; Domenico Cempella, Managing Director; Franco Raffaele, Financial Control Director; Giovanni Sebastiani, Flight Operations Director; Enzo Giuntoli, Commercial Director; Claudio Carli, Personnel Director.

HQ Airport & Main Base: Rome Fiumicino, with a further hub at Milan.

Radio callsign: ALITALIA/TEAM ALITALIA

Designator: AZ/AZA (Alitalia), NOV (Team Alitalia)

Employees: Flight-crew: 1,448; Cabin

Modern twin-jets such as this Alitalia 767-300ER have taken over many long-haul routes from tri-jets and even the older 747s.

staff: 3,827; Ground staff: 11,575; Total: 16,850.

Main destinations served: Almost 30 domestic destinations, plus Accra, Algiers, Amsterdam, Ankara, Athens, Bangkok, Barcelona, Beijing, Berlin, Bogotá, Bombay, Boston, Brussels, Bucharest, Budapest, Buenos Aires, Cairo, Caracas, Casablanca, Chicago, Cologne/Bonn, Copenhagen, Dakar, Delhi, Dublin, Düsseldorf, Frankfurt, Geneva, Hamburg, Helsinki, Hong Kong, Istanbul, Johannesburg, Lagos, Lima, Lisbon, London Heathrow, Los Angeles, Luxor, Lyons, Madrid, Malaga, Malta, Manila, Marseilles, Melbourne, Mexico City, Miami, Montreal, Moscow, Munich, Nairobi, New York JFK, Nice, Nuremberg, Oporto, Oslo, Paris CDG, Prague, Rio de Janeiro, Santiago de Chile, Santo Domingo, São Paulo, Seoul, Seville, Singapore, Stockholm, Stuttgart, Sydney, Tirana, Tokyo, Toronto, Tunis, Valencia, Vienna, Warsaw, Zürich.

Annual turnover: US $4,541 million (£2,752 million)

Aircraft km pa: 279.3 million

Revenue passenger km pa: 34,556.2 million

Cargo tonne km pa: 2,758,590

LINKS WITH OTHER AIRLINES
A 30 per cent interest in Malév (qv), 45 per cent in Eurofly (qv), and 24.6 per cent in Air Europe Italy (qv), with Alitalia Team and Alitalia Express being developed as wholly-owned low cost and

feeder operations.
Code-sharing with American Airlines (qv), British Midland (qv), Canadian Airlines (qv), Continental Air Lines (qv), Gulf Air (qv), Korean Air (qv), and Royal Air Maroc (qv).
Freight marketing alliance with Nippon Cargo Airlines (qv).

FLEET
10 Boeing 747-200/200F
8 McDonnell Douglas MD-11
6 Boeing 767-300ER
17 Airbus A321-100 (Alitalia Team)
90 McDonnell Douglas MD-80
5 McDonnell Douglas MD-82
10 Fokker 70 (Alitalia Team/Alitalia Express)
5 ATR 72 (Alitalia Team/Alitalia Express)
9 ATR 42 aircraft (Alitalia Team/Alitalia Express)
plus 23 A320/A321 outstanding

EUROFLY

Eurofly SpA

Incorporated: 1989

HISTORY
Eurofly was formed in May 1989 and commenced operations the following February, flying inclusive tour charters within Europe and to North Africa and the Middle East. It is owned 45 per cent each by Alitalia (qv) and Olivetti, with the remaining 10 per cent held by San Paolo Finance.

Executive Directors & Officers: Angelo Fornasari, Chairman & Managing Director; Giampiero Gabotto, President.

HQ Airport & Main Base: HQ at Aeroporto Citta di Torino, main operational base is Milan Orio al Serio.

Radio callsign: SIRIOFLY

Designator: EEZ

LINKS WITH OTHER AIRLINES
Alitalia (qv) has a 45 per cent interest.

FLEET
4 McDonnell Douglas MD-82/83 (leased)
2 McDonnell Douglas DC-9-51

MERIDIANA

Meridiana SpA

Incorporated: 1963

HISTORY
Meridiana was founded as Alisarda in March 1963, and commenced air taxi and light charter operations the following year. Alisarda started its first scheduled services in 1966 and soon established a network of services, initially from Olbia in northern Sardinia, but later from Cagliari and Catania. Having developed into a substantial carrier, the need arose for a new third level operator, and in 1986 Alisarda and Alitalia (qv) established Avianova as a joint venture, although the operations of the latter were absorbed into Alitalia in 1996.

The current title was adopted in 1991 to match a similarly named Spanish operator formed by air taxi and air charter airlines to take advantage of deregulation of air transport in Europe, but the Spanish airline, Meridiani Air, had to suspend operations the following year. Since then Meridiana has continued to grow. It is one of the few airlines able to operate jet aircraft from Florence (most operators have to use Pisa), and remains completely privately-owned.

Executive Directors & Officers: Franco Trivi, President, Managing Director & Director General; Steve Forte, Commercial Director.

HQ Airport & Main Base: Olbia, with further bases at Cagliari, Catania, and Palermo.

Radio callsign: MERAIR

Designator: IG/ISS

Employees: Flight-crew: 182; Cabin staff: 224; Engineering: 6; Ground staff: 946; Total: 1,143.

Main destinations served: Amsterdam, Barcelona, Bergamo, Bologna, Brindisi, Cagliari, Catania, Florence, Frankfurt, Genoa, Geneva, Lyons, London Gatwick, Milan Linate, Munich, Naples, Nice, Olbia, Palermo, Paris CDG, Pisa, Rome Fiumicino, Turin, Venice, Verona, Zürich.

Revenue passenger km pa: 1,522.3 million

Cargo tonne km pa: 2.5 million

FLEET
9 McDonnell Douglas MD-82
6 McDonnell Douglas DC-9-51
4 British Aerospace 146-200

Ivory Coast – TU

AIR AFRIQUE

Société Aérienne Africaine Multinationale

Incorporated: 1961

HISTORY
Air Afrique was established in 1961 to provide an international airline for a large number of French colonies as they became independent, on the assumption that none of these would be able to support an international airline of its own. The states consisted of Benin, Burkina Faso (originally Upper Volta), Cameroon, Central African Republic, Chad, Congo, Gabon, Ivory Coast, Mauritania, Niger, Senegal, and Togo, each of which contributed 7.2 per cent of the share capital, with Sodetraf (Société pour le Développement du Transport Aérien en Afrique) holding the remainder. The airline was at first established in Cameroon.

Initially it operated Douglas DC-8s, and there was a marketing and technical alliance with French airline UTA. Cameroon left the consortium in 1971, causing the base to move to the Central African Republic; Chad also left in 1972 and Gabon in 1977.

Today Air Afrique is based in the Ivory Coast and is owned 70.4 per cent by the remaining states, with Air France (qv) having 12.6 per cent, and DHL (qv) 3.2 per cent. In turn, Air Afrique has shareholdings in Air Mauritania, Air Mali, and Air Burkina.

Executive Directors & Officers: Yves Roland Bellecart, President & Director General; Dalmoade Licien, Commercial Director; Pierre Agbogba, Operations Director; A. N'Diaye, Technical Director.

HQ Airport & Main Base: Abidjan

Radio callsign: AIRAFRIC

Designator: RK/RKA

Employees: 5,000

Main destinations served: The capitals of the member states plus Bordeaux, Gran Canaria, Johannesburg, Lagos, Lyons, Marseilles, New York JFK, Paris CDG, and Rome.

LINKS WITH OTHER AIRLINES
Air France (qv) has a 12.6 per cent stake, and DHL (qv) 3.2 per cent.
Air Afrique has a 20 per cent stake in Air Mauritania, 46 per cent in Air Mali, and 17 per cent in Air Burkina.
Code-sharing with South African Airways (qv); Swissair (qv), and TAP Air Portugal (qv).

FLEET
2 Airbus A300-600 (leased)
3 Airbus A300B4
10 Airbus A310-300
1 Boeing 737-200C (leased)
1 Antonov An-12 (wet-leased)

Jamaica – 6Y

AIR JAMAICA

Air Jamaica

Incorporated: 1968

HISTORY
Air Jamaica was formed in October 1968 and commenced operations the following April from Kingston to both Miami and New York JFK. Ownership was initially divided between the Jamaican Government and Air Canada (qv), but in 1980 it became completely state-owned.

Expansion saw the introduction of a service to London operated jointly with British Airways (qv) and using one of that airline's aircraft. Most of the emphasis, however, was placed on the North American market, largely with tourism to Jamaica in mind. In 1994 the airline was privatised, and since then it has undergone considerable modernisation, although the government still retains an interest.

A subsidiary, Air Jamaica Express, originally known as Trans Jamaican Airlines, provides feeder services with a single AI(R) ATR 42 and three Fairchild Dornier Do.228s. In 1997 a marketing alliance was agreed with Delta Air Lines (qv).

Executive Directors & Officers:
Gordon Stewart, Chairman & Chief

Executive Officer; A.P. Chappell, President & Chief Operating Officer; Ainsley B. Campbell, Financial Director; Captain P. Cousins, Operations Director; Roy Beazley, Maintenance Director; Ray Austin, Marketing Director; B. Hall-Alleyne, Personnel Director.

HQ Airport & Main Base: Kingston, with a further base at Montego Bay.

Radio callsign: JULIET MIKE

Designator: JM/AJM

Employees: 1,607

Main destinations served: Atlanta, Baltimore, Chicago, Fort Lauderdale, Grand Cayman, London Heathrow, Miami, New York Newark, New York JFK, Nassau, Orlando, Philadelphia.

LINKS WITH OTHER AIRLINES
Marketing alliances with Delta Air Lines (qv), TWA (qv), United Airlines (qv), and US Airways (qv).
A service to Toronto uses an Air Canada (qv) aircraft and is operated jointly.

FLEET
6 Airbus A310-300
4 Airbus A320-200
2 Boeing 727-200Adv
2 McDonnell Douglas MD-83

Japan – JA

AIR NIPPON

Air Nippon Co Ltd

Incorporated: 1974

HISTORY
Air Nippon was founded in 1974 as Nihon Kinkyori Airways by All Nippon Airways (qv), Toa Domestic (predecessor of Japan Air System (qv)), and Japan Airlines (qv), to operate the less heavily used domestic services. The airline has since become Air Nippon, reflecting its outright ownership by All Nippon Airways.

Executive Directors & Officers: Akio Kondo, Chairman; Takahide Yamada, President; Yuichi Takakishi, Deputy President & Executive Vice-President; Takesi Kuauhara, Chief Operating Officer; Koji Akaike, Chief Financial Officer; Mitsutoshi Hirota, Director General; Tosaka Takahashi, Engineering & Maintenance Director; Hitoshi Nakashima, Personnel Director.

HQ Airport & Main Base: Tokyo Haneda

Radio callsign: ANK AIR

Designator: EL/ANK

Employees: 1,306

Main destinations served: 25 domestic destinations.

Annual turnover: Included in Air Nippon figures.

LINKS WITH OTHER AIRLINES
A subsidiary of All Nippon Airways (qv). Marketing alliances with All Nippon Airways and Eva (qv).

FLEET
20 Airbus A320 (leased)
9 Boeing 737-200
10 Boeing 737-500
12 NAMC YS-11 (leased)

ANA – ALL NIPPON AIRWAYS

All Nippon Airways Co Ltd

Incorporated: 1952

HISTORY
All Nippon Airways dates from 1952, the first year that Japanese ownership and operation of commercial aircraft was permitted after World War Two, operations beginning in December 1953 as Japan Helicopter and Airplane. From the start, the airline operated scheduled services. Growth was aided by a number of mergers and acquisitions, merging with Far Eastern Airlines in 1957, and then acquiring Fujita Airlines in 1963, Nakanihon Air Services in 1965, and Nagasaki Airways in 1967. This contributed towards the airline becoming the second-largest in Japan, and ninth-largest in the world on the basis of annual turnover. The present title was adopted followed the merger with Far East Air Transport.

Early growth was confined to domestic routes, with Japan Airlines (qv) having a monopoly of international services up to its privatisation in 1986. Since that time ANA has developed an extensive network of international services, beginning with a Tokyo–Guam service in 1986. By 1989 services had been introduced between Tokyo and London Gatwick, and a service to Paris was introduced the following year. A network of international alliances was quickly established to help accelerate the growth of its international services. Domestic operations were not neglected, however, and today ANA has more than 50 per cent of Japan's domestic air travel market.

In 1974 the airline was one of the founders of Air Nippon (qv), which today is a wholly-owned subsidiary, operating domestic services as feeders into the ANA trunk network. Ownership of ANA itself is spread between a large number of Japanese financial institutions, and the Nagoya Railroad.

Executive Directors & Officers: Takaya Sugiura, Chairman; Seiji Fukatsu, President & Chief Executive Officer; Kazuhiko Komiya, Senior Managing Director, Finance; Mitsuo Iijima, Senior Managing Director, Executive Office; Hiroshi Sakabe, Managing Director, Flight Operations; Tetsuya Kubo, Managing Director, Engineering & Maintenance; Masahiro Kinoshita, Managing Director, IT; Yoshiyuki Nakamachi, Managing Director, Corporate Planning; Kanij Kimura, Managing Director, Human Resources; Yuzuru Masumoto, Managing Director, General Affairs; Osamu Nagahata, Managing Director, Marketing; Kenichi Sugihara, Managing Director, Tokyo; Mitsuo Ota, Managing Director, Associated Business Development; Koji Yamashita, Managing Director, Airport Operations.

HQ Airport & Main Base: Tokyo, with further hubs at Fukuoka and Osaka Kansei.

Radio callsign: ALL NIPPON

Designator: NH/ANA

Employees: 14,396

Main destinations served: More than 30 domestic destinations, plus Bangkok, Beijing, Bombay, Brisbane, Dalian, Delhi, Frankfurt, Guam, Hong Kong, Kuala Lumpur, London Heathrow, Los Angeles, New York JFK, Paris CDG, Rome, Shanghai, Seoul, Singapore, Sydney, Tsingtao, Washington.

Annual turnover: US $9,074 million (£5,500 million)

Passengers pa: 39.7 million

LINKS WITH OTHER AIRLINES
Air Nippon (qv) is a subsidiary.
A 13.2 per cent interest is held in Nippon Cargo Airlines (qv).
Marketing alliances with Air Canada (qv) and Japan Airlines (qv), and code-sharing with Ansett Australia (qv), Austrian Airlines (qv), British Airways (qv), Cathay Pacific (qv), Delta Air Lines (qv), Malaysian Airlines (qv), Singapore Airlines (qv), Swissair (qv), and US Airways (qv).

FLEET
18 Boeing 747-400
6 Boeing 747-200B

14 Boeing 747SR
9 Boeing 777-200
40 Boeing 767-300
25 Boeing 767-200
23 Airbus A320-200

JAA

Japan Asia Airways Co Ltd

Incorporated: 1975

HISTORY

Japan Asia Airways was formed by Japan Airlines (JAL) (qv) in 1975 for operations between Japan and Taiwan, removing any obstacles which might have prevented JAL from operating to Beijing, because of Chinese Communist objections to businesses which recognised the regime in Taiwan. Initially its aircraft were wet-leased from the JAL fleet, but later JAA assumed responsibility for purchasing its own aircraft. JAL has a 91 per cent stake in the airline, which also uses a variation of the JAL colour scheme on its aircraft.

Since its formation, the airline has extended its range of destinations to include other popular centres in Asia.

Executive Directors & Officers: Noboru Okamura, Chairman; Kozo Miyasaka, President; Akira Hayakawa, Vice-President; Osamu Mitsuyasa, Senior Managing Director, Maintenance; Tetsuo Sawada, Managing Director, Traffic; Hiromitsu Sawada, Managing Director, Corporate Planning; Yasushi Kawano, Sales Director.

HQ Airport & Main Base: Tokyo Narita

Radio callsign: ASIA

Designator: EG/JAA

Employees: Flight-crew: 101; Cabin staff: 442; Engineering: 30; Ground staff: 312; Total: 885.

Main destinations served: Tokyo, Nagoya, Okinawa, and Osaka to Denpasar (Bali), Hong Kong, Jakarta, Kaohsiung, Taipei.

Annual turnover: US $452.7 million (£274.3 million)

Revenue passenger km pa: 2,825.4 million

Cargo tonne km pa: 139,182

LINKS WITH OTHER AIRLINES Japan Airlines (qv) has a 91 per cent interest.

FLEET
1 Boeing 747-300

2 Boeing 747-200B
1 Boeing 747-100
1 McDonnell Douglas DC-10-40 (leased)
3 Boeing 767-200

JAPAN AIR CHARTER

Japan Air Charter

Incorporated: 1990

HISTORY

Established in 1990 as the air charter subsidiary of Japan Airlines (qv), Japan Air Charter commenced operations the following year. The fleet is small, with aircraft wet-leased as required from other companies in the same group, which can mean operations with five or more Boeing 747-200Bs and four or more McDonnell Douglas DC-10-40s at any one time.

Executive Directors & Officers: Shinzo Sudo, Chairman & President; Tesuo Kubota, Senior Managing Director, Flight Operations; Yasuo Wakuta, Executive Vice-President.

HQ Airport & Main Base: Tokyo

Radio callsign: JAPAN CHARTER

Designator: JZ/JAZ

Annual turnover: Included in Japan Airlines figures

LINKS WITH OTHER AIRLINES Japan Airlines has an 82 per cent interest.

FLEET
5 Boeing 747
4 McDonnell Douglas DC-10-40

JAPAN AIR COMMUTER

Japan Air Commuter Co Ltd

Incorporated: 1983

HISTORY

The feeder network operator for Japan Air System (qv), Japan Air Commuter has a fleet of turboprop aircraft and operates from two hubs, at Kagoshima and Osaka.

Executive Directors & Officers: Yoshitomi Oti, President; Masaki Oka, Executive Vice-President; Shizuo Shigeru, Senior Vice-President & General Manager; Kaoru Haradome, Vice-President, Maintenance & Administration.

HQ Airport & Main Base: Kagoshima,

with a further hub at Osaka.

Radio callsign: COMMUTER

Designator: 3X/JAC

Employees: 416

Main destinations served: Operates to 16 destinations.

Annual turnover: Included in Japan Air System figures

LINKS WITH OTHER AIRLINES A subsidiary of Japan Air System (qv).

FLEET
11 NAMC YS-11-500
10 Saab 340B (leased from Japan Air System)

JAPAN AIR SYSTEM

Japan Air System Co Ltd

Incorporated: 1971

HISTORY

Originally formed in 1971 as Toa Domestic Airlines, Japan Air System (JAS) operates the largest network of scheduled domestic air services within Japan, as well as operating charters throughout Asia, and, more recently, scheduled services to China and Korea. It was founded on the merger of Toa Airways with Japan Domestic Airlines, which was founded in 1964. The present title was adopted in 1988, with a new corporate identity.

Shareholders include a number of industrial groups, including the Kinki Nippon Railway and Japan Airlines (qv), each of which holds 9 per cent of the shares. A subsidiary is Japan Air Commuter (qv).

Executive Directors & Officers: Hiromi Funabiki, President; Michihiko Matsuo, Executive Vice-President; Minoru Morikawa, Executive Vice-President; Shiro Oshima, Senior Vice-President, Engineering & Operations; Kiyoje Kume, Managing Director & Vice-President; Kazuo Tonomura, Managing Director & Vice-President, Corporate Planning; Masashi Ueda, Managing Director & Vice-President, Cargo & Mail Sales; Mitsuo Komatsubara, Managing Director & Vice-President, Finance & Accounting; Akio Komura, Managing Director & Vice-President, Marketing & Sales; Yasuo Toda, Managing Director & Vice-President, International Planning, Personnel, Purchasing; Isamu Tanaka, Director & Counsellor.

HQ Airport & Main Base: Tokyo

Japan Air System is another user of the Boeing 777, mainly on its growing network of international routes.

Haneda, with further hubs at Osaka and Sapporo.

Radio callsign: AIR SYSTEM

Designator: JD/JAS

Employees: Flight-crew: 987; Cabin staff: 1,447; Engineering: 1,166; Ground staff: 4,450; Total: 5,959.

Main destinations served: More than 30 domestic destinations, plus Tokyo Narita to Seoul, and Osaka Kansai to Hong Kong, Guangzhou.

Annual turnover: US $3,086 million (£1,870 million)

Aircraft km pa: 103.1 million

Revenue passenger km pa: 13,735 million

Cargo tonne km pa: 2,516,3 million

LINKS WITH OTHER AIRLINES
Japan Airlines (qv) has a 9 per cent interest.

A large Airbus A300 fleet is operated by Japan Air System, which has the three main variants of this aircraft in service.

Japan Air Commuter (qv) is a subsidiary.

FLEET
7 Boeing 777-200IGW
19 Airbus A300-600R
9 Airbus A300B2
8 Airbus A300B4
12 McDonnell Douglas MD-90-30
8 McDonnell Douglas MD-87
26 McDonnell Douglas MD-81

Japan Airlines is one of those which have a significant air freight business, often requiring dedicated freight aircraft rather than just using the underfloor holds. Here a Boeing 747-200F is being loaded through the nose.

JAPAN AIRLINES

Japan Airlines

Incorporated: 1951

HISTORY

The world's third-largest airline, Japan Airlines, or JAL, was formed in 1951, during the Korean War, when permission was granted by the Supreme Commander,

Allied Powers, for the operation of domestic air services by a Japanese airline, but only on condition that the aircraft and crews would be supplied by a non-Japanese operator. Five companies bid for the right to start services, and Japan Airlines was selected on condition that it formed a union with its four competitors to strengthen the enterprise.

Japan Airlines had a predecessor, Dai-

Nippon Airways, which had been formed in 1938 on the amalgamation of the Japan Air Transport Company and several smaller operators. Although the airline was not formally disbanded until the end of World War Two in 1945, its wartime operations were increasingly limited and had to be curtailed before the end of hostilities because of the acute shortage of fuel.

The first services of JAL were operated by Martin 202s of Northwest Orient Air Lines – now Northwest (qv) – flights between Tokyo and Sapporo and Tokyo and Osaka commencing on 25 October, with some extending to Fukuoka. This arrangement lasted for exactly a year, until the first Japanese-owned and crewed aircraft – Douglas DC-4s – entered service on 25 October 1952. The new airline ordered two de Havilland Comet 2s, but did not take delivery after the failure of the de Havilland Comet 1 in a series of accidents. JAL's next aircraft, the first of which were delivered in 1953, were Douglas DC-6B Cloudmasters, and after route-proving throughout the rest of the year, a new service was opened between Tokyo and San Francisco in February 1954, with the aircraft operating via Wake Island and Honolulu. Meanwhile the Japanese Government had taken a 50 per cent share in the airline to increase its capital for expansion, this being later increased to 58 per cent.

A service from Tokyo to Hong Kong via Okinawa was inaugurated in 1955, and at the end of the year Douglas DC-8 jet airliners were ordered, followed by an order for DC-7C piston-engined airliners in April 1956! The DC-7Cs entered service on the Tokyo–San Francisco route early in 1958.

An in-flight shot of a JAL McDonnell Douglas MD-11, easily distinguishable from the earlier DC-10 by the winglets.

Services had by this time extended as far as Bangkok, reached via Singapore. While consolidation of services in Asia and across the Pacific continued, a Tokyo–Paris service was started in 1960, flying over the North Pole in a Boeing 707 belonging to Air France. The first Douglas DC-8 jet airliners arrived later in the year, and were used initially on services from Tokyo to the west coast of the United States, although later they were also used on the polar routes to Paris, Amsterdam, and London. For less busy services, the smaller Convair 880 entered service in 1961.

During the early-1960s the airline also developed freight services, initially using converted DC-4s, while later, in 1965, DC-8-55F mixed passenger and cargo aircraft were introduced. JAL participated in the formation of Southwest Airlines, now Japan TransOcean Air (qv), in 1967, when the airline was formed to improve air services between Japan and the Ryukyu Islands, including Okinawa. As the decade progressed, Boeing 727s were introduced, followed by Boeing 747s in 1970. However, the airline's first trans-Siberian services, via Moscow to Paris, launched that same year, were operated by Douglas DC-8-62s. One of the innovations made by the airline was the use of the specially developed Boeing 747SR, a high-capacity short-range variant of the 747 with 498 seats, first operated on the Tokyo–Okinawa service in 1973. Seven years later an even higher-capacity version, with 550 seats, was introduced on the same route. JAL was also amongst the first to operate Boeing 747 freighters, and today it has the world's largest fleet of Boeing 747s.

In 1975 political difficulties between Communist China and Taiwan led to the formation of JAA (Japan Asia Airways) (qv) specifically for services between Japan and Taiwan. JAL took a 91 per cent stake in this company, as well as a 9 per cent stake in Japan Domestic Airways (qv).

JAL's shares were launched on the Tokyo stock market in 1986, as the first stage in privatisation of the airline. It lost its monopoly on international services the same year, and All Nippon Airways started to compete for these. The government sold its remaining shares in 1987. Reacting to changes in travel patterns elsewhere, JAL established a charter subsidiary, Japan Air Charter (qv), in 1990.

Today, Japan Airlines is owned by a number of Japanese financial institutions, primarily banks and insurance companies. It has interests in a number of major Japanese airlines, and in tour operators

One of JAL's new Boeing 777-200s.

and ground-handling. Marketing alliances of various kinds exist with a number of the world's major airlines. The McDonnell Douglas DC-10-40 fleet is being converted to freighters and replaced by a mix of Boeing 767s and 777s.

Executive Directors & Officers:
Susumu Yamaji, Chairman; Akira Kondo, President; Akio Kuono, Executive Vice-President; Shinzo Suto, Senior Managing Director, Passengers; Yoshihiko Murata, Senior Managing Director, Operations & Engineering; Isao Keneko, Senior Managing Director, Human Resources; Fumio Kuwano, Managing Director, IT; Satoshi Hirano, Managing Director, Executive Office; Yukio Ohtani, Managing Director, The Americas; Zenta Yokoyama, Managing Director, Planning; Toshio Shiota, Managing Director, Western Japan; Masahide Ochi, Managing Director, Facilities & Administration; Yoichiro Takada, Senior Vice-President, Engineering & Maintenance; Sadao Hara, Senior Vice-President, Public Relations; Toshiki Okazaki, Senior Vice-President, Eastern Japan.

HQ Airport & Main Base: Tokyo Narita (international) and Tokyo Haneda

Radio callsign: JAPANAIR

Designator: JL/JAL

Employees: Flight-crew: 2,600; Cabin staff: 5,600; Ground staff: 10,800; Total: 19,000.

Main destinations served: Akita,

Amsterdam, Anchorage*, Atlanta, Bangkok, Beijing, Brisbane, Cairns, Chicago, Denpasar (Bali), Fairbanks*, Frankfurt, Fukuoka, Fukushima, Guam, Hakodate, Hiroshima, Ho Chi Minh City, Hong Kong, Honolulu, Istanbul, Jakarta, Kagoshima, Komatsu, Kona, Kuala Lumpur, Kumamoto, London Heathrow, Los Angeles, Madrid, Manila, Matsuyama, Mexico City, Milan, Miyazaki, Moscow, Nagasaki, Nagoya, New Delhi, New York JFK, Niigata, Obihiro, Oita, Okinawa Naha, Osaka Itami, Osaka Kansai, Paris CDG, Pusan, Rome, Saipan, San Francisco, São Paulo, Sapporo, Sendai, Seoul, Shanghai, Singapore, Sydney, Vancouver, Yamagata, Memambetsu, Kochi.
* cargo only.

Annual turnover: US $16,422.5 million (£9,953 million)

Revenue passenger km pa: 77,228.6 million

Cargo tonne km pa: 3,989.8 million

Passengers pa: 30,197,904

LINKS WITH OTHER AIRLINES
Has interests in Japan Asia Airways (90.5 per cent), Japan TransOcean (51 per cent), Japan Air Charter (82 per cent), and Japan Air System (9 per cent). Code-sharing with Air France (qv), Air New Zealand (qv), Canadian Airlines (qv), KLM (qv), Thai International (qv), Varig (qv), and Vietnam Airlines (qv). Cargo joint operations with Air France,

On the less busy routes JAL uses the Boeing 767 in both -200 and -300 variants.

British Airways* (qv), and Lufthansa* (qv).
Shared frequent flyer programmes with Air France and American Airlines (qv).

FLEET
32 Boeing 747-400 (plus 18 on order)
4 Boeing 747-300SR
9 Boeing 747-300
8 Boeing 747-200F
19 Boeing 747-200B
6 Boeing 747-100
10 McDonnell Douglas MD-11
14 McDonnell Douglas DC-10-40 (being converted to freighters)
5 Boeing 777-200 (plus 7 on order)
17 Boeing 767-300 (plus 4 on order)
3 Boeing 767-200
9 Boeing 737-400 (2 wet-leased from Japan TransOcean Air)
plus 5 Boeing 777-300 on order

JAPAN TRANSOCEAN

Japan TransOcean Air

Incorporated: 1967

HISTORY
Originally founded in 1967 as Southwest Airlines with the backing of Japan Airlines (qv), which took a 51 per cent stake, the new airline took over the services to Okinawa and the Ryukyu islands which had hitherto been operated by Air America. A subsidiary, Ryukyu Air Commuter, operates feeder services into the main hubs from the smaller islands.

Executive Directors & Officers: Keiivhi Inamine, Chairman; Michio Okuno, President; Yukinobu Ariga, Managing Director & Senior Vice-President; Eiji Mikami, Senior Vice-President, Corporate Planning; Norio Ogo, Senior Vice-President, Maintenance & Engineering; Wakatsu Oshiro, Executive Vice-President; Seizo Kuroda, Executive Vice-President; Kenji Ono, Vice-President, Finance; Masami Seiki, Vice-President, Sales.

HQ Airport & Main Base: Naha, Okinawa, with a further hub at Miyako.

Radio callsign: JAI OCEAN

Designator: NU/JTA

Employees: 750

Main destinations served: Naha, Miyako, Nagoya, and Tokyo, with a substantial number of destinations within the Ryukyu Islands.

LINKS WITH OTHER AIRLINES
Japan Airlines holds a 51 per cent interest.
Ryukyu Commuter is a subsidiary.

FLEET
1 Boeing 767-200 (leased from Japan Airlines)
3 Boeing 737-400 (plus 2 leased to Japan Airlines)
9 Boeing 737-200
5 NAMC YS-11-500
4 de Havilland DHC-6 Twin Otter (operated by Ryukyu Commuter)
2 Pilatus Britten-Norman BN-2B Island (operated by Ryukyu Commuter)

NIPPON CARGO AIRLINES

Nippon Cargo Airlines

Incorporated: 1978

HISTORY
A Japanese scheduled and charter cargo airline, Nippon Cargo Airlines was formed in 1978 but did not commence operations until 1985, largely due to delays in obtaining government approval. The airline's shareholders include All Nippon Airways (qv) and the Mitsui OSK shipping line.

Executive Directors & Officers: Jiro Nemoto, Chairman; Toyochiro Nakada, President; Takeshi Kurachi, Vice-President, Engineering & Maintenance.

HQ Airport & Main Base: Tokyo Narita

Radio callsign: NIPPON CARGO

Designator: KZ/NCA

Employees: 500

Main destinations served: Amsterdam, Anchorage, Bangkok, Chicago, Hong Kong, Los Angeles, Milan, Nagoya, New York JFK, San Francisco, Seoul, Singapore.

LINKS WITH OTHER AIRLINES
All Nippon Airways (qv) has a 13.2 per cent interest.

FLEET
7 Boeing 747-200F
1 Boeing 747-100F

Jordan – JY

ROYAL JORDANIAN

Royal Jordanian Airlines

Incorporated: 1963

HISTORY
Originally known as Alia Royal Jordanian Airlines, with Alia meaning 'high flying', the airline was founded and commenced operations in 1963 with a fleet of two Handley Page Heralds and a Douglas DC-7. It replaced an earlier operation, Air Jordan. The first routes were from Amman to Jerusalem (at that time partly within Jordan), Beirut, Cairo, and Kuwait. Initially ownership was divided equally between private interests and the state, but today it is completely state-owned.

The first jet equipment, Sud Aviation Caravelles, entered service in 1965, with operations extended to Rome that year, and to Paris and London in 1966.

The current title was adopted in 1986. It is possible that Royal Jordanian might be privatised in the near future.

Executive Directors & Officers: Basel Jardaneh, Chairman; Nadar Dahabi, President & Chief Executive Officer; Suhail Al-Baho, Financial Director; Shabo Bisso, Operations Director; Hazaa Irteimeh, Technical Director; Talat Ramzi, Marketing Director; Abed Al-Rahim Khasawneh, Director, Fuel; Mohammed Kalimat, Director, Purchasing; Nabiha Abdul-Haq, Personnel Director.

HQ Airport & Main Base: Amman

Radio callsign: JORDANIAN

Designator: RJ/RJA

Employees: 5,050

Main destinations served: Abu Dhabi, Aden, Amsterdam, Ankara, Aqaba, Baghdad, Bahrain, Bangkok, Beirut, Belgrade, Berlin, Brussels, Cairo, Calcutta, Casablanca, Colombo, Damascus, Delhi, Dhahran, Doha, Dubai, Frankfurt, Geneva, Istanbul, Jakarta, Jeddah, Karachi, Kuala Lumpur, Larnaca, London Heathrow, Madrid, Montreal, Muscat, New York JFK, Paris CDG, Riyadh, Rome, Sana'a, Singapore, Toronto, Tunis, Vienna.

LINKS WITH OTHER AIRLINES
Marketing alliance with Air Canada (qv).

FLEET
5 Lockheed L-1011-500 TriStar
4 Airbus A310-300
2 Airbus A310-200
3 Boeing 707-320 (leased)
3 Airbus A320-200

Kazakhstan – UN

AIR KAZAKHSTAN

Air Kazakhstan/Kazakhstan National Airways

Incorporated: 1992

HISTORY
A former Aeroflot (qv) division which has become the national airline of Kazakhstan on the latter achieving independence, Air Kazakhstan was initially known as Kazair, but during 1996 was restructured and renamed. During 1995 and 1996 the first western aircraft were introduced to its fleet, and further additions can be expected as funding permits. The country has substantial natural resources. Both domestic and international services are operated.

Executive Directors & Officers: Amantai B. Zholdybaev, President.

HQ Airport & Main Base: Alma-Ata

Radio callsign: AIR KAZAKHSTAN

Designator: K4/KZK

Employees: approx 30,000

Main destinations served: An extensive internal network and services throughout the former Soviet Union, as well as international services to Frankfurt.

FLEET
1 Boeing 747SP
5 Boeing 767-300
7 Ilyushin Il-86
4 Ilyushin Il-76TD
1 Antonov An-72
10 Tupolev Tu-134
29 Yakovlev Yak-40
5 Yakovlev Yak-42D
8 Antonov An-30
9 Antonov An-26
22 Antonov An-24

Kenya – 5Y

AIRKENYA

Airkenya Aviation

Incorporated: 1985

HISTORY
A privately-owned airline, Airkenya was formed in 1985 on the merger of Air Kenya and Sunbird Aviation. It operates scheduled and charter services within Kenya, mainly to tourist centres.

Executive Directors & Officers: John Buckley, Managing Director.

HQ Airport & Main Base: HQ at Nairobi, with bases at Nayuki and Nyeri.

Radio callsign: AIRKENYA

Designator: QP

Employees: 240

Main destinations served: Serves ten domestic destinations, including Nairobi, Mombasa, and Masai Mara.

FLEET
2 de Havilland Dash 7
1 Fokker F-27-200 Friendship
2 Short 360-30

2 Douglas DC-3
7 de Havilland DHC-6 Twin Otter
3 Beech Baron B55

EAGLE AVIATION

International African Eagle

Incorporated: 1986

HISTORY
Eagle Aviation operates a network of regional routes from its base at Mombasa on the coast of Kenya, mainly to domestic destinations but also to Zanzibar. It plans to operate further regional international services in the near future.

Executive Directors & Officers: Captain Gilbert M. Kibe, Chairman; Charles K. Muthama, Managing Director; Kiran C. Patel, Financial Director & Chief Pilot.

HQ Airport & Main Base: Mombasa

Radio callsign: MAGNUM

Designator: Y4/EQA

Employees: 115

Main destinations served: Kilimanjaro, Kisumu, Lamu, Masai Mara, Nairobi, Zanzibar.

FLEET
1 ATR 42-320
4 Let L-410A

KENYA AIRWAYS

Kenya Airways

Incorporated: 1977

HISTORY
Kenya Airways came into existence in 1977, founded by the Kenyan Government following the collapse of East African Airways, which had operated since 1946 with the assistance of BOAC (British Overseas Airways Corporation) and had been owned by BOAC Associated Companies and the governments of Kenya, Uganda, Tanganyika and Zanzibar (later Tanzania).

The new airline's first flight was on 4 February 1977, from London Heathrow to Nairobi, using a Boeing 707, one of three such aircraft in the fleet. While the 707s were used on services to Europe, African and domestic services used a McDonnell Douglas DC-9-30, a Boeing 720, and two Fokker F-27 Friendships. The airline's growth was helped by the increasing importance of Kenya as a tourist destination.

A Boeing 737-300 of Kenya Airways rolls away from the camera.

In 1996 Kenya Airways was privatised, and it is now quoted on the Nairobi Stock Exchange. KLM (qv) bought 26 per cent of its shares, and a marketing alliance also exists between the two carriers.

Executive Directors & Officers: Isaac Omolo Okero, Chairman; Brian Davies, Managing Director; Malcolm Naylor, Finance Director; George Kivindyo, Commercial Director; Steve Clarke, Technical Director; David Namu, Director of External Affairs; Ben Mtuweta, Director of Corporate Affairs; Lewis Kamu, Legal Director.

HQ Airport & Main Base: Nairobi Embakasi Airport, but the main base/hub is Nairobi Jomo Kenyatta International Airport.

Radio callsign: KENYA

Designator: KQ/KQA

Employees: Flight-crew: 114; Cabin staff: 236; Engineering: 507; Ground staff: 1,607; Total: 2,464.

Main destinations served: Addis Ababa, Bombay, Bujumbura, Cairo, Copenhagen, Dar-es-Salaam, Dubai, Entebbe, Harare, Jeddah, Johannesburg, Karachi, Khartoum, Kigali, Kisumu, Lilongwe, London Heathrow, Lusaka, Malindi, Mombasa, Paris, Rome, Seychelles, Stockholm, Zanzibar.

Revenue passenger km pa: 1,837.5 million

Cargo tonne km pa: 47.8 million

LINKS WITH OTHER AIRLINES
KLM (qv) owns 26 per cent.

FLEET
3 Airbus A310-300 (1 leased)
3 Boeing 737-300 (leased)
3 Fokker 50

Korea (South) – HL

ASIANA

Asiana Airlines, Inc

Incorporated: 1988

HISTORY
Asiana Airlines was formed as Seoul Air International by its present owners, the Kumho Group, in 1988, with the encouragement of the South Korean Government, which wanted the country to have a second major airline. Initially it operated scheduled domestic services and international charters, building up a fleet of Boeing 737s, but in 1990 it moved into international scheduled services, initially to destinations in Japan and China. The present title was adopted in advance of the start of international services. It received its first wide-bodied aircraft, a Boeing 767 and a Boeing 747, in November 1991, and introduced a service from Seoul to Los Angeles.

In a single decade the airline has grown from nothing to become not only South Korea's second-largest airline, but also one of the top 40 airlines in the world by annual turnover. It has alliances of various kinds with a number of other major international airlines.

Executive Directors & Officers: Sam Koo Park, President & Chief Executive Officer; Young Han Choi, Executive Vice-President, Planning & Administration; Chan Bup Park, Executive Vice-President, Marketing & Sales; Hoon Shin, Executive Vice-President, Systems; Cha Dong Huh, Executive Vice-President, Maintenance & Engineering; Chang Soo Lee, Managing Director, Traffic; Keun Sik Park, Managing Director, USA; Sang Hwan Park, Managing Director, Seoul; Byung Ryool Yoo, Managing Director, Passenger Sales; Ho Sun Suh, Managing Director, Flight Operations; Yong Dae Kwon, Managing Director, Marketing; Jae Suk Yoon, Managing Director, Cabin Crew; Won Joon Choe, Managing Director, Software R&D; Ock Kee, Managing Director, Finance; Tae Jae Lee, Managing Director, Catering; Duk Young Kim, Managing Director, Strategic Planning; Hong Lae Kim, Managing Director, Public Relations; Noh Pil Park, Managing Director, MIS; Jae Hoon Bae, Managing Director, Airports; Jong Hoon Park, Managing Director, Beijing; Sang Kyun Suh, Managing Director, Japan; Kyu Nam Ahn, Managing Director, Facilities & Environment.

HQ Airport & Main Base: Kimpo International, Seoul

Radio callsign: ASIANA

Designator: OZ/AAR

Employees: Flight-crew: 756; Cabin staff: 1,552; Engineering: 837; Ground staff: 3,350; Total: 6,495 (excluding Asiana Airport, Inc).

Main destinations served: More than 20 domestic destinations, plus Seoul to Bangkok*, Beijing*, Brussels, Cairns, Changchun, Detroit, Frankfurt, Fukuoka*, Guam, Guangzhou, Hiroshima, Ho Chi Minh City, Hong Kong, Honolulu, Istanbul, Khabarovsk, Los Angeles, Macau, Manila, Matsuyama, Nagoya, New York JFK, Okinawa, Osaka*, Saipan, San Francisco, Seattle, Sendai, Shanghai, Singapore, Sydney, Takamatsu, Tashkent, Tokyo, Toyama, Vienna.
* also served from Pusan.

Annual turnover: US $1,498 million (£907.9 million)

Revenue passenger km pa: 12,890 million

Cargo tonne km pa: 1, 289 million

Passengers pa: 846,759

LINKS WITH OTHER AIRLINES
Code-sharing with Northwest (qv) and Qantas (qv).

FLEET
3 Boeing 777-200IGW*
2 Boeing 777-300*
6 Boeing 747-400 Combi
2 Boeing 747-400
1 Boeing 747-400F
3 Airbus A330-300*
2 Airbus A330-200ER*
7 Boeing 767-300ER
10 Boeing 767-300
1 Boeing 767-300F
18 Airbus A321-100*
17 Boeing 737-400
6 Boeing 737-300 (may be replaced by A321 deliveries)
of which aircraft 22 are leased
*in course of delivery

KOREAN AIR

Korean Air Lines

Incorporated: 1962

HISTORY
Korean Air was founded in 1962 as the successor to Korean National Airlines, which had dated from 1948. Initially the new airline was owned by the Korean Government, but it was acquired by the present owners, the Hanjin Group, in 1969. It is one of the 20 largest airlines in the world in terms of annual turnover, and one of the three largest in Asia. It operates an extensive domestic network as well as a large international network, which includes a substantial number of scheduled cargo services, reflecting the country's status as one of the 'tiger economies' of Asia.

Executive Directors & Officers:
Choong Hoon Choo, Chairman & Chief Executive Officer; Yan-Ho Cho, President & Chief Operating Officer; Nam Ho, Director; Tae Hee Lee, General Counsel; Yi Taek Shim, Executive Vice-President, Aerospace; Tai Won Lee, Executive Vice-President, Corporate Planning; Soo Ho Cho, Executive Vice-President, Sales & Marketing; Yoiung Han Cho, Senior Vice-President, Finance; Hee Kyoon Cheon, Senior Vice-President, Maintenance & Engineering.

HQ Airport & Main Base: Seoul

Radio callsign: KOREANAIR

One of Korean Air's Boeing 777s climbs away.

Designator: KE/KAL

Employees: 17,500

Main destinations served: Some 15 domestic destinations, plus Amsterdam, Anchorage, Aomori, Atlanta, Auckland, Bahrain, Bangkok, Basle*, Beijing, Bombay, Boston, Brisbane, Brussels*, Cairo, Chicago, Christchurch, Colombo*, Dallas, Delhi*, Denpasar (Bali), Dubai*, Frankfurt, Fukuoka, Ho Chi Minh City, Hong Kong, Honolulu, Jakarta, Jeddah, Johorubaru*, Kagoshima, Kuala Lumpur, Kumamoto, London Heathrow, Los Angeles, Macao, Madras*, Madrid, Manila, Milan*, Moscow, Nadi, Nagasaki, Nagoya, New York Newark, New York JFK, Nihata, Oita, Okayama, Paris CDG, Penang*, Portland*, Qingdao, Rome, Saipan, San Francisco, São Paulo, Sapporo, Shanghai, Shenzen*, Shenyang, Singapore, Sydney, Tel Aviv, Tienjin, Tokyo, Toronto, Vancouver, Vladivostok, Washington, Zürich.
* also used by all-cargo services.

Annual turnover: US $4,341 million (£2,630.9 million)

LINKS WITH OTHER AIRLINES
Marketing alliances with Air France (qv), Air New Zealand (qv), Alitalia (qv), Ansett New Zealand (qv), Delta Air Lines (qv), Garuda Indonesia (qv), Japan Airlines (qv), Saudi Arabian (qv), and Vietnam Airlines (qv).

FLEET
31 Boeing 747-400
3 Boeing 747-300
12 Boeing 747-200F

4 Boeing 777-200
4 Boeing 777-300
2 Airbus A330-200
4 Airbus A330-300
3 McDonnell Douglas MD-11
2 McDonnell Douglas MD-11F
33 Airbus A300-600R
2 Airbus A300B4
11 McDonnell Douglas MD-82
3 McDonnell Douglas MD-83

Kuwait – 9K

KUWAIT AIRWAYS

Kuwait Airways Corporation

Incorporated: 1954

HISTORY
It was as the Kuwait National Airways Company that Kuwait Airways commenced operations in 1954 with two Douglas DC-3 aircraft on routes to Iraq, Syria, the Lebanon, Jordan, and Iran. The airline was an immediate success, and added two Handley Page Hermes aircraft the following year, and in 1957 these were joined by Douglas DC-4s. The name of the company was changed in 1957 to the Kuwait Airways Company. BOAC (British Overseas Airways Corporation) became responsible for its technical management in 1958, for five years.

Although it had been formed as a 50:50 venture between the state and private interests, ownership passed to the state in 1962, when the current title was adopted. The airline introduced its first jet aircraft – a leased de Havilland Comet 4 – the same year, and three of these aircraft were later purchased, eventually being joined by Hawker Siddeley Trident 1Es and Boeing 707s.

Despite the considerable wealth of Kuwait and its pivotal position on routes between the East and Europe, the airline has suffered mixed fortunes due to the aggressive posture adopted towards Kuwait by Iraq. Although a threatened invasion during the early 1960s was prevented by the prompt action of British forces, the country was overrun by Iraq in August 1990. Many of the airline's aircraft were caught on the ground in Kuwait and seized, while the airline's management set up a temporary head office in Cairo, the remaining aircraft – four Boeing 747-200 Combis, a Boeing 767, and three Boeing 727s – operated a temporary service from Cairo to Bahrain, Dubai, and Jeddah.

The airline has now recovered from the invasion, and operates a modern fleet. To diversify from its small base, a 20 per cent stake has been taken in an Indian operator, Jet Airways (qv).

Executive Directors & Officers: Ahmad Hamad Al Mishari, Chairman & Managing Director; Ahmad Faisal Al-Zabin, Director General; Hesham Al-Gharabally, Planning Director; Captain Suleimann Al-Wazzan, Operations Director; Maleeha Hussain Al-Ayyer, Human Resources Director; Saleh Al-Askar, IT Director; Abdul Wahhab Boodai, Engineering Director; Barrak Al-Sabeen, Marketing Director; Rashad Al-Rumeh, Ground-Handling Director; Moubarak Al-Maskati, Flight Services Director; Abdul Sattar Satara, Legal Director.

HQ Airport & Main Base: Kuwait

Radio callsign: KUWAITI

Designator: KU/KAC

Employees: 4,760

Main destinations served: Abu Dhabi, Alexandria, Amsterdam, Athens, Bahrain, Bangkok, Beirut, Bombay, Cairo, Casablanca, Colombo, Copenhagen, Damascus, Dakar, Delhi, Dhahran, Doha, Dubai, Frankfurt, Geneva, Istanbul, Jakarta, Jeddah, Karachi, Larnaca, London Heathrow, Luxor, Madrid, Malaga, Manila, Munich, Muscat, Nice, Paris CDG, Riyadh, Rome, Sharjah, Shiraz, Singapore, Trivandrum, Tehran.

LINKS WITH OTHER AIRLINES
Has a 20 per cent shareholding in Jet Airways (qv).

FLEET
2 Boeing 747-200B Combi

2 Boeing 777-200
4 Airbus A340-300
5 Airbus A300-600R
3 Airbus A310-300
3 Airbus A320-200

Kyrgyzstan – EX

KYRGYZSTAN AIRLINES

Kyrgyzstan Aba Yolduru National Airlines

Incorporated: 1992

HISTORY
A former Aeroflot (qv) division, Kyrgyzstan Airlines is now the national airline following the break up of the Soviet Union. Strong links remain with Aeroflot.

Executive Directors & Officers: Croskul B. Kuttabaev, General Director.

HQ Airport & Main Base: Bishkek

Radio callsign: KYRGHYZ

Designator: K2/KGA

Main destinations served: The main points within the Commonwealth of Independent States.

LINKS WITH OTHER AIRLINES
Marketing alliance and code-sharing with Aeroflot (qv).

FLEET
14 Tupolev Tu-154B/M
6 Tupolev Tu-134
24 Yakovlev Yak-40

Laos – RDLP

LAO AVIATION

Lao Aviation

Incorporated: 1991

HISTORY
Formed in 1991, Lao Aviation is the national airline, but ownership is spread amongst import-export agencies and China Travel Air Service, based in Hong Kong. Both domestic and international services are operated.

Executive Directors & Officers: Ouneheuane Saditthein, President; Hu Chang, Managing Director.

HQ Airport & Main Base: Vientiane

Radio callsign: LAO

Designator: QV/LAO

Main destinations served: About a dozen domestic destinations, plus Bangkok, Chiangmai, Hanoi, Ho Chi Minh City, Kunming, Phnom Penh, Yangon.

FLEET
1 Boeing 737-200 (leased)
2 ATR 42 (leased)
6 HAMC Y-12
4 XAC Y-7

Latvia – YL

AIR BALTIC

Air Baltic

Incorporated: 1995

HISTORY
One of the newer airlines to emerge from the ruins of the former Soviet empire, Air Baltic is a joint venture between the state, SAS (qv), and other interests. The state decided that Air Baltic would become the national carrier, taking over from Latavio, which had been a former Aeroflot division. The airline has concentrated on establishing a fleet of European aircraft.

Executive Directors & Officers: Rudi Peter Schwab, President & Chief Executive Officer; K.R. Forsman, Senior Vice-President, Finance; G. Agren, Senior Vice-President, Flight Operations; U. Nystrom, Senior Vice-President, Technical Operations; M. Petersen, Senior Vice-President, Marketing; D. Arbidane, Senior Vice-President, Human Resources; O. Korse, Senior Vice-President; Government & Public Affairs; A. Zobens, Senior Vice-President, Quality Management.

HQ Airport & Main Base: Riga

Radio callsign: AIR BALTIC

Designator: BT/BTI

Employees: Flight-crew: 31; Cabin staff: 42; Engineering: 39; Ground staff: 91; Total: 203.

Main destinations served: Copenhagen, Frankfurt, Geneva, Helsinki, Kiev, London Heathrow, Minsk, Stockholm, Tallin, Vilnius, Warsaw.

Revenue passenger km pa: 23.8 million

Passengers pa: 30,155

Above: *Air Baltic has a small fleet of modern western aircraft, including two Saab 340As.*

Right: *Both the RJ85 and its smaller sister, the RJ70, are used by Air Baltic. This is the RJ70.*

LINKS WITH OTHER AIRLINES
SAS has a 29 per cent shareholding. Code-sharing with SAS (qv) and Lufthansa (qv).

FLEET
2 Avro RJ85
2 Avro RJ70 (leased)
2 Saab 340A (leased)
1 Saab 2000

Lebanon – OD

MEA – MIDDLE EAST AIRLINES

Middle East Airlines Airliban SARL

Incorporated: 1945

HISTORY
Middle East Airlines was founded in 1945 and commenced operations in 1946 with a fleet of three de Havilland Rapide biplanes, quickly establishing routes from Beirut to Baghdad, Aleppo, Cairo, Lydda, Haifa, Damascus, and Amman by the middle of the year, so that two Douglas DC-3s had to be acquired. The crisis in Palestine in 1948 forced the termination of the Haifa and Lydda services, but the impact of this was offset by new services to Ankara and Istanbul. A third DC-3 was acquired the following year and the Rapides were sold.

In 1949 Pan American World Airways acquired a 36 per cent interest in the airline, providing three more DC-3s. This arrangement lasted until 1955, when BOAC (British Overseas Airways Corporation) took a 48.5 per cent shareholding and assisted with the purchase of three Vickers Viscounts and a new main-

tenance base. In 1960 BOAC leased two de Havilland Comet 4s to the airline while it awaited delivery of its own aircraft. Meanwhile MEA had also expanded into the air freight business, initially with a Bristol Freighter and then with three Avro Yorks. The agreement with BOAC ended in 1961 once MEA started to experience competition from BOAC's sister airline, BEA (British European Airways).

For two years MEA operated without foreign backing, and even took a 30 per cent shareholding in Jordan Airways, but in 1963 Air France (qv) took a 30 per cent stake in MEA and it was merged with Air Liban, in which the French airline had a controlling interest. Air Liban had operated Douglas DC-4s on services to Europe and West Africa. Once again, the choice of associate had a bearing on MEA's choice of equipment, with Sud Aviation Caravelles joining the fleet.

MEA's operations have been frequently disrupted by the unstable political and military situation in the Middle East. One of the worst incidents came on 28 December 1968, when an Israeli attack on the airport at Beirut resulted in a Viscount, a Boeing 707, three Comets, and two Caravelles being destroyed, along with a leased Vickers VC10. The airline started the long process of reconstruction, acquiring Lebanese International Airways in 1969, and later buying Boeing 747s. Yet worse was to come, for between 1975 and 1990 civil war in the Lebanon saw Beirut International Airport closed for some 800 days.

Nevertheless, in 1992 further reconstruction was assisted by the award of a 20-year exclusivity right to operate as a commercial airline in the Lebanon, effectively making MEA the official flag carrier. Today, the main shareholder is the Central Bank of Lebanon, indirectly making the airline state-owned. Code-sharing arrangements are in place with a number of major airlines.

Top: *Despite the difficulties suffered by the Lebanon in recent years, Middle East Airlines has managed to survive, and is updating its image. This is an artist's impression of an Airbus A321-100 in the new colour scheme.*

Middle: *Compare the previous picture with this one of a Middle East Airlines Boeing 747-200 Combi in the old colour scheme . . .*

Bottom: *. . . or this A310 on the ground at Beirut – in the past not such a safe place to be.*

Executive Directors & Officers: Khaled Salam, Chairman & President; Youssef Lahoud, Managing Director.

HQ Airport & Main Base: Beirut

Radio callsign: CEDAR JET

Designator: ME/MEA

Employees: Flight-crew: 323; Cabin staff: 161; Engineering: 1,012; Ground staff: 2,373; Total: 3,869.

Main destinations served: Abidjan, Abu Dhabi, Accra, Amman, Athens, Bahrain, Berlin, Bombay, Brussels, Bucharest, Cairo, Colombo, Copenhagen, Damascus, Dhahran, Doha, Dubai, Frankfurt, Geneva, Istanbul, Jeddah, Kano, Kuala Lumpur, Lagos, Larnaca, London Heathrow, Milan Linate, Nice, Paris CDG, Riyadh, Rome, São Paulo, Sydney, Zürich.

Annual turnover: US $239.1 million (£144.9 Million)

Aircraft km pa: 10.9 million

Revenue passenger km pa: 1,173.7 million

Cargo tonne km pa: 46.3 million

LINKS WITH OTHER AIRLINES
Code-sharing with Air Afrique (qv), British Airways (qv), Malaysia Airways (qv), and Nigeria Airways (qv).

FLEET
3 Boeing 747-200 Combi
3 Airbus A310-300 (leased)
3 Airbus A310-200 (leased)
6 Boeing 707-320
3 Airbus A321-100 (leased)
2 Airbus A320-200 (leased)

Libya – 5A

LIBYAN ARAB AIRLINES

Jamahiriya Libyan Arab Airlines

Incorporated: 1964

HISTORY
Originally founded as Kingdom of Libya Airlines, the present title was adopted in 1971 after the monarchy was overthrown in a coup. A ban on all flights to and from Libyan airspace has been imposed by the United Nations and this, together with previous embargoes on equipment, mean that the current operational status of the airline is uncertain.

Executive Directors & Officers: Mohamed Saad Aissa, Chief Executive Officer.

HQ Airport & Main Base: Tripoli

Radio callsign: LIBAIR

Designator: LN/LAA

FLEET
21 Ilyushin Il-76TD
5 Lockheed L-100-20 Hercules
3 Boeing 707-320
8 Boeing 727-200
3 Fokker F-28-4000 Fellowship
12 Fokker F-27-600 Friendship
2 Fokker F-27-500 Friendship
1 Fokker F-27-400 Friendship

Lithuania – LY

AIR LITHUANIA

Lithuanian State Airlines

Incorporated: 1991

HISTORY
Air Lithuania was founded in 1991 and started operations the following February, with a flight from Vilnius to Budapest. The airline was the former Kaunas Division of Aeroflot (qv).

Executive Directors & Officers: Kestutis Auryla, Chairman & Director

General; Janina Sinkeviciene, Financial Director; Tomas Laurinaitis, Commercial Director; Evaldos Petkus, Operations Director; Antanas Marcinkevicius, Technical Director.

HQ Airport & Main Base: Kaunas, but main hub is at Vilnius.

Radio callsign: LITHUANIA AIR

Designator: TT/LIL

Main destinations served: Billund, Budapest, Hamburg, Kristiansand, Oslo, Prague, Tallin.

FLEET
1 Tupolev Tu-134A
1 ATR 42-300
6 Yakovlev Yak-40
2 Saab 340B (leased)

Luxembourg – LX

CARGOLUX

Cargolux Airlines International SA

Incorporated: 1970

HISTORY
Cargolux was founded in 1970 by a consortium consisting of Luxair (qv), Loftleidir Icelandic Airlines, the Salen Shipping Group, and a number of other private interests. The first aircraft was a Canadair

It may be a small country, but Luxembourg has two airlines, including the all-freight carrier Cargolux. Here are two of that airline's Boeing 747 freighters, with a 747-400 nearest the camera, and cargo-handling equipment in the foreground.

Another load is swallowed by a Cargolux Boeing 747-200F.

CL-44, a stretched and licence-built variant of the Bristol Britannia with Rolls-Royce Tyne engines, which incorporated a swing-tail for easier loading of large items. Eventually the airline had five of these before they were supplemented and then replaced by Douglas DC-8 freighters, which enabled it to extend its scheduled operations to the United States.

The first Boeing 747-200F was delivered in 1979, followed by a second aircraft in 1980. The first of a number of strategic alliances was established in 1982 with China Airlines (qv). Cargolux also moved into passenger charters in 1983, operating two 747s and a DC-8 on Hadj pilgrim flights. Lufthansa (qv) acquired a 24.5 per cent shareholding in 1987, while Luxair (qv) increased its stake to the same level. The airline became the first operator of the Boeing 747-400 freighter in 1993, and remains the only European operator of this aircraft.

Executive Directors & Officers: Roger Sietzen, Chairman; Heiner Wilkens, President & Chief Executive Officer; Robert Arendal, Senior Vice-President, Sales, Marketing & Cargo Services; Jean-Donat Calmes, Senior Vice-President, Finance & Administration; Eyolfur Hauksson, Senior Vice-President, Operations/Chief Pilot; Jean-Claude Schmitz, Senior Vice-President, Maintenance & Engineering.

HQ Airport & Main Base: Luxembourg Findel

Radio callsign: CARGOLUX

Designator: CV/CLX

Employees: Flight-crew: 175; Engineering: 210; Ground staff: 503; Total: 888.

Main destinations served: Abu Dhabi, Bangkok, Damascus, Detroit, Dubai, Hong Kong, Houston, Istanbul, Johannesburg, Karachi, Keflavik, Komatsu, Kuala Lumpur, Kuwait, Los Angeles, Madras, Mexico City, New York, Prestwick, San Francisco, Santiago de Chile, São Paulo, Seattle, Singapore, Taipei, plus other destinations on charter.

Annual turnover: US $396.6 million (£240.4 million)

Cargo tonne km pa: 2,021 million

LINKS WITH OTHER AIRLINES
Lufthansa (qv) and Luxair (qv) each have 24.5 per cent interests.
Code-share with Lufthansa.
Exchange of space with China Airlines (qv).

FLEET
4 Boeing 747-400F
4 Boeing 747-200F

LUXAIR

Société Anonyme Luxembourgeoise de Navigation Aérienne

Incorporated: 1962

HISTORY
Luxair was founded in 1962 as the national airline for the Grand Duchy of Luxembourg, with ownership shared between the government, the steel industry, and the banks. Its predecessor Luxembourg Airlines was supported by a British company, Scottish Airways, between 1948 and 1951, and then by Seaboard World Airlines, an American company, until 1960.

Initially Luxair's fleet consisted of a Vickers Viscount 810 and three Fokker F-27 Friendships, while the route network consisted of the main centres in northwestern Europe, including London and Paris. Today it has a more extensive route network, although given the small size of Luxembourg and its small population it is not surprising that no wide-bodied aircraft are operated. A subsidiary, Luxair Commuter, operates the shorter and less busy routes, while the airline also has an interest in the Luxembourg-based air cargo airline, Cargolux (qv). Lufthansa (qv) has a 13 per cent share in the airline.

Executive Directors & Officers: Gust Graas, Chairman; Roger Sietzen, President; Jean-Pierre Walesch, Vice-President, Finance; Jean Poeckes, Vice-President, Operations; Marc Galowich, Vice-President, Technical.

HQ Airport & Main Base: Aéroport de Luxembourg

Radio callsign: LUXAIR

Designator: LG/LUX

Employees: 1,240

Main destinations served: Alicante, Athens, Barcelona, Bastia, Berlin Templehof, Copenhagen, Faro, Frankfurt, Geneva, Gran Canaria, Hamburg, Ibiza, Larnaca, Lisbon, London Heathrow, London Stansted, Madrid, Malaga, Manchester, Milan, Munich, Nice, Palma de Mallorca, Paris CDG, Prague, Rimini, Rome, Strasbourg, Venice, Vienna.

LINKS WITH OTHER AIRLINES
Lufthansa (qv) owns 13 per cent. Luxair owns Luxair Commuter, and has a 24.5 per cent stake in Cargolux (qv).

FLEET
2 Boeing 737-400
4 Boeing 737-500

4 Fokker 50
3 Embraer EMB-120 Brasilia (operated by Luxair Commuter)

Macau

AIR MACAU

Air Macau

Incorporated: 1994

HISTORY
Formed in 1994, Air Macau started operations in 1995 with the support of the Portuguese colonial authorities, who have declared that the airline will be the sole designated carrier for the colony for the next 25 years. Macau will follow Hong Kong and face a transfer of authority to China in the future, so it is perhaps not surprising that the China National Aviation Corporation is the single largest shareholder, with 51 per cent, against just 5 per cent for the local administration and 25 per cent for TAP Air Portugal (qv).

The airline plans to develop Macau as a hub for Asian air services using a new airport as an alternative to Hong Kong. It is also under pressure from the authorities to expand its route network beyond China and Taiwan.

Executive Directors & Officers: Wang Guixiang, Chairman; Dr Leonel Miranda, President; Zhou Yunda, Chairman & Commercial Director; Gao Jincal, Operations Director; Captain Jaime Caldas, Flight Operations Director; Carlos Pimental, Engineering & Maintenance Director; Jose Onofre, Ground Operations Director; Dominic Ching, Marketing Director; Liao Wei, Personnel Director.

HQ Airport & Main Base: Macau

Radio callsign: AIR MACAU

Designator: NX/AMU

Employees: 480

Main destinations served: Bangkok, Beijing, Haikou, Kaohsiung, Qingdao, Taipei, Wuhan, Xiamen.

LINKS WITH OTHER AIRLINES
TAP Air Portugal has a 25 per cent shareholding.
Marketing alliance with EVA Airways (qv).

FLEET
4 Airbus A321-100 (at least one leased)
2 Airbus A320-200 (leased)

Macedonia – Z3

AVIOIMPEX

Avioimpex Makedonija Airways

Incorporated: 1992

HISTORY
Avioimpex was founded in 1992 on the break-up of the former Yugoslavia and began operating workers' charter flights to a number of European destinations. Scheduled flights have been introduced in addition to a number of regular charter flights, and the airline has been adding western aircraft types to its fleet. It is the operating division of the Interimpex Group.

Executive Directors & Officers: Ilija Smilev, Managing Director; Dobri Jakimov, Commercial Manager; Alexandar Moysov, Technical Manager.

HQ Airport & Main Base: Skopje

Radio callsign: AVIOIMPEX

Designator: M4/AXX

Employees: Flight-crew: 17; Cabin staff: 39; Engineering: 7; Ground staff: 97; Total: 160.

Main destinations served: Copenhagen, Gothenburg, Istanbul, Ljubljana, London, Moscow, Paris, Rome, Vienna, Zagreb.

Annual turnover: US $29.5 million (£17.9 million)

Aircraft km pa: 4.2 million

Passenger km pa: 255.4 million

Cargo tonne km pa: 991,000

Passengers pa: 194,539

LINKS WITH OTHER AIRLINES
Code-sharing with Adria Airways (qv).

FLEET
2 McDonnell Douglas MD-81
1 McDonnell Douglas DC-9-33
2 Tupolev Tu-154M (wet-leased)
1 Yakovlev Yak-42 (wet-leased)

Avioimpex is re-equipping with western aircraft, with this McDonnell Douglas DC-9 and two MD-81s taking over from Tupolev and Yakovlev types.

PALAIR

Palair Macedonian

Incorporated: 1991

HISTORY
Founded in 1991 as a regional scheduled service airline, Palair has also undertaken charter flights throughout Europe and is currently developing a European scheduled service network.

Executive Directors & Officers: Bitoljana Vanja, Chairman; Peter Balog, Chief Operating Officer; Selim Selim, Director General; Beader Valeria, Operations Director; Nikolic Branislav, Technical Director.

HQ Airport & Main Base: Skopje

Radio callsign: PALAIR

Designator: 3D/PMK

Employees: approx 400

Main destinations served: Amsterdam, Berlin, Copenhagen, Frankfurt, Geneva, Istanbul, Munich, Rome, Zürich.

FLEET
1 British Aerospace One-Eleven 500
2 Fokker 100
2 Fokker F-28 Fellowship

Madagascar – 5R

AIR MADAGASCAR

Société Nationale Malgache de Transports Aériens

Incorporated: 1962

HISTORY
The nationalised carrier of Madagascar, Air Madagascar was founded in 1962 by the newly-independent Malagasy Republic with the support of Air France (qv), which still retains a 3.5 per cent shareholding today. It was formed to replace a local operator, Madair. In addition to operating throughout Madagascar it also operates to countries in Africa, and to Europe using a single Boeing 747, giving it an unusually wide range of capacity.

Executive Directors & Officers: Emmanuel Rakotovahiny, President; Jacky Randriamsay, Director General; Besoa Rolland Razafimaharo, Finance Director; Harilala Ranaivomampianina, Operations Director; Rolland Ranjatoelina, Marketing Director.

HQ Airport & Main Base: Antananarivo

Radio callsign: AIR MADAGASCAR

Designator: MD/MDG

Employees: 1,248

Main destinations served: Domestic destinations, plus Comoros Islands, Djibouti, Frankfurt, Johannesburg, Mauritius, Nairobi, Paris, Reunion, Seychelles, Zürich.

LINKS WITH OTHER AIRLINES
Air France (qv) has a 3.5 per cent interest.

FLEET
1 Boeing 747-200B Combi
1 Boeing 737-300
2 Boeing 737-200
2 British Aerospace 748
2 ATR 42
4 de Havilland DHC-6 Twin Otter

Malaysia – 9M

MALAYSIA AIRLINES

Malaysia Airlines Berhad

Incorporated: 1971

HISTORY
Malaysia Airlines can trace its history back to the formation of Malayan Airways in 1937 as a joint venture between Imperial Airways, Straits Steamship, and Ocean Steamship. Operations did not begin until after the end of World War Two, commencing with a service from Singapore to Penang via Kuala Lumpur in 1947. When the new state of Malaysia was formed incorporating Singapore, the airline changed its name in 1963 to Malaysian Airways, but in 1966 the governments of Malaysia and Singapore acquired a joint majority stake in the airline and had it renamed Malaysia-Singapore Airlines. It was restructured and renamed yet again after the ending of the agreement between the two governments in 1971, becoming Malaysian Airline System, or MAS. The present title was adopted in 1987.

Ownership of the airline rests with a number of financial institutions and investment agencies, as well as with Royal Brunei Airlines (qv). It has an extensive domestic and international network.

Executive Directors & Officers: Dato Tajudin Ramli, Chairman; Wan Malek Ibrahim, Managing Director; S. Suppiah, Finance Director; Bashir Ahmad, Commercial Director; Captain Mohd Khamil, Director, Flight Operations; Noor Amirudiin Nordin, Director, Engineering; Bakhtiar Affandi Md Ariffin, Director, Administration & Facilities; Shamin Ahmad Mohamed Ishak, Director, Sales; Baharuddin Ngah, Director, Cargo; Abdullah Mat Zaid, Director, Catering Services; Daud Abdul Kadir, Director, Human Resources.

HQ Airport & Main Base: Kuala Lumpur

Radio callsign: MALAYSIA

Designator: MH/MAS

Employees: 19,616

Main destinations served: Almost 40 domestic destinations, including Penang, plus Adelaide, Amman, Amsterdam, Auckland, Bandar Seri Begawan, Bangkok, Beijing, Beirut, Brisbane, Buenos Aires, Cairns, Canberra, Cape Town, Cebu, Chiang Mai, Christchurch, Colombo, Dacca, Darwin, Davao, Delhi, Denpasar (Bali), Dubai, Frankfurt, Fukuoka, Guangzhou, Hanoi, Hat Yai, Ho Chi Minh City, Hong Kong, Istanbul, Jeddah, Johannesburg, Kaohsiung, Karachi, Los Angeles, London Heathrow, Macau, Madras, Madrid, Manila, Melbourne, Mexico City, Munich, Nagoya, New York JFK, Osaka, Paris CDG, Perth, Phuket, Phnom Penh, Pontianak, Rio de Janeiro, Rome, Singapore, Surabaya, Sydney, Taipei, Tokyo Narita, Ujang Padang, Vancouver, Vienna, Zürich.

Annual turnover: US $2,594 million (£1,572.1 million)

LINKS WITH OTHER AIRLINES
Royal Brunei (qv) has a 10 per cent shareholding.
Subsidiaries include a 40 per cent stake in Royal Air Cambodge (qv).
Marketing alliances with Ansett Australia (qv), Ansett New Zealand (qv), British Midland (qv), Cathay Pacific (qv), Singapore Airlines (qv), and Virgin Atlantic (qv).

FLEET
20 Boeing 747-400 (plus 3 on order)
12 Airbus A330-300
8 Boeing 777-200IGW (plus 4 on order)
3 Boeing 777-300
3 McDonnell Douglas MD-11 (leased)
2 McDonnell Douglas MD-11F (leased)
41 Boeing 737-400 (5 leased to other airlines)
2 Boeing 737-300F
9 Boeing 737-500
10 Fokker 50 (2 leased to other airlines)
6 de Havilland DHC-6 Twin Otter

TRANSMILE AIR

Transmile Air Services

Incorporated: 1992

HISTORY
Formed in 1992, Transmile Air commenced operations in 1993, initially on passenger and cargo charter flights, but a number of scheduled services have since been introduced within Malaysia and to neighbouring states. The airline is privately-owned.

Executive Directors & Officers: Tan Sri Zainol Mahmood, Chairman; Gan Boon Aun, Chief Executive Officer; Khiudin Mohd, General Manager, Finance; Othman B. Abas, General Manager, Engineering & Ground Operations; Captain Jawaharlal Ratilal, General Manager, Flight Operations.

HQ Airport & Main Base: Kuala Lumpur

Radio callsign: TRANSMILE

Designator: 9P/TSE

Employees: approx 550

Main destinations served: Charter and scheduled operations to some 30 destinations within Malaysia, Singapore and Indonesia.

FLEET
3 Boeing 737-200
3 Boeing 737-200QC
1 Boeing 737-200F
4 Cessna 208B Grand Caravan II

Malta – 9H

AIR MALTA

Air Malta Co Ltd

Incorporated: 1973

HISTORY
Air Malta was founded in 1973 and commenced operations in April 1974 with the assistance of Pakistan International Airlines (qv), which also wet-leased it two Boeing 720 airliners. It had been founded by the Maltese Government as the successor to The Malta Airlines, which had comprised the Malta Airways Company and an associate, Air Malta, which had been formed in 1946 with BOAC (British Overseas Airways Corporation) holding a 34 per cent interest, which passed to BEA (British European Airways) in 1948. The Malta Airlines did not have a fleet of their own; instead BEA services from the UK to

Air Malta has two of these Airbus A320-200s, but is currently seeking more Boeing 737-300s.

Malta generally passed through Rome and Naples, at which point the flight designators changed to Malta Airlines.

The new Air Malta's scheduled services at the outset included London Heathrow, Birmingham, Manchester, Rome, Frankfurt, Paris, and Tripoli. The fleet of wet-leased aircraft grew, but in March 1983 it introduced the first of three Boeing 737s purchased new from the manufacturer, which were later joined by another two aircraft of the same type.

Air Malta has obvious limits set on its expansion by the small size of its home market, with less than 400,000 people. It was involved with a British charter airline, Excalibur Airways, founded in 1992 to take over the operations of Trans European Airways, but this has since ceased operations. More recently, in 1995, Air Malta helped found an Italian regional airline, AZZURRAair, based at Bergamo, which has three Avro RJ85s, although these are being replaced by three smaller ex-Air Malta RJ70s.

The fleet has grown steadily since 1983, undertaking charters as well as scheduled services to almost 40 destinations in Europe, North Africa, and the Middle East. Meanwhile the fleet has grown to 11 aircraft, although its future composition will be interesting since it is replacing its Avro RJ70s with a larger aircraft offering greater flexibility, possibly suggesting further Airbus A320s, although more Boeing 737-300s appear to be an interim measure.

In 1995 the airline introduced a direct Malta–New York service, using space on a Balkan Bulgarian (qv) service. A subsidiary, Malta Air Charter, operates a helicopter service between Malta and its smaller sister island of Gozo using Mil Mi-8 helicopters.

Executive Directors & Officers: Louis Grech, Chairman & Chief Executive Officer; Ray Sladden, Divisional Co-ordinator, Finance; Joe Capello, Divisional Co-ordinator, Commercial; Wilfred Borg, Divisional Co-ordinator, Operations.

HQ Airport & Main Base: Luqa

Radio callsign: AIR MALTA

Designator: KM/AMC

Employees: 1,758

Main destinations served: Abu Dhabi, Amsterdam, Bahrain, Berlin Tegel, Birmingham, Brussels, Budapest, Cairo, Casablanca, Catania, Copenhagen, Damascus, Dubai, Dublin, Düsseldorf, Frankfurt, Geneva, Glasgow, Hamburg, Istanbul, Larnaca, Lisbon, London Heathrow, London Gatwick, Lyon, Manchester, Marseilles, Milan, Monastir, Munich, Oslo, Palermo, Paris Orly, Rome, Stockholm, Tunis, Vienna, Zürich.

Passengers pa: 1.44 million

LINKS WITH OTHER AIRLINES
A subsidiary is Malata Air Charter. Marketing alliance with Balkan Bulgarian (qv).

FLEET
2 Airbus A320-200
3 Boeing 737-300
2 Boeing 737-200Adv
4 Avro RJ70 (3 passed to AZZURRAair,
1998)

Mauritius – 3B

AIR MAURITIUS

Air Mauritius

Incorporated: 1967

HISTORY
Air Mauritius was founded in 1967 as the country's national carrier with the support of Air France (qv), Air India (qv), and BOAC, all of which invested in the airline and initially provided block space on their aircraft. In 1977, the airline assumed responsibility for operating its own services, and has now developed a route network embracing Africa, Australia, Asia, and Europe.
 The Mauritius Government has a 51 per cent majority stake in the airline.

Executive Directors & Officers: Sir H.K. Tirvengadum, Chairman & Managing Director; S.K. Gujadhur, Director, Internal Audit; S. Seegobin, Commercial Director; R. Appa, Director, Operations; V.K. Chidambaram, Director, Planning & Information Systems; V. Poonoosamy, Director, Legal & International Affairs; J. Gentil, Maintenance Director; A.K. Huajadhur, Personnel Director.

HQ Airport & Main Base: Sir Seewoosagur Ramgoolam International Airport, Mauritius

Radio callsign: AIRMAURITIUS

Designator: MK/MAU

Employees: 1,481

Main destinations served:
Antananarivo, Bombay, Brussels, Durban, Frankfurt, Geneva, Harare, Hong Kong, Johannesburg, Kuala Lumpur, London Heathrow, Melbourne, Moroni, Munich, Nairobi, Paris CDG, Perth, Reunion, Rome, Singapore, Vienna, Zürich.

LINKS WITH OTHER AIRLINES
Air France has a 12.8 per cent interest, British Airways 12.8 per cent, Air India 8.5 per cent.
Marketing alliances with Air France (qv), Air India (qv), Air Madagascar (qv), British Airways (qv), Condor (qv), and Singapore Airlines (qv).

FLEET
4 Airbus A340-300 (2 leased)
2 Boeing 767-200ER
2 Avro ATR 42
2 Bell 206B JetRanger

Mexico – XA

AERO CALIFORNIA

Aéro California SA de CV

Incorporated: 1982

HISTORY
Originally founded in 1982 as a regional airline, operating from La Paz in Baja California, the initial fleet included Douglas DC-3s which were later joined by a Convair 340 Metropolitan and small Cessna and Beech twins. Today the route network has extended, and reaches as far north as Los Angeles in the United States and south to Mexico City.

Executive Directors & Officers: Raul A. Archiga, Chairman & President; Alexander Gorgelos, Vice-President, Marketing & Commercial.

HQ Airport & Main Base: La Paz, Baja California

Radio callsign: AEROCALIFORNIA

Designator: JR/SER

Employees: 1,800

Main destinations served: Almost 20 destinations, mainly in Mexico.

FLEET
16 McDonnell Douglas DC-9

AEROCARIBE

Aérocaribe SA de CV

Incorporated: 1975

HISTORY
Originally formed by private investors as a regional airline serving Mexican centres in Yucatan, Aérocaribe was bought by Mexicana (qv) in 1990 and is now part of the CINTRA Group, owners of Mexicana and Aéroméxico (qv). The airline operates feeder flights for Mexicana as Mexicana Inter. In addition to scheduled services it also handles charters.

Executive Directors & Officers: Jaime Valenzuela Tamariz, President; Captain Fernando Paredes, Vice-President, Operations; Austin Gaona, Vice-President, Maintenance.

HQ Airport & Main Base: Merida International Airport, Yucatan

Radio callsign: AEROCARIBE

Designator: QA (except when using Mexicana MX)

Employees: 356

Main destinations served: Almost 20 domestic destinations plus charter flights.

Annual turnover: Included in Aéroméxico/Mexicana figures.

Passengers pa: 727,600

LINKS WITH OTHER AIRLINES
Operates Mexicana Inter flights.

FLEET
4 McDonnell Douglas DC-9-15
6 Fairchild FH-227

AEROEXO

Aéroejecutivo SA de CV

Incorporated: 1977

HISTORY
A small passenger charter airline, Aéroexo operates a fleet of Boeing 727s.

Executive Directors & Officers: Alejandro Morales, President & Chief Executive Officer.

HQ Airport & Main Base: HQ is at Garza Garcia, base is at Monterrey.

Radio callsign: AEROEXO

Designator: SX/AJO

Employees: 300

FLEET
5 Boeing 727-200
1 Boeing 727-100

AEROLITORAL

Servicios Aéreos Litoral SA de CV

Incorporated: 1989

HISTORY
Founded in 1989, Aérolitoral became a subsidiary of Aéroméxico (qv) in 1990 and has served as the parent airline's feeder operator since, using Aéroméxico flight numbers.

Executive Directors & Officers: Alfonso Pasquel, Chairman; Carlos Trevino, President; Raul Saenz, Vice-President, Commercial; Cesar Garcia, Vice-President, Operations; Raul Zabre,

Aerolitoral is a subsidiary of Aeroméxico, and carries that airline's colour scheme. This is a Fairchild Metro.

Vice-President, Technical; Gerardo Esquer, Vice-President, Administration; Francisco Dominguez, Vice-President, Human Resources.

HQ Airport & Main Base: Nueva León, but the main base/hub is Monterrey.

Radio callsign: COSTERA

Designator: SLI (or Aéroméxico AM/AMX)

Employees: 569

Main destinations served: More than 20 domestic destinations.

Annual turnover: Included in the Aéroméxico/Mexicana figures.

Passengers pa: 639,000

LINKS WITH OTHER AIRLINES
A subsidiary of Aéroméxico (qv), and uses Aéroméxico flight numbers.

FLEET
14 Fairchild Metro III
13 Fairchild Metro 23
6 Saab 340B

AEROMAR

Transportes Aéromar SA de CV

Incorporated: 1987

HISTORY

Aéromar was formed in 1987 and has taken over a number of shorter and less busy services previously operated by Aéroméxico (qv). It has a marketing alliance with both Aéroméxico and Mexicana (qv).

Executive Directors & Officers: Carlos Autrey, Chairman; Zvi Katz, Chief Executive Officer; Juan I. Steta, Director General; Javier Warnholtz, Vice-President, Commercial; Juan M. Rodriguez Anza, Vice-President, Planning.

HQ Airport & Main Base: Aéropuerto International, Mexico City, and Monterrey.

Radio callsign: TRANS-AEROMAR

Designator: VW/TAO

Employees: 530

Main destinations served: Some 15 destinations mainly in Mexico, but with some operations into the USA.

Passengers pa: 370,000

LINKS WITH OTHER AIRLINES
Marketing alliances with Aéroméxico (qv), Mexicana (qv), and United Airlines (qv).

FLEET
2 ATR 42-500
6 ATR 42-320

AEROMEXICO

Aérovías de México SA de CV

Incorporated: 1988

HISTORY

Although Aéroméxico only dates from 1988 it can trace its origins to as early as 1934, when Aéronaves de México was formed with a small fleet of Beech aircraft.

The airline was granted an experimental permit by the Mexican Government in September of that year to operate a scheduled service between Mexico City and Acapulco, now Mexico's bustling main tourist resort but then just a small fishing village. The licence for this service was later made permanent.

In 1940 Pan American World Airways acquired a 40 per cent interest in Aéronaves, and in 1941 services were inaugurated to Mazatlan and La Paz (Mexico). No less important, in 1940 the airline also made the first of many acquisitions, buying Transportes Aéreos de Pacifico, following this in 1943 with the acquisition of Taxi Aéreo de Oaxaca, giving Aéronaves a route network to the north, west, and south of Mexico City. When Líneas Aéreas Jesus Sarabia collapsed in 1944 Aéronaves also acquired this airline's route rights.

A major acquisition came in 1952, when a major domestic operator, LAMSA (Líneas Aéreas Mexicanas SA), which also dated from 1934, was acquired following United Air Lines' (qv) decision to dispose of its interest in the company. This gave Aéronaves important routes in both north and central Mexico. Further expansion in the north followed in 1954 with the acquisition of Aérovías Reforma, taking the route network right to the border with the United States, which proved useful given the great difficulty encountered in obtaining international route permits. One route taken over with Aérovías Reforma was Mexico City to Tijuana, a town on the border just 30 miles from San Diego in California, and this became the airline's most important route at the time, to the extent that two Lockheed Constellations were leased from Pan American to operate the service, while the rest of the fleet consisted of Douglas DC-3s and DC-4s.

The airline finally received permission to operate its first international route in 1957, the same year that Pan American disposed of its shareholding to Mexican interests. The first route was from Mexico City to New York, and marked a change of emphasis for the airline away from domestic and towards international route development. The grant of the international permit had probably been helped by Aéronaves forming Aérolineas Mexicanas the previous year, at government request, as a carrier intended to operate unprofitable but socially necessary services.

This promising progress was arrested in 1959 by a strike by Mexican airline pilots. The impact on Aéronaves was so devastating that it had to be nationalised to remain operational. A government administrator was appointed to ensure that the

One of the largest aircraft in the Aeroméxico fleet is this Boeing 767-300ER.

airline avoided losses and covered its expenses, and a reorganisation followed, with greater standardisation of the fleet, which now comprised Douglas DC-3s and DC-6s, plus two new Bristol Britannia 302s. Domestic air fares were increased to more commercially realistic levels, and a Douglas DC-8 was ordered for the prestigious New York service.

Aeroméxico is one of the many airlines to operate Boeing 757s – often on routes into the United States.

Aéronaves was not the only airline to suffer from the pilots' strike, and in 1960 it acquired two bankrupt airlines, Aérolineas Mexicanas and Trans Mar de Cortes. The former was the airline established by Aéronaves to operate many unprofitable routes, but in the latter it gained a valuable route to Los Angeles. The following year Aéronaves acquired Aérovías Guest when it bought the SAS (qv) interest in that airline. This not only gave the company routes into South America, but a profitable Mexico City–Miami service as well. Nevertheless, a shortage of suitable aircraft meant that some of the Aérovías Guest routes had to be temporarily suspended. By the mid-1960s Aéronaves was operating a fleet in which the Douglas DC-3 still played a prominent part, having a dozen of these aircraft in service as well as five Douglas DC-8s and nine DC-9s.

The difficulties facing any airline which attempts to do, if not everything, then at least everything ranging from local domestic feeder services through to intercontinental operations, was eventually recognised, and in 1970 a government plan saw domestic airlines rationalised into an integrated air transport system under Aéronaves de México, and organised into eight smaller carriers, many of which today operate under Aéroméxico flight numbers.

Two years later the current title was adopted, and the airline continued to operate until 1988, when it was declared bankrupt by the Mexican Government, its only shareholder at the time. A bank was appointed as liquidator and prepared a six-month recovery programme. The much-reduced airline which subsequently

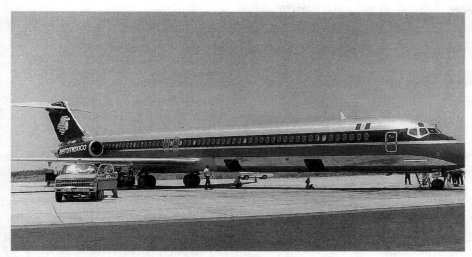

One of Aeroméxico's substantial MD-80 fleet is ready for loading.

emerged was renamed Aerovías de México, but retained the name Aeroméxico for trading purposes. A consortium of business interests took a majority shareholding. In 1996 CINTRA, a Mexican trading group, acquired 99.2 per cent of Aeroméxico's shares and 99.9 per cent of its rival, Mexicana (qv). While the two airlines continue to operate with their separate identities, this effectively puts Mexican commercial aviation into one group, along with AéroPeru (qv). Other group companies in Mexico include Aérolitoral (qv), Aérocaribe (qv) and Aéromexpress, with the latter operating freight terminals, although it also has two leased Boeing 727 freighters.

Executive Directors & Officers:
Ernesto Martens, Chairman & Chief Executive Officer; Alfonso Pasquel, President; Victor Bernal, Senior Vice-President, Finance; Manuel Reyes, Senior Vice-President, Operations; Alberto Castrejon, Senior Vice-President, Passenger Services; Jorge Wheatley, Senior Vice-President, Systems & Communications; Arturo Barahona, Senior Vice-President, Commercial; Jared Harckham, Senior Vice-President, Commercial Planning; Gustavo Struck, Senior Vice-President, Business Development; Rafeal Ruiz, Senior Vice-President, International Sales; Jose Robles, Senior Vice-President, Administration.

HQ Airport & Main Base: Aéropuerto International, Mexico City, with additional bases/hubs at Guadalajara, Monterrey, and Tijuana.

Radio callsign: AEROMEXICO

Designator: AM/AMX

Employees: Flight-crew: 589; Cabin staff: 1,164; Ground staff: 3,763; Total: 5,516.

Main destinations served: Almost 20 domestic destinations, plus Atlanta, Austin, Boston, Dallas/Fort Worth, Detroit, El Paso, Frankfurt, Houston, Lima, Los Angeles, Madrid, Miami, New Orleans, New York JFK, Orlando, Paris CDG, Philadelphia, Phoenix, San Antonio, San Diego, San Francisco, São Paulo, Tucson, Washington

Annual turnover: US $1,949.4 million (£1,181.5 million) (includes turnover for Aeroméxico, Mexicana and subsidiaries)

Revenue passenger km pa: 8,883 million

Passengers pa: 6.9 million

LINKS WITH OTHER AIRLINES
Sister company of Mexicana (qv).
Aérolitoral (qv) and Aéromexpress are subsidiaries.
Code-sharing with Delta Airlines (qv) and AéroPeru (qv).

FLEET
1 Boeing 767-300ER (leased)
2 Boeing 767-200 (leased)
6 Boeing 757-200 (leased)
10 McDonnell Douglas MD-82 (leased)
4 McDonnell Douglas MD-83 (leased)
2 McDonnell Douglas MD-87 (leased)
10 McDonnell Douglas MD-88 (leased)
18 McDonnell Douglas DC-9-32 (14 leased)

MEXICANA

Corporacíon Mexicana de Aviación de CV

Incorporated: 1921

HISTORY
Mexico's oldest airline and today one of the two largest, Mexicana was founded in 1921 as Compania Mexicana de Transportes Aéreos, taking its present name in 1924. It is the second oldest airline in the Americas and claims to be the fourth oldest in the world, with 75 years of continuous operation.

It has developed a route network within Mexico and to North America, as well as to destinations in Central America and the Caribbean. In 1990 it acquired Aérocaribe (qv), which operates many of its feeder services as Mexicana Inter. Privatised in 1989 after a spell in state control, Mexicana is now part of the CINTRA Group, which took a 99.9 per cent stake in the airline and which also owns Aeroméxico (qv). At present both Aeroméxico and Mexicana are operated as separate companies.

Executive Directors & Officers:
Fernando Flores, President & Chief Executive Officer; Luis Villegas, Executive Vice-President, Finance & Administration; Captain Jaan Albrecht, Executive Vice-President, Commercial; Orcar Arguello, Executive Vice-President, Technical.

HQ Airport & Main Base: Aéropuerto International, Mexico City, with an additional base/hub at Guadalajara.

Radio callsign: MEXICANA

Designator: MX/MXA

Employees: 5,800

Main destinations served: Some 30 domestic destinations, plus Baltimore, Chicago, Dallas/Fort Worth, Denver, Guatemala City, Havana, Los Angeles, Miami, New York JFK, Philadelphia, San Antonio, San Francisco, San José, San Juan, Seattle, Tampa/St Petersburg.

Annual turnover: US $1,949.4 million (£1,181.5 million) (includes turnover for Aeroméxico, Mexicana and subsidiaries)

Revenue passenger km pa: 8,371 million

Passengers pa: 6.4 million

LINKS WITH OTHER AIRLINES
Owns Aérocaribe (qv), which operates Mexicana Inter.
Code-sharing with United Air Lines (qv).

FLEET
3 Boeing 757-200 (leased)
14 Airbus A320 (2 leased)
22 Boeing 727-200 (2 leased)
10 Fokker 100 (leased)

Moldova – ER

AIR MOLDOVA

Air Moldova

Incorporated: 1992

HISTORY
Flag carrier of the newly independent Republic of Moldova, Air Moldova is based on the former local Aeroflot (qv) division.

Executive Directors & Officers:
Viacheslav F. Gyrlia, Director General.

HQ Airport & Main Base: Chisinau

Radio callsign: AIR MOLDOVA

Designator: 9U/MLD

Main destinations served: Bucharest, Donetsk, Ekatarinburg, Frankfurt, Krasnodar, Mineralnye Vody, Minsk, Moscow, Murmansk, Samara, Sochi, St Petersburg, Tbilisi, Volgograd.

FLEET
7 Tupolev Tu-154B
11 Tupolev Tu-124
4 Antonov An-26
7 Antonov An-24

Mongolia

MIAT – MONGOLIAN AIRLINES

Mongolyn Irgeniy Agaaryn Teever

Incorporated: 1956

HISTORY
Mongolian Airlines was formed by the Mongolian Government in 1956, with assistance from Aeroflot (qv). Because of the country's considerable poverty the fleet is mainly old and of Russian and Chinese origin, although one of three Boeing 727-200s was donated by Korean Air (qv).

Executive Directors & Officers: Manjiin Dhagva, Director General; Darjaagiyn Surenhorloo, Managing Director.

HQ Airport & Main Base: Ulan Bator

Radio callsign: MONGOL AIR

Designator: OM/MGL

Main destinations served: An extensive domestic network, plus Beijing, Hohhoy, Irkutsk, Moscow, Sofia.

FLEET
3 Boeing 727-200
1 Antonov An-30
3 Antonov An-26
12 Antonov An-24
5 Harbin Y-12
3 Mil Mi-8T

Morocco – CN

RAM ROYAL AIR MAROC

Cie Nationale de Transport Aériens/Royal Air Maroc

Incorporated: 1953

HISTORY
Morocco's national airline, Royal Air Maroc was founded in 1953 as Compagnie Chrefienne on the merger of Air Maroc with Air Atlas. Both airlines had been experiencing financial difficulties, and the merger had been instigated by the government to both strengthen the two airlines and eliminate duplication on some routes. Air France (qv) and Aviaco (qv), the Spanish domestic carrier, provided assistance and took token shares in the new airline.

Of the two predecessor airlines, Air Atlas was slightly the older, having been founded in 1946 under the sponsorship of the French Resident-General as a domestic operator, but with some services to southern France. The initial fleet consisted of ten war-surplus Junkers Ju.52/3ms, supplemented by some French Martinets for the shorter routes, the Junkers being replaced in 1948 by Douglas DC-3s for the busiest routes, from Casablanca to Bordeaux and Marseilles.

Air Maroc had been formed a year later, in 1947, but did not start charter operations until 1948, using Douglas DC-3s. Scheduled services started in 1949, and at the time of the merger with Air Atlas it was operating from Casablanca to Paris and Geneva.

On its formation, the new airline was owned 34 per cent by the government, with Air France having a similar shareholding. It was recognised officially as the national airline in 1956, on the eve of Moroccan independence, when the present title was adopted. The level of state ownership grew steadily, with the share rising to 64 per cent by the early-1960s, and today it is owned 92.7 per cent by the Moroccan Government.

It operated DC-3s throughout the 1950s, subsequently replacing these with Sud Aviation Caravelles and Fokker F-27s. The route network has grown steadily, helped by a growth in tourism. At one stage domestic services were hived off to a subsidiary airline, Royal Air Inter, but this has been re-absorbed and today RAM operates both domestic and international services, including inclusive tour charters.

Executive Directors & Officers:
Mohammed Hassad, Chairman & President; Abderrafih Tahiri, Director General; Camel Bekkari, Director, Operations; Mohammed Benchekroun, Director, Administration; Nour Eddine Layt, Director; Commercial; Rafik Hamayed Elmili, Director, Technical; Mohammed Ballatig, Director, Maintenance; Jai Hokimi, Director, IT; Ali Sebti, Director, Flight Services.

HQ Airport & Main Base: Casablanca, with bases at Tangier and Marrakech.

Radio callsign: MOROCAIR

Designator: AT/RAM

Employees: 5,360

Main destinations served: 13 domestic destinations, plus Abidjan, Algiers, Amsterdam, Athens, Bamako, Barcelona, Bastia, Bordeaux, Brussels, Cairo, Conakry, Copenhagen, Dakar, Düsseldorf, Frankfurt, Geneva, Istanbul, Las Palmas, Libreville, Lille, Lisbon, London Heathrow, Madrid, Malabo, Malaga, Marseilles, Milan, Montreal, Munich, Nantes, New York JFK, Nice, Nouakchott, Oran, Paris CDG, Rio de Janeiro, Rome, Strasbourg, Toulouse, Tripoli, Tunis, Vienna, Zürich.

LINKS WITH OTHER AIRLINES
Air France (qv) has a 4 per cent interest, Iberia (qv) has 2 per cent.

FLEET
1 Boeing 747-400
1 Boeing 747-200 Combi
2 Boeing 757-200
2 Boeing 707-320
2 Boeing 727-200
7 Boeing 737-400
4 Boeing 737-300
2 Boeing 737-200
6 Boeing 737-500
2 AI(R) ATR 42-300
plus 9 Boeing 737-800 on order

Mozambique – C9

LAM

Linhas Aéreas de Moçambique

Incorporated: 1936

HISTORY
Originally founded under Portuguese colonial rule in 1936, LAM commenced operations in 1937 as DETA (Direçcao de Exploraçao dos Transportes Aéreos), a division of the Railways, Harbours and Airways Administration. Following independence the original title was retained until 1980, when the current name was adopted. The airline remains in state ownership. Most of its services are domestic, but it also operates international services to neighbouring countries and to Lisbon.

Executive Directors & Officers: Jose Ricardo Zuzarte Viegas, Director General.

HQ Airport & Main Base: Maputo, with some international services operated via or extended to Beira.

Radio callsign: MOZAMBIQUE

Designator: TM/LAM

Employees: Flight-crew: 47; Cabin staff: 70; Engineering: 185; Ground staff: 969; Total: 1,271.

Main destinations served: Half-a-dozen domestic destinations, including Beira, plus Harare, Johannesburg, Lisbon, Matsapa.

Aircraft km pa: 3.1 million

Revenue passenger km pa: 259.9 million

Cargo tonne km pa: 5.4 million

LINKS WITH OTHER AIRLINES
Code-sharing agreements with TAP Air Portugal (qv), Air Malawi, and Air Zimbabwe (qv).

FLEET
1 Lockheed L-1011 TriStar (leased from TAP)
2 Boeing 737-200
1 Fokker 100 (leased)
4 CASA C-212
4 Partenavia P68C
2 Beech King Air

Myanmar (formerly Burma) – XY, XZ

MYANMAR AIRWAYS

Myanmar Airways

Incorporated: 1948

HISTORY
Originally founded in 1948 as Union of Burma Airways, the airline became Burma Airways in 1972 and adopted the present title in 1989, when the country changed its name. For most of its history it has been government-owned.

Executive Directors & Officers: Captain Thura U Win Myint, Managing Director; Pe Thuang, General Manager.

HQ Airport & Main Base: Yangon (formerly Rangoon)

Radio callsign: UNIONAIR

Designator: UB/UBA

Employees: 1,100

Main destinations served: Domestic network, plus Bangkok and Singapore.

FLEET
2 Boeing 737-400 (leased from Malaysia Airlines (qv))
2 Fokker F-28-4000 Fellowship
1 Fokker F-28-1000 Fellowship
6 Fokker F-27-600 Friendship
1 Fokker F-27-400 Friendship
2 Eurocopter SA.330 Puma

Nepal – 9N

NECON AIR

Necon Air

Incorporated: 1992

HISTORY
Necon Air operates domestic and international scheduled services as well as charter flights.

Executive Directors & Officers: Anoop S.J.B. Rana, Chairman; D.M. Rajbhandari, Managing Director; D.R. Koiraia, Operations Director.

HQ Airport & Main Base: Kathmandu

Radio callsign: NECONAIR

Designator: 3Z/N4C

Main destinations served: Domestic destinations and charters, plus Bagdogra, Calcutta, Dhaka, Gorakhpur, Lucknow, Patna.

FLEET
5 British Aerospace 748
1 Cessna 208 Caravan I

NEPAL AIRWAYS

Nepal Airways

Incorporated: 1992

HISTORY
Formed in 1992 to operate domestic services and international air charters, Nepal Airways has a small route network based on the capital, Kathmandu.

Executive Directors & Officers: B. Sharma, General Manager.

HQ Airport & Main Base: Kathmandu

Designator: 7E

Main destinations served: About half-a-dozen domestic destinations, plus air charters.

FLEET
3 HAMC Y-12
2 British Aerospace 748

ROYAL NEPAL

Royal Nepal Airlines

Incorporated: 1958

HISTORY
Royal Nepal Airlines was formed by the Nepalese Government in 1958 to take over domestic services and also the routes from India to Nepal which had been operated by Indian Airlines (qv). The airline was the first to place the Boeing 757-200 Combi in service.

Executive Directors & Officers: Bhubaneshwor Daibagya, Executive Chairman; Pradeep Panday, Deputy Managing Director; R.R. Upadhaya, Director, Finance; Captain D.M.S. Rajbhandari, Director, Operations; Geeta Keshary, Director, Commercial; Bal Ram Tandukar, Director, Ground Operations; V.M. Saud, Director, Engineering; B.N. Shrestha, Director, Technical.

HQ Airport & Main Base: Kathmandu

Radio callsign: ROYAL NEPAL

Designator: RA/RNA

Employees: 2,200

Main destinations served: Almost 40 domestic destinations, plus Bangkok, Bombay, Calcutta, Delhi, Frankfurt, Hong Kong, London Heathrow, Paris CDG, Singapore.

FLEET
1 Airbus A310-300
2 Boeing 757-200
2 British Aerospace 748-2A
7 de Havilland DHC-6 Twin Otter
1 Pilatus PC-6 Turbo Porter

Netherlands – PH

AIR HOLLAND

Air Holland Charter BV

Incorporated: 1991

HISTORY
Air Holland was formed in 1991 as a charter airline, mainly in the inclusive tour market, but it was also initially involved in the early transatlantic operations of Air Guadeloupe (qv). Today it operates inclusive tour charters from the Netherlands to destinations in the Mediterranean, the Canary Islands, and Portugal.

Executive Directors & Officers: Dr van Berckel, President; Mijl van Berckel, Executive Director.

HQ Airport & Main Base: Amsterdam Schiphol

Radio callsign: ORANGE

Designator: GG/AHR

Employees: 400

Main destinations served: Inclusive tour charter flights.

FLEET
3 Boeing 757-200
3 Boeing 737-300

KLM CITYHOPPER

KLM CityHopper

Incorporated: 1991

HISTORY
KLM CityHopper operates KLM's (qv) domestic network and the less heavily used and shorter European services. It was formed in 1991 on the merger of KLM's regional subsidiary, NLM, which dated from 1966, with Netherlines, which KLM had acquired in 1988. It is owned 100 per cent by KLM.

Executive Directors & Officers: F.J. van Pallandt, Managing Director; H.K. de Brujin, Deputy Managing Director.

HQ Airport & Main Base: Schiphol, Amsterdam, plus Eindhoven and Rotterdam.

Radio callsign: CITY

Designator: KL/KLC (or KL/KLM)

Employees: 500

Main destinations served: Domestic destinations, plus many of the shorter routes on the KLM network, including many international flights from Eindhoven and Rotterdam.

Annual turnover: Included in KLM figures

LINKS WITH OTHER AIRLINES
A subsidiary of KLM (qv).

FLEET
2 Fokker 100
12 Fokker 70
13 Fokker 50
5 Saab 340B

KLM ROYAL DUTCH AIRLINES

Koninklijke Luchvaart Maatschappij NV

Incorporated: 1919

HISTORY
Formed in 1919 at the Hague, KLM operated its first scheduled service between Amsterdam and London the following year using a single-engined two-passenger biplane, making this the oldest scheduled air service in the world to be operated by the same company. It introduced services from Amsterdam to other major European cities before commencing the world's first intercontinental air service in 1929, between Amsterdam and Jakarta in Indonesia (then a Dutch colony), using a Fokker F-VIIB trimotor. KLM was the first European airline to operate the Douglas DC-2 and DC-3 before the outbreak of World War Two, and in 1946 it introduced its first transatlantic services using Douglas DC-4s from a fleet of 18 of these aircraft, with 30 DC-3s for European services.

Post-war the airline expanded its interests in other ways. In 1965 KLM Helikopters (now KLM/ERA Helicopters) was launched, in time for the massive growth in offshore oil and gas exploration in the North Sea. A year later a domestic subsidiary, NLM, now KLM Cityhopper (qv), was launched, separating international and domestic services, although this airline now also undertakes some of the less busy European scheduled services for its parent. In 1988 NetherLines, a Dutch regional carrier, was acquired. KLM also built up a shareholding in the British regional carrier KLMuk (qv), before acquiring this airline outright in 1997. An 80 per cent stake in Transavia (qv) has also been taken, as well as a 50 per cent stake in Martinair (qv) and a 26 per cent stake in Kenya Airways (qv). Before this, in 1989 KLM was amongst the first to create a transatlantic alliance, taking 19 per cent of the shares in the US airline Northwest (qv), with which it also operates a code-share arrangement; however, KLM has now agreed to dispose of its shares in Northwest, selling these of in four tranches by the year 2000.

Today, in terms of annual turnover KLM is the thirteenth-largest airline in the world, and fifth-largest in Europe, despite the rel-

KLM was a pioneer of intercontinental travel, and today's Boeing 747-400s are a far cry from the Fokker F.VII/3M trimotors of the early days.

The Boeing 737-400s of KLM are a common sight on the airline's European routes. This one is named after the explorer Henry Hudson.

atively small size of its home market. At its Amsterdam Schiphol hub, KLM has introduced a 'wave system' of arrivals and departures, to provide better onward connections between incoming and departing flights, and KLMuk (formerly Air UK) and KLM Cityhopper services are included in the system.

For most of its post-war existence the airline was owned 50.5 per cent by the state, with the remainder in private hands, but the state involvement has been reduced, and a major share offering in 1994 means that the state now owns just 38.2 per cent of KLM. In 1997 KLM took a 30 per cent stake in Braathens SAFE (qv).

Executive Directors & Officers: Pieter Bouw, President & Chief Executive Officer; Leo van Wijk, Managing Director & Chief Operating Officer; Rob Abrahamsen, Chief Financial Officer; Cees van Woudenberg, Chief Human Resources Officer.

HQ Airport & Main Base: Schiphol, Amsterdam

Radio callsign: KLM

Designator: KL/KLM

Employees: Flight-crew: 1,700; Cabin staff: 6,000; Engineering: 4,500; Ground staff: 13,800; Total: 26,000.

Main destinations served: (includes KLM Cityhopper) Aarhus, Abu Dhabi, Accra, Adelaide, Almaty, Amman, Antwerp, Athens, Atlanta, Baku, Bahrain, Bangkok, Barcelona, Basle/Mulhouse, Beijing, Beirut, Berlin, Birmingham, Bologna, Bombay, Bremen, Brisbane,

Bristol, Brussels, Bucharest, Budapest, Buenos Aires, Cairns, Calcutta, Canberra, Cairo, Cape Town, Cardiff, Casablanca, Chicago O'Hare, Colombo, Conakry, Copenhagen, Cork, Curaçao, Damascus, Dar-es-Salaam, Delhi, Denpasar (Bali), Detroit, Dhahran, Dubai, Düsseldorf, Eindhoven, Frankfurt, Freetown, Geneva, Gothenburg, Guatemala City, Guayaquil, Guernsey, Hamburg, Hannover, Harare, Helsinki, Ho Chi Minh City, Hong Kong, Houston, Innsbruck, Istanbul, Jakarta, Jeddah, Jersey, Johannesburg, Kano, Karachi, Kilimanjaro, Khartoum, Kiev, Kuala Lumpur, Kuwait, Lagos, Larnaca, Lilongwe, Lima, Lisbon, Lome, London Heathrow, Los Angeles, Lusaka, Lyon, Maastricht, Madrid, Malmö, Manila, Melbourne, Memphis, Mexico City, Milan, Minneapolis/St Paul, Montreal, Moscow, Munich, Muscat, Nairobi, New York JFK, Nice, Oporto, Osaka Kansei, Oslo, Paphos, Paris CDG, Prague, Rio de Janeiro, Rome, Rotterdam, Quito, Salzburg, San Francisco, San José, San Juan, Sana'a, Santiago de Chile, São Paulo, Seoul, Singapore, Southampton, St Maarten, St Petersburg, Stavanger, Stockholm, Strasbourg, Stuttgart, Surabaya, Sydney, Taipei, Tehran, Tel Aviv, Tokyo Narita, Toronto, Toulouse, Vancouver, Venice, Vienna, Warsaw, Zürich.

Annual turnover: US $5,952 million (£3,607.3 million)

Revenue passenger km pa: 45,531 million

Cargo tonne km pa: 3,813 million

Passengers pa: 12,339 million

LINKS WITH OTHER AIRLINES
Strategic alliance with Northwest (qv), in which KLM has a 20 per cent stake. Owns 100 per cent of KLMuk (qv) and KLM Cityhopper (qv), plus 50 per cent of Martinair (qv), 80 per cent of Transavia (qv), and 40 per cent of ALM Antillean.

FLEET
5 Boeing 747-400
15 Boeing 747-400 Combi
3 Boeing 747-300
10 Boeing 747-300 Combi
10 McDonnell Douglas MD-11
10 Boeing 767-300ER
19 Boeing 737-400
17 Boeing 737-300
2 Fokker 100 (operated by KLM Cityhopper)
12 Fokker 70 (operated by KLM Cityhopper)
13 Fokker 50 (operated by KLM Cityhopper)
5 Saab 340B (operated by KLM Cityhopper)

MARTINAIR

Martinair Holland NV

Incorporated: 1958

HISTORY
Martinair takes its name from its founder, Martin Schroder, who founded it in 1958 as Martin's Air Charter. Schroder had previously operated Piper and Auster aircraft on air taxi work and pleasure flights. Initially the airline wet-leased aircraft as required, but in 1961 an ex-BEA Douglas DC-3 Pionair was purchased, and a Douglas DC-4 and a de Havilland Dove soon followed. in addition to air charters and executive flights the airline soon started to undertake contract flying for KLM (qv).

Eventually KLM acquired an interest in the company, initially at just 28.8 per cent, a larger shareholder being the Royal Nedlloyd shipping group with 49.2 per cent. Martinair has the distinction of operating and maintaining a Fokker 70 Fellowship used by the Dutch Royal Family and by members of the government, having previously also handled this work on a Fokker F-28 Fellowship.

In addition to a growing inclusive tour charter business, the airline moved into low-cost scheduled transatlantic flights during the late-1980s, and unusually continued its executive charters as well. Today, Martinair continues to offer the mix of scheduled, inclusive tour charter, contract, and executive flying, while ownership is now divided equally between

KLM and Nedlloyd, although the founder remains its chairman.

Executive Directors & Officers: Martin Schroder, Chairman; Dr A. Verberk, Managing Director.

HQ Airport & Main Base: Schiphol, Amsterdam

Radio callsign: MARTINAIR

Designator: MP/MPH

Employees: 2,360

Main destinations served: Ad hoc and inclusive tour charters, plus scheduled flights to Bangkok, Bridgetown, Calgary, Cancun, Denver, Edmonton, Holguin, Ibiza, Isla Margarita, Las Palmas, Los Angeles, Malaga, Miami, Montego Bay, New York Newark, Oakland, Orlando, Palma de Mallorca, Phuket, Puerto Plata, Puerto Vallarta, Punta Cana, San Juan, Santo Domingo, Seattle, Tampa, Tenerife, Toronto, Varadero.

Annual turnover: US $692.7 million (£419.8 million)

Revenue passenger km: 945.9 million

Cargo tonne km pa: 1,520.2 million

LINKS WITH OTHER AIRLINES
KLM (qv) owns 50 per cent of the shares.

FLEET
2 Boeing 747-200C
1 Boeing 747-200F
4 McDonnell Douglas MD-11CF
1 McDonnell Douglas MD-11F
6 Boeing 767-300ER (1 leased)
1 Fokker 70 (owned by the Dutch Government)
1 Dornier Do.228-212 (fitted as surveillance aircraft)
2 Cessna Citation VI
plus a number of smaller aircraft for training

SCHREINER AIRWAYS

Schreiner Airways

Incorporated: 1945

HISTORY
Originally founded in 1945, Schreiner has been heavily involved in the operation of flying schools, including one for professional commercial and military pilots opened in 1968. The company's airline operations centre around operating a fleet of aircraft on behalf of major oil companies and other airlines.

Executive Directors & Officers: Evart van Schaik, Managing Director; Egbert van der Grijp, Deputy Managing Director; Richard Freiwald, Commercial Director; Nico Hemmer, Engineering Director; Jan Verhulst, Personnel Director.

HQ Airport & Main Base: HQ at Leiden, operations include Maastricht.

Radio callsign: SCHREINER

Designator: AW/SCH

FLEET
8 de Havilland Dash 8-300
3 de Havilland Dash 8-100
9 de Havilland DHC-6 Twin Otter
4 British Aerospace 125
16 Aérospatiale Dauphin
2 Eurocopter AS355 Ecureil

TRANSAVIA

Transavia Airlines NV

Incorporated: 1966

HISTORY
Transavia was established in 1966 as an air charter operator, initially operating a fleet of five Douglas DC-6s, to which a Boeing 707-320 was soon added for transatlantic charters. Originally known as Transavia Holland, the present title was adopted in 1986. The airline took the opportunity of greater freedom in air transport to introduce scheduled services to European destinations during the late-1980s. KLM (qv) acquired a 40 per cent interest in 1991, which it has more recently doubled to 80 per cent.

Executive Directors & Officers: Peter J. Legro, President & Chief Executive Officer; I. Meyer, Operations Director.

HQ Airport & Main Base: Schiphol, Amsterdam

Radio callsign: TRANSAVIA

Designator: HV/TRA

Employees: 1,100

Main destinations served: Inclusive tour charter flights, plus Alicante, Barcelona, Djerba, Faro, Funchal, Las Palmas, Lisbon, London Gatwick, Malaga, Malta, Nice, Tenerife, Palma de Mallorca.

LINKS WITH OTHER AIRLINES
KLM (qv) has an 80 per cent interest.

FLEET
4 Boeing 757-200
14 Boeing 737-300
plus 8 Boeing 737-800 on order

AIR NELSON

Air Nelson Ltd

Incorporated: 1986

HISTORY
Air Nelson evolved from a flying school and air taxi operation, starting scheduled services in 1986. It has since been acquired by Air New Zealand (qv), and as Air New Zealand Link it operates services which are unprofitable for the parent airline's larger aircraft.

Executive Directors & Officers: Steve Wilkes, Chief Executive Officer.

HQ Airport & Main Base: Nelson

Designator: RLK

Employees: 455

Main destinations served: Upwards of 15 destinations.

Annual turnover: Included in Air New Zealand figures.

LINKS WITH OTHER AIRLINES
A wholly-owned subsidiary of Air New Zealand (qv).

FLEET
12 Saab 340A/B* (operated on Air New Zealand Link)
12 Fairchild Metroliner (operated on Air New Zealand Link)
9 Embraer EMB-110 Bandeirante (operated on Air New Zealand Link)
*The Saab 340A fleet is being 'rolled over', replaced by second-hand Saab 340Bs as these become available.

AIR NEW ZEALAND

Air New Zealand Ltd

Incorporated: 1940

HISTORY
Originally founded in 1940 as Tasman Empire Airways Ltd, or TEAL, Air New Zealand (ANZ) was originally owned by the governments of Australia, New Zealand, and the United Kingdom, and was intended to operate air services between New Zealand and Australia. Ownership was left with the governments of these two countries in 1954, when the UK withdrew, although co-operation with BOAC continued. During the early years of its existence TEAL operated flying-boats, although these

were later replaced by Lockheed Electras. Australia withdrew from the partnership in 1961, and in 1965 the present title was adopted. The airline began to expand at this time, introducing Douglas DC-8s and developing routes to the Far East and the United States in addition to those to Australia. Later McDonnell Douglas DC-10s supplemented and then replaced the DC-8s.

It did not operate domestic services for many years, because a domestic airline that was also owned by the government – New Zealand National Airways (trading as National Airways) – had been formed after World War Two. ANZ bought stakes in Mount Cook Airline (qv) and SAFEAIR, with the latter flying Bristol 170 Freighters on vehicle ferry and livestock flights across the Cook Straits between the South and North Islands. National Airways, by this time operating a fleet of Boeing 737s, was merged into ANZ in 1978.

ANZ was privatised in 1988, with Brierley Investments taking 35 per cent, Qantas (qv) 19.9 per cent, American Airlines (qv) 7.5 per cent, and Japan Airlines (qv) 7.5 per cent. Brierley have since increased their share to 41.8 per cent, and while Qantas retains its stake, both American and JAL have sold theirs. More recently, in 1996, ANZ has acquired a 50 per cent shareholding in Ansett Australia (qv), which forced the Ansett Group to sell its share in Ansett New Zealand (qv) to prevent a domestic monopoly emerging.

Today, Air New Zealand has an extensive network, reaching almost 30 domestic points as well as destinations in Australia, South-East Asia, the United States, and Europe. Feeder services are operated under the name Air New Zealand Link by a subsidiary, Air Nelson (qv).

Executive Directors & Officers: Bob Matthew, Chairman; James McCrea, Managing Director & Chief Executive Officer; Robert Nazarian, Chief Financial Officer; Mike Flanagan, Director, Strategic Planning; Ron Tannack, General Manager Operations, International; Paul Bowe, General Manager, National Airline; Peter Clark, General Manager, Mount Cook; Grant Lilly, General Manager, New Zealand & Australia; Peter Elmsly, General Manager, Cargo; Ian Diamond, General Manager, Engineering; Garth Briggs, General Manager, Information Services; Brendan Fitzgerald, General Manager, Terminal Services; John Gribble, General Manager, Portfolio Businesses; Graeme McDowall, General Manager, Government & International Affairs; Tony Marks, General Manager, Sales & Marketing International; Trevor Rainham, General Manager, Catering.

HQ Airport & Main Base: Auckland

Radio callsign: NEW ZEALAND

Designator: NZ/ANZ

Employees: 9,929

Main destinations served: Serves 28 domestic points as well as flights from Auckland, Christchurch and Wellington to international destinations including Apia, Bangkok, Brisbane, Cairns, Denpasar (Bali), Frankfurt, Fukuoka, Hobart, Hong Kong, Honolulu, London Heathrow, Los Angeles, Melbourne, Nadi, Nagoya, Norfolk Island, Noumea, Osaka, Papeete, Perth, Rarotonga, Seoul, Singapore, Sydney, Tonga.

Annual turnover: US $2,002 million (£1,213.3 million)

Revenue passenger km pa: 1,655 million

Passengers pa: 6,591,000

LINKS WITH OTHER AIRLINES
Qantas (qv) has a 19.9 per cent shareholding.
ANZ has a 50 per cent shareholding in Ansett Australia (qv), and owns Air Nelson (qv) and Mount Cook Airline (qv).

FLEET
6 Boeing 747-400 (4 leased)
5 Boeing 747-200 (1 leased)
9 Boeing 767-300ER (4 leased)
3 Boeing 767-200ER (leased)
11 Boeing 737-200 (5 leased)
7 ATR 72 (operated on Air New Zealand Link)
12 Saab 340A (operated on Air New Zealand Link)
12 Fairchild Metroliner (operated on Air New Zealand Link)
9 Embraer EMB-110 Bandeirante (operated on Air New Zealand Link)
plus 6 Boeing 737-300 on order

ANSETT NEW ZEALAND

Ansett New Zealand Ltd

Incorporated: 1985

HISTORY
Originally founded in 1985 as Newmans Air, this airline adopted its present title in 1987 after becoming part of the Ansett Group, and operated as a subsidiary of Ansett Australia (qv). Ownership passed from Ansett to News Corporation in 1996 after Air

New Zealand bought TNT's 50 per cent shareholding in Ansett in order to maintain competition on domestic air services.

Executive Directors & Officers: Doddrell, Chief Executive Officer; Marko Bogoievski, Chief Financial Officer.

HQ Airport & Main Base: Auckland

Designator: AN

Employees: 1,200

Main destinations served: Serves 12 domestic destinations including Auckland, Wellington, Christchurch, and Nelson.

LINKS WITH OTHER AIRLINES
Marketing alliances with Cathay Pacific (qv), Malaysia Airlines (qv), and United Airlines (qv).

FLEET
9 British Aerospace 146-300
1 British Aerospace 146-200QC
4 de Havilland Dash 8-100

MOUNT COOK AIRLINE

Mount Cook Airline Ltd

Incorporated: 1920

HISTORY
Originally founded in 1920 as New Zealand Aero Transport, Mount Cook has evolved into a domestic scheduled service operator which is now wholly-owned by Air New Zealand (qv), and with many of its services operated under the Air New Zealand Link banner. Since its acquisition by ANZ it has been steadily replacing its British Aerospace 748s, of which it had eight at one stage.

Executive Directors & Officers: Peter Clark, General Manager.

HQ Airport & Main Base: Christchurch

Radio callsign: MOUNTCOOK

Designator: NM/NZM (or Air New Zealand NZ/ANZ)

Employees: 300

Main destinations served: More than a dozen domestic destinations.

Annual turnover: Included in the figures for Air New Zealand.

LINKS WITH OTHER AIRLINES
A wholly-owned subsidiary of Air New Zealand (qv).

FLEET
7 ATR 72 (operated on Air New Zealand
Link)
3 British Aerospace 748
3 Pilatus PC-6 Turbo Porter
plus Cessna and Piper light aircraft for air
taxi/sight seeing flights.

Nigeria – 5N

FLASH AIRLINES

Flash Airlines

Incorporated: 1992

HISTORY
A subsidiary of MK Airlines (qv), Flash
operates cargo services to the UK.

HQ Airport & Main Base: Benin City

Radio callsign: FLASH

Designator: 7K/FSH

Main destinations served: London
Stansted.

LINKS WITH OTHER AIRLINES
A subsidiary of MK Airlines (qv).

FLEET
5 McDonnell Douglas DC-8-50 (possibly
provided by MK)

KABO AIR

Kabo Air

Incorporated: 1980

HISTORY
A Nigerian domestic airline, Kabo Air was
founded in 1980 and commenced operations the following year, developing a network of services from its base at Kano and
using two Boeing 727s and a McDonnell
Douglas DC-8. The airline also undertakes
international charters, including pilgrimage flights to Saudi Arabia. It is named
after its founder, the current chairman.

Executive Directors & Officers: Alhaji
Dan Kabo, Chairman; Thomas Barnabas,
Managing Director; Alhaji Mohammed D.
Hassan, Director, Hadj Affairs.

HQ Airport & Main Base: Kano

Radio callsign: KABO

Designator: KO/QNK

Main destinations served: Scheduled
flights linking ten domestic destinations,
plus international charters.

FLEET
2 Boeing 747-100 (leased)
6 Boeing 727-200
2 Boeing 727-100
3 British Aerospace One-Eleven 400
7 British Aerospace One-Eleven 200

MAINA AIR

Maina Air

Incorporated: 1994

HISTORY
Maina Air operates passenger and cargo
charters, and has a small domestic
scheduled network.

Executive Directors & Officers: Usman
Lawan, Chairman; Kingston McGreen,
Managing Director.

HQ Airport & Main Base: Lagos

Radio callsign: MAINA AIR

Designator: MNI

Main destinations served: International
charters plus a five point domestic route
network.

FLEET
1 Ilyushin Il-76
5 Tupolev Tu-134
2 Yakovlev Yak-42

NIGERIA AIRWAYS

Nigeria Airways Ltd

Incorporated: 1958

HISTORY
Nigeria Airways dates from 1958, when it
was formed to take over the routes operated from Nigeria by the West African
Airways Corporation, or WAAC, which had
been formed in 1946 by the governments
of Nigeria, the Gold Coast (now Ghana),
Sierra Leone, and Gambia, when these
were all British colonies.

The core of the initial West African
routes were those which had been developed by the Royal Air Force during World
War Two. In Nigeria the airline also took
over the Lagos–Kano service of Nigeria Air
Services, and then added extensions from
Lagos to Freetown, Bathurst, and Dakar. A
further boost came in 1950, when the
British Colonial office called upon the airline to operate a trans-Africa service to
Khartoum, and for this and the Dakar service the airline purchased a number of
Bristol Wayfarers, the all-passenger
version of the Bristol 170 Freighter. The

remaining routes at this time were oper-
ated by de Havilland Doves. In 1956 the
Wayfarers were replaced by much older
Douglas DC-3s and by de Havilland
Herons, which were also replaced shortly
afterwards by DC-3s.

The new Nigeria Airways inherited this
fleet and continued to operate it until
1963, when the first of the airline's Fokker
F-27 Friendships arrived, initially working
the Lagos–Dakar service but then gradually taking over the domestic services as
well. Even before its foundation, from
1957 a 'pool' service was operated from
Lagos to London with BOAC (British
Overseas Airways Corporation), using the
latter's aircraft; initially Canadair
Argonauts (licence-built DC-4s with Rolls-
Royce Merlin engines) were used, followed briefly by Boeing Stratocruisers,
then Bristol Britannias, de Havilland
Comet 4s, and then Vickers VC.10s. This
arrangement soon had its counterpart in a
service between Lagos and New York,
operated with Pan American World
Airways using that airline's Douglas
DC-8s.

Ownership of Nigeria Airways at the
time of its creation in 1958 was with the
Nigerian Government (51 per cent), BOAC
(32.6 per cent), and Elder Dempster Lines,
but in 1961 the Government took complete control of the airline, which it retains
to this day. Under its new ownership the
airline started to acquire its own jet equipment, initially Boeing 707s and then
Boeing 737s, later adding Airbus A310 and
McDonnell Douglas DC-10 aircraft. This
rapid expansion, fuelled by a booming
economy with revenue from crude oil production, nevertheless resulted in a period
of financial difficulties during the late-
1980s, which called for reorganisation and
other remedial measures, reducing the
workforce and suspending unprofitable
services.

Today, the airline maintains a considerable network of domestic services as well
as routes to a number of neighbouring
states. Intercontinental services are confined to a few major destinations.

Executive Directors & Officers: Group
Captain Peter N. Gana, Managing
Director.

HQ Airport & Main Base: Murtala
Muhammed Airport, Lagos

Radio callsign: NIGERIA

Designator: WT/NGA

Employees: 4,600

Main destinations served: Domestic
destinations throughout Nigeria, plus
Abidjan, Accra, Amsterdam, Banjul,

Conakry, Cotonou, Douala, Jeddah, Kinshasa, Libreville, Lone, London Heathrow, Rome, New York JFK.

FLEET
1 McDonnell Douglas DC-10-30
2 Airbus A310-200
1 Boeing 707-320C
5 Boeing 737-200

North Korea – P

AIR KORYO

Air Koryo

Incorporated: 1955

HISTORY
Air Koryo, the airline of the People's Republic of North Korea, was founded in 1955, taking over from SOKAO, a joint Soviet-Korean airline founded in 1950. Initially the new airline was known as Chosonminhang Korean Airways, but the present title was adopted in 1994. It is primarily domestic scheduled airline, although there is a limited international network, and international freight charters are flown. Given the state of the North Korean economy, it is not clear how many of the airline's aircraft are operational.

Executive Directors & Officers: Kim Yo Ung, Director General.

HQ Airport & Main Base: Pyongyang

Radio callsign: AIR KORYO

Designator: JS/KOR

Employees: 2,500

Main destinations served: Domestic destinations plus international scheduled flights from Pyongyang to: Bangkok, Beijing, Khabarovsk, Moscow.

FLEET
3 Ilyushin Il-76MD
4 Ilyushin Il-62M
4 Tupolev Tu-154B
2 Tupolev Tu-134B
4 Ilyushin Il-18
8 Antonov An-24

Norway – LN

See also Scandinavia

BRAATHENS SAFE

Braathens South American & Far East Airtransport A/S

Incorporated: 1946

HISTORY
Norway's largest airline, Braathens SAFE takes its name from its founder, Ludvig Braathen, a Norwegian shipowner. It was formed in 1946 and three Douglas DC-4

Skymasters were delivered the following year for the airline to commence charter flying. The movement of ships' crews was initially a major part of the business, and early flights were between Europe and the Middle East, these being gradually extended to the Far East. In 1949 the airline was awarded a five-year licence to fly from Norway to the Far East, the journey taking four days. Occasional charter flights were operated to Caracas in Venezuela.

Domestic air services started in 1952 using de Havilland Herons, which were soon supplemented, and eventually replaced, by Douglas DC-3s. The services to the Far East were abandoned in 1954 on the expiry of the original licence because of Norway's involvement in SAS (qv). Although the Far East scheduled services were lost, the airline continued to operate charter flights, eventually replacing the DC-4s with pressurised DC-6s, while the DC-3s were in turn replaced on the domestic routes by turboprop Fokker F-27 Friendships and, later, the jet Fokker F-28 Fellowship. Occasionally Fokker 50 aircraft are chartered from Norwegian Air Shuttle, which operates four of these aircraft and acts as a sub-carrier for several airlines in Northern Europe.

Today an all-Boeing 737 fleet is operated on domestic and international scheduled flights, with a substantial inclusive tour charter operation to resorts in the Mediterranean and the Canary Islands which account for a sixth of the airline's annual revenue. It bought a 50 per cent

This Boeing 737-400 of Braathens SAFE carries the airline's web-site address.

The most numerous version of the Boeing 737 in the Braathens' fleet is the -500, shown here over the type of terrain which makes air transport so vital within Norway.

share in Transwede Airways (qv) in 1996 and may exercise its option to purchase the remainder. During 1997 KLM (qv) acquired a 30 per cent interest in Braathens, reducing the family interest to 38.8 per cent.

Executive Directors & Officers: Arve Johnsen, Chairman; Erik G. Braathen, President & Chief Executive Officer; Geir Olsen, Senior Vice-President; Per Christiansen, Vice-President, Finance; Anders C. Fougli, Vice-President, Commercial; Svein Solberg, Vice-President, Operations; Svein K. Bertheussen, Vice-President, Technical & Maintenance; Ole Jacob Ostberg, Vice-President, Ground Operations; H. Orfeldt Pedersen, Vice-President, Electronic Data Processing; Audun Tjomsland, Vice-President, Corporate Affairs; Halfdan Haaland, Vice-President, Personnel.

HQ Airport & Main Base: Fornebu, Oslo

Radio callsign: BRAATHENS

Designator: BU/BRA

Employees: Flight-crew: 600; Cabin staff: 300; Engineering: 600; Ground staff: 2,500; Total: 4,000.

Main destinations served: Alesund, Alicante, Bergen, Billund, Bodo, Harstad/Narvik, Haugesund, Kristiansand, London Gatwick, Longyearbyen, Malaga, Molde, Murmansk, Newcastle, Rome, Roros, Stavanger, Stockholm, Tromsø, Trondheim, plus a coastal route from Stavanger to Tromsø, calling at intermediate points.
London Gatwick and Newcastle are also served from Bergen and Stavanger.

Annual turnover: US $615.8 million (£373.2 million)

Aircraft km pa: 5,106 million

Revenue passenger km pa: 3,110 million

Cargo tonne km pa: 507 million

LINKS WITH OTHER AIRLINES
Owns 50 per cent of Transwede (qv). KLM (qv) has a 30 per cent interest in Braathens.
Code-sharing with Finnair (qv).
Marketing co-operation with British Airways (qv).

FLEET
6 Boeing 737-700 (being delivered 1998–2000) (plus 10 options)
8 Boeing 737-400
21 Boeing 737-500
Of the above, 15 aircraft are owned and 12 leased

FRED OLSEN'S AIR TRANSPORT

Fred Olsen Flyselskap ASA

Incorporated: 1946

HISTORY
A subsidiary of the shipping line of the same name, Fred Olsen's Air Transport undertakes air freight charters and contract operations.

Executive Directors & Officers: Fredrik Hirsh, General Manager.

HQ Airport & Main Base: Oslo, Fornebu

Radio callsign: FREDOLSEN

Designator: FO/FOF

Employees: 110

Main destinations served: Ad hoc and contract freight charters.

FLEET
6 Lockheed L-188 Electra
1 British Aerospace 748

WIDEROE

Widerøe's Flyveselskap

Incorporated: 1934

HISTORY
Norway's oldest airline, Widerøe was formed in 1934 and operates mainly scheduled domestic services, although there are also services to neighbouring countries and charter operations. It acquired Norsk Air in 1989. At one time Widerøe counted amongst its shareholders Fred Olsen (qv), Braathens SAFE (qv), and SAS (qv).
A subsidiary is Widerøe Norsk Air, which operates three Embraer EMB-120 Brasilias.

Executive Directors & Officers: Brad Mikkelsen, President; Bjorn Eriksen, Vice-President, Operations; Gunnar Orskaug, Vice-President, Commercial; Dagfiuu Danielsen, Vice-President, Technical.

HQ Airport & Main Base: HQ at Bodo, but main bases are Bergen and Sandefjord.

Radio callsign: WIDEROE

Designator: WF/WIF

Employees: 700

Main destinations served: More than 40 airports in Norway and neighbouring countries, including Copenhagen, Gothenburg, and Oslo.

FLEET
3 de Havilland Dash 8-300
15 de Havilland Dash 8-100
3 de Havilland Dash 7
3 Embraer EMB-120 Brasilia (operated by Wideroe Norsk Air)
1 de Havilland DHC-6 Twin Otter

Oman – A40

OMAN AIR

Oman Aviation Services

Incorporated: 1981

HISTORY

Founded by the merger of what had been Gulf Air's Light Aircraft Division and Oman International Services, for the first ten years or so of its existence Oman Air operated domestic services within the Sultanate. In recent years the network has grown to include other Gulf destinations and the Indian sub-continent. Ownership is varied, with the Sultanate holding 35 per cent and private individuals the remainder.

Executive Directors & Officers: Sheikh Salin bin Abdulla Al Ghazali, Chairman; M. Bamukhalef, General Manager.

HQ Airport & Main Base: Muscat

Radio callsign: OMAN AIR

Designator: WY/OMA

Employees: 2,400

Main destinations served: Serves six domestic destinations, plus Colombo, Dubai, Karachi, Kuwait, Trivandrum.

FLEET
3 Airbus A320-200
4 Fokker F-27-500 Friendship
1 de Havilland DHC-6 Twin Otter
1 Cessna Citation II

Pakistan – AP

AERO ASIA INTERNATIONAL

Aero Asia International

Incorporated: 1993

HISTORY
A private enterprise carrier, Aero Asia International operates a small group of scheduled services and charter flights using aircraft leased from Tarom (qv).

Executive Directors & Officers: Ashfaq A. Jan, Chief Executive Officer; Arshad Jalil, Managing Director.

HQ Airport & Main Base: Karachi

Radio callsign: AERO ASIA

Designator: E4/RSO

Employees: 500

Main destinations served: Karachi to six domestic destinations.

FLEET
1 Boeing 707-300C (leased)
6 Rombac One-Eleven 500 (leased)

Largest aircraft in the PIA (Pakistan International) fleet are Boeing 747-200s for intercontinental services.

PIA PAKISTAN

Pakistan International Airlines Corporation

Incorporated: 1954

HISTORY
Pakistan International Airlines was established in 1954, commencing operations with a single Lockheed Super Constellation which operated a direct service between West and East Pakistan (now Bangladesh). The following year the airline merged with Orient Airways at the behest of the Pakistani Government, creating the present Pakistan International Airlines Corporation. It was also in 1955 that the airline introduced its first international service, operating Lockheed Constellations from Karachi to London via Cairo and Rome, while Douglas DC-3s operated domestic services.

Turboprop operations started in 1959 with the arrival of the airline's first Vickers Viscounts, and in 1960 these were joined by Fokker F-27 friendships, which started to replace the DC-3s. Jet operations began in 1960 using a wet-leased Boeing 707 from Pan American, and a service between Karachi and New York was introduced in 1961. PIA's own Boeing 720s were introduced in 1962. The difficult nature of the terrain in East Pakistan meant that fixed wing operations were difficult, so in 1962, PIA introduced three Sikorsky S-61 helicopters to the network, although by 1966 traffic, and the runways, had improved sufficiently for fixed-wing operations to take over. Meanwhile, in 1963 PIA had become the first airline from the non-Communist world to operate to Beijing.

During the late-1960s the fleet was improved with the delivery of Boeing 707-320s and Hawker Siddeley Trident 1E airliners, although the Tridents were later sold to CAAC, the Communist Chinese airline of the day.

The war of December 1971 between Pakistan and India saw East Pakistan break away and establish itself as an independent nation, thus at a stroke cutting off a significant part of PIA's domestic network and forcing changes to some international services as well. PIA was then, from 1972 onwards, closely involved with the founding and early years of Air Malta (qv), seconding a management team to the airline and wet-leasing two Boeing 720s in 1973, the same year that the first McDonnell Douglas DC-10s were delivered. Two years later the first Boeing 747s were introduced, initially using leased aircraft.

In addition to its connection with Air Malta, PIA was also involved in establishing Somali Airlines (qv) and Yemen Airways, predecessor of today's Yemenia (qv).

Today PIA continues to operate an intensive domestic network – having resisted the fashion towards passing the less busy routes to a subsidiary or a franchisee – as well as a growing international network. The fleet has become a mixture of Boeing and Airbus types, supported by Fokker F-27s and de Havilland Twin Otters. It is owned 56 per cent by the state, with the remainder of the shares held by private institutions, further privatisation having been postponed for the time being.

Executive Directors & Officers: Shahid Khagan Abbabi, Chairman; M. Nawaz

The large capacity of the Airbus A300B4 is useful on PIA's regional routes, especially to the Gulf.

Tiwana, Managing Director; Arshad Mahmud, Deputy Managing Director, Finance; Dr S. Mir Muhammad Shah, Deputy Managing Director, Planning, Monitoring & Control; Jalaluddin, Director, Finance; Badshah Gul, Director, Corporate Planning; Jawaid Akhtar Khan, Director, Flight Services; S.M. Tareen, Director, Marketing; Kaleem Malik, Director, Airport Services; Shahid Islam, Director, Information Systems; Captain S.S. Zaman, Director, Flight Operations; Imran A. Khan, Director, Stores & Purchases; Ali Abbas Brohi, Director,

General Services; Salam Khan, Director, Engineering & Maintenance; Air Vice-Marshal Muhammad Afzal, Director, Precision Engineering & Maintenance; Captain Humayun Jameel, General Manager, Administration.

HQ Airport & Main Base: Karachi, with additional hubs at Islamabad, Lahore, and Peshawar.

Radio callsign: PAKISTAN

Designator: PK/PIA

Employees: Flight-crew: 759; Cabin staff:

1,893; Engineering: 819; Ground staff: 18,206; Total: 20,977.

Main destinations served: 36 domestic destinations, plus Abu Dhabi, Al-Ain, Almaty, Amman, Amsterdam, Ashkabad, Athens, Baku, Bahrain, Bangkok, Beijing, Bombay, Cairo, Chicago O'Hare, Colombo, Copenhagen, Damascus, Dhahran, Delhi, Dhaka, Doha, Dubai*, Frankfurt*, Istanbul*, Jakarta, Jeddah, Kathmandu, Kuala Lumpur, Kuwait, London Heathrow, Male, Manchester, Manila, Moscow, Muscat, Nairobi, New York JFK, Paris CDG, Ras Al Khaimah, Riyadh, Rome, Sharjah, Singapore, Tehran, Tokyo, Toronto, Washington, Yangon (Rangoon), Zürich.
* freighter service also.

Annual turnover: US $860 million ($521.2 million)

Aircraft km pa: 72.5 million

Revenue passenger km pa: 10,382.4 million

Cargo tonne km pa: 1,408.3 million

Passengers pa: 5.5 million

FLEET
8 Boeing 747-200B
9 Airbus A300B4 (2 leased)
6 Airbus A310-300
2 Boeing 707-320F
6 Boeing 737-300
13 Fokker F-27-200/400 Friendship
2 de Havilland DHC-6 Twin Otter

PIA also operates the A300's smaller sister, the A310-300.

Panama – HP

AEROPERLAS

Aérolineas Pacifico Atlantico SA

Incorporated: 1969

HISTORY
Grandly named, reflecting the country's strategic position between two continents and two oceans, AéroPerlas was founded in 1969 by the Panamanian Government and remained in state hands until 1987, when it was sold to Raul Espinosa. More recently it has acquired another airline, Alas Chircanas, and absorbed its equipment and services. Operations are primarily domestic scheduled and international charter.

Executive Directors & Officers: George Novey, Chairman, President & Chief Executive Officer; Eduardo Stagg, General Manager & Chief Operating Officer.

HQ Airport & Main Base: Panama City

Radio callsign: AEROPERLAS

Designator: WL/APP

Employees: 260

Main destinations served: Some 15 domestic destinations.

LINKS WITH OTHER AIRLINES
Marketing alliance with American Airlines (qv).

FLEET
7 Short 360-200
1 Embraer EMB-110 Bandeirante
6 de Havilland DHC-6 Twin Otter

COPA

Compañia Panameña de Aviación SA

Incorporated: 1944

HISTORY
Founded by Pan American in 1944, COPA started scheduled services in 1947. It later became Panamanian-owned and has outlived its founding airline. Domestic and international scheduled services are operated, as well as international charters.

Executive Directors & Officers: Alberto Motta, Chairman & President; Pedro Heilbron, Vice-President.

HQ Airport & Main Base: Panama City

Radio callsign: COPA

Designator: CM/CMP

Employees: 1,260

Main destinations served: A small domestic network, plus Bogotá, Guatemala City, Kingston, Managua, Mexico City, Miami, Montego Bay, Port-au-Prince, Quito, San José, San Juan, San Salvador, Santo Domingo.

FLEET
13 Boeing 737-200Adv

Papua New Guinea – P2

AIR NUIGINI

Air Nuigini

Incorporated: 1973

HISTORY
Air Nuigini was founded in 1973 as a joint venture between the New Guinea Government, with 60 per cent of the shares, and the then three main Australia airlines: Qantas (qv), with 12 per cent; Ansett (qv), with 16 per cent; and TAA Trans Australia, with 12 per cent. It eventually became completely government-controlled (through a National Airlines Commission) after the Qantas and TAA shares had been purchased in 1976, followed by those of Ansett in 1980.

There is an extensive domestic network, reflecting the difficult terrain of the island, with regional international services. Plans to privatise the airline have been postponed.

Executive Directors & Officers: Joseph Tauvasa, Chairman; Moses Maladina, Managing Director; Captain Paun Nonggo'r, Operations Director; John Lynch, Engineering & Maintenance Director; Simon Foo, Director, Commercial/Customer Services.

HQ Airport & Main Base: Port Moresby

Radio callsign: NUIGINI

Designator: PX/ANG

Employees: 363

Main destinations served: More than 20 domestic destinations including Rabaul, plus Brisbane, Cairns, Hong Kong, Manila, Singapore, Sydney.

LINKS WITH OTHER AIRLINES
Marketing alliances with Philippine Airlines (qv), Singapore Airlines (qv), and Solomon Islands Airways.

FLEET
2 Airbus A310-300
2 Fokker F-28-4000 Fellowship
6 Fokker F-28-1000 Fellowship
2 de Havilland Dash 7

Paraguay – ZP

LAPSA AIR PARAGUAY

Lineas Aéreas Paraguayas SA

Incorporated: 1962

HISTORY
LAPSA, the national airline of Paraguay, was founded in 1962 and commenced operations in August 1963. Initially it was operated by air force officers and operated only on domestic services, but an international network was also developed whilst still under air force control. The airline has since passed into civilian hands, and this process was accelerated by the sale of an 80 per cent stake to a consortium organised by the Ecuadorian airline SAESA (qv) in 1994.

Executive Directors & Officers: Miguel Candia, Managing Director; Oscar Johansen, Chief Financial Officer; Anibal Gomez de la Fuerte, Vice-President, Operations; Javier Hikecthier, Vice-President, Route Planning; Francisco Rey, Vice-President, Fleet Planning.

HQ Airport & Main Base: Asunscion

Designator: PZ/LAP

Employees: 1,000

Main destinations served: Domestic services, plus Brussels, Buenos Aires, Frankfurt, Lima, Madrid, Miami, Montevideo, Rio de Janeiro, Santa Cruz de la Sierra, São Paulo, Santiago de Chile.

LINKS WITH OTHER AIRLINES
SEATA (qv) has an 80 per cent shareholding.
Marketing alliances with AéroPeru (qv), Aérolineas Argentinas (qv), and LAN Chile (qv).

FLEET
2 Airbus A310-300
3 Airbus A320-200
2 Boeing 737-200
2 Fokker 100

AERO CONTINENTE

Compañia Aéro Continente

Incorporated: 1992

HISTORY
A passenger charter airline operating domestic and international flights, Aéro Continente is owned by the Zevallos family.

Executive Directors & Officers:
Fernando Zevallos, President; Sara Zevallos, Vice-President, Finance; Milagros Zevallos, Vice-President, Commercial; Ricardo Zevallos, Vice-President, Maintenance.

HQ Airport & Main Base: Lima

Radio callsign: AERO CONTINENTE

Designator: N6/ACQ

Employees: 500

Main destinations served: Charters.

FLEET
1 Lockheed L-1011 TriStar
3 Boeing 727-100
3 Boeing 737-200
1 Fokker F-28 Fellowship
2 Fairchild FH-227

AERONAVES DEL PERU

Aéronaves del Peru

Incorporated: 1965

HISTORY
Founded in 1965, Aéronaves did not begin operations until 1971. Its business is primarily international cargo charters, but there is a regular service via Iquitos to Miami.

Executive Directors & Officers: Alfredo Zanatti, President.

HQ Airport & Main Base: Lima

Designator: XX/WPL

Main destinations served: International cargo charter, plus Lima and Iquitos to Miami.

FLEET
1 McDonnell Douglas DC-8-61F
1 McDonnell Douglas DC-8-50F
2 Boeing 707-320C

AEROPERU

Empresa de Transporte Aéro del Peru

Incorporated: 1973

HISTORY
Peru's national airline, AéroPeru was founded by the Peruvian Government in 1973 on the merger of SATCO, which had been operated by the Peruvian Air Force, and TANS. SATCO dated from 1931, when it had been founded as Lineas Aéreas Nacionales, later becoming TAM (Transportes Aéreos Militares). In 1960 TAM was divided into SATCO to operate trunk routes, and TANS to provide feeder services.

AéroPeru was denationalised in 1981, since when CINTRA, owners of Aéromexico (qv) and Mexicana (qv), acquired a 47 per shareholding, although the airline is reported as having negative equity.

Executive Directors & Officers:
Roberto Abusada, President; Luis Ballen, Chairman, Finance; Jaan Albrecht, Vice-President, Operations; Manuel Cordero, Vice-President, Maintenance; Alejandro Gomez Monroy, General Manager.

HQ Airport & Main Base: Lima

Radio callsign: AEROPERU

Designator: PL/PLI

Employees: 1,280

Main destinations served: Eight domestic destinations including Iquitos, plus Asuncion, Bucaramanga, Bogotá, Buenos Aires, Cali, Cochabamba, Guatemala City, La Paz, Maracaibo, Mexico City, Panama City Tocumen, Quito, Rio de Janeiro, Santa Cruz (Bolivia), Santiago Comordoro, São Paulo.

Revenue passenger km pa: 1,664 million

Passengers pa: 1 million plus

LINKS WITH OTHER AIRLINES
Code-sharing and frequent flyer programme with Aéromexico (qv).

FLEET
2 Boeing 757-200 (leased)
3 Boeing 727-200 (leased)
3 Boeing 727-100
1 Fokker F-28-1000

AMERICANA

Americana de Aviación

Incorporated: 1991

HISTORY
Primarily a domestic scheduled airline, Americana also operates international charters.

Executive Directors & Officers:
Leandro Chiok, Chairman; Augusto Dalmau, Commercial Director; Guido Zavalaga, Operations Director.

HQ Airport & Main Base: Lima

Radio callsign: AMERICANA

Designator: 8A/ANE

Main destinations served: Domestic scheduled.

FLEET
3 Boeing 727-200
4 Boeing 727-100

FAUCETT PERU

Compañia de Aviación Faucett

Incorporated: 1928

HISTORY
One of the oldest airlines in Latin America, Faucett takes its name from its founder, the eponymous American Elmer J. Faucett. Throughout its existence it has been primarily a domestic scheduled carrier, and is today Peruvian-owned.

Executive Directors & Officers: Roberto Leigh, President; Juan Carlos Nunez, General Manager; Fernando Nunez, Vice-President, Finance; Rebeca Menacho Puelles, Vice-President, Commercial.

HQ Airport & Main Base: Lima

Radio callsign: CHARLIE FOXTROT

Designator: CF/CFP

Employees: 1,000

Main destinations served: Serves 15 domestic destinations, including Iquitos, and operates internationally from Lima and Iquitos to Miami.

FLEET
1 Lockheed L-1011 TriStar 1
1 Boeing 727-100
4 Boeing 737-200
3 Boeing 737-100

ABOITIZ AIR TRANSPORT

Aboitiz Air Transport Corporation

Incorporated: 1988

HISTORY

Aboitiz Air Transport is a domestic and regional international air charter operator, owned by its chairman.

Executive Directors & Officers: Jon Ramon Aboitiz, Chairman.

HQ Airport & Main Base: Manila

Radio callsign: ABAIR

Designator: BO/BOI

FLEET
1 Lockheed L-100 Hercules
7 NAMC YS-11

AIR PHILIPPINES

Air Philippines Corporation

Incorporated: 1995

HISTORY

A relatively new airline, Air Philippines was founded in 1995, and operations started the following year. Scheduled domestic and international charter flights are operated.

Executive Directors & Officers:
General Lizandro Abadia, Chairman; Major-General Rodolfo S. Estrellado, President & Chief Executive Officer; General Jovenar N. Reambillo, Chief Operating Officer; Sherwin T. Gatchalian, Senior Vice-President, Finance & Treasury; Atty. Cristina Portia B. Mojica, Senior Vice-President, Corporate Affairs & Administration; Captain Mario Jesus M. Calma, Vice-President, Operations; Morris B. Pineda, Vice-President, Finance; Danilo F. Celis, Vice-President, Marketing & Services; Colonel Edilberto H. Platon, Vice-President, Special Projects; Annabele H. Mayor, Vice-President, Corporate Planning; Alex C. Patrana, Vice-President, Safety & Security; Atty. Arthur Ponzaran, Corporate Secretary.

HQ Airport & Main Base: HQ at Subic Bay International Airport, main hub at Manila.

Radio callsign: ORIENT PACIFIC

Designator: 3G/GAP

Employees: Flight-crew: 56; Cabin staff: 114; Engineering: 60; Ground staff: 286; Total: 600.

Main destinations served: Manila to Cebu, Cotabato, Davao, Iloilo, Kalibo, Legaspi, Naga, Puerto Princesa, Subic Bay, Zamboanga.

Aircraft km pa: 2.3 million

Revenue passenger km pa: 344,536 million

Cargo tonne km pa: 6,053.7 million

FLEET
9 Boeing 737-200
4 NAMC YS-11

PAL PHILIPPINE AIRLINES

Philippine Airlines Corporation

Incorporated: 1941

HISTORY

Although Philippine Airlines (or PAL) was founded in February 1941 and commenced operations in March, services had to be abandoned on the outbreak of World War Two in the Pacific, and the subsequent Japanese occupation of the Philippines. Services restarted in 1946, and the airline was soon operating an extensive domestic network as well as international services. However, the latter were dropped in 1954 and the airline spent the next eight years concentrating on its domestic routes. The return to international services in 1962 saw routes established initially to other destinations in the Far East, and then to the United States, before spreading to Europe. The airline used a fleet of Douglas DC-8s for its longer-haul routes during the 1960s and 1970s, augmented by British Aerospace One-Elevens and 748s on domestic and regional services.

Today the airline's main investor is PR Holdings, a group of Philippine financial institutions, with 67 per cent of the shares, while the Philippine Government holds a 33 per cent stake. The current fleet is mainly of Boeing and Airbus manufacture, with the McDonnell Douglas MD-11 fleet, leased from World Airways (qv), cut from four to two in 1997 when PAL withdrew its services from Manila to Los Angeles and New York Newark. It is the world's 50th largest airline on the basis of annual turnover.

Executive Directors & Officers: Lucio Tan, Chairman; José Antonio Garcia, President; Romeo David, Executive Vice-President; Jamie J. Bautista, Senior Vice-President & Chief Financial Officer; Avelino L. Zapanta, Senior Vice-President, Sales; Antonio V. Ocampo, Senior Vice-President, Corporate Counsel; Ernesto C. Garcia, Senior Vice-President, Planning; Manolo E. Aquino, Senior Vice-President, Administration & Procurement; Pastor C.

Pangilinan, Senior Vice-President, Service Support; Ponciano B. Tuano, Senior Vice-President, Engineering & Maintenance.

HQ Airport & Main Base: Manila

Radio callsign: PHILIPPINE

Designator: PR/PAL

Employees: 14,525

Main destinations served: More than 20 domestic destinations, plus Amsterdam, Bandar Seri Begawan, Bangkok, Brisbane, Dhahran, Dubai, Frankfurt, Guam, Ho Chi Minh City, Hong Kong, Honolulu, Karachi, Kuala Lumpur, London Heathrow, Melbourne, Paris CDG, Riyadh, Rome, San Francisco, Seoul, Singapore, Sydney, Taipei, Tokyo.

Annual turnover: US $1,074 million (£650.9 million)

FLEET
10 Boeing 747-400
2 McDonnell Douglas MD-11 (leased from World Airways)
3 Boeing 747-200
10 Airbus A340-300
4 Airbus A340-200
8 Airbus A330-300
12 Airbus A300B4
12 Airbus A320-200
11 Boeing 737-300
10 Fokker 50

Poland – SP

LOT POLISH AIRLINES

LOT – Polski Linie Lotnicze

Incorporated: 1929

HISTORY

Poland's state-owned flag carrier, LOT was formed by the Polish Government in 1929 to take over two private enterprise airlines, Aerolot and Aero, both of which dated from the early-1920s. The two airlines had operated domestic services, and LOT continued these before introducing its first international service in 1930, operating to neighbouring states in Eastern Europe and, later, Greece. Steady progress was made during the 1930s, and by the outbreak of World War Two in Europe in 1939 LOT's network had reached many European capitals and the airline had a modern fleet of Douglas DC-2s and Lockheed Electras.

Operations were suspended following

the German and Soviet invasion of Poland, although many aircraft had been flown to the United Kingdom once the invasion started. LOT was reformed in March 1945 using ex-Polish Air Force Lisunov Li-2s – DC-3s built under licence in the Soviet Union – and operations were supported by Soviet technical assistance. The route network expanded throughout the late-1940s and the 1950s, although, as a reflection of the changed political scene, services to Warsaw Pact destinations took precedence. Some Convair 240s were acquired, but aircraft of Soviet manufacture predominated in the fleet, starting with Ilyushin Il-12 and Il-14 airliners, followed by Ilyushin Il-18s before the first jets, Tupolev Tu-134s, arrived, followed in turn by the long-range Ilyushin Il-62. By the early-1970s the route network extended throughout Europe and the Middle East.

After the break-up of the Warsaw Pact western equipment started to appear in the fleet, including Boeing 767s for transatlantic operations. However, foreign exchange problems and the relatively high capital cost of new European and American aircraft meant that Tupolev Tu-154s and Antonov An-24s still figured prominently in the fleet for some years.

Although the state still owns LOT, the airline's status has been changed to a limited company in order to permit eventual privatisation. The fleet is now formed entirely of modern western aircraft. In July 1997 a low-cost feeder operation, EUROLOT, was established, to which LOT's eight ATR 72-200 aircraft have been transferred.

Executive Directors & Officers: Jan Litynski, President; Bazyli Samojlik, Vice-President, Finance; Tadeusz Postepski, Vice-President, Commercial; Andrzej Skodownik, Vice-President, Operations, & Director, Technical.

HQ Airport & Main Base: Warsaw

Radio callsign: POLLOT

Designator: LO/LOT

Employees: 4,100

Main destinations served: Serves six domestic destinations, plus Amsterdam, Athens, Bangkok, Beirut, Belgrade, Berlin, Budapest, Bucharest, Brussels, Cairo, Casablanca, Chicago O'Hare, Copenhagen, Damascus, Dubai, Düsseldorf, Frankfurt, Geneva, Hamburg, Helsinki, Larnaca, London Heathrow, Milan, Moscow, New York JFK, New York Newark, Oslo, Paris CDG, Rome, Sofia, Split, Stockholm, Vienna, Zagreb, Zürich.

LINKS WITH OTHER AIRLINES
Marketing alliance with American Airlines (qv) and DHL (qv) (freight).

FLEET
3 Boeing 767-300ER
2 Boeing 767-200
6 Boeing 737-400
4 Boeing 737-300
6 Boeing 737-500
8 AI(R) ATR 72-300 (operated by EUROLOT)

Portugal – CS

PORTUGALIA

Companhia Portuguesa de Transportes Aéreos SA

Incorporated: 1990

HISTORY
A private enterprise Portuguese airline, Portugalia was founded in 1990 and operates scheduled and charter flights, mainly from Lisbon but also from Faro and Oporto.

Executive Directors & Officers: João Ribiro da Fonseca, Chairman, President & Chief Executive Officer.

HQ Airport & Main Base: Lisbon, with further bases at Faro and Oporto.

Radio callsign: PORTUGALIA

Designator: NI/PGA

Employees: 577

Main destinations served: Domestic services, plus charters throughout Europe.

FLEET
6 Fokker 100
1 Avro RJ70
3 Embraer EMB-145

SATA AIR ACORES

Servicion Açoreano de Transports Aéreos SA

Incorporated: 1941

HISTORY
This airline for the Azores in the North Atlantic started out in 1941 as a study group, when local people founded the Azorean Society of Aeronautic Study, or Sociedada Açoreana de Estudos Aéreos. Its first services did not commence until 1947, when a Beechcraft AT11 was introduced on an internal service within the islands. The following year a de Havilland

Dove was added to the fleet, where it remained until 1971 – by which time a Douglas DC-3 Dakota was also operated – and was then replaced by a British Aerospace 748 turboprop airliner.

The airline was taken over by the Azores regional government in 1980, when the current title was adopted. It continued to develop, and today runs services to all of the islands within the Azores, as well as operating charter flights to Europe and the United States. It is likely to be privatised in the near future.

Executive Directors & Officers: Manual Antonio Carvalho Cansado, President; Antonio Mauricio do Couto Tavares de Sousa, Vice-President.

HQ Airport & Main Base: Ponta Delgada

Radio callsign: SATA

Designator: SP/SAT

Employees: Flight-crew: 25; Cabin staff: 14; Engineering: 64; Ground staff: 352; Total: 455.

Main destinations served: Serves all nine islands in the Azores, plus charters to Europe, especially Lisbon, Madeira, as well as Boston and Toronto.

Annual turnover: US $31.3 million (£19 million)

Aircraft km pa: 1,634,349

Revenue passenger km pa: 59.1 million

Cargo tonne km pa: 5,763,962

FLEET
1 Boeing 737-300 (leased)
3 British Aerospace ATP
1 Dornier Do.228 (leased)

TAP AIR PORTUGAL

Transportes Aéreos Portugueses SA

Incorporated: 1944

HISTORY
Portugal's national carrier, TAP was founded in 1944 by the Portuguese Government, although operations did not begin until two years later, when Douglas DC-3s started flying between Lisbon and Madrid, and, later the same year, to the colonies of Angola and Mozambique. The European network expanded during the late-1940s, reaching London in 1949. Douglas DC-4s were introduced for the longer-haul routes, especially to southern

Africa. In 1953 the airline was given private company status, allowing its directors greater commercial freedom.

The important colonial services were much improved in 1955 with the arrival of three Lockheed Super Constellations, which displaced the three DC-4s for other duties, while six DC-3s remained in the fleet. The purchase of modern aircraft proved difficult for what was at the time one of Western Europe's poorest nations, so in 1959 a pool arrangement was reached with BEA (British European Airways) on the Lisbon–London route, enabling both airlines to use BEA's Vickers Viscounts. This was followed by a similar arrangement with Air France (qv) on the Lisbon–Paris service using the French airline's Sud Aviation Caravelles. Another pool agreement came the following year, using Douglas DC-7Cs of Panair do Brasil on the Lisbon–Rio de Janeiro route.

TAP eventually introduced its own jet equipment in 1962, when the first of three Caravelles entered service. These were followed by Boeing 707-320s in 1966, and by Boeing 727s in 1968. The airline was nationalised in 1975 following political upheaval in Portugal. The name was changed to TAP Air Portugal in 1978. It became a public limited company in 1991, although the state is still the majority shareholder.

Executive Directors & Officers: Eng Manuel Ferreira Lima, President; Dr Orlanda Sampaio, Secretary General; Dr Mario Matos, Finance Director General; Eng Eduardo Branco, Commercial Director General; Captain Luis Faria, Flight Operations Director General; Dr Rogerio Fidalgo, Ground-Handling Director General; Dr Rocha Pimental, Personnel Director General; Eng Jorge Sobral, Maintenance & Engineering Director General; Dr Marques da Cruz, Corporate Planning & Control Director General.

HQ Airport & Main Base: Lisbon

Radio callsign: AIR PORTUGAL

Top: *Largest aircraft in the TAP Air Portugal fleet are the airline's four Airbus A340-300s, one of which is seen awaiting passengers at Lisbon.*

Middle: *The Airbus A310-300 has a long range, useful for operations into Africa or the busier European routes.*

Bottom: *Airbus A320-200s operate alongside Boeing 737s on TAP's European routes.*

Designator: TP/TAP

Employees: Flight-crew: 448; Cabin staff: 1,155; Engineering: 1,567; Ground staff: 4,278; Total: 7,448.

Main destinations served: Abidjan, Amsterdam, Athens, Azores, Barcelona, Berlin, Bissau, Bologna, Brazzaville, Brussels, Caracas, Copenhagen, Curaçao, Dakar, Faro, Frankfurt, Geneva, Hamburg, Johannesburg, Kinshasa, London, Luanda, Luxembourg, Lyons, Madeira, Madrid, Maputo, Milan, Munich, New York JFK, Nice, Oporto, Oslo, Paris CDG, Recife, Rio de Janeiro, Rome, Sal, Salvador de Bada Bahia, Santo Domingo, São Paulo, São Tomé, Stockholm, Vienna, Zürich.

Annual turnover: US $1,097 million (£664.8 million)

Aircraft km pa: 90.4 million

Cargo tonnes pa: 72.8 million

Passengers pa: 4,029,061

LINKS WITH OTHER AIRLINES
Code-sharing with Aer Lingus (qv), Air Afrique (qv), British Midland (qv), Delta Airlines (qv), Hamburg Airlines (qv), LAM, Luxair (qv), Portugalia (qv), South African Airways (qv), and TAAG (qv).

FLEET
4 Airbus A340-300
5 Airbus A310-300 (leased)
6 Airbus A320-200 (leased)
10 Boeing 737-300 (leased)
3 Boeing 737-200Adv (leased)
1 Boeing 737-200C (leased)
4 Airbus A319
plus 14 on order, which may replace some 737s

Qatar – A7

QATAR AIRWAYS

Qatar Airways

Incorporated: 1993

HISTORY
The national airline of Qatar is privately-owned and dates from 1993, although operations did not begin until January 1994. It operates international services as far afield as London and Osaka.

Executive Directors & Officers: Dr Saeed Al-Suleiman, Chief Executive Officer.

HQ Airport & Main Base: Doha

Radio callsign: QATARI

Designator: Q7/QTR

Employees: 500

Main destinations served: Abu Dhabi, Bangkok, Cairo, Dubai, Khartoum, Kuwait, London Gatwick, Madras, Manila, Muscat, Osaka, Sharjah, Taipei, Tokyo, Trivandrum.

FLEET
2 Boeing 747-100SR
2 Airbus A300-600R
3 Boeing 727-200Adv

Romania – YR

DAC AIR

DAC Air

Incorporated: 1996

HISTORY
A regional airline, DAC Air has an ambitious plan to develop domestic services and also to serve destinations in neighbouring countries with a fleet of de Havilland Dash 8s and, eventually, Canadair regional jets.

HQ Airport & Main Base: Bucharest

Radio callsign: DACFLIGHT

Designator: GCP

Main destinations served: Up to 12 domestic destinations.

LINKS WITH OTHER AIRLINES
Tarom (qv) is believed to have a minority shareholding.

FLEET
4 de Havilland Dash 8

ROMAVIA

Romavia Romanian Aviation Company

Incorporated: 1991

HISTORY
Romania's other state-owned airline, Romavia is owned by the Ministry of National Defence and its primary role was originally intended to be the operation of government VIP flights. The natural extension of this service has been the operation of aircraft on behalf of major industrial groups or banks. It has since developed into operating charter flights and has acquired the rights for scheduled services from Bucharest and Constanta to a number of destinations in Europe, North

Africa, the Gulf, and Pakistan. It remains to be seen whether such a small country facing considerable economic and infrastructural problems can maintain two international airlines.

Executive Directors & Officers: Iuliu Adrian Goleanu, Director General; Sorin Rabaea, Executive Director.

HQ Airport & Main Base: Bucharest

Radio callsign: AEROMAVIA

Designator: VQ/RMV

Employees: 350

Main destinations served: Charter flights to Europe, North Africa, the Gulf, and Pakistan, plus scheduled flights to a number of destinations, including Copenhagen, London Gatwick, London Stansted, St Petersburg, Sofia.

FLEET
1 Boeing 707-320C
1 Ilyushin Il-18D
3 Rombac One-Eleven 500
2 Mil Mi-8
1 Bell 412 (operated on behalf of Columna Bank)
1 Bell 222SP (operated on behalf of Columna Bank)
1 Bell 407 (operated on behalf of ANA-Industries)

TAROM

Transporturile Aeriene Romane

Incorporated: 1946

HISTORY
In common with many other East European national airlines, Tarom was founded in 1946 with Soviet assistance, with the USSR holding a half share in the airline. It replaced a pre-war airline, LARES, which had been formed in 1932 by the Romanian Government and ceased operations in 1939. Full ownership and control of Tarom passed to Romania in 1954, and the period which followed saw steady expansion, with the initial fleet of Lisunov Li-2 aircraft replaced by Ilyushin Il-14 airliners. Later equipment included Ilyushin Il-18s, the first turboprops introduced in 1962, and Antonov An-24s.

The first jet equipment – British Aerospace One-Elevens – entered service in 1968, and subsequently these aircraft were assembled under licence in Romania as Rombac One-Elevens. The decision may have had much to do with the ending of One-Eleven production in the UK and the desire of the Romanian

Government to establish an aircraft industry, or it may have been due to the growing rift between Romania and the Warsaw Pact nations, which saw the country increasingly aligned with Communist China. Tarom has leased and wet-leased Rombac One-Elevens to other airlines, and in the past a major user of these aircraft was Ryanair (qv).

The end of Communist dictatorship in Romania has seen many more western types enter service with Tarom, which is developing a comprehensive European and intercontinental network. There is just one domestic route. A subsidiary, Liniile Aeriene Romane (LAR), was formed in 1975 to provide feeder services, and today continues in this role, as well as undertaking charter flights, using two Beech 1900Ds. Although Tarom may well be privatised in the future, at present ownership rests with the State Ownership Fund and the oddly-named Private Ownership Fund.

Executive Directors & Officers:
Nicolae Brutaru, President; V. Gontsa, Chairman; Gheorghe Racaru, Chief Executive Officer; Ion Badescu, Vice-President, Finance.

HQ Airport & Main Base: Otopeni Airport, Bucharest

Radio callsign: TAROM

Designator: RO/ROT

Employees: 3,500

Main destinations served:
Bucharest–Baneasa, plus Abu Dhabi, Amman, Amsterdam, Athens, Bahrain, Bangkok, Barcelona, Beijing, Beirut, Belgrade, Berlin, Bologna, Brussels, Budapest, Cairo, Calcutta, Chicago O'Hare, Copenhagen, Delhi, Düsseldorf, Frankfurt, Istanbul, Karachi, Kiev, Kishinev, Kuwait, Larnaca, London Heathrow, London Stansted, Madrid, Male, Milan, Moscow, New York JFK, Paris CDG, Prague, Rome, Shannon, Sofia, Stockholm, Stuttgart, Tel Aviv, Thessaloniki, Verona, Vienna, Warsaw, Zürich.

FLEET
2 Airbus A310-300
7 Tupolev Tu-154B
2 Boeing 707-320C
6 Antonov An-24
5 Boeing 737-300
7 Rombac One-Eleven 500
2 ATR 42

Russian Federation – RA

One can either be very optimistic or very pessimistic about the state of commercial aviation in the Russian Federation, which, with the Ukraine, constitutes the rump of the former Soviet Union. The real point is, of course, that so much civil aviation in these countries is commercial in name only, with operators having to learn how to operate in a market economy and forget all that they ever learnt about the old Soviet-style command economy. For much of its history Aeroflot (qv) was operated on military lines and was almost indistinguishable from the Soviet Air Force's transport elements.

In essence, the history of Aeroflot is the history of Russian civil aviation. The dramatic political and economic changes which swept through the old Soviet Union have resulted in Aeroflot itself fragmenting. The result for what is left – Aeroflot Russian International Airlines – has been beneficial. New equipment has been acquired, and travellers report that, happily, Aeroflot is no longer the airline it used to be. For the rest, the consequences have varied. Many of the 'new' Russian airlines whose history began within the old Aeroflot have themselves failed to survive, and many of those which remain continue to struggle through lean and uncertain times, faced with poor infrastructure, elderly equipment, fuel shortages, poor productivity, and a simple lack of comprehension over what it takes to survive and prosper.

The airlines do not have the market to themselves. In addition to military-operated airlines, perhaps not too dissimilar from those which were once commonplace in Latin America, many research institutes faced with reduced budgetary support from the Russian Government have put their own aircraft into the charter market. Some industrial concerns have followed suit, although, to be fair, in the case of the Ukrainian aircraft manufacturer Antonov this has been an astute move; but Antonov is leading in a niche market.

In an attempt to emulate western success, and perhaps reconcile socialism with capitalism, many Russian airlines have substantial employee shareholdings. There are also a number of genuinely new airlines, and some of these show real potential, the most notable examples being Volga-Dnepr (qv), which has shown spectacular growth in a short time and established a reputation to match, and Transaero (qv). One or two former Aeroflot divisions, such as Aviation Enterprise Pulkovo (qv) and Don Airlines (qv), also demonstrate what can be achieved by switching from one politico-economic system to another.

In a country such as the Russian Federation aviation is not a luxury, but a necessity. The vast distances, the harsh climate, and the difficult terrain combine to give aviation a distinct advantage over other forms of transport. In the far northern wastes, road and railway construction is often simply not an option, with marshland in summer and extreme cold Arctic temperatures in winter. The failure of the so-called 'Stalin Railway' in northern Siberia proves the point.

The leading Russian airlines have been given separate entries, but the uncertain situation is such that the following list and brief fleet details is subject to change at short notice. In many ways Russian civil aviation needs consolidation, but consolidating back into the old over-centralised system will not work in such a large and diverse country. Nevertheless, strong regional groupings need to emerge. At present so many Russian airlines take the name of their home airport for their own title that there is sometimes difficulty in distinguishing between operators at the same base. This is an unusual feature of the post-Aeroflot era – there are few examples in the West of airlines adopting airport names, one of the few examples being the old Midway Airlines (not to be confused with the current airline of that name) based at Chicago's second airport.

Abakan Air Enterprise – Abakan Aviapredpriatie
6 Tupolev Tu-154
5 Antonov An-24
2 Let L-410
10 Mil Mi-12
5 Mil Mi-8

Aerokuznetsk-Novokuznetsk Airline
9 Tupolev Tu-154B/M
5 Antonov An-24
5 Antonov An-26
10 Mil Mi-8
9 Mil Mi-2

Aerolik Airline
1 Tupolev Tu-154M
1 Ilyushin Il-18
3 Yakovlev Yak-40

Aerovolga
4 Tupolev Tu-154M
1 Yakovlev Yak-42
1 Yakovlev Yak-40

ALK Kuban Airlines
5 Tupolev Tu-204
1 Tupolev Tu-154M
6 Antonov An-26
10 Antonov An-24
12 Yakovlev Yak-42D
3 Let L-410

Arkhangelsk 2nd United Air Detachment
22 Antonov An-2
30 Let L-410
9 Mil Mi-26
19 Mil Mi-8
14 Mil Mi-6
10 Mil Mi-2

Astrakhan Airlines – Astrakhan Avialinski
5 Tupolev Tu-134
9 Antonov An-24
13 Antonov An-2
2 Yakovlev Yak-42D
15 Kamov Ka-26

Atlant Soyuz Airlines
8 Ilyushin Il-76TD
1 Ilyushin Il-62
1 Tupolev Tu-154B
1 Antonov An-12

ATRAN – Aviatrans Cargo Airlines
6 Ilyushin Il-76TD
3 Antonov An-32
5 Antonov An-26
7 Antonov An-12

Atruvera Aviation
5 Ilyushin Il-76TD

Aviakor Air Transport – Aviakor – Proizvodstavenno Kommercheskaya Aviatransportnaya
2 Antonov An-74
1 Antonov An-26
1 Antonov An-24
1 Antonov An-12
1 Yakovlev Yak-40
1 Mil Mi-8

Avianergo
1 Ilyushin Il-76TD
1 Antonov An-74
4 Tupolev Tu-154M
1 Tupolev Tu-134M
2 Yakovlev Yak-40
4 Mil Mi-8

Aviaobschemash Shareholders' Air Company
1 Ilyushin Il-76
2 Antonov An-32
7 Antonov An-26
3 Antonov An-24
8 Antonov An-12
2 Yakovlev Yak-40

Aviastar
3 Antonov An-26
1 Antonov An-12
2 Antonov Yak-40

AVL Arkhangelsk Airlines – Arkhangelskie Vozdushnye Linie
2 Ilyushin Il-114
5 Tupolev Tu-154M
14 Tupolev Tu-134

14 Antonov An-26
12 Antonov An-24

Baikal Avia – Baikal Aviakompaniya
7 Ilyushin Il-76
17 Tupolev Tu-154M
7 Antonov An-26
11 Antonov An-24
8 Antonov An-12
12 Antonov An-2
11 Mil Mi-8/17

BAL Bashkiri Airlines – Bashkiri Avialinii
12 Tupolev Tu-154B/M
5 Tupolev Tu-134A
6 Antonov An-28
10 Antonov An-24
49 Antonov An-2
14 Mil Mi-8
24 Kamov Ka-26

Barnaul State Aviation Enterprise
3 Ilyushin Il-76TD
4 Tupolev Tu-154B
5 Antonov An-26
1 Antonov An-24
25 Antonov An-2
12 Yakovlev Yak-40
8 Let L-410
5 Mil Mi-8
5 Mil Mi-2

Belgorod State Air Enterprise
10 Yakovlev Yak-40
28 Antonov An-2
13 Kamov Ka-26

Bratsk Air Enterprise
5 Tupolev Tu-154B/M
11 Yakovlev Yak-40
12 Antonov An-2
7 Mil Mi-8

Bugulma Air Enterprise
15 Yakovlev Yak-40

Buryat Airlines
1 Tupolev Tu-154
3 Antonov An-26
10 Antonov An-24
24 Antonov An-2
2 Let L-410
15 Mil Mi-8
15 Mil Mi-2

Bykovo Avia
6 Antonov An-26
10 Antonov An-24
10 Yakovlev Yak-40

Central Districts Airlines – Avialinii Tsentralnikh Raionov
6 Antonov An-26
2 Antonov An-24
3 Yakovlev Yak-42
5 Mil Mi-8/17

Cheboksary Air Enterprise – Cheboxsrskoe A/P
5 Tupolev Tu-134

6 Antonov An-24
26 Antonov An-2

Chelal-Chelyabinsk Airline – Chelyabinsk Chief Aviation Enteprise
6 Tupolev Tu-154
3 Tupolev Tu-134
4 Yakovlev Yak-40
7 Yakovlev Yak-42

Cheremshanka Airline
7 Antonov An-24
23 Yakovlev Yak-40
19 Let L-410
6 Mil Mi-26
12 Mil Mi-8/17
5 Mil Mi-6
2 Mil Mi-2

Chita-Avia
7 Tupolev Tu-154B/M
1 Antonov An-28
1 Antonov An-26
3 Antonov An-24
8 Antonov An-2
6 Mil Mi-8/17
1 Mil Mi-2

Dagestan Airlines – Avialinii Dagestana
2 Tupolev Tu-154M
6 Antonov An-24
4 Antonov An-2
4 Mil Mi-8

DAK-Far Eastern Aviation – Khabarovsk United Air Detachment
2 Ilyushin Il-96M
22 Ilyushin Il-62M
25 Tupolev Tu-154B/M
10 Antonov An-26
19 Antonov An-24

Dobrolet Airline
4 Ilyushin Il-76TD
1 Antonov An-26

Domodedovo Airlines
3 Ilyushin Il-96-300
5 Ilyushin Il-76TD
45 Ilyushin Il-62M
3 Ilyushin Il-18

East Line Aviation
1 Ilyushin Il-86
5 Ilyushin Il-76
2 Antonov An-12

Elf Air
4 Ilyushin Il-76
1 Ilyushin Il-18
3 Tupolev Tu-134
1 Antonov An-26
1 Antonov An-12
1 Yakovlev Yak-40

ELIIP Ermolinksi Flight Test Research Institute – Ermolinskoe Letnoe Ispitatelno-Issledovatelskoe Predpriyativ
1 Antonov An-26

1 Antonov An-24
4 Antonov An-12

Flight Detachment 223 – 223 Letny Otryad
6 Ilyushin Il-62M
11 Tupolev Tu-154M
14 Tupolev Tu-134
6 Ilyushin Il-18
4 Antonov An-26
5 Antonov An-24
2 Antonov An-12
1 Mil Mi-8

Gosnil GA
1 Ilyushin Il-62M
1 Tupolev Tu-154M
1 Tupolev Tu-134
3 Ilyushin Il-18
1 Antonov An-30
2 Antonov An-12

Gromov Air
2 Ilyushin Il-76TD
2 Tupolev Tu-154A
1 Ilyushin Il-18
2 Antonov An-12
2 Yakovlev Yak-40

Izhavia – Izhevsk Air Enterprise
4 Tupolev Tu-134
3 Antonov An-26
4 Antonov An-24
1 Yakovlev Yak-42
3 Antonov An-2

Kalingrad United Air Detachment
2 Tupolev Tu-154M
9 Tupolev Tu-134

Kirov Airlines – Kirovskoe A/P
3 Tupolev Tu-134
2 Antonov An-26
5 Antonov An-24
40 Antonov An-2
9 Mil Mi-2

KMV Airlines – Kavkazia Mineralne Vody Mineralovodskoe
14 Tupolev Tu-154
5 Tupolev Tu-134
33 Antonov An-2

Kogalymavia Open Co – Kogalimavia
6 Tupolev Tu-154B/M
1 Yakovlev Yak-40
4 Mil Mi-8
1 Mil Mi-2

Kolpashevo State Airline – Kolpashevskoe GAP
15 Antonov An-28
5 Yakovlev Yak-40
47 Antonov An-2
37 Mil Mi-8/17
7 Mil Mi-2

Kolyma Avia – Kolima Avia Aviapredriyatie
2 Antonov An-26
10 Antonov An-24

Kolymo-Indigirski Airlines
3 Antonov An-74
5 Antonov An-26
14 Antonov An-2
6 Mil Mi-8

Komi Avia
36 Tupolev Tu-134
20 Antonov An-28
10 Antonov An-26
20 Antonov An-24
9 Yakovlev Yak-40
3 Antonov An-12
62 Antonov An-2
8 Mil Mi-26
4 Mil Mi-10
55 Mil Mi-8/17
18 Mil Mi-6
50 Mil Mi-2

Komsomolsk na Amure APO
2 Ilyushin Il-76TD
2 Tupolev Tu-134
2 Antonov An-32
1 Antonov An-26
3 Antonov An-12
2 Mil Mi-8

Korsar Airline – Aviakompaniya Korsar
1 Ilyushin Il-76TD
5 Tupolev Tu-154
3 Tupolev Tu-134
1 Antonov An-12
2 Yakovlev Yak-40

Krasair – Krasnoyarsk Avia
1 McDonnell Douglas DC-10-30F
4 Ilyushin Il-86
12 Ilyushin Il-76TD
7 Ilyushin Il-62
22 Tupolev Tu-154
6 Antonov An-26
8 Yakovlev Yak-40
20 Antonov An-2

Krylo Avia – Krylo Aviakompania
1 Ilyushin Il-76
2 Antonov An-31
1 Antonov An-26
1 Yakovlev Yak-40

Kurgan State Airline – Kurganskoe Gosudartsvennoe
1 Tupolev Tu-154B
2 Antonov An-26
8 Antonov An-24
2 Antonov An-2
1 Kamov Ka-32

Lipetsk Airlines – Lipetsk State Air Company
3 Yakovlev Yak-42
11 Yakovlev Yak-40
40 Antonov An-2
24 Mil Mi-2

Magadan Air Charter – Magadanaerogruz
7 Antonov An-12
3 Ilyushin Il-76

Magadan Airline – Magadanski Avialinii
8 Tupolev Tu-154B/M

Magnitogorsk State Air Enterprise
4 Antonov An-26
6 Antonov An-24
6 Antonov An-2

Minsk Flight Detachment No 1
12 Tupolev Tu-154 (believed to be included in Belavia (qv) fleet)

Minskavia-Minsk Flight Detachment No 2
4 Antonov An-26
6 Antonov An-24
4 Yakovlev Yak-40 (believed to be included in Belavia (qv) fleet)

Mirni Air Enterprise
3 Ilyushin Il-76TD
4 Antonov An-26
10 Antonov An-24
14 Antonov An-2
3 Mil Mi-26
27 Mil Mi-8

Murmansk Airline – Murmanskoe GAP
4 Tupolev Tu-154M
3 Antonov An-2
4 Mil Mi-8
12 Mil Mi-2
9 Kamov Ka-32

Myachkova Airline – Myachkovskoe AP
10 Antonov An-30
1 Antonov An-26
4 Mil Mi-8/17
2 Mil Mi-2

Nadym State Airline – Naimskoe Gosudarstvennoe Aviapredprivatie
3 Antonov An-74
1 Yakovlev Yak-40
5 Antonov An-2
28 Mil Mi-8/17

Nizhegorod Airlines – Nizhegorodsky
8 Tupolev Tu-154
6 Tupolev Tu-134
1 Antonov An-26
5 Antonov An-24
29 Antonov An-2

North Eastern Cargo Airlines
3 Ilyushin Il-76TD
3 Antonov An-12

Omsk Airline – Omskavia
7 Tupolev Tu-154M
2 Antonov An-26
4 Antonov An-24
9 Antonov An-2
4 Mil Mi-2

Orenburg Airlines – Orenburgskoe Gosudarstvennoe
4 Tupolev Tu-154B
6 Tupolev Tu-134A

5 Antonov An-24
30 Antonov An-2
6 Mil Mi-8

**Penza United Air Detachment –
Penzenskii Obedinenny Aviaotrad**
1 Antonov An-26
9 Antonov An-24
2 Antonov An-12
29 Antonov An-2

**Perm State Air Enterprise – Permskoe
Gosudartsvennoe**
1 Tupolev Tu-204
4 Tupolev Tu-154
5 Tupolev Tu-134
3 Antonov An-26
3 Antonov An-24

Pskov Airline
5 Antonov An-26
10 Antonov An-24
15 Antonov An-2

RDS Avia
3 Antonov An-74
2 Antonov An-26

Rossiya Airlines
2 Antonov An-124 Ruslan
2 Tupolev Tu-204
2 Ilyushin Il-96-300
13 Ilyushin Il-62
11 Tupolev Tu-154M
17 Tupolev Tu-134
3 Ilyushin Il-18
7 Yakovlev Yak-40
11 Mil Mi-8/17
1 Mil Mi-2

Ryazan Airlines – Ryazan Avia Trans
3 Antonov An-24
12 Let L-410VP
50 Antonov An-2
6 Mil Mi-2

**Rzhevka Leningrad Region Air
Company**
5 Antonov An-30
2 Antonov An-26
3 Antonov An-24
7 Antonov An-2

**Saak Stavropol Stock Airline – Saak
Gem Aviakompaniya**
3 Tupolev Tu-134
1 Antonov An-26
11 Antonov An-24
3 Yakovlev Yak-40
33 Antonov An-2
6 Mil Mi-8/17
27 Kamov Ka-26

Sakha Avia National Air Company
4 Ilyushin Il-76TD
11 Tupolev Tu-154B/M
1 Antonov An-74
6 Antonov An-26
21 Antonov An-24

15 Antonov An-12
1 Let L-410
1 Antonov An-2
1 Mil Mi-8
1 Mil Mi-2

Sakhaviatrans Airline
2 Ilyushin Il-76
3 Antonov An-26
4 Antonov An-12

**Samara Airlines – Aviacompania
Samara**
3 Ilyushin Il-76
16 Tupolev Tu-154B/M
8 Tupolev Tu-134A
3 Yakovlev Yak-40
4 Antonov An-12

Samarkand United Air Detachment
2 Tupolev Tu-154M
1 Antonov An-26
12 Antonov An-24
1 Yakovlev Yak-40
20 Antonov An-2

Saravia
5 Antonov An-24
9 Yakovlev Yak-42D
13 Let L-410
15 Mil Mi-2

SAT Airlines – Sakhalinski Aviatrassy
2 Boeing 737-200
3 Antonov An-26
8 Antonov An-24
1 Yakovlev Yak-40
2 Mil Mi-8
3 Mil Mi-2

Si Air – Kemerov Airline
2 Tupolev Tu-154
8 Antonov An-26
5 Antonov An-24

Sibavia – Siberia Airline
7 Ilyushin Il-86
13 Tupolev Tu-154B/M
1 Antonov An-32
4 Antonov An-26
4 Antonov An-24

Sibaviatrans Air Co
2 Antonov An-74
2 Antonov An-32
2 Yakovlev Yak-40
1 British Aerospace 125-700
6 Mil Mi-8

Simbirsk Aero Air Company
1 Ilyushin Il-86
2 Ilyushin Il-76TD
2 Ilyushin Il-62M
8 Tupolev Tu-154B/M
2 Tupolev Tu-134
5 Yakovlev Yak-42
6 Yakovlev Yak-40
26 Antonov An-2

Sochi Airlines
1 Ilyushin Il-76

1 Tupolev Tu-154M
1 Boeing 727-200
2 Tupolev Tu-134
1 Antonov An-26
1 Antonov An-24
1 Antonov An-12

Spair Air Transport
3 Ilyushin Il-76TD
3 Tupolev Tu-154
1 Ilyushin Il-18
2 Antonov An-24
3 Antonov An-12

**Special Cargo Airlines – Spetsialnie
Gruzovie Avialinii**
2 Antonov An-26
5 Antonov An-1
4 Antonov An-2
5 Mil Mi-8/17
3 Kamov Ka-26

**Sverdlovsk 2nd Air Enterprise –
Sverdlovskoe Aviapredpriat**
2 Antonov An-28
19 Antonov An-2
19 Mil Mi-8/17
14 Mil Mi-2

Trans-Charter Airlines
1 Antonov An-74
3 Antonov An-32
1 Yakovlev Yak-40

Tula Airlines – Tulskoe
2 Antonov An-26
5 Antonov An-24

Tupolev-Aerotrans Air Co
2 Ilyushin Il-76
3 Tupolev Tu-154
5 Tupolev Tu-134

**Tuvinsk Airlines – Tuvinskie
Aviatsionne Linii**
10 Yakovlev Yak-40
10 Let L-410
12 Antonov An-2
5 Mil Mi-8

Tyumenaviatrans
4 Tupolev Tu-154M
2 Antonov An-26
4 Yakovlev Yak-40
3 Mil Mi-26
14 Mil Mi-8/17
(see also Tyumen Airlines (qv))

Ural Airline 3 – Uralskoe UGA
4 Ilyushin Il-86
17 Tupolev Tu-154B/M
3 Antonov An-26
3 Antonov An-24
6 Antonov An-12

Uralinteravia
6 Ilyushin Il-76TD

UST Ilimsk Airline
1 Tupolev Tu-154
3 Yakovlev Yak-40

2 Antonov An-24
3 Antonov An-2

Veteran Airlines
17 Ilyushin Il-76
5 Antonov An-12

Vitiaz Aviatransport
2 Ilyushin Il-76
4 Tupolev Tu-154M

Vladivostok Avia
3 Ilyushin Il-76TD
8 Tupolev Tu-154B/M
4 Yakovlev Yak-40
7 Mil Mi-8/17
1 Mil Mi-2
6 Kamov Ka-32

Volga Airlines
5 Tupolev Tu-134
5 Yakovlev Yak-42
2 Yakovlev Yak-40
5 Antonov An-2

Vologada State Air Enterprise
6 Antonov An-28
1 Antonov An-26
14 Yakovlev Yak-40
24 Antonov An-2
3 Mil Mi-8
15 Mil Mi-2

Voronezh Joint Stock Aircraft Company
13 Tupolev Tu-134
10 Antonov An-24
2 Yakovlev Yak-42D
28 Antonov An-2

Voronezh Shareholder Aircraft Society
2 Ilyushin Il-76
1 Antonov An-26
1 Antonov An-24
1 Antonov An-12
1 Antonov An-2

Yeniseisk Airline – Yeniseiskoe
6 Antonov An-26
10 Let L-410VP
17 Antonov An-2
11 Mil Mi-8
9 Mil Mi-2

Zenit Airline
2 Ilyushin Il-76
2 Antonov An-12
1 Yakovlev Yak-40

AEROFLOT – ARIA

Aeroflot Russian International Airlines

Incorporated: 1932

HISTORY
At one time the world's largest airline, albeit run more on military than commercial lines, Aeroflot is still one of the top 40 in terms of annual turnover. In recent years its activities have become more confined with the break-up both of the former Soviet system – thereby enabling the airline to become more commercial – and of Aeroflot itself, into many regional or state airlines. Gone too are the days when Aeroflot handled everything, from air taxis and crop-spraying to long-haul airline operation.

Its immediate predecessor was Dobroflot, formed in 1923 at the start of the first five-year plan on the merger of several small pioneering airlines. Dobroflot's routes covered 6,000 miles when, in 1932, Aeroflot was formed and took it over. Expansion was rapid thereafter, albeit almost entirely on domestic services, until the German invasion in 1941 halted many services, subsequent activity being reduced in favour of supporting Russia's war effort.

Extensive military assistance from the United States during the war years saw the Douglas C-47 – the military variant of the DC-3 – provided for Soviet use, and this aircraft was subsequently produced under licence in the Soviet Union as the Lisunov Li-2. The Li-2 formed the backbone of the airline's fleet after the war ended, with large numbers remaining in service throughout the 1950s, even after Russian aircraft such as the Ilyushin Il-12 and Il-14 had entered service. For many years all Aeroflot aircraft were single or twin-engined types, since travel was restricted to senior government and Communist Party officials, and it was not considered worth spending scant resources on aircraft of Douglas DC-4 or DC-6 type.

Following World War Two and the Russian occupation of Eastern Europe, Aeroflot was the chosen instrument for Soviet participation in the national airlines then being established throughout the countries of what later became the Warsaw Pact. Most of these airlines were formed with standard packages of Li-2s.

Aeroflot's first jet was the twin-engined Tupolev Tu-104, introduced in 1956 and first seen in the west during a state visit to the United Kingdom. A shorter range version of the Tu-104 was the Tu-124, while turboprop aircraft followed soon afterwards, with the Ilyushin Il-18 and the Antonov An-24 and An-114. These aircraft were followed by the second generation of jet airliners, including the Tupolev Tu-134 and Tu-154, equating to the Douglas DC-9 and Boeing 727 respectively, and by the Ilyushin Il-62, an aircraft of strikingly similar appearance to the Vickers VC-10. The airline operated the unsuccessful Tupolev Tu-144 supersonic jet airliner for a short period, although this never saw service on international routes.

In recent years the much-reduced Aeroflot has become more commercial, with operations confined to what might be regarded as the domestic trunk routes and international services, developing a more extensive network than hitherto. The airline is still controlled by the Russian Government, but the state's shareholding has been reduced to 51 per cent, with the remainder being held by the airline's employees. Further steps towards privatisation may be taken during 1998. Russian and Ukrainian aircraft types still predominate in the fleet, but increasing numbers of western aircraft are in service, although whether this continues will depend on the airline's success in earning foreign currency – a compromise might be Russian aircraft with western engines and avionics. In 1997 Aeroflot decided to re-establish itself on a broader domestic network, using Moscow Sheremetyevo as a hub.

Two Boeing 777-200s have been leased for seven years to cover for delays in deliveries of the new Ilyushin Il-86.

Executive Directors & Officers: Yevgeni Shaposhnikov, General Director; Nikolai Glushkov, Deputy Director General; Alexander Azeev, Deputy Director General, Finance; Alexander Krasnenker, Deputy Director General, Commercial; Genndi Anikaev, Deputy Director General, Maintenance; Mikhail Denisov, Deputy Director General, Computer Systems; Anatoly Lazukin, Deputy Director General, Personnel; Vladimir Antonov, Director General, Security.

HQ Airport & Main Base: Moscow, but with further bases/hubs at St Petersburg.

Radio callsign: AEROFLOT

Designator: SU/AFL

Employees: 15,000

Main destinations served: Abu Dhabi, Accra, Addis Ababa, Amman, Amsterdam, Anchorage, Ankara, Antananarivo, Athens, Bamako, Bangkok, Barcelona, Beijing, Beirut, Belgrade, Berlin, Bombay, Bratislava, Brazzaville, Brussels, Bucharest, Budapest, Buenos Aires, Cairo, Calcutta, Casablanca, Chicago, Cologne/Bonn, Colombo, Conakry, Copenhagen, Cotonou, Dacca, Dakar, Damascus, Frankfurt, Geneva, Gothenburg, Hamburg, Helsinki, Hong Kong, Istanbul, Jakarta, Johannesburg, Kabul, Karachi, Kathmandu, Khabarovsk, Kuala Lumpur, Kuwait, Larnaca, Leipzig, Lima, Lisbon, Lome, London Heathrow, Los Angeles, Luanda, Lusaka, Luxembourg, Ljubljana, Madrid, Malta, Marseilles, Mexico City, Miami, Milan,

Montreal, Munich, Nairobi, New York JFK, Novosibirsk, Nurengri, Osaka, Oslo, Ougadougou, Paris CDG, Phnom Penh, Prague, Rio de Janeiro, Rome, St Petersburg, Sal, San Francisco, Sana'a, Santiago de Chile, São Paulo, Seattle, Seoul, Shanghai, Shannon, Sharjah, Singapore, Skopje, Sofia, Stockholm, Sydney, Tehran, Tel Aviv, Tokyo, Tunis, Ulan Bator, Venice, Vienna, Warsaw, Washington, Yakutsk, Zagreb, Zürich.

Annual turnover: US $1,478 (£895.8 million)

LINKS WITH OTHER AIRLINES
Lufthansa (qv) is assisting with the expansion of Moscow Airport.

FLEET
1 Antonov An-124-100
10 Airbus A310-300
2 Boeing 767-300ER
26 Ilyushin Il-96-300M/T
18 Ilyushin Il-86
2 Boeing 777-200 (leased)
18 Ilyushin Il–76T/TD
29 Tupolev Tu-154B/M
10 Boeing 737-400

AVIATION ENTERPRISE PULKOVO

Aviation Enterprise Pulkovo

Incorporated: 1932

HISTORY
Originally a part of Aeroflot (qv), since the break up that airline's regional network Pulkovo has remained in state hands. Nevertheless, it is also one of the more successful of the former Aeroflot divisions, operating to many destinations outside Russia. After autonomy from Aeroflot it was initially known as the Pulkovo Aviation Concern, but has now adopted the current title.

Executive Directors & Officers: Boris Demchenko, General Director; Boris Gudkovich, Finance Director; Nikolay Kolesov, Operations Director; Sergev Belov, Airline Director; Nikolai Shipil, Commercial Director.

HQ Airport & Main Base: Pulkovo Airport, St Petersburg

Radio callsign: PULKOVO

Designator: Z8/PLK

Employees: Aircrew: 790; Engineering:

930; Others: 5,280; Total: 7,000.

Main destinations served: Amsterdam, Athens, Barcelona, Berlin, Brussels, Budapest, Bourgas, Copenhagen, Düsseldorf, Frankfurt, Hamburg, Helsinki, Larnaka, London Heathrow, Luxembourg, Madrid, Milan, Munich, Oslo, Paris CDG, Paphos, Prague, Rome, Saloniki, Shannon, Sofia, Stockholm, Tel Aviv, Varna, Vienna, Warsaw, Zürich.

Passenger km pa: 3,448 million

FLEET
9 Ilyushin Il-86
7 Tupolev Tu-154M
17 Tupolev Tu-154B
10 Tupolev Tu-134
4 Antonov An-12

DONAVIA

Don Airlines Joint-Stock Aviation Company

Incorporated: 1993

HISTORY
Able to trace its origins back to 1925, Donavia operated within the Aeroflot (qv) organisation before being restructured and relaunched as a private enterprise airline in 1993, owned 51 per cent by its employees and 20 per cent by the state. It is one of Russia's larger airlines, operating mainly on domestic routes but with a few international destinations, where further growth can be expected.

Executive Directors & Officers: Pavel Duznikov, Director General; Galina Gorochova, Financial Director; Micheal Kritsky, Commercial Director; Yuri Lebedev, Maintenance Director; Vladimir Demianov, Personnel Director.

HQ Airport & Main Base: Rostov-on-Don

Radio callsign: DONAVIA

Designator: D9/DNV

Employees: 2,000

Main destinations served: Ashkhabad, Dubai, Düsseldorf, Kalingrad, Khabarovsk, Minsk, Moscow Vnukovo, Novosibirsk, Omsk, Samara Bratsk, St Petersburg, Tashkent, Tchita, Tyumen, Ufa Irkutsk, Yerevan.

FLEET
16 Tupolev Tu-154B
8 Tupolev Tu-134

5 Antonov An-12
10 Yakovlev Yak-40

TRANSAERO

Transaero Airlines AP
Incorporated: 1990

HISTORY
Commencing operations in November 1991, this was the first truly private enterprise Russian airline, and the first with non-Aeroflot origins to gain approval for scheduled services, first within Russia and then internationally. Its first international service was from Moscow to Tel Aviv, and was inaugurated in November 1993.

Lacking any inherited aircraft, the airline has been able to concentrate on creating a fleet which is almost entirely western in origin, initially using leased older aircraft which are now being up-dated as new aircraft are delivered. It is likely that some of the new aircraft will be Russian-built Ilyushin Il-96Ms, easing the financial burden of concentrating solely on more expensive western equipment, and doubtless also reflecting the fact that the Ilyushin and Yakovlev design bureaux are both shareholders, along with the Aerotrans and Ikar joint stock companies, Aeronavigation, and the Loriel Partnership. The airline has also followed the western fashion of establishing a commuter or feeder subsidiary, Transaero Express.

Executive Directors & Officers: Alexander Pleshakov, Chairman & President; Sergey Frantsev, Deputy Director General, Finance; Nikolai Kozevnikov, Deputy Director General, Operations; Boris Gulnitsky, Deputy Director General, Commerce; Alexander Basyuk, Deputy Director General, Maintenance.

HQ Airport & Main Base: Moscow Sheremetyevo

Radio callsign: TRANSOVIET

Designator: UN/TSO

Employees: 2,400

Main destinations served: Akmola, Almaty, Baku, Berlin, Ekarinburg, Elat, Frankfurt, Irkutsk, Kiev, Kishinev, Krasnoyarsk, Karaganda, London Gatwick, Los Angeles, Lvov, Minsk, Nizhnevartovsk, Novosibirsk, Norlisk, Odessa, Omsk, Paris CDG, Riga, Sochi, St Petersburg, Tashkent, Tel Aviv, Vladivostok.

LINKS WITH OTHER AIRLINES
Transaero Express is a subsidiary. Code-sharing with Riar of Latvia.

Russia's Tyumen Airlines has several of these Ilyushin Il-76 freighters in its fleet.

FLEET
3 McDonnell Douglas DC-10-30
1 Ilyushin Il-86
5 Boeing 757-200 (leased)
5 Boeing 737-200 (leased)
plus unconfirmed orders for Boeing 767s
and 737-600s, and Ilyushin Il-96Ms

TYUMEN AIRLINES

Tyumen Airlines/Tyumenskie Avialinii

Incorporated: 1968

HISTORY
Tyumen Airlines was formed in 1968 as a
division of Aeroflot (qv), operating services to and from the East Siberian region,
where it is now the largest carrier.
International services started in 1989.

Executive Directors & Officers: Yuri
Ermolaev, Director.

HQ Airport & Main Base: Roshino
Airport, Tyumen

Radio callsign: AIR TYUMEN

Designator: 7M/TYM

Employees: Flight-crew: 180; Cabin staff:
100; Engineering: 500; Ground staff:
2,220; Total: 3,000.

Main destinations served: Destinations
within the Russian Federation and the
Ukraine, as well as services to the United
Kingdom, Bulgaria, China, France,
Greece, Spain, Turkey, and the United
Arab Emirates.

Aircraft km pa: 41 million
Revenue passenger km pa: 2,112 million

Cargo tonne km pa: 4.4 million

FLEET
5 Ilyushin Il-76TD
16 Tupolev Tu-154B/M
16 Tupolev Tu-134
6 Antonov An-26
17 Antonov An-24
9 Antonov An-12

VNUKOVO AIRLINES

Vnukovski Avialinii

Incorporated: 1993

HISTORY
Formerly part of Aeroflot (qv), and named
after its home airport, Vnukovo is credited
with being amongst the leaders in privatisation of the former Aeroflot divisions. It
operates scheduled air services from
Moscow to the southern areas of both
Russian and the other constituent states of
the former Soviet Union, as well as world-
wide charters. There are also a number of
services to destinations outside the former
Soviet Union, including Athens and
Barcelona. Vnukovo has a number of firsts
to its credit, being the first airline to operate the Tupolev Tu-154 tri-jet, the Ilyushin
Il-86, and the Tupolev Tu-204.

Executive Directors & Officers: Y.P.
Kashitsin, General Manager; V.
Soukhatchev, Chief Financial Officer; I.
Akindeyev, Commercial Director; M.V.
Bulanov, Technical Director.

HQ Airport & Main Base: Moscow
Vnukovo

Radio callsign: VNUKOVO

Designator: V5/VKO

Employees: 1,300

Main destinations served: World-wide
charters plus scheduled flights to some
40 destinations in the southern states of
the former Soviet Union, and to Athens,
Barcelona, and Istanbul.

FLEET
22 Ilyushin Il-86

6 Tupolev Tu-204 (including one operated for Perm)
28 Tupolev Tu-154B/M

VOLGA-DNEPR CARGO

Volga-Dnepr Airlines

Incorporated: 1990

HISTORY

The first airline without its origins in Aeroflot to be able to undertake heavy and outsized cargo charters, Volga-Dnepr was founded in 1990 and commenced operations in 1991. The shareholders include the Aviastar Joint Stock Company, Motor Sich, and the Ukrainian-based Antonov Design Bureau, builders of the largest aircraft in commercial use, the Antonov An-124 Ruslan. Volga now also operates scheduled cargo services. The airline has been extremely successful in carving out a specialised niche for itself, and has enhanced its marketing efforts through an agreement with the British freight airline, HeavyLift (qv). Annual cargo tonnage has risen from 35,655 tonnes in 1993 to 50,851 in 1996.

Executive Directors & Officers: Alexey Isaikin, President & Chief Executive Officer; Vladimir Gridnev, Vice-President; Sergey Shklyanik, Deputy General Director; Victor Merkulov, Flight Operations Director; Gregory Stilbans, Commercial Director; Victor Tolmachov, Technical Director; Konstantin Zorin, Financial Director-Chief Accountant.

HQ Airport & Main Base: Ulyanovsk

Radio callsign: VOLGA-DNEPR

Designator: VI/VDA

Employees: Flight-crew: 158; Engineering: 279; Others: 537; Total: 974.

Main destinations served: World-wide cargo charters, plus scheduled cargo to Moscow, Shenyang, Shenzhen, Tianjin. Passenger service Ulyanovsk–Moscow.

Cargo tonnes pa: 50,851

Above: *Not a traffic jam, but the 107 cars which participated in the 1993 London--Sydney rally, which two Volga-Dnepr Antonov An-124 Ruslans moved between Ankara and Delhi, and then again between Bombay and Perth.*

Below: *This is how they did it – cars parked on two decks, three abreast on the lower deck.*

Mil Mi-17 helicopters (the successor to the Mi-8) can be taken in one gulp, and had folding rotor blades been fitted, probably without removing the rotor. More than one helicopter can be carried.

LINKS WITH OTHER AIRLINES
Marketing and operational alliance with HeavyLift (qv).

FLEET
7 Antonov An-124-100 Ruslan (operated jointly with HeavyLift)
4 Ilyushin Il-96T (plus 2 on option)
2 Tupolev Tu-204-120 (leased from Scirocco)
4 Ilyushin Il-76TD (3 leased)
1 Antonov An-32
1 Yakovlev Yak-40

SAUDI ARABIAN AIRLINES

Saudi Arabia Airlines Corporation

Incorporated: 1945

HISTORY
The largest airline in the Middle East,

Saudi Arabian Airlines was formed in 1945 by the Saudi Arabian Government with assistance from TWA (Trans World Airlines) (qv), and initially undertook charter flights using Douglas DC-3s. Scheduled services began in 1947, initially on domestic routes which were soon extended to neighbouring states. While Bristol Wayfarers – passenger-carrying versions of the Bristol 170 Freighter – were introduced in 1951, for the first 20 years of the airline's history there was a marked preference for Douglas products.

Left: *Another unusual Ruslan load – taking four mobile television stations, based on Mercedes goods vehicles, from Frankfurt to Seoul.*

Below: *Volga-Dnepr also has smaller aircraft, such as this Ilyushin Il-76TD; but smaller is a relative term!*

The first jets, Boeing 727s, were introduced in 1962.

The airline has enjoyed considerable growth, due not so much to the size of the Saudi population as to the country's booming oil economy which has led to substantial numbers of expatriate workers being employed, most of whom are contracted to use the airline's services, on which no alcohol is served. Although the airline does receive some benefit from pilgrims travelling to Mecca, most of this traffic is handled by non-Saudi charter airlines. For a period the fleet name Saudia was used, but the airline, which remains in state hands, has now reverted to its full title.

Two unusual aspects of its operations are that a number of aircraft are operated on behalf of the Saudi Government, or Royal family, for VIP use, and that, in contrast to many large airlines today, there is no separate feeder or commuter operation. In addition to its fleet of commercial aircraft the airline also owns its own training aircraft, including Piper Archers and Beechcraft Bonanzas.

Executive Directors & Officers: Prince Sultan Bin Abdul Aziz, Chairman; Dr Khaled A. Ben-Bakr, Director General.

HQ Airport & Main Base: Jeddah, with further bases/hubs at Dhahran and Riyadh.

Radio callsign: SAUDI (SAUDI GREEN for VIP flights)

Designator: SV/SVA

Employees: 28,000

Main destinations served: Almost 30 domestic destinations, plus Abu Dhabi, Addis Ababa, Algiers, Amman, Amsterdam, Ankara, Asmara, Brussels*, Damascus, Delhi, Dhaka, Doha, Dubai, Frankfurt, Geneva, Islamabad, Istanbul, Johannesburg, Jakarta, London Heathrow, Manila, Milan*, Muscat, Nairobi, New York JFK, Nice, Orlando, Paris CDG, Rome, Sana'a, Seoul, Sharjah, Singapore, Taipei*, Tokyo*, Tunis, Washington.
* cargo services

Annual turnover: US $2,500 million (£1,515 million)

FLEET
5 Boeing 747-400
11 Boeing 747-300 (1 owned by the Government)
2 Boeing 747-200F (leased)
7 Boeing 747-100
3 Boeing 747SP (1 owned by the Government)
23 Boeing 777-200 (in course of delivery)
4 McDonnell Douglas MD-11F

17 Lockheed L-10ll TriStar 200
2 Lockheed L-1011 TriStar 500 (2 owned by the Government)
11 Airbus A300-600
1 Boeing 757 (owned by the Government)
29 McDonnell Douglas MD-90 (in course of delivery)
2 Boeing 707-320C (owned by the Government)
20 Boeing 737-200 (1 owned by the Government) (being replaced by MD-90s)

Other aircraft operated on behalf of the Government include
6 Grumman Gulfstream IV
5 Gulfstream III
4 Gulfstream II
2 Dassault Falcon 900
1 de Havilland Canada DHC-6 Twin Otter

Scandinavia

SAS COMMUTER

SAS Commuter

Incorporated: 1989

HISTORY
Formed in 1989 to take over SAS's (qv) shorter routes as well as a number of services within the three participating countries, SAS Commuter has the same 3:2:2 division of ownership between Sweden, Denmark, and Norway as its parent. Services are divided and branded into three sections known as 'Norlink', 'Eurolink', and 'Swelink'.

Executive Directors & Officers: Ole Pedersen, Chief Executive Officer; Kenneth Marx, Director, Business & Finance; Leif Overskott, Director, Operations; Claus Albrechtsen, Director, Technical; Jytte Ryde, Director, In-Flight Service; Tore Olsen, Director, Norway; Kjell Sundstrom, Director, Sweden; Soren Boje, Director, Human Resources.

HQ Airport & Main Base: Copenhagen, with further bases/hubs at Oslo and Stockholm. Maintenance divided between Copenhagen and Trondheim.

Radio callsign: SCANDINAVIAN

Designator: SK/SAS

Employees: Flight-crew: 276; Cabin staff: 185; Engineering: 76; Ground staff: 63; Total: 600.

Main destinations served: 'Norlink': Alta, Bardufoss, Bodo, Evenes, Kirkenes, Lakselv, Tromsø, Trondheim.
'Eurolink': Aalborg, Berlin, Billund, Cologne, Copenhagen, Gdansk, Gothenburg, Hamburg, Kalingfrad, Karup, Luxembourg, Oslo, Prague,

SAS Commuter operates more than 20 Fokker 50s, such as this one on a Eurolink service flying over Denmark.

Poznan, Stavanger, Szczecin.
'Swelink': Angelholm, Jonkoping, Kalmar, Karlstad, Kristianstad, Norrkoping, Orebro, Skelleftea, Tampere, Turku, Vaasa, Väasterås, Vaxjo.

Annual turnover: Included in SAS figures

LINKS WITH OTHER AIRLINES
Operates as part of SAS (qv).

FLEET
22 Fokker 50 (9 leased)
6 Saab 2000 (leased)
Aircraft have national registrations
15 de Havilland Dash 8-400

SAS
SCANDINAVIAN
AIRLINES SYSTEM

Scandinavian Airlines System

Incorporated: 1946

HISTORY
One of the world's largest airlines, SAS dates from the merger of three airlines – the Danish DDL, the Swedish ABA, and the Norwegian DNL – in 1946. Of these, the Danish airline DDL was the oldest, dating from 1919, although in common with DNL, which dated from 1927, operations had been suspended completely after the German invasion of these countries during World War Two. The Swedish airline, ABA, dated from 1924 and had

maintained limited operations during wartime because of Swedish neutrality.

From the outset the new airline was owned in the proportions of 3:2:2 by Sweden, Denmark, and Norway respectively, with each national share being divided 50:50 between the state and private investors. More recently, however, the names of the shareholding national airlines have been changed to SAS Sweden AB, SAS Danmark AS and SAS Norge ASA.

Initially SAS was only concerned with transatlantic operations and was known as OSAS (Overseas Scandinavian Airlines System), but the participating airlines merged their European networks into ESAS (European Scandinavian Airlines System) in 1948, and in 1951 ESAS and OSAS were merged to form the current airline. The intercontinental operations of Braathens SAFE (qv) were added to those of OSAS before the merger.

SAS soon expanded its route network into Africa and Asia. It also worked hard to make a virtue of its geographical position, which some might have viewed as being isolated on the fringes of northern Europe. In 1954 it made air transport history by inaugurating the first air service over the North Pole, using Douglas DC-6Bs on a service to the West Coast of the United States. This was followed by a DC-7C service in 1957, which cut the Europe–Japan journey time in half. Ten years later SAS became the first European airline to operate via Tashkent in what was then the USSR but is now Uzbekistan, cutting 1,350 miles off the journey from Copenhagen to Bangkok and Singapore.

Its DC-6s and DC-7s had been complemented by Convair 440 Metropolitans on the European services, but these were later replaced by Sud Aviation Caravelles. SAS for many years proved to be a loyal customer for Douglas and later McDonnell Douglas, also buying Douglas DC-8 long-haul airliners, DC-9s to replace the Caravelles, and then DC-10s, before moving onto the MD series. More recently, however, it has concentrated on Boeing 767s for its long-haul operations and is introducing Boeing 737-600s for its less busy European routes.

The airline's links with the Far East saw it play a leading role in the establishment of Thai Airways (qv) in 1959, in which for many years SAS held a substantial stake, although this was subsequently reduced from its initial 30 per cent to 15 per cent before the Thai Government bought out the SAS holding in 1977.

Originally it was not intended that SAS should operate domestic services, although it did acquire a 50 per cent holding in the Swedish domestic airline, Linjeflyg, and a 25 per cent interest (now increased to one-third) in Greenlandair (qv) has been held for many years. Nevertheless, the formation of SAS Commuter (qv) in 1989 saw expansion onto domestic services, while Linjeflyg's operations were absorbed by SAS in 1993, some of this airline's routes being passed to SAS Commuter. Linjeflyg had been founded in 1957 as a domestic airline to operate passenger and newspaper delivery flights, and quickly established a 38-point domestic network. The airline expanded into operating inclusive tour holiday charter flights, which made a convenient fit with the domestic scheduled services. By the time it came to be merged into SAS, Linjeflyg was operating eight Boeing 737-500s and 16 Fokker F-28-4000s, as well as four leased Saab 340s, and had another six 737-500s on order.

In 1988 SAS took a 24.9 per cent shareholding in Airlines of Britain Holdings, owners of British Midland (qv), and has since built this up to 40 per cent, but it has relinquished the right to a 40 per cent shareholding in the new British Regional Airlines (qv). British Midland has taken over some SAS routes, notably Glasgow to Copenhagen. Spanair (qv) is a joint venture between SAS, with 49 per cent, and a Spanish travel group. The airline is a founder-member of the 'Star Alliance', which brings together frequent flyer programmes and other services for Air Canada (qv), Lufthansa (qv), Thai International (qv), United Airlines (qv), and, in late-1997, Varig (qv), as well as SAS.

The McDonnell Douglas MD-90 is likely to remain with SAS for some time, while older DC-9s are being replaced by Boeing 737s.

Executive Directors & Officers: Hugo Schroder, Chairman; Jan Stenberg, President & Chief Executive Officer; Gunnar Reitan, Executive Vice-President & Chief Financial Officer; Vagn Soerensen, Senior Vice-President, Business Division; Otto Lagarhus, Senior Vice-President, Production Division; Bjorn Boldt-Christmas, Senior Vice-President, Information Systems; Hans Erik Stuhr, Senior Vice-President, Station Services; Peter Forssman, Senior Vice-President, Public Relations.

HQ Airport & Main Base: Stockholm, with the main hub at Copenhagen and a further base at Oslo.

Radio callsign: SCANDINAVIAN

Designator: SK/SAS

Employees: Aircrew: 5,000; Engineering: 3,200; Ground staff:12,300; Total: 20,500.

Main destinations served: Aalborg, Aarhus, Alicante, Alta, Amsterdam, Arkhangelsk, Athens, Bangkok, Barcelona, Bardufoss, Beijing, Bergen, Berlin, Bodo, Borlange, Brussels, Budapest, Chicago O'Hare, Cologne/Bonn, Delhi, Dublin, Düsseldorf, Evenes, Frankfurt, Gdansk, Gothenburg, Hamburg, Hanover, Haugesund, Helsinki, Hong Kong, Istanbul, Jonkoping, Kalingrad, Kalmar, Kangerlussaq, Karup, Kiev, Kirkenes, London Heathrow, Longyearbyen, Luxembourg, Lyons, Madrid, Malmö, Manchester, Marseilles, Milan, Moscow, Munich, Nice, New York JFK, Norrkoping, Osaka Kansai, Paris CDG, Pori, Poznan, Prague, Riga, Rome, Singapore, St Petersburg, Stavanger, Stuttgart, Tallinn, Tromsø, Trondheim, Turin, Vaasa, Västerås, Vaxjo, Venice, Vilnius, Warsaw, Zagreb, Zurich.

Annual turnover: US $5,246 million (£3,179.4 million)

LINKS WITH OTHER AIRLINES
Interests in British Midland (qv) (40 per cent), Greenlandair (qv) (33.3 per cent), and Spanair (qv) (49 per cent).
Star Alliance member with Air Canada (qv), Lufthansa (qv), Thai International (qv), United Airlines (qv), and Varig (qv). Marketing alliance with Icelandair (qv).

FLEET
14 Boeing 767-300ER
8 McDonnell Douglas MD-90
18 McDonnell Douglas MD-87
2 McDonnell Douglas MD-83
12 McDonnell Douglas MD-82
38 McDonnell Douglas MD-81
20 McDonnell Douglas DC-9-41 (being

replaced by Boeing 737s)
9 Boeing 737-500 (plus 32 on order)
Aircraft have national registrations

Serbia – YU

JAT YUGOSLAV AIRLINES

Jugoslovenski Aerotransport

Incorporated: 1946

HISTORY
Now the airline of newly-independent Serbia following the break-up of Yugoslavia and the resultant war, JAT was originally founded in 1946 by the Yugoslav Government. A predecessor airline, Aeropout, had ceased operations shortly after the outbreak of World War Two. JAT commenced operations in 1947, initially operating a small fleet of Douglas DC-3s on domestic routes, but international services to Czechoslovakia, Hungary, and Romania were introduced before the year was out.

The international services were suspended the following year, but restarted in 1949, only to have the routes into eastern Europe suspended yet again in 1950 after Yugoslavia declared itself independent of what had emerged as a Soviet Bloc. The airline's route development then reflected this policy change, with priority given to establishing services to major centres in Western Europe. Eventually services to Prague and East Berlin were reinstated.

The airline also looked to western suppliers for its equipment, starting with an order for Convair 440 Metropolitans in 1954, and also ordered Douglas DC-6Bs at the same time. Nevertheless, in 1957 a number of Ilyushin Il-14s were also obtained. Jet aircraft were introduced in 1962, in the form of JAT's first delivery of Sud Aviation Caravelles. These were later augmented and eventually replaced by Douglas DC-9s.

Encouraged by Yugoslavia's growing popularity as a tourist destination JAT continued to expand, obtaining Boeing 727-20Advs and 737-300s, as well as McDonnell Douglas DC-10s. This steady progress was thrown sharply into reverse in the early-1990s with the start of hostilities between the different communities within Yugoslavia following the disintegration of the latter. Serbia had taken 51 per cent of the airline's shares on the break-up of the country, and following United Nations sanctions against Serbia

because of the its part in the conflict JAT was reduced to operating just two domestic routes from Belgrade.

The return of peace has meant that JAT's international route network is now being reinstated, albeit slowly.

Executive Directors & Officers: Ziko Petrovic, Director-General, President & Chief Executive Officer.

HQ Airport & Main Base: Novi Beograd (Belgrade)

Radio callsign: JAT

Designator: JU/JAT

Employees: 6,800

Main destinations served: Athens, Beirut, Bucharest, Cairo, Chicago, Dubai, Larnaca, London Heathrow, Malta, Melbourne, Montreal, Moscow, New York JFK, Paris CDG, Rome, Singapore, Tel Aviv.

FLEET
1 McDonnell Douglas DC-10-30
8 Boeing 727-200 Adv
2 Boeing 737-300
2 Boeing 737-200
7 McDonnell Douglas DC-9-32
3 ATR 72-200

Singapore – 9V

SILK AIR

Silk Air Ltd

Incorporated: 1989

HISTORY
Originally founded in 1989 as Tradewinds, using two leased Boeing 737-300s, Silk Air soon became a wholly-owned subsidiary of Singapore Airlines (qv). The present title was adopted in 1992. Many of its services are operated on behalf of its parent airline, while it has marketing alliances with a number of regional carriers.

Executive Directors & Officers: Chew Choon Serf, Chairman; Michael Chan, General Manager.

HQ Airport & Main Base: Singapore

Radio callsign: SILKAIR

Designator: MI/SLK

Employees: 490

Main destinations served: Cebu, Kunming, Langkawi, Lombok, Manado, Medan, Padang, Pekanbaru, Phnom Penh, Phuket, Solo, Tioman, Ujang Pandang, Vientiane, Xiamen.

Annual turnover: Included in figures for Singapore Airlines.

LINKS WITH OTHER AIRLINES
Wholly-owned by Singapore Airlines. Marketing alliances with Bouraq Airlines (qv), Merpati Air (qv), and Sempati Air (qv).

FLEET
5 Boeing 737-300
2 Fokker 70

SINGAPORE AIRLINES

Singapore Airlines Ltd

Incorporated: 1972

HISTORY
For almost the first quarter-century of its operations, the history of Singapore Airlines was inextricably tied up with that of Malaysian Airlines (qv). The present title was not adopted until 1972, after the ending the previous year of the agreement between the governments of Singapore and Malaysia which had created the relatively short-lived Malaysia-Singapore Airlines.

Initially Singapore Airlines was a nationalised concern, but the state's holding has been steadily reduced, largely as a result of the airline seeking additional capital from private investors to fund its

With no domestic services, Singapore Airlines is a completely international operator, with many long-haul routes. Largest aircraft in the fleet are its Boeing 747-400s, some of which may be available for leasing.

expansion. Despite the small size of Singapore and the absence of any domestic routes, the airline is one of the world's top 20 airlines in terms of annual turnover, and is the third-largest in Asia, a reflection both of the rapid economic growth achieved by Singapore, and the pivotal position of the country as a hub.

The airline has made a number of investments elsewhere in the air transport industry, including Singapore Aircraft

Leasing Enterprise, which is a joint venture with Boullioun Aviation Services, for which a substantial number of Boeing 777s and Airbus A320s are being delivered. It now owns Silk Air (qv), as well as having small interests in both Swissair (qv) and Delta Air Lines (qv), which have small shareholdings in Singapore Airlines as part of a strategic partnership. The Singapore Government stake is now just over 50 per cent.

The Airbus A340-300E is marketed by Singapore Airlines as the 'Celestar'.

Well away from its base is this Singapore Airlines A310-300, which is probably a leased aircraft, given the French 'F' registration.

Executive Directors & Officers: S. Dhanaban, Chairman; Cheong Choong Kong, Deputy Chairman & Chief Executive Officer; Chew Choon Seng, Deputy Managing Director, Administration; Michael Tan Jiak Ngee, Deputy Managing Director, Commercial; Chew Leng Seng, Deputy Managing Director, Technical.

HQ Airport & Main Base: Singapore

Radio callsign: SINGAPORE

Designator: SQ/SIA

Employees: 27,516

Main destinations served: Adelaide, Amsterdam, Athens, Auckland, Bandar Seri Begawan, Bangkok, Beijing, Berlin, Brisbane, Brussels, Cairns, Chiang Mai, Christchurch, Copenhagen, Darwin, Denpasar (Bali), Frankfurt, Fukuoka, Guangzhou, Hangzhou, Hanoi, Hat Yai, Hiroshima, Ho Chi Minh City, Hong Kong, Jakarta, Kaohsiung, Kota Kinabalu, Kuantan, Kuching, London Heathrow, Los Angeles, Madrid, Macau, Manchester, Manila, Melbourne, Nagoya, New York JFK, Osaka, Paris CDG, Penang, Perth, Port Moresby, Rome, San Francisco, Sendai, Seoul, Shanghai, Surabaya, Sydney, Taipei, Tokyo, Vancouver, Vienna, Yangon, Zürich.

A number of other destinations are served by Silk Air (qv).

Annual turnover: US $4,782.2 million (£2,898.3 million)

Revenue passenger km pa: 54,692.5 million

Cargo tonne km pa: 4,348.6 million

Passengers pa: 12,022,000

LINKS WITH OTHER AIRLINES
Owns Silk Air (qv). Owns 5 per cent of Delta Air Lines (qv) and 2.7 per cent of Swissair (qv).
Delta Air Lines has a 2.7 per cent interest and Swissair has 0.6 per cent.
A strategic alliance exists with these airlines, with Silk Air also undertaking a number of SIA operations.

FLEET
36 Boeing 747-400 'Megatop' (plus 8 on order) (l leased out)
3 Boeing 747-300 'Big Top' (may be replaced by 747-400 arrivals)
3 Boeing 747-300 Combi
8 Boeing 747-400F 'Mega Ark'
8 Airbus A340-300E 'Celestar' (plus 9 on order)
16 Boeing 777 (in course of delivery) (6 for Singapore Aircraft Leasing)
17 Airbus A310-300
6 Airbus A310-200
24 Airbus A320-200 (in course of delivery) (most for Singapore Aircraft Leasing)

Slovakia – OM

TATRA AIR

Tatra Air

Incorporated: 1990

HISTORY
The national airline of Slovakia, Tatra Air was established in 1990 and commenced operations in April 1991, taking over the Bratislava routes which had hitherto been operated by CSA (qv) before the division of Czechoslovakia. Assistance was at first provided by Crossair (qv), the initial fleet included three Let L-410s and two Saab 340As obtained from this airline. Tatra Air has grown considerably since its formation, with its international services handled by a fleet of Boeing 737-300s.

Executive Directors & Officers: Bohuslav Huraj, Director General.

HQ Airport & Main Base: Bratislava
Radio callsign: TATRA

Designator: QS/TTR

Employees: 500

Main destinations served: Berlin, Frankfurt, Geneva, Kosice, Munich, Prague, Sliac, Stuttgart, Tatry/Popra, Vienna, Zürich.

LINKS WITH OTHER AIRLINES
Marketing Alliances with CSA Czech Airlines (qv) and Swissair (qv).

FLEET
6 Boeing 737-300 (leased)
2 Saab 2000
2 Saab 340A

South Africa – ZS

COMAIR

Commercial Airways

Incorporated: 1946

HISTORY
Originally founded in 1946, Comair did not begin operations until 1948, and has since developed a network of domestic services which has recently been extended to neighbouring states. An important element in the airline's business has been the development of safari tours. At one time it operated a service to Gabarone for South African Airways, but the airline is now a British Airways (qv) franchisee. The fleet, which as late as 1991 consisted of a Douglas DC-3 and four Fokker F-27 Friendships, now includes Boeing jets. In 1997 Comair acquired a 25 per cent stake in state-owned SunAir.

Executive Directors & Officers: D. Novick, Chairman; P van Hoven, Managing Director; B. van der Linden, Commercial Director; N. Vlok, Airline Operations Director.

HQ Airport & Main Base: Johannesburg

Radio callsign: COMMERCIAL

Designator: CAW

Employees: Flight-crew: 140; Cabin staff: 160; Engineering: 50; Ground staff: 600; Total: 950.

Main destinations served: Cape Town, Durban, Gabarone, Harare, Hoodspruit, Manzini, Port Elizabeth, Richards Bay, Skukuza, Victoria Falls, Windhoek.

LINKS WITH OTHER AIRLINES
A British Airways (qv) franchisee.

FLEET
2 Boeing 727-200 (leased)
6 Boeing 737-200
2 Fokker F-27-200 Friendship
2 ATR 42 (leased)

SA AIRLINK

Airlink Airlines

Incorporated: 1992

HISTORY
SA Airlink came into existence in 1992, taking over the services of bankrupt Link Airways and initially operating a mixed fleet including four ATR 42s, two Metroliners, a Dornier Do.228, and two Piper Navajo Chieftains. It took its present title in 1995 when it entered into an alliance with South African Airways (qv), operating commuter or feeder services and complementing the operations elsewhere in South Africa of SA Express (qv).

Executive Directors & Officers: Richard Charter, Chairman; Barrie Webb, Joint Managing Director; Roger A. Foster, Joint Managing Director; Patrick Kleu, Financial Director; Duke Morosi, Operations Director.

HQ Airport & Main Base: Johannesburg

Radio callsign: LINK

Designator: 4Z/LNK

Employees: 352

Main destinations served: Bloemfontein, Durban, Margate, Mmabatho, Nelspruit, Phalaborwa, Pietersburg, Pietmaritzburg, Plettenberg, Sun City, Umtata.

LINKS WITH OTHER AIRLINES
Operates in a marketing alliance with South African Airways and SA Express (qv).

FLEET
11 British Aerospace Jetstream 41
2 Dornier Do.228

SA EXPRESS

South African Express Airways

Incorporated: 1993

HISTORY
SA Express was founded in December 1993 and commenced operations the following April. It was intended from the start as a commuter airline to feed into the trunk domestic services of South African

Airways (qv), and also to take over routes which could not be served economically by jet aircraft. South African Airways acquired a 20 per cent stake in the new airline, while the main shareholder is Thebe Investments with 51 per cent. In addition to the South African Airways connection the airline also has a marketing alliance with SA Airlink (qv).

Executive Directors & Officers: Bell Deluce, Chief Executive Officer; Israel Skosana, Deputy Chief Executive Officer; Andre Viljoen, Chief Operating Officer.

HQ Airport & Main Base: Johannesburg

Radio callsign: EXPRESSWAYS

Designator: YB/EXY

Employees: 328

Main destinations served: Bloemfontein, Cape Town, Durban, East London, George, Kimberley, Port Elizabeth, Richards Bay, Upington, Walvis Bay.

LINKS WITH OTHER AIRLINES
South African Airways (qv) has a 20 per cent stake.
Marketing alliance with South African Airways and SA Airlink (qv).

FLEET
8 de Havilland Dash 8-300
8 Canadair CRJ-200ER plus 2 on order

SAFAIR

Safair Freighters

Incorporated: 1970

HISTORY
South Africa's main freight airline, Safair was formed in 1970 as a subsidiary of the state-owned shipping line, Safmarine, which still owns it today. It operates world-wide on a charter basis, as well as having a domestic network. Its fleet has varied over the years, and has included a Boeing 707 and British Aerospace 146s, but today it has settled on the Boeing 727 and Lockheed Hercules.

Executive Directors & Officers: Ralph Boettler, Chief Executive Officer.

HQ Airport & Main Base: Johannesburg

Radio callsign: CARGO

Designator: FA/SFR

Employees: 240

Main destinations served: Charters world-wide, plus scheduled services to

Africa's largest airline, South African Airways has a new identity, replacing its famous 'springbok' with the colours of the new national flag, as shown on this Boeing 747-400.

Cape Town, Durban, East London, George, Johannesburg, Port Elizabeth, Walvis Bay.

FLEET
9 Lockheed L-100-30 Hercules
8 Boeing 727-200F

SOUTH AFRICAN

South African Airways
Incorporated: 1934

HISTORY
Africa's largest airline, South African Airways (or SAA) was originally founded in 1934 when the South African Government acquired Union Airways, a privately-owned airline unable to keep pace with the capital demands of rapid growth. It was soon enlarged by the acquisition of South West African Airways in 1935. South West African had also been privately-owned and dated from 1932. The mainstay of the new airline's fleet was the Junkers F.13, later supplemented by Junkers Ju.52/3m trimotors and then

Ju.86s, with a sizeable fleet of Lockheed Lodestars also pressed into service before the outbreak of World War Two. Wartime demands for aircraft and aircrew, and the difficulty in obtaining spares for the German-built aircraft, meant that all services were suspended in 1940, and the serviceable aircraft taken over by the South African Air Force. A limited number of services were reinstated in 1944, in recognition of the significance of air transport in a large country.

Post-war a service to London was started in 1945, with the airline operating the surviving Lockheed Lodestars and Douglas DC-3s on domestic services and Douglas DC-4s and Avro Yorks on the longer-haul routes. Lockheed Constellations were introduced in 1950, being replaced by Douglas DC-7Bs in 1956. Meanwhile de Havilland Comet I jet airliners had been leased from BOAC in 1953, and were flown with South African crews until the aircraft were grounded after a spate of serious accidents. Much greater success was experienced with a fleet of Vickers Viscount turboprop airliners, first introduced in 1956 and used on services within South Africa and to neighbouring states.

South African Airways entered the jet age permanently in 1960, with Boeing 707s. The extra range of these aircraft soon came to be valued after a number of newly independent African states banned the use of their airspace by South African aircraft, leading to the European services having to be re-routed via the Cape Verde Islands, at that time a Portuguese colony. The new routes, nevertheless, proved popular with passengers.

Airbus A320-200s are used on regional routes, including the 'golden triangle' between Cape Town, Johannesburg, and Durban.

Short-haul jet airliners eventually replaced the Viscounts, with Boeing 727s and then 737s entering service, while long-haul routes came to be taken over by the Boeing 747. At the other end of the scale the less heavily-used domestic services had most of their DC-3s replaced by Hawker Siddeley, later British Aerospace, HS 748 twin turboprop airliners.

Political change in South African has eased the airline's operating conditions considerably, and also led to a massive growth in competition with more than 80 foreign airlines now operating into the country's airports, as opposed to a mere handful during the final days of apartheid. A visible alteration has been the change from the airline's well-known blue cheat line and orange tail with a springbok symbol, to an all-white fuselage and a tailplane design incorporating the colours of the new national flag. Unusually, especially for a large national airline, the fleet includes aircraft maintained in active preservation, including DC-3s, DC-4s, and a Ju.52/3m.

SAA is owned by Transnet, a state-owned company. In turn, it has a 20 per cent stake in SA Express (qv), which operates feeder services, and a marketing alliance with SA Airlink (qv), another feeder operator. The airline is being prepared for privatisation in the near future.

Executive Directors & Officers: Prof Louise A. Tager, Chairman; S.J. Macozoma, Managing Director.

HQ Airport & Main Base: Johannesburg International, with additional hubs/bases at Cape Town and Durban.

Radio callsign: SPRINGBOK

Designator: SA/SAA

Employees: Flight-crew: 650; Cabin staff: 2,000; Engineering: 3,000; Ground staff: 5,150; Total: 10,800.

Main destinations served: Abidjan, Accra, Amsterdam, Bangkok, Blantyre, Bloemfontein, Bombay, Buenos Aires, Bulawayo, Cape Town, Dar-es-Salaam, Dubai, Durban, Düsseldorf, East London, Frankfurt, George, Harare, Hong Kong, Ilha do Sal, Johannesburg, Kinshasa, Lilongwe, London Heathrow, Luanda, Lusaka, Maputo, Mauritius, Miami, Munich, Nairobi, New York JFK, Perth, Port Elizabeth, Rio de Janeiro, São Paulo, Singapore, Sydney, Taipei, Tel Aviv, Victoria Falls, Windhoek, Zürich.

Annual turnover: US $1,416 million (£858.2 million)

Passengers pa: 6 million

LINKS WITH OTHER AIRLINES
Marketing alliances with Lufthansa (qv), SA Express (qv), and SA Airlink (qv). Owns 20 per cent interest in SA Express.

FLEET
6 Boeing 747-400
4 Boeing 747-300
5 Boeing 747-200B
1 Boeing 747-200F
7 Boeing 777-200
8 Airbus A300B4
7 Airbus A320-200
13 Boeing 737-200
2 Douglas DC-4
2 Douglas DC-3
1 Junkers Ju52/3m

Spain – EC

AIR NOSTRUM

Air Nostrum SA

Incorporated: 1994

HISTORY
Privately-owned Air Nostrum was formed in 1994 to operate scheduled services from Valencia to other major Spanish cities, the Balearic Islands, and southern France.

Executive Directors & Officers: Carlos Bertomeu, Chairman.

HQ Airport & Main Base: Valencia

Designator: YW/RQQ

Main destinations served: Biarritz, Bilbao, Ibiza, Madrid, Menorca, Nice, Palma de Mallorca, Vitoria.

FLEET
15 Fokker 50
4 ATR 72-200

AIR TRACK

Air Track SA

Incorporated: 1986

HISTORY
Originally founded in 1986, Air Track began operations the following year as Air Truck, offering air charter services. The present title was taken in 1996. A subsidiary is Líneas Aéreas Navarras, which uses Air Track's three ATR 42s on scheduled passenger services from Pamplona in northern Spain.

Executive Directors & Officers: Gerardo Herrerro, Chairman; José

Pamies, Managing Director; Emelio Nunez, Financial Director; Javiel Villanneva, Commercial Director; Juan Llort, Operations Director; Jaime Gonzala, Maintenance Director; Ramon Villanneva, Engineering Director; Christian Herrero, Personnel Director.

HQ Airport & Main Base: Madrid, with a base at Pamplona

Radio callsign: AIR TRUCK

Designator: ZH/TPK

Employees: approx 200

Main destinations served: Pamplona to Madrid, Barcelona.

LINKS WITH OTHER AIRLINES
Owns Líneas Aéreas Navarras.

FLEET
3 ATR 42-300

AVIACO

Aviaco – Aviacion y Comercio SA

Incorporated: 1948

HISTORY
Spain's main domestic airline, Aviaco was formed in 1948 by a group of businessmen in Bilbao, in northern Spain, as an all-cargo charter airline using Bristol 170 Freighters. Scheduled passenger services followed in 1950, initially from Bilbao to Madrid and Barcelona, and before long the airline was establishing services from the mainland to the Balearic Islands and to the Canaries. Major expansion of the domestic route network followed with services based on Madrid, and jet equipment was introduced during the early-1960s, initially using Sud Aviation Caravelles leased from Sabena (qv).

An unusual feature of its operations during the 1960s was the vehicle ferry service from Barcelona to Palma de Mallorca, on the largest of the Balearic Islands, using Aviation Trader Carvairs, which were converted Douglas DC-4s.

Acquisition of a substantial shareholding in Aviaco by Iberia (qv) enabled the airline to take over some of Iberia's domestic services, leaving that airline with a presence on the major trunk routes, such as Madrid to Barcelona. A number of internal services are operated on behalf of Iberia. Today Aviaco operates a fleet of McDonnell Douglas DC-9s and MD-88s, and is owned 32.9 per cent by Iberia and 67 per cent by SEPI, the state-owned industrial group which controls Iberia itself.

Spain's main domestic airline is Aviaco, although international charters are also flown, using aircraft such as this McDonnell Douglas MD-88.

Executive Directors & Officers: Xabier de Irala, Chairman; Juan Losa, General Manager; Enrique Marote, Business Director; Jesus Revilla, Operations Director; José Salas, Economic Director; Juan F. Miranda, Technical Director; Juan Martinez, Industrial Director.

HQ Airport & Main Base: Madrid, with further bases/hubs at Barcelona and Zaragoza.

Radio callsign: AVIACO

Designator: AO/AYC

Employees: Flight-crew: 360; Cabin staff: 480; Engineering: 200; Ground staff: approx 760; Total: 1,800.

Main destinations served: Almeria, Alicante, Asturias, Barcelona, Bilbao, Fuerteventura, Gran Canaria, Granada, Ibiza, Jeréz, Lanzarote, Las Palmas, Malaga, Menorca, Murcia, Palma de Mallorca, Pamplona, San Sebastian, Santander, Seville, Tenerife, Valencia, Valladolid, Vigo, Zaragoza.

Annual turnover: US $429.1 million (£260 million)

Aircraft km pa: 34.3 million

Revenue passenger km pa: 2,460.75 million

LINKS WITH OTHER AIRLINES
Iberia (qv) has a 32.9 per cent interest, with code-sharing and joint marketing. Code-sharing with British Airways (qv).

FLEET
24 McDonnell Douglas MD-87
13 McDonnell Douglas MD-88
19 McDonnell Douglas DC-9

BINTER

Binter Canarias SA

Incorporated: 1988

HISTORY
Established in 1988, Binter Canarias commenced operations the following year, taking over many of the routes within the Canary Islands hitherto operated by Iberia (qv) and Aviaco (qv). Iberia has a controlling interest in the airline, which now also operates to Madeira.

Executive Directors & Officers: Javier Alvarez, President; Luis Gonzalez, Director General; Alfredo Iglesias, Financial Director; Victor Siberio, Commercial Director; Rafael Lopez, Maintenance Director.

HQ Airport & Main Base: Tenerife Norte

Radio callsign: BINTER

Designator: NT/IBB

Employees: 500

Main destinations served: El Hiero, Fuerteventura, Funchal, Gran Canaria, Las Palmas, Lanzarote.

Annual turnover: Included in figures for Iberia

Revenue passenger km pa: 317 million

LINKS WITH OTHER AIRLINES
A low-cost subsidiary of Iberia.

FLEET
4 McDonnell Douglas DC-9

6 ATR 72
4 CASA/IPTN CN-235

BINTER MEDITERRANEO

Binter Mediterraneo SA

Incorporated: 1989

HISTORY
A low cost operation established by Iberia (qv) to operate short routes from Malaga to Almeria and Valencia in Spain, and to Melilla and Ceuta in North Africa.

Executive Directors & Officers: Javier Alvarez Gonzale, President; Leopoldo Iglesia Lachia, Director General.

HQ Airport & Main Base: Malaga

Radio callsign: BINTER

Designator: AX/BIM

Employees: 120

Main destinations served: Almeria, Ceuta, Melilla, Valencia.

Annual turnover: Included in figures for Iberia.

Revenue passenger km pa: 44 million

LINKS WITH OTHER AIRLINES
A subsidiary of Iberia.

FLEET
5 CASA/IPTN CN-235

FUTURA

Futura International Airways SA

Incorporated: 1989

HISTORY
Founded in 1989 by Aer Lingus (qv) and Spanish tour operating interests, Futura began charter operations in 1990. Initially Aer Lingus held a 25 per cent interest, but this has since increased to 85 per cent.

Executive Directors & Officers: Leo Guckian, Chief Executive Officer; Bruno Claeys, Commercial Director; Juan Payo, Operations Director; Roman Pane, Maintenance Director.

HQ Airport & Main Base: Palma de Mallorca

Radio callsign: FUTURA

Designator: FH/FVA

Employees: 550

Main destinations served: Inclusive tour charter flights to Spanish resorts, especially those in the Balearics, from the main European centres.

LINKS WITH OTHER AIRLINES
Aer Lingus has an 85 per cent interest.

FLEET
8 Boeing 737-400

IBERIA

Iberia Airlines – Linéas Aéreas de España SA

Incorporated: 1927

HISTORY
Spain's national airline Iberia was originally founded in 1927 as Iberia Air Transport. In 1929 it was merged with two other Spanish airlines, CETA and Union Aérea Espanola, to create CLASSA, and a majority shareholding in this new airline was taken by the Spanish Government. CLASSA was in turn acquired in 1931 by a newly-established state-owned carrier, LAPE. These manoeuvres failed to establish a solid footing for air transport in Spain, largely because of the impact of the Spanish Civil War, which saw many routes suspended and aircraft requisitioned for the war effort by both sides, leaving LAPE in severe financial and operational difficulties by 1938.

The present Iberia was formed in 1938 to acquire the equipment and services of LAPE, and re-establish domestic and inter-

One of Iberia's Boeing 747-200Bs used on long-haul services.

national services suspended during the Civil War. The initial fleet consisted almost entirely of Junkers Ju.52/3M trimotors. Initially it was a mixed enterprise, with the Spanish Government holding a 51 per cent majority stake, but the difficulties experienced during World War Two – despite Spanish neutrality – resulted in the state acquiring the private shareholdings. Wartime services were limited to links with Portugal, Spanish Morocco, and Spain's offshore islands.

Post-war, Iberia began a programme of expansion, acquiring a new fleet of Douglas DC-3s for internal and European

services, and then DC-4s for longer-distance operations, including the airline's first transatlantic services. The DC-4s were augmented and then replaced by Lockheed Super Constellations on the longer routes, while the DC-3s remained on domestic services but were replaced on European routes by Convair 440 Metropolitans. The airline's first jet equipment, Douglas DC-8s for the transatlantic routes, were introduced in 1961, while Sud Aviation Caravelles were introduced on European routes in 1962. A fleet of Fokker F-27 Friendship airliners was introduced in 1967 to replace the DC-3s on domestic routes.

Iberia also has eight Airbus A340s, ideal for 'long thin' routes.

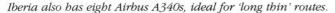

As the jet age progressed Iberia operated a mix of Boeing and Douglas types, notably the Boeing 727 and 747 and different marks of Douglas DC-9. In more recent years it has also operated aircraft of Airbus manufacture, as well as the Boeing 757.

After Iberia took a shareholding in the Spanish domestic carrier Aviaco (qv) many domestic services were handed over to the latter, although Iberia continued to maintain a presence on the trunk routes. Iberia also took a 20 per cent stake in the Argentine airline Aérolineas Argentinas (qv) when it was privatised in 1990. Another South American carrier in which Iberia has a substantial interest is Viasa (qv) of Venezuela. There is also a token 2 per cent stake in Royal Air Maroc (qv). Iberia itself is owned by the state holding company SEPI, itself a major shareholder in Aviaco.

In recent years Iberia has been struggling to control costs and reduce its dependence on state support, which has come under increasing scrutiny by the European Commission. It may even be that the stake in Aérolineas Argentinas may have to be sold. In a further attempt to contain costs Iberia has participated in the creation of low cost regional carriers such as Binter Canarias, and a new airline, Viva Air (qv), operating both scheduled and charter flights for the leisure market. A marketing alliance with American Airlines (qv) was agreed in 1997.

The Spanish Government intends to privatise Iberia by 1999.

Executive Directors & Officers: Xabier de Irala Estevez, President & Chairman; Angel Mullor Parrondo, Director General; Enrique Dupuy de Lome Chavarri, Director, Finance; Martin Cuesta Vivar, Director, Organisation & Human Resources; José Maria Fariza Batanero, Director, Control & Administration; Enrique Donaire Rodriguez, Director, Commercial; Javier Arraiza Martinez-Marina, Director, Operations; Sergio Turrion Barbado, Director, Industrial Relations.

HQ Airport & Main Base: Madrid, with a further hub/base at Barcelona.

Radio callsign: IBERIA

Designator: IB/IBE

Employees: Flight-crew: 1,922; Cabin staff: 3,637; Engineering: 1,514; Ground staff: 19,147; Total: 26,220.

Main destinations served: Alicante, Amsterdam, Asuncion, Athens, Berlin, Bilbao, Bogotá, Brussels, Buenos Aires, Cairo, Cancun, Caracas, Copenhagen, Dakar, Dublin, Düsseldorf, Frankfurt, Geneva, Guatemala, Hamburg, Havana, Istanbul, Las Palmas, Lima, Lisbon, London Heathrow, London Gatwick, Malabo, Malaga, Managua, Manchester, Marseilles, Mexico City, Milan, Montevideo, Montreal, Moscow, Munich, New York JFK, Nice, Oporto, Quito, Palma de Mallorca, Panama City, Paris CDG, Paris Orly, Rio de Janeiro, Rome, San José, San Juan, San Pedro de Sula, San Salvador, Santa Cruz de Tenerife, Santiago de Chile, Santiago de Compostela, Santo Domingo, São Paulo, Seville, Stockholm, Stuttgart, Tangiers, Tel Aviv, Tokyo, Tunis, Valencia, Venice, Vienna.

Annual turnover: US $3,502 million (£2,122.4 million)

Revenue passenger km pa: 25,931 million

LINKS WITH OTHER AIRLINES
Interests in other airlines include Viva (qv), 99.4 per cent; Viasa (qv), 45 per cent; Ladeco (qv), 37.5 per cent; Aviaco (qv), 32.9 per cent; Aérolinas Argentinas, 20 per cent; and Royal Air Maroc (qv), 2 per cent.

FLEET
4 Boeing 747-200B (1 leased)
4 McDonnell Douglas DC-10
12 Airbus A340 (leased)
8 Airbus A300B4 (2 not operational)
10 Boeing 757-200 (leased)
3 McDonnell Douglas DC-8 (1 leased, 2 chartered to Cargosur)
28 Boeing 727-200A (5 leased)
8 Airbus A321
22 Airbus A320 (11 leased)
9 Boeing 737 (7 leased) (operated by Viva Air (qv))
24 McDonnell Douglas MD-87 (7 leased)
13 McDonnell Douglas MD-88 (operated by Aviaco (qv))
6 ATR
8 CASA/IPTN CN-235 (1 leased, 2 operated by Binter Canarias (qv), 2 by Austral (qv))

OASIS

Oasis International Airlines

Incorporated: 1988

HISTORY
Originally founded as Andalusair, Oasis is a Spanish inclusive tour charter operator, flying into the main Spanish resorts from major centres elsewhere in Europe, and also flying from Spain to resorts in the Caribbean. It has a stake in small Mexican charter airline Aérocancum, with which it exchanges aircraft at peak periods, using Aérocancum's McDonnell Douglas MD-83s during the European summer peak.

Executive Directors & Officers: Antonio Mara, President & Managing Director.

HQ Airport & Main Base: Madrid

Radio callsign: OASIS

Designator: OB/ANN

Employees: 280

Main destinations served: Inclusive tour charters to the main Spanish resorts from points elsewhere in Europe, and charters from Spain to the Caribbean.

LINKS WITH OTHER AIRLINES
An interest in Aérocancum, with an operational alliance.

FLEET
1 Airbus A310-300
3 McDonnell Douglas MD-83
1 McDonnell Douglas MD-82

PAN AIR

Pan Air Linéas Aéreas SA

Incorporated: 1987

HISTORY
A freight specialist, Pan Air was founded in 1987 and commenced operations the following year, initially operating a Fokker F-27 Friendship on cargo charters. It became part of the TNT (qv) air freight network, with TNT acquiring a 25 per cent stake which has since increased to 49 per cent. The fleet now consists of British Aerospace 146 aircraft, including the QT 'quiet trader' versions.

Executive Directors & Officers: Nicolas Valero, President; David Robinson, Director General.

HQ Airport & Main Base: Madrid

Radio callsign: SKYJET

Designator: PA/PNR

Employees: 140

Main destinations served: Charter and TNT contract cargo operations throughout Europe, North Africa, and the Middle East, including services from Spain to the TNT hub at Cologne/Bonn.

LINKS WITH OTHER AIRLINES
TNT (qv) has a 49 per cent interest.

One of the airlines making the most of European deregulation in the air and on the ground is Spanair, which has almost 20 of these McDonnell Douglas MD-83s.

FLEET
1 British Aerospace 146-300QT
6 British Aerospace 146-200QT
2 British Aerospace 146-100QC
(convertible pax/cargo)

SPANAIR

Spanair SA

Incorporated: 1986

HISTORY
Spanair was founded in 1986 as a joint venture between the Viajes Marsans travel agency group and SAS (qv), and began charter operations in 1988 using a single McDonnell Douglas MD-83, with most of the flights being inclusive tour charters from mainland European centres to the Balearic Islands. Scheduled services started in 1994, the same year that Spanair moved into ground-handling, hitherto the preserve of Iberia (qv) and Aviaco (qv). Although based at Palma de Mallorca, the main hub for its growing scheduled network is Madrid.

Executive Directors & Officers:
Gonzalo Pascual, Chairman; Carlos Bravo, Managing Director; Eduardo Aranda, Deputy Managing Director; Juan Bonilla, Financial Director; Javier Muela, Operations Director; Tirso Gonzalez, Maintenance & Engineering Director; Ricardo R. Roda, Commercial Director; Ola Ohlsson, Passenger Services Director; Frank Badino, Scheduled Flights Director.

HQ Airport & Main Base: Palma de
Mallorca, with bases/hubs at Madrid and Barcelona.

Radio callsign: SUNWING

Designator: JK/SPP

Employees: Flight-crew: 220; Cabin staff: 425; Engineering: 91; Ground staff: 1,101 (includes ground-handling); Total: 1,837.

Main destinations served: Charter flights to and from more than 100 airports in Europe and the Americas to mainland Spain, the Balearics, and the Canaries.
Scheduled flights, mainly from Madrid, to Barcelona, Bilbao, Copenhagen*,

Lanzarote, Las Palmas*, London Gatwick, Mahon, Malaga*, Palma de Mallorca, Santiago de Compostela*, Tenerife*.
* also from Barcelona.

Annual turnover: US $309.6 million (£187.7 million)

Aircraft km pa: 21.6 million

Revenue passenger km pa: 3,483.2 million

Cargo tonne km pa: 13.1 million

Passengers pa: 3.4 million

LINKS WITH OTHER AIRLINES
SAS (qv) has a 49 per cent shareholding.

FLEET
2 Boeing 767-300ER (leased)
2 McDonnell Douglas MD-87 (leased)
17 McDonnell Douglas MD-83 (leased)

VIVA AIR

Vuelos Internacionales de Vacaciones SA

Incorporated: 1988

HISTORY
Originally formed by Iberia (qv) and Lufthansa (qv) as a special 'vacation' airline, Viva Air is now owned more than 90 per cent by Iberia. It operates charter flights and international scheduled flights from points throughout Europe to the main Spanish holiday destinations. It is meant to be a low cost operation to

For longer distance charters, Spanair has two Boeing 767-300ERs.

counter Iberia's traditionally high labour costs.

Executive Directors & Officers: Manuel Rodriguez Gimeno, President; José M. de Calis Bores, Director General; Julio Larruba, Director, Commercial; Alvaro Epinosa de los Monteros, Director, Finance; Luis Seco Lopez, Director, Operations; Rufino Velasco, Director, Technical.

HQ Airport & Main Base: Palma de Mallorca

Radio callsign: VIVA

Designator: FV/VIV

Employees: approx 500

Main destinations served: Scheduled services from the main European capitals to the Balearic Islands, plus charter flights.

Annual turnover: Included in figures for Iberia.

Revenue passenger km pa: 1,544 million

LINKS WITH OTHER AIRLINES
Iberia owns 99.4 per cent of Viva's shares.

FLEET
9 Boeing 737-300

Sri Lanka – 4R

AIR LANKA

Air Lanka Corporation

Incorporated: 1979

HISTORY
Air Lanka was formed as the national airline of Sri Lanka in 1979, wholly-government owned, to take over the operations of Air Ceylon, which had been established by the government in 1947. Air Ceylon had initially operated three Douglas DC-3s on services within Ceylon and to India. Services to London and Sydney followed in 1949 after the airline entered into an operating agreement with Australian National Airways (ANA), and two Douglas DC-4s were obtained for these routes. In 1951 the airline was restructured, becoming a corporation rather than a department of the Ministry of Communications & Works, and under the new arrangement the Ceylon Government held 51 per cent of the shares and ANA the remainder. ANA's interest was purchased in 1955 by KLM

(qv), and from 1956 onwards a service was also operated to Amsterdam.

The agreement with KLM was terminated in 1961, when the airline became wholly-government owned and had to suspend operations other than those within Ceylon and to India until BOAC (British Overseas Airways Corporation) was able to start a London–Colombo service in association with Air Ceylon, initially using one of BOAC's de Havilland Comet 4s, later replaced by a Vickers VC10.

Its own jet equipment arrived soon afterwards, with a Hawker Siddeley Trident 1E for services to India, while turboprop Hawker Siddeley (later British Aerospace) HS 748s and Nord 262s were used on internal services (alongside two surviving DC-3s) and those to southern India. After the ending of the agreement with BOAC the French independent airline UTA provided management assistance, and services once again extended to Europe and Australia, using a Douglas DC-8.

The change of name and restructuring in 1979 also reflected the new name adopted for Ceylon. The network continued to expand, with the airline's first wide-bodied aircraft – Lockheed TriStars – while a Boeing 737-200 was acquired for the shorter routes. In place of the agreements with UTA, BOAC, and KLM, today Air Lanka has marketing alliances with a number of airlines in the Indian sub-continent, the Gulf, and South-East Asia. Privatisation is a possibility in the near future.

Executive Directors & Officers: Sepala Attygalle, Chairman; S.A. Chandrasekara, Chief Financial Officer.

HQ Airport & Main Base: Colombo

Radio callsign: AIR LANKA

Designator: UL/ALK

Employees: 4,000

Main destinations served: Abu Dhabi, Amsterdam, Bahrain, Bangkok, Bombay, Delhi, Dhahran, Dubai, Frankfurt, Fukuoka, Hong Kong, Jeddah, Karachi, Kuala Lumpur, Kuwait, London Heathrow, Madras, Male, Muscat, Paris CDG, Riyadh, Rome, Singapore, Tiruchirapelli, Tokyo, Trivandrum, Vienna, Zürich.

LINKS WITH OTHER AIRLINES
Code-sharing with Gulf Air (qv), Malaysia Airlines (qv), and Middle East Airlines (qv), and revenue-sharing with Indian Airlines (qv) and Pakistan International (qv).

FLEET
3 Airbus A340-300
1 Lockheed L-1011 TriStar 100
2 Lockheed L-1011 TriStar 50

2 Lockheed L-1011 TriStar 500
2 Airbus A320-200

Sudan – ST

SUDAN AIRWAYS

Sudan Airways Corporation

Incorporated: 1946

HISTORY
Sudan Airways was founded in 1946 by the Sudanese Government-owned Sudan Railways System, beginning operations in 1947 with the assistance of a British company, Airwork, at that time also involved in airline operations. Initially three de Havilland Dove light transports operated on domestic services, linking the more important Sudanese centres. The route network subsequently expanded, so that by 1960 Sudan Airways was operating to a number of important points in the Middle East, still with four Doves, augmented by seven Douglas DC-3s and a single Vickers Viscount turboprop airliner.

Three Fokker F-27 Friendship airliners were introduced in 1962, and in 1963 the airline received its first jet equipment, the first of two de Havilland Comet 4Cs, which enabled it to extend its route network south to Nairobi and north to Frankfurt and London. The Comets were joined by Boeing 707s in 1974, with the first short-haul jets, Boeing 737s, the following year.

Executive Directors & Officers:
Mukhtar Osman, General Manager; Faisal Mukhtar, Deputy General Manager; Y.E. Khaleel, Deputy General Manager; A. Elkheir, Finance Director; R.J. Belal, Commercial Director; O.H. Higazie, Operations Director; E. Mekki, Engineering Director; A. Idris, Administrative Director.

HQ Airport & Main Base: Khartoum

Radio callsign: SUDANAIR

Designator: SD/SUD

Employees: 2,400

Main destinations served: Domestic services, plus Abu Dhabi, Addis Ababa, Cairo, Damascus, Doha, Dubai, Frankfurt, Jeddah, Johannesburg, Kano, London Heathrow, Muscat, Nairobi, N'Djamena, Riyadh, Rome, Sana'a, Sharjah.

FLEET
1 Airbus A300B4-200
2 Airbus A310-300
3 Boeing 707-320C

1 Airbus A320-200
2 Boeing 737-200C
2 Fokker 50
3 de Havilland DHC-6 Twin Otter

Sweden – SE

See also Scandinavia

AIR SWEDEN

West Air Sweden AB

Incorporated: 1963

HISTORY
Originally founded in 1963 as an air taxi operator under the name of Abal Air, the name was changed to Time Air Sweden in 1990 and to West Air Sweden in 1993 – trading as Air Sweden – as the airline graduated to scheduled services. Executive charters are still operated, and patient transport is another aspect of the charter business.

Executive Directors & Officers: Gustaff Thureborn, President; Mikeal Heed, Vice-President, Flight Operations.

HQ Airport & Main Base: Karlstad

Radio callsign: AIR SWEDEN

Designator: PT/SWN

Main destinations served: Scheduled services linking some ten destinations within Sweden, plus charters.

FLEET
7 British Aerospace 748
2 IAI 1124 Westwind

NORDIC EUROPEAN

Nordic East Airways AB

Incorporated: 1991

HISTORY
Primarily an inclusive tour charter operator, Nordic European Airways also has plans to enter the scheduled service market. It is owned by Gunnar Ohlsson, its current chairman.

Executive Directors & Officers:
Gunnar Ohlsson, Chairman; Carl-Johas Stahle, President; Cammilla Lennhammer, Commercial Director; Joe Edlund, Operations Director; Robert Svedenbrant, Maintenance Director.

HQ Airport & Main Base: Stockholm Arlanda

Radio callsign: NORDIC

Designator: N7/NOD

Main destinations served: Charters to southern European, North African, and Middle East resorts.

FLEET
2 Lockheed L-1011 TriStar
2 Boeing 757-200
1 Boeing 737-400
1 Boeing 737-300

SKYWAYS

Skyways AB

Incorporated: 1987

HISTORY
Skyways was originally founded in 1987 as Avia, operating internal commuter or feeder services with a fleet of Short 330s and 360s. In 1991 it acquired another commuter operator, Salair, which also dated from 1987 and operated a fleet of three Saab 340s. Today Skyways has a fleet of Fokker and Saab aircraft and operates scheduled services within Sweden and to nearby countries.

Executive Directors & Officers: Sven Salen, Chairman; Jan Palmer, President & Managing Director; Jan Olor Bergling, Senior Vice-President; Christoffer Olsson, Vice-President, Operations; Soren Roos, Vice-President, Commercial & Marketing; Claes Norden, Vice-President, Maintenance & Technical.

HQ Airport & Main Base: Linkoping, with a further base at Stockholm-Arlanda.

Radio callsign: SKY EXPRESS

Designator: JZ/SKX

Employees: 380

Main destinations served: Arvidsjaur, Borlange, Copenhagen, Gallivare, Kramfors, Lycksele, Orebro, Pori, Storuman, Trollhattan, Vilhelmina, Visby.

FLEET
8 Fokker 50
10 Saab 340A

SUNWAYS

Sunways Airlines AB

Incorporated: 1994

HISTORY
Formed in 1994, Sunways commenced operations in 1995 with three Boeing 757s on inclusive tour charters to destinations in the Mediterranean, the Canaries, Portugal, the Middle East, and India.

Executive Directors & Officers:
Richard W. Hjelt, Chairman; Engin Gulmez, Managing Director; Robert Saflund, Operations Director; Krister Nalund, Engineering Director; Mikael Norgren, Technical Director.

HQ Airport & Main Base: Stockholm Arlanda

Radio callsign: SUNWAYS

Designator: SWY

Employees: 360

Main destinations served: Inclusive tour charters to Europe, Africa, and India.

FLEET
4 Boeing 757-200

TRANSWEDE

Transwede Airways AB

Incorporated: 1985

HISTORY
Originally founded in 1985 by NRT Nordisk as an inclusive tour charter airline, Transwede moved into scheduled services with a service from Stockholm to London Gatwick in 1991. At one time operating long-haul charters, this aspect of the business was split off in 1996 to a new airline, Transwede Leisure (qv), leaving Transwede to develop scheduled services within Sweden and to neighbouring countries. Ownership was transferred to Transwede Holdings and Braathens SAFE (qv), with each holding 50 per cent, and it is likely that Braathens will exercise its option to take full control of Transwede.

Executive Directors & Officers: Per Odegaard, President & Chief Executive Officer.

HQ Airport & Main Base: Stockholm Arlanda

Radio callsign: TRANSWEDE

Designator: TQ/TWE

Employees: 300

Main destinations served: Halmstad, Jonkoping, Lulea, Sundsvall, Umea.

LINKS WITH OTHER AIRLINES
Braathens SAFE (qv) holds 50 per cent.

FLEET
5 Fokker 100

TRANSWEDE LEISURE

Transwede Leisure AB

Incorporated: 1996

HISTORY
A relatively new airline, owned by the Transpol Group of tour operators. It was formed to take over the inclusive tour charter business of Transwede (qv) and in 1998 ownership passed to Britannia Airways (qv).

HQ Airport & Main Base: Stockholm Arlanda

Designator: TQ/TWE

Main destinations served: Inclusive tour charters to destinations in the Caribbean, Mediterranean, North Africa, Portugal, and the Canaries.

FLEET
2 Boeing 757-200
3 McDonnell Douglas MD-83
1 McDonnell Douglas MD-87

Switzerland – HB

AIR ENGIADINA

Air Engiadina

Incorporated: 1987

HISTORY
Air Engiadina was founded in 1987 to operate scheduled services from the Swiss Federal capital, Berne, where the airport is limited in the size of aircraft which can be operated. A domestic and international network has been developed, including services to London City. Some services are operated on behalf of Crossair (qv).

Executive Directors & Officers:
Dietmar Leitgeb, President & Chief Executive Officer; Charles Schnider, Managing Director; H.P. Kaufman, Operations Director.

Radio callsign: ENGIADINA

Designator: RQ/RQX (or LX for Crossair)

HQ Airport & Main Base: Berne, with an additional base at Zürich.

Employees: 120

Main destinations served: Amsterdam, Brno, Dublin, Eindhoven, Elba, Frankfurt,

Crossair started operations with aircraft such as Saab 340 turboprops, following these with the stretched Saab 2000, shown here.

London City, Manchester, Munich, Reus, Roh, Vienna.

LINKS WITH OTHER AIRLINES
Operates some flights for Crossair (qv).

FLEET
5 Fairchild Dornier 328-110

CROSSAIR

Crossair

Incorporated: 1975

HISTORY
Originally founded in 1975, Crossair did not commence operations until 1979, initially operating domestic services. Swissair (qv) acquired a significant minority stake in 1988, and has since increased this to a majority, 56.1 per cent shareholding, with a 59.8 per cent voting share. Crossair was the first operator of the Saab 340 regional turboprop, and has since developed into providing international and domestic feeder services for Swissair, as well as flying some of the parent airline's less busy routes, or even in some cases sharing routes with the larger operator by operating these outside peak periods.

In 1995 Balair/CTA's aircraft and services were transferred to Crossair by Swissair, taking the former into the inclusive tour charter market. In April 1996 a

Inevitably, Crossair soon required jet aircraft, such as these Avro RJ85s, known as 'Jumbolinos' to Crossair passengers.

Crossair has taken over many of Swissair's European routes, and also Balair's charters, for which a fleet of McDonnell Douglas MD-82/83s is operated in the airline's clean and attractive colour scheme.

new McDonnell Douglas MD-83 for inclusive tour charter operations was delivered in the colours of McDonald's, the hamburger chain.

By contrast, this Crossair MD-83 in all-over advertising for hamburgers is not everyone's idea of how an airliner should look.

Executive Directors & Officers:
Philippe Bruggisser, Chairman; Moritz Suter, Vice-Chairman, President & Chief Executive Officer; Thomas Hofmann, Executive Vice-President, Commercial & Finances; Dr Jurgen Termin, Executive Vice-President, Corporate Controlling; Fritz Grotz, Executive Vice-President, Technical & Operations; Josef Felder, Executive Vice-President, Product Management.

HQ Airport & Main Base: Basle, with a further base/hub at Lugano.

Radio callsign: CROSS AIR

Designator: LX/CRX (except when operating Swissair flights)

Employees: 2,280

Main destinations served: Many of the destinations on the Swissair list.

Annual turnover: US $501.2 million
(£303.8 million)

Cargo tonnes pa: 4,550,958

Passengers pa: 3,974,676

LINKS WITH OTHER AIRLINES
Swissair has a 56.1 per cent controlling
interest.
Some services are operated by Air
Engiadina (qv).

FLEET
4 McDonnell Douglas MD82 (leased)
4 McDonnell Douglas MD83 (leased)
12 Avro RJ100 'Jumbolino' (8 leased)
4 Avro RJ85 'Jumbolino'
24 Saab 2000 'Concordino' (12 leased)
15 Saab 340B Cityliner (4 leased)

FARNER

Farner Air Transport

Incorporated: 1984

HISTORY
Founded in 1984, Farner operates regular
express parcels services and light freight
air charters mainly within Europe, including work for the oil industry and humani-
tarian organisations. The original fleet,
which included Cessna 404s and Embraer
Bandeirantes, has grown to all-cargo
Fokker Friendships.

Executive Directors & Officers: Guy
Girard, Managing Director.

HQ Airport & Main Base:
Basle/Mulhouse

Radio callsign: FARNER

Designator: FAT

Main destinations served: Operates to
the main European freight/parcels hubs,
including Cologne/Bonn, Paris CDG, and
Southend.

FLEET
6 Fokker F27-500 Friendship
2 Fokker F27-400 Friendship

SWISSAIR

Swiss Air Transport Company/
Schweizerische Luftverkehr AG

Incorporated: 1931

HISTORY
Despite the small size and population of
Switzerland, Swissair is the world's 11th,

and Europe's fourth, largest airline by
annual turnover. Its history dates from the
merger of Balair of Basle and Ad Astra
Aero of Zürich in 1931. Ad Astra was the
older of the two, dating from 1919, when
it had appeared as the Ad Astra Swiss Air
Transport Company, operating in competition with the Aero-Gesellschaft Comte
Mittelholzer & Co and Avion Tourisme,
which it acquired in 1920. The acquisition
led to the airline being named Ad Astra
Aero Tourisme, or Ad Astra Aero, operating a fleet of 16 aircraft. Balair dated from
1925.

At the outset Swissair had a fleet of 13
aircraft, mainly of Fokker manufacture.
New aircraft were not long in arriving,
with the single-engined, four passenger
Lockheed Orion being introduced in 1932
for the Zürich–Munich–Vienna service. In
1934 Curtiss Condor biplane airliners were
introduced, and on these Swissair became
the first European airline to employ
female cabin attendants. A year later all-
year operations started on the
Zürich–Basle–London service, using
Douglas DC-2s.

Operations had to be suspended on the
outbreak of World War Two in Europe,
despite Swiss neutrality, both for safety
reasons and to conserve fuel. By this time
Swissair's fleet consisted of five Douglas
DC-3s, three DC-2s, a de Havilland DH-89
Dragon Rapide, a Fokker F-VIIa, and a
Comte AC-4 – slightly smaller in terms of
aircraft numbers than eight years earlier,

but showing a massive advance in
capacity. Operations were resumed in
1945 following the end of the war, when
the fleet was enlarged by the addition of
several more DC-3s. The airline introduced its first four-engined aircraft,
Douglas DC-4s, in 1946, and in 1949
these launched Swissair's first transatlantic
service linking Geneva and New York.
By this time Swissair had become the
national airline of Switzerland, although
not a nationalised airline, since a 1947
agreement enabled the airline to become
the official flag carrier in return for the
state taking a 30 per cent shareholding.

Swissair became a loyal supporter of
Douglas aircraft after receiving its DC-4s,
introducing first DC-6Bs and then DC-7Cs
on its longer-haul routes, although the
absence of Douglas from the short-haul
market for many years following the DC-
3, and the unsuccessful DC-5, meant that
Convair 440 Metropolitans were the
choice for the European routes. Swissair's
first jet airliners, Douglas DC-8s, were
introduced in 1960, and were later joined
by Convair 990 Coronado airliners for the
less busy long-haul routes, and by Sud
Aviation Caravelles for the European
services, although these too were in due
course replaced by Douglas DC-9s.

In 1958 Swissair entered into a collaborative agreement with SAS (Scandinavian
Airlines System) (qv), covering the pooling of certain intercontinental services and
technical collaboration, since the two air-

*Swissair has long been a keen purchaser of McDonnell Douglas products, having intro-
duced the Douglas DC-2 to Europe. This is an MD-11.*

The long and the short of it – an Airbus A320-200 (middle) is flanked by the stretched A321-100 and the more recent shortened A319, the smallest member of the Airbus family.

lines had almost identical fleets. This agreement was superseded in 1968 by another involving SAS, Swissair, and KLM (qv), allowing for collaboration on the DC-9 and the newly-introduced Boeing 747. Under this Swissair maintained all of the DC-9 engines along with the airframes of its own aircraft and those of KLM, while KLM maintained the airframes of all three fleets' 747s and SAS maintained the engines. All three airlines became customers for the Douglas DC-10.

Swissair obtained a share of the fast-growing air charter market by taking a controlling interest in a charter airline, Balair, which despite its name had no link with the original airline of that name and had started charter operations as recently as 1957. In 1988 a 38 per cent shareholding was acquired in a new Swiss regional airline, Crossair (qv), a 3 per cent interest also being taken in Austrian Airlines (qv). In 1993 Balair merged with CTA (Compagnie de Transport Aérien), and in 1995 the merged Balair-CTA's operations were transferred to Crossair, in which Swissair now has a 56.1 per cent interest.

A significant cross-border acquisition in recent years was a 49.5 per cent stake in Sabena (qv). Other alliances, such as those with Delta Air Lines (qv) and Singapore Airlines (qv), were marked by cross-shareholdings.

Recently the decision has been taken to concentrate intercontinental services on Zürich, rather than dividing these with Geneva, although both airports still operate European services. Crossair operates a number of the less busy routes on behalf of Swissair.

Executive Directors & Officers:
Hannes Goetz, Chairman; Philippe Bruggisser, President & Chief Executive Officer; Jeffrey G. Katz, Chief Operating Officer.

HQ Airport & Main Base:
Zürich, with a further European base/hub at Geneva.

Radio callsign:
SWISSAIR

Designator:
SR/SWR

Employees:
Flight-crew: 1,100; Cabin staff: 3,900; Engineering: 2,700; Ground staff: 2,780; Total: 9,480.

Main destinations served: Abidjan, Abu Dhabi, Accra, Amsterdam, Athens, Atlanta, Bamako, Bangkok, Banjul, Barcelona, Basle/Mulhouse, Beijing, Beirut, Belgrade, Berlin Templehof, Birmingham*, Bombay, Boston, Bratislava, Brazzaville, Brussels, Bucharest, Budapest, Buenos Aires, Cairo, Calgary/Banff, Cape Town, Chicago O'Hare, Cologne/Bonn*, Copenhagen, Dakar, Dar-es-Salaam, Delhi, Douala, Dubai, Düsseldorf, Edinburgh*, Frankfurt, Gothenburg, Graz, Guernsey*, Hamburg*, Hannover*, Harare, Helsinki, Hong Kong, Istanbul, Izmir, Jeddah, Jersey*, Johannesburg, Karachi, Kinshasa, Lagos, Larnaca, Las Palmas, Leipzig*, Lisbon, Ljubljana, London City*, London Heathrow, Los Angeles, Lugano*, Luxembourg, Lyons*, Madrid, Malaga, Malta, Manila, Marseilles*, Milan*, Montreal, Moscow, Munich, Munster/Osnabruck*, Muscat, Nairobi, New York JFK, New York Newark, Nice*, Nuremberg, Oporto, Osaka Kansai, Oslo*, Palma de Mallorca*, Paris CDG, Philadelphia, Prague*, Rio de Janeiro, Riyadh, Rome*, Rostock*, St Petersburg,

These days Swissair passengers are more likely to fly on an Airbus than a McDonnell Douglas aircraft, with Airbus A330-200s on medium and long-haul routes . . .

Santiago de Chile, São Paulo, Seoul, Shanghai, Singapore, Sofia, Stockholm, Stuttgart*, Taipei, Tehran, Tel Aviv, Thessaloniki, Tirana, Tokyo Narita, Tunis, Turin*, Valencia*, Vienna, Warsaw, Zagreb. * includes flights by Crossair.

Annual turnover: Swissair US $3,462.3 million (£2,098.4 million)
SAir Group US $6,646 million (£4,027.9 million)

Aircraft km pa: 195.9 million

Revenue passenger km pa: 27,573.4 million

Cargo tonne km pa: 1,634.9 million

LINKS WITH OTHER AIRLINES
A 56.1 per cent interest in Crossair (qv), with code-sharing and some Crossair flights carrying Swissair designator. Strategic alliance marked by a 49.5 per cent interest in Sabena (qv). Other strategic alliances marked by reciprocal shareholdings with Delta (qv) and Singapore Airlines (qv), Swissair having a 4.6 per cent share in Delta (and Delta a 4.5 per cent stake in Swissair) and a 0.6 per cent share in Singapore Airlines (which has a 2.7 per cent stake in Swissair).
A 10 per cent interest in Austrian Airlines (qv).

. . . and members of the A320 'family' on shorter routes.

FLEET
5 Boeing 747-300
12 McDonnell Douglas MD-11 (plus 3 on order)
8 Airbus A310-300 (at least one in BalairCTA livery for long-haul low-cost holiday flights)
8 Airbus A321-100
20 Airbus A320-200
8 Airbus A319-100
plus 9 Airbus A330-200 on order

TEA

TEA Switzerland AG

Incorporated: 1988

HISTORY
TEA Switzerland was one of the TEA group of airlines, an ambitious plan which saw charter airlines established using the TEA name in most of the main air charter markets across Europe. The airline was rescued by its directors when TEA collapsed, and its main shareholder is now Air Finance.

Executive Directors & Officers: Ernst Staehelin, Chairman; Markus Seiler, Managing Director; Jean-Jacques Boissin, Financial Director; Ernst Preiswerk, Commercial Director; Jean-Marc Thevenaz, Flight Operations Director; Hans-Ruedi Meyer, Ground Operations Director; Jean-Pierre Dreyfus, Technical Director; Daniela Gyger-Thommen, Personnel Director.

HQ Airport & Main Base: Basle/Mulhouse

Radio callsign: TOPSWISS

Designator: BH/TSW

Main destinations served: Inclusive tour charter operations to destinations in Europe, North Africa, and Asia.

Passengers pa: 560,000

FLEET
5 Boeing 737-300
2 Boeing 737-700

Syria – YK

SYRIANAIR

Syrian Arab Airlines

Incorporated: 1961

HISTORY
The history of air transport in Syria pre-

dates the formation of Syrian Arab Airlines in 1961, going back to a private venture airline, Syrian Airways, which commenced operations on domestic routes in 1947. This airline soon encountered difficulties, and in 1948 had to suspend operations, which did not begin again until 1951, when it received the support of Pan American World Airways. The first international routes, to neighbouring capitals, were not introduced until 1953.

The creation of the short-lived United Arab Republic of Egypt and Syria in 1960 led to the merger of Syrian Airways with the state-owned Egyptian airline, Misrair, to create United Arab Airways. On the division of the United Arab Republic in 1961 the Syrian Government had to quickly re-establish an airline, creating Syrian Arab Airlines, which initially operated a mixture of elderly piston-engined aircraft on domestic routes, including Douglas DC-3s, DC-4s, and DC-6s. Jet airliners were soon introduced in the form of three Sud Aviation Caravelles, with which services to European capitals were steadily introduced during the 1960s.

Syrian Arab Airlines now has an extensive international network, and a limited domestic network serving just three airports from its base in Damascus. The route network and the fleet has tended to reflect a close alliance with the former Eastern Bloc, although some western aircraft types are in service. The arrival of three Airbus A320s may see the final retirement of the remaining two Caravelles, or the Tu-134 fleet.

Executive Directors & Officers: Major General Omar Rida, Chairman & Managing Director; Nabil Raifaat Sami, Deputy Managing Director; Marwan Jazairi, Financial Director; Burhan Ramo, Commercial Director; Captain Adnan Shujan, Flight Operations Director; Walid Shaban, Technical Director; Ibrahim Ashi, Marketing Director; Dr Farouk Salibi, Planning Director; Nawaf Azzam, Administration Director.

HQ Airport & Main Base: Damascus

Radio callsign: SYRIANAIR

Designator: RB/SYR

Employees: 3,700

Main destinations served: Three domestic airports, plus Abu Dhabi, Algiers, Athens, Bahrain, Bombay, Budapest, Cairo, Dhahran, Delhi, Doha, Dubai, Istanbul, Jeddah, Karachi, Kuwait, Larnaca, London Heathrow, Madrid, Moscow, Munich, Paris CDG, Prague, Riyadh, Rome, Sana'a, Sharjah, Sofia, Stockholm, Tunis.

FLEET
2 Boeing 747SP
3 Tupolev Tu-154M
3 Airbus A320-200
6 Boeing 727-200
4 Tupolev Tu-134B
2 Sud Aviation Caravelle
6 Yakovlev Yak-40
5 Antonov An-26
1 Antonov An-24

Taiwan – B

CHINA AIRLINES

China Airlines

Incorporated: 1959

HISTORY
Although sometimes mistaken for the national airline of China – now Air China (qv), but previously CAAC – China Airlines is the national airline of Taiwan, the only part of China not to have succumbed to Communist rule after World War Two. Although at the time state-owned through the China Aviation Development Foundation, the airline was not officially recognised as the national flag carrier until 1965.

It is now one of the top 40 airlines in the world by annual turnover. A subsidiary is Mandarin Airlines, which operates flights to Sydney, Auckland, and Vancouver with a fleet of three aircraft. In 1996 China Airlines acquired a 42 per cent stake in Formosa Airlines (qv), the main Taiwanese domestic carrier. The China Aviation Development Foundation stake has meanwhile been reduced to 62 per cent.

Executive Directors & Officers: Chiang Hung, Chairman; Chun Fan Fu, President; Hung-Hsiang Sun, Director, Marketing & Planning; Wu Chien Min, Director, Engineering & Maintenance.

HQ Airport & Main Base: Taipei

Radio callsign: DYNASTY

Designator: CI/CAL

Employees: 8,167

Main destinations served: Abu Dhabi*, Amsterdam*, Anchorage*, Bangkok*, Chicago O'Hare, Dallas/Fort Worth*, Denpasar (Bali), Dubai, Frankfurt, Fukuoka, Hanoi, Ho Chi Minh City, Hong Kong*, Honolulu, Jakarta, Johannesburg, Kaohsiung, Kuala Lumpur, Los Angeles, Luxembourg*, Manila, Nagoya, New York JFK*, Okinawa, Penang, Phuket, San Francisco, Seoul, Singapore*, Tokyo*.
* also served by cargo flights.

Annual turnover: US $1,848 million (£1,120 million)

Revenue passenger km pa: 18,696 million

Cargo tonne km pa: 2,396.8 million

Passengers pa: 6,996,000

LINKS WITH OTHER AIRLINES
Owns Manadarin Airlines 100 per cent,

Exotic tail-planes for China Airlines. A Boeing 747 is posed for a loading shot at Taipei.

This is how China Airlines sees its new Boeing 737-800s.

has a 40 per cent stake in, and a code-sharing agreement with Formosa Airlines (qv), and a 19 per cent stake in Far Eastern Air Transport (qv).

Marketing alliances with Continental Airlines (qv), Garuda Airlines (qv), and Vietnam Airlines (qv), and freight space-sharing with Cargolux (qv), Japan Asia Airways (qv), and Martinair (qv).

FLEET
14 Boeing 747-400 (at least 2 leased)
7 Boeing 747-200F (4 wet-leased)
4 Boeing 747SP (2 leased)
5 McDonnell Douglas MD-11
7 Airbus A300-600R
6 Airbus A300B4
2 Airbus A320-200 (wet-leased)
6 Boeing 737-800
4 Boeing 737-400 (leased)
3 Boeing 737-200

EVA AIR

Eva Airways

Incorporated: 1989

HISTORY
Founded in 1989 by the Evergreen Corporation, a shipping conglomerate, Eva Airways began operations in 1991 as Taiwan's first private enterprise international airline, at first using two leased Boeing 767-300ERs. Initially assistance was received from several airlines, including British Airways (qv), Alitalia (qv), All Nippon (qv), and Thai International (qv).

Its first destinations were in the Far East, but a route to the United States was opened in 1993. The network has now extended to several points in Europe after tremendous growth which has seen this still relatively young company projected into the world's top 50 airlines in terms of annual turnover.

Executive Directors & Officers: S.C. Cheng, Chairman; Richard Huang, President; Hansen Chen, Executive Vice-President; David Wang, Vice-President, Engineering & Maintenance.

HQ Airport & Main Base: Taipei

Radio callsign: EVA AIR

Designator: BR/EVA

Employees: 5,200

Main destinations served: Amsterdam, Anchorage, Auckland, Bangkok, Brisbane, Cebu, Denpasar (Bali), Fukuoka, Ho Chi Minh City, Hong Kong, Honolulu, Jakarta, Kaohsiung, Kuala Lumpur, London, Los Angeles, Macau, Maldives, Manila, Melbourne, New York JFK, New York Newark, Panama City, Paris CDG, Penang, Phnom Penh, Phuket, San Francisco, Seattle, Singapore, Suurabaya, Sydney, Vienna.

Annual turnover: US $ 1,282 million (£777.0 million)

LINKS WITH OTHER AIRLINES
Owns 51 per cent of UNI Air (qv) and 25 per cent of Great China Airlines (qv). Marketing alliances with All Nippon Airways (qv), Ansett Australia (qv),

Continental Airlines (qv), Garuda (qv), and UNI Air (qv).

FLEET
10 Boeing 747-400
2 Boeing 747-400 Combi
3 McDonnell Douglas MD-11F
5 McDonnell Douglas MD-11
5 Boeing 767-300ER
4 Boeing 767-200
3 McDonnell Douglas MD-90

FAR EASTERN AIR TRANSPORT

FAT Far Eastern Air Transport

Incorporated: 1957

HISTORY
Originally founded as a charter airline, Far Eastern Air Transport moved into scheduled services in 1965, operating to the main Taiwanese cities. China Airlines (qv) has acquired a 19 per cent shareholding.

Executive Directors & Officers: Captain Y.L. Lee, President; C.Y. Lee, Director, Finance; S.C. Chang, Director, Development & Planning; Captain S. Chiu, Director, Operations; N. Jang, Director, Maintenance; Y.C. Yen, Director, Sales & Traffic; M.C. Yang, Director, Administration; F.B. Lee, Director, Personnel.

HQ Airport & Main Base: Taipei

Designator: EF/FEA

Employees: 1,440

Main destinations served: Hualien, Kaohsiung, Kinmen, Makung, Tainan, Taitung.

LINKS WITH OTHER AIRLINES
China Airlines (qv) has a 19 per cent stake.

FLEET
3 Boeing 757-200
2 McDonnell Douglas MD-83
7 McDonnell Douglas MD-82
5 Boeing 737-200

FORMOSA AIRLINES

Formosa Airlines

Incorporated: 1966

HISTORY
Founded in 1966 as a crop-spraying com-

Great China Airlines operates de Havilland Dash 8-300s on domestic routes from Taipei.

pany, Formosa Airlines is now a domestic carrier. In 1996 China Airlines (qv) acquired a 42 per cent interest, and the two airlines now code-share on certain domestic routes.

Executive Directors & Officers: Kuo-Hsiung Kao, Chairman; Chang Ming-Chin, Chief Financial Officer.

HQ Airport & Main Base: Taipei

Designator: HU/FOS

Main destinations served: A number of domestic destinations, including Kaohsiung, are served by scheduled services.

LINKS WITH OTHER AIRLINES
China Airlines (qv) has a 42 per cent stake.

FLEET
2 Fokker 100
4 Fokker 50
6 Saab 340B
3 Saab 340A
5 Fairchild Dornier 328

GREAT CHINA AIRLINES

Great China Airlines

Incorporated: 1966

HISTORY
Originally founded as an agricultural crop-spraying company, Great China Airlines started operating domestic scheduled services in 1990, initially using a single de Havilland Dash 8-100, although another five of these aircraft followed soon afterwards. Today the airline, in which Eva Air (qv) has a 25 per cent interest, operates an extensive domestic route network, taking a claimed 10 per cent of the Taiwanese domestic market. Its first jet equipment, a McDonnell Douglas MD-90, was introduced in 1996. The new Canadair Regional Jets may replace some of the Dash 8-300 fleet, although Formosa Airlines is also the launch customer for the new Dash 8-400.

Executive Directors & Officers: Peter Szu, Chairman; James Jeng, President; Charles Wu, Director, Executive Vice-President; Paul Hu, Director of Finance; K.C. Ho, Director, Quality Control; P.R. Chiao, Director, Flight Operations; H.Y. Chiu, Director, Maintenance; I.I. Yen, Director, Administration.

HQ Airport & Main Base: Sung Shan (domestic airport), Taipei

Designator: IF/GCA

Employees: Flight-crew: 85; Cabin staff: 120; Engineering: 110; Ground staff: 410; Total: 730.

Great China Airlines also has a solitary McDonnell Douglas MD-90 for charters.

Main destinations served: Kaohsiung, Kinmen, Makung, Pintung, Taichung, Tainan, plus some routes between these places.

Annual turnover: US $6.3 million (£3.8 million)

Revenue passenger km pa: 336.2 million

Cargo tonne km pa: 0.2 million

Annual aircraft km: 9.5 million

LINKS WITH OTHER AIRLINES
Eva Air (qv) has a 25 per cent interest.

FLEET
1 McDonnell Douglas MD-90
12 de Havilland Dash 8-300
plus 6 Canadair CRJ-700 and 8 de Havilland Dash 8-400 on order

TRANS-ASIA

Trans-Asia Airways Corporation

Incorporated: 1951

HISTORY
Originally founded in 1951 as Foshing Airlines, using Douglas DC-3s to operate from Kaohsiung to Taipei and Makung on the Pescadore Islands, the name Trans-Asia was taken in 1992 to reflect a major expansion into regional charter flights. The fleet expanded quickly from just four ATR 42s to include Airbus A320 and A321 aircraft, as well as ATR 72s for an expanded domestic network.

Executive Directors & Officers: Charles Lin, Chairman.

HQ Airport & Main Base: Taipei

Designator: GE/TNA

Employees: 1,400

Main destinations served: Regional charters plus a domestic network serving eight points, and international scheduled services to Cebu, Manila, Surabaya, and Phnom Penh.

FLEET
2 Airbus A321-100
6 Airbus A320-200
12 ATR 72
3 ATR 42

UNI AIR

UNI Airways Corporation

Incorporated: 1988

HISTORY
Originally founded in 1988, UNI Air commenced operations the following year as Makung Airlines, operating from Makung in the Pescadore Islands to Taipei and Kaohsiung. The initial fleet included the last two British Aerospace HS 748s to be built, and these were soon joined by two British Aerospace 146-300s. The new Taiwanese international carrier, Eva Air (qv), subsequently acquired a 51 per cent interest in the company. The present title was adopted later, reflecting the significance of other routes in the airline's growing network. Charter flights are also undertaken.

Executive Directors & Officers: Frank Hsu, Chairman; Joseph Lin, President; Jinn-Shyon Chem, Executive Vice-President, Operations; P.J. Hsu, Executive Vice-President, Engineering & Maintenance; C.H. Kung, Senior Vice-President, Finance.

HQ Airport & Main Base: Kaohsiung

Designator: B7/MKO

Employees: 970

Main destinations served: International charter flights plus domestic scheduled services to a number of destinations including Taipei and Makung.

LINKS WITH OTHER AIRLINES
Eva Air (qv) owns 51 per cent of the shares.
Marketing alliances with Eva Air and Great China Airlines (qv).

FLEET
3 McDonnell Douglas MD-90
5 British Aerospace 146-300
2 British Aerospace HS 748

Tajikistan – EY

TAJIK AIR

Tajikistan Airlines

Incorporated: 1992

HISTORY
A former Aeroflot (qv) division, Tajik Air was formed in 1992 after Tajikistan became independent from the former Soviet Union. Scheduled and charter flights are operated for passengers and freight. A subsidiary airline is Khojand Air Enterprise.

Executive Directors & Officers: Mirzo A. Mastangulov, Director General.

HQ Airport & Main Base: Dushanbe

Radio callsign: TAJIKISTAN

Designator: 7J/TZK (TIL – International)

Employees: Flight-crew: 250; Cabin staff: 100; Engineering: 120; Ground staff: 3,470; Total: 3,940.

Main destinations served: Aini, Almaty, Ashkhabad, Bishkek, Horog, Karachi, Khudjand, Mashhad, Moscow, Novosibirsk, Piyndjikent, Samara, Sharjah, St Petersburg, Uralsk.

Annual turnover: US $20 million (£12.1 million) (Tajik Air figs)

Aircraft km pa: 5.3 million

Revenue passenger km pa: 355.8 million

Cargo tonne km pa: 7.9 million

LINKS WITH OTHER AIRLINES
Khojand Air Enterprise is a subsidiary.

FLEET
3 Tupolev Tu-154M
11 Tupolev Tu-154B
6 Tupolev Tu-134
15 Yakovlev Yak-40
3 Antonov An-28
2 Antonov An-26
6 Antonov An-24
5 Mil Mi-8

Tanzania – 5H

AIR TANZANIA

Air Tanzania

Incorporated: 1977

HISTORY
Air Tanzania was formed in 1977 following the collapse of East African Airways, to take over Tanzania's share of the routes which the latter had hitherto operated. East African had been founded in 1946 with the financial and operational support of BOAC (British Overseas Airways Corporation) and the governments of Kenya, Uganda, Tanganyika, and Zanzibar, with the last two merging after independence to form Tanzania. Initially it had operated internal services in what were Britain's East African colonies, but it had moved into international services in 1957 with a Canadair DC-4M, a Canadian-built DC-4 with Rolls-Royce Merlin engines. This aircraft was superseded by first a Bristol Britannia, later a de Havilland Comet 4, and eventually by four

Vickers Super VC10s. An unusual feature of the airline, which it shared with SAS (qv), was that aircraft were registered in different member states.

Initially Air Tanzania concentrated on developing a network of domestic services and regional services to neighbouring states, but today its routes extend as far as Aden and Johannesburg. It is controlled by the Tanzanian Government, while it in turn has a 10 per cent stake in Alliance Airlines – African Joint Service (qv), a venture involving Air Tanzania and Uganda Airlines, both governments, and South African Airways (qv). During 1998 the equipment and routes of Air Tanzania and Uganda Airlines will be transferred to Alliance.

Executive Directors & Officers: Joseph Mungai, Chairman; Joseph S. Marandus, Chief Executive Officer & Managing Director; Abubakar Yakubu, Director of Finance & Administration; Peter M. Matumula, Commercial Director; A. Willilo, Operations Director; John Gwaseko, Technical Director.

HQ Airport & Main Base: Dar-es-Salaam

Radio callsign: TANZANIA

Designator: TC/ATC

Employees: approx 800

Main destinations served: More than ten domestic destinations, plus Aden, Djibouti, Dubai, Entebbe, Gabarone, Harare, Johannesburg, Lusaka, Mombasa, Nairobi.

LINKS WITH OTHER AIRLINES
Marketing alliances with Air Malawi and Alliance (qv), and a 10 per cent stake in the latter.

FLEET
2 Boeing 737-200C
3 Fokker F-27-600 Friendship

Tatarstan

TATARSTAN AIRLINES

Avialinii Tatarstana

Incorporated: 1992

HISTORY
As with most airlines operating in what was once the Soviet Union, Tatarstan Airlines is a former Aeroflot (qv) division, or at least part of one, having originated in Aeroflot's Aerovolga Division. It is now the national airline of recently-independent Tatarstan, and is owned by the state.

Executive Directors & Officers: Vasili M. Nesterov, General Director.

HQ Airport & Main Base: Kazan

Main destinations served: Services within Tatarstan and to centres in the former USSR.

FLEET
3 Tupolev Tu-154B
1 Boeing 727-100
6 Yakovlev Yak-42
1 Yakovlev Yak-40
1 Antonov An-26
6 Antonov An-24

Thailand – HS

BANGKOK AIR

Bangkok Airways Co Ltd

Incorporated: 1986

HISTORY
Originally founded in 1968 as Sahakol Air, Thailand's first privately-owned airline, Bangkok Air started as a charter airline with a single nine-seat aircraft, mainly supporting the oil, natural gas exploration, and timber industries. The business was restructured and renamed in 1986 and moved into scheduled domestic air services. One unusual feature of the airline's operations is that it has built and opened its own airports on the island of Samui and at Sukhothai, to tap the lucrative tourist potential of these destinations.

Executive Directors & Officers: Dr Prasert Prasarttong-Osoth, President & Chief Executive Officer; Group Captain Charoon Peetong, Vice-President, Airports; Puttipong Prassarttong-Osoth, Vice-President, Operations; Thavatvong Thanasumitra, Vice-President, Finance; Pradit Theekakul, Vice-President, Administration; Rudi Fischer, Vice-President, Sales; Marc Kirner, Vice-President, Technical.

HQ Airport & Main Base: Bangkok

Radio callsign: BANGKOK AIR

Designator: PG/BKP

Employees: Flight-crew: 38; Cabin staff: 39; Engineering: 48; Ground staff: 410; Total: 535.

Main destinations served: Bangkok to seven domestic destinations, including Phuket, as well as some cross-country routes, and Samui–Singapore.

Aircraft km pa: 5.1 million

Revenue passenger km pa: 236.9 million

Bangkok Air builds and operates its own airports at tourist destinations – here is one of their ATR 72-200s at Samui.

LINKS WITH OTHER AIRLINES
Interline agreements with 18 international airlines.

FLEET
6 ATR 72-200 (leased)
1 ATR 42-320 (leased)

THAI AIRWAYS

Thai Airways International Public Co Ltd

Incorporated: 1959

HISTORY
Thai Airways was founded in 1959 as a joint venture between Thailand's domestic carrier, Thai Airways Company, and SAS (Scandinavian Airlines System) (qv), with the latter taking a 30 per cent interest. The new airline took over the external routes and equipment of TAC when it commenced operations in 1960, the equipment consisting of Douglas DC-6Bs. These were followed by leased Sud Aviation Caravelles and Convair 990 Coronados, which quickly replaced the DC-6Bs so that Thai could eventually claim to have the first all-jet fleet of any airline in Asia. A network of services was developed, initially serving destinations in South-East Asia but gradually extending to Japan and Australia. By the early-1970s the airline had standardised its equipment on several different variants of the Douglas DC-8, ranging from the 140-seat DC-8-30 through to the 200-seat DC-8-63.

The SAS stake was steadily reduced over the years, and the airline became fully Thai-owned in 1977 when the Thai Government acquired SAS's remaining shares. The Thai Airways Company's domestic services were absorbed in 1988, adding 11 more aircraft to what was, by then, Thai's own fleet of 30 wide-bodied aircraft. Privatisation began in 1991, with a stock exchange listing and a share offer which reserved 5 per cent of the new shares for the airline's employees. The airline is likely to become a completely privatised enterprise shortly.

It is a founder-member of the 'Star Alliance', which brings together frequent flyer programmes and other services for Air Canada (qv), Lufthansa (qv), SAS (qv), United Airlines (qv) and, in late-1997, Varig (qv), as well as Thai Airways.

Executive Directors & Officers:
Siripong Thongyai, Chairman; Thamnoon Wanglee, President; Flight Lieutenant Prija Thawornpradit, Executive Vice-President, Operations; Jothin Pamon-Montri, Senior Vice-President, Quality & Safety Control; Flight Lieutenant Chusak Bhachaiyud, Senior Vice-President, Technical; Nares Hovatanakul, Senior Vice-President, Aviation Support; Squadron Leader Pongsawit Punyindu, Senior Vice-President, General Assignment; Squadron Leader Payoon Puakpong, Senior Vice-President, Flight Operations; Bhisit Kuslayanon, Senior Vice-President, Commercial; Amnuay Chanya, Vice-President, Finance.

HQ Airport & Main Base: Bangkok

Radio callsign: THAI

Designator: TG/THA

Employees: 22,136

Main destinations served: More than 20 domestic destinations, including Phuket, are served, plus Amsterdam, Athens, Auckland, Bandar Seri Bagawan, Beijing, Brisbane, Brussels, Calcutta, Chiang Mai, Colombo, Copenhagen, Delhi, Denpasar (Bali), Dhaka, Dubai, Frankfurt, Fukuoka, Guangzhou, Hanoi, Ho Chi Minh City, Hong Kong, Istanbul, Jakarta, Kaohsiung, Karachi, Kathmandu, Kuala Lumpur, Kunming, Lahore, London Heathrow, Los Angles, Madrid, Manila, Melbourne, Munich, Muscat, Nagoya, Osaka, Paris CDG, Penang, Perth, Phnom Penh, Rome, Seoul, Shanghai, Singapore, Stockholm, Surabaya, Sydney, Taipei, Tokyo, Yangon, Zürich.

Annual turnover: US $3,088 million (£1,871.5 million)

Revenue passenger km pa: 29,226 million

Cargo tonne km pa: 1,266 million

Passengers pa: 14.3 million

LINKS WITH OTHER AIRLINES
Major marketing alliance with Air Canada (qv), Lufthansa (qv), SAS (qv), and United Air Lines (qv).
Marketing alliance with Air New Zealand (qv), Ansett Australia (qv), and Japan Airlines (qv).

FLEET
8 Boeing 777-200
9 Boeing 747-400
2 Boeing 747-300
4 Boeing 747-200
8 Airbus A330-300
4 McDonnell Douglas MD-11
7 Airbus A300B4
16 Airbus A300-600
2 Airbus A310-200
11 Boeing 737-400
5 British Aerospace 146-300
2 ATR 72
2 ATR 42

BWIA INTERNATIONAL

BWIA International Airways

Incorporated: 1940

HISTORY
Originally founded in 1940 as one of the TACA group of airlines, this company was acquired by British South American Airways (BSAA) in 1947, with ownership passing to BOAC (British Overseas Airways Corporation) shortly afterwards when ownership of BSAA passed to BOAC after the failure of the former's Avro Tudor airliners. The title of British West Indian Airways, or BWIA, was taken in 1948. Another BOAC acquisition, British Caribbean Airways, was merged into BWIA in 1949.

After Britain's West Indian colonies were granted independence, the Trinidad Government took a 90 per cent stake in BWIA in 1961, acquiring the airline outright six years later, while the airline developed services to North American destinations using a fleet of Boeing 707s. Another airline, Trinidad & Tobago Air Services (TTAS), was formed by the Trinidad Government in 1974 to provide inter-island and local services, and in 1980 TTAS and BWIA were merged.

The airline has been effectively privatised in recent years, with the Trinidad & Tobago Government now owning just 15.5 per cent and private investors holding the remainder. In 1995 BWIA took a 29.2 per cent stake in LIAT (qv).

Executive Directors & Officers: Giles Pilatreault, Chief Executive Officer; Anderson Begg, Deputy Chief Executive Officer & Operations Director; Brenda Billy, Financial Director; Hilton Wharfe, Director, Maintenance & Engineering; Beatrix Carrington, Director, Marketing & Sales; Gilberto Duarte, Director, Cargo; Agna da Costa-Vieria, Director, Inflight Services; Mitra Mahabir, Director, Inventory & Logistics; Dennis Phillip, Director, Corporate Development & Government Affairs.

HQ Airport & Main Base: Piarco International Airport, Port of Spain

Radio callsign: WEST INDIAN

Designator: BW/BWA

Employees: 2,600

Main destinations served: Antigua,

Barbados, Caracas, Frankfurt, Grenada, Georgetown, Kingston, London Heathrow, Miami, New York JFK, St Lucia, St Maarten, Toronto.

LINKS WITH OTHER AIRLINES
Holds a 29.2 per cent stake in LIAT (qv).

FLEET
4 Lockheed L-1011 TriStar 500
2 Airbus A321-100
5 McDonnell Douglas MD-83

Tunisia – TS

NOUVELAIR TUNISIE

Nouvelair Tunisie

Incorporated: 1989

HISTORY
Tunisia's first charter airline, Nouvelair Tunisie was founded in 1989 and started operations the following year as Air Liberté Tunisie, an associate of Air Liberté (qv), which at that time was also confined to charters. The airline is now owned by the Tunisian Travel Service, and the present title was adopted in 1994. Nouvelair specialises in inclusive tour charter flights into Tunisia from major European centres.

Executive Directors & Officers: Aziz Milad, Chairman; Slahdine Kastalli, General Manager; Mohsen Nasra, General Manager.

HQ Airport & Main Base: Aeroport International Habib Bourguiba, Monastir

Radio callsign: NOUVELAIR

Designator: BJ/LBT

Employees: Flight-crew: 92 (116 summer); Cabin staff: 64 (88 summer); Engineering: 19; Ground staff: 362; Total: 537 (657 summer).

Main destinations served: Operates from most European countries, including the UK, on inclusive tour charter flights to Tunisian resorts.

Annual turnover: US $48 million (£29.1 million)

Aircraft km pa: 5.7 million

Revenue passenger km pa: 819 million

Annual passengers: 464,500

FLEET
4 McDonnell Douglas MD-83 (leased)

TUNISAIR

Société Tunisienne de l'Air

Incorporated: 1948

HISTORY
Tunisair was founded in 1948 with the support of Air France (qv), and until Tunisian independence in 1957 the French airline was the major share-holder. The initial fleet consisted of Douglas DC-3s for domestic services. The connection with Air France remained even after independence, with the French airline having a 49 per cent interest and the Tunisian Government holding the majority 51 per cent. International services were developed, initially to France, using Douglas DC-4s which were later joined by Sud Aviation Caravelle jet airliners.

Today the airline operates a mixed Boeing and Airbus fleet on scheduled and charter services, with the latter generally being for inclusive tour operators, reflecting Tunisia's popularity as a holiday destination. The Tunisian Government owns 45.2 per cent of Tunisair's shares and is the largest single shareholder, while Air France now has just 5.6 per cent.

Executive Directors & Officers: Tahar Belhadj Ali, Chairman & General Manager; Jilani Chouk, Financial Director; Jemaa Cheouch, Operations Director; Hei Hadj Mohamed, Engineering Director; Hechemi Siaoud, Marketing Director; Mohamed Hadj Sassi, Marketing Director; Moncef Badiss, Director, Sales; Abdelkerim Ouertani, Director, Central Products; Taoufik Baklouti, Personnel Director.

HQ Airport & Main Base: Tunis Carthage

Radio callsign: TUNAIR

Designator: TU/TAR

Employees: 7,300

Main destinations served: A limited domestic network, plus Abu Dhabi, Algiers, Amman, Amsterdam, Athens, Barcelona, Berlin Schonefeld, Bordeaux, Brussels, Cairo, Casablanca, Copenhagen, Dakar, Damascus, Düsseldorf, Frankfurt, Geneva, Hamburg, Istanbul, Jeddah, Lille, Lisbon, London Heathrow, Lyons, Madrid, Marseilles, Milan, Munich, Nice, Palermo, Paris Orly, Prague, Rome, Strasbourg, Toulouse, Vienna, Warsaw, Zurich.

LINKS WITH OTHER AIRLINES
Air France has a 5.6 per cent stake.

FLEET
1 Airbus A300B4

8 Airbus A320-200
7 Boeing 727-200
4 Boeing 737-200
4 Boeing 737-500
plus orders for Airbus A319 and Boeing 737-600 aircraft

Turkey – TC

AIR ALFA

Air Alfa Hava Yollari

Incorporated: 1992

HISTORY
A Turkish charter airline specialising in the inclusive tour market, Air Alfa dates from 1992.

Executive Directors & Officers: Ahmed Yasaroglu, Commercial Director.

HQ Airport & Main Base: Istanbul

Designator: H7/LFA

Main destinations served: Inclusive tour charters to Turkish resorts, mainly from centres in Belgium, France, Germany, Italy, and the Netherlands.

FLEET
4 Airbus A300B4
2 Boeing 727-200
2 Airbus A321-100

ISTANBUL AIRLINES

Istanbul Hava Yollari

Incorporated: 1985

HISTORY
Istanbul Airlines was established in 1985 and began operations the following year, carrying inclusive tour charter passengers into Turkish resorts from elsewhere in Europe. Initially the fleet comprised Sud Aviation Caravelles, which were later joined by Boeing 737s. Today an all-Boeing fleet is operated.

Executive Directors & Officers: Safi Ergin, General Manager.

HQ Airport & Main Base: Ataturk Airport, Instanbul

Radio callsign: ISTANBUL

Designator: IL/IST

Employees: 1,650

Main destinations served: Charter flights from major European centres to Turkish resorts.

FLEET
31 Boeing 757-200
8 Boeing 727-200
8 Boeing 737-400

SUNEXPRESS

SunExpress Aviation

Incorporated: 1990

HISTORY
SunExpress was established in 1990 as a joint venture between Lufthansa (qv) and THY Turkish Airlines (qv) to cater for the inclusive tour charter market from elsewhere in Europe to resort destinations in Turkey. Shareholdings are divided 60 per cent THY and 40 per cent Lufthansa.

Executive Directors & Officers: Atilla Celebi, Chairman; Florian Hamm, Managing Director & Operations Director; Guralp Alpay, Deputy Managing Director; Michael Buck, Commercial Director; Andreas Gherman, Technical Director.

HQ Airport & Main Base: Oktay Airport, Antalya

Designator: XQ/SXS

Employees: approx 400

Main destinations served: Inclusive tour charter flights from the main centres in Europe, and especially Germany, to Turkish resorts.

LINKS WITH OTHER AIRLINES
THY Turkish Airlines (qv) has a 60 per cent interest, and Lufthansa (qv) has 40 per cent.

FLEET
2 Boeing 737-400
3 Boeing 737-300

THY TURKISH AIRLINES

THY Turk Hava Yollari/Turkish Airlines

Incorporated: 1933

HISTORY
The origins of Turkish Airlines, or THY, date from the formation in 1933 of Devlet Hava Yollari (Turkish State Airlines), which was operated as a branch of the air force. This operation continued for more than 20 years, with the airline gathering a fleet of Douglas DC-3s for domestic services, mainly between Istanbul and Ankara, and to other destinations in the Middle East. THY itself was created in

A THY Turkish Airlines Boeing 737-400 lands while a Tupolev Tu-154 of another airline taxies in the background.

1956 to take over DHY's services and equipment, and initially ownership was split between the Turkish Government, with 94 per cent, and BOAC (British Overseas Airways Corporation), holding the remaining 6 per cent.

A fleet of five Vickers Viscount 700 turboprop airliners was introduced in 1957 for international services, and these were joined in 1960 by ten Fokker F-27 Friendships, although unusually the order was split equally between the F-27 and the US-built Fairchild FH-227 version. The DC-3s remained on a number of domestic services meanwhile, until in 1968, after leasing a Douglas DC-9-10 from the manufacturer, THY introduced three Douglas DC-9-30s, allowing the DC-3s to be withdrawn. The airline later added Boeing 707s (for the introduction of long-haul services) and Fokker F-28 Fellowships. Meanwhile, the BOAC interest was gradually reduced so that for some years the airline has been owned 98.2 per cent by the state Public Participation Administration, with the remaining shares in private hands.

A regional airline – Turk Hava Tasimaciligi, or THT – was established in 1989, and the following year THY took 64 per cent of the shares, intending to operate THT as a feeder. Initially THT operated two Antonov An-24RVs, but these were soon joined by the first two of four British Aerospace ATPs, or Jetstream 61s as they were later renamed. In 1993 THT's operations were absorbed into those of THY.

Executive Directors & Officers: Atilla Celebi, President & Chief Executive Officer; Yusuf Bolayirli, Vice-President, Technical; S. Sevgi Gumustekin, Vice-President, Planning & Support; Vural Akgun, Vice-President, Administration;

Oktay Oztekin, Vice-President, Flight Operations; Ilknur Ezgu, Vice-President, Finance; Gurol Yuksel, Vice-President, Commercial; Mujdat Yucel, Vice-President, Ground Operations.

HQ Airport & Main Base: Ataturk Airport, Istanbul, but a further base is at Ankara.

Radio callsign: TURKAIR

Designator: TK/THY

Employees: Flight-crew: 644; Cabin staff: 982; Engineering: 155; Ground staff: 6,888; Total: 8,668.

Main destinations served: 30 domestic destinations, plus Abu Dhabi, Almaty, Amman, Amsterdam, Ashkhabad, Athens, Bahrain, Baku, Bangkok, Basle/Mulhouse, Beijing, Berlin Schonefeld, Berlin Tegel, Bishkek, Brussels, Bucharest, Budapest, Cairo, Cape Town, Cologne/Bonn, Copenhagen, Damascus, Dubai, Düsseldorf, Frankfurt, Geneva, Hamburg, Hanover, Jakarta, Jeddah, Johannesburg, Karachi, Kiev, Kuala Lumpur, Kuwait, London Heathrow, Lyons, Madrid, Manchester, Milan, Moscow, Munich, New York JFK, Nice, Nuremberg, Odessa, Osaka Kansai, Paris CDG, Paris Orly, Prague, Riyadh, Rome, Sarajevo, Singapore, Sofia, Stockholm, Strasbourg, Stuttgart, Tashkent, Tbilisi, Tehran, Tel Aviv, Tirana, Tokyo Nairita, Tunis, Vienna, Zürich.

Annual turnover: US $1,040.3 million (£630.5 million)

Aircraft km pa: 109.4 million

Revenue passenger km pa: 12,305 million

THY is another operator of the long-range Airbus A340-300.

One of THY's fleet of Airbus A310s – the airline operates both the A310-200 and the -300.

Cargo tonne km pa: 171.8 million

LINKS WITH OTHER AIRLINES
Marketing alliances with Czech Airlines (qv), Swissair (qv), and Japan Air Lines (qv).
Has a 60 per cent interest in SunExpress (qv) and 50 per cent in Kibris Turkish Airlines (qv).

FLEET
5 Airbus A340-300
7 Airbus A310-300
7 Airbus A310-200
3 Boeing 727-200F
26 Boeing 737-800*
28 Boeing 737-400
2 Boeing 737-500 (leased)
10 Avro RJ-100
4 Avro RJ-70
* in course of delivery from June, 1998 until 2002, replacing 737-400/500 fleet

Turkmenistan – EZ

KHAZAR

Khazar Airline

Incorporated: 1940

HISTORY
Khazar Airline commenced operations in 1940 as the local Krasnovodsk Division of Aeroflot (qv). It became a subsidiary of the national airline, Turkmenistan Airlines (qv), in 1992, after Turkmenistan left the former Soviet Union, and the present title was adopted the same year after its home base changed its name from Krasnovodsk to Turkmenbashy. The airline is state-owned.

Executive Directors & Officers: Anatoli Kurdiukov, Director General.

HQ Airport & Main Base: Turkmenbashy

Radio callsign: KHAZAR

Designator: KHR

Employees: approx 900

Main destinations served: Destinations within the former Soviet Union, and local feeder services for Turkmenistan Airlines.

LINKS WITH OTHER AIRLINES
A subsidiary of Turkmenistan Airlines (qv).

FLEET
5 Antonov An-26
1 Antonov An-24
3 Antonov An-2

TURKMENISTAN AIRLINES

Turkmenistan Airlines

Incorporated: 1992

HISTORY
Based on the former Aeroflot (qv) divisions within Turkmenistan, Turkmenistan Airlines is the national airline and also operates as a holding company for other airlines in the country, including Khazar Airline (qv). Although Russian and Ukrainian equipment continues to predominate in the fleet, western types are being introduced. The British Aerospace 125 is used for VIP duties.

Executive Directors & Officers: Aleksi Bonarev, General Director.

HQ Airport & Main Base: Ashkhabad

Radio callsign: TURKMENISTAN

Designator: T5/TUA

Main destinations served: Domestic services, plus destinations within the former Soviet Union.

LINKS WITH OTHER AIRLINES
Subsidiaries include Khazar Airline (qv).

FLEET
2 Ilyushin Il-76TD
1 Boeing 757-200
12 Tupolev Tu-154B
3 Boeing 737-300
4 Yakovlev Yak-42
14 Antonov An-24
20 Mil Mi-8
3 Mil Mi-6

Uganda – 5X

ALLIANCE AIRLINES

Alliance Airlines – African Joint Air Service

Incorporated: 1996

HISTORY
Alliance Airlines commenced operations in 1997 as a joint airline for Uganda and Tanzania, with backing from South African Airways (qv), who provided the first aircraft, a wet-leased Boeing 747SP. In 1998 the airline will absorb the operations of Uganda Airlines and Air Tanzania. The airline is owned 40 per cent by South African

Airways, ten per cent each by Uganda Airlines and Air Tanzania, and five per cent each by the governments of Uganda and Tanzania.

Directors: Adrian Sibo, Chairman; Christo Roodt, Managing Director.

HQ Airport & Main Base: Kampala

Radio callsign: JAMBO

Designator: Y2/AFJ

Main destinations served: Dar-es-Salaam and Entebbe to Bombay and London Gatwick, as well as domestic and regional services.

LINKS WITH OTHER AIRLINES
South African Airways has a 40 per cent interest.

FLEET
1 Boeing 747SP
3 Boeing 737-200C (2 ex-Air Tanzania/1 ex-Uganda Airlines)
1 Boeing 737-500 (ex-Uganda Airlines)
3 Fokker F-27-600 (2 ex-Air Tanzania/1 ex-Uganda Airlines)

Ukraine – UR

As with the Russian Federation, the Ukraine has a substantial number of airlines which have their origins in either divisions of the old Soviet Aeroflot, or of quasi-military operations similar to those once so prevalent in Latin America. True, there are many fewer Ukrainian airlines, but the country is that much smaller, and although far more prosperous than most of the former Soviet Union the currency with which to obtain more reliable and economic western aircraft remains in short supply.

The three main Ukrainian airlines can be taken as Air Ukraine (qv), Ukraine International (qv) and, of course, the Antonov Design Bureau (qv), which has ensured the survival of its An-124 Ruslan project by well considered marketing alliances outside the country. The remaining airlines will have a much harder task in securing a stable long-term future, and details of some of these are not completely reliable due to the sometimes poor availability of their equipment. Two airlines, Dneproavia and Lvov, are subsidiaries of Air Ukraine.
Brief details of the other Ukrainian airlines are as follows:

Air Urga/International Joint Stock Company-Air Urga
8 Antonov An-26
8 Antonov An-24

Crimea Air/Krymavia
4 Antonov An-26
10 Antonov An-24

Dneproavia Airline
7 Yakovlev Yak-42
5 Yakovlev Yak-40
7 Antonov An-26

Khors Air Company
10 Ilyushin Il-76
1 Antonov An-24
4 Antonov An-12

Kiev United Air Detachment/Zhuliani
1 Yakovlev Yak-40
1 Let L-410
1 Antonov An-24
3 Antonov An-2

UNA/Southern Independent Air Co
2 Boeing 737-400
2 Boeing 737-300

Veteran Air Company
15 Ilyushin Il-76MD (2 of these are
believed to be water bombers for forest
fire-fighting)

AIR UKRAINE

Avialinii Ukraini

Incorporated: 1992

HISTORY
Formed as a direct result of the break-up
of the former Soviet Union, Air Ukraine's
operations were developed under Aeroflot
(qv) after the Ukrainian Soviet Socialist
Republic became part of the USSR in 1923.
In terms of the number of aircraft and
employees, this is one of the world's
largest airlines, but not so in terms of
annual turnover. In addition to its role as
a commercial airline, Air Ukraine is
responsible for the operation of the country's main airports, and to some extent it
still bears a closer resemblance to the old
Aeroflot and the Chinese CAAC than to
western ideas of a commercial airline. The
airline plans expansion, especially on the
North Atlantic and to the Far East, using
western equipment, including Boeing
767s introduced in late-1997, but at present the bulk of its fleet consists of Russian
and Ukrainian types, and there is a
marked absence of the latest types, such
as the Ilyushin Il-96 and Tupolev Tu-204.
Air Ukraine is the country's national airline and has not been privatised, while
many of the most important destinations in
western Europe are being served by
Ukraine International Airlines (qv), in which
the state has a majority stake. Nevertheless,

the prospects are better than for many airlines in the former Soviet Union inasmuch
as the country was by far the most fertile
and prosperous part of the USSR, with mineral and oil deposits. A subsidiary, formed
in 1963, is Dneproavia Airline, which
appears to have a quasi-military structure,
as has another subsidiary, Lvov Airline.

Executive Directors & Officers: Ilyin
Viacheslav, President; Sergei Mailutin,
First Vice-President.

HQ Airport & Main Base: Kiev, with
further hubs at Donetsk, Kharkov, Lvov,
Odessa.

Radio callsign: AIR UKRAINE

Designator: 6U/UKR

Employees: 40,000

Main destinations served: Destinations
throughout the Ukraine and the former
Soviet Union, as well as Bangkok,
Beijing, Chicago O'Hare, Delhi, Prague.

LINKS WITH OTHER AIRLINES
Owns Dnepravia Airline (qv) and Lvov
Airline (qv).

FLEET
3 Boeing 767-200ER (leased)
7 Ilyushin Il-62
35 Tupolev Tu-154B/M
3 Airbus A320-200 (leased)
2 Ilyushin Il-18
28 Tupolev Tu-134
1 Boeing 737-200
21 Yakovlev Yak-42
15 Yakovlev Yak-40
1 Antonov An-72
4 Antonov An-32
10 Antonov An-30
14 Antonov An-26
52 Antonov An-24
9 Let L-410

ANTONOV

Antonov Design Bureau

Incorporated: 1923

HISTORY
The Antonov Design Bureau first moved
into aircraft operations in 1989, reaching
an agreement with Air Foyle (qv) under
which the British cargo airline marketed
the capabilities of the Antonov An-124
Ruslan, still the largest aircraft in commercial service today. The move into operating aircraft, as opposed to their design and
construction, was vital for the company's
survival faced with the sudden collapse of
its traditional markets in the former Soviet

Union, and the lack of funds for aircraft
development. It has proven to be so successful that Antonov took an interest in
Volga-Dnepr (qv), the Russian heavy lift
specialist, and has since moved into the
market on its own account.
Although the Antonov An-225, an even
larger six-engined development of the
An-124, is supposed to be in the fleet,
development of this aircraft has stopped
due to funding problems, and it is highly
unlikely to be available commercially for
some time yet.

Executive Directors & Officers: Anatoli
Bulianenko, General Director.

HQ Airport & Main Base: Kiev

Radio callsign: ANTONOV BUREAU

Designator: ADB

Main destinations served: Ad hoc
cargo charters world-wide.

LINKS WITH OTHER AIRLINES
Shareholding in Volga-Dnepr (qv).
Marketing alliance with Air Foyle (qv).

FLEET
1 Antonov An-225 (unlikely to be
operational)
6 Antonov An-124 Ruslan
1 Antonov An-74
2 Antonov An-72
3 Antonov An-22
3 Antonov An-12

UKRAINE INTERNATIONAL AIRLINES

Ukraine International Airlines

Incorporated: 1992

HISTORY
Although not officially the national airline
of the newly-independent Ukraine,
Ukraine International is a joint venture
between the Ukrainian Government with
a 68.4 per cent interest, aircraft leasing
specialists Guinness Peat Aviation with
13.2 per cent, and a partnership of
Austrian Airlines (qv) and Swissair (qv)
holding the remaining 18.4 per cent. A relatively modest operation compared with
Air Ukraine (qv), it nevertheless has western aircraft and expertise, as well as the
prime destinations in western Europe,
which suggests that this could become the
leading Ukrainian airline in the long term.

Executive Directors & Officers: Vitaly

Heavy loads such as these could not be moved by road because of their size, but present little difficulty for the Antonov An-124 Ruslan.

Construction equipment is one of the cargo mainstays of the An-124 fleet world-wide.

M. Potyomski, President; Richard W. Creagh, Deputy President.

HQ Airport & Main Base: Kiev

Radio callsign: UKRAINE INTERNATIONAL

Designator: PS/AUI

Employees: 500

Main destinations served: Kiev to Amsterdam, Barcelona, Berlin, Brussels, Donetsk, Dnepropetrovsk, Frankfurt, London Gatwick, Lvov, Manchester, Munich, Paris CDG, Odessa, Rome, Vienna, Zürich.

LINKS WITH OTHER AIRLINES
Austrian Airlines (qv) and Swissair (qv) hold 18.4 per cent of the airline's shares.

FLEET
2 Boeing 737-300 (leased)
2 Boeing 737-200 (leased)
1 Antonov An-12 (leased)

United Arab Emirates – A6

EMIRATES

Emirates Airline

Incorporated: 1985

HISTORY
Established in 1985 as an international airline for the United Arab Emirates by the Government of Dubai, Emirates has developed an extensive internal and international route network with a modern fleet, reflecting the prosperity of the region.

Executive Directors & Officers: Sheikh Ahmed bin Saeed Al Maktoum, Chairman; Maurice Flanagan, Managing Director; Tim Clark, Chief Director, Airline; Gary Chapman, Chief Director, Group services.

HQ Airport & Main Base: Dubai

Radio callsign: EMIRATES

Designator: EK/UAE

Employees: approx 2,000

Main destinations served: Abu Dhabi, Amman, Athens, Bandar Abbas, Bangkok, Beirut, Bombay, Cairo, Colombo, Comores, Damascus, Delhi, Dhahran, Dhaka, Doha, Istanbul, Jakarta, Jeddah, Johannesburg, Karachi, Kuala Lumpur, Kuwait, Larnaca, London Heathrow, London Gatwick, Manila, Manchester,

Melbourne, Muscat, Nairobi, Nice, Paris CDG, Riyadh, Sana'a, Singapore, Tehran, Zürich.

Annual turnover: US $1,000 million (£606.1 million)

LINKS WITH OTHER AIRLINES
Code-sharing with United Airlines (qv).

FLEET
6 Airbus A300-600R
10 Airbus A310-300
plus 16 Airbus A330-200 for delivery 1999–2002 (4 per year)

United Kingdom – G

AIR ATLANTIQUE

Atlantic Air Transport Ltd
Incorporated: 1969

HISTORY
Air Atlantique was originally founded in 1969 as a Jersey-based aircraft sales and service company and air taxi operator, General Aviation Services. The first aircraft was a Cessna 336, which was soon joined by two other light aircraft, both Cessnas. The sales and service aspects of the business were hived off in 1974, leaving the company free to concentrate on air taxi work, standardising on the Cessna 310. The name Air Atlantique was adopted later that year. Operations started in the UK two years later, using two Douglas Dakota aircraft on general freight and aerial survey work throughout Europe. In 1979 two Douglas DC-6s were used briefly for livestock flights to Europe and Africa.

Major expansion occurred in 1981, with the Dakota fleet expanding to eight aircraft, and a new base at Blackpool Airport. In mid-1984 the business was transferred from Jersey to London's Stansted Airport, but the development of Stansted as London's third airport forced a further move to a permanent home at Coventry Airport in the West Midlands.

A major part of the airline's business is the operation of two Dakotas and five of the much smaller Britten-Norman Islander aircraft on marine pollution control duties for the British Department of Transport. This work has been carried out since 1987, and the aircraft were involved with the aftermath of both the *Baer* and *Sea Empress* incidents off Shetland and South Wales respectively, with the aircraft flying at just five metres above the surface of the sea during spraying runs. Although the company operates freight and passenger charter flights within the UK and into Europe, its most high profile activity is the operation of Atlantic Historic Flight, offering pleasure flights in a number of aircraft, including not only the Dakota but also such rare types as the Percival Prentice, de

Most airlines are proudest of their newest aircraft, but Air Atlantique, or Atlantic Air Transport, follows the opposite policy, with aircraft such as this de Havilland Rapide in demand.

Havilland DH89A Rapide, and the Scottish Aviation Twin Pioneer.

Executive Directors & Officers:
Michael J.H. Collett, Chairman; W. James Foden, Group Managing Director; Captain Raymond S. Johnson, Managing Director.

HQ Airport & Main Base: Coventry

Radio callsign: ATLANTIC

Designator: NL/AAG

Employees: Flight-crew: 55; Cabin staff: 4; Engineering: 80; Ground staff: 71; Administration and sales: 40; Total: 250.

LINKS WITH OTHER AIRLINES
Subsidiaries include Atlantic Cargo; Atlantic Airways; Air Caernarfon; Highland Airways; Atlantic Historic Flight.

Air Atlantique's C-47/DC-3 fleet is used for pleasure flights, and for spraying dispersant onto oil spillages.

Setting the world record for the single heaviest item carried by air is this Antonov An-124 Ruslan operated by Air Foyle, taking a new 109 tonne diesel electric locomotive from London, Ontario, to Dublin. With the equipment necessary to handle the load and keep it in place, the total shipment weighed more than 146 tonnes.

FLEET
5 Lockheed L-188 Electra
2 Douglas DC-6
8 Douglas DC-3
1 Shorts 360
1 Hunting Percival Pembroke
1 Fairchild Metro III
2 Reims/Cessna F406 Caravan II
3 Pilatus/Britten-Norman BN-2 Islander
1 de Havilland Rapide
1 Cessna 500 Citation
3 Cessna 404 Titan
2 Cessna 402C
3 Cessna 310
1 Percival Prentice I

AIR FOYLE

Air Foyle Limited

Incorporated: 1978

HISTORY
One of the relatively small number of airlines to be named after its founder, Christopher Foyle, Air Foyle started life as an air taxi operator in 1978, using a single Piper Aztec. Although the early operations centred around passenger traffic, in 1979 the company became involved in overnight light cargo and parcels traffic for clients such as Skypack – now part of TNT (qv) – and Datapost. By 1981 the fleet had grown to four aircraft. The basis for the present airline was soon established after the award of a contract by TNT to carry express freight traffic from Birmingham to Hanover and Nuremberg in Germany, for which Air Foyle acquired two Handley Page Herald turboprop aircraft, replacing these as traffic grew with a BAC One-Eleven and a Boeing 737-200 in quick change configuration. When TNT acquired a fleet of British Aerospace 146QT freighters (QT standing for 'quiet trader'), Air Foyle won the contract to operate a fleet of these aircraft in the UK and Europe for the Australian-based cargo company.

Expansion into heavier cargo operations followed an inspection of the Antonov An 124-100 Ruslan at the 1987 Paris Air Show. The aircraft, the largest in commercial operation, offered new opportunities for air freight, but it took two years of persistent negotiations before the then Russian president, Mikhail Gorbachev, became involved and authorised a presidential decree allowing the manufacturer to become an aircraft operator, breaking the monopoly of Aeroflot (qv) in air transport. Starting in 1989, Air Foyle was operating four Ruslans on world-wide charters within a year, and the

Gulf War of 1991 accelerated this growth still further as the company moved a wide variety of cargoes, including mobile field hospitals and power generators, into Saudi Arabia. Turnover shot up from US $5 million to over US $25 million as a result.

Today, Air Foyle has sales and operational links with several airlines in the former Soviet Union and can offer a wide variety of cargo aircraft. Recognising the difference between its operations, Air Foyle has two divisions, Air Foyle-TNT and Air Foyle-Antonov. Air Foyle-TNT operates nine British Aerospace 146QT freighter aircraft on a night-scheduled freight network, with the aircraft used for daytime charters for other customers, including the transport of racehorses during most summer weekends. The other division operates up to six Ruslans on behalf of the Antonov Design Bureau, carrying a wide range of cargoes on charter, such as America's Cup yachts, railway locomotives, and oil drilling equipment. Loads have included the heaviest single piece of cargo carried by air – a turbine weighing 135.2 tonnes – from Düsseldorf to Delhi, and the largest-ever commercial load carried by air, when a diesel electric railway locomotive and supporting equipment was moved from London, Ontario, to Dublin.

Aircraft are usually operated in the colours of clients such as TNT or the Antonov Design Bureau.

Executive Directors & Officers: W.R. Christopher Foyle, Chairman & Managing Director; Peter D.C. Sorby, Commercial & Finance Director.

HQ Airport & Main Base: London Luton Airport

Radio callsign: CUTLASS

Designator: GS/UPC

Main destinations served: On behalf of TNT from Birmingham, Edinburgh, Liverpool, and London Stansted to Belfast, Begramo, Billund, Cologne, Copenhagen, Dublin, Gothenburg, Malmö, Milan, Oslo, Shannon and Stavanger; plus ad hoc charters during daylight and at weekends. On behalf of Antonov, world-wide heavy freight charters.

Cargo tonnes pa: In excess of 50,000

Annual turnover: US $52.8 million (£32 million)

LINKS WITH OTHER AIRLINES
Aircraft operated on behalf of TNT of Australia and Antonov Design Bureau of the Ukraine.

FLEET
6 Antonov An-124-100 Ruslan (on behalf of Antonov)
2 Antonov An-22 (on behalf of Antonov)
3 Antonov An-12 (on behalf of Antonov)
4 Ilyushin 76-TD (on behalf of Khors, Ukraine (qv))
3 British Aerospace 146-200QT (on behalf of TNT Express parcel)
6 British Aerospace 146-300QT (on behalf of TNT Express parcel)

AIR FOYLE CHARTER AIRLINES

Air Foyle Charter Airlines

Incorporated: 1994

HISTORY
Part of the Air Foyle (qv) Group, Air Foyle Charter Airlines was established in 1994 to operate passenger aircraft, assisting tour operators wishing to establish their own 'in-house' inclusive tour charter airline, or financial institutions wishing to put into revenue-earning service aircraft lying idle between leases. The first customer was Sunseeker Leisure, and since then the company has helped establish Airworld and Sabre Airways, whilst more recently it has taken over support for Virgin Express (qv) and the British-based 'no frills, low cost' airline EasyJet (qv). Aircraft are usually operated in the colours of client airlines.

Executive Directors & Officers: W.R. Christopher Foyle, Chairman & Managing Director; Peter D.C. Sorby, Commercial & Finance Director.

HQ Airport & Main Base: London Luton Airport

Radio callsign: BROADSWORD

Designator: GS/UPD

Employees: Flight-crew: 90; Cabin staff: 1; Engineering: 2; Administration and sales: 10; Total: approx 100.

Main destinations served: London Heathrow to Brussels; London Luton to Aberdeen, Amsterdam, Barcelona, Edinburgh, Glasgow, Inverness, Nice.

Annual turnover: US $13.2 million (£8 million)

LINKS WITH OTHER AIRLINES
Operates aircraft on behalf of EasyJet and Virgin Express.

FLEET
5 Boeing 737-300
2 Boeing 737-200

Air 2000, one of Britain's leading inclusive tour charter airlines, has adopted a new and very much brighter colour scheme in recent years, as seen on this Airbus A320.

AIR 2000

Air 2000 Ltd

Incorporated: 1987

HISTORY

Air 2000 was formed in 1987 as an inclusive tour charter airline based in Manchester, initially operating two Boeing 757s. Three years later a second base was opened at Gatwick, Britain's main departure point for holiday charter flights. Meanwhile the fleet continued to expand, mainly through the addition of further Boeing 757s, although a Boeing 737 was operated for a short period. In 1996, taking advantage of the liberalisation of air transport within the European Union, a further base was opened at Dublin in the Irish Republic. Recently the airline's first scheduled services have been introduced to Cyprus.

Today the airline operates a fleet of 13 Boeing 757s, augmented by four of the smaller Airbus A320s. A new corporate identity was unveiled in October 1996, the entire fleet being rebranded during the following winter season.

Air 2000 is a wholly-owned subsidiary of First Choice Holidays plc.

Executive Directors & Officers: Peter Long, Chairman; Ken Smith, Managing Director; Richard Roberts, Commercial Director; Nigel Addison Smith, Finance Director; Glenda Lamont, Customer Services Director; Gareth Cunningham, Engineering Director; Captain Robert Screen, Director Flight Operations.

HQ Airport & Main Base: Manchester, with extensive operations from London Gatwick and Dublin.

Radio callsign: JETSET

Designator: DP/AMM

Employees: Flight-crew: 234; Cabin staff: 859; Engineering: 55; Administration and sales: 216; Total: 1,370.

Main destinations served: Charter flights to popular tourist destinations in the Mediterranean, Madeira, and the Canaries, as well as scheduled services to Cyprus.

No. of passengers pa: 4.3 million

FLEET
4 Airbus A320 (leased)
13 Boeing 757 (leased)

AIR UK

See KLMuk

AIRTOURS

Airtours International

Incorporated: 1986

HISTORY

Airtours commenced operations in 1991 as the airline subsidiary of the Airtours group, whose other activities included inclusive tour operations, including Airtours Holidays, Aspro Holidays, Suncruises, Tradewinds, and the Going Places travel agency chain. The fleet originally included McDonnell Douglas MD-83s, but is now composed of Airbus A320s, and Boeing 757s and 767s. Airtours absorbed Inter European Airways in 1993, and in 1996 the parent company acquired Spies, the Scandinavian leisure group, which also gave it ownership of Premiair (qv), the largest charter airline in Scandinavia.

Executive Directors & Officers: Michael Lee, Chief Executive; Gene

Airtours is another major operator of the Airbus A320 on inclusive tour charter flights from British airports.

Mashlan, Operations Director; Clive Darlaston, Finance Director; Bryan Deavall, Commercial Director; Captain David Parson, Flight Operations Director; Robin Walling, Ground Services Director; Patsy Plested, Cabin Services Director; Merv Davies, Engineering Director; Captain Colin Penny, Planning/IT Director.

HQ Airport & Main Base: Manchester, but flights are also operated out of many other major UK airports.

Radio callsign: TOURJET

Designator: VZ/AIH

Employees: Flight-crew: 300; Cabin staff: 1,000; Engineering: 15; Ground staff: 25; Administration and sales: 160; Total: 1,500.

Main destinations served: Holiday destinations on a charter basis, including destinations in North America, the Mediterranean, Canaries, the Indian Ocean, Thailand, and Australia.

Revenue passenger km pa: 13,136 million

Cargo km pa: 43.3 million

Annual turnover: US $578 million (£350 million)

LINKS WITH OTHER AIRLINES
Joint purchasing agreements are in force with Premiair.

FLEET
10 Airbus A320 (leased)
7 Boeing 757-200 (leased)
3 Boeing 767-300ER (leased)

AIRWORLD

Airworld Aviation Ltd
Incorporated: 1993

HISTORY
Airworld commenced operations in 1994, operating Airbus A320 aircraft on behalf of its parent company, Sunworld, itself a subsidiary of the famous travel agency network Thomas Cook. In common with most 'in-house' airlines, charters are also carried for other companies. The airline is

the first British operator of the Airbus A321, a stretched version of the A320.

Executive Directors & Officers: Shaun Dewey, Managing Director; Jackie Bedlow, Finance Director; Shaun Monnery, Commercial Director; Tony Saville, Technical Operations Director.

HQ Airport & Main Base: London Gatwick, but operations are also conducted from Bristol, Cardiff, and Manchester.

Radio callsign: ENVOY

Designator: RL/AWD

Employees: Aircrew: 80 plus; Total: approx 300.

Main destinations served: Mainly holiday destinations in the Mediterranean area.

FLEET
5 Airbus A320
2 Airbus A321-200 plus 2 on order.

AURIGNY

Aurigny Air Services Limited
Incorporated: 1968

HISTORY
Taking its name from the French word for the Channel Island of Alderney, Aurigny Air Services was founded in 1968 when British United Channel Islands Airways decided to withdraw the air service between Alderney and Guernsey. Its first

Aurigny's bright yellow Britten-Norman Trislanders provide vital links between the Channel Islands, often at very high frequencies. This is G-JOEY, the hero in a book for children!

aircraft was the appropriately-named Britten-Norman Islander. The airline then took over what has now become its busiest route, the inter-island service between Jersey and Guernsey, which at the time was served only by morning and evening British European Airways' flights – today the service is half-hourly at peak periods and hourly off-peak throughout the day. Operations were initially intended to operate on a 'no-booking, turn-up and take-off' shuttle system, but passengers soon showed a preference for a reservation-based booking system.

The twin-engined Islanders were soon replaced by the stretched tri-motor Trislander; eventually a fleet of eight was assembled and routes operated between the three largest Channel Islands and to France and the British mainland. Since the Trislander is no longer in production, Aurigny's engineering subsidiary, Anglo-Normandy Engineering, located a kit of parts to produce a ninth Trislander, the fleet having meanwhile also been strengthened by the addition of a Short 360 airliner.

The type of low-cost lifeline air service pioneered by Aurigny has been the model for many others world-wide, and the airline helps train personnel for other airlines operating in remote areas, such as the Falklands. Aurigny also claims to have been the first airline to have an aircraft sponsored, when G-OTSB was sponsored by a bank in 1984; another aircraft, G-JOEY, features in a series of books for young children.

Executive Directors & Officers: Andrew Round, Managing Director; Peter O'Donovan, Financial Director; John Cadolet, Operations Director.

HQ Airport & Main Base: Guernsey; with aircraft and crew also based at Jersey and Alderney.

Radio callsign: AYLINE

Designator: GR/AUR

Employees: Flight-crew: 30 plus; Cabin staff: 5; Engineering: 60 plus; Administration and sales: 20; Total: 150.

Main destinations served: Jersey to Guernsey; Jersey to Alderney, Caen, Dinard; Guernsey to Alderney, Cherbourg, Dinard; Alderney to Southampton.

No. of passengers pa: 300,000

LINKS WITH OTHER AIRLINES Ground-handling in Guernsey for British Airways (qv) and franchisees British Midland (qv) and Lufthansa (qv).

FLEET
9 Britten-Norman/Pilatus Britten-Norman Trislander
1 Short 360

BAC EXPRESS

BAC Express Airlines Ltd

Incorporated: 1992

HISTORY
BAC Express Airlines started life as BAC Aircraft in 1992, the name being changed in 1995. The early fleet included two Handley Page Heralds, an Embraer Bandeirante, a Shorts 330, and a Shorts 360. These aircraft were used on regular postal charters for the Royal Mail, while ad hoc passenger and freight charters were also operated. Today the airline operates a mixed fleet of aircraft of Fokker and Shorts manufacture, and continues to operate for the Royal Mail and express courier companies, as well as having aircraft available for ad hoc passenger and freight charters, or for wet-lease on scheduled services.

Executive Directors & Officers: Mike Forsyth, Managing Director; Captain Eric Blacklock, Operations Director; Jon Stratfull, Commercial Director.

HQ Airport & Main Base: London Stansted, but aircraft are operated from many major airports throughout the UK.

Radio callsign: RAPEX

Designator: RPX

Employees: 60

Main destinations served: Destinations mainly within the UK.

FLEET
3 Fokker F-27-500
1 Shorts 360-100
4 Shorts 360-200
4 Shorts 360-300

BRITANNIA

Britannia Airways Ltd

Incorporated: 1962

HISTORY
One of the world's largest inclusive tour charter airlines, Britannia dates from 1962, when Euravia (London) commenced operations from Luton Airport, using three former El Al (qv) Lockheed Constellations carrying holiday-makers for its parent, Universal Sky Tours. The airline was one of the first to be started by a tour operator, a practice which has since become commonplace. The fleet of Constellations rapidly grew to eight aircraft. In 1964 Britannia started to re-equip with Bristol Britannia turboprop airliners, and the present title was adopted.

Thomson Industrial Holdings, now the International Thomson Organisation, acquired Universal Sky Tours and Britannia in 1965. The business continued to develop, aided partly by the convenient location of its home airport, and before long charters were also being flown from Glasgow, Manchester, and Newcastle. During the winter months trooping flights

Once operating an all-Boeing 737 fleet, today Britannia is primarily a Boeing 767 operator, as seen here.

for the British Ministry of Defence provided additional work, and the airline also undertook charters carrying pilgrims to Mecca, so that by the late-1960s some 20 per cent of receipts were in foreign currency. The fleet of Bristol Britannias eventually totalled seven before these were supplemented and then replaced by Boeing 737-200s, the first of which were delivered in 1968, when they were the first 737-200s to be operated in Europe. Twenty years later, the Boeing 737-200 and 737-300 fleet amounted to almost 30 aircraft, and the airline was operating out of 20 UK airports.

In 1988 the former Universal Sky Tours, by now renamed Thomson Holidays, bought Horizon Travel and its subsidiary, the East Midlands-based Orion Airways, whose operations were soon integrated into those of Britannia. By this time Britannia was already re-equipping with larger aircraft – Boeing 767s – and these were followed by the smaller Boeing 757. The highly competitive nature of the package holiday market meant that the largest possible aircraft were necessary so that tour operators could enjoy the economies of scale. The larger aircraft also opened up longer distance inclusive tour operations for Britannia, operating initially to Florida and then, as the market developed, other destinations throughout the world.

Over the years Britannia, once the world's largest charter airline, has seen this position challenged by other airlines, many of them also owned by tour operators in effect hoping to copy Britannia's success. In 1997 the airline moved into the German market, initially with two Boeing 767-300ERs in 1998, Transwede Leisure (qv) was acquired, and is being renamed Britannia Airways AB.

Executive Directors & Officers: Roger Burnell, Managing Director; Robert G. Parker Eaton, Deputy Managing Director; Peter Buckingham, Marketing & Operations Director; Richard J. Manley, Finance Director; John Roberts, Personnel Director; Andy Reynolds, Systems Director; Bernard Newton, Technical Director; Paul Bradley, Director Flight Crew; Captain C. Sharples, Director Flight Safety.

HQ Airport & Main Base: London Luton

Radio callsign: BRITANNIA

Designator: BY/BAL

Employees: Aircrew: 2,000; Engineering: 650; Ground staff: 550; Total: 3,200.

Main destinations served: Operates from 16 UK airports to more than 100 destinations throughout the world.

FLEET
5 Boeing 757-200
14 Boeing 767-200
6 Boeing 767-200ER
6 Boeing 767-300ER (plus 4 on option)

BRITISH AIRWAYS

British Airways plc

Incorporated: 1972

HISTORY
Carrying more international passengers than any other airline, British Airways, or BA, is also one of just two airlines cur-

rently operating supersonic air services. Its long history began in 1924, when four small airlines – Handley Page Transport, Instone Air Line, Daimler Hire, and British Marine Air Navigation – were merged to form Imperial Airways with a combined fleet of just 18 aircraft. While initially the airline developed services to Europe, it soon established a network of services throughout the British Empire using a combination of landplanes and flying-boats, reaching Basra in the Persian Gulf by 1927, Karachi in 1929, Nairobi and Cape Town in 1932, Calcutta, Rangoon, and Singapore in 1933, and Brisbane in 1935. The complete journey on the Australian service took 12½ days, and the

It is said that a corporate identity is the single visual image of an organisation, so what can be made of the different fin designs for British Airways?

route often had to be altered to avoid world trouble spots. The Singapore-Brisbane section was operated by the then newly-formed Qantas (qv).

Other airlines had meanwhile been established in the UK, and in 1935 three of these – Hillman's Airways, Spartan Air Lines, and United Air Lines – merged to form British Airways, which operated landplanes mainly on routes between the UK and Europe.

The growth of Imperial Airways was given added impetus after 1937 when the British Government introduced the Empire Air Mail Scheme, which enabled all letters between the countries of the British Empire to be sent by air at a rate of 1½d (0.625p) per half-ounce, or US 3 cents at the exchange rate of the day. To handle this growing volume of air mail, Imperial took the unprecedented step of ordering 28 of the new Short S.23 Empire flying-boats off the drawing board, without a prototype aircraft. The first of these aircraft entered service on 31 October 1936, reducing the UK–Australia journey to nine days. The Empire flying-boats would later take part in experiments in in-flight refuelling and, with Pan American World Airways, conducted successful trials for transatlantic flying-boat services.

Both Imperial Airways and British Airways were nationalised in 1939 as a result of the previous year's Cadman Report, which recommended a single British international airline. The new merged airline, British Overseas Airways Corporation (BOAC), commenced operations in 1940. While air services were drastically reduced during World War Two, BOAC maintained its African network and a new service from Cape Town to Australia via Ceylon. Liberator bombers were used on the North Atlantic to return ferry pilots to Canada and the United States. Modified de Havilland Mosquito fighter-bombers were used to fly ball-bearings from Sweden to Scotland, flying over enemy-held territory.

Post-war, the airline concentrated on inter-continental services, while domestic and European services passed to a new airline, British European Airways (BEA).

BOAC's fleet became increasingly land-plane-dominated, and the last flying-boats left the fleet in the early 1950s. The airline was the first to introduce jet airliners in 1952, but their de Havilland Comet I jets had to be withdrawn in 1954 after several disasters. Nevertheless, the much improved de Havilland Comet 4 enabled BOAC to launch the first transatlantic jet air services in 1958.

Meanwhile, BEA had been the first air-line to introduce turboprop aircraft after successful trials with the prototype Vickers Viscount in 1951. The airline also experimented with the carriage of mail, and then passengers, by helicopter. A subsidiary, BEA Helicopters, was formed in 1964 to operate helicopter services to the Isles of Scilly, but the main boost to the helicopter operations came with the discovery of oil and natural gas in the North Sea.

While BOAC developed satellite airlines in Africa and the Caribbean, BEA became involved with regional airlines in England and Wales through involvement in BKS Air Services (which later changed its name to North East Airlines) and Cambrian Airways, eventually establishing a subsidiary, British Air Services, to co-ordinate these two companies. In 1969 a charter subsidiary, BEA Airtours, was formed. Throughout its existence BEA also oper-ated a network of German domestic services radiating out of West Berlin, since East German airspace was closed to airlines other than those of the four occupying powers.

At the beginning of the 1970s history repeated itself when another government-appointed committee, the Edwards Committee, recommended the merger of BEA and BOAC. A holding company for both airlines was established in 1972, while the merger itself was implemented

Showing one of the many new designs on its tail is one of BA's Boeing 747-400s.

in 1974, when the new British Airways appeared. The main subsidiaries included British Airtours and British Airways Helicopters.

Since the merger, British Airways has continued the tradition of 'firsts', by introducing transatlantic supersonic services with the Anglo-French Concorde airliner, while its 'no reservation' shuttle services on the UK domestic trunk routes were the first of their kind outside the United States. In 1987 BA became the first European nationalised flag-carrier to be privatised. The following year it bought its main British rival, British Caledonian, which was encountering financial difficulties, and merged that airline's charter activities with those of British Airtours under the Caledonian Airways name. Four years later BA acquired another Gatwick-based airline, Dan Air.

BA sold off British Airways Helicopters in 1986, when it became British International Helicopters (qv), and in 1995 sold Caledonian Airways (qv). Nevertheless, its history since privatisation has been mainly one of acquisition to establish a global airline. In 1992 BA bought 49 per cent holdings in both France's leading regional airline, TAT European Airlines (qv) – later increasing this to 100 per cent – and in Germany's Delta Air Regionalflug, which was renamed Deutsche BA (qv). The following year BA acquired a 25 per cent holding in USAir, leading to code sharing on USAir flights to 38 cities in the United States. Later in 1993 it acquired a 25 per cent interest in the Australian airline, Qantas (qv). A smaller acquisition during this period was the West Country airline Brymon Airways (qv). BA has also acquired a 49 per cent interest in the Gibraltar airline GB Airways.

Rationalisation has included selling BA's package holiday operations to Owners Abroad (now the First Leisure Group, owners of Air 2000 [qv] in 1990, and its engine-overhaul plant in Wales to General Electric in 1991.

Expansion has also included franchise operations with smaller regional airlines operating their aircraft in BA livery on flights with BA designators operated by staff wearing BA uniforms. Current franchise partners include not only the wholly-owned Brymon, but also Loganair (qv), British Regional Airways (qv) as the successor to Manx Airlines (Europe) – a subsidiary of Manx Airlines (qv) – CityFlyer Express (qv), Maersk Air (UK) (qv), TAT (qv), and SUN-AIR. Using three Airbus A320s, in 1997 British Mediterranean Airways took over BA's services from London to Amman, Beirut, and Damascus,

becoming a franchisee. BA is also involved in Airline Management (AML) – a low-cost joint venture based at Gatwick – to which it is transferring five Boeing 777s to replace McDonnell Douglas DC-10s inherited from British Caledonian; these aircraft will retain BA aircrew and livery until at least 1999. A 'low cost, no frills' operation started at London Stansted in April 1998, using four Boeing 737-300s for services to Amsterdam, Paris, and Madrid under the name of Go Airways (qv).

Currently BA is completing a major global alliance with the world's largest airline, American Airlines (qv). This will entail selling off the BA's interest in USAir. During 1997 a controversial new corporate identity was introduced, part of which entails having no standardised identity on the tails of the company's aircraft.

Executive Directors & Officers: Sir Colin Marshall, Chairman & CEO; Sir Michael Angus, Deputy Chairman; Robert Ayling, Chief Executive; Derek Stevens, Chief Financial Officer; Martin George, Director of Marketing; David Holmes, Director of Corporate Resources; Colin Matthews, Managing Director, BA Engineering; John Patterson, Director of Strategy; Peter White, Director of Sales; Charles Gurassa, Director of Passenger Business; Captain Mike Jeffery, Director of Flight Crew; Roger Maynard, Director of Investments and Joint Ventures; Valerie Scoular, Director of Customer Service; Mike Street, Director of Operations.

HQ Airport & Main Base: London Heathrow, but there are also extensive operations from London Gatwick, Manchester, and Birmingham.

Radio callsign:
BEALINE/SPEEDBIRD/SHUTTLE

Designator: BA/BAW

Employees: Flight-crew: 3,450; Cabin staff: 12,562; Engineering: 10,407; Ground staff: 21,268; Administration and sales: 5,096; Total: 53,783.

Main destinations served: Flights from London Heathrow – except for (g): flights from both Heathrow and Gatwick; or (G): flights from Gatwick only – but the main UK, European, and some North American destinations are also served from Manchester and Birmingham: Aberdeen (g), Abidjan (G), Abu Dhabi (g), Accra (G), Amman, Amsterdam, Antigua (G), Antwerp* (g), Athens (g), Atlanta (G+), Bahrain, Baku (G), Baltimore (G), Bangkok, Barbados (g), Barcelona, Basle/Mulhouse, Beijing, Beirut, Belfast International, Belgrade (G), Berlin, Bermuda (G+), Bilbao,

Bogota, Bologna, Bombay, Bordeaux (G), Boston, Bremen (G), Brisbane, Brussels (g), Bucharest (G), Budapest, Buenos Aires, Cairo, Calcutta, Cape Town, Caracas, Charlotte (G), Chicago, Cologne, Copenhagen (g), Dallas/Fort Worth (G+), Damascus, Dar-es-Salaam (G), Delhi, Detroit, Dhahran, Dhaka, Dubai, Durban, Düsseldorf (g*), Edinburgh (g), Entebbe (G), Faro (G), Frankfurt (g), Gabarone, Geneva (g), Genoa (G), Glasgow (g), Gothenburg (g), Grand Cayman (G), Grenada (G), Guernsey* (G), Hamburg (g), Hanover, Harare (G), Helsinki, Hong Kong, Houston (G), Inverness, Islamabad (G), Istanbul, Jakarta, Jeddah, Jersey (g*), Johannesburg, Kano (G), Kiev (G), Kingston (G+), Kuala Lumpur, Kuwait, Lagos (G), Larnaca, Leipzig, Lilongwe (G), Lisbon, Los Angeles, Lourdes/Tarbes (G), Lusaka (G), Luxembourg, Lyon (g*), Madras, Madrid (g), Malaga (G), Manchester (g), Manila, Marseilles (G), Mauritius (G), Melbourne, Mexico City, Miami (g), Milan (g), Montego Bay (G+), Montpellier (G), Montreal, Moscow (g), Munich (g), Muscat, Nagoya, Nairobi (G), Naples (G), Nassau (G), Newcastle (g*), Newquay, New York JFK (g) and Newark, Nice (g), Orlando (G), Oporto, Osaka, Oslo (g), Paris CDG (g) and Orly, Perpignan (G), Perth (Australia), Philadelphia, Pisa, Phoenix (G), Pittsburgh (G), Plymouth, Port of Spain (G), Prague, Río de Janeiro, Riyadh, Rome (g), Rotterdam* (G), St Lucia (G), St Petersburg, San Diego (G), San Francisco, San Juan (G), Santiago, Seattle, Seoul, Seychelles (G), Singapore, Sofia (G), Stockholm (g), Stuttgart, Sydney, Taipei†, Tampa (G), Tehran, Tel Aviv (g), Thessaloniki, Tokyo, Toronto (b), Toulouse (G), Turin, Vancouver, Venice, Verona (G), Vienna (g), Warsaw, Washington, Zürich (g).
Key: * = service operated by a franchisee; † = British Asia Airways; (g*) = Gatwick service operated by franchisee, Heathrow by BA; + = service operated by BA aircraft and crew as part of Airline Management joint venture.

Revenue passenger km pa: 96,163 million

Cargo tonne km pa: 3,476 million

Passengers carried pa: 32,272 million

Annual turnover: US $13,792 million (£8,359 million)

LINKS WITH OTHER AIRLINES
BA is a member of the Galileo reservations system.
BA's subsidiary airlines are Brymon Airways (qv) and TAT (qv).

BA has shareholdings in Air Mauritius (12.8%), Deutsche BA (49%), and Qantas (25%). Stake in USAir is being sold. BA franchise airlines include Brymon Airways (qv), CityFlyer Express (qv), Loganair (qv), TAT (qv), SUN-AIR, British Mediterranean Airways, and British Regional Airlines (qv).

FLEET

7 Aérospatiale/BAe Concorde
10 Airbus A320 (plus 59 A319/A320 on order)
33 Boeing 737-200A (being replaced by additional 737-300s)
34 Boeing 737-400
11 Boeing 737-300 (leased, with additional aircraft on order)
15 Boeing 747-100
16 Boeing 747-200B
46 Boeing 747-400 (plus 16 on order)
48 Boeing 757-200
28 Boeing 767-300ER
7 Boeing 777-200
2 McDonnell Douglas DC-10-30
9 Boeing 777-200IGW
14 British Aerospace ATP
5 de Havilland Canada DHC-7-100 (operated by Brymon)
6 de Havilland Canada DHC-8 (operated by Brymon)

BRITISH AIRWAYS EXPRESS

See companies listed below

Incorporated: 1995

HISTORY

British Airways Express was established by British Airways (qv) in 1995 as a franchise operation, with participating airlines adopting British Airways liveries, uniforms, and flight designators. The airlines currently operating within this grouping include two of the three British Regional Airlines (Group) companies, British Regional Airlines (qv) and Business Air (qv), as well as TAT (qv), CityFlyer Express (qv) and SUN-AIR of Scandinavia. Brymon Airways (qv) also carries BA livery.

The concept is one which has been pioneered by major airlines in the United States, and enables large carriers, with the high overheads which seem to be almost inescapable on major intercontinental networks, to reach smaller communities by enjoying the lower costs of smaller regional airlines. For the regional airlines involved the marketing expenditure of the major carrier seems to increase traffic volume rapidly.

Radio callsign: SPEEDBIRD

Designator: BA/BAW

BRITISH INTERNATIONAL

Brintel Helicopters Ltd

Incorporated: 1993

HISTORY

British International Helicopters can trace its origins to the formation by British European Airways of the BEA Helicopter Experimental Unit in 1947, which initially used an S-51 helicopter for experimental postal services and subsequently operated Westland WS-55 Whirlwinds on passenger feeder services to airports, although these were withdrawn in 1956 as an economy measure. During 1953, with heavy flooding in the Netherlands, two of the S-51s were used to rescue 76 people.

BEA Helicopters was formed in 1964, and within a few years was operating Sikorsky S-61 helicopters, mainly in support of the North Sea oil and gas industry. It also operated Britain's only scheduled helicopter service, between Penzance and the Isles of Scilly off the south-western tip of Cornwall. Between 1971 and 1983 a Sikorsky S-61N was operated on behalf of the British Coastguard service out of Aberdeen, saving more than 260 people during this period. At one stage large Boeing Chinook helicopters were also operated on behalf of the oil and gas industry. Although the helicopter operation survived the merger of BEA and BOAC into British Airways (qv), becoming British Airways Helicopters, the company was subsequently sold as BA endeavoured to concentrate on its core scheduled airline operations, becoming British International Helicopters in 1986. The present title was adopted in 1995.

In 1996 the company acquired Cardiff-based Veritair, operators of light helicopters in support of police forces, including South Wales Police. Today, British International continues to operate helicopters in support of the oil and gas industries, and has developed a cost-effective aerial crane service for the construction industry.

Executive Directors & Officers: Paul Conway, Managing Director; Steve Stubbs, Operations Director.

HQ Airport & Main Base: Aberdeen, with other bases at Sumburgh (Shetland), Penzance, and Cardiff.

Radio callsign: BRINTEL

Designator: UR/BIH

Employees: Flight-crew: 103; Cabin staff: 7; Engineering: 139; Ground staff:78; Administration and sales: 45; Total: 372.

Main destinations served: Penzance to St Mary's; Penzance to Tresco.

Although scheduled helicopter services were pioneered in the UK, the only service which survives today is that from Penzance to the Isles of Scilly operated by British International. Here a Sikorsky S-61 loads at Penzance for St Mary's.

Hours flown pa: 22,000

Annual turnover: US $78,643,950
(£47,663,000)

LINKS WITH OTHER AIRLINES
Owned by CHC Helicopter Corporation
(Canada).
Reciprocal training links with Helikopter
Service of Norway.

FLEET
12 Sikorsky S-61N
1 Sikorsky S-61NM
1 Sikorsky S-76A
8 Eurocopter AS.332L Super Puma
2 Eurocopter AS.332C-L Super Puma
1 Eurocopter AS.355
1 Eurocopter BO.105

BRITISH MIDLAND

British Midland Airways Limited

Incorporated: 1938

HISTORY
Within a span of 60 years British Midland
has grown from operating a small flying
school at Burnaston, near Derby, to
become first a major British domestic airline, and then, within the last ten years, a
significant major international airline. The
original company was known as Air
Schools, providing pilot training, and during World War Two its schools at Derby
and Wolverhampton trained some 14,000
pilots. As the demand for pilot training

reduced with the return of peace and the
availability of ex-service pilots for airlines,
the company diversified into ad hoc charters for both passengers and cargo, initially using eight-seat de Havilland Rapide
biplanes. The name was soon changed to
Derby Aviation, but the first scheduled
service did not come until 1953, when a
Dragon Rapide operated from
Wolverhampton to Jersey in the Channel
Islands. Other routes soon followed, with
services from Derby as well as
Wolverhampton, and the small Rapides
were soon replaced by larger Douglas
DC-3 Dakotas and the four-engined
Handley Page Marathon, albeit still with
just 20 seats. The Marathons were soon
replaced by three Canadair DC-4M
Argonauts for the rapidly growing inclusive tour charter market. A further name
change came in 1959, when the airline
became Derby Airways.

During the early post-war period British
commercial aviation had been dominated
by the big nationalised companies, British
European Airways and British Overseas
Airways Corporation, with private enterprise airlines being allowed charters and
confined to a minor role on scheduled
services, often as 'associates' of the state
carriers. The establishment of an Air
Transport Licensing Board in 1960 prepared the way for greater opportunities
for the private sector.

In 1965 Derby Airways moved to the
new East Midlands Airport at Castle
Donington and changed its name to
British Midland Airways, adopting a two-

tone blue and white livery. More modern
aircraft were soon acquired, starting in
1967 with Vickers Viscount turboprop airliners. Shortly afterwards British Midland
started its first service to a London airport
with a route from Teesside to Heathrow.

Boeing 707 aircraft were also operated
for a time during the 1970s, and the airline
provided an 'instant airline' start-up service for newly independent nations wishing to have their own national airline,
helping to start 25 airlines over a seven-
year period. In 1978 the airline was purchased by the present chairman, Sir
Michael Bishop, and two partners, from
the previous owners Minster Assets, which
had acquired British Midland ten years
earlier. The new owners then set out to
establish the airline as a major competitor
on the domestic trunk routes from
London's Heathrow Airport to Belfast,
Glasgow, and Edinburgh. Although the
initial application for licences was made in
1979, strong objections from British
Airways (qv) meant that it was not until
1982 that the first services could be operated to Glasgow, with Edinburgh services
following in 1983 and those to Belfast in
1984. A fleet of McDonnell Douglas DC-9s
was acquired to operated the new routes.

In 1985 a new blue and white livery
with red lettering was adopted, although
this has since been modified. A new holding company, Airlines of Britain Holdings,
was established in 1987, to take into
account the company's ownership of the
main Scottish airline, Loganair (qv) and
the rapidly expanding Manx Airways (qv),
while the following year Scandinavian
Airlines System (SAS) (qv) took a 24.9 per
cent stake in ABH. In 1986, British
Midland inaugurated a Heathrow–
Amsterdam service. New Boeing 737 airliners started to augment, and then
replace, the DC-9s throughout the late-
1980s and early-1990s, with Fokker 100
airliners also being introduced. When SAS
increased its holding to 40 per cent in
1994, British Midland took over that airline's Glasgow–Copenhagen service,
increasing the flights to twice daily and
then introducing a daily call at Edinburgh.
The airline has reintroduced two-class air
travel to British domestic flights as well as
on its European network.

Today, British Midland is the second
largest user of London's Heathrow Airport,
and has code-share arrangements with a
number of international airlines. The other
ABH subsidiaries, which also came to
include Business Air in 1986, transferred
to a new company, British Regional
Airlines (qv), in 1997 although Business
Air also operates the British Midland
Commuter Service.

*British Midland has made it its business to compete with British Airways, first on the UK
trunk routes and more recently on the main European routes from London. Until
recently the backbone of its fleet has been the Boeing 737, of which a -300 is shown here.*

In recent years the airline has used Boeing 737s, but in 1998 the first of an order of Airbus A320/321s entered service; these may replace some of the older Boeing 737s.

Executive Directors & Officers: Sir Michael Bishop, Chairman; Austin Reid, Managing Director; Captain Bill Gilmour, Operations Director; Alex Grant, Sales & Marketing Director; Nigel Turner, Finance Director; Graham Norman, Commercial Director.

HQ Airport & Main Base: London Heathrow is the main base, but the HQ airport is East Midlands.

Radio callsign: MIDLAND

Designator: BD/BMA

Employees: 4,600

Main destinations served: London Heathrow to Amsterdam, Belfast, Brussels, Dublin, Edinburgh, Frankfurt, Glasgow, Leeds/Bradford, Nice, Palma de Mallorca, Paris, Prague, Teesside, Zürich. London Luton to Jersey. East Midlands to Aberdeen, Amsterdam, Belfast, Brussels, Dublin, Edinburgh, Faro, Glasgow, Guernsey, Jersey, Malaga, Nice, Palma de Mallorca, Paris. Belfast to Jersey, Birmingham to Brussels and Jersey, Glasgow to Copenhagen and Jersey.

No. of passengers pa: 6.1 million (of which 5.6 million scheduled service)

Annual turnover: US $976 million (£591.5 million), including British Regional Airlines (qv)

LINKS WITH OTHER AIRLINES
SAS has a 40 per cent shareholding in British Midland.
Code-sharing agreements are in place with Air Canada (qv), Air Lanka (qv), Air New Zealand (qv), Alitalia (qv), Austrian Airlines (qv), Cathay Pacific (qv), Gulf Air (qv), Iberia (qv), Lufthansa (qv), Malaysia Airlines (qv), Royal Brunei (qv), SAS (qv), TAP (qv), United Airlines (qv), Virgin Atlantic (qv).

FLEET
3 Airbus A321-100 (plus 7 on order)
3 Airbus A320-200 (plus 8 on order; can be changed to A321)
7 Boeing 737-300 (some may be replaced by A320/321)
5 Boeing 737-400
12 Boeing 737-500
3 Fokker 70
4 Fokker 100
9 Saab 304

BRITISH REGIONAL AIRLINES

British Regional Airlines Ltd

Incorporated: 1990

HISTORY
British Regional Airlines came into existence in 1990 as Manx Airlines (Europe), a subsidiary of Manx Airlines (qv), set up to develop the parent company's growing network of operations based outside the Isle of Man. A growing number of services were based on Cardiff, Manchester, and Southampton, with services from the last two being boosted in 1994 by the transfer of Loganair (qv) operations outside Scotland. The following year Manx Airlines (Europe) became a British Airways Express (qv) franchise-holder, adopting British Airways colour schemes, uniforms, and flight designators.

The current title was adopted in 1996, reflecting further growth in the network after British Airways decided to withdraw its operations within Scotland, handing these over to British Regional Airlines. Shortly afterwards Loganair's operations were incorporated into British Regional Airlines.

Initially the fleet was largely based on British Aerospace ATP, Jetstream 31 and 41, and Shorts 360 aircraft, but this soon included a British Aerospace 146 and a Saab SF340, while the smaller Jetstream 31s were soon replaced by more of the larger 41s. In 1997 British Regional Airlines became the first British operator of the new Embraer 145 regional jet aircraft.

Manx Airlines had been for many years a subsidiary of Airlines of Britain Holdings (ABH), along with British Midland (qv) and Loganair (qv), while in 1996 ABH also took over Aberdeen-based Business Air (qv), which in 1997 became part of British Regional Airlines (Holdings), a new company set up as a parent for both British Regional Airlines, as an operating company, and Manx Airlines. Loganair, which had been operated as part of British Regional Airlines, was bought-out by its management early in 1997 and left the BRAL Group.

Executive Directors & Officers: Sir Michael Bishop, Chairman; Terry Liddiard, Managing Director; Paul Neilson, Finance Director; Mike Bathgate, Commercial Director; Captain Norman Brewitt, Operations Director, Ian Woodley, Director.

HQ Airport: East Midlands International (holding company only)

Main Base: Isle of Man (Ronaldsway) Airport

Radio callsign: BRITISH

Designator: BA/BRT

Employees: Flight-crew: 99; Cabin staff: 73; Engineering: 128; Ground staff: 250; Total: 550.

Main destinations served: Manchester to Belfast City, Belfast International, Berlin, Cardiff, Cork, Guernsey, Hanover, Jersey, Knock, Londonderry, London Stansted, Shannon, Southampton, Waterford.
Glasgow to Aberdeen, Belfast City, Belfast International, Benbecula, Cardiff, Donegal, Guernsey*, Inverness, Islay, Kirkwall, Londonderry, Southampton, Sumburgh, Stornoway.
Edinburgh to Belfast City, Blackpool*, Cardiff, Inverness, Jersey*, Kirkwall, Newcastle, Southampton, Sumburgh, Wick.
Southampton to Aberdeen, Belfast City, Belfast International, Brussels, Guernsey, Leeds/Bradford.
Aberdeen to Belfast City, Belfast International, Cardiff, Kirkwall, Leeds/Bradford, Sumburgh.
Belfast City to Cardiff, Liverpool, London Luton, Newcastle.
Cardiff International to Brussels, Guernsey*, Newcastle, Paris CDG.
Inverness to Kirkwall, Stornoway, Sumburgh.
Benbecula to Stornoway, Blackpool to Jersey*, Brussels to Guernsey, Kirkwall to Sumburgh, Lerwick to Unst, London Stansted to Waterford, Sumburgh to Unst, Sumburgh to Wick.
Key: * = summer only.

Passengers pa: 1,038,173

LINKS WITH OTHER AIRLINES
British Airways Express franchise holder
British Midland Commuter operator.

FLEET
1 British Aerospace 146-200
10 Embraer 145 (plus 10 on option)
12 British Aerospace ATP
12 British Aerospace Jetstream 41
6 Shorts 360
1 Saab SF340 (leased from Business Air)

BRITISH WORLD

British World Airlines Ltd

Incorporated: 1963

HISTORY
British World Airlines can trace its history

Until recently British World operated the world's largest fleet of Vickers Viscounts, but these are now being retired, including this Viscount 800.

services to and from Guernsey and Jersey in the Channel Islands. The new airline then attempted to pioneer deep penetration vehicle air ferries flying deeper into Europe, but these were less successful because of the relatively high costs.

The combined airline eventually left the British United Group following its merger with Caledonian Airways (qv), and became British Air Ferries, changing ownership again in 1971. The airline moved into passenger and freight charters, acquiring a large fleet of Vickers Viscount aircraft. During the late-1980s the airline suffered a spell of Administration, the British equivalent of the United States Chapter 11 bankruptcy protection, but emerged from this in 1989. The current name was adopted in 1993.

Today British World operates passenger and freight charters, and wet-leases its aircraft to other airlines. Air freight services are operated on behalf of Parcel Force, part of the Post Office, and operates charters on behalf of the oil industry from Aberdeen, where two ATR 72s replaced three Viscounts in 1995 before being replaced in turn by two British Aerospace ATPs. In 1997 an ex-Cathay Pacific Lockheed TriStar was added to the fleet, and is operated under wet-lease to Classic Airways.

Executive Directors & Officers: Roger Pinnington, Chairman; Robert Sturman, Chief Executive; John Deether, Finance Director; Captain J. Vanderbeek, Operations Director; Mike Sessions, Sales Director.

HQ Airport: Southend

back to the formation of Silver City Airways in 1946, operating an Avro Lancastrian, a conversion for commercial use of the famous World War Two Lancaster heavy bomber. The new airline soon established itself by pioneering the world's first vehicle air-ferry services, introducing Bristol Freighters on short cross-Channel services between the south of England and northern France.

A major competitor soon emerged on these services in the form of Channel Air Bridge, which, in 1960, became part of the new British United Airways. Silver City Airways, in which by this time the P&O shipping group had a substantial interest, was acquired by British United in 1962, after which a reorganisation put the former Silver City and Channel Air Bridge routes and aircraft into a specialised division, British United Air Ferries. By this time the network included services from Southend to the Netherlands and Belgium as well as to France, while there were also

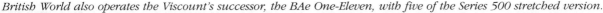

British World also operates the Viscount's successor, the BAe One-Eleven, with five of the Series 500 stretched version.

British World has two ATR 72s, originally bought for oil industry charters between Aberdeen and the Shetlands, but now available for other work following the arrival of BAe ATPs.

Main Base: London Stansted Airport, with other bases at London Gatwick, Manchester, and Aberdeen.

Radio callsign: BRITWORLD

Designator: VF/BWL

Employees: Flight-crew: 69; Cabin staff: 80; Engineering: 193; Ground staff: 5; Administration and sales: 73; Total: 420.

Main destinations served: Ad hoc and inclusive tour charter operations within Europe, as well as regular parcels operations for Parcel Force and passenger flights from Aberdeen to Shetland for the oil industry.

Passengers pa: 412, 742

Cargo tonne km pa: 8,744,200

FLEET
1 Lockheed L-1011 TriStar 100
5 British Aerospace One-Eleven 500 (leased)
7 British Aerospace 146-200/300 (leased from USAir and operated on behalf of Debonair (qv))
3 Vickers Viscount 800
2 British Aerospace ATP (leased)
2 ATR 72 (leased)

BRYMON AIRWAYS

Brymon European Airways Ltd

Incorporated: 1972

HISTORY
Brymon Airways takes its name from that of the two founders, William Bryce, a New Zealander, and Chris Amon. Operations started in 1972 using a nine-passenger Britten-Norman Islander, flying to the Isles of Scilly and Jersey from the company's base at Newquay and from Plymouth. The following year Brymon moved its base to Plymouth and obtained a larger aircraft in the form of a 20-seat de Havilland Canada Twin Otter. A Plymouth–Guernsey service was also introduced that year.

In the years that followed, Cork and Exeter were added to the network, and a major step forward came in 1977, when the airline took over the British Midland (qv) Newquay to London Heathrow route, replacing the Vickers Viscounts used by BM with a smaller Handley Page Herald. Services from Plymouth to London Gatwick were introduced two years later, using Twin Otters. The restricted length of the runway at Plymouth had limited the development of services from that airport, but this changed in 1982, when Brymon introduced the short take-off and landing (STOL) de Havilland Canada Dash 7, initially for use on an oil industry charter because of the aircraft's ability to use another short runway at Unst in Shetland, the UK's most northerly airport. Brymon's Dash 7 was also used in experiments to prove the feasibility of an airport in London's docklands, encouraging the future development of what is now London City Airport.

A number of changes of ownership followed during the next few years. In 1983 de Havilland Canada bought a 75 per cent stake in Brymon from the founders, while three years later ownership passed to The Plimsoll Line, a company owned 40 per cent by British Airways (qv), and in which the Danish airline Maersk Air (qv) acquired a 40 per cent stake in 1988 before TPL acquired Birmingham European Airways.

Brymon launched flights from London City Airport to both Paris and Plymouth in 1987. Three years later further expansion started with the introduction of the de

Still in the old British Airways colour scheme is this de Havilland Dash 8-300 turboprop of Brymon Airways.

Havilland Dash 8, and a new network of routes from Bristol to Glasgow, Edinburgh, and Paris, with a feeder service between Plymouth and Bristol. The following year services from Bristol were introduced to Aberdeen, Jersey, and Newcastle. A short-lived merger of the two TPL subsidiaries followed in 1992, but this was reversed the following year, leaving Maersk with Birmingham European, while Brymon became a wholly-owned subsidiary of British Airways, adopting the parent company's livery and flight designators.

Further expansion followed the acquisition by BA, although by this time the airline was no longer operating to London City Airport. Services were introduced from Newcastle and Southampton to Paris. In 1997 services from Newquay and Plymouth to London Heathrow were switched to London Gatwick, allowing a 25 per cent increase in flights. Despite the growth in the scheduled network, Brymon continues to operate oil industry-related charters out of Aberdeen.

Executive Directors & Officers: Gareth Kirkwood, Managing Director.

HQ Airport & Main Base: Plymouth City Airport, with the main operations out of or via Bristol Lulsgate, and charter operations from Aberdeen.

Radio callsign: BRYOPS

Designator: BA/BRY

Employees: Flight-crew: 94; Cabin staff: 87; Engineering: 82; Ground staff: 63; Administration and sales: 30; Total: 355.

Main destinations served: Bristol to Aberdeen, Cork, Edinburgh, Glasgow, Guernsey, Jersey, London Gatwick, Newcastle, Paris, Plymouth. Plymouth to Aberdeen*, Cork, Edinburgh*, Glasgow*, Guernsey, Jersey, London Gatwick, Newcastle*, Paris. Newcastle to Aberdeen, Frankfurt, Paris, Southampton. Southampton to Paris. * via Bristol.

Passenger miles pa: 158 million

Annual turnover: US $82.5 million (£50 million)

LINKS WITH OTHER AIRLINES
Brymon is a wholly-owned subsidiary of British Airways, and links with other airlines as for British Airways.

FLEET
9 de Havilland Canada Dash 8-300
2 de Havilland Canada Dash 7-110*
* Based at Aberdeen for oil industry charters under contract to Scatsta.

BUSINESS AIR

Business Air Ltd

Incorporated: 1987

HISTORY
Business Air dates from 1987, when it was formed by Ian Woodley to fly daytime charters for the North Sea oil industry and to undertake charters for the Royal Mail at night, using a small fleet of Embraer Bandeirante aircraft. Soon thereafter scheduled services were started, linking Aberdeen to Dundee and Manchester, and Aberdeen to Esbjerg in Denmark. New investors in 1990, including Crossair (qv), enabled the airline to buy larger Saab SF340 aircraft. The new investors doubled their stake to just over 30 per cent in 1992, and this encouraged Business Air to introduce new scheduled services linking Edinburgh and Aberdeen with the East Midlands and, later, Manchester. Business Air launched a service from Frankfurt to London City Airport in 1993, operating the aircraft on behalf of Lufthansa (qv).

The collaboration with Lufthansa led to the German airline taking a 38 per cent shareholding in Business Air the following year, and this was matched by Crossair. Further services were added to the network, including flights from Belfast and Glasgow to Manchester, which, with the flights from other Scottish cities, were timed to provide connections with Lufthansa flights to and from Germany.

Ian Woodley bought back the shares held by Lufthansa and Crossair in 1996, and for a while the airline was completely independent until, later the same year, it was acquired by Airlines of Britain Holdings, owners of British Midland (qv). After restructuring ownership passed to British Regional Airlines (Holdings) the following year.

In addition to its own routes, the airline provides wet-leasing capacity for both British Regional Airlines (qv) and British Midland, and continues the BA-146 Frankfurt–London City services for Lufthansa, with a weekend Frankfurt–Glasgow service as well.

Executive Directors & Officers: Ian Woodley, Managing Director; Graeme Ross, Commercial Director; Stewart Adams, General Manager.

HQ Airport & Main Base: Aberdeen

Radio callsign: GRANITE

Designator: II/GNT

Employees: Flight-crew: 103; Cabin staff: 43; Engineering: 7; Ground staff: 56; Administration and sales: 16; Total: 245.

Main destinations served: Aberdeen to Dundee, Edinburgh, Esbjerg, Manchester. Manchester to Edinburgh, Glasgow. Dundee to Edinburgh.

LINKS WITH OTHER AIRLINES
Operates services for Lufthansa and British Midland Connector.
British Airways franchisee.
Marketing partnership with Lufthansa and code-share with Continental Airlines (qv).

FLEET
8 Saab SF-340A
2 Saab SF-340B
1 British Aerospace 146-200
(British Regional and Manx each have one SF 340 leased in, and further aircraft are leased to British Midland.)

CALEDONIAN

Caledonian Airways Ltd

Incorporated: 1988

HISTORY
Although the name of Caledonian Airways can be traced back to the formation of the airline of that name in 1961, the present airline's links with the original are tenuous. The original Caledonian Airways was founded to operate North Atlantic passenger charters, with the original intention that it should eventually become the Scottish international airline. In the event, the airline's business became increasingly London Gatwick-based, operating first a single Douglas DC-7C, then four Bristol Britannias, and then two Boeing 707-399s. A scheduled service between Glasgow and Barcelona was licensed, but never operated. Nevertheless, during the early 1970s the airline merged with British United Airways to form British Caledonian Airways (or 'BCAL'), which at its peak operated a mixed fleet of BAC One-Elevens, Boeing 707s and Vickers VC10s on a route network which included destinations in Africa and South America, as well as New York and Los Angeles, and also served many of the main European destinations as well as the UK domestic trunk routes from its London Gatwick base.

McDonnell Douglas DC-10 and Airbus A320 airliners were also introduced, and a route swap with British Airways (qv) saw the South American routes exchanged for a number of destinations in the Middle East, before mounting economic difficulties saw British Caledonian taken over by British Airways in 1988. In the subsequent reorganisation the scheduled services and their aircraft were absorbed by BA, while the charter operations were combined with those of BA's charter subsidiary, British Airtours, and the combined charter operation was renamed Caledonian Airways.

The present company was acquired from British Airways by Inspirations, a British inclusive tour operator, in 1994. Operations are entirely charter, and primarily for inclusive tour operators.

Executive Directors & Officers:
Eamonn Mullaney, Chairman and Managing Director; Jane Huntley, Finance Director; David Newell, Operations Director; George Blundell-Pound, Commercial Director; Brian Bradbury, Engineering Director; Nigel Tarr, Customer Services Director.

HQ Airport & Main Base: London Gatwick

Radio callsign: CALEDONIAN

Designator: KG/CKT

Employees: Flight-crew: 153; Cabin staff: 493; Engineering: 11; Ground staff: 170; Total: 827.

Main destinations served: Inclusive tour charters to destinations within Europe and the Mediterranean fringe, the Canaries, North America and the Caribbean, Pacific and Indian Ocean areas.

LINKS WITH OTHER AIRLINES
Peach Air is a subsidiary.

FLEET
3 Airbus A320 (leased from Kawasaki)
3 McDonnell Douglas DC-10-30 (1 leased from British Airways)
5 Lockheed L-1011-50 TriStars

CHANNEL EXPRESS

Channel Express (Air Services) Ltd

Incorporated: 1978

HISTORY
Channel Express was founded in 1978 as Express Air Services, commencing air freight operations using Handley Page Herald freighters on services between Bournemouth's Hurn Airport and the Channel Islands. During the early-1980s a number of Royal Mail contracts were obtained and the present name was adopted. Other traffic developed, with the airline introducing its own special cooling plant in Guernsey to prepare cut flowers

for air transport to the British mainland. While the Herald fleet grew, until eventually Channel Express had eight upgraded and refurbished 'Super' Heralds, larger aircraft were seen to hold the key to the future, and the airline was the first to place Lockheed L-188C Electra freighters on the British register. The arrival of the Electras saw the airline begin to take an increasing share of the overnight parcels and freight market within the UK and Europe.

In recent years Fokker F-27 Friendship freighters have been added to the fleet, and in 1997 the airline introduced the Airbus A300B4-100F freighter, as launch customer for the British Aerospace conversion of this type, able to carry loads of up to 45 tonnes. In addition to its own contracts, Channel Express also provides additional freight capacity for other airlines throughout Europe and the Middle East.

The airline is part of the Dart Group's Aviation Division.

Executive Directors & Officers: Philip Meeson, Managing Director; Ian Doubtfire, Deputy Managing Director; Andy Menzies, Technical Director; Antony Sainthill, Director A300 programmes.

HQ Airport & Main Base: Bournemouth International Airport

Radio callsign: CHANNEX

Designator: LS/EXS

Employees: Flight-crew: 115; Engineering: 70; Ground staff: 25; Administration and sales: 70; Total: 280.

Main destinations served: Jersey and Guernsey to destinations throughout the UK; Post Office contracts and contracted parcels services throughout Europe; ad hoc charters in Europe and the Middle East.

Cargo tonnes pa: 140,000

Annual turnover: US $47.355 million (£28.7 million)

FLEET
5 Fokker F-27-500F Friendship (1 leased from Jersey European Airways (qv))
3 Fokker F-27-600F Friendship
5 Lockheed L-188 Electra
1 Airbus A300B4-100F
2 Airbus A300B4-200F

CITYFLYER EXPRESS

CityFlyer Express Ltd

Incorporated: 1991

HISTORY
Formed in 1991 as Euroworld Airways to take over routes from London Gatwick freed by the collapse of Air Europe, the present title was adopted the following year. The airline was amongst the first to become British Airways Express franchisees, but ownership rests with the directors and the 3i investment bank.

All aircraft carry British Airways Express

CityFlyer Express is a BA franchisee, and its aircraft all carry BA colours. This is one of the airline's Avro RJ100s.

CityFlyer Express also operates ATR 72s, again in BA colours, mainly from London Gatwick.

livery and crew wear BA uniforms, while BA flight designators are used.

Executive Directors & Officers: Robert Wright, Chairman; Brad Burgess, Managing Director; Chris Simpson, Finance Director; Jim Bond, Operations Director; Malcolm Coupar, Commercial Director; Dennis McQuoid, Flight Operations Director.

HQ Airport & Main Base: London Gatwick

Radio callsign: FLYER

Designator: FD/BA/CFE

Employees: Flight-crew: 152; Cabin staff: 193; Engineering: 64; Ground staff: 77; Administration and sales: 31; Total: 517.

Main destinations served: London Gatwick to Amsterdam, Antwerp, Bremen, Cologne/Bonn, Cork, Dublin, Düsseldorf, Guernsey, Jersey, Leeds/Bradford, Luxembourg, Newcastle, Rotterdam.

Passenger km pa: 525 million

Annual turnover: US $148.5 million (£90 million)

LINKS WITH OTHER AIRLINES
Operates as a British Airways franchisee and uses BA flight designators.

FLEET
5 ATR 42 (leased)
5 ATR 72 (leased)
5 Avro RJ100 (leased)

DEBONAIR

Debonair Airways Ltd

Incorporated: 1995

HISTORY
Debonair commenced operations in 1996 with a small fleet of British Aerospace 146 airliners leased from British World Airlines (qv), and operated under that airline's air operator's certificate. The airline is a 'no frills' low-cost scheduled operator, whose first routes are mainly international.

Executive Directors & Officers:
Franco Mancassola, Chairman & Chief Executive; Richard Clapson, Finance Director; Stu Grieve, Operations Director; John Tenner, Maintenance Director.

HQ Airport & Main Base: London Luton

Radio callsign: DEBONAIR

Designator: 2G/DEB

Employees: 174

Main destinations served: London Luton Airport to Barcelona, Copenhagen, Düsseldorf, Mönchengladbach, Madrid, Munich, Newcastle, Rome.

LINKS WITH OTHER AIRLINES
Operates under British World Airlines' AOC.

FLEET
7 British Aerospace 146-200 (all leased)

EASYJET

easyJet Airline Ltd

Incorporated: 1995

HISTORY
The first low cost 'no frills' airline to begin operations within Britain, EasyJet started with operations out of London Luton Airport along the British domestic trunk routes to Edinburgh and Glasgow. International services have followed. Initially the airline used the AOC of GB Airways, but has since transferred to Air Foyle Charter Airlines (qv), who also provide flight-crew.

Executive Directors & Officers:
Steliosa Haji-Ioannu, Chairman; Ray Webster, Managing Director; Nick Manoudakis, Finance Director; Nick Hartley, Director.

HQ Airport & Main Base: London Luton

Radio callsign: EASY

Designator: U2/EZY

Employees: 200

Main destinations served: London Luton to Aberdeen, Amsterdam, Barcelona, Edinburgh, Glasgow, Inverness, Nice.

LINKS WITH OTHER AIRLINES
Uses AOC of Air Foyle Charter Airlines.

FLEET
10 Boeing 737-300 (plus 6 more in 1999)

EUROPEAN AVIATION

European Aviation Air Charter

Incorporated: 1994

HISTORY
Commencing operations in 1994 with three British Aerospace One-Eleven 500s, European Aviation Air Charter has since expanded its fleet to 15 such aircraft. Ad hoc passenger and cargo charters, and wet-leasing operations to other airlines, are operated from airports throughout the UK and Europe, while the main base is at Bournemouth International Airport on the south coast of England. In 1997 a One-Eleven 500 was wet-leased to EuroScot Express for a service from Bournemouth to Glasgow and Edinburgh.

Executive Directors & Officers: P.G. Stoddart, Chairman; W. O'Neil, Managing Director; John Lailey, Finance Director; Captain Owen Wright, Operations Director; T. Fox, Commercial Director; S. Aston, Personnel Director.

HQ Airport & Main Base: Bournemouth International Airport

Radio callsign: EUROCHARTER

Designator: EAF

Employees: Aircrew: 70; Engineering: 65; Ground staff: 15; Total: 150.

Main destinations served: Ad hoc charters throughout Europe.

FLEET
23 British Aerospace One-Eleven 500

FLYING COLOURS

Flying Colours Airlines Ltd

Incorporated: 1995

HISTORY
Founded in 1995, Flying Colours commenced inclusive tour charter operations in 1997 with a single leased Boeing 757-200. The airline was founded by Erroll Cossey, former head of Air 2000 (qv) and the Flying Colours Leisure Group, the parent company for a number of British tour operators.

Executive Directors & Officers: Erroll Cossey, Chairman; Jeremy Muller, Managing Director.

HQ Airport & Main Base: Manchester, with London Gatwick as a further base.

Radio callsign: FLYING

Designator: FLY

Main destinations served: World-wide inclusive tour charters.

FLEET
4 Boeing 757-200ER (leased)
1 Boeing 757-200 (leased)
1 Airbus A320-200 (leased)

GB AIRWAYS

GB Airways Ltd

Incorporated: 1981

HISTORY
GB Airways was originally formed in 1931, as a subsidiary of the Gibraltar-based shipping and travel group M.H. Bland, carrying the name Gibraltar Airways. Early opera-

tions were to Tangier, giving the airline the world's fastest intercontinental service with a flight taking just 15 minutes. Flights were also operated to London, using a wet-leased Britannia Airways (qv) Boeing 737. The name GB Airways was taken in 1981, as the airline prepared to broaden its area of operations and moved its base to London Gatwick. It gradually developed a route network to destinations in the Mediterranean, and to Portugal and Madeira. In 1995 the airline became a British Airways (qv) franchise operator, adopting the livery, uniforms, and flight designators of the larger airline and enabling BA to re-establish its presence on routes such as those to Malta which it had surrendered previously.

Executive Directors & Officers: Joseph J. Gaggero, Chairman; James Gaggero, Deputy Chairman; John Osborne, Managing Director; John Hawkins, Finance Director; Peter Kenworthy, Commercial Director; Valerie Gooding, Director.

HQ Airport & Main Base: London Gatwick

Radio callsign: GEEBEE AIRWAYS

Designator: GBL

Employees: Aircrew: 160; Engineering: 10; Ground staff: 110; Total: 280.

Main destinations served: London Gatwick to Casablanca, Gibraltar, Lisbon, Malta, Madeira, Tangier, Tunis.

LINKS WITH OTHER AIRLINES
British Airways franchise partner.

FLEET
3 Boeing 737-300
5 Boeing 737-400

GILL AIRWAYS

Gill Aviation Ltd

Incorporated: 1969

HISTORY
Gill Air commenced charter operations in 1969 from its base at Newcastle, and expanded into scheduled services in 1989, the year that MB Holdings acquired the airline. The fleet, at one time entirely composed of different marks of Shorts 360 commuter airliners, now includes a mix of Shorts and ATR types. Services have been operated to London Gatwick from both Newcastle and Teesside in the past, but it now operates Newcastle to London Stansted and most London Stansted to Paris flights on behalf of Air UK (qv).

Gill Air is now a subsidiary of New Aviation Holdings.

Executive Directors & Officers: W. Price, Chairman; Malcolm Hart, Managing Director; Captain Walter Casey, Operations Director & Chief Pilot; Colin Pollard, Commercial Director; A. Spreadborough, Engineering Director.

HQ Airport & Main Base: Newcastle International Airport

Radio callsign: GILLAIR

Designator: 9C/GIL (was originally GX/GIL)

Employees: Flight-crew: 60; Cabin staff: 41; Engineering: 87; Ground staff: 112; Total: 300.

Main destinations served: Newcastle to Aberdeen, Belfast, Düsseldorf, Guernsey, Jersey, Manchester, Wick.
Aberdeen to Wick.
On behalf of Air UK: London Stansted to Newcastle, Paris.

LINKS WITH OTHER AIRLINES
Operates services on behalf of Air UK.

FLEET
2 ATR 42-300
2 ATR 72-202
3 Shorts 360-100
2 Shorts 360-200
2 Shorts 360-300

GO

Go Airways Ltd

Incorporated: 1998

GO is the new 'low cost, no-frills' subsidiary of British Airways (qv). Based at London Stansted Airport, it is developing a network of routes from Stansted to destinations in mainland Europe. The initial fleet consists of eight Boeing 737-300s leased from GECAS and previously operated by Philippine Airlines (qv). Services started in April 1998.

Executive Directors & Officers: Barbara Cassani, Chief Executive.

HQ Airport & Main Base: London Stansted

FLEET
8 Boeing 737-300 (leased)

HEAVYLIFT

HeavyLift Cargo Airlines Ltd

Incorporated: 1978

HISTORY

HeavyLift commenced operations in 1980, initially from Southend Airport in Essex, where the company still has its main maintenance base, before later moving to London's new third airport at Stansted. A wide variety of aircraft has been operated over the years including the 'Guppy' conversions of the Canadair CL-44, but the airline was firmly established as the first British carrier of difficult or outsized loads when it acquired the bulk of the Royal Air Force's fleet of Shorts SC-5 Belfast transports. The composition of the fleet has closely followed the demands of the air charter market, and in 1989 both Lockheed Hercules and Boeing 707 freighters were added, the former to boost the company's operations in Europe and to provide for loads below the capacity of the Belfasts.

In more recent years HeavyLift has become another operator of the large Antonov (qv) An-124 Ruslan, which it operates in conjunction with the manufacturer, while it introduced two Airbus A300B4 freighter conversions in 1997.

The airline is a wholly-owned subsidiary of Trafalgar House, a group perhaps best known for its former ownership of Cunard, but with extensive interests in construction and transport.

Executive Directors & Officers:

Michael Hayles, Managing Director; Graham Pearce, Commercial Director.

HQ Airport & Main Base: London Stansted

Radio callsign: HEAVYLIFT

Designator: NP/HLA

Employees: 145

Main destinations served: Ad hoc world-wide freight charters.

FLEET

9 Antonov An-124 Ruslan (wet-leased from Antonov (qv))
2 Airbus A300B4F
1 Antonov An-12
2 Ilyushin Il-76
1 Lockheed L-100-30 Hercule

HUNTING

Hunting Cargo Airlines Ltd

Incorporated: 1972

HISTORY

Originally formed as Air Bridge Carriers, or ABC, Hunting's first aircraft were former BEA Hawker Siddeley Argosy freighters – an unusual four-engined, twin-boom aircraft – which the company operated mainly on freight services to and from the Channel Islands. The Argosy fleet was soon replaced with Vickers Merchantmen, freight conversions of BEA's Vanguard airliners, before these were complemented, and then replaced, by Lockheed L-188C Electra freighters.

Originally a subsidiary of Field Aviation, itself part of the Hunting Group, the airline took its present title in 1992. Although the airline has an extensive charter business, the bulk of its operations are scheduled cargo services, either on its own behalf or for other carriers, including TNT (qv), for which Hunting Cargo operates four of the Boeing 727-200F freighters which it first introduced in 1994. The airline is planning to introduce an Airbus A300 freighter conversion.

Executive Directors & Officers: G.H.
Williams, Chairman; M.P. Timson, Managing Director; A. Humphreys, Technical Director; N.I.L. Ferguson, Director; S. Rafferty, Director.

HQ Airport & Main Base: East Midlands Airport

Radio callsign: HUNTING

Designator: AG/ABR

Employees: 240

Main destinations served: East Midlands and other airports to Belfast, Bergamo, Brussels, Cologne, Coventry, Dublin, Frankfurt, Glasgow, London Heathrow, London Luton, Manchester, Nuremburg, Shannon, Southend, Stuttgart.

LINKS WITH OTHER AIRLINES

Four Boeing 727s operated on behalf of TNT.

FLEET

6 Lockheed L-188C Electra
10 Boeing 727-200F
plus 1 Airbus A300 freighter conversion on order.

JERSEY EUROPEAN

Jersey European Airways Ltd

Incorporated: 1979

HISTORY

Formed by a merger of Jersey-based Intra Airways, dating from 1967, and the passenger operations of Express Air Services of Bournemouth, Jersey European started operations in 1979 using Douglas DC-3 Dakotas. These were soon replaced by more modern Embraer Bandeirantes and de Havilland Twin Otters, aircraft of a size well-suited to traffic flows from the Channel Islands to many mainland destinations at the time. Meanwhile another

Many of the major airlines on both sides of the Atlantic have had their colours on aircraft in the BAe 146/Avro RJ family, but few look quite as attractive as this Jersey European 146-200.

airline, Spacegrand Aviation, based in Blackpool in the north-west of England, was developing from an air taxi operation to a regional scheduled carrier, building up a network of services from Blackpool to Belfast, Dublin, and the Isle of Man. Spacegrand's parent company, the Walker Steel Group, acquired Jersey European in 1983 and merged the two companies under the Jersey European name in 1985, with headquarters at Exeter Airport.

The combined airline started to introduce new routes, including services from Exeter to Belfast and London Heathrow to Toulouse and Lyons as an Air France Express franchisee. There are also interlining arrangements with a number of major airlines.

Executive Directors & Officers: Barry Perrott, Chief Executive; Jim French, Chief Operating Officer/Deputy Chief Executive; David Quick, Chief Financial Officer; Michael Wood, Operations Director; Simon Newton Chance, Managing Director, JEA Engineering.

HQ Airport & Main Base: Exeter, with bases at Belfast, Birmingham, Guernsey, Jersey, London Gatwick, London Heathrow.

Radio callsign: JERSEY

Designator: JY/JEA

Employees: Flight-crew: 129; Cabin staff: 164; Engineering: 270 (Jersey European Engineering); Ground staff: 52; Administration and sales: 200; Total: 545 (excluding Jersey European Engineering).

Main destinations served: Belfast City to Birmingham, Blackpool, Bristol, Derry, Exeter, Isle of Man, Jersey, Leeds/Bradford, London Gatwick. Belfast International to Blackpool, London Stansted. Birmingham to Glasgow, Guernsey, Jersey, Paris CDG. Blackpool to Isle of Man. Exeter to Dublin, Guernsey, Jersey. London Gatwick to Belfast City, Guernsey, Jersey.

Aircraft km pa: 9,623,000

Passenger km pa: 507,425,000

Cargo tonne km pa: 537,000

Annual turnover: US $110.389 million (£66.872 million)

LINKS WITH OTHER AIRLINES
Interline agreements with Air Seychelles, Air Zimbabwe (qv), Alitalia (qv), Aviaco (qv), American Airlines (qv), Air Baltic (qv), Continental Airlines (qv), Delta Air Lines (qv), Emirates (qv), Iberia (qv), GB Airways (qv), Lauda-Air (qv), Maersk Air (qv), Qatar Airways (qv), Northwest Airlines (qv), TWA (qv), Virgin Atlantic (qv).

Operates London Heathrow to Toulouse and Lyons as Air France Express franchisee.

FLEET
3 British Aerospace 146-100 (1 leased)
7 British Aerospace 146-200 (all leased)
2 British Aerospace 146-300 (1 leased)
7 Fokker F-27-500
3 Shorts 360

KLMuk

KLMuk Ltd

Incorporated: 1980

HISTORY
Renamed KLMuk in January 1998, the former Air UK was probably the leading British regional airline, and had been formed in 1980 on the merger of four smaller airlines – Air Anglia, Air Wales, Air West, and British Island Airways. While Air Wales and Air West were relative newcomers, Norwich-based Air Anglia had already established a strong network of routes along the east coast of England and Scotland as far north as Aberdeen, with services to Amsterdam, while the Douglas DC-3/C-47 Dakotas used on the original services had been replaced by more modern turbine aircraft. Oldest and largest of the founding airlines, however, was British Island Airways (BIA), which had been formed from the old British United Airways (Channel Islands) and British United Airways (Manx) operations. The origins of these services had been in the formation of Jersey Airlines after the end of World War Two, with the company being acquired by the then comparatively new British United in 1962.

After its creation, Air UK embarked on a programme of rationalisation and development, remaining a major operator to Amsterdam and along the east coast, and retaining the Channel Islands services which had been the core activity for BIA. The London Gatwick services to Edinburgh and Glasgow of British Caledonian, the successor to British United, were eventually taken over when that airline was acquired by British Airways (qv), but these have been dropped in recent years as British Airways has moved back onto these routes to support its growing Gatwick hub. The airline also developed its route network into Amsterdam, with KLM (qv) taking an increasingly large stake in the airline, and the two airlines enjoying code-sharing, through-booking, and other arrangements before KLM eventually acquired the remaining interest in Air UK from British Air Transport Holdings during 1997.

Air UK was to the forefront in developing Stansted, London's fourth airport, as a hub, and this has now displaced Norwich as the airline's main base. On leaving London Gatwick, the airline has replaced its Gatwick services with the first domestic trunk operations into London City Airport, flying from Glasgow and Edinburgh into this new airport in London's docklands, and international services are also being developed from London City.

Over the years the fleet has changed, with the original mixture – which included Handley Page Heralds and Fokker F-27 Friendships – being replaced by Fokker F-50s and 100s, while the airline was an early major purchaser of the British Aerospace 146 series, the world's quietest jet airliner and the *only* jet airliner allowed to operate into London City. A number of Short 360s were operated for a period. Modernisation of the turboprop fleet was delayed by the collapse of Fokker, but KLMuk has now introduced four AI(R) ATR 72-210s instead.

The airline moved into the air charter market with a 60 per cent stake in a charter airline, Air UK Leisure, in 1992, but this has since been sold and renamed Leisure International (qv). The airline's engineering wing, Air UK Engineering, although also likely to be renamed, is now operated as a separate company and has its own board of directors.

Today, KLMuk is the largest non-Dutch-based user of Amsterdam's Schiphol Airport, as well as the major scheduled carrier from London Stansted. In 1998 it was the first airline to operate from the new Sheffield City Airport, flying Fokker 50s to Amsterdam.

Executive Directors & Officers: Henry Essenberg, Chief Executive Officer; John Derbyshire, Chief Financial Officer; Philip Chapman, Planning & Industry Affairs Director; Len Nutter, Technical Director; Tony Le Masurier, Customer Services Director.

HQ Airport & Main Base: London Stansted, but there are extensive operations out of Aberdeen, Edinburgh, and Norwich.

Radio callsign: UKAY

Designator: UK/UKA

Employees: approx 2,000

Main destinations served: London

Stansted to Aberdeen, Amsterdam, Brussels, Copenhagen, Düsseldorf, Edinburgh, Frankfurt, Glasgow, Guernsey (LHR), Hamburg, Inverness, Jersey, Maastricht (e), Milan, Munich, Newcastle (g), Paris CDG (1), Zürich (2).
Amsterdam to Aberdeen, Belfast International, Birmingham, Bristol (k), Cardiff (k), Edinburgh, Glasgow, Guernsey, Humberside, Inverness, Jersey, Leeds/Bradford, London City, London Stansted, Manchester, Newcastle, Norwich, Sheffield City, Southampton (k), Teesside.
Aberdeen to Amsterdam, Bergen, Humberside, London Stansted, Norwich, Stavanger, Teesside.
London City to Amsterdam, Dublin (c), Edinburgh, Glasgow, Malmö (m), Rotterdam.
Leeds/Bradford to Amsterdam, Edinburgh, Guernsey.
Key: (1) some services operated by another airline under contract; (2) service operated by another airline; (c) operated by CityJet; (e) operated by Air Excel; (g) operated by Gill Air (qv); (k) operated by KLM (qv); (m) operated by Malmö Aviation.

Passengers pa: approx 4 million

Annual turnover: US $470 million (£285 million)

SUBSIDIARIES
Air UK Engineering, with 450 employees and annual turnover of around US $66 million (£40 million).

LINKS WITH OTHER AIRLINES
A wholly-owned subsidiary of KLM Royal Dutch Airlines (qv), with links with the other airlines shown above.
Code-sharing with VLM on Rotterdam–London City.

FLEET
1 Boeing 737-400
15 Fokker 100
10 British Aerospace 146-300
1 British Aerospace 146-100
9 Fokker F-50
4 AI(R) ATR 72-210

LEISURE INTERNATIONAL

Leisure International Airways Ltd

Incorporated: 1992

HISTORY
Leisure International Airways commenced operations in 1993 as a sister airline of Air UK Leisure, which had started five years earlier. Two Boeing 767s formed the initial fleet, complementing the seven smaller Boeing 737-400 aircraft operated by Air UK Leisure. The operations of the two airlines were merged in 1997 under the Leisure International Airways name, with ownership now in the hands of the Unijet Group.

Executive Directors & Officers: C.J. Parker, Chairman; J.D. Dixon, Deputy Chairman; Philip Ovenden, Managing Director; I. Jones, Commercial Director; Captain D.L. Henry, Flight Operations Director; S. Carson, Director; Peter Brown, Director.

HQ Airport & Main Base: London Gatwick

Designator: ULE

Employees: 160

Main destinations served: Ad hoc and inclusive tour passenger charters worldwide.

FLEET
2 Airbus A321-100 (plus 2 on order)
2 Airbus A320-200
2 Boeing 767-300ER

LOGANAIR

Loganair Ltd

Incorporated: 1962

HISTORY
Originally billed as 'Scotland's airline', Loganair has seen many changes of ownership, but throughout has managed to maintain the vital 'lifeline' services linking the Scottish islands to the mainland or to larger islands.
Loganair did not start life as an airline at all. When operations commenced in 1962 it was as the aviation division of a civil engineering company, Duncan Logan (Contractors). Initially a single Piper Aztec was used to carry the company's staff to construction sites and to meetings, but the demand for this type of service in Scotland – with its mountains, heavily indented coastline and many island groups – was such that Loganair soon started to offer an air taxi service to other organisations. A regular service between Edinburgh and Dundee was operated for a while, and in 1964 the company won the contract to provide a regular newspaper service to Benbecula and Stornoway.
By the end of the 1960s it was operating two Piper Aztecs, two Britten-Norman BN-2 Islanders, a Beech 18, and a Piper Cherokee Six: The Beech 18 is now preserved in the Scottish Aviation Museum at East Fortune. Regular services had been introduced to Orkney in 1967, and to Shetland the following year, in each case linking the outlying islands with the Orkney and Shetland 'mainlands'. Apart from the newspaper contracts, there was also a regular weekday operation flying computer cards from Glasgow to Blackpool for the Post Office Savings Bank.
Out of the initial varied fleet, the aircraft which did most to transform travel in the more remote parts of the Scottish islands were the Islanders. Using these to serve sparsely populated communities was more economic than using passenger-carrying ferries, leaving heavy items to less frequent cargo sailings while passengers, mail, newspapers, and light freight went by air. For a while Loganair also operated the Islander's larger cousin, the stretched three-engined Trislander. The Islander also proved to be the ideal aircraft for the Scottish Air Ambulance Service, operated under contract by Loganair.
Financial difficulties led to Loganair being taken over by the National Commercial Bank in 1968, with ownership passing to the Royal Bank of Scotland following a merger. Control later passed to Airlines of Britain Holdings, and later to British Regional Airlines (qv), while for a time the airline was managed by Manx Airlines (qv), before a management buy-out early in 1997. The Manx Airlines involvement followed a period when Loganair had set up a hub operation at Manchester, followed by one at Southampton, attempting to expand beyond the confines of the Scottish market in what proved to be a costly experiment. Loganair lost its external routes in 1994, and by the end of 1995 its management had been largely taken over by Manx.
During this period the fleet changed. Islanders remained popular on the Orkney and Shetland internal services and for the air ambulance flights, but the Trislanders were replaced by de Havilland Canada DHC-6 Twin Otters for flights to and between the Western Isles. British Aerospace Jetstream 31 and 41 aircraft were introduced for some of the external services and also for flights from Glasgow and Edinburgh to the Northern Isles. Larger aircraft in the form of British Aerospace ATPs were also obtained for flights from Glasgow and Edinburgh to Manchester and Belfast, while two British Aerospace 146 airliners were operated for a short period out of Manchester on routes to Brussels and the Channel Islands. Shorts 360 were introduced for some of

the busier routes to the islands, and it was eventually hoped that these would replace the older Twin Otters, but the 360 proved too heavy for some routes, and especially those to Barra, where aircraft have to land on the beach at low tide. The Jetstreams and ATPs passed to Manx under the ABH-inspired reorganisation of 1994.

In 1996 British Airways (qv) announced that it was pulling out of Scottish internal services, and operation of these passed to Loganair and British Regional Airlines, operating as British Airways Express franchise partners.

Loganair is now concentrating on the Scottish internal services which it knows so well. The management buy-out has not affected the airline's status as a BA franchise partner. Apart from using the beach at Barra, other features of the airline's operations include the world's shortest air service, between Westray and Papa Westray, on the Orkney internal services, with a flight scheduled to take just two minutes – but timed by a television reporter at 100 seconds!

Executive Directors & Officers: Scott Grier, Chairman; Trevor Bush, Managing Director; Captain Iain J. Hazzard, Flight Operations Director.

HQ Airport & Main Base: Glasgow Airport, but aircraft are also based at Kirkwall (Orkney) and Lerwick (Shetland).

Radio callsign: LOGAN

Designator: LC/LOG (or BA/BAW)

Main destinations served: Glasgow to Barra, Campbeltown, Islay, Tiree. Kirkwall to Eday, North Ronaldsay, Papa Westray, Sanday, Stronsay, Westray. Lerwick to Fair Isle, Foula, Out Skerries, Papa Stour, Unst. Barra to Benbecula and Stornoway.

Passengers pa: approx 260,000

LINKS WITH OTHER AIRLINES
British Airways Franchise Partner.

FLEET
5 Pilatus Britten-Norman BN-2 Islander
1 de Havilland Canada DHC-6 Twin Otter
1 Shorts 360

MAERSK AIR

Maersk Air Ltd

Incorporated: 1983

HISTORY
A subsidiary of the Danish airline Maersk Air (qv), the British company of the same name operates under a franchise agreement with British Airways (qv). The airline traces its history to the founding in 1983 of Birmingham Executive Airways, which aimed to provide business class scheduled air services from that city. Birmingham Executive started operations with three British Aerospace Jetstream 31 aircraft, two of which had just 12 seats instead of the usual 18 or 19, but the third had standard seating and even at that early date operated in British Airways livery, usually on services from Birmingham to Aberdeen. Early scheduled services included Birmingham to Copenhagen and Stuttgart.

In 1988 the airline was acquired by The Plimsoll Line, in which British Airways and Maersk Air each had a 40 per cent interest, and the name changed the following year to Birmingham European Airways, often marketing itself as 'BEA', less than a decade after the disappearance of the old British European Airways into BA! The fleet also changed, with two Shorts 360 and five British Aerospace One-Eleven 400 aircraft – in normal scheduled seating configuration – eventually being operated, while the route network expanded to include Amsterdam, Belfast, Cork, Copenhagen, Milan, Newcastle and Stuttgart.

The Plimsoll Line eventually acquired the West Country airline Brymon (qv), and in 1992 the two airlines were merged to form Brymon European Airways. This new airline operated for just a short time, however, and in 1993 The Plimsoll Line and Brymon European were broken up, leaving Brymon to become a wholly-owned subsidiary of British Airways, while the Birmingham operations became Maersk Air UK, later becoming a British Airways franchisee.

The current fleet is a mixture of Canadair CRJ-200 regional jets, which replaced former British Airways One-Eleven 500s, and Boeing 737-500s. The airline is also planning to introduce additional CRJs, including some of the stretched CRJ-700 variety. A subsidiary, Maersk Air Engineering, provides maintenance services for a number of airlines as well as for Maersk itself.

Executive Directors & Officers:
Flemming Knudsen, Managing Director.

HQ Airport & Main Base: Birmingham International Airport

Radio callsign: BLUESTAR

Designator: MSK (or BA/BAW)

Employees: 400

Main destinations served: The airline operates a substantial proportion of British Airways flights out of Birmingham.

Passengers pa: 451,000

LINKS WITH OTHER AIRLINES
A British Airways franchisee.
Subsidiary of Maersk Air, Denmark.

FLEET
4 Boeing 737-500
3 Canadair CRJ-200
1 British Aerospace Jetstream 41
3 British Aerospace Jetstream 31 (2 leased to European Airways, Newcastle) plus further CRJs on order.

MANX

Manx Airlines Ltd

Incorporated: 1982

HISTORY
Although Manx Airways dates from 1982, the airline can trace its history back to the formation of Manx Air Charter in 1947, using just two de Havilland Dragon Rapide biplanes. The following year five Dragon Rapides were being operated. Scheduled services started in 1950, with a route from the Isle of Man to Carlisle in the north of England. Further scheduled services followed, with services to Newcastle and Renfrew, near Glasgow, by 1953, when the Manx Airlines name was adopted and the fleet comprised four Dragon Rapides and two of the much larger Douglas DC-3 Dakotas. In 1956 the airline was acquired by the British Aviation Services Group, and two years later it was absorbed into Silver City Airways, marking the disappearance of the 'Manx Airlines' name. When Silver City became part of British United Airways, a restructuring led to the emergence of a British United Airways (Manx) operation, mainly operating Handley Page Heralds on services to and from the island and across the Irish Sea.

The present company was established in 1982 with the support of British Midland (qv) and Air UK (qv). Manx Airlines' initial fleet included an ex-British Midland Vickers Viscount and two Fokker F-27 Friendships, as well as an Embraer Bandeirante, while the route network was based on the Isle of Man and Irish Sea operations of both airlines, who saw the creation of the new airline as a means of achieving viable operations on what was then a notoriously seasonal network of short routes. Later the airline became a major part of Airlines of Britain Holdings,

Manx had a mainly turboprop fleet until the first EMB-145s were introduced in 1997, prior to which its solitary jet was this BAe 146-200.

and in 1986 took over British Midland's Liverpool to London Heathrow service, by which time the Shorts 360 commuter liner was the mainstay of the fleet.

A wide variety of regional aircraft has been operated by the airline since its formation, and in many ways these have reflected developments in the aircraft available to regional airlines. Manx was the first British airline to operate the Saab SF340, initially using it on the Liverpool–London service, as well as the British Aerospace Jetstream 31 and larger Jetstream 41, and then the British Aerospace ATP. The company was one of the first to put British Aerospace 146 airliners onto domestic services within the British Isles, initially on its Isle of Man to London Heathrow service, where it replaced a leased BAC One-Eleven.

In 1995 Manx assumed the management of the Scottish airline Loganair (qv), which at the time was also an ABH subsidiary.

Expanding operations led to bases being established at Manchester, Cardiff, and Southampton. Recognising the differences between these services and those operating to and from the Isle of Man, the company initially split its operations into two divisions, Manx Airlines and Manx Airlines (Europe). To enhance the marketing of the Manx Airlines (Europe) services, in early 1995 these and the Loganair operation became British Airways (qv) franchisees, operating under the name of British Airways Express, using BA designators, and with the aircraft carrying British Airways Express livery and the crews wearing BA uniforms. In 1996 further restructuring led to the renaming of Manx Airlines (Europe) as British Regional Airlines (qv), absorbing the operations of Manx Airlines (Europe) and the other companies in what was ABH with the exception of British Midland. Although British Regional Airlines and Manx Airlines are managed as a single company, Manx as an Isle of Man-registered company is a separate legal entity, with aircraft on operations to and from the Isle of Man remaining in Manx colours, and Manx flight designators are used.

Executive Directors & Officers: Sir Michael Bishop, Chairman; Terry Liddiard, Managing Director; Paul Neilson, Finance Director; Mike Bathgate, Commercial Director; Captain Norman Brewitt, Operations Director, Ian Woodley, Director.

HQ Airport & Main Base: Isle of Man (Ronaldsway) Airport

Radio callsign: MANX

Designator: JE/MNX

Employees: Flight-crew: 88; Cabin staff: 61; Engineering: 118; Ground staff, including Administration and sales: 239; Total: 506.

Passengers pa: 574,316

Main destinations served: Isle of Man to Birmingham, Cardiff, Dublin, Glasgow, Jersey, Leeds/Bradford, Liverpool, London Heathrow, London Luton, Manchester, Newcastle, Southampton. Cardiff to Dublin, Jersey, Cork to Jersey, London Luton to Kerry.

LINKS WITH OTHER AIRLINES
A subsidiary of British Regional Airlines (Holdings) Limited.

FLEET
2 British Aerospace 146-200
3 British Aerospace ATP
2 Embraer EMB-145
1 Saab SF340 (leased from Business Air (qv))

MK AIRLINES

MK Airlines

Incorporated: 1990

HISTORY
MK started operations in 1991 as MK Air Cargo with a McDonnell Douglas DC-8-54F and a DC-8-55F, operating from Gatwick to destinations in Africa, usually via Accra in Ghana. The airline is now based at London Stansted and has five DC-8 freighter conversions, while there are two subsidiary companies, MK Airlines Ghana and Flash Airlines in Nigeria. As a specialist in scheduled operations between the UK and Africa, MK has alliances with a number of major airlines. Aircraft are available for ad hoc charters, and passengers can be carried since the current fleet is composed of quick change passenger/cargo aircraft.

Executive Directors & Officers:
Captain Michael Kruger, Chief Executive & Managing Director; Mark Rose, Finance Director.

HQ Airport & Main Base: London Stansted, with bases in Luxembourg and Accra.

Designator: 7G/MKA

Employees: Flight-crew: 55; Engineering: 35; Ground staff:15; Total: 105.

Main destinations served: London Stansted/Ostend/Luxembourg to Accra, Hirare, Kano, Lagos, Nairobi.

LINKS WITH OTHER AIRLINES
Owns Flash Airlines (qv), Nigeria. Alliances with Air Malawi, Air Namibia, British Airways (qv), Icelandair (qv), Lan Chile (qv).

FLEET
1 McDonnell Douglas DC-8-55 Combi
4 McDonnell Douglas DC-8-55QF

MONARCH

Monarch Airlines Ltd

Incorporated: 1967

HISTORY

Monarch Airlines commenced operations from London Luton Airport in 1968, initially using two Bristol Britannia turboprop airliners, although these were later joined by BAC One-Elevens. The early aircraft were replaced by more modern types during the 1970s, while the airline continued to concentrate on inclusive tour charters to Europe, and especially to destinations in the Mediterranean. Long haul services started in 1988, using Boeing 757-200ERs on charter flights to Florida, and in 1990 charters to New York and Boston were introduced. A small scheduled network was also being developed by this time, with flights from Luton to Mahon, Malaga, and Tenerife.

Today, Monarch operates out of a number of UK airports, and has further developed its scheduled network. A modern fleet is operated with aircraft mainly of Airbus and Boeing manufacture. It has an extensive engineering subsidiary, Monarch Aircraft Engineering, which undertakes work for the airline and for third party customers.

Executive Directors & Officers:
D.L. Bernstein, Managing Director; R.J. Kirby, Managing Director, Engineering; M.J. Ellingham, Finance Director; Captain M. Poole, Operations Director; M.J. Dovey, Commercial Director; J. Bonner, Personnel Director.

HQ Airport & Main Base: London Luton, although most flights operate from London Gatwick or Manchester.

Radio callsign: MONARCH

Designator: ZB/MON

Employees: 2,200

Main destinations served: Inclusive tour and ad hoc charters world-wide from a number of airports, but mainly London Gatwick, London Luton, and Manchester, plus scheduled services from London Luton to: Alicante, Gibraltar, Malaga, Menorca, Palma de Mallorca, Tenerife.

FLEET
2 McDonnell Douglas DC-10-30
4 Airbus A300-600R
2 Airbus A321-200 (1 leased)
7 Airbus A320-200
7 Boeing 757-200

SUCKLING

Suckling Airways Ltd

Incorporated: 1986

HISTORY

Suckling commenced operations in 1986 with a single Dornier Do228 operating between the airline's home base of Ipswich and Amsterdam, with a domestic route later being introduced between Ipswich and Manchester. During the early 1990s the main base was transferred from Ipswich to Cambridge, a more central point for passengers from East Anglia, and recently a secondary base has been opened at London Luton. The airline has taken over a number of routes discarded by larger airlines, including the Edinburgh–Norwich service of Air UK (qv). Meanwhile the fleet has grown to include the larger Dornier Do328-100, as well as additional Do228-200s.

Executive Directors & Officers:
Captain R.G. Suckling, Chief Executive & Managing Director; Mrs M.V.W. Suckling, Marketing Director.

HQ Airport & Main Base: Cambridge, with further services operated from London Luton.

Radio callsign: SUCKLING

Designator: CB/SAY

Employees: Flight-crew: 20; Cabin staff: 20; Engineering: 9; Ground staff: 21; Total: 70.

Main destinations served: Cambridge to Amsterdam, Manchester.
London Luton to Amsterdam, Paris, Waterford.
London Stansted to Rotterdam, Edinburgh to Norwich.

FLEET
2 Fairchild Dornier Do328-100
4 Fairchild Dornier Do228-200

TITAN

Titan Airways

Incorporated: 1988

HISTORY

Titan Airways began air charter operations in 1988, and within a couple of years was operating an Embraer Bandeirante, two Shorts 330s, and a Shorts 360 from its main base at London Stansted. The fledgling airline was sold to its management in 1992, and since then it has continued steady growth, offering contract and ad hoc passenger and freight charters throughout Europe as well as in North Africa and the Middle East. Titan often undertakes charters for scheduled airlines, many of these at short notice.

Executive Directors & Officers: Gene H. Wilson, Managing Director; Brian Donald, Commercial Director; G. Baguley, Operations Director.

HQ Airport & Main Base: London Stansted Airport

Radio callsign: ZAP

Designator: T4/AWC

Employees: 82

Main destinations served: Ad hoc and contract charters.

FLEET
2 British Aerospace 146-200QC
2 ATR 42-300
1 Shorts 360-300
1 Cessna Citation 1

TNT

TNT International Aviation Services Ltd

Incorporated: 1987

HISTORY

TNT has developed a world-wide network of overnight scheduled freight services, using locally-based airlines to operate its aircraft, which carry the TNT livery. Participating airlines can market the aircraft for cargo or, in the case of the quick change variants, passenger operations during the day and at weekends, provided that the aircraft are always available for their night duties. The initial services were introduced to Europe, with a major hub at Cologne in Germany, while a similar operation has been established in Asia based on Manila in the Philippines. In 1997 the Cologne hub was moved to Liège in Belgium. Airlines participating in this operation include Air Foyle (qv), Hunting Cargo (qv), and Pacific East Asia (qv). The main aircraft operated are British Aerospace 146 QT ('quiet trader') because of this aircraft's low noise levels.

Executive Directors & Officers: Tom Storey, Managing Director.

HQ Airport & Main Base: HQ is at Windsor, the main hubs are Liège and Manila, but aircraft are based with the participating operators.

Radio callsign: NITRO

Designator: NTR

Employees: 100 (primarily sales and administration)

Main destinations served: From Liège to Arlanda, Barcelona, Belfast, Billund, Birmingham, Budapest, Cologne, Copenhagen, Dublin, Edinburgh, Glasgow, Gothenburg, Helsinki, Linz, Liverpool, Luton, Lyons, Madrid, Manchester, New York, Nuremburg, Paris CDG, Valencia, Vienna, Zaragoza.

LINKS WITH OTHER AIRLINES
Aircraft operated by Air Foyle, Eurowings (qv), Hunting Cargo (qv), Malev (qv), Pacific East Asia Cargo (qv), and Sterling Europe (qv).

FLEET
12 British Aerospace 146-200/300QT (8 Air Foyle, 2 Eurowings, 2 Pacific East Asia Cargo)
1 Boeing 727-200 (Sterling Europe)
4 Boeing 727-200F (Hunting Cargo)
1 Boeing 737-200F (Pacific East Asia Cargo)

VIRGIN ATLANTIC

Virgin Atlantic Airways

Incorporated: 1984

HISTORY

Britain's second largest long-haul airline, Virgin Atlantic Airways was founded in 1984 by Richard Branson, and was intended to be an offshoot of his popular music businesses. The first aircraft was a Boeing 747, used for a service from London Gatwick to New York Newark Airport. Two years later a second route was introduced, to Miami, and a second aircraft acquired. The third and fourth aircraft arrived in 1988, and the following year a service from Gatwick to Tokyo was inaugurated. In 1991 the airline was allowed to operate its first flights from London Heathrow, initially operating to Los Angeles, New York JFK, and Tokyo, while maintaining services from Gatwick.

The sale of Virgin Music in 1992 resulted in a pledge to invest the proceeds in the further development of the airline, which started to franchise its name the same year, with a service from Gatwick to Athens operated under the Virgin name by South East European Airways, although this service was transferred to Heathrow in 1993. A further franchise operation began in 1994 with a service from London City Airport to Dublin operated by CityJet. Meanwhile Virgin Atlantic had introduced the first Airbus A300-300 aircraft to be operated by a British airline.

Further routes followed, and a change of corporate identity marked the airline's tenth anniversary. During 1995 Virgin Atlantic entered into a number of marketing alliances, first with Malaysia Airlines (qv), then with Delta Air Lines (qv), followed by a code-share with British Midland (qv), and a partnership arrangement with Malaysia Airlines and Ansett Australia (qv). The airline took advantage of growing liberalisation of the European air travel market in 1995 to launch a Dublin–Brussels service in conjunction with CityJet, but the franchise was terminated by mutual agreement the following year after Virgin acquired Euro Belgian

Virgin Atlantic started life with early model Boeing 747s, but in recent years has been expanding and modernising with aircraft such as this Airbus A340-300.

Airlines, a low cost Brussels-based operator, which it renamed Virgin Express (qv). The first Virgin services to South Africa were launched that year, with a Heathrow–Johannesburg flight. The arrangement with Delta Air Lines ended in 1997, and was replaced by a similar arrangement with Continental Airlines (qv).

For the future, Virgin Atlantic's declared aim is to double the existing fleet with 16 stretched A340-600s, due to be delivered in 2002, mainly for the Far East and US West Coast routes, and another two A340-300s. The A340-600s are intended to have double beds and showers.

The airline might seek a stock exchange listing during 1998.

Executive Directors & Officers: Richard Branson, Chairman & Chief Executive; Nigel Primrose, Finance Director; Roy Gardner, Flight Operations Director; Paul Griffiths, Commercial Director; Frances Farrow, Corporate Services Director; Steve Ridgway, Customer Services Director; David Tait, Overseas Director.

HQ Airport & Main Base: London Gatwick. Other bases are London Heathrow and Manchester.

Radio callsign: VIRGIN

Designator: VS/VIR

Employees: Flight-crew: 474; Cabin staff: 1,794; Engineering: 415; Ground staff: 1,031; Administration and sales: 417; Total: 4,131.

Main destinations served: London Heathrow to Athens, Hong Kong, Johannesburg, Kuala Lumpur*, Los Angeles, Miami, New York JFK, New York Newark, San Francisco, Tokyo, Washington.
London Gatwick to Athens, Boston, New York Newark, Orlando.
Manchester to Orlando.
* operated by Malaysia Airlines

Revenue tonne km pa: 1,973.5 million

Passengers pa: 2,292,417

LINKS WITH OTHER AIRLINES
Code-sharing arrangements with British Midland, Continental, Sun Air, Malaysia.

FLEET
5 Boeing 747-200
1 Boeing 747-100
5 Boeing 747-400 (leased)
10 Airbus A340-300 (leased)
1 Airbus A320-200 (leased)

United States – N

AIR CARGO CARRIERS

Air Cargo Carriers, Inc

Incorporated: 1986

HISTORY
Formed in 1986, Air Cargo Carriers uses a small fleet of Shorts aircraft to operate feeder cargo charters for major airlines, operating throughout North America and the Caribbean.

Executive Directors & Officers: James Germek, President/Director of Operations; David Koen, Director of Maintenance; John Montgomery, Vice-President, Maintenance.

HQ Airport & Main Base: Milwaukee

Radio callsign: NIGHT CARGO

Designator: UN/SNC

Employees: 22

Main destinations served: Cargo charters throughout the United States, Canada, and the Caribbean.

FLEET
3 Shorts 360-100
1 Shorts 330-200
8 Shorts 330-100
5 Shorts SC-7 Skyvan

AIR RESORTS

Air Resorts Airlines, Inc

HISTORY
A regional charter airline carrying both passengers and cargo, Air Resorts has a fleet of Convair Metropolitans, including a number of the 580 turboprop conversion. The airline's parent company is Flight Trails.

Executive Directors & Officers: Ted Vallas, President; Joe Morgan, Operations Director; James Biggie, Maintenance Director; Joanne Russo, Inflight Services Director.

HQ Airport & Main Base: Carlsbad

Radio callsign: AIR RESORTS

Designator: AR/ARZ

Main destinations served: Charters throughout North America.

FLEET
4 Convair 580
5 Convair 440
3 Convair 340

AIR SOUTH

Air South Airlines, Inc

Incorporated: 1994

HISTORY
A relatively recent arrival, Air South operates scheduled passenger services from Columbia in South Carolina with a fleet of Boeing 737-200s. The airline entered Chapter 11 Bankruptcy Protection in September 1997.

Executive Directors & Officers: John P. Tague, Chairman, Chief Executive Officer & President; John Affeltranger, Senior Vice-President & Chief Operating Officer; Lisa Cooke, Financial Director; Serre Fedor, Maintenance Director; Richard Brunner, Airport Operations Director; Usto Schultz, Vice-President, Maintenance; Tom Volz, Vice-President, Marketing.

HQ Airport & Main Base: Columbia

Radio callsign: KHAKI BLUE

Designator: WV/KKB

Employees: 558

Main destinations served: Atlanta, Charleston, Chicago Midway, Greenville/Spartanburg, Jacksonville, Miami, Myrtle Beach, New York JFK, Norfolk/Virginia Beach, Savannah/Hilton Head Island.

LINKS WITH OTHER AIRLINES
A marketing alliance exists with Kiwi International (qv).

FLEET
7 Boeing 737-200

AIR TRANSPORT INTERNATIONAL

Air Transport International, Inc

Incorporated: 1979

HISTORY
Originally founded as US Airways, this airline soon changed its name to Interstate Airlines. Originally an air cargo specialist supporting the express parcels sector, it included UPS (qv) amongst its early clients. The present title was adopted in

1988, a year after the airline had filed for Chapter 11 Bankruptcy Protection. In 1994 it absorbed the operations and assets of ICX International Cargo Express. The current fleet is entirely of McDonnell Douglas manufacture, including convertible passenger/cargo Combis, while the original express parcels traffic has been augmented by contracts with manufacturing industry and the US Department of Defense.
ATI is currently owned by Active Aero/USA Jet.

Executive Directors & Officers: Chuck Adami, Executive Vice-President & General Manager; Jim Young, Controller; Jerry Zerkel, Vice-President, Technical Services; Rich Carlson, Operations Director; Gerry Horoth, Maintenance Director; Wade Johnson, Cargo Sales & Services Director; Eric Korth, Passenger Sales & Service Director.

HQ Airport & Main Base: Little Rock

Radio callsign: AIR TRANSPORT

Designator: 8C/ATN

Employees: 500

Main destinations served: World-wide cargo charters.

FLEET
11 McDonnell Douglas DC-8-71F
5 McDonnell Douglas DC-8-63F
6 McDonnell Douglas DC-8-62 Combi
2 McDonnell Douglas DC-8-62F
1 McDonnell Douglas DC-8-61F

AIR WISCONSIN

Air Wisconsin, Inc

Incorporated: 1965

HISTORY
In 1993 Air Wisconsin was purchased by three of its present executives – Geoffrey Crawley, William Jordan and Patrick Thomson – from United Airlines (qv), after United had acquired the airline in early 1992. It was originally started in 1965, operating scheduled commuter services that summer. The first jet equipment, consisting of British Aerospace 146-200s, appeared in 1983, and the airline became a United Express operator in 1986. In 1991 Air Wisconsin purchased another United Express operator, Denver-based Aspen Airways, which had originally been founded as an air taxi operator in 1953. At the time of the acquisition, Aspen had disposed of many of its routes to Mesa Airlines (qv), and was operating four British Aerospace 146-100 and ten Convair 580s on

the remaining scheduled services and some charters. This fleet matched Air Wisconsin's ten 146s, five British Aerospace ATPs, 14 Fokker F 27s, and a single Shorts 360.

Today, Air Wisconsin operates an all-jet fleet, which has been rationalised to consist of just BAE 146s, albeit of all three sizes. The route network reaches more than 30 airports in the midwest and eastern United States, operating mainly from Denver.

Executive Directors & Officers: Geoffrey Crawley, President & Chief Operating Officer; William Jordan, Executive Vice-President, Administration; Patrick Thomson, Executive Vice-President, Operations; Kevin Reinhalter, Vice-President, Maintenance; Gary Marsh, Vice-President, Operations.

HQ Airport & Main Base: Headquarters is Appleton, Wisconsin, but the hubs are Chicago O'Hare, Denver, and Washington Dulles.

Radio callsign: AIR WISCONSIN

Designator: ZW/AWI

Main destinations served: 31 airports on the United Express network.

LINKS WITH OTHER AIRLINES
Part of United Express.

FLEET
2 British Aerospace 146-100
12 British Aerospace 146-200
5 British Aerospace 146-300

AIRBORNE EXPRESS

Airborne Express, Inc

Incorporated: 1980

HISTORY
The operating name of parent company Airborne Freight Corporation, Airborne Express was founded in 1980 when the corporation acquired Midwest Air Charter. It has seen steady expansion since, and currently operates a substantial fleet of Boeing 767, McDonnell Douglas DC-8 and DC-9, and NAMC YS-11 aircraft flying on weekday night cargo services throughout North America, with charters world-wide. It seems likely that at the top end, the future fleet will be standardising on Boeing 767 freighter conversions, replacing the DC-8 freighters.

Subsidiary companies include ABX Air, Sky Courier, and Advanced Logistical Services.

Executive Directors & Officers: Carl Donaway, President; Bob Morgenfield, Senior Vice-President, Flight Operations; Tom Poynter, Senior Vice-President, Ground Operations; Joe Hete, Senior Vice-President, Administration; Dennis A. Manibusan, Senior Vice-President, Maintenance; Mike Kuli, Vice-President, Business Development; Robert Carter, Senior Corporate Director, Human Resources.

HQ Airport & Main Base: Wilmington Air Park

Radio callsign: ABEX

Designator: GB/ABX

Employees: 6,900

Main destinations served: Airports throughout the United States, plus world-wide charters.

FLEET
6 Boeing 767-200F (plus 6 on order and options for 10-15)
10 McDonnell Douglas DC-8-61
6 McDonnell Douglas DC-8-62
13 McDonnell Douglas DC-8-63
23 McDonnell Douglas DC-9-41
18 McDonnell Douglas DC-9-31
16 McDonnell Douglas DC-9-32
6 McDonnell Douglas DC-9-33F
3 McDonnell Douglas DC-9-32F
2 McDonnell Douglas DC-9-15
9 NAMC YS-11A-200

AIRTRAN AIRLINES

AirTran Airlines, Inc

Incorporated: 1993

HISTORY
AirTran Airlines was originally founded as Valujet, a 'low cost, no frills' operator, with its main base at Atlanta. Growth proved to be rapid, and by early-1996 the airline had 48 McDonnell Douglas DC-9 aircraft, and hubs at Boston, Orlando, and Washington, in addition to Atlanta. Following a fatal accident, caused by the inadvertent loading of dangerous cargo, Valujet was grounded in June 1996, and only allowed to resume operations on a reduced scale in September, initially with a fleet of 15 DC-9s.

In mid-1997 agreement was reached over a merger between Valujet and Airways, owners of AirTran Airways (qv), under which the Valujet operation will become AirTran Airlines, and while both airlines will use separate operating certificates initially, an outright merger is likely. Meanwhile the former Valujet McDonnell

Douglas DC-9s now carry the same livery as AirTran's Boeing 737-200s.

Before suspending operations, Valujet had placed the first order for the McDonnell Douglas MD-95 100-seat regional airliner. Fifty of these aircraft, now renamed the Boeing 717-200, are still on order, although it remains to be seen whether the airline will take them all.

Executive Directors & Officers: Lewis Jordan, Chairman; Joseph Corr, President & Chief Executive Officer; Steve Nevin, Senior Vice-President Finance & Chief Financial Officer; Tommy Kalil, Senior Vice-President, Customer Service/Operations; Jim Jenson, Senior Vice-President, Maintenance & Engineering; Ponder Harrison, Senior Vice-President, Sales & Marketing; Mike Acks, Vice-President & Controller; John Souders, Vice-President, Flight Operations; Bob Zoller, Vice-President, Technical Operations; John Auch, Vice-President, Inflight Services; Bob Toth, Vice-President, Quality Assurance; David Gentry, Vice-President, Heavy Maintenance; Dave Ulmer, Vice-President, Planning; Gil Morgan, Vice-President, Contracts; Louise Laughlin, Vice-President, People.

HQ Airport & Main Base: Atlanta

Radio callsign: CRITTER

Designator: J7/VJA

Employees: 1,500

Main destinations served: Boston, Charlotte, Chicago, Columbus, Fort Lauderdale, Jackson, Jacksonville, Kansas City, Newport News/Norfolk, Orlando, Pittsburgh, Raleigh/Durham, Savannah, Washington.

LINKS WITH OTHER AIRLINES
Operations being merged with those of AirTran Airways (qv).

FLEET
15 McDonnell Douglas DC-9-30 (with plans to return more to service, at least doubling the fleet by 1999)
50 Boeing 717-200 (on order for delivery 1999 onwards)

AIRTRAN AIRWAYS

AirTran Airways, Inc

Incorporated: 1994

HISTORY
Originally founded as Conquest Sun

Airlines, the present title was adopted in 1994. AirTran, in which Northwest Airlines (qv) had a 30 per cent shareholding at one time, subsequently became the operating subsidiary of its parent Airways Corporation, and flies scheduled passenger services from its main base at Nashville. During 1997 agreement was reached over a merger between Valujet, a pioneer of 'low cost, no frills' scheduled operations, and Airways, under which the Valujet operation will become AirTran Airlines (qv), and while both airlines will use separate operating certificates initially, an outright merger is likely. Meanwhile the former Valujet McDonnell Douglas DC-9s now carry the same livery as AirTran's Boeing 737-200s.

Executive Directors & Officers: Robert D. Swenson, Chairman, President & Chief Executive Officer; Mark Rinder, Chief Financial Officer; Klaus Guersch, Vice-President, Operations; Carl Millican, Vice-President, Maintenance; Gus Carbonell, Vice-President, Planning; Cathy Hoag, Vice-President, Sales, Marketing & Customer Service; Eric Hanson, Sales & PR Director; Allison Mainhart, Director of Inflight.

HQ Airport & Main Base: Orlando

Radio callsign: MANATEE

Designator: FL/MTE

Employees: 500

Main destinations served: Albany, Cincinnati, Hartford, Knoxville, Nashville, Newburgh, Omaha, Providence, Syracuse, Tampa.

FLEET
10 Boeing 737-200

ALASKA

Alaska Airlines, Inc

Incorporated: 1932

HISTORY
The main airline operating within and to Alaska, Alaska Airlines dates from 1932, when it was founded as McGhee Airways, before later taking the name Alaska Star Airlines and finally adopting the present title in 1944. Throughout its history it has followed a pattern of acquisition of smaller airlines, including Horizon Air (qv) in 1986 – which retains its identity as sister company in the same Alaska Air Group – and most recently, in 1987, Jet America. In recent years the end of the Cold War

has resulted in services being introduced to Russia.

In common with many inter-state and international carriers, especially in the United States, a commuter airline network has been established feeding traffic from 60 small communities into Alaska Airlines' hubs, using aircraft operated by Bering Air, Era Aviation (qv), LAB Flying Services, and Peninsula Airways, as well as those of Horizon Air, operating under the name of Alaska Airlines Commuter Service. In turn, Alaska Airlines has a code-sharing agreement with Northwest Airlines (qv).

Executive Directors & Officers:
John F. Kelly, Chairman, President & Chief Executive Officer; Harry Lehr, Senior Vice-President, Planning & Finance; Robin Kruegar, Staff Vice-President, Chief Finance & Treasurer; Mike Swannigan, Vice-President, Flight Operations; John Fowler, Vice-President, Maintenance; William L. MacKay, Staff Vice-President, Public Affairs; William Ayer, Vice-President, Marketing & Planning; Edward White, Vice-President, Customer Service; Steven Hamilton, Vice-President, Legal; Marjorie Laws, Vice-President, Corporate Affairs and Corporate Secretary.

HQ Airport & Main Base: Seattle, with further hubs at Anchorage and Portland.

Radio callsign: ALASKA

Designator: AS/ASA

Employees: 6,500

Main destinations served: Bellingham, Bethel, Boise, Burbank, Cordova, Fairbanks, Glacier Bay, Juneau, Ketchikan, Khabarovsk, Kotzebue, Los Angeles, Los Cabos, Magadan, Mazatlan, Nome, Oakland, Ontario (California), Orange County, Palm Springs, Petersburg, Petropavlovsk-Kamchatski, Phoenix, Prudhoe Bay, Puerto Vallarta, San Francisco, San Diego, San Jose, Sitka, Spokane, Toronto, Tucson, Vladivostok, Wrangell, Yakutat.

Annual turnover: US $1,592 million (£996.6 million); includes turnover of other Alaska Air Group operators, including Horizon Air.

LINKS WITH OTHER AIRLINES
Code-share with Northwest Airlines (qv), and with members of the Alaska Airlines Commuter Service.

FLEET
26 Boeing 737-400 (plus 12 on order)
9 McDonnell Douglas MD-82
31 McDonnell Douglas MD-83

ALLEGHENY COMMUTER

Allegheny Commuter Airlines, Inc

Incorporated: 1941

HISTORY
Although Allegheny Commuter Airlines was founded in 1941, the restrictions of World War Two meant that the new airline could not begin operations until 1946, when it commenced charter operations as Reading Aviation Services, operating from the town of that name. The first scheduled commuter or regional services were not introduced until 1957, using the title of Reading Airlines. A further name change occurred in 1968, when the title Suburban Airlines was adopted.

In 1973 a long-term contract began with Allegheny Airlines, predecessors of US Airways (qv), to provide feeder services, with Suburban becoming a member of the Allegheny Commuter network, itself in turn the precursor of today's US Airways Express (qv). Initially Suburban provided feeder services at high frequency to Philadelphia and Newark. Allegheny became USAir in 1979, and in 1986 acquired Suburban, which then adopted its current title and became a USAir Express carrier. Allegheny Commuter has a dense network of services within Pennsylvania and Virginia, as well as operations into Maryland, New York State, Massachusetts and Washington DC.

The fleet has evolved since being in US Airways ownership, with the mixture of Fokker F-27 Friendships and Shorts 330/360s of the late-1980s gradually being replaced so that the present fleet has a backbone of de Havilland Dash 8s, Beech 1900Cs, and just four of the Shorts 330/360 series. There are 48 airports on the Allegheny Commuter network. US Airways Express branding is carried by the aircraft, and US Airways Express designators are used.

Executive Directors & Officers:
William C Clark, President.

HQ Airport & Main Base: Harrisburg International Airport

Radio callsign: ALLEGHENY

Designator: ED/ALO

Main destinations served: Allegheny serves 48 destinations, mainly in the north-east United States.

Annual turnover: Merged into US Airways total.

LINKS WITH OTHER AIRLINES
A wholly-owned subsidiary of US Airways (qv), operating as a US Airways Express carrier.

FLEET
36 de Havilland Dash 8
13 Beech 1900C
2 Shorts 330
2 Shorts 360

ALOHA

Aloha Airlines, Inc

Incorporated: 1946

HISTORY
The largest operator within the Hawaiian islands, Aloha was founded in 1946 as Trans-Pacific Airlines. It proudly claims to be the only airline serving ten of the smaller airports within Hawaii, as well as offering high frequency services between the major Hawaiian airports. An unusual aspect of Aloha's operations is a weekly charter from Honolulu to Christmas Island.

The airline has been privately-owned since 1987, when it became a subsidiary of the locally-based Aloha Airgroup, which has interests in aviation engineering and support services, and also owns a small airline, Aloha Island Air, trading as Island Air, which was originally founded as Princeville Airways.

The fleet is highly standardised, with 17 Boeing 737-200s.

Executive Directors & Officers:
Han H. Ching, Chairman; Glenn R. Zander, President & Chief Executive Officer; Randal M. Okita, Director, Internal Audit; Brenda F. Cutwright, Senior Vice-President & Chief Financial Officer; Michael S. Cohen, Senior Vice-President, Operations; Stephanie Ackerman, Staff Vice-President, Corporate & Government Affairs; Joseph E. Hale, Senior Vice-President, Marketing; Karl Freienmuth, Vice-President, Maintenance; Albert Pattison, Vice-President, Human Resources.

HQ Airport & Main Base: Honolulu

Radio callsign: ALOHA

Designator: AQ/AAH

Employees: 2,275

Main destinations served: Airports on Hawaii, Kauai, Maui, and Oahu, as well as services to smaller airports and islands, often operated in conjunction with Island Air.

LINKS WITH OTHER AIRLINES
Marketing alliance and code-share with United Airlines.
Marketing alliance with Canadian Airlines International and Island Air.

FLEET
17 Boeing 737-200

AMERICA WEST AIRLINES

America West Airlines, Inc

Incorporated: 1981

HISTORY
Founded in 1981, in the mood of optimism which followed deregulation of air transport in the United States in 1978, America West Airlines commenced operations in 1983, with three Boeing 737-200 aircraft flying from its main base at Phoenix to Colorado Springs, Los Angeles, Arizona, and Wichita. A service was also operated to Kansas City, but this was discontinued after a year. Steady expansion followed, with the fleet growing to 21 aircraft in just two years, and to almost 50 in 1987, when it took delivery of its first Boeing 757. The Australian airline Ansett (qv) held a 20 per cent interest in the company from 1987 until 1994. America West itself bid for the Eastern Shuttle, operated along the Washington–New York–Boston corridor by Eastern Air Lines, in 1989, seeking the route and 21 Boeing 757 aircraft, but was unsuccessful despite increasing its offer. By this time operations out of Las Vegas had grown to the extent that this had become a second hub, complementing the airline's main base at Phoenix.

The first Boeing 747s were introduced in 1990. At the other end of the scale, the airline had also been accumulating a small fleet of de Havilland Canada DHC-8s, operated for some years on routes which were either less busy or had airfields with shorter runways. In 1991 Airbus A320 airliners were introduced to the fleet. While by this time America West's route network covered much of the United States, coast-to-coast, it was not until 1991 that the first international route was opened, to Nagoya in Japan, although this was transferred to Northwest Airlines (qv) after just 15 months. Nevertheless, the growing airline was kept busy at this period helping to bring American military personnel home from Kuwait and Saudi Arabia after the Gulf War. A code-sharing agreement with Aéroméxico (qv) in 1992 preceded

America West's introduction of services to Mexico City. The same year saw the introduction of a commuter franchise operation, America West Express (qv).

In 1993 America West celebrated the fact that it was the only survivor of 150 airlines which had been founded following deregulation, though in common with many older airlines it was by this time under the protection of Chapter 11 Bankruptcy Protection (the US equivalent of British administrative receivership, or 'administration'). America West finally emerged from Chapter 11 in August 1994. New investors in the airline at this stage included Continental Airlines (qv) and Mesa (qv), owners of the regional airlines constituting America West Express. Later that year, America West and Continental introduced a code-sharing arrangement on a number of routes.

A service to Vancouver in Canada was launched in 1995, along with additional services to Mexico. Operations out of Columbus had by this time grown to the extent that the airport gained 'mini-hub' status.

Today, America West is the ninth largest airline in the United States, operating as a 'low cost, low fare' airline, albeit with the availability of first class accommodation on its flights. The network covers more than 50 airports in the United States, as well as a number in Canada and Mexico and another 17 operated by America West Express; 19 more are reached through the code-sharing arrangement with Continental. The fleet is well standardised, and appears to be moving from Boeing to Airbus products. The airline is owned by the America West Holdings Corporation, and as a result of a reorganisation America West Vacations has been moved from being a subsidiary of the airline to being a separate division of the holdings corporation.

America West was amongst the first airlines to paint aircraft in themed colour schemes, dedicating aircraft to individual states or to sports teams, and in one case to its ground staff.

Executive Directors & Officers:
William A. Franke, Chairman; Richard R. Goodmanson, President & Chief Executive Officer; Ronald A. Aramini, Vice-President, Operations.

HQ Airport & Main Base: Phoenix, with an additional hub at Las Vegas and mini-hubs at Des Moines and Columbus.

Radio callsign: CACTUS

Designator: HP/AWE

Employees: 11,000

AMERICA WEST AIRLINES *Commemorative Aircraft Cards*

NEVADA

OHIO

ARIZONA

PHOENIX SUNS

THE PHOENIX SUNS

TEAMWORK

ARIZONA DIAMONDBACKS

Identifying America West's livery must be difficult, with so many of its aircraft painted to demonstrate support for sports teams or the people of a particular state. In fact the picture at top right is in the airline's official corporate colour scheme.

Main destinations served:
Albuquerque, Anchorage, Atlanta, Austin, Baltimore, Boston, Burbank, Chicago Midway, Chicago O'Hare, Cleveland, Colorado Springs, Columbus, Dallas/Fort Worth, Denver, Detroit, El Paso, Fort Myers, Houston, Indianapolis, Kansas City, Las Vegas, Long Beach, Los Angeles, Miami, Milwaukee, Minneapolis/St Paul, New York JFK, New York La Guardia, Newark, Oakland, Omaha, Ontario (California), Orange County, Orlando, Philadelphia, Phoenix, Portland, Reno, Sacramento, Salt Lake City, San Antonio, San Diego, San Francisco, San Jose, Seattle, St Louis, Tampa, Tucson, Washington Dulles, Washington National, Wichita.

Annual turnover: US $ 1,740 million (£1,055 million)

LINKS WITH OTHER AIRLINES
Code-share arrangements with Continental Airlines and Mesa Airlines.

FLEET
21 Boeing 737-200 (being replaced by new A319/320s)
40 Boeing 737-300 (some may be replaced by new A320s)
14 Boeing 757
22 Airbus A319 (in course of delivery)
50 Airbus A320-200 (in course of delivery)

AMERICA WEST EXPRESS

Desert Sun Airlines/Mountain West Airlines

Incorporated: 1992

HISTORY
America West Express was established in 1992 as a regional feeder network through a code-sharing arrangement with Mesa Airlines (qv), initially using the Phoenix services of Desert Sun Airlines. The service now reaches 18 airports, including the hubs of Phoenix, Des Moines, and Fresno. The fleet is predominantly the relatively small Beech 1900C/D feeder airliner, but Desert Sun operates two Fokker 70s, and Mountain West (qv) has Embraer Bandeirantes and de Havilland Canada Dash 8s as well.

Executive Directors & Officers:
William A. Franke, Chairman & Chief Executive Officer; Maurice Myers, President & Chief Operating Officer; Alphonse E. Frei, Senior Vice-President, Finance; Don Monteith, Senior Vice-President, Operations; Martin J. Whalen, Senior Vice-President, General Counsel; John Garel, Senior Vice-President, Sales & Marketing Programmes.

HQ Airport & Main Base: Phoenix, with additional hubs at Des Moines and Fresno.

Designator: HP/AWE

Main destinations served: Bullhead City/Laughlin, Des Moines, Durango, Farmington, Flagstaff, Fresno, Gallup, Grand Junction, Gunnison, Kingman, Lake Havasu City, Montrose, Palm Springs, Phoenix, Prescott, Santa Barbara, Sierra Vista/Fort Huachuca, Yuma.

LINKS WITH OTHER AIRLINES
The operating companies are wholly-owned subsidiaries of Mesa Air (qv) Group.

FLEET
Aircraft belong to the operating companies.

The world's largest airline, American operates well over 500 aircraft, including this Boeing 767, dubbed the 'Luxury Liner' by the airline.

AMERICAN

American Airlines, Inc

Incorporated: 1934

HISTORY
Currently the world's largest airline, American Airlines has a long history in which it has often been instrumental in drawing up the specifications of many successful airliner types, including the Douglas DC-3, DC-7 and DC-10, the Convair 340 and the Convair 990 development of the Convair 880, and the Lockheed Electra.

As with so many larger airlines, American's history is that of the amalgamation of many smaller airlines. The formation of the Aviation Corporation in 1929 involved the acquisition of several small, often single route, airlines. The oldest of these, the Robertson Aircraft Corporation, which operated a Chicago–St Louis–Omaha service, dated from 1921, and was acquired through its parent company, the Universal Aviation Corporation. Most of the other airlines had been founded between 1926 and 1929, and they included: Canadian Colonial Airways (operating New York–Montreal); Central Air Lines (Kansas City–Wichita–Tulsa); Continental Airlines (Cleveland–Louisville); Colonial Air Transport (New York–Boston, Albany–Buffalo–Cleveland); Embry-Riddle Aviation Corporation (Chicago–Cincinnati); Gulf Air Lines (Atlanta–Houston–New Orleans); Interstate Airlines (Chicago–Atlanta, St Louis–Evansville); Northern Air Lines (Cleveland–Chicago–Kansas City); Texas Air Transport (Dallas–Galveston); and the Universal Aviation Corporation (Tulsa–Dallas). Some of these airlines had been subsidiaries of larger concerns.

The Aviation Corporation established American Airways as its operating company in 1930, with the task of rationalising the wide assortment of equipment and integrating the widely scattered network of services. Whilst this was being done, American continued to make further acquisitions, so that in 1930 Standard AirLines with its Los Angeles–El Paso service was acquired from its parent, Western Air Express, while from E.L. Cord in 1932 American bought Century Air Lines, with a network of routes in the midwest, and Century Pacific Lines. An Act of Congress in 1934 forced the Aviation Corporation to isolate its manufacturing and operating interests, and as a result American Airlines was formed as a separate operating entity the same year. The new airline started life with a network of services stretching across the United States, from the Pacific to the Atlantic coasts, and from Canada to close to the border with Mexico.

American spent the remaining years until the outbreak of World War Two consolidating and expanding its domestic network. In 1942 licences were obtained for services from El Paso and Dallas to Mexico City, but due to wartime equipment shortages and flight-crews being conscripted these services could not be introduced until after the war ended, and the number

American also has a substantial fleet of Airbus A300-600Rs.

of flight-crew conscripted into the armed forces. Looking further afield, the airline obtained a 51 per cent interest in American Export Airlines (AEA), a company which, though formed in 1937 to operate services to Europe and countries around the Mediterranean, had only managed to

obtained a temporary permit for a service to Lisbon by 1940. Yet in October 1945, just two months after the end of World War Two, AEA was able to introduce the first commercial New York–London landplane service, using Douglas DC-4s. AEA changed its name to American Overseas

Airlines in 1948, the same year that American increased its stake to 62 per cent. However, two years later the company was sold to Pan American World Airways, an old rival, almost certainly as a result of difficulties encountered in obtaining sufficient overseas bilateral rights.

The 1950s saw a further period of rationalisation for American Airlines, dropping many small communities from its network, and handing these over to the feeder or local service airlines – companies which would be known as 'commuters' today. Some 30 years later, deregulation of air transport in the United States would see much of this repeated. The rationalisation was in effect a reshaping of the network, with airlines such as American becoming major transcontinental and, eventually, intercontinental carriers. Steps towards this end included the introduction of a Chicago–San Francisco service in 1955, which was followed later by a non-stop New York–San Francisco route. A merger with what was then another major United States airline, Eastern Air Lines, was mooted during the early-1960s and approved by shareholders of both companies, but vetoed by the Civil Aeronautics Board in

Dubbed the 'Super 80', this is one of American's fleet of 260 McDonnell Douglas MD-80s.

1963. Sadly, Eastern then suffered an uncertain three decades before finally ceasing operations in 1991, after a dramatic slimming down and disposal of routes and assets, which included selling its Caribbean and South American operations to American Airlines.

American grew through other acquisitions, buying AirCal in 1986 to gain a network of services along the West Coast of the United States. During the same decade, major advances were made in developing both a transatlantic network and a transpacific network. Its five main hubs at Dallas/Fort Worth (its main base), Chicago, Nashville, Raleigh/Durham, and San Juan, were joined by a sixth hub at San Jose. Realising that an airline geared for the busier and longer routes is almost invariably at a disadvantage, in 1987 the airline created the American Eagle (qv) system of feeder airlines, and AMR Corporation – by this time the holding company for American Airlines – spent US $150 million (£90 million) acquiring five airlines: Air MidWest, AVAir, Command Airways, Simmons Airlines, and Wings West. The airline may acquire the US Airways Shuttle (qv) from troubled US Airways, and if it does so it is likely to operate this as an integral part of the American Airlines operation.

Today, American's distinctive silver aircraft with their blue and red cheat lines, can be seen at 164 airports world-wide. Code-share alliances have been in force since 1992, when an arrangement was made with South African Airways (qv), followed by one with British Midland Airways (qv), although the latter may be dropped as the alliance with British Airways (qv) has been provisionally approved by regulators on both sides of the Atlantic.

Executive Directors & Officers: Robert L. Crandall, Chairman, President & Chief Executive Officer; Don Carty, Executive Vice-President, Operations; Gerard Arpey, Senior Vice-President, Finance & Planning/Chief Financial Officer; Michael W. Gunn, Senior Vice-President, Marketing; Hans Mirka, Senior Vice-President, International; Peter Dolara, Senior Vice-President, Miami, Caribbean & Latin America; David Kruse, Senior Vice-President, Maintenance & Engineering; Donald O'Hare, Senior Vice-President, Domestic Field Services; Anne H. McNamara, Senior Vice-President, General Counsel; Jayne Ellison, Vice-President, Human Resources.

HQ Airport & Main Base: Dallas/Fort Worth, with additional hubs at Chicago O'Hare, Miami, and San Juan.

Radio callsign: AMERICAN

Designator: AA/AAL

Employees: Flight-crew: 9,000; Cabin staff: 20,000; Engineering: 5,725; Ground staff: approx 56,000; Total: 90,000.

Main destinations served: Acapulco, Albany, Albuquerque, Amarillo, Antigua, Aruba, Asuncion, Atlanta, Austin, Bakersfield, Baltimore, Barranquilla, Belize City, Belo Horizonte, Bermuda, Birmingham (Alabama), Birmingham (England), Bogota, Boston, Bridgetown, Brussels, Buenos Aires, Buffalo/Niagara Falls, Burbank, Calgary/Banff, Cali, Cancun, Caracas, Casa de Campo/La Romana, Charlotte, Chicago O'Hare, Cincinnati, Cleveland, Colorado Springs, Columbus, Curaçao, Dallas/Fort Worth, Dayton, Denver, Des Moines, Detroit, Durango, El Paso, Fort Lauderdale, Fort Myers, Frankfurt, Fresno, Glasgow, Grand Cayman, Greensboro, Grenada, Guadalajuato, Guatemala City, Guayaquil, Gunnison, Harrisburg, Hartford/Springfield, Honolulu, Houston Intercontinental, Huntsville/Decatur, Indianapolis, Jackson Hole, Jacksonville, Kahului, Kansas City, Kingston, La Paz, Las Vegas, Leon-Guanajuato, Lima, Little Rock, London Gatwick, London Heathrow, Long Beach, Long Island, Los Angeles, Los Cabos, Louisville, Madrid, Managua, Manchester, McAllen, Memphis, Mexico City, Miami, Milan, Minneapolis/St Paul, Montego Bay, Monterrey, Montevideo, Montreal, Nashville, New Orleans, New York JFK, New York La Guardia, Newburgh/Stewart, Newark, Norfolk/Virginia Beach, Oakland, Oklahoma City, Omaha, Ontario (California), Orange County, Orlando, Ottawa, Palm Springs, Panama City, Paris Orly, Philadelphia/Wilmington, Phoenix/Scottsdale, Pittsburg, Port-au-Prince, Port of Spain, Portland, Providence/Newport, Providenciales, Puerto Plata, Puerto Vallarta, Quito, Raleigh/Durham, Reno, Richmond, Rio de Janeiro, Rochester (Minnesota), Rochester (New York), Sacramento, St Croix, St Louis, St Lucia, St Maarten, St Thomas, Salt Lake City, San Antonio, San Diego, San Francisco, San Jose, San Juan, San Pedro Sula, San Salvador, Santa Cruz (Bolivia), Santiago (Chile), Santo Domingo, São Paulo, Seattle/Tacoma, Steamboat Springs, Stockholm, Syracuse, Tampa/St Petersburg, Tegucigalpa, Tokyo Narita, Toronto, Tucson, Tulsa, Vail, Vancouver, Washington National, Washington Dulles, West Palm Beach, White Plains, Wichita, Zürich.

Annual turnover: US $17,753 million (£10,760 million); includes American Eagle

LINKS WITH OTHER AIRLINES

Code-shares with ALM (qv), Avianca (qv), British Midland Airways (qv), BWIA (qv), Canadian Airlines (qv), China Airlines (qv), China Eastern (qv), El Al (qv), Gulf Air (qv), LAPSA (qv), Lone Star (qv), LOT Polish Airlines (qv), Philippine (qv), Qantas (qv), Singapore Airlines (qv), South African Airways (qv), TACA (qv), and Transaero (qv).

FLEET

35 Airbus A300-600R
41 Boeing 767-300ER
22 Boeing 767-200ER
8 Boeing 767-200
90 Boeing 757-200
81 Boeing 727-200
75 Fokker F-100
15 McDonnell Douglas MD-11
5 McDonnell Douglas DC-10-30
11 McDonnell Douglas DC-10-10
260 McDonnell Douglas MD-80
plus 75 Boeing 757-800 on order.

AMERICAN EAGLE

AMR Eagle, Inc

Incorporated: 1986

HISTORY

American Eagle was established by American Airlines' (qv) parent, AMR, in 1986, to provide a network of feeder services linking smaller communities into major airport and, of course, the major hubs of the American Airlines network. Although the network was initially a franchise operation, four airlines have been acquired and all operate under the American Eagle name and with American Airlines designators. The airlines are Executive Airlines (qv), Flagship Airlines (qv), Simmons Airlines, and Wings West Airlines (qv).

American Eagle shares the headquarters of American Airlines.

Executive Directors & Officers: Daniel Garton, President; Tom R. Del Valle, President, Executive Airlines; Dave Kennedy, President, Flagship Airlines; Ralph Richardi, President, Simmons Airlines; Mary Jordan, President, Wings West Airlines; Pete Pappas, Senior Vice-President, Planning; Will Folger, Vice-President, Finance; John Nick, Vice-President, Corporate Services; Mike Costello, Vice-President, Employee Relations; Greg Hall, Vice-President, Maintenance & Engineering; Lance

American Eagle's fleet of more than a hundred Saab 340Bs is operated by the four subsidiary airlines.

American Eagle, the feeder network for American Airlines, operates both the ATR 42 and the stretched ATR 72, shown here.

American Eagle has a large number of the new Canadair CRJ-700 Regional Jets on order, with deliveries starting in 2001.

McDonald, Vice-President, Operations; Joel Chusid, Vice-President, Marketing.

HQ Airport & Main Base: Dallas/Fort Worth, plus Chicago O'Hare, Los Angeles, Miami, Nashville, New York JFK, Raleigh/Durham, and San Juan.

Radio callsign: EAGLE FLIGHT

Designator: AA/EGF

Employees: Aircrew: 3,500; Engineering: 60; Ground staff: 5,500; Total: approx 9,100

Main destinations served: Albany, Abilene, Alexandria, Amarillo, Anguilla, Antigua, Bakersfield, Baltimore, Baton Rouge, Beaumont/Port Arthur, Bloomington, Boston, Buffalo/Niagara Falls, Bryon/College Station, Carlsbad, Casa de Campo, Castries/St Lucia, Cedar Rapids/Iowa City, Champagne, Chicago O'Hare, Cincinnati, Cleveland, Columbus, Corpus Christi, Dallas/Fort Worth, Dayton, Des Moines, Dominica, Dubuque, Evansville, Fayetteville, Fort-de-France, Fort Myers, Fort Smith, Fort Wayne, Freeport, Fresno, George Town (Bahamas), Governor's Harbour, Grand Rapids, Green Bay, Harlingen, Hartford/Springfield, Houston-Hobby, Indianapolis, Jackson, Jacksonville, Kalimazoo, Key West, Killeen/Fort Hood, LaCross, Lafayette, Lake Charles, Lansing, Laredo, Las Vegas, Lawton/Fort Sill, Little Rock, Longview, Los Angeles, Lubbock, Madison, Marathon, Marsh Harbour, Mayaguez, Memphis, Miami, Midland/Odessa, Milwaukee, Moline, Monterey, Montreal, Naples, Nashville, Nassau, New York JFK, Oklahoma City, Orange County, Orlando, Ottawa, Palm Springs, Peoria, Philadelphia/Wilmington, Pittsburgh, Pointe-a-Pitre, Ponce, Port-au-Prince, Providence/Newport, Puerto Plata, Punta Cana, Raleigh/Durham, Rochester, St Croix, St Kitts/Nevis, St Louis, St Maarten, St Thomas, St Vincent, San Angelo, San Antonio, San Diego, San Francisco, San Juan, San Luis Obispo, Santa Barbara, Santo Domingo, Sarasota/Bradenton, Shreveport, South Bend, Springfield (Illinois), Springfield/Branson (Mississippi), Syracuse, Tampa/St Petersburg, Texarkana, Tabago, Toledo, Tortola/Virgin Goreda, Traverse City, Tulsa, Tyler, Waco, Wasau/Stevens Point, Washington Dulles, Washington National, West Palm Beach, Wichita, Wichita Falls.

FLEET
64 ATR 72 (plus 58 options)
42 Embraer EMB-145LR (in course of delivery to end 1999)
56 ATR 42

11 SAAB 340A
115 SAAB 340B/340B
plus 25 Canadair CRJ-700 on order from 2001

AMERICAN INTERNATIONAL

Kalitta American International Airways, Inc

Incorporated: 1972

HISTORY
Operating as American International or AIA, Kalitta American International Airways was formed in 1972 as Connie Kalitta Services, named after its founder Conrad Kalitta. The airline confined itself to domestic passenger and cargo operations until 1984, when it moved into international cargo charter work. Further expansion occurred in 1983, when AIA started to operate the scheduled services of Zantop International Airlines (qv) under the name of American International Freight.

An unusually wide variety of aircraft is operated, providing the flexibility to meet widely varied customer needs. Scheduled and charter passenger and freight services are offered. Unusual aircraft still in the fleet include Beech 18Ts, and the relatively rare HFB Hansa Jet.

During 1997 the airline acquired the Kitty Hawk Group (qv).

Executive Directors & Officers: Conrad Kalitta, Chairman & Chief Executive Officer; Tom Jones, Director of Operations; Alex Cameron, Executive Director, Maintenance; Jane Phifer, Vice-President, Finance.

HQ Airport & Main Base: Willow Run Airport, Ypsilanti, Michigan

Radio callsign: CONNIE

Designator: CB/CKS

Employees: 3,000, including 600 flight-crew

FLEET
19 McDonnell Douglas DC-8
16 Boeing 727
8 Lockheed L-1011 TriStar freighters
5 Boeing 747-100F
3 Boeing 747-200 Combi
17 Learjet 22/24
2 Learjet 35/36
3 HFB Hansa Jet
3 Mitsubishi Mu-2
1 British Aerospace 125
10 Beech 18T

AMERICAN TRANS AIR

American Trans Air, Inc

Incorporated: 1973

HISTORY
American Trans Air was founded in 1973 to manage the Ambassadair Travel Club, and it was not until 1981 that the airline became a Common Air Carrier, able to develop charter and scheduled services. A holding company, Amtran, was established to take over the airline in 1984. Today, it operates a fleet of 44 aircraft out of three hub airports.

Executive Directors & Officers: George Mikelsons, Chairman & Chief Executive Officer; Kenneth K. Wolff, Executive Vice-President & Chief Financial Officer; James W. Hlavacek, Executive Vice-President; Randy E. Marlar, Vice-President, Maintenance.

HQ Airport & Main Base: Indianapolis, with bases/hubs also at Chicago Midway and New York La Guardia.

Radio callsign: AMTRAN

Designator: TZ/AMT

Employees: 3,750

Main destinations served: Operates scheduled and charter flights, mainly passenger, to destinations including Fort Lauderdale, Fort Myers, Honolulu, Las Vegas, Milwaukee, Orlando, Riga, St Croix, St Petersburg (US), St Thomas, Sarasota/Bradenton, Salt Lake City, San Juan.

FLEET
20 Boeing 727-200
14 Boeing 757-200
13 Lockheed L-1011 TriStar

AMERIJET INTERNATIONAL

Amerijet International, Inc

Incorporated: 1974

HISTORY
This Fort Lauderdale-based airline operates scheduled and charter cargo services on domestic and international routes, although mainly in an around the Caribbean and Central American areas.

Executive Directors & Officers: David Bassett, President; Joseph Garvia, Chief

Financial Officer; Larry Borneman, Maintenance Director; Wayne Perry, Personnel Director; Ann Prochaska, Vice-President, Finance; Peter Steele, Vice-President, Flight Operations; Irving Schumacher, Vice-President, Maintenance; Pamela Rollins, Vice-President, Strategic Planning.

HQ Airport & Main Base: Fort Lauderdale

Radio callsign: AMERIJET

Designator: JH/AJT

Employees: 487

Main destinations served: Antigua, Aruba, Atlanta, Barbados, Belize, Cancun, Caracas, Chicago, Curaçao, Dominica, Fort de France, Georgetown, Grenada, Guadalajara, Houston, Los Angeles, Merida, Mexico City, Miami, Montserrat, New York, Point-a-Pitre, Porlamar, Port-au-Prince, Port of Spain, Puerta Plata, St Kitts, St Lucia, St Maarten, St Vincent, San Juan, Santo Domingo, Toronto, Valencia (Venezuela).

FLEET
9 Boeing 727-200C
5 Boeing 727-100C

ARROW AIR

Arrow Air, Inc

Incorporated: 1947

HISTORY
Founded in 1947 by George Bachelor, Arrow has twice suspended operations, resuming these in 1981 and again in 1995. Originally operating passenger and cargo charters, passenger operations ended in 1986 to leave the airline to concentrate on cargo charters and scheduled cargo services from Miami. While McDonnell Douglas DC-8s still form the backbone of the fleet, the first TriStar was introduced in 1996 and more have been added since, suggesting that this may be Arrow Air's freighter for the future.

Executive Directors & Officers:
Terrence Fensome, President & Chief Executive Officer; Jacabo Bolivar, Operations Director; Phil Wester, Vice-President, Finance & Accounting; Ken Wilson, Vice-President, Maintenance & Engineering; Ed Lesko and Jon D. Bachelor, Vice-Presidents, Sales.

HQ Airport & Main Base: Miami International

Radio callsign: BIG A

Designator: JW/APW

Employees: 335

Main destinations served: Charter cargo operations plus scheduled cargo services from Miami to Atlanta, Bogota, Costa Rica, Guayaquil, New York, Panama, Quito, San Juan.

FLEET
3 Lockheed L-1011-200F TriStar
6 McDonnell Douglas DC-8-62
3 McDonnell Douglas DC-8-63F

ASA ATLANTIC SOUTHEAST AIRLINES

Atlantic Southeast Airlines, Inc

Incorporated: 1979

HISTORY
Atlantic Southeast Airlines was established in 1979 with the primary aim of providing short-haul or regional services from its base at Atlanta. Given this operating philosophy, and the presence of Delta Air Lines, it is not surprising that ASA was one of the first smaller airlines to establish links with a major one, creating the Delta Connection service in 1984. Aircraft operate with the branding 'Delta Connection' along the fuselage, but with ASA on the tail. Operating in a niche market, ASA has been consistently profitable and has enjoyed rapid growth, with a second hub opening at Dallas/Fort Worth in 1986. A hub operation at Memphis developed with the introduction of services between 1983 and 1985, but this was discontinued in 1986. The launch customer for Embraer's successful EMB-120 Brasilia, ASA has also operated the smaller Embraer EMB-110 Bandeirante, while larger aircraft have included the de Havilland Dash 7.

The airline has been introducing a large number of Canadair Regional Jets.

Executive Directors & Officers: George F. Pickett, Chairman & Chief Executive Officer; John W. Beiser, President; Ronald V. Sapp, Vice-President, Finance & Treasurer; T. M. Shanahan, Vice-President, Flight Operations; Sam J. Watts, Vice-President, Sales & Customer Services; William H. Hinson, Vice-President, Technical Services.

HQ Airport & Main Base: Atlanta, with a further hub at Dallas/Fort Worth. Maintenance bases are Macon and Texarkana.

Radio callsign: ASEA

Designator: EV/ASE

Employees: Flight-crew: 500; Cabin staff: 800; Engineering: 10; Ground staff: 1,540; Administration and sales: 150; Total: 3,000.

Main destinations served: Atlanta to Albany, Alexandria, Asheville, Augusta, Brunswick, Chattanooga, Charleston, Charlotte, Columbus (Georgia), Columbus/Starkville/West Point (Mississippi), Dothan, Evansville, Fayetteville, Florence, Fort Walton Beach, Gainesville, Greensboro/High Point, Greenville/Spartanburg, Gulfport, Jackson, Jacksonville, Lafayette, Lexington, Louisville, Lynchburg, Macon, Meridian, Montgomery, Myrtle Beach, Panama City, Pensacola, Roanoke, Tallahassee, Tri-Cities, Valdosta, Wilmington.
Dallas/Fort Worth to Alexandria, Amarillo, Beaumont/Port Arthur, Columbus/Starkville/West Point (Mississippi), Corpus Christi, Fayetteville, Fort Smith, Houston Intercontinental, Killeen, Lafayette, Lawton, Lubbock, Meridian, Monroe, Oklahoma City, San Antonio, Shreveport, Texarkana, Tulsa, Wichita, Wichita Falls.

Passenger miles pa: 874 million

Passengers pa: 3.63 million

Annual turnover: US $375.3 million (£227.45 million)

LINKS WITH OTHER AIRLINES
Operates all services under the Delta Connection name.

FLEET
63 Embraer EMB-120 Brasilia (4 leased)
12 ATR 72-210 (leased)
30 Canadair Regional Jets (plus options on another 60)

ATLANTIC COAST AIRLINES

Atlantic Coast Airlines, Inc

Incorporated: 1989

HISTORY
Atlantic Coast Airlines is a United Express (qv) carrier, and has grown rapidly since it was first formed in 1989. It established the first scheduled international service out of Stewart International Airport in 1992, when it started operations to Toronto in Canada. Earlier operations had been

based on what was then Atlantic Coast's main hub, at Washington Dulles.

The fleet is highly standardised on British Aerospace Jetstreams, with the larger 41 gradually taking over from the Jetstream 31.

Executive Directors & Officers: E. Edward Acker, Chairman; Kerry B. Steen, President & Chief Executive Officer; Paul Tate, Chief Financial Officer; Ken Latour, Operations Director; John Cross, Maintenance Director; Larry Murray, Human Resources Director; Phillip Keller, Marketing Director; Angie Shermer, Sales Director.

HQ Airport & Main Base: Washington Dulles, with hubs at Atlanta and Dallas/Fort Worth

Radio callsign: BLUERIDGE

Designator: DH/BLR

Employees: 1,350

Main destinations served: 39 airports from Atlanta and 25 airports from Dallas/Fort Worth.

LINKS WITH OTHER AIRLINES
United Express carrier.

FLEET
22 Canadair CRJ
36 British Aerospace Jetstream 41
30 British Aerospace Jetstream 31

ATLAS AIR

Atlas Air, Inc

Incorporated: 1992

HISTORY
Although still a relatively young airline, Atlas Air – a subsidiary of Atlas Holdings – has ambitious plans in the air freight market, concentrating on creating a fleet of 24 Boeing 747 freighters for long-haul international operations out of New York JFK. It enables major airlines to outsource their trunk cargo operations, effectively operating these services for them while they concentrate on sales and marketing of cargo traffic. In 1998 the airline introduced its first aircraft bought new from the manufacturer, these being the first deliveries from an order for ten Boeing 747-400Fs.

Executive Directors & Officers:
Michael Chowdry, Chairman & Chief Executive Officer; George Mumane, Executive Vice-President & Chief Operating Officer; Clark H. Onstad, Senior Vice-President & General Counsel.

HQ Airport & Main Base: New York JFK

Radio callsign: GIANT

Designator: 5Y/GTI

Employees: 200 plus

Main destinations served: New York JFK to Anchorage, Hong Kong, Khaborovs, plus trunk services for major airlines.

LINKS WITH OTHER AIRLINES
Client airlines include China Airlines (qv), Emirates (qv), KLM (qv), Lufthansa (qv), and Varig (qv).

FLEET
4 Boeing 747-400F (plus 6 on order 1999–2001)
13 Boeing 747-200F
1 Boeing 747-100F

BARON AVIATION

Baron Aviation Services, Inc

HISTORY
Baron Aviation Services uses a substantial fleet of Cessna 208 Caravan light freighters to provide feeder services into the Federal Express (qv) network. In addition five Douglas DC-3 freighters are operated, mainly on cargo charters.

Executive Directors & Officers: C.E. Schmidt, President; Lee Maples, Vice-President.

HQ Airport & Main Base: Rolla National Airport, Vichy, Missouri

Radio callsign: SHOW-ME

Designator: BVN

LINKS WITH OTHER AIRLINES
Most operations are on behalf of Federal Express.

FLEET
5 Douglas DC-3
34 Cessna 208 Caravan

BROOKS FUEL

Brooks Fuel, Inc

HISTORY
One of the more unusual airlines, this company specialises in the carriage of fuel to remote sites in Alaska which suffer from poor surface communications.

HQ Airport & Main Base: Fairbanks

FLEET
2 McDonnell Douglas DC-7
9 McDonnell Douglas DC-4
1 Beech 18

BURLINGTON AIR EXPRESS

Burlington Air Express, Inc

Incorporated: 1972

HISTORY
Since its formation, Burlington Air Express has developed into a specialist in scheduled and charter cargo operations, including providing integrated logistics services for companies in other sectors.

Executive Directors & Officers: Joseph Farrell, Chairman & Chief Executive Officer; Dennis Eittreim, President, Americas; Steve Dearnley, President, International; Robert Arovas, Chief Financial Officer; Larry Van Pelt, Vice-President, Marketing.

HQ Airport & Main Base: HQ is Irvine, California, but main base is Toledo.

Designator: 8W

Main destinations served: Destinations throughout North America, including Mexico, on a contract and ad hoc charter basis.

LINKS WITH OTHER AIRLINES
Provides freight forwarding for Air Transport International (qv), American International (qv), and Kitty Hawk (qv).

FLEET
17 McDonnell Douglas DC-8
14 Boeing 727
1 Boeing 737

BUSINESS EXPRESS

Business Express, Inc

Incorporated: 1981

HISTORY
Originally a passenger charter operator, Business Express started scheduled operations in 1984, and two years later acquired Pilgrim Airlines. Today it is a regional or commuter operator, with its aircraft and flights operated on behalf of Delta (qv) – as part of the Delta Connection (qv) network – and, more recently, Northwest (qv), as part of Northwest Airlink (qv).

In 1996 Business Express had to file for Chapter 11 Bankruptcy Protection in order to continue services.

Executive Directors & Officers: James McManus, Chairman & Chief Executive Officer; Bill Dusold, Director, Maintenance; Warren Wilkinson, Director, Marketing and Sales; E. McGill, Executive Vice-President; Mark Hahn, Vice-President, Finance; Roy Spencer, Vice-President, Operations; Chet Hooper, Vice-President, Maintenance; Jeff Hawkins, Vice-President, Passenger Services; F. Aruvolo, Vice-President, Marketing.

HQ Airport & Main Base: HQ at Portsmouth, New Hampshire, with operational hubs at Boston Logan and Minneapolis/St Paul.

Radio callsign: BIZEX

Designator: SW/GAA

Employees: 1,500

Main destinations served: More than 30 airports in the north-east United States and Canada, including many winter sports seasonal operations.

LINKS WITH OTHER AIRLINES
Member of Delta Connection and Northwest Airlink.

FLEET
20 Saab 340B
17 Saab 340A
16 Beech 1900C
plus 20 Embraer EMB-135 on order.

CARNIVAL AIR LINES

See PanAm

CCAIR

CC Air, Inc

Incorporated: 1984

HISTORY
Part of the US Airways Express (qv) network, CCAIR was founded in 1984 at Charlotte in North Carolina. The route network extends to 23 communities in eight states, 14 routes being shared with US Airways (qv), parent of US Airways express.

Executive Directors & Officers:
Kenneth W. Gann, President & Chief Executive Officer; Leigh Phillips & Dirk Ruehle, Directors, Finance; Ken Humphries, Director, Operations; Brian

Billings, Director, Maintenance; Mike Halcomb, Director, Marketing; Carletta Sullivan, Director, Personnel; Peter J. Sistare, Vice-President, Operations & Maintenance; Eric Montgomery, Vice-President, Finance.

HQ Airport & Main Base: Charlotte

Designator: ED/CDL (US Airways Express)

Employees: 640

Main destinations served: Asheville, Athens (Ohio), Augusta, Baltimore, Charleston, Cincinnati, Columbus, Greenbriar/Lewisburg, Greenville (North Carolina), Greenville/Spartanburg, Hickory, Huntington, Jacksonville, Kinston, Lexington, Lynchburg, Norfolk, Pinehurst/Southern Pines, Raleigh/Durham, Rocky Mount/Wilson, Shenandoah Valley, Winston Salem.

LINKS WITH OTHER AIRLINES
US Airways Express (qv) carrier.

FLEET
4 de Havilland Dash 8-100
9 Shorts 360
14 British Aerospace Jetstream 31

CHAUTAUQUA AIRLINES

Chautauqua Airlines, Inc

Incorporated: 1973

HISTORY
Chautauqua Airlines was founded in 1973 and commenced operations the following year. It is now a part of the US Airways Express (qv) network.

Executive Directors & Officers:
Timothy L. Coon, President & Chief Executive Officer; John Weibel, Chief Financial Officer; Captain Barry Confer, Director of Flight Operations; Bernard Kirchhoff, Director, Personnel; James I. Muroski, Vice-President, Maintenance & Operations; Ronald L. Graff, Vice-President, Technical; Michael Suckow, Vice-President, Strategic Planning; Jerome L. Balsano, Vice-President, Stations; Mickey Bowman, Vice-President, Marketing.

HQ Airport & Main Base: Indianapolis

Radio callsign: CHAUTAUQUA

Designator: CHQ

Employees: 510

Main destinations served:
Akron/Canton, Altoona, Buffalo, Champaign, Cleveland, Columbus, Dayton, Detroit, Evansville, Fort Wayne, Grand Rapids, Hagerstown, Johnstown, Kansas City, Lancaster, Milwaukee, Nashville, Newark, Pittsburgh, South Bend, Syracuse.

LINKS WITH OTHER AIRLINES
US Airways Express carrier.

FLEET
12 Saab 340
17 British Aerospace Jetstream 31
4 Fairchild Metro III
plus 20 Embraer EMB-145 on order.

CONTINENTAL

Continental Airlines, Inc

Incorporated: 1934

HISTORY
Currently the twelfth largest airline in the world, and sixth largest in the United States, Continental's history started with the formation of Varney Speed Lines in 1934, the present title being adopted in 1937. The first services operated between El Paso in Texas and Pueblo, Colorado. A major step forward for Continental occurred in 1981, when Texas Air – the parent company of another airline, Texas International – acquired a controlling interest in Continental, and the following year the two airlines were merged using the Continental name. Texas International's history had dated from the airline's formation in 1940, but because of wartime restrictions and shortages of aircraft and aircrew, scheduled operations did not start until 1947, using the name of Trans-Texas Airways until the title Texas International was adopted in 1969.

The new and enlarged Continental acquired a number of other airlines, including Frontier Airlines in late-1986, and both New York Air and People Express in 1987. Further regional acquisitions led to the formation of a wholly-owned regional subsidiary, Continental Express (qv), in 1987. By this time the airline had expanded into international operations, primarily on routes across the Pacific.

Nevertheless, this rapid expansion was not without its problems. In 1983 Continental filed for Chapter 11 Bankruptcy Protection (the US equivalent of Administration), with a dramatic cut in the route network from 78 airports to just 25, while the number of employees was cut by almost two-thirds, from 12,000 to

Continental has come through some difficult years, but it has emerged as being still one of the world's major airlines. This is one of its McDonnell Douglas DC-10-30s.

4,200. These drastic measures quickly paid off, and by 1985 Continental was able to put a plan of reorganisation before the Bankruptcy Court and emerged from Protection the following year. Continental again sought Chapter 11 Protection in 1990, emerging on this occasion in 1993, this time with fresh investments from Air Partners and Air Canada (qv), although the latter's investment has been substantially reduced.

During its second spell of Protection, Continental sold its Seattle to Tokyo rights to American Airlines (qv), but acquired rights from Newark (sometimes called New York Newark) to Frankfurt, Madrid, and Munich, and from Houston to Paris.

The fleet, which had become highly diversified, was rationalised during the second spell of Protection, with the airline reducing the number of types operated, losing its Airbus A300s and Boeing 747s.

Today it consists entirely of Boeing and McDonnell Douglas types. Continental is accelerating the replacement of its older aircraft to reap the benefits of up-to-date models which are quieter and more economical to operate.

The airline has expanded over the years and in addition to its original hub at Houston now has substantial hubs at Cleveland, Denver, and Newark, with mini-hubs for its Pacific services at Honolulu and Guam.

Executive Directors & Officers:
Gordon Bethune, Chairman & Chief Executive Officer; Greg Benneman, President & Chief Operating Officer; Larry Kellner, Senior Vice-President & Chief Financial Officer; C.D. McLean, Senior Vice-President, Operations; Raymond Valeika, Senior Vice-President, Technical Operations; John Nelson, Executive Vice-President, Marketing; Charles T. Goolsbee, Executive Vice-President, Corporate Affairs; Thomas Kalil, Senior Vice-President, Customer Service; Robert Allen, Senior Vice-President, Human Resources; Sam Ashmore, Senior Vice-President, Civic/Airport Affairs.

HQ Airport & Main Base: Houston,

One of more than 20 Boeing 757-200s in the Continental fleet.

with hubs also at Cleveland, Denver, Newark, Guam, and Honolulu.

Radio callsign: CONTINENTAL

Designator: CO/COA

Employees: 43,000

Main destinations served: Houston Intercontinental to Acapulco, Albuquerque, Amsterdam, Atlanta, Austin, Baltimore, Belize, Bermuda, Bogota, Boston, Cancun, Charleston, Chicago O'Hare, Cleveland, Colorado Springs, Columbus, Corpus Christi, Cozumel, Dallas/Fort Worth, Denver, Detroit, El Paso, Fort Lauderdale, Fort Myers, Frankfurt, Greensboro, Guadalajara, Guam, Guatemala City, Guayaquil, Hartford/Springfield, Honolulu, Indianapolis, Ixtapa, Jacksonville, Kansas City, Las Vegas, Leon, Lima, London Gatwick, Lubbock, Los Cabos, Louisville, Managua, Mazatlan, McAllen/Rio Granda Valley, Mexico City, Miami, Midland/Odessa, Milwaukee, Minneapolis/St Paul, Monterrey, Nashville, Nassau, New Orleans, New York La Guardia, New York Newark, Norfolk, Oklahoma City, Omaha, Ontario (California), Orange County, Orlando, Panama City, Paris CDG, Pensacola, Philadelphia, Portland, Puerto Vallarta, Raleigh/Durham, Rochester, San Salvador, San Antonio, San Diego, San Francisco, San Jose, San Jose (Costa Rica), Salt Lake City, Seattle, St Louis, Tampa/St Petersburg, Tegucigalpa, Tuka, Tucson, Washington Dulles, Washington National, West Palm Beach, Vancouver, plus Calgary and Toronto through code-share with Air Canada.
Cleveland to Atlanta, Boston, Chicago O'Hare, Chicago Midway, Dallas/Fort Worth, Denver, Fort Myers, Hartford/Springfield, Kansas City, Las Vegas, Los Angeles, Louisville, Minneapolis/St Paul, New Orleans, New York La Guardia, Newark, Orlando, Philadelphia, Providence, San Diego, Seattle, Salt Lake City, San Francisco, St Louis, Tampa/St Petersburg, Tucson, Washington Dulles, Washington National.
New York Newark to Amsterdam, Anchorage, Antigua, Bermuda, Birmingham (England), Bogota, Boston, Buffalo, Cleveland, Colorado Springs, Columbus, Charleston, Charlotte, Chicago O'Hare, Chicago Midway, Cincinnati, Cleveland, Colorado Springs, Columbus, Dayton, Daytona Beach, Dallas/Fort Worth, Denver, Düsseldorf, Fort Lauderdale, Frankfurt, Greensboro, Greenville/Spartanburg, Guayaquil, Honolulu, Indianapolis, Jacksonville, Kansas City, Las Vegas, Lima, Lisbon,

London Gatwick, Los Angeles, Madrid, Manchester, Mexico City, Miami, Milan, Minneapolis/St Paul, Montreal, Nashville, New Orleans, Orange County/Santa Ana, Orlando, Paris CDG, Pensacola, Phoenix, Portland, Quito, Raleigh/Durham, Richmond, Rio de Janeiro, Rome, Salt Lake City, San Antonio, San Diego, San Francisco, San Juan, São Paolo, Sarasota, Seattle, St Louis, St Maarten, Tampa/St Petersburg, Toronto, Washington Dulles, Washington National, West Palm Beach.
From Honolulu to Guam, Johnston Island, Kosrae, Kwajalein, Los Angeles, Majuro, New York Newark, Pohnpei, San Francisco, Tokyo Narita, Truk.
From Guam to Sapporo, Denpasar Bali, Fukuoka, Hong Kong, Johnston Island, Kaohsung, Koror, Kosrae, Majuro, Manila, Nagoya, Osaka, Saipan, Sendai, Seoul, Taipei, Tokyo Narita, Truk, Yap.

Passenger miles pa: 41,914 million

Passengers pa: 38.3 million

Annual turnover: US $6,360 million (£3,855 million)

LINKS WITH OTHER AIRLINES
Code-share with Air Canada.
Marketing alliance with Air Micronesia (qv).

FLEET
33 Boeing 727-200
13 Boeing 737-100
18 Boeing 737-200
65 Boeing 737-300
37 Boeing 737-500
25 Boeing 757-200
12 Boeing 767-300

5 Boeing 777
28 McDonnell Douglas DC-9-30
1 McDonnell Douglas DC-10-10
16 McDonnell Douglas DC-10-30
6 McDonnell Douglas MD-81
56 McDonnell Douglas MD-82
6 McDonnell Douglas MD-83

CONTINENTAL EXPRESS

Continental Express, Inc

Incorporated: 1987

HISTORY
A wholly-owned subsidiary of parent airline Continental Airlines (qv), Continental Express was formed in 1987 following Continental's acquisition of a regional carrier, People Express. The initial services included not only those of People Express, but also of some earlier regional acquisitions, including part of the route network of Frontier Airlines, while People Express itself had acquired Britt Airways and PBA the year before its acquisition.

The airline has grown rapidly and now operates feeder services from Continental's three main hubs at Houston, Cleveland, and New York Newark. The fleet has grown to around a hundred aircraft, with a substantial number of Embraer EMB-145 regional jets being introduced in 1997, providing improved comfort and faster sector times as well as offering greater flexibility between Continental and Continental Express services on some 'long and thin' routes.

Continental Express has a small fleet of ATR 72s.

The Embraer EMB-145, for which Continental Express has almost 200 options, has brought jet speeds and comfort to many feeder routes.

The slightly unusual shape of the Beech 1900D's fuselage is intended to provide greater headroom.

Executive Directors & Officers: David Siegel, President; Jerry Losness, Chief Operating Officer; Bob Brayton, Vice-President, Flight Operations; John Prestifilipo, Vice-President, Maintenance; Leon Kinloch, Vice-President, Marketing; Chuck Coble, Vice-President, Airport Services.

HQ Airport & Main Base: Houston, with hubs at Cleveland and New York Newark. Maintenance at Qualitron Hangar, Houston.

Radio callsign: CONTINENTAL

Designator: CO/COA

Employees: Flight-crew: 930; Cabin staff: 330; Engineering: 297; Ground staff: 585; Administration and sales: 236; Total: 2,378.

Main destinations served: Houston to Alexandria, Baton Rouge, Beaumont/Port Arthur, Brownsville, Bryan College Station, Corpus Christi, Gulfport/Biloxi, Harlingen, Houston/Ellington Field, Houston/Hobby Field, Jackson, Killeen, Lafayette, Lake Charles, Little Rock, McAllen, Memphis, Monroe, Monterrey, Shreveport, Tyler, Waco.
Cleveland to Akron, Albany, Allentown, Atlantic City, Buffalo, Cincinnati, Columbus, Detroit, Erie, Flint, Fort Wayne, Grand Rapids, Greensboro, Hartford, Kalamazoo, Knoxville, Lansing, Lexington, Louisville, Milwaukee, Minneapolis, Norfolk, Pittsburgh, Raleigh/Durham, Richmond, Rochester, Saginaw, South Bend, Syracuse, Toledo, Washington Dulles, White Plains, Wilkes Barre/Scranton, Youngstown.
New York Newark to Albany, Allentown, Atlantic City, Baltimore, Bangor, Binghampton, Buffalo, Burlington, Charlottesville, Harrisburg, Hartford/Springfield, Hyannis, Ithaca, Manchester (Kentucky), Martha's Vineyard, Milwaukee, Nantucket, New Haven, New York La Guardia, Philadelphia, Portland, Providence, Richmond, Roanoke, Rochester, Savannah, Syracuse, Washington Dulles, Washington National, Wilkes Barre/Scranton, Worcester.

Aircraft miles pa: 1,750.6 million

Passenger miles pa: 904 million

LINKS WITH OTHER AIRLINES
Wholly-owned subsidiary of Continental Airlines, using that airline's colour scheme and flight designators.

FLEET
25 Embraer EMB-145 (plus options for 175)

32 Embraer EMB-120 Brasilia
38 ATR 42
3 ATR 72
25 Beech 1900D
All aircraft are owned, although some
additional EMB-145s may be leased.

CORPORATE AIR

Corporate Air, Inc

HISTORY
Corporate Air is a regional feeder specialising in charter and scheduled light freight
and packages, with its scheduled operations feeding into the Federal Express (qv)
network. For the airline's size, a very wide
variety of aircraft is operated.

Executive Directors & Officers:
Michael Overstreet, Chairman; Linda
Overstreet, President; Roger Gray,
Director, Operations; Robert McIver, Vice-
President, Flight Operations; Jim
Savastano, Vice-President, Maintenance.

HQ Airport & Main Base: Billings Logan
International Airport, Montana

Radio callsign: AIR SPUR

Designator: DN/CPT

LINKS WITH OTHER AIRLINES
Federal Express feeder carrier.

FLEET
1 Douglas DC-4
9 Douglas DC-3
2 Fokker F-27-600 Friendship
1 Convair 580
1 Convair 340
3 Shorts 360
3 Shorts 330
4 Embraer EMB-110 Bandeirante
4 de Havilland DHC-6-300 Twin Otter
1 Beech 1900C
2 Beech 99A
1 Cessna 414 Chancellor
17 Rockwell Aero Commander
4 Piper PA-31 Navajo Chieftain

DELTA AIR LINES

Delta Air Lines, Inc

Incorporated: 1924

HISTORY
Today one of the world's largest airlines,
and third largest in the United States, Delta
was originally founded not as an airline
but as a crop spraying company. Its
history dates from the formation in 1924,
at Macon in Georgia, of Huff Daland Crop

Dusters by one C.E. Wolman. This was the
world's first aerial crop-spraying company,
brought into existence to combat the boll
weevil, a persistent pest which frequently
devastated the cotton crop in the southern
United States.

Airline operations started in 1929, after
the company had changed its name to
Delta Air Service. Three Travelaire mono-
planes entered service between Dallas,
Texas, and Jackson, Missouri, on a route
which was later extended to Atlanta,
which became Delta's main base. The
route network grew steadily during the
years up to the outbreak of World War
Two, and a succession of more advanced
aircraft entered service, including Stinson
As and Douglas DC-2s, the immediate predecessor of the famous DC-3.

Post-war, Delta made rapid progress,
aided by three major acquisitions. First of
these was Chicago & Southern Airlines,
which dated from 1934 and passed to Delta
in 1953. Almost 20 years later a more significant acquisition was that of Northeast
Airlines in 1972. Northeast had been
founded in 1933 under the name of Boston-
Maine Airways, using two Stinson trimotors,
and by the time of its acquisition by Delta
possessed a route network stretching from
Montreal in the north to Miami in the south.
The third major acquisition was that of
Western Airlines in 1987, which finally pro-
pelled Delta into the position of third largest
US airline. Western also helped expand
Delta's network on the Pacific coast. Older
than the other two airlines, Western had
been founded in 1925 as Western Air
Express, operating a Douglas M-2 biplane
between Los Angeles and Salt Lake City.

During its early years Delta remained
primarily a North American operator, with
routes throughout the United States and
across the borders into Canada and
Mexico. Expansion into the Caribbean area
followed, and during the 1980s transatlantic operations began to the main
European hubs. A major leap forward
occurred in 1991, when Delta took over no
less than 21 routes from the by then
defunct Pan American World Airways, and
then added a further 17 destinations later
in the year, mainly in Europe. These
moves meant that a seventh US hub was
added to the six then in operation, with
New York JFK joining those at Atlanta,
Cincinnati, Dallas/Fort Worth, Los Angeles,
Orlando, and Salt Lake City. Portland and
a European feeder hub at Frankfurt in
Germany have since followed.

In common with other major carriers,
Delta has franchised smaller regional airlines to provide feeder services into its
major hubs, in this case operating under
the Delta Connection (qv) name.

Executive Directors & Officers: Loe
Mullin, President & Chief Executive;
Gerald Grinstein, Chairman; Maurice
Worth, Chief Operating Officer; Edward
H. West, Controller; Harry C. Alger,
Executive Vice-President, Operations;
Maurice W. Worth, Executive Vice-
President, Customer Service; Thomas J.
Roeck, Senior Vice-President & Chief
Financial Officer; Robert W. Coggin,
Senior Vice-President, General Counsel;
Rex A. McClelland, Senior Vice-President,
Corporate Services; Ray Valeika, Senior
Vice-President, Technical Operations;
Paul G. Matsen, Senior Vice-President,
Corporate Planning; D. Scott Yohe, Senior
Vice-President, Government Affairs; W.E.
Doll, Senior Vice-President, Cargo; Vicki
B. Escara, Senior Vice-President, Airport
Customer Service; Jenny Poole, Senior
Vice-President, Inflight Service; Thomas
Slocam, Senior Vice-President, Corporate
Communications; Robert W. Coggan,
Senior Vice-President, Marketing; Vince
Caminiti, Senior Vice-President, Sales &
International; Robert G. Adams, Senior
Vice-President, Personnel; J.G. Matthews,
Treasurer; Anthony Charaf, Director,
Engine Maintenance; Fred Buttrell,
Director, TOC Materials; J.C. Niscard,
Director, Health Services; R.M. Bell,
Director, Schedule Development; Brenda
Barnes, Director, Investor Relations; D.W.
Blisset, Director, Market Analysis; J.L.
Chapline, Director, Frequent Flyer; W.D.
Berry, Director, Corporate
Communications.

HQ Airport & Main Base: Atlanta, with
additional hubs at Cincinnati, Dallas/Fort
Worth, Frankfurt, Los Angeles, New York
JFK, Orlando, Portland, and Salt Lake
City.

Radio callsign: DELTA

Designator: DL/DAL

Employees: 59,100

Main destinations served: Delta serves
some 200 destinations within the United
States, Canada, and Mexico, plus trans-
atlantic flights to Amsterdam, Athens,
Barcelona, Berlin, Brussels, Bucharest,
Budapest, Copenhagen, Dublin,
Frankfurt, Helsinki, Istanbul, Lisbon,
London Heathrow, Madrid, Manchester,
Munich, Paris CDG, Prague,
St Petersburg, Rome, Shannon, Stuttgart,
Vienna, Warsaw, Zürich.

Annual turnover: US $12,251 million
(£7,425 million)

LINKS WITH OTHER AIRLINES
Delta Connection is Delta's commuter
system.

Code-share with ARIA (qv), Aéroméxico (qv), All Nippon Airlines (qv), Austrian Airlines (qv), Korean Airlines (qv), MALEV (qv), Sabena (qv), Scenic Airlines, Singapore Airlines (qv), Swissair (qv), TAP Air Portugal (qv), Varig (qv), Vietnam Airlines (qv), Virgin Atlantic (qv).

FLEET
15 McDonnell Douglas MD-11
55 Lockheed L-1011 TriStar
33 Boeing 767-300ER
26 Boeing 767-300
15 Boeing 767-200
98 Boeing 757
129 Boeing 727-200 (some will be replaced by 737-700/800 order)
70 Boeing 737-700/800 (in course of delivery)
13 Boeing 737-300
54 Boeing 737-200 (some will be replaced by 737-700/800 order)
31 McDonnell Douglas MD-90-30
120 McDonnell Douglas MD-88

DELTA CONNECTION

HISTORY
Delta Connection is the feeder or commuter operation of Delta Air Lines (qv), feeding into the airline's major hubs. The main carriers participating in the scheme include Atlantic Southeast (qv), Business Express (qv), Comair, and Skywest Airlines (qv).

DHL

DHL Airways, Inc

Incorporated: 1969

HISTORY
Part of the international DHL Group, DHL Airways takes its name from the initials of the three founders – Adrian Dalsye, Larry Hillblom, and Robert Lynn – who established the company originally to expedite the movement of bills of lading between Hawaii and San Francisco. Using the name DHL Worldwide Express, the company is today one of the leading carriers of express cargo and urgent documents world-wide, generally using its own aircraft, and those of subsidiaries such as European Air Transport (qv) in Belgium. Marketing arrangements exist with both Japan Airlines (qv) and Lufthansa (qv), while a joint venture with Sinotrans has

seen the service extended to 26 Chinese centres, in addition to 14 hubs world-wide and another 12 hubs and 76 airports in the United States.

Executive Directors & Officers: Patrick Foley, Chairman, Chief Executive Officer & President; Vic Guinasso, Chief Operating Officer; George Gonzalez, Director, Operations & Transportation; Steve Waller, Senior Vice-President, Field Operations; Bill Smart, Chief Financial Officer.

HQ Airport & Main Base: Cincinnati

Radio callsign: DAHL

Designator: ER/DHL

Main destinations served: Scheduled services from 12 US hubs to 76 airports, plus 14 international hubs world-wide.

LINKS WITH OTHER AIRLINES
Marketing alliances with Japan Air Lines (qv) and Lufthansa (qv).
Joint venture with Sinotrans.
Subsidiaries include European Air Transport (qv).

FLEET
1 Airbus A300B4F (plus 8 on order)
7 McDonnell Douglas DC-8-73F
11 Boeing 727-100C
6 Boeing 727-200
7 Boeing 727-200Adv
10 Fairchild Expediter
1 Learjet 35A
1 Bell JetRanger

EMERY WORLDWIDE

Emery Worldwide Airlines, Inc

Incorporated: 1946

HISTORY
Although founded in 1946 as Emery Air Freight, for more than 30 years Emery used aircraft chartered from other carriers or pre-booked space on scheduled services, before finally operating aircraft on its own account in 1980. In 1989 it was acquired by Consolidated Freightways, whose subsidiary CF Airfreight was merged into Emery Air Freight to create Emery Worldwide. Today, Emery operates as a subsidiary of CNF Transportation.

In common with many air freight carriers, the fleet is comprised mainly of McDonnell Douglas DC-8 and Boeing 727 aircraft converted to the freight role. Almost half the 727 fleet is used on a major US Mail contract.

Executive Directors & Officers: David I. Beatson, President & Chief Executive Officer; William H. Scherrer Jr, Senior Vice-President & Chief Executive Officer EWA; Gary Kowalski, Vice-President, Strategic Planning & Quality; John Coletti, Vice-President, Controller EWA; Peter Quantrill, Vice-President, Europe, Middle East & Africa; Roger Piazza, Vice-President, North America; Chutta Ratnathicam, Vice-President, International; Douglas J. Eoster, Vice-President, Sales & Marketing.

HQ Airport & Main Base: HQ at Redwood City, California, but hubs are at Dayton, Ohio, and Brussels in Belgium.

Radio callsign: EMERY

Designator: EB/EWW

Employees: 900

Main destinations served: Regular scheduled freight services with 580 agents and service centres throughout the US, including those linked by road haulage, and operations into 95 countries world-wide.

FLEET
34 McDonnell Douglas DC-8F (several different types)
50 Boeing 727-100/200F (of which 24 used on US Mail services)

EMPIRE

Empire Airlines , Inc

Incorporated: 1977

HISTORY
Empire Airlines operates cargo and light freight services under contract to organisations needing a regular service, and on ad hoc charters, all primarily within the United States.

Executive Directors & Officers: M.E. Speide, President & Chief Executive Officer; Tom Kammers, Director, Maintenance; Victor Walyters, Vice-President, Operations.

HQ Airport & Main Base: Main base is in Idaho

Designator: EM/CFS

Employees: 140

FLEET
10 Fokker F-27 Friendship
1 Fairchild FH-227
2 Fairchild Metro III
40 Cessna Caravan

ERA

Era Aviation, Inc

Incorporated: 1983

HISTORY
A regional commuter airline, Era participates in the Alaska Airlines (qv) Commuter Service, carrying passengers and cargo out of its main hub at Anchorage, while operations from Bethel form part of the Alaska Airlines Village Service, the latter using de Havilland DHC-6 Twin Otter aircraft.

Executive Directors & Officers: Charles W. Johnson, President; Cathy Antush, Financial Director; James Vande Voorde, Operations Director; Ray Anthony, Maintenance Director; Joseph Sprague, Marketing Director; Karla Grumman, Personnel Director.

HQ Airport & Main Base: Anchorage, with a further hub at Bethel

Radio callsign: ERAH

Designator: 7H/ERA

Employees: 330

Main destinations served: Anchorage to Cordova, Homer, Iliamna, Kenai, Kodiak, Valdez, etc.
  Bethel to small Alaskan communities.

LINKS WITH OTHER AIRLINES
Participates in the Alaskan Airlines (qv) Commuter Service.

FLEET
2 de Havilland Dash 8
5 Convair 580
10 de Havilland DHC-6 Twin Otter
plus 2 EMB-145 on order.

EVERGREEN

Evergreen International Airlines, Inc

Incorporated: 1975

HISTORY
Originally founded in 1924 as Johnson Flying Service, Evergreen adopted its existing title in 1975. Air cargo is carried under contract for other airlines, and ad hoc cargo charters are also available, operating world-wide. Major clients include both the US Mail and United Parcels Service, or UPS (qv). In contrast to many air freight carriers, the fleet is centred around conversions of the Boeing 747.

Executive Directors & Officers: Delford M. Smith, Chairman; Larry K. Lane, President; Ronald A. Lane, Chief Executive Officer, Vice-President, Marketing; Michael Clark, Chief Financial Officer; Peter Smith, Vice-President, Finance; Penn Stohr, Vice-President, Operations; Robert Welch, Vice-President, Maintenance.

HQ Airport & Main Base: Oregon

Radio callsign: EVERGREEN

Designator: EZ/EIA

Employees: 450

Main destinations served: Operations are world-wide, and include a regular New York JFK to Hong Kong service. Most services are ad hoc charter or contract charter for other airlines.

LINKS WITH OTHER AIRLINES
Operates on a contract basis for United Parcels Service, or UPS (qv).

FLEET
8 Boeing 747-100F
4 Boeing 747-200B/C
8 McDonnell Douglas DC-9F

EVERTS AIR FUEL

Everts Air Fuel, Inc

Incorporated: 1980

HISTORY
Everts Air Fuel uses a fleet of veteran, mainly ex-USAF, aircraft to carry fuel to remote locations in both Alaska and Canada. The fleet includes one of the few twin-boom Fairchild Flying Boxcars still operational.

Executive Directors & Officers:
Clifford R. Everts, President; W. Everts, Vice-President.

HQ Airport & Main Base: Fairbanks, Alaska

Employees: 44

FLEET
4 Douglas DC-6
1 Fairchild C-119 Flying Boxcar
4 Curtiss C-46 Commando

EXECUTIVE AIRLINES

Executive Airlines, Inc (AMR American Eagle)

Incorporated: 1989

HISTORY
Originally known as Executive Air Charter, providing corporate aircraft services at San Juan in Puerto Rico, the company moved into regional scheduled services before becoming an American Eagle franchisee in 1986. Three years later it became a subsidiary of AMR American Eagle (qv), since which time the fleet has changed with the disposal of the CASA 212s used on regional services, and the Cessna 402 and two Riley Herons – conversions of de Havilland Herons – used for executive charters. A large fleet of Shorts 360s was built up, but these have now been replaced by ATR 42s and 72s. All aircraft carry American Eagle branding.

Executive Directors & Officers: Thomas del Valle, President; Kevin K. Craig, Vice-President, Finance; Ken Durst, Vice-President Maintenance & Engineering; Jose Machado, Vice-President, Flight Operations; Curt Reimer, Vice-President, Field Services and Marketing.

HQ Airport & Main Base: San Juan

Designator: AA/AAL, with occasional use of NA

Employees: 1,800

Main destinations served: See American Eagle (qv).

LINKS WITH OTHER AIRLINES
Subsidiary of AMR American Eagle, and uses the same flight designators.

FLEET
More than 30 ATR 42/72 aircraft from the American Eagle fleet
11 Shorts 360

EXPRESS

Express Airlines, Inc

Incorporated: 1985

HISTORY
Operating out of its main base at Memphis and another at Minneapolis, Express Airlines is a member of the Northwest Airlink (qv) regional feeder operation for Northwest Airlines (qv). The network has grown so that Express reaches 52 airports spread across 22 states. The company is a subsidiary of Phoenix Airline Services, owned by its President, Michael Brady.

Executive Directors & Officers:
Michael J. Brady, President & Chief Executive Officer; Glenn Schaab, Chief Financial Officer; Terry Harvel, Operations Director; Steve Lutjemeyer,

Maintenance Director; Jeff MacKinney, Senior Vice-President; Jim Wides, Vice-President, Operations; Doug Shockey, Vice-President, Maintenance; Phillip Reed, Vice-President, Marketing.

HQ Airport & Main Base: HQ at Atlanta, with main hubs at Memphis and Minneapolis

Radio callsign: FLAGSHIP

Designator: 9E/FLG

Employees: 1,500

Main destinations served: Services reach 52 cities as part of the Northwest Airlink network.

LINKS WITH OTHER AIRLINES
Member of Northwest Airlink (qv) network.

FLEET
11 Saab 340B
25 Saab 340
22 British Aerospace Jetstream 31

EXPRESS ONE INTERNATIONAL

Express One International, Inc

Incorporated: 1980

HISTORY
Originally founded in 1980 as Jet East International, Express One adopted its current title in 1983. It is primarily a charter cargo carrier specialising in short notice operations, but it also operates under contract to the US Parcels Service from Indianapolis, and to DHL to Brussels. Passenger charters are also available.

Executive Directors & Officers: Alinda H. Wikert, Chairman; James R. Wikert, Chief Executive Officer; Keven Good, President & General Manager; Skip Spence, Operations Director; Bobby Raper, Maintenance Director.

HQ Airport & Main Base: Dallas/Fort Worth, with further bases at Indianapolis, Minneapolis/St Paul, Brussels (Belgium).

Radio callsign: LONGHORN

Designator: EO/LHN

Employees: 500

Main destinations served: Belgium, and destinations throughout North America and the Caribbean.

LINKS WITH OTHER AIRLINES
Operates under contract to DHL (qv) and EAT European Air Transport (qv).

FLEET
15 Boeing 727-200F
5 Boeing 727-100F
5 McDonnell Douglas DC-9-30

FEDERAL EXPRESS

Federal Express, Inc

Incorporated: 1971

HISTORY
The world's largest air freight operator, Federal Express was founded in 1971 by Frederick Smith, who is still Chairman and President today. Operations started two years later, using a fleet of Dassault Falcon 20 business jets to carry documents overnight across the United States. Although a substantial fleet of aircraft and a strong route network was quickly established, the major catalyst in the development of Federal Express, or FedEx as it is often known, was deregulation of the American air cargo market in 1977. Deregulation allowed FedEx to operate larger aircraft, and, building on its existing route network, a fleet of Boeing 727 and McDonnell Douglas DC-10 aircraft was created. In 1986 operations to Europe began with services to London and Brussels.

In 1989 FedEx bought the then largest air cargo operator, Flying Tiger, giving the company an extensive intercontinental operation into Europe, Asia, and South America. The Flying Tiger Line had been founded immediately after the end of World War Two by a group of former USAAF war veterans who had fought as the 'Flying Tigers' in Burma and China. Initially 'Flying Tigers', as the airline was usually known, operated Budd Conestogas, but these were soon replaced by Douglas C-47 Dakotas and C-54 Skymasters retired from US military service. In 1949 Flying Tigers gained authority to operate scheduled cargo services across the United States from coast-to-coast, with its main base being at Los Angeles.

While using large wide-bodied aircraft on the trunk routes, FedEx has not lost its link with small aircraft and the package market, using a very large fleet of some 300 small Cessna Caravan aircraft on feeder services which are operated under contract by the cargo equivalent of the commuter airlines. Operations within specific target markets have often been developed through the acquisition of locally-based package or document carriers, such as Lex Wilkinson in the UK in 1986. Currently the largest aircraft in the fleet are McDonnell Douglas MD-11s, following the run down of the Boeing 747 freighter fleet

with the transfer of the five remaining aircraft to Lufthansa (qv) in 1998.

Executive Directors & Officers:
Frederick W. Smith, Chairman, Chief Executive Officer & President; Alan B. Graf, Executive Vice-President & Chief Financial Officer; Theodore L. Weise, Executive Vice-President, Worldwide Customer Operations; Dennis H. Jones, Senior Vice-President & Chief Information Officer; Joseph C. McCarty, Senior Vice-President, Latin America & Caribbean; T. Michael Glenn, Senior Vice-President, Worldwide Marketing, Customers Services & Corporate Communications; Kenneth R. Masterson, Senior Vice-President, General Counsel & Secretary; David J. Bronczek, Senior Vice-President, Europe, Asia, Pacific; Tracy R. Schmidt, Senior Vice-President, Air Ground Terminal & Transportation; David F. Rebholz, Senior Vice-President, Americas & Caribbean; William Fraine, Senior Vice-President, Global Sales & Trade Services; Gilbert D. Mook, Senior Vice-President, Central Support Services; James A. Perkins, Senior Vice-President & Chief Personnel Officer.

HQ Airport & Main Base: Memphis, with additional hubs at Chicago, Dallas/Fort Worth, Frankfurt, Indianapolis, London Stansted, Los Angeles, Newark, Oakland, Paris, and a gateway at Anchorage.

Radio callsign: FEDEX

Designator: FX/FDX

Employees: 127,000

Main destinations served: Destinations in 210 countries.

LINKS WITH OTHER AIRLINES
Feeder aircraft are operated on behalf of FedEx by a number of airlines, including Baron Aviation (qv), Corporate Air (qv), Mountain Air Cargo, Union Flights, and Wigins Airways.

FLEET
19 McDonnell Douglas MD-11
23 McDonnell Douglas DC-10-30F
13 McDonnell Douglas DC-10-10F
36 Airbus A300-600F
26 Airbus A310-200F
163 Boeing 727F
32 Fokker F-27 Friendship
309 Cessna 208 Caravan

FINE AIRLINES

Fine Airlines, Inc

Incorporated: 1992

HISTORY
Named after its founder, Frank Fine, Fine Airlines carries cargo on scheduled and charter flights from the United States to countries in and bordering the Caribbean.

Executive Directors & Officers: Frank Fine, President & Chief Executive Officer; Terry Sullivan, Financial Director; Tony Philips, Director, Interline; Elvis Brazil, Personnel Director; Barry H. Fine, General Manager & Senior Vice-President; Hector Ponte, Vice-President, Commercial; John D. Zappia, Vice-President, Maintenance; Hugh Nash, Vice-President, Marketing.

HQ Airport & Main Base: Miami

Radio callsign: FINE AIR

Designator: FB/FBF

Employees: 800

Main destinations served: Miami to airports within the Caribbean and bordering countries, including Colombia and Venezuela. Authority has been sought for operations to Peru and Brazil.

LINKS WITH OTHER AIRLINES
Marketing agreements with ATC/Aéro Transcolumbiana de Carga and Aéromar Airlines.

FLEET
4 McDonnell Douglas DC-8-61F
8 McDonnell Douglas DC-8-54F
4 McDonnell Douglas DC-8-51F

FLAGSHIP AIRLINES

Flagship Airlines, Inc

Incorporated: 1987

HISTORY
Originally known as Nashville Eagle, a regional carrier, the company became an American Eagle (qv) franchisee in 1986, and a subsidiary of AMR American Eagle the following year, when the present title was adopted. One of the largest constituent parts of American Eagle, Flagship's aircraft all use the American Eagle branding and flight designators. A large fleet of British Aerospace Jetstream 31s is being replaced by more ATR 42s and SAAB 340Bs.

Flagship's main base is at Nashville, but it also operates from the American Eagle hubs at Miami, New York JFK, and Raleigh/Durham.

Executive Directors & Officers: John Hayes, President; Peggy Arnold, Vice-President, Finance; Ed Criner, Vice-President, Operations; Douglas Shockey, Vice-President, Maintenance; Mark Marudas, Vice-President, Field Services; Tina Mishko, Vice-President, Personnel.

HQ Airport & Main Base: Nashville, with additional hubs at Miami, New York JFK, and Raleigh/Durham.

Radio callsign: FLAG

Designator: AA/AAL, plus occasionally 8N/FSX

Employees: 3,600

Main destinations served: 83 cities on the American Eagle network.

LINKS WITH OTHER AIRLINES
A wholly-owned subsidiary of AMR American Eagle, using their branding and designators.

FLEET
More than 80 AI(I) ATR 42 and SAAB 340B aircraft from the American Eagle fleet.

FLORIDAGULF AIRLINES

FloridaGulf Airlines, Inc

Incorporated: 1991

HISTORY
FloridaGulf Airlines is a wholly-owned subsidiary of Mesa Air Group (qv), and operates feeder services as part of the US Airways Express (qv) system, with aircraft carrying the branding of US Airways (qv) (formerly USAir) and using the same flight designators. All services are operated within the United States, primarily on the eastern seaboard.

Executive Directors & Officers: Dick Paquette, President; Clint McQueen, Vice-President, Passenger Services; Jens Malmbarg, Vice-President, Flight Operations; Brad Kuhns, Vice-President, Maintenance.

HQ Airport & Main Base: Jacksonville, with hubs at Boston, New Orleans, Philadelphia, Orlando, and Tampa.

Designator: US/MAG

Employees: 700

Main destinations served: Atlantic City, Baltimore, Bangor, Baton Rouge, Birmingham, Bridgeport, Charleston, Daytona Beach, Elmire, Fort Lauderdale, Fort Myers, Fort Walton, Gainesville, Groton, Hagerstown, Hartford, Hyannis, Ithaca, Jackson, Jacksonville, Key West, Lancaster, Lebanon, Little Rock, Marathon, Martha's Vineyard, Manchester, Melbourne, Miami, Monroe, Nantucket, New Haven, New York, Panama City, Pensacola, Preque Isle, Reading, Sarasota, Savannah, Shreveport, Tallahassee, West Palm Beach, Wilkes-Barre, Williamsport.

LINKS WITH OTHER AIRLINES
Wholly-owned by Mesa Air Group, and operates as part of the US Airways Express network.

FLEET
40 Beech 1900D
9 Embraer EMB-120 Brasilia

FOUR STAR AIR CARGO

Four Star Aviation, Inc

Incorporated: 1982

HISTORY
A regional air cargo specialist, Four Star Aviation operates both charters and scheduled cargo services from its base at St Thomas, in the US Virgin Islands. Interline agreements exist with several of the major US airlines, as well as with British Airways (qv) and Lufthansa (qv).

Executive Directors & Officers: J.J. McCarthy, President; Nikki Colon, Director, Operations; Curtis R. White, Vice-President.

HQ Airport & Main Base: HQ at Cyril E. King Airport, St Thomas, US Virgin Islands; main base at San Juan, Puerto Rico.

Radio callsign: FOUR STAR

Designator: HK/FSC

Employees: 45

Main destinations served: San Juan to Boringuen, St Croix Island, St Thomas, Santo Domingo, Tortola.

LINKS WITH OTHER AIRLINES
Interline with American Airways (qv), Arrow Air (qv), British Airways (qv), Continental Airlines (qv), Delta Airlines (qv), Federal Express (qv), Fine Airlines (qv), Lufthansa (qv), and US Airways (qv).

FLEET
4 Convair 440
5 Douglas DC-3

FRONTIER

Frontier Airlines, Inc

Incorporated: 1994

HISTORY
Frontier Airlines operates from the new Denver International Airport, and was formed to take advantage of a massive reduction in flights to and from that airport by Continental Airlines (qv). During 1997 a merger was agreed with Western Pacific (qv), but was called off three months later.

Executive Directors & Officers: B. Larae Orullian, Chairman; Sam Addoms, President & Chief Executive Officer; Elissa Potucek, Controller & Treasurer; Jimmie Wyche, Executive Vice-President, Operations; Wayne Eliot, Engineering Director; Roland Mease, Purchasing Director; John Herschner, Personnel Director; Art Voss, Vice-President & General Counsel; Jon Bartram, Vice-President, Maintenance; William Durlin, Vice-President, Technical; Jeff Potter, Vice-President, Marketing.

HQ Airport & Main Base: Denver

Radio callsign: FRONTIER FLIGHT

Designator: F9/FFT

Employees: 750

Main destinations served: Denver to Albuquerque, Chicago Midway, El Paso, Las Vegas, Los Angeles, Minneapolis, Omaha, Phoenix, St Louis, Salt Lake City, San Diego, San Francisco, Seattle.

LINKS WITH OTHER AIRLINES
Marketing alliance with Continental Airlines (qv).

FLEET
14 Boeing 737-300
2 Boeing 737-200A
5 Boeing 737-200

GREAT AMERICAN

Great American Airways, Inc

Incorporated: 1979

HISTORY
Originally a domestic cargo and passenger charter airline, Great American Airways expanded onto international services in 1993.

Executive Directors & Officers: Ken Damask, Vice-President & General Manager; Richard K. Stephan, Senior Vice-President; Steve Branum, Director, Operations; Jim Nickelson, Director, Maintenance; Robb Steele, Director, Quality Control.

HQ Airport & Main Base: Reno, Nevada

Radio callsign: GREAT AMERICAN

Designator: MV/GRA

Employees: 100

Main destinations served: International and domestic passenger and freight charter operations.

FLEET
3 McDonnell Douglas MD-87
1 McDonnell Douglas MD-82
3 McDonnell Douglas DC-9-15

GREAT LAKES

Great Lakes Aviation, Inc

Incorporated: 1979

HISTORY
Although founded in 1979, Great Lakes Aviation did not commence operations until 1982. The airline soon joined the United Express (qv) network, and in 1995 entered into a marketing alliance with Midway Airlines (qv) under the name of Midway Connection. Some services are also operated under the Arizona Airways Express banner. In addition to the scheduled network, Great Lakes provides passenger and freight charter and fixed base (ie general aviation support) services.

Executive Directors & Officers: Douglas G. Voss, Chairman & Chief Executive Officer; Dick Fontaine, President & Chief Operating Officer, Vice-President, Marketing; Al Maxson, Chief Financial Officer; Kurt Franklin, Director, Maintenance; Jeff Davis, Director, Training & Operations; Sara Sherlock, Director, In-Flight; Dave Thomas, Director, Marketing; Jim Nazaarkewich, Vice-President, Maintenance.

HQ Airport & Main Base: Spencer, Iowa

Radio callsign: LAKES AIR

Designator: ZK, UA, or JI/GLA

Employees: 1,250

Main destinations served: Almost 80 destinations in the upper midwest and south-west USA.

LINKS WITH OTHER AIRLINES
Operates as Arizona Airways Express.

Marketing alliances with Midway Connection (qv) and United Express (qv).

FLEET
30 Beech 1900C
8 Beech 1900D
12 Embraer EMB-120 Brasilia

GULFSTREAM

Gulfstream International Airlines, Inc

Incorporated: 1988

HISTORY
Gulfstream International Airlines was founded in 1988, and operations began in 1991, initially using a Cessna 402 to provide an 'on demand' air taxi service between Miami and Cap Haitien, Haiti. The founder was a former Eastern Air Lines captain, Thomas Cooper, who remains the proprietor and Chief Operating Officer today.

The company has since expanded and provides a network of short scheduled passenger services from points in Florida to the closer Caribbean resort destinations. The fleet includes a mixture of Beech 1900 and Shorts 360 aircraft. A code-share arrangement exists with United Airlines (qv).

Executive Directors & Officers: Thomas L. Cooper, President & Chief Executive Officer; C. Wray, Director, Maintenance; Pete Taggart, Director, System Control; Wayne Modny, Director, Quality Control; L. Leeman, Director, Personnel; Dee Buchanan, Director, In-Flight Services; Doug Wolfe, Director, Stations; Tiffany Thompson, Director, Gulfstream Holidays; Richard M. Draina, Senior Vice-President, Flight Operations; Betty Lerner, Senior Vice-President, Administration; Peter Clements, Senior Vice-President, Training & Safety; Roger F. Larreur, Senior Vice-President, Passenger Service; Pierre Galoppi, Senior Vice-President, Market Planning; Tony Gattone, Senior Vice-President, Sales & Marketing.

HQ Airport & Main Base: Miami, with services also from Orlando and Tampa.

Radio callsign: GULF FLIGHT

Designator: 3M/GFT

Employees: 640

Main destinations served: Freeport, Fort Lauderdale, Gainesville, Jacksonville, Key West, Marsch Harbour, Nassau, North Eleuthera, Tallahassee, Treasure Cay, West Palm Beach.

LINKS WITH OTHER AIRLINES
Code-share with United Airlines (qv).

FLEET
5 Shorts 360
22 Beech 1900C

HAWAIIAN

Hawaiian Airlines, Inc.

Incorporated: 1929

HISTORY
Hawaiian Airlines dates from 1929, when it was formed as Inter-Island Airways, commencing operations on 11 November with flights from Honolulu's John Rodgers Airport, on the island of Oahu, to Maui and Hawaii itself. Given the absence of runways on most of the islands at the time, and a route network almost entirely over water, the choice of aircraft settled on two Sikorksy S-38 eight-passenger amphibians. Schedules were far less frequent than today, with three round trips per week on each of the inaugural routes. Frequencies and destinations increased steadily, nevertheless, and in 1935, with the support of a new inter-island airmail contract, a fleet of 16-passenger Sikorsky S-43s were introduced.

The present title was adopted in 1941, a year during which, almost on the eve of America's involvement in World War Two, Douglas DC-3s were introduced to the fleet. Although most of these aircraft had seating for 24 passengers, the airline became heavily involved with air cargo operations to the other islands following the outbreak of war. All inter-island traffic was placed under military control, and Hawaiian received the first air cargo certificate to be issued by the Civil Aeronautics Board.

Post-war, Hawaiian introduced its first pressurised aircraft, Convair 340s, to the inter-island routes, and in 1958 acquired a Douglas DC-6 for transpacific US military charters. Douglas DC-9 jet airliners were introduced in 1966, reducing many of the sector times on the inter-island routes to just 20 to 30 minutes. The charter market was not overlooked, and in 1984 Hawaiian moved into the long-haul charter market with three McDonnell Douglas DC-8 jet airliners, before later introducing the first scheduled routes outside of the islands, to American Samoa and Tonga. The following year five Lockheed L-1011 TriStars were introduced for long-haul charter and scheduled services, with the first of these to the US West Coast beginning that year when a route was opened to Los Angeles, with San Francisco and Seattle being added to the network early in 1986.

In 1993 Hawaiian agreed to a programme of co-operation with American Airlines (qv), including marketing and technical support, leading to the replacement of the TriStars with McDonnell Douglas DC-10s, maintained by American. More recently the airline has seen Japan Air Lines (qv) take an 8.5 per cent stake in Hawaiian, while Northwest Airlines (qv) has taken a 25 per cent interest, with a marketing agreement signed in 1996.

Executive Directors & Officers: Bruce Nobles, President & Chief Executive Officer; Irving Fluke, Senior Director; Steve van Ribbink, Senior Vice-President, Finance & Chief Financial Officer; Peter Jenkins, Senior Vice-President, Marketing & Sales; Glen L. Stewart, Senior Vice-President, Transpacific; Andrew Availone, Vice-President, Flight Operations; George E. Barnes, Vice-President, Maintenance & Engineering.

HQ Airport & Main Base: Honolulu

Radio callsign: HAWAIIAN

Designator: HA/HAL

Employees: Flight-crew: 281; Cabin staff: 643; Engineering: 300; Ground staff: 802; Administration and sales: 517; Total: 2,543.

Main destinations served: Within the Hawaiian islands, Lihue (Kauai), Kahului (Maui), Hoolehua (Molokai), Lanai, Kona (Hawaii), Hilo (Hawaii).
Kapalua (Maui) served through a code-share with Mahalo Air.
Also Honolulu to Las Vegas, Los Angeles, Papaeete (Tahiti), Pago Pago (American Samoa), Portland, San Francisco, Seattle. There are also charter flights to the US mainland.

Aircraft miles pa: 19 million plus

Passenger miles pa: 3,324 million

Cargo tonne-km pa: 392.4 million

LINKS WITH OTHER AIRLINES
Code-share with American Eagle (qv) and Reno Air (qv).
Northwest Airlines (qv) has a 25 per cent interest, Japan Air Lines (qv) an 8.5 per cent interest.
Marketing alliance with Northwest Airlines.

FLEET
10 McDonnell Douglas DC-10-10
13 McDonnell Douglas DC-9-50

HORIZON AIR

Horizon Air Industries, Inc

Incorporated: 1981

HISTORY
Part of the Alaska Air Group since 1986, Horizon Air dates from 1981, when it was formed as a small regional carrier. Another airline, Air Oregon, was acquired in 1982, allowing Horizon to become one of the largest regional airlines on the north-west Pacific coast of the United States. Further expansion followed in 1984, when

Hawaiian Airlines operates ten McDonnell Douglas DC-10-10s, mainly on routes to the mainland of the United States.

Transwestern was acquired and Horizon introduced its first jet equipment, Fokker F-28 Fellowships.

A marketing alliance exists with Alaska Airlines (qv) – the other major airline in the Alaska Air Group – and with Northwest Airlines (qv). The network now extends north and south of the airline's Seattle base, and includes destinations as far south as California, and north to Canada.

Executive Directors & Officers: George Bagley, Chairman; Thomas Geharter, Senior Vice-President; Glenn S. Johnson, Vice-President, Finance; Art Thomas, Vice-President, General Counsel & Secretary; Daniel Scott, Vice-President, Operations; Jeffrey D. Pinneo, Vice-President, Passenger Service; Kenneth L. Hobby, Vice-President, Maintenance; Patrick F. Zachwieja, Vice-President, Marketing.

HQ Airport & Main Base: Seattle, with additional bases and hubs at Boise, Portland, and Spokane.

Radio callsign: HORIZON AIR

Designator: AS/QXE

Employees: 3,000

Main destinations served: Bellingham, Billings, Bozeman, Butte, Calgary, Edmonton, Eugene, Eureka/Arcata, Great Falls, Helena, Idaho Falls, Kalispell, Klamath Falls, Lewiston, Medford, Missoula, Moses Lake, North Bend, Oakland, Pasco, Pendleton, Pocatello, Port Angeles, Pullman, Redding, Redmond, Sacramento, San Jose, Sun Valley, Twin Falls, Vancouver, Victoria, Walla Walla, Wenatche, Yakima.

Annual turnover: Included in Alaska Airlines figure

LINKS WITH OTHER AIRLINES
Marketing alliances with Alaska Air (qv) and Northwest Airlines (qv).

FLEET
5 Fokker F-28-4000 Fellowship
9 Fokker F-28-1000 Fellowship (leased)
23 de Havilland Dash 8-100 (leased)
25 de Havilland Dash 8-200/300 (leased), plus 45 options
14 Fairchild Metro III

KITTY HAWK

Kitty Hawk Group, Inc

Incorporated: 1976

HISTORY
Kitty Hawk has operated domestic cargo and passenger charter flights within the United States since 1976, when it was formed as Kitty Hawk Airways. In 1997 it was taken over by the Kalitta Group, owners of American International Airlines (qv).

Executive Directors & Officers: Tom Christopher, Chairman & Chief Executive Officer; Tilmon Reeves, President & Chief Operating Officer; James G. Doyle, Director, Business Development; Tej Raj, Vice-President, Operations; Robert Grober, Vice-President, Maintenance.

HQ Airport & Main Base: Dallas/Fort Worth, with an additional base at Detroit.

Radio callsign: AIR KITTY HAWK/CARGO HAWK

Designator: KR/KHA or KHC

Employees: 225

FLEET
6 Boeing 747F
8 Lockheed L-1011 TriStar F
22 Boeing 727-200
5 McDonnell Douglas DC-9-15
11 Convair 600
3 Convair 640

KIWI

Kiwi International Airlines, Inc

HISTORY
Owned by former employees of Pan Am, Midway, and Eastern Airlines, Kiwi operates regional and domestic scheduled and charter air services from its main base at New York Newark. The airline entered Chapter 11 Bankruptcy Protection in 1996, enabling it to continue operations, and emerged in late-1997, announcing a plan to expand the fleet and eventually introduce Airbus A320-200 freighters.

Executive Directors & Officers: Russell Thayer, Chairman; Jerry Murphy, President & Chief Executive Officer.

HQ Airport & Main Base: New York Newark

Radio callsign: KIWI AIR

Designator: KP/KIA

Employees: 1,000

Main destinations served: Atlanta, Chicago, Midway, Orlando, Tampa, West Palm Beach.

LINKS WITH OTHER AIRLINES
Marketing alliance with Air South (qv).

FLEET
16 Boeing 727-200 (leased)

MAHALO

Mahalo Air, Inc

Incorporated: 1994

HISTORY
Originally known as Island Express Air, Mahalo Air operates a fleet of ATR 42 aircraft on routes within the Hawaiian Islands, these aircraft having replaced a fleet of Fokker F-27 Friendships. The airline entered Chapter 11 Bankruptcy Protection in July 1997.

Executive Directors & Officers: Michael D. Yocum, Chairman, President & Chief Executive Officer; Robert Lavesque, Director, Maintenance; William J. Slaz, Vice-President, Finance; Scott Crosier, Vice-President, Operations; Joseph J. Hutchings, Vice-President, Administration; Elizabeth Pape, Vice-President, Customer Service; Douglas Caldwell, Vice-President, Marketing; David T. Querio, Vice-President, Maintenance.

HQ Airport & Main Base: Honolulu

Radio callsign: MAHALO

Designator: 8M/MLH

Employees: 300

Main destinations served: Honolulu to Kahului, Kona, Molokai.

LINKS WITH OTHER AIRLINES
Marketing alliances with Hawaiian Airlines (qv) and Northwest Airlines (qv).

FLEET
7 ATR 42

MESA AIR GROUP

Incorporated: 1980

HISTORY
Mesa Air Group is the holding company for a group of regional airlines, most of which are franchisees for major American airlines, with aircraft carrying the branding and using the flight designators of the larger airlines. One of the constituent airlines, Mountain West, was originally known as Mesa Airlines, but the name was changed to avoid confusion.

The six airline divisions, with their alliances, are: Air Midwest – US Airways (qv); Desert Sun Airlines – America West (qv); FloridaGulf Airlines (qv) – US Airways; Liberty Express – US Airways; Mountain West Airlines (qv) – United (qv) and America West; and WestAir Commuter

Airlines (qv) – United. There are also technical support and pilot training divisions within the group.

Claiming to be the largest independent regional carrier based in New Mexico, in 1997 Mesa introduced 16 Canadair Regional Jets, marking a major advance in the services offered.

Executive Directors & Officers: Larry L. Risley, Chairman & Chief Executive Officer; Clark Stevens, President & Chief Operating Officer; Mike Lewis, President, Mountain West Airlines; Rolly Bergeson, President, WestAir; Bob Dynan, President, Liberty Express; Dick Pacquette, President, FloridaGulf; George Lippemeier, President, Desert Sun; Steve Jackson, Chief Financial Officer; Michael Ferverda, Senior Vice-President, Flight Operations; Arlo Clough, Senior Vice-President, Technical Services; Ben Harrison, Vice-President, Planning & Pricing; Gary Risley, Vice-President, Legal Affairs; Grady Reed, Vice-President, Safety, Sarah Pitcher, Vice-President, Corporate Communications.

HQ Airport & Main Base: Farmington, New Mexico, with hubs at Albuquerque, Boston, Denver, Des Moines, Florida/Southeast, Fresno, Kansas City, Los Angeles, Philadelphia, Pittsburgh, Phoenix, Portland, San Francisco, Seattle.

Radio callsign: AIR SHUTTLE

Designator: YV/ASH, but individual airlines and franchise arrangements may have different designators.

Employees: 4,100

Main destinations served: See individual airlines, but 166 airports are served altogether.

Passengers pa: 6.5 million

LINKS WITH OTHER AIRLINES
Individual airlines code-share and act as regional commuter or express franchisees for America West (qv), US Airways (qv) (formerly USAir) and United Air Lines (qv).

FLEET
21 Jetstream 31 (some of these may have been retired)
118 Beech 1900
10 de Havilland Canada Dash 8
2 Fokker 70
16 Canadair Regional Jet
32 Embraer EMB-120 Brasilia

MIAMI AIR

Miami Air International, Inc.

Incorporated: 1991

HISTORY
Miami Air International was founded in 1991 as a supplemental, or charter, passenger carrier, a type of airline operation which is still less common in the United States than in the United Kingdom and Europe. Operations extend throughout the United States and to some 30 countries. The fleet is standardised on one aircraft type, the Boeing 727-200, which streamlines maintenance and marketing. The airline is privately owned.

Executive Directors & Officers: Ross Fischer, President; George Lyall, Chief Executive Officer; Brian Fitzgerald, Chief Financial Officer; Jim Proia, Director of Operations; Robert Conser, Vice-President, Sales & Marketing.

HQ Airport & Main Base: Miami

Radio callsign: BISCAYNE

Designator: GL/BSK

Destinations Served: Passenger charters, mainly within the United States, Canada and the Caribbean area.

FLEET
7 Boeing 727-200

MIDWAY

Midway Airlines, Inc

Incorporated: 1993

HISTORY
Not to be confused with an earlier airline of the same name based at Chicago Midway which operated between 1976 and 1991, Midway Airlines dates from 1993, and is based at Durham in North Carolina. The airline is a subsidiary of the Zell/Chilmark Fund, which purchased its parent company, Midway Airlines Corporation, in 1994.

Executive Directors & Officers: Jerry Jacob, Chairman; John Selvaggio, President & Chief Executive Officer; Jonathan Waller, Senior Vice-President; Steven Westberg, Chief Financial Officer; Hale Quigley, Director of Training; Teri Steele, Marketing Director; Gina Selvaggio, Human Resources Director; Tom Duffy, Senior Vice-President, Maintenance; Joanne Smith, Senior Vice-President, Marketing; Dave Vance, Vice-President, Operations.

HQ Airport & Main Base: Raleigh/Durham, North Carolina

Radio callsign: MIDWAY

Designator: JI/MDW

Employees: 880

Main destinations served: Raleigh/Durham to Baltimore, Boston, Cancun, Charleston, Columbia, Columbus, Fort Lauderdale, Greenville, Hartford/Springfield, Hilton Head, Jacksonville, Los Angeles, Myrtle Beach, Nashville, New York La Guardia, New York Newark, Norfolk, Orlando, Philadelphia, Tampa, Washington National, West Palm Beach.

LINKS WITH OTHER AIRLINES
Marketing alliances with American Airlines (qv) and Great Lakes Aviation (qv).

FLEET
1 Airbus A320 (plus 4 on order for late-1998 delivery)
12 Fokker 100
plus 10 Canadair CRJ-700 for delivery from 2000

Miami Air operates seven of these Boeing 727-200s on passenger charter services.

MIDWEST EXPRESS

Midwest Express Airlines, Inc

Incorporated: 1984

HISTORY

A subsidiary of Kimberley-Clark through holding company K-C Aviation, Midwest Express has developed a network of services from its main hub at Milwaukee since 1984, and now has additional hubs at Kansas City and Omaha. In recent years the fleet has grown to include smaller aircraft, Beech 1900s, in addition to the McDonnell Douglas DC-9s which have been the mainstay of the airline for most of its existence.

Executive Directors & Officers:
Timothy Hoeksema, President, Chairman & Chief Executive Officer; Roland Breunig, Chief Financial Officer; Daniel Sweeney, Director, Passenger Services; Dennis Crabtree, Senior Vice-President, Operations; Brenda Skelton, Senior Vice-President, Marketing & Customer Services; Rex Kessler, Vice-President, Maintenance.

HQ Airport & Main Base: Milwaukee, with additional hubs at Kansas City and Omaha.

Radio callsign: MIDEX

Designator: YX/MEP

Employees: 1,775

Main destinations served: Appleton, Atlanta, Boston, Cleveland, Columbus, Dallas/Fort Worth, Denver, Fort Lauderdale, Fort Myers, Grand Rapids, Las Vegas, Los Angeles, Madison, Michigan, Missouri, Nebraska, New York, Ohio, Ontario (California), Orlando, Philadelphia, Phoenix, San Diego, San Francisco, Tampa, Toronto, Washington, Wisconsin.

FLEET
16 McDonnell Douglas DC-9-32
2 McDonnell Douglas MD-88
15 Beech 1900

MILLION AIR

Million Air, Inc

Incorporated: 1983

HISTORY

Named after its founders, Ernesto and Juan Million, Million Air is an inter-national and domestic cargo carrier which undertakes ad hoc and contract charters, including charters for other airlines, while scheduled route approvals are held for services from the airline's base at Miami to a number of destinations in South America. The airline received authority for passenger operations in 1991.

Executive Directors & Officers: Juan B. Million, Chairman & Director of Operations; Ernesto Million, President; John F. Bonner, Vice-President & General Manager; Angel D. Tinoco, Director of Maintenance; Lester Lowe, Director of Quality Control.

HQ Airport & Main Base: Miami

Radio callsign: MILL AIR

Designator: OX/OXO

Employees: 175

Main destinations served: Charter destinations within the Americas, while approvals are held for scheduled services from Miami to a number of destinations in South America.

FLEET
1 Lockheed L-1011-200 TriStar freighter
2 McDonnell Douglas DC-8-71
1 McDonnell Douglas DC-8-54F
3 Boeing 707-320F

MOUNTAIN WEST AIRLINES

Mountain West Airlines

Incorporated: 1982

HISTORY

Originally formed as Mesa Airlines, the name was changed to avoid confusion with the different airline operations belonging to the Mesa Air Group (qv). A major advance was the acquisition of most of the scheduled services operated out of Denver by Aspen Airways, another United Express operator, in 1991. Unusually, the airline has three distinct operational identities, operating as Mesa Airlines out of the Albuquerque hub, as America West Express (qv) at Columbus and Phoenix, and as United Express (qv) in Denver and Los Angeles, serving a total of 71 airports, all within the United States. It uses the flight designators of its franchisers when appropriate.

Executive Directors & Officers: Mike Lewis, Vice-President; Micky Moman, Vice-President, Flight Operations; Gary McCracken, Vice-President, Maintenance.

HQ Airport & Main Base: Albuquerque, plus Columbus, Denver, Los Angeles, and Phoenix.

Designator: YV/HP/UA

Employees: 1,390

Main destinations served: See America West Express (qv) and United Express (qv).

LINKS WITH OTHER AIRLINES
Operates regional feeder services for America West (qv) and United Airlines (qv).
Wholly-owned by Mesa Air Group.

FLEET
47 Beech 1900
7 de Havilland Canada Dash 8
10 Embraer EMB-120 Brasilia

NORTHERN AIR CARGO

Northern Air Cargo, Inc

Incorporated: 1956

HISTORY

Claiming to be Alaska's first scheduled air cargo carrier, Northern Air Cargo was founded in 1956 by Robert Sholton and Maurice Carlson, and commenced operations a year later. The route network covers some 30 points throughout Alaska, which, being sparsely populated and having a rugged terrain, is ideal for air transport. For many years Douglas DC-6 freighters have provided the backbone of the fleet, including rare swing-tailed examples. More recently a Boeing 727-100F has also been added.

Executive Directors & Officers: Mary Sholton, President; Rita Sholton, Chief Executive Officer; Marjorie McLaren, Vice-President, Finance; Leonard Kirk, Vice-President, Operations.

HQ Airport & Main Base: Anchorage

Radio callsign: NORTHERN AIR CARGO

Designator: HU/NAC

Employees: 225

Main destinations served: Scheduled operations reach some 30 airfields throughout Alaska, while ad hoc and contract charters are also undertaken.

FLEET
1 Boeing 727-100F
11 Douglas DC-6A
1 Douglas DC-6B (tanker)
2 Douglas DC-6ST (swing tail)

NORTHWEST

Northwest Airlines, Inc

Incorporated: 1926

HISTORY

America's fourth largest airline, Northwest's history dates from 1926, when it was formed as Northwest Airways, not taking the present title until 1934. The airline remained primarily a regional carrier until after World War Two, when expansion saw the route network spread coast-to-coast across the United States and reach destinations in Canada. At this stage the strategy was for international expansion to concentrate on services from the United States to the Far East, and although the airline's legal title remained unchanged, for many years aircraft, advertising, and tickets carried the name 'Northwest Orient'. The first transpacific route operated in 1947, from Detroit and New York through Anchorage and Shemya, in Alaska, to Tokyo, Seoul, Shanghai, and Manila, initially using Douglas DC-4s which were soon replaced by the larger and faster Boeing Stratocruisers.

The ambitious expansion across the Pacific soon ran into trouble. First, in 1949, the conflict between Communist and Nationalist forces in mainland China saw Shanghai dropped from the route. In 1950 the invasion of South Korea by North Korea resulted in services to Seoul being dropped. However, these problems were more than compensated for by Northwest being selected as the prime contractor for the Korean Airlift by the United States Government. The following year a service was introduced to Hong Kong, initially through a connection with a Hong Kong Airways flight.

Reorganisation in 1985 led to the formation of a holding company, NWA, which became the owner of Northwest and a number of other subsidiaries. The following year Northwest took over Republic Airlines, expanding its domestic services within the United States still further. Although Republic itself only dated from 1979, it had been the result of a merger between North Central Airlines (originally founded in 1948 as Wisconsin Central Airlines) and Southern Airways (founded in 1949 and based in Atlanta). Republic had acquired Hughes Airwest in 1980, an airline which had been formed in 1968 as Airwest on the merger of several small airlines and was acquired by the Hughes Air Corporation in 1970.

Northwest expanded onto the North Atlantic in 1979, with a cargo service from New York and Boston to Glasgow Prestwick in Scotland. A few weeks later passenger services were introduced from New York and Detroit to Copenhagen and Stockholm. The following year services to London, Oslo, Hamburg, and Shannon were introduced.

In 1989 Northwest was itself acquired for US $3.65 million by a group of investors, known as Wings Holdings, headed by Alfred Checchi, Gary Wilson, and Fred Malek, but became a publicly-quoted company once again in 1994, with the employees holding a 27 per cent interest and KLM Royal Dutch Airlines (qv) holding 19 per cent, while Alfred Checchi and Gary Wilson, now co-chairmen, still retain 11 per cent. The relationship with KLM, once regarded as a model example of airline co-operation and enjoying anti-trust immunity status from the United States Government, has since fallen foul of disagreements over ultimate control of the airline. These were resolved in 1997 by an agreement that KLM should sell all of its shares in Northwest in four tranches by 2000.

Today, Northwest operates a substantial route network within the United States, plus transpacific and transatlantic routes. Marketing alliances exist with a number of regional airlines who operate feeder or commuter services under the Northwest Airlink (qv) banner.

Executive Directors & Officers: Al Checchi, Co-Chairman; Gary Wilson, Co-Chairman; John H. Dasburg, President & Chief Executive Officer; James P. Reinnoldt, Regional Managing Director, Southeast Asia & China; Mickey Foret, Executive Vice-President & Chief Financial Officer; Michael E. Levine, Executive Vice-President, Marketing & International; Donald A. Washburn, Executive Vice-President, Customer Service & Operations; Joseph E. Francht, Senior Vice-President, Finance & Treasurer; Richard Hirst, Senior Vice-President, General Counsel; John S. Kern, Senior Vice-President, Operations & Safety; Philip Haan, Senior Vice-President, International; David Wookey, Senior Vice-President, Atlantic; H. Clayton Foushee, Vice-President, Flight Operations; Chris Doan, Vice-President, Technical Operations; Joseph D. Vreeman, Vice-President, Engineering & Quality Assurance; Frank Jauregui, Vice-President, Line Maintenance; Jeff McClelland, Vice-President, Planning & Finance-Technical Operations; Marilyn Rogers, Vice-President, Customer Service Ground Operations/Central; William Slattery, Vice-President, Cargo.

HQ Airport & Main Base: Minneapolis/St Paul, with additional hubs at Detroit, Memphis, and Tokyo Narita.

Radio callsign: NORTHWEST

Designator: NW/NWA

Employees: 47,536

Main destinations served: Some 105 cities throughout most of the United States, plus Amsterdam, Bangkok, Beijing, Manila, Frankfurt, Fukuoka, Guam, Hong Kong, Jakarta, London Gatwick, Nagoya, Osaka, Paris, Saipan,

Originally intending to operate in the north-west of the United States, and then across the Pacific, Northwest's Boeing 747-400s can now be seen on both sides of the Atlantic.

Seoul, Shanghai, Singapore, Taipei, Tokyo.

Employees: Flight-crew: 9,000

Annual turnover: US $9,881 million (£5,988 million)

Revenue passenger km pa: 109,822.6 million

Cargo tonne km pa: 3,545.3 million

Passengers pa: 52.7 million

LINKS WITH OTHER AIRLINES
Alliance with KLM Royal Dutch Airlines (qv).
Marketing alliances with Alaska Airlines (qv), Asiana (qv), Eurowings (qv), Hawaiian (qv), Pacific Island Aviation (qv), Air New Zealand (qv), Mahalo Air (qv), and Horizon Air (qv).

FLEET
14 Boeing 747-400
20 Boeing 747-200B
8 Boeing 747-200F
21 McDonnell Douglas DC-10-40
11 McDonnell Douglas DC-10-30
60 Boeing 757-200 (plus 17 on order)
40 Boeing 727-200
8 Airbus A330 (plus 8 on order)
60 Airbus A320-200 (plus 10 on order)
8 McDonnell Douglas MD-80
35 McDonnell Douglas DC-9-50
12 McDonnell Douglas DC-9-40
106 McDonnell Douglas DC-9-30
22 McDonnell Douglas DC-9-10

NORTHWEST AIRLINK

The branding carried by aircraft operating commuter or regional feeder services into the Northwest Airlines (qv) route network. Participating airlines include Express Airlines (qv), Horizon Air (qv), Mesaba Airlines, and Business Express (qv).

PANAM

PanAm, Inc

Incorporated: 1927 and 1993

HISTORY
The old Pan American World Airways, or Pan Am, went into liquidation in 1991 after several years of declining fortunes. The name and trademark were obtained in 1993 by Martin Shugrue and Charles Cobb, and a new airline was created with five Airbus A300B4-200s, operating low-fare services starting with routes from New

York to Los Angeles and San Francisco in 1996, which were soon joined by services from New York to Chicago and Miami.

Pan American World Airways had originally been founded in 1927 as Pan American Airways, when Juan Trippe put two Fokker F-VII/3M trimotors on a route between Key West in Florida and Havana in Cuba, just 90 miles away. A year later the new airline was flying across the Caribbean to South America, using the new Sikorsky S-38 amphibian, the first of many Sikorsky and Boeing aircraft to be designed to meet the airline's requirements. Further expansion into South America came in 1929, when an agreement with the W.R. Grace company led to the formation of a joint venture, Pan American-Grace Airways, or PANAGRA, to develop services to South America, and especially to the west coast. In 1966 PANAGRA was sold to the now defunct Braniff.

Meanwhile, Pan American had retained the famous aviation pioneer, Charles Lindbergh – who had flown the first solo non-stop crossing of the Atlantic – to chart courses for transatlantic and transpacific services. The first flights were in 1935 across the Pacific with the Martin M-130 flying-boat *China Clipper*, and in 1939 across the Atlantic with the Boeing 314 flying-boat *Dixie Clipper*, operating jointly with the Short Empire flying-boats of Imperial Airways, predecessor of British Airways (qv). Post-war, Pan Am became a major force on the North Atlantic, and for many years did not have a domestic network. Instead it acquired American Overseas Airlines in 1950, and acquired significant holdings in airlines in Latin America and the Philippines. A domestic network finally came with the take-over of Miami-based National Airlines.

Pan Am had not been exclusively a flying-boat operator, and in 1933 had introduced the Boeing 247, often regarded as being the first modern airliner. This aircraft persuaded TWA to encourage Douglas to proceed with the DC-1 and its successors. Later, in 1940, Pan Am was one of just two operators of the Boeing 307, the first pressurised airliner, its main rival TWA (qv) being the other. Other 'firsts' attributed to the old Pan Am were the first 'round-the-world' service in 1947, using a Lockheed Constellation, and the first order for an American jet airliner, the Boeing 707, in 1955. The 1980s were to see the airline disposing of assets and reducing its route network, even before the traumatic destruction of a Pan Am Boeing 747 over southern Scotland in late 1988 by a terrorist bomb.

The new PanAm has moved quickly to

consolidate its position in an effort to acquire critical mass. In mid-1996 it made a successful bid for Carnival Air Lines, which had been formed in 1988 following the purchase of Pacific Interstate Airlines. Carnival has been seeking permission to operate between the United States and Lima, in Peru, in addition to its existing network.

Executive Directors & Officers: Charles Cobb, Chairman; Reuben Wertheim, Chairman (Carnival); Daniel Ratti, President; Lew Graham, Chief Financial Officer; Captain Thomas Peters, Vice-President, Operations; Richard Sartini, Vice-President, Maintenance; Hector Burga, Vice-President, Marketing & Sales.

HQ Airport & Main Base: New York and Fort Lauderdale, with further hubs at Miami, West Palm Beach, and New York Newark.

Radio callsign: PANAM

Designator: KW/CAA or PA/PXA

Employees: approx 1,600

Main destinations served: New York to Chicago, Los Angeles, Miami, San Francisco.
Fort Lauderdale/Miami to Aguadilla, Islip, Los Angeles, Nassau, Newburgh, New York Newark, Orlando, Ponce, San Juan, Tampa, White Plains.

LINKS WITH OTHER AIRLINES
Code-share with Iberia (qv) and joint flight with Ladeco (qv), inherited from Carnival, with PanAm having marketing alliances with Icelandair (qv) and Olympic Airways (qv).

FLEET
11 Airbus A300B4
6 Boeing 727-200
9 Boeing 737-400 (leased)
5 Boeing 737-200

PARADISE ISLAND AIRLINES

Paradise Island Airlines, Inc

HISTORY
Paradise Island Airways operates scheduled and charter passenger and freight services from its base at Fort Lauderdale in Florida, as a participant in the US Airways Express (qv) network.

Executive Directors & Officers: Tom Sullivan, Chairman & Chief Executive Officer; John W. Presburg, President &

Chief Operating Officer; Amy Farrington, Financial Director; Bob Peloquin, Vice-President, Operations; Debbie Webb, Vice-President, Sales, Marketing & Administration.

HQ Airport & Main Base: Fort Lauderdale

Radio callsign: PARADISE ISLAND

Designator: PDI

LINKS WITH OTHER AIRLINES
US Airways Express (qv) carrier.

FLEET
6 de Havilland Dash 7

PIEDMONT

Piedmont Airlines, Inc
Incorporated: 1931

HISTORY
Originally founded in 1931 as Henson Aviation, Piedmont was absorbed in 1989 by USAir, predecessor of US Airways (qv), and subsequently became a USAir Express – now US Airways Express (qv) – carrier. Aircraft carry US Airways Express colours and flights use the US Airways Express designators.

Executive Directors & Officers: John F. Leonard, President & Chief Executive Officer; Robert Murrel, Vice-President, Finance; Stephen R. Farrow, Vice-President, Flight Operations; William J. Farmery, Vice-President, Maintenance; Mark W. Fischer, Vice-President, Customer Service.

HQ Airport & Main Base: Salisbury-Wicomico, Maryland

Radio callsign: PIEDMONT

Designator: US/PDT

Employees: 1,643

Main destinations served: More than 40 destinations on the US Airways Express network, from Toronto in Canada to points in Florida, and offshore to the Bahamas.

Annual turnover: Included in figure for US Airways (qv).

LINKS WITH OTHER AIRLINES
Subsidiary of US Airways and participant in US Airways Express network.

FLEET
3 de Havilland Dash 7
46 de Havilland Dash 8-100
10 de Havilland Dash 8-200

POLAR AIR CARGO

Polar Air Cargo, Inc
Incorporated: 1993

HISTORY
Polar Air Cargo provides international freight forwarders and their agents with an all-freight contract scheduled service. The airline was founded in 1993 with just two Boeing 747 freighters, but now has 17. Charter services are available world-wide, while scheduled services are operated within the United States, to Latin America, and across the Atlantic and the Pacific.

Executive Directors & Officers: Edwin H. Wallace, Chairman & Chief Executive Officer; Mark S. West, President; Brian C. Daggett, Chief Financial Officer; Grant Ledford, Vice-President, Operations; Jill Muckenthaler, Controller; Jack T. Kane, Executive Vice-President; Kevin Montgomery, Vice-President, Government & Industry Affairs; Richard Scholl, Vice-President, Maintenance & Engineering; Alex Milovec, Vice-President, Terminal Services; Michael W. English, Vice-President, Asia-Pacific Region; Gary Runyon, Vice-President, Sales, The Americas; Gregory Meadowns, Director, Charter Sales; Lynn Stauffer, Director, System Control; Cathy West, Director, Corporate Communications.

HQ Airport & Main Base: Long Beach

Radio callsign: POLAR TIGER

Designator: PO/PAC

Employees: 475

Main destinations served: Anchorage, Atlanta, Auckland, Buenos Aires, Chicago, Columbus, Hong Kong, Honolulu, Los Angeles, Melbourne, New York JFK, Miami, Moscow, Prestwick, Santiago, Seoul, Singapore, Sydney, Taipei.

FLEET
12 Boeing 747-100F
5 Boeing 747-200F

PSA

PSA Airlines, Inc
Incorporated: 1979

HISTORY
Originally known as Jetstream International Airlines after the aircraft used on the initial regional services, PSA was acquired by USAir in 1988 and adopted its present title in 1995. The airline's operations are fully integrated with those of the US Airways Express (qv) network.

Executive Directors & Officers: Richard Pfennig, President; Albert F. Schroeck, Vice-President, Finance; Timothy J. Keuscher, Vice-President, Operations; Patrick Brady, Vice-President, Maintenance.

HQ Airport & Main Base: Dayton, Ohio

Designator: US/JIA

Employees: 945

Main destinations served:
Akron/Canton, Burlington, Charlotte, Charleston (South Carolina), Charleston (Wyoming), Cincinnati, Columbia, Evansville, Flint, Greenville/Spartansburg, Hartford, Huntsville, Ithaca, Kalamazoo, Knoxville, Lansing, Manchester (Kentucky), New Haven, Philadelphia, Pittsburgh, Portland, Raleigh/Durham, Reading, Richmond, Roanoke, South Bend, Toledo, Tri-City Airport, Fairfax, Washington Dulles, Washington National, White Plains, Williamsport.

Annual turnover: Included in figures for US Airways (qv).

LINKS WITH OTHER AIRLINES
Member of US Airways Express network.

FLEET
30 Fairchild Dornier 328
17 British Aerospace Jetstream 31
3 Embraer EMB-120 Brasilia

REEVE ALEUTIAN

Reeve Aleutian Airways, Inc
Incorporated: 1932

HISTORY
Originally named after its founder when operations began in 1932, Reeve Aleutian Airways adopted its current title in 1951, marking the beginning of scheduled passenger services between Alaska and the Aleutian Islands. Services today include destinations in Alaska, with charter flights further afield.

Executive Directors & Officers: Richard Reeve, Chairman & President; Allyn Wilson, Director, Maintenance; David Tredway, Senior Vice-President, Maintenance; David Jensen, Vice-President, Administration.

HQ Airport & Main Base: Anchorage

Radio callsign: REEVE

Designator: RV/RVV

Employees: 240

Main destinations served: Anchorage to Adak, Attu, Bethel, Cold Bay, Dillingham, King Salmon, Port Hedien, Pribilof Islands, Sand Point, Shemya, Unalska/Dutch Harbor.

LINKS WITH OTHER AIRLINES
Marketing alliance with Alaska Airlines (qv).

FLEET
2 Boeing 727-100QC
3 Lockheed L-188 Electra

RENOWN

Renown Aviation, Inc

Incorporated: 1982

HISTORY
A charter and scheduled cargo operator, Renown Aviation commenced operations in 1982.

Executive Directors & Officers: Captain Terry Cedar, President; Captain John Hutchins, Director, Operations; Kenneth Davis, Director, Quality Assurance; Ronald Simpson, Vice-President, Maintenance.

HQ Airport & Main Base: Santa Maria, California

Radio callsign: RENOWN

Designator: RG/RGS

Employees: approx 90

Main destinations served: Scheduled, contract, and ad hoc cargo charters in the United States and Mexico.

FLEET
1 Lockheed L-188A Electra
1 Lockheed L-188C Electra
4 Convair 580
2 Convair 440
2 Convair 340
4 Convair 240

RYAN INTERNATIONAL

Ryan International Airlines, Inc

Incorporated: 1972

HISTORY
Founded in 1972 as Ryan Aviation by the eponymous Ronald Ryan, the airline established itself as a scheduled and charter operator carrying passengers and cargo before being sold. It was bought back by Ronald Ryan in 1989 and began operations for the US Postal Service from Indianapolis under contract to Emery Worldwide Airlines (qv), using a fleet of Boeing 727s and McDonnell Douglas DC-9s. The DC-9 fleet is now considerably reduced, and further acquisitions may centre around the Boeing 737.

Executive Directors & Officers: Ronald Ryan, President & Chief Executive Officer; Jeffrey Crippen, Executive Vice-President & General Manager; Danny Looney, Vice-President, Operations; Raymond Thomas, Vice-President, Technical Services.

HQ Airport & Main Base: HQ at Wichita, Kansas, with a hub at Indianapolis.

Radio callsign: RYAN INTERNATIONAL

Designator: HS/RYN

Employees: 650

LINKS WITH OTHER AIRLINES
Contractor to Emery Worldwide Airlines (qv).

FLEET
9 Boeing 727-200F
24 Boeing 727-100FL
1 Boeing 737-100
3 McDonnell Douglas DC-9-15

SHUTTLE BY UNITED

United Shuttle, Inc

Incorporated: 1994

HISTORY
United Airlines' (qv) bid to counter growing competition from low cost airlines such as Southwest Airlines (qv), Shuttle by United commenced operations in 1994, and has developed with full employee support. Despite having a head office in Illinois, the main area of business is on the US West Coast, with hubs at Los Angeles, Oakland, and San Francisco. Services are entirely short-haul, and during 1997 United converted its Denver–Phoenix and Denver–Las Vegas routes to Shuttle by United operation, while an entirely new route between Los Angeles and Tucson was introduced.

Executive Directors & Officers: George Chelius, Chairman & Chief Executive Officer; Amoas Kazzaz, President.

HQ Airport & Main Base: Los Angeles, with further hubs at Oakland and San Francisco.

Radio callsign: UNITED SHUTTLE

Designator: UA/UAL

Main destinations served: Boise, Burbank, Denver, Eugene, Las Vegas, Los Angeles, Medford, Oakland, Ontario (California), Phoenix, Portland, Reno, Sacramento, Salt Lake City, San Diego, San Francisco, Santa Barbara, Seattle, Spokane, Tucson.

LINKS WITH OTHER AIRLINES
A wholly-owned subsidiary of United Airlines (qv).

FLEET
23 Boeing 737-300
24 Boeing 737-500

SIERRA PACIFIC

Sierra Pacific Airlines, Inc

Incorporated: 1976

HISTORY
Sierra Pacific was founded as a charter carrier, and acquired by Mountainwest Aviation – not to be confused with Mountain West Airlines (qv), part of Mesa Air Group (qv) – in 1978. Mountainwest adopted the Sierra name for the merged operations in 1981. The airline is owned by its President, G.M. Thorsrud.

Executive Directors & Officers: G.M. Thorsrud, President; Captain A. Adyono, Director.

HQ Airport & Main Base: Tucson, Arizona

Radio callsign: SIERRA PACIFIC

Designator: SI/SPA

FLEET
2 Boeing 737-200
4 Convair 580

SIMMONS AIRLINES

Simmons Airlines, Inc (AMR American Eagle)

Incorporated: 1974

HISTORY
America's largest regional airline, Simmons Airlines was formed in 1974 and

started operating regional services in 1978. It became an American Eagle (qv) franchisee in 1986, and was acquired by AMR American Eagle two years later. In 1992, Simmons acquired the assets and services of Metroflight Airlines from the Metro Airlines holding company. Metroflight had earlier (1990) taken over the operations of Chaparral. Since becoming part of AMR American Eagle, Simmons's fleet has been standardised, losing its Embraer Bandeirantes, while the large fleet of Shorts 360s which Simmons and the other American Eagle airlines once operated have now been replaced by a mixture of AI(R) 42s and 72s, and Saab 340s.

Executive Directors & Officers: Peter Piper, President; John Boyd, Vice-President, Finance; Lance McDonald, Vice-President, Flight Operations; Dave Ewing, Vice-President, Airline Services; Charles Rathbun, Vice-President, Maintenance & Engineering; Tricia Frank, Vice-President, Marketing.

HQ Airport & Main Base: Dallas/Fort Worth, with a second hub at Chicago O'Hare.

Designator: AA/AAL, and occasionally MQ

Main destinations served: 52 airports on the American Eagle network.

Passengers pa: 2.9 million

LINKS WITH OTHER AIRLINES
A wholly-owned subsidiary of AMR American Eagle, whose branding and flight designators are used.

FLEET
27 ATR 42
30 ATR 72
11 SAAB 340A
24 SAAB 340B
These aircraft are included in the total given for American Eagle.

SKYWEST

Skywest Airlines, Inc

Incorporated: 1972

HISTORY
Skywest originally started as a small air charter and air taxi company, with a fleet which included four-seat single-engined Piper Cherokee Arrows. The move into scheduled services came in 1974, since when the airline has developed into a strong regional carrier. It acquired its first Embraer EMB-120 Bandeirante aircraft in

Operating as a Delta Connection member, Skywest has ten Canadair Regional Jets in service.

1987, and this type now constitutes the backbone of its fleet.

Acquisitions of other airlines have speeded Skywest's growth, including SunAir of Palm Springs in 1984, and Scenic Airlines of Las Vegas in 1993. In many ways Scenic's history parallels that of Skywest, although dating from 1967 when it had a single five-seat aircraft. In 1969 Scenic introduced the first automated air tour narration system, and in 1981 was the pioneer of aircraft simulators for regional aircraft. It is now the largest sightseeing aircraft operator in the world, carrying up to half-a-million passengers annually in a fleet of Cessnas and Twin Otters, with the latter modified with larger windows than the standard aircraft.

Whilst maintaining its independence, Skywest itself has followed the majority of airlines of its type in the United States by establishing operational and marketing alliances with major airlines, in this case with Delta (qv), which has a 15 per cent interest, operating as the 'Delta Connection' at Salt Lake City; and with Continental (qv) at Los Angeles, operating as the 'Continental Connection'. In each case, Delta DL and Continental CO designators are used on these flights.

The airline has accelerated many of its services with the recent introduction of the new Canadair Regional Jet from both of its hubs, which also provide opportunities for operating longer distance services.

Executive Directors & Officers: Jerry C. Atkin, Chairman, President & Chief Executive Officer; Bradford R. Rich, Vice-President, Finance; Rob B. Reber, Chief Operating Officer; Michael J. Kraupp, Vice-President, Controller; Brad Holt, Vice-President, Flight Operations; Michael Gibson, Vice-President, Maintenance; Steven L. Hart, Vice-President, Market Development; Eric D. Christensen, Vice-President, Planning; Dale Merrill, Vice-President, Human Resources.

HQ Airport & Main Base: St George, with maintenance at Salt Lake City, and hubs at Salt Lake City and Los Angeles.

Radio callsign: SKYWEST

Designator: OO/SKW

Employees: Flight-crew: 542; Cabin staff: 280; Engineering: 238; Ground staff: 871; Administration and sales: 211; Total: 2,142.

Main destinations served: Salt Lake City to Albuquerque, Billings, Boise, Bozeman, Butte, Casper, Cody, Colorado Springs, Elko, Grand Junction, Helena, Idaho Falls, Jackson Hole, Las Vegas, Lewiston/Clarkston, Missoula, Pasco, Pocatello, Portland, Rapid City, Reno, St George, San Francisco, Sun Valley, Tucson, Twin Falls, Vancouver, Vernal, West Yellowstone.
Los Angeles to Bakersfield, Burbank, Fresno, Imperial/El Centro, Monterey, Ontario (California), Orange County, Palm Springs, Phoenix, Sacramento, San Diego, San Jose, San Luis Obispo, Santa Barbara, Santa Maria, Yuma.

Annual turnover: US $232.7 million (£141 million)

Aircraft miles pa: 1,371 million

Passenger miles pa: 703.3 million

Cargo pa: 3.9 million lbs (1.8 million kg)

LINKS WITH OTHER AIRLINES
Code-sharing with Delta Airlines (qv) as 'Delta Connection' and with Continental Airlines (qv) as 'Continental Connection.' Delta has a 15 per cent interest in Skywest.

Skywest owns Scenic Airlines of Las Vegas.

FLEET
50 Embraer EMB-120 Brasilia (33 leased)
10 Canadair Regional Jets (leased)

SOUTHERN AIR TRANSPORT

Southern Air Transport, Inc

Incorporated: 1947

HISTORY
Formed in 1947, Southern Air Transport is a specialised air cargo operator, operating on ad hoc and contract charters to take outsize items of freight to areas where surface transport would be impractical. A more recent addition to the company's operations has been the low-level spraying of chemical dispersents and insecticides. Operations are for forwarders, businesses, other airlines, and governmental and international relief and aid agencies. The fleet includes 14 Lockheed L-100 Hercules, able to operate with the minimum of ground support.

During the late-1980s the airline purchased Lockheed's Hercules flight training centre at Marietta in Georgia.

Executive Directors & Officers: James H. Bastian, Chairman; William G. Langton, President; David P. Mulligan, Executive Vice-President; Michael M. Hartley, Senior Vice-President, Operations; Stephen J. Van Gordon, Senior Vice-President, Technical Services; Asa C. Hemperley, Senior Vice-President, Sales; Robert Mason, Vice-President, Finance; Larry Twitchell, Vice-President, Flight Operations; John L. Palo, Vice-President, Defense Programs & Government Relations; Kenneth O. Wilson, Vice-President, Technical Services; Crystal Bergstrom, Vice-President, Sales; Garry Eakins, General Counsel.

HQ Airport & Main Base: Rickenbacker Airport, Columbus, Ohio

Radio callsign: SOUTHERN AIR

Designator: SJ/SJM

Employees: 600

Main destinations served: Worldwide charters.

FLEET
4 Boeing 747-200F
14 Lockheed L-100 Hercules
3 McDonnell Douglas DC-8-73F
1 McDonnell Douglas DC-8-71F

SOUTHWEST

Southwest Airlines Corporation

Incorporated: 1971

HISTORY
The largest low fares airline – the fastest growing sector in air transport – in the world, Southwest Airlines dates from 1971, and today is the eighth largest American airline. It was originally formed as Air Southwest, but the present title was adopted before operations commenced. A fleet of three Boeing 737-200s, surplus because of the recession, were obtained at a discount, and operated the 'Texas triangle' routes, linking Dallas Love Field, Houston, and San Antonio. Flights to Houston were eventually concentrated on the old Houston Hobby Airport, neglected by the larger airlines, while the airline fought a successful battle to continue using Dallas Love Field, despite pressure from airport operators and the airline industry to move to the then new Dallas/Fort Worth.

The fleet remained at three for the first two years, after a fourth aircraft had to be returned due to restrictions on the airline flying charters outside Texas, but a fourth aircraft finally joined the fleet in 1974. The route network also started to grow, with the Rio Grande Valley being added in 1975, and Corpus Christi, Lubbock, Midland/Odessa, El Paso, and Austin in 1977, during which the fleet doubled from five to ten aircraft, still standardising on the Boeing 737-200. A Boeing 727-200 was leased from Braniff for two years in 1978, while the route network grew to include Dallas and Amarillo. The rate of growth continued to accelerate into the 1980s, including an order for ten new Boeing 737-300s, while more Boeing 727-200s were leased before being replaced by the new 737-300s. By the end of 1984 the airline was operating 54 aircraft.

Southwest acquired a competitor, Muse Air, in 1985, renaming it TranStar Airlines the following year, operating a fleet of McDonnell Douglas MD-80 series aircraft. Unfortunately TranStar passed into liquidation in 1987.

Despite its rapid growth, even as late as 1988 Southwest was still inaugurating services to airports abandoned by other airlines, and in that year it became the first airline in more than 40 years to operate into Detroit City Airport. Sadly, five years later the airline had to move to the other Detroit airport because promised runway improvements were not made.

Southwest is the world's largest low fare airline, with more than 260 aircraft, including this Boeing 737-300, of which almost 200 are in service.

A further acquisition came in 1993, when Morris Air Corporation of Salt Lake City, another 737 operator, was acquired. By this time Southwest was operating 178 aircraft.

Today, Southwest Airlines has survived more than a quarter of a century of low cost air travel, and outlived rivals such as Braniff, which in its early days had attempted to undercut the new airline. The fleet is highly standardised on Boeing 737s, and the airline is the launch customer for the new generation 737-700, which may replace some of the older 737-200s. Southwest claims to have been the pioneer of ticket-less air travel.

Executive Directors & Officers: Herbert D. Kelleher, Chairman, President & Chief Executive Officer; Gary A. Barron, Vice-President, Chief Operations Officer; Gary C. Kelly, Vice-President, Finance; Alan S. Davis, Vice-President, Internal Audit; Paul E. Sterbenz, Vice-President, Flight Operations; Luke J. Gill, Vice-President, Maintenance & Engineering; James C. Wimberley, Vice-President, Ground Operations; John G. Denison, Vice-President, Corporate Services; Carolyn R. Bates, Vice-President, Reservations; Colleen C. Barrett, Vice-President, Customers; Dave Ridley, Vice-President, Marketing & Sales; Ginger C. Hardage, Vice-President, Public Relations & Corporate Communications.

HQ Airport & Main Base: Dallas Love Field, with hubs at Chicago Midway, Houston Intercontinental, Oakland, and Phoenix.

Radio callsign: SOUTHWEST

Designator: WN/SWA

Employees: 22,944

Main destinations served:
Albuquerque, Amarillo, Austin, Baltimore, Birmingham, Boise, Burbank, Chicago Midway, Cleveland, Columbus, Corpus Christi, Dallas Love Field, Detroit Metropolitan, El Paso, Fort Lauderdale, Harlingen, Houston Hobby, Houston Intercontinental, Indianapolis, Jacksonville, Kansas City, Las Vegas, Little Rock, Los Angeles, Louisville, Lubbock, Midland/Odessa, Nashville, New Orleans, Oakland, Oklahoma City, Omaha, Ontario (California), Orange County, Orlando, Phoenix, Portland, Providence, Reno, Sacramento, St Louis, Salt Lake City, San Antonio, San Diego, San Francisco, San Jose, Seattle, Spokane, Tampa, Tucson, Tulsa.

Annual turnover: US $3,406 million (£2,064 million)

Passenger miles pa: 27,083 million

Passengers pa: 49.6 million

FLEET
43 Boeing 737-200
191 Boeing 737-300
25 Boeing 737-500
4 Boeing 737-700
(of the above, 120 are owned and the remainder are leased)
There are outstanding orders for a further 46 Boeing 737-600/700/800 aircraft, with options for a further 63 737-600/700/800s.

SPIRIT

Spirit Airlines, Inc

Incorporated: 1992

HISTORY
A domestic passenger operator, Spirit Airlines commenced operations in 1992 and is now moving into scheduled operations.

Executive Directors & Officers:
Edward Homfeld, President; Robert Moreland, General Manager; Mark Kahan, Executive Vice-President, Marketing; Victoria Moreland, Senior Director, Sales & Services.

HQ Airport & Main Base: HQ is at Eastpointe, Michigan

Radio callsign: SPIRIT WINGS

Designator: NK/SWG

Employees: 450

Main destinations served: Resort destinations in continental United States.

FLEET
4 McDonnell Douglas DC-9-40
5 McDonnell Douglas DC-9-30
1 McDonnell Douglas DC-9-20

SUN COUNTRY

Sun Country Airlines, Inc

Incorporated: 1983

HISTORY
Originally formed in 1983 by employees of the former Braniff Airways, Sun Country is a charter or supplemental passenger and cargo airline, with some scheduled operations, which was acquired by the Minnesota Corporation in 1988. Operations extend to destinations in Canada, Mexico, and the Caribbean countries, as well as within the United States.

Executive Directors & Officers: John Barry, Chairman; Gregory Smith, Vice-Chairman; John Skiba, President & Chief Executive Officer; Thomas Schmidt, Chief Financial Officer; John Thomas, Vice-President, Operations; Charley Beers, Vice-President, Maintenance; Mike Finney, Vice-President, Military Operations & Planning; Glenn Nording, Vice-President, Cargo; Dale Kariya, Vice-President, Customer Service; Karl Freienmuth, Chief Administrative Officer.

HQ Airport & Main Base:
Minneapolis/St Paul

Radio callsign: SUN COUNTRY

Designator: SY/SCX

Employees: 1,100

FLEET
2 McDonnell Douglas DC-10-10
3 McDonnell Douglas DC-10-15
10 Boeing 727-200

TOLAIR

Tolair Services , Inc

Incorporated: 1981

HISTORY
Tolair commenced operations in 1981, initially with just one Cessna 182 for the movement of packages and other urgent light cargo. Today it operates scheduled and charter cargo services from San Juan in Puerto Rico, using a varied fleet of Douglas, Convair, Beech, and Cessna aircraft. The airline is owned by Jorge Toledo and Lisa Rossello.

Executive Directors & Officers: Jorge R. Toledo, Chairman & President; Lisa L. Rossello, Executive Vice-President & Chief Financial Officer; Stanley Santiago, Maintenance Director.

HQ Airport & Main Base: San Juan, Puerto Rico

Radio callsign: TOLAIR

Designator: TOL

Employees: 63

Main destinations served: Caribbean and southern United States.

FLEET
3 Convair 240
5 Douglas DC-3
3 Beech 18
1 Fairchild Metro II
5 Cessna 402

TOWER AIR

Tower Air, Inc

Incorporated: 1982

HISTORY
Tower was formed to take over the passenger services of Metro International Airways, which had operated from New York to Tel Aviv via Brussels, with the new airline's first flights to these cities in 1983. Today it operates international and domestic scheduled and charter flights for passengers and cargo.

Executive Directors & Officers: Morris Nachtomi, Chairman & Chief Executive Officer; Michael Savage, Chief Financial Officer; Bill Cain, Vice-President, Maintenance; Chris Frankel, Vice-President, Marketing; Anne Aktabowski, Vice-President, Ground Operations.

HQ Airport & Main Base: New York JFK

Radio callsign: TEE AIR

Designator: FF/TOW

Employees: 1,400

Main destinations served: New York JFK to Amsterdam, Berlin, Bombay, Cologne, Los Angeles, Miami, Paris, San Juan, Tel Aviv, plus charters.

FLEET
8 Boeing 747-100
2 Boeing 747-100F
8 Boeing 747-200B

TRANS AIR LINK

Trans Air Link, Inc

Incorporated: 1979

HISTORY
Miami-based Trans Air Link operates both scheduled and chartered freight flights.

Executive Directors & Officers: Gary Balnicki, President; Gary Naumer, Director of Operations.

HQ Airport & Main Base: Miami International

Radio callsign: SKY TRUCK

Designator: TY/GJB

Employees: 60

Main destinations served: Miami International to Freeport, Nassau, St Croix, St Maarten, St Thomas, San Juan, plus charters.

FLEET
1 Douglas DC-7CF
4 Douglas DC-6

TRANS STATES AIRLINES

Trans States Airlines, Inc

Incorporated: 1982

HISTORY
Originally founded as Resort Air, Trans States Airlines became a franchised regional feeder for TWA (qv) in 1985, using TWA's designators. The Trans World Express operations of Airmidwest were acquired in 1991, and in 1995 the airline took over the operations of Trans World Express, the renamed Pan Am Express acquired by TWA four years earlier.

Executive Directors & Officers: Hulas Kanodia, President; Gerald Wigmore, Vice-President, Finance; Craig Tompkins, Vice-President, Flight Operations; Al Blosse, Vice-President, Maintenance; Rick Leach, Vice-President, Customer Service; William R. Mishk, Marketing Director.

HQ Airport & Main Base: St Louis

Radio callsign: WATERSKI

Designator: 9N/LOF or TW/TWA

Employees: approx 1,000

Main destinations served: Baltimore, Birmingham, Bloomington, Boston, Burlington, Cape Girardeau, Cedar Rapids, Champaign, Chicago Meigs Field, Chicago Midway, Columbia, Decatur, Evansville, Fayetteville, Fort Smith, Fort Leonard Wood, Fresno, Hartford, Joplin, Knoxville, Lexington, Lincoln, Louisville, Memphis, Madison, Marion, Moline, Paduca, Peoria, Quincy, Sioux City, South Bend, Springfield City, Waterloo.

LINKS WITH OTHER AIRLINES
Operates Trans World Express network for TWA (qv), as well as having marketing alliances with Air Alaska (qv), Northwest Airlines (qv), and US Airways (qv).

FLEET
8 ATR 42
3 ATR 72
32 British Aerospace Jetstream 31
25 British Aerospace Jetstream 41

TWA TRANS WORLD

Trans World Airlines, Inc

Incorporated: 1930

HISTORY
With a history dating back to 1925, Trans World Airlines – or TWA, as it is more usually called – is the seventh largest United States Airline. The earliest of TWA's predecessors, Western Air Express, was formed in 1925 to take advantage of the opportunities offered when Congress passed the so-called Kelly Act, which allowed US Mail contracts to be let to privately-owned companies, having up to then been operated by the United States Post Office. Competition for the early contracts was intense, with more than 5,000 applicants, and Western was one of just five companies to be successful in winning a contract, being awarded the route between Los Angeles and Salt Lake City, a distance of 575 miles. A variety of equipment was operated on the route during the early years, including the Douglas Cruiser biplane and Fokker trimotors.

Amongst the other American airlines operating at the time were Maddux Airlines, flying Fokkers from Los Angeles to San Diego and San Francisco, and Transcontinental Air Transport, or TAT, an airline formed in 1929. TAT operated an early trans-USA rail and air service, and retained Charles Lindbergh – who had flown the first solo crossing of the Atlantic – as a consultant. Control of Maddux passed to Transcontinental in 1929, while Western Air Express acquired Standard Airlines, another Los Angeles operator. It was in 1930 that TAT-Maddux and part of Western Air Express merged to form Transcontinental and Western Air Express, which soon became known as 'TWA', even though it was to be another 20 years before the present title was adopted. The other part of Western Air Express became Western Airlines, for many years a major operator in North America.

Unlike Pan American, or Pan Am (qv), its rival for many years, TWA's development was initially confined to domestic routes, and – again in contrast to Pan Am – TWA concentrated on landplane operation rather than flying-boats or amphibians. Spurred on by the challenge presented by Pan AM's purchase of Boeing 247 landplanes, TWA pressed Douglas to pursue an alternative, the DC-1 and DC-2. TWA operated both the Douglas DC-2, generally regarded as being one of the first modern airliners, and its more famous successor, the DC-3, before becoming, in 1940, the first to fly the world's first pressurised airliner, the Boeing 307 Stratoliner, of which just ten were built (five each for TWA and Pan Am) before the demands of wartime production and operation saw production stopped. This aircraft gave TWA its first experience of over-water operation, as the aircraft and their TWA crews were pressed into war service.

Before the outbreak of World War Two, TWA had also co-operated with Lockheed on a new long distance airliner, the Constellation, and this aircraft saw the airline inaugurate its first intercontinental service in 1946, between New York and Paris with a refuelling stop at Shannon in Ireland. Reflecting the growing sphere of operation, the airline's name was changed to Trans World Airlines in 1950.

Throughout the 1950s TWA continued to develop, introducing the Lockheed Super Constellation and subsequently embracing the jet age with the Boeing 707 and, on domestic routes and European feeder services in the 1960s, the 727, so that at one time the airline was the world's largest operator of Boeing aircraft. Later, Lockheed L-1011 TriStars were introduced and, on short-haul routes, Douglas DC-9s, followed by the McDonnell Douglas MD-80 series.

In 1979 the airline was acquired by the Trans World Corporation, only to be sold in 1984, when TWA once again became an autonomous company. Eighteen months later, in September 1985, TWA was taken over by a New York investor, Carl Icahn, who acquired 52 per of the airline's shares.

In common with many of the older-established US airlines, TWA then passed through a difficult period. The difficulties partly reflected the economic cycle of the air transport industry, but also the difficulties in competing on international routes against airlines in Europe, and elsewhere, which were in state-ownership and, at the time, often-heavily subsidised by their taxpayers. TWA survived these problems, even though many of its contemporaries could not. Some of its services, including some into London, were sold. In addition the airline twice sought Chapter 11 Bankruptcy Protection (equivalent to British Administration) in four years, before finally emerging from this in 1995 after a financial restructuring which saw TWA employees receive some 30 per cent of the airline's shares in return for wage and benefit concessions.

Despite these difficulties, the airline managed to make progress. In 1991 TWA acquired Pan Am Express from the liquidator of its old rival, renaming the operation Trans World Express and boosting feeder services into the New York JFK and La Guardia hubs. The new subsidiary had started life as Ransom Airlines in 1967, and between 1970 and 1982 had operated as part of the Allegheny Commuter System. Between 1984 and 1986 it became a franchisee of Delta (qv), under the 'Delta Connection' branding, before being bought by Pan Am

and renamed Pan Am Express in 1986. At the time of its acquisition by TWA, the airline was operating 11 AI(R) ATR 42s, eight British Aerospace Jetstream 31s, and eight de Havilland Canada Dash 7s. TWA, meanwhile, had already established a 'Trans World Express' operation, using the franchised services of seven smaller airlines, including Trans State Airlines (qv), who took over the routes of TWA's new acquisition when it ceased operations in November 1995.

Today, TWA operates a comprehensive network of services out of its main hubs at New York JFK and St Louis, serving more than a hundred US domestic destinations and a transatlantic network serving Europe and the Middle East.

Executive Directors & Officers: Gerald Gitner, Chairman & Chief Executive Officer; David Kennedy, Chief Operations Officer; Michael Palumbo, Senior Vice-President, Finance & Chief Financial Officer; Rod Brandt, Senior Vice-President, Marketing & Planning; Charles Thibaudeau, Senior Vice-President, Employee Relations; William Compton, Vice-President, Operations; Scott Gibson, Vice-President, Corporate Affairs & Strategy; Rich Roberts, Vice-President, Operations; Renee Vischer, Vice-President, Maintenance & Engineering.

HQ Airport & Main Base: St Louis, with a second major hub at New York JFK

Radio callsign: TWA

Designator: TW/TWA

Employees: 25,000

Main destinations served: Over 100 US destinations plus an extensive transatlantic network to Europe and the Middle East.

Annual turnover: US $3,554 million (£2,154 million)

LINKS WITH OTHER AIRLINES
Trans States Airlines (qv) operates the Trans World Express network.

FLEET
39 Boeing 727-200
10 Boeing 747-100
4 Boeing 747-200B
20 Boeing 757-200
12 Boeing 767-200
2 Boeing 767-300
11 Lockheed L-1011 TriStar
58 McDonnell Douglas DC-9
30 McDonnell Douglas MD-82
23 McDonnell Douglas MD-83
10 Airbus A330

UNITED AIRLINES

United Airlines, Inc

Incorporated: 1934

HISTORY
At one time the largest airline in the free world, United is today the world's, and America's, second largest airline in terms of sales. In common with many of the oldest airlines, United can trace its history back to the merger of several of the early pioneering airlines, of which Varney Air Lines was the first, formed in 1926. Varney's initial operations were providing feeders to the transcontinental air mail service, at that time operated by the US Mail. The small Swallow biplanes used by Varney were limited to the carriage of mail.

The other three airlines which were eventually to form United had also been created for the transfer of air mail to private contractors, and all dated from 1927. Boeing Air Transport, owned by the eponymous aircraft manufacturer, had been awarded the contract for San Francisco–Chicago, National Air Transport received Chicago–New York, and Pacific Air Transport operated the Seattle–Los Angeles feeder service. Boeing hastened its latest commercial design, the 40A, into service for the air mail contract, and using this aircraft could accommodate passengers as well as mail. The next step forward for these services were Boeing and Ford Trimotor aircraft capable of carrying up to 14 passengers, and these arrived in 1929. The following year Boeing introduced stewardesses and meal service on its flights.

The first steps towards consolidation had already occurred by this time, with Boeing taking over Pacific Air Transport as early as 1928, as a step towards single carrier operation of the transcontinental service, and in 1930 it also acquired both Varney and National. A new company, United Aircraft and Transport, was formed to manage the merged airlines in July 1931, and this soon acquired a fifth company, Stout Airlines, with services from Detroit to Chicago and Cleveland. In 1933, the year that Boeing introduced the 247 – the first twin-engined, all-metal low-wing airliner – an Act of Congress forbade the grouping of manufacturing and operating interests: The following year saw United Airlines, although at first known as United Air Lines, founded as an independent company, completely divorced from Boeing.

In its first year the new airline suffered a major setback, with the loss of several of

One of the world's largest airlines, United has almost 40 Boeing 777s in service or on order.

its US Mail contracts as these were put out to fresh tender. Nevertheless, United managed to continue its expansion throughout the 1930s and into the early-1940s, until the outbreak of World War Two slowed progress from late-1941 onwards. Nevertheless, United soon renewed its growth once hostilities ended, and in 1946 introduced its first route away from the continental United States with a service to Hawaii. Six years earlier the Civil Aeronautics Board had forbidden a proposed merger between United and Western Airlines, but in 1946 United took over Western's Los Angeles–Denver route.

As befits a major airline, United can claim a number of firsts in its history. In 1947 it was first with the Douglas DC-6 pressurised airliner, a development of the earlier unpressurised DC-4. It was also first with the earliest Douglas jet airliner, the DC-8, in 1959, and again with the Super DC-8, or DC-8-61 series, in 1967. In between, United was first with the Boeing 720 in 1960 and the 727 in 1962, while being the first and only American airline to operate Sud Aviation's Caravelle jet airliner, which it introduced in 1961. Most recently, it was the launch customer for the Boeing 777, which it introduced in 1995.

Another major development in 1961 saw United acquire Capital Airlines, another major American carrier, which was in financial difficulties after very protracted negotiations with United, lasting some years, over the terms of a merger.

The scale of the merger can be judged by the fact that Capital, despite its problems, immediately boosted United's annual sales figure by 25 per cent. Just as United had been the sole United States purchaser of the Caravelle, Capital had been the sole purchaser of the Vickers Viscount, the world's first successful turboprop airliner (although Trans Canada, predecessor of Air Canada (qv), also had a large fleet of this aircraft), and the merger bought almost 50 of these into the United fleet.

The difficulties facing other airlines at different periods contributed to United's further growth in the post-war period. A major expansion by United came with the acquisition in 1986 of Pan American's historic Pacific Division, the subject of much pioneering in long-distance over-water flights during the late-1930s. It was also in 1986 that United introduced United Express (qv), using the services of a number of regional airlines to provide feeder services into United's hubs, of which the most important was Chicago. Other hubs also developed, aided in 1991 by the acquisition of Pan American's Latin American network, with United commencing operations to Latin America out of Los Angeles, Miami, and New York JFK in 1992. Operations to the Caribbean and then to South America had been behind the formation of Pan Am in 1927, and reinforced by the absorption of the joint venture airline PANAGRA (Pan American-Grace Airways) in 1966, and by the Miami-based National Airlines in 1979, which had

effectively given Pan Am a domestic route network for the first time.

One of the United Express operators was Air Wisconsin (qv), which United bought in January 1992. This was sold again some 18 months later to Air Wisconsin's present management team. The airline remains a United Express carrier.

Although United was spared many of the traumas experienced by the other 'first generation' major United States airlines, in 1994 a majority of its employees took a 55 per cent shareholding in return for concessions on working practices. The airline took this opportunity to launch a low cost operation, Shuttle by United (qv), which it is intending to build up to 130 aircraft, as a counter to the growing number of new low cost operators.

Today, United is the world's largest employee-owned business, and carries more passengers on a greater number of international flights than any other United States airline. Even so, it serves more than a hundred destinations within the United States, in addition to a large number of international destinations, although a number of these are reached through code-sharing arrangements with other airlines, such as Air Canada (qv) and Ansett Australia (qv). It is a founder-member of the 'Star Alliance', which brings together frequent flyer programmes and other services for Air Canada (qv), Lufthansa (qv), SAS (qv), Thai International (qv) and, in 1997, Varig (qv), as well as United.

Executive Directors & Officers: Gerald Greenwald, Chairman & Chief Executive Officer; John A. Edwardson, President & Chief Operating Officer; Joseph R. O'Gorman, Executive Vice-President, Operations & Administration; Stuart I. Oran, Executive Vice-President, Corporate Affairs & General Counsel; Douglas A. Hacker, Senior Vice-President & Chief Financial Officer; Hart A. Langer, Senior Vice-President, Flight Operations; Rono J. Dutta, Senior Vice-President, Planning; David A. Coltman, Senior Vice-President, Marketing; Christopher D. Bowers, Senior Vice-President, International; James E. Goodwin, Senior Vice-President, North America; Sara A. Fields, Senior Vice-President, Onboard Service; William Hobgood, Senior Vice-President, People; Andrew P. Studdert, Senior Vice-President & Chief Information Officer; Amaos Kazzar, Vice-President, Shuttle by United; Louis J. Mancini, Vice-President, Engineering & Technical Support; Donald U.D. Utecht, Vice-President, Line Maintenance; John D. Kiker, Vice-President, Corporate Communications.

HQ Airport & Main Base: Chicago O'Hare, with additional hubs at Denver, San Francisco, and Washington Dulles.

Radio callsign: UNITED

Designator: UA/UAL

Employees: Flight-crew: 9,053; Cabin staff: 20,670; Engineering: 25,906; Ground staff: 34,724; Total: 90,353.

Main destinations served: Almost a hundred domestic destinations, plus the following international cities: Abu Dhabi, Adelaide, Amman, Amsterdam, Antigua, Antofagasta, Arica, Auckland, Bandar Seri Begawan, Bangkok, Beijing, Belo Horizonte, Berlin, Bonn, Brisbane, Brunei, Brussels, Budapest, Buenos Aires, Cairns, Cairo, Calgary, Canberra, Caracas, Cardenas, Christchurch, Cologne, Concepción, Copenhagen, Copiapo, Curaçao, Delhi, Dubai, Düsseldorf, Frankfurt, Freeport, Geneva, Gothenburg, Governor's Harbour, Grand Cayman, Guatemala City, Guayaquil, Hamburg, Hannover, Helsinki, Hong Kong, Huatulco, Jeddah, Kiev, Kingston, Kuala Lumpur, Kuwait, Lazaro, La Serena, Lima, London Heathrow, Madrid, Manila, Marsh Harbour, Melbourne, Mexico City, Milan, Montego Bay, Monterrey, Montevideo, Morelia, Munich, Naples, Nassau, Nice, Osaka, Oslo, Panama City, Paris, Perth, Phuket, Port Moresby, Prague, Puerto Montt, Punta Arenas, Queretaro, Quito, Rio de Janeiro, Rome, St Kitts, Saipan, Salina Cruz, San Jose, San Luis Potosi, San Salvador, Santiago, São Paulo, Seoul, Shanghai, Singapore, Sydney, Taipei, Tokyo, Toronto, Trinidad, Vancouver, Vienna, Wellington, Zürich, plus Halifax, Ottawa, and Quebec City code-shared with Air Canada (qv).

Annual turnover: US $16,362 million (£9,916 million)

Revenue passenger km pa: 186.56 billion

Cargo tonnes pa: 2.53 billion

Passengers pa: 81,639,185

LINKS WITH OTHER AIRLINES
Star Alliance member with Air Canada (qv) (including code sharing), Lufthansa (qv), SAS (qv), Thai International (qv), and Varig (qv).
Marketing alliances with Ansett Australia (qv), Emirates (qv), and Royal Brunei (qv).
Owns Shuttle by United.
Several airlines operate under the United Express (qv) banner.

FLEET
30 Boeing 747-400 (plus 17 on order)
9 Boeing 747-200
12 Boeing 747-100
26 Boeing 777-200 (plus 10 on order)
25 McDonnell Douglas DC-10-10
4 McDonnell Douglas DC-10-30
4 McDonnell Douglas DC-10-30F
19 Boeing 767-200
25 Boeing 767-300ER (plus 6 on order)
92 Boeing 757-200
40 Airbus A320 (plus 11 on order)
75 Boeing 727-200
14 Airbus A319 (plus 14 on order)
60 Boeing 737-200
101 Boeing 737-300
57 Boeing 737-500

UNITED EXPRESS

United Express

Incorporated: 1986

HISTORY
United Express first appeared in 1986, and is the franchise for airlines operating regional and feeder services into United Airlines (qv) main hubs. The airlines involved are independent of United ownership, and include companies in the Mesa Airlines (qv) Group, as well as Air Wisconsin (qv), Atlantic Coast (qv), and Great Lakes (qv). Full details are found under these airlines.

Main hubs: Denver, Los Angeles, Portland, San Francisco, and Seattle.

Radio callsign: UNITED

Designator: UA/UAL

FLEET
34 Beech 1900D
10 de Havilland Canada Dash 8
20 Embraer EMB-120 Brasilia
21 British Aerospace Jetstream 31

UPS

United Parcels Service, Inc

Incorporated: 1988

HISTORY
One of the world's largest parcel and package delivery operations, with a scheduled network to some 200 countries, UPS first ventured into the air express parcels service in 1929, operating on the West Coast of the United States until 1931. The company did not return to air transport until 1953, when it established a two-day 'UPS-Air' service between major American cities using aircraft belonging to other operators. In 1981 UPS entered the next day overnight market, using its own aircraft but with crews provided by other operators, before finally establishing its own airline in 1988. The original two-day 'UPS-Air' service has now been rebranded as '2nd Day Air delivery', as an economy option to the 'Next Day Air' delivery service.

The current fleet includes Boeing and McDonnell Douglas aircraft, but the large number of new Boeing 757 and 767 aircraft entering service or on option suggests that the older Boeing 727 and McDonnell Douglas DC-8 fleets may be replaced in due course.

Executive Directors & Officers: Tom Weidemeyer, President & Chief Operating Officer; Edwin H. Reitman, President, UPS Europe; Steve Staruch, Personnel Director; Pete Dalmares, Vice-President, Finance; John Beystehner, Vice-President, Operations; Jerry Coyle, Vice-President, Maintenance; Don Herbert, Vice-President, Marketing; Doug Kuelpman, Vice-President, Public Affairs.

HQ Airport & Main Base: Louisville, with additional hubs at Cologne/Bonn, Dallas, Hamilton, Hong Kong, Miami, Montreal, Ontario (California), Philadelphia, and Singapore.

Radio callsign: UPS

Designator: 5X/UPS

Employees: 335,000 (includes handling and ground transport staff; Aircrew: 1,850.

Main destinations served: Major airports in some 200 countries, plus an extensive feeder network.

FLEET
15 Boeing 747-200F
20 Boeing 767-300F (plus 30 options)
65 Boeing 757-200F (plus 41 options)
52 McDonnell Douglas DC-8
51 Boeing 727-100QF
8 Boeing 727-200C

US AIRWAYS

US Airways, Inc

Incorporated: 1939

HISTORY
US Airways changed its name from USAir in 1997, the latest in many changes of name since its formation in 1939 as All American Aviation. The name was changed first to Allegheny Airlines in 1953, and to USAir in 1979. The original airline was founded to operate air mail feeder and delivery services in Pennsylvania, Maryland, and West Virginia, but after World War Two it developed a strong network of passenger and cargo services, helped by a number of significant acquisitions including Lake Central Airlines in 1968, Mohawk Airlines – which had introduced the British Aerospace One-Eleven to North America – in 1972, Piedmont Airlines in 1988, and Pacific Southwest Airlines in 1989.

The parent company, the USAir Group, also owns a number of smaller airlines, and these form the core of US Airways Express (qv), the airline's regional feeder operation, which also includes a number of franchised airlines.

US Airways has had a difficult recent history, attempting to follow the other major airlines in cutting costs. British Airways (qv) acquired a 24 per cent stake in 1993, but the relationship has been uneasy and BA has disposed of its shareholding, preferring instead to press ahead with an alternative arrangement with American Airlines (qv). During 1997 the airline cut a number of unprofitable routes and reduced its fleet by 22 aircraft.

A major element in the USAir Group portfolio of airlines is the US Airways Shuttle (qv), which shares the branding of US Airways, although not the flight designators as yet. There is the possibility that

this might be sold to American Airlines (qv). Meanwhile US Airways is attempting to launch a 'low fare, no frills' operation, provisionally known as US2, subject to the agreement of the unions.

The fleet includes aircraft of Boeing, McDonnell Douglas, and Fokker manufacture, with a very ambitious order for 120 Airbus A320 and options for up to 280 more. This suggests that the fleet will become increasingly standardised, possibly with the older McDonnell Douglas DC-9s and then the older Boeing 737-200s being replaced by the A320s as these arrive.

Executive Directors & Officers:
Stephen M. Wolf, Chairman & Chief Executive Officer; Rakesh Gangwal, President; Lawrence M. Nagin, Executive Vice-President & General Counsel; John W. Harper, Chief Financial Officer; W. Thomas Lagow, Executive Vice-President, Marketing; Robert Oaks, Senior Vice-President, Operations; Robert Fornaro, Senior Vice-President, Planning.

HQ Airport & Main Base: HQ is at Arlington, Virginia, with operational bases/hubs at Baltimore, Charlotte, Philadelphia, and Pittsburgh.

Radio callsign: US AIR

Designator: US/USA

Employees: 42,000

Main destinations served: Domestic network, including US Airways Express operations, reaches almost 200 airports, plus an international network which includes Athens, Bermuda, Cancun, Frankfurt, Grand Cayman, London Gatwick, London (Ontario), Madrid, Munich, Ottawa, Paris, Rome, St Maarten, Toronto.

Annual turnover: US $8,142 million (£4,935 million) including other airline operations of the USAir Group.

LINKS WITH OTHER AIRLINES
US Airways Express (qv) network, US Airways Shuttle (qv).

FLEET
12 Boeing 767-200ER
34 Boeing 757-200
54 Boeing 737-400
85 Boeing 737-300 (plus 40 on order)
64 Boeing 737-200A
31 McDonnell Douglas MD-80
72 McDonnell Douglas DC-9-30
40 Fokker 100
13 Fokker F-28-4000
plus orders and options for up to 400 Airbus A320

US AIRWAYS EXPRESS

This is the commuter/feeder operation of US Airways (qv), and includes four airlines within the USAir Group – Allegheny Commuter (qv), Piedmont (qv), PSA (qv), and Metrojet – as well as Air Midwest, CCAIR (qv), Chautauqua (qv), Commutair, Florida Gulf (qv), Liberty Express, and Paradise Island Airlines (qv).

US AIRWAYS SHUTTLE

Shuttle, Inc

Incorporated: 1992

HISTORY
US Airways Shuttle was the pioneer of the 'no booking' shuttle service which has since been emulated by British Airways (qv) and Air France (qv). The origins of the service lay with the now defunct Eastern Air Lines, who founded the service in 1964. After Eastern's demise, the service was sold in 1988 by Eastern's parent, the Texas Air Group, to millionaire Donald Trump, who renamed it the Trump Shuttle and re-commenced operations in 1989. USAir Group bought the operation in 1992, but there has been speculation in the industry that the operation might be sold to American Airlines (qv).

A fleet of Boeing 727 aircraft is dedicated to the service.

Executive Directors & Officers: Terry V. Hallcom, President & Chief Executive Officer; Michael Kopya, Operations Director; Paul Marks, Marketing Director.

HQ Airport & Main Base: New York La Guardia

Radio callsign: US SHUTTLE

Designator: TB/USS

Employees: 620

Destinations served: New York La Guardia to Washington National; New York La Guardia to Boston.

Annual turnover: Included in US Airways (qv) figure.

LINKS WITH OTHER AIRLINES
Part of the USAir Group, parent of US Airways and US Airways Express (qv).

FLEET
12 Boeing 727-200
1 Boeing 727-100

USA JET

USA Jet Airlines, Inc

Incorporated: 1979

HISTORY
A subsidiary of the Active Aero Group, USA Jet Airlines operates an on-demand cargo charter service, as well as contract operations for major companies, including the Ford Motor Company.

Executive Directors & Officers: Martin R. Goldman, President & Chief Executive Officer; David B. Hermelin, Senior Vice-President; Brian Hermelin, Chief Operating Officer.

HQ Airport & Main Base: Willow Run Airport, Belleville, Michigan, with subsidiary hubs at El Paso, Little Rock and Memphis.

Radio callsign: JET USA

Designator: U7/JUS

Employees: 320

FLEET
26 McDonnell Douglas DC-8-60
7 McDonnell Douglas DC-9-15F
15 Dassault Falcon 20

VALUJET

See AirTran Airlines

VANGUARD

Vanguard Airlines, Inc

Incorporated: 1994

HISTORY
A relatively new regional airline operating scheduled passenger services from Kansas City.

Executive Directors & Officers: John Tague, Chairman, President & Chief Executive Officer; Bill Garrett, Chief Financial Officer; Irene Goosley, Operations Director; Randy Smith, Marketing Director; Bill McKinney, Vice-President, Operations; Ron McClennan, Vice-President, Maintenance; Steve Schlaghter, Vice-President, Marketing.

HQ Airport & Main Base: Kansas City

Radio callsign: VANGUARD AIR

Designator: NJ/VGD

Employees: 453

Main destinations served: Kansas City to Atlanta, Chicago Midway, Dallas/Fort Worth, Denver, Des Moines, Fort Myers, Las Vegas, Los Angeles, Miami, Minneapolis/St Paul, Orlando, San Francisco, Tampa, Wichita.

FLEET
2 Boeing 737-300
9 Boeing 737-200

VISCOUNT

Viscount Air Service, Inc

Incorporated: 1980

HISTORY
A passenger charter airline, Viscount Air Service has continued operations since seeking Chapter 11 Bankruptcy Protection in 1996.

HQ Airport & Main Base: Tucson, Arizona

Radio callsign: VISCOUNT AIR

Designator: VCT

FLEET
1 Boeing 727-200
1 Boeing 727-100
11 Boeing 737-200

WESTERN PACIFIC

Western Pacific Airlines, Inc

Incorporated: 1994

HISTORY
Originally founded as Commercial Air, Western Pacific (or WestPac) is a low fare scheduled passenger and cargo airline based at Colorado Springs. A fleet of Boeing 737s is expanding rapidly. A merger was agreed with Frontier Airlines (qv) during 1997, but was called off three months after the initial agreement.

Executive Directors & Officers: Edward R. Beauvais, Chairman; Richard Peiser, President & Chief Executive Officer; George Leonard, Chief Financial Officer & Vice-President; Carl Lowman, Financial Director; Roger Gray, Maintenance Director; Timothy D. Komberec, Vice-President, Flight Operations; Nolan Wiley, Vice-President, Maintenance; Donald Applegart, Vice-President, Information Technology; Martin Wax, Vice-President, Purchasing; Glenn Goldberg, Vice-President, Human Resources.

HQ Airport & Main Base: Colorado Springs

Radio callsign: KOMSTAR

Designator: W7/KMR

Employees: 1,400

Main destinations served: Colorado Springs to Atlanta, Chicago Midway, Dallas/Fort Worth, Houston, Indianapolis, Kansas City, Los Angeles, Miami, New York Newark, Oklahoma City, Orlando, Phoenix, Portland, San Diego, San Francisco, Seattle, Tulsa, Washington Dulles.

LINKS WITH OTHER AIRLINES
Mountain Air Express is a subsidiary.

FLEET
21 Boeing 737-300

WINGS WEST AIRLINES

Wings West Airlines, Inc (AMR American Eagle)

Incorporated: 1981

HISTORY
Originally starting operations as a regional airline in 1981, Wings West soon grew a network which covered the seven western states, and in 1986 joined the American Eagle (qv) system. The airline became a wholly-owned subsidiary of AMR American Eagle in 1989, and since then the network has expanded beyond the original seven states. The fleet at one time included almost 30 British Aerospace Jetstream 31s, but is now highly standardised with more than 40 Saab 340Bs.

Executive Directors & Officers: Robert Cordes, President; Paula Dooley, Vice-President, Finance; Mike Lewis, Vice-President, Operations; Gene Hahn, Vice-President, Maintenance & Engineering.

HQ Airport & Main Base: San Luis Obispo, California

Designator: AA/AAL, while RM is occasionally used

Employees: 1,400

Main destinations served: 33 cities on the American Eagle network, mainly in California, Alabama, Arkansas, Louisiana, Mississippi, Missouri, Nevada, Tennessee, and Texas.

LINKS WITH OTHER AIRLINES
Wholly-owned subsidiary of AMR American Eagle, whose branding and designators are used.

Marketing alliances with Reno Air (qv) and Canadian Airlines International (qv).

FLEET
41 SAAB 340B (included in the list for American Eagle).

WORLD AIRWAYS

World Airways, Inc

Incorporated: 1948

HISTORY
World Airways is a major US supplemental, or charter, airline. Originally formed in 1948, it was not immediately successful, amassing liabilities of US $250,000 by 1950, when it was bought by Edward Daly for just US $50,000 (£17,540 at the time). Starting with a fleet of two twin-engined Curtiss C-46 transports, the airline mainly concentrated on military charter work, expanding so that by 1962 the original fleet had grown to eight Douglas DC-6s and 11 Lockheed Constellations. With the advent of jet equipment during the early-1960s, the airline expanded onto North Atlantic charter operations for the inclusive tour holiday market, and by 1969 the fleet comprised eight Boeing 707-373s and six Boeing 727QCs, the latter being rapid conversion passenger/cargo aircraft.

In 1979 World Airways introduced scheduled low fare transcontinental air services, linking New York Newark and Baltimore/Washington DC with Los Angeles and Oakland. Further scheduled expansion arose in 1981, with services from New York/Newark to London Gatwick and Frankfurt, and the US domestic network was extended to include Honolulu. Three years later Edward Daly, who controlled 81 per cent of the airline's capital, died. In the years following his death the airline saw a period of retrenchment, closing down the scheduled services in September 1986, even though these comprised the bulk of its business by that time, and concentrating instead on freight charter work. Today it handles both passenger and freight charters, including contract and ad hoc work, as well as wet-leasing activity. Customers for contract passenger services include Philippine Airlines (qv) and VASP (qv).

Executive Directors & Officers: T. Coleman Andrews, Chairman; Charles W. Pollard, President; Ahmad Khatib, Deputy President; Ralph Masino, Financial Director; Michael Savage, Chief Financial Officer; Katherine Larson, Marketing Director; Vance Fort, Senior Vice-President, Government & Legal Affairs;

Joseph J. Shallcross, Senior Vice-President, Technical Services; Peter Villano, Vice-President, Flight Operations; Jim Smith, Vice-President, Maintenance; Sandy Rederer, Vice-President, Marketing; Bob Perry, Vice-President, Sales & Schedule Planning; Joe Fralick, Vice-President, Cargo Sales/Service; Steve Berger, Vice-President, Passenger Sales/Service; Howard Thrall, Vice-President, Asian Sales.

HQ Airport & Main Base: New York Newark

Radio callsign: WORLD

Designator: WO/WOA

Employees: 800

Main destinations served: Ad hoc and contract charters, and wet-lease operations.

LINKS WITH OTHER AIRLINES
The Malaysian registered company MHS Berhard Holdings, part of Malaysian Airlines (qv), owns 17 per cent of World Airways.

FLEET
2 McDonnell Douglas MD-11ER
2 McDonnell Douglas MD-11CF
1 McDonnell Douglas MD-11F
4 McDonnell Douglas MD-11 (2 leased to Philippine Airlines, 2 to VASP)
6 McDonnell Douglas DC-10-30F (1 leased to VASP)

ZANTOP

Zantop International Airlines, Inc

Incorporated: 1972

HISTORY
Named after the founding family, Zantop was formed in 1972 as a contract cargo airline, with its main market in the motor industry in the United States. In 1978 Zantop was allowed to operate ad hoc cargo charters throughout the United States, and two years later moved into scheduled cargo services, acquiring the air cargo operations of Hawaiian Airlines (qv). Zantop itself was taken over by American International Airlines in 1994.

Executive Directors & Officers: Duane A. Zantop, Chairman; James Zantop, President; Peter Howarth, Executive Vice-President; Robert Weir, Vice-President, Operations; Edward Bahn, Vice-President, Maintenance.

HQ Airport & Main Base: Willow Run Airport, Ypsilanti, Michigan

Radio callsign: ZANTOP

Designator: VK/ZAN

Employees: 755

Main destinations served: Albany, Ashville, Atlanta, Baltimore, Boston, Buffalo, Charlotte, Chicago, Cincinnati, Cleveland, Dallas/Fort Worth, Dayton, Detroit, Fort Wayne, Grand Rapids, Hartford, Houston, Indianapolis, Jackson, Kansas City, Little Rock, Los Angeles, Memphis, Minneapolis/St Paul, Nashville, New York JFK, New York Newark, Norfolk, Philadelphia, Richmond, Rochester, St Louis, Shreveport, South Bend, Syracuse.

LINKS WITH OTHER AIRLINES
A subsidiary of American International Airlines (qv).

FLEET
1 McDonnell Douglas DC-8-62F
2 McDonnell Douglas DC-8-54F
17 Lockheed L-188 Electra
11 Convair 640

Uzbekistan – UK

UZBEKISTAN AIRWAYS

Uzbekistan Havo Yullari

Incorporated: 1992

HISTORY
Uzbekistan's national airline, Uzbekistan Airways was founded in 1992 and based on the former Aeroflot divisions in Tashkent and Samarkand. Although still state-owned, since its independence the airline has developed services to destinations outside the former Soviet Union and introduced western aircraft types to its fleet, doubtless hoping to develop the area's tourist potential. The fleet still includes a majority of former-Soviet types, but most of these are relatively modern, although the An-24 and Yak-40 fleet is being replaced by RJ85s.

Executive Directors & Officers: Arslan G. Ruzmetov, Director General; Egambergen M. Palvanov, Technical Director; Stanislav M. Siumbaev, Deputy Director, Finance.

HQ Airport & Main Base: Tashkent, with a further base/hub at Samarkand.

Radio callsign: UZBEK

Designator: 6Y/UZB

Employees: 16,500

Main destinations served: Domestic destinations, and destinations in the CIS, plus Delhi, Istanbul, Jeddah, Karachi, Kuala Lumpur, London Heathrow, Tel Aviv.

FLEET
2 Airbus A310-300
2 Boeing 767-300ER
1 Boeing 757-200
10 Ilyushin Il-86
19 Ilyushin Il-76TD
12 Ilyushin Il-62
3 Tupolev Tu-154M
3 Avro RJ85
28 Yakovlev Yak-40 (possibly not all operational)
23 Antonov An-24 (possibly not all operational)
5 Antonov An-12

Venezuela – YV

AEROEJECUTIVOS

Aéroejecutivos

Incorporated: 1986

HISTORY
Venezuela's passenger charter airline, Aéroejecutivos operates charters throughout the Americas.

HQ Airport & Main Base: Caracas

Radio callsign: VENEJECUTIV

Designator: VE/VEJ

Main destinations served: Inclusive tour and ad hoc charters throughout the Americas.

FLEET
12 Boeing 727-200
2 Boeing 727-100

ASERCA

Aéroservicios Carabobo

Incorporated: 1958

HISTORY
Aserca operates domestic and regional passenger charter flights and a small network of domestic scheduled services from its base at Valencia in Venezuela.

Executive Directors & Officers: Simeon Garcia, President; Winston Rochard, Vice-President, Commercial; Jesus E. More, Vice-President, Maintenance.

HQ Airport & Main Base: Valencia (Venezuela)

Radio callsign: AROSCA

Designator: R7/OCA

Main destinations served: About six destinations, including Maracaibo.

FLEET
11 McDonnell Douglas DC-9-30

AVENSA

Aérovias Venezolanas

Incorporated: 1943

HISTORY
Avensa was founded in 1943 with the support of Pan American, which bought 30 per cent of its shares. Services started on domestic routes in 1944, but international services did not start until 1955. In 1961 the international services of Avensa and another airline, LAV, were transferred to newly created Viasa (qv), although Avensa was allowed a proportion of the 45 per cent of Viasa's shares reserved for the private sector. In 1946 Pan Am's interest was acquired by the state-owned Corporacion Venezolana de Fomento, and the airline has since become wholly-state owned.

HQ Airport & Main Base: Caracas

Radio callsign: AVE

Designator: VE/AVE

Employees: 2,800

Main destinations served: Serves some 20 domestic destinations from Caracas.

FLEET
2 Boeing 757-200
9 Boeing 727-200
6 Boeing 727-100
2 Boeing 737-200
4 McDonnell Douglas DC-9-50
1 McDonnell Douglas DC-9-30
2 Convair 580

VIASA

Viasa Venezuelan International Airways/Venezolana Internacional de Aviacion

Incorporated: 1961

HISTORY
Viasa was founded in 1961 to take over the international services operated by two airlines, Avensa (qv) and LAV, leaving these to concentrate on domestic routes.

The new airline was owned 55 per cent by the Venezuelan Government, with Avensa and LAV each having a share of the remaining 45 per cent. Initially it received technical and managerial assistance from KLM (qv), and the fleet also reflected the KLM connection, operating Douglas DC-8s, which were soon joined by DC-9s and, later, DC-10s. It developed a route network including the main destinations in the Americas, while services to Europe were operated in a pooling arrangement with KLM and Iberia (qv).

In recent years Iberia has acquired a 45 per cent stake. The airline suspended services temporarily in January 1997, ready for a major reorganisation.

Executive Directors & Officers: José Campinas, President; Javier Martinez, Deputy President; Marcos Pinter, Executive Vice-President; José Pascuali, Vice-President, Finance; Maruja Correa, Vice-President, Commercial.

HQ Airport & Main Base: Caracas

Radio callsign: VIASA

Designator: VA/VIA

Employees: 2,000

Main destinations served: Aruba, Bogotá, Buenos Aires, Cancun, Cartagena, Frankfurt, Havana, Lima, London Heathrow, Madrid, Miami, Milan, Oporto, Paris CDG, Quito, Rio de Janeiro, Rome, San José, Santiago de Compostela, São Paulo, Santa Domingo, St Maarten, Zürich.

LINKS WITH OTHER AIRLINES
Iberia (qv) holds a 45 per cent interest.

FLEET
5 McDonnell Douglas DC-10
7 Boeing 727-200

Vietnam – XV

VIETNAM AIRLINES

Vietnam Airlines

Incorporated: c1955

HISTORY
Vietnam Airlines has its origins in the General Civil Aviation Administration of Vietnam, formed after the French withdrawal in 1954 and after the Viet Cong had seized power in the north. Operations during the Vietnam War were severely

restricted by American air power. Since the American withdrawal from Vietnam, however, an extensive network of domestic services has been established, as well as a growing number of international destinations, initially within South-East Asia and, more recently, as far afield as Australia and Japan. The title of Hang Khong Vietnam was adopted for a number of years, but the current title has since been assumed.

Originally the fleet reflected assistance from the Soviet Union, with Antonov, Ilyushin, Tupolev, and Yakovlev aircraft being operated, but over the past few years there has been a strong preference for western types. The airline is completely state-owned.

Executive Directors & Officers: Le Luc Tu, Director General.

HQ Airport & Main Base: Hanoi, with a further hub/base at Ho Chi Minh City.

Designator: VN/HVN

Employees: 6,000

Main destinations served: More than a dozen domestic destinations, plus Bangkok, Guangzhou, Hong Kong, Jakarta, Kaohsiung, Kuala Lumpur, Manila, Melbourne, Osaka, Phnom Penh, Seoul, Singapore, Sydney, Taipei, Tokyo, Vientiane.

FLEET
5 Boeing 767-300ER
1 Boeing 767-200
10 Airbus A320-200 (leased)
12 Tupolev Tu-134
4 Yakovlev Yak-40
4 ATR 72
2 Fokker 70

Yemen – 7O

YEMENIA

Yemen Airways

Incorporated: 1963

HISTORY
Yemen Airways was founded in 1963 as the national airline of North Yemen, and in 1996 absorbed Alyemda-Democratic Yemen Airlines, which dated from 1961 and was the airline of the People's Republic of South Yemen, formerly Aden. The bringing together of the two airlines was long delayed by disagreements between the two territories which were exacerbated by the Gulf War. Yemenia had originally been known as Yemen Airways

when it was first formed, and became Yemen Airways on nationalisation in 1972.

The fleets of the two airlines were broadly compatible, since both operated a mixture of Boeing and de Havilland aircraft, although Alyemda also had Tupolev and Antonov types in service. The merged airline is owned 51 per cent by the new united Republic of Yemen Government, and 49 per cent by the Kingdom of Saudi Arabia.

Executive Directors & Officers: Hassan Abdo Sohbi, Chairman; Ali Allbagdadi, Director, Finance; Captain Abdulkhalek Alkadi, Director, Flight Operations; Ahmed H. Alhaddad, Director, Technical; Abdulwali K. Tarboosh, Director, Corporate Planning; Yahya Hassan Suwayd, Director, Administration.

HQ Airport & Main Base: Sana'a, with a secondary hub at Aden.

Radio callsign: YEMENI

Designator: IY/IYE

Employees: 4,200

Main destinations served: A domestic network covers eight destinations, with international services, mainly from Sana'a, to Abu Dhabi, Addis Ababa, Amman, Asmara, Bahrain, Beirut, Bombay, Cairo, Damascus, Djibouti, Doha, Dubai, Frankfurt, Jeddah, Karachi, Khartoum, Larnaca, London Gatwick, Madrid, Moscow, Paris CDG, Riyadh, Rome, Sharjah.

LINKS WITH OTHER AIRLINES
Marketing alliances with Air India (qv), Cathay Pacific (qv), Gulf Air (qv), Lufthansa (qv), and TWA (qv).

FLEET
4 Airbus A310-300
4 Boeing 727-200
3 Boeing 737-200
4 de Havilland Dash 7-100
2 de Havilland DHC-6 Twin Otter

Zaire – 9Q

AIR ZAIRE

Société Air Zaire

Incorporated: 1961

HISTORY
Air Zaire has suspended operations following the civil war which raged until 1997. It was originally founded as Air Congo in 1961 after the Congo had gained

its independence the previous year, and adopted its present title ten years later when the country changed its name to Zaire. The airline had been operating two Boeing 737-200s, a McDonnell Douglas DC-10, and two McDonnell Douglas DC-8s at the time operations were suspended. Sabena (qv) and the Zairean Government were examining the prospects for creating a new airline before the civil war ended.

HQ Airport & Main Base: Kinshasa

Radio callsign: AIR ZAIRE

Designator: AZR

ZAIRE EXPRESS

Zaire Express

Incorporated: 1994

HISTORY
A subsidiary of Express Cargo, Zaire Express was founded in 1994 and operates scheduled passenger services in addition to scheduled and ad hoc charter cargo services. A marketing alliance existed with Air Zaire (qv) before that airline suspended operations during the civil war.

Executive Directors & Officers: Jose Eendundo, President; Stavros Papaionnou, Chief Executive Officer.

HQ Airport & Main Base: Kinshasa

Designator: EO/EZR

Main destinations served: Domestic scheduled plus ad hoc international charter.

LINKS WITH OTHER AIRLINES
Marketing alliances with Air Zaire (qv) and Sabena (qv).

FLEET
3 Boeing 707-320
2 Boeing 737-200
3 British Aerospace One-Eleven 500

ZAIREAN

Zairean Airlines

Incorporated: 1981

HISTORY
Zairean Airlines operates a network of scheduled services throughout Zaire, and ad hoc charters throughout Africa. The current operational status is uncertain following the civil war, but a number of aircraft have been leased out to other operators. The airline is owned by Alfred Sommerauer, its Director General.

Executive Directors & Officers:
Captain Alfred Sommerauer, Director
General.

HQ Airport & Main Base: Kinshasa

Radio callsign: ZAIREAN

Designator: ZAR

Main destinations served: Domestic
destinations plus international ad hoc
charters.

FLEET
1 Boeing 707-320
1 Boeing 707-420 (leased out)
1 Boeing 727-100 (leased out)
1 Vickers Viscount 700
2 Piper Seneca

Zimbabwe – Z

AIR ZIMBABWE

Air Zimbabwe

Incorporated: 1961

HISTORY

Air Zimbabwe was originally founded in
1961 as Air Rhodesia, and from the outset
was owned by the then Rhodesian
Government. It was formed initially to
take over the services operated by the former Central African Airways Corporation
(CAAC), which had been founded after
World War Two with assistance and
investment by BOAC (British Overseas
Airways Corporation) and the then
Federation of Rhodesia and Nyasaland.
The breaking up of the federation into
three separate countries on Northern
Rhodesia and Nyasaland gaining independence also marked the end for CAAC.

The new airline found itself initially
operating a fleet of Douglas DC-3s and
Vickers Viscounts. The route network
included domestic services and destinations in South Africa and the neighbouring
Portuguese territories of Angola and
Mozambique. Services to what had been
Northern Rhodesia and Nyasaland – by
this time Zambia and Malawi respectively
– were soon suspended following
Rhodesia's Unilateral Declaration of
Independence and the application of
sanctions against the country by most of
the international community. Sanctions
also inhibited traffic growth and new
equipment, so it was not until 1973 that
the airline obtained its first jet airliners,
three Boeing 720s.

Air Rhodesia became Air Zimbabwe
Rhodesia in 1978 after sanctions ended,
and in 1980 assumed its present title,
reflecting the country's new name. Since
independence the airline has undertaken a
modernisation programme, partly spurred
on by a growing tourist trade.

Executive Directors & Officers: D.M.
Zamchiya, Chairman; M.M. Ndubiwa,
Deputy Chairman; Huttush R. Muringi,
Managing Director; C. Tapambwa,
Finance Director; P. Chikumba,
Operations Director; P. Chakauya,
Marketing & Customer Services Director;
N. Masuku, Human Resources &
Administration Director.

HQ Airport & Main Base: Harare

Radio callsign: AIR ZIMBABWE

Designator: UM/AZW

Employees: 920

Main destinations served: Bulawayo,
Cape Town, Durban, Frankfurt,
Gaborone, Hwange, Johannesburg,
Kariba, Larnaca, Liliongwe, London

Gatwick, Lusaka, Manzini, Mauritius,
Nairobi, Perth, Sydney, Victoria Falls,
Windhoek.

LINKS WITH OTHER AIRLINES
Marketing alliances with Air Malawi and
Qantas (qv).

FLEET
2 Boeing 767-200ER
2 Boeing 707-320B
3 Boeing 737-200
1 British Aerospace 146-200
2 Fokker 50

ZIMBABWE EXPRESS

Zimbabwe Express Airlines

Incorporated: 1994

HISTORY

Zimbabwe Express is a relatively new
operator with a small domestic scheduled
network largely centred around the growing market for air services to the main
tourist destinations. Charters are also
undertaken.

Executive Directors & Officers: Evans
Ndebele, Managing Director.

Radio callsign: ZIM EXPRESS

Designator: Z7/EZX

Main destinations served: Kariba and
Victoria Falls.

FLEET
2 Boeing 727-100
1 British Aerospace 146-200
2 British Aerospace 748

PART TWO

AIRLINER MANUFACTURERS AND THEIR AIRCRAFT

AERO INTERNATIONAL (REGIONAL) – AI(R)

AI(R) was a short-lived European joint venture established to combine the product ranges of Avions de Transport Regional (qv), or ATR, originally formed by Aerospatiale of France and Alenia of Italy, and the regional aircraft of British Aerospace (qv), which had hitherto been marked under the Avro and Jetstream names. The object of the exercise was to counter fierce competition in this market, which has seen many new manufacturers emerge in the developing nations, often with substantially lower labour costs. Initially some difficult decisions were made, with BAe ceasing production of its successful Jetstream 31 19-seat feeder liner after 446 had been built (64 of them by the aircraft's original manufacturer, Handley Page), Jetstream 41 29-seat feeder liner after 106 had been built, and the slow selling Jetstream 61, which had originally started life as the ATP, or Advanced Turboprop, a 64-68 passenger aircraft of which fewer than 60 had been sold and competed directly with the ATR 72. The ATP had been developed from the earlier BAe 748, which had started life as the Avro 748, later becoming the Hawker Siddeley HS 748 before being absorbed by BAe, and which had been a successful aircraft in the 46-56 seat range.

On the other hand, BAe's Avro RJ series was intended to continue, especially after the collapse of Fokker, manufacturer of the rival Fokker 70 and 100 airliners. At one time, many believed that AI(R) had the potential to become the regional arm of Airbus (qv), anxious to extend its product range downwards as well as upwards in size. This would have been complicated by some differences in the membership of the two joint ventures.

ATR – AVIONS DE TRANSPORT REGIONAL

A joint venture between Aerospatiale of France and Alenia of Italy, ATR produces two successful turboprop airliners, the ATR 42 and 72, both of which are intended for regional services.

The Aircraft
ATR 42/72: The original ATR 42 first flew

Aero International (Regional), or AI(R), had two families of aircraft originating with the original AI partners and British Aerospace. The British Aerospace contribution was the 146/RJ family, and here is a THY Turkish Airlines RJ100 in flight.

in 1984 and entered service in late-1985, with the stretched ATR 72 following almost four years later. The ATR 42 takes 50 passengers in four-abreast layout at 76cm pitch, while the ATR 72 carries up to 74. Twin Pratt & Whitney Canada PW120 series turboprops of between 1,490kW and 2,050kW power the aircraft, which have a range of up to 1,000km (625 miles). These two aircraft have been extremely successful, with more than 330 ATR 42s and almost 200 ATR 72s delivered.

AVRO

Resurrecting an old name in British aircraft manufacturing, Avro took over the family of four-engined regional jet airliners developed by British Aerospace, Avro's sole shareholder, as the 146, and with a number of refinements and improvements produced these as the RJ, for 'regional jet' family. The choice of Avro as a name is curious, for except for the 748 twin turboprop, Avro's history as an airliner manufacturer was less than illustrious, given that the York had been a development of the Lancaster bomber, using that aircraft's aerodynamic surfaces, and the failure of the Tudor.

The Aircraft
RJ70/85/100/115: This family of four-engined aircraft is based on the BAe 146 series, originally designed by Hawker Siddeley but shelved before nationalisation led to the creation of BAe. More than 200 146s were delivered, as the 146-100, -200, and -300, and carrying between 70 and 128 passengers depending on seat pitch and whether five- or six-abreast seating was specified. As a general rule,

Continental Express operates aircraft that were from the other side of the AI(R) operation, including this ATR 42.

American and Australian airlines specified five abreast, and European airlines six abreast. The airliner claimed to be the quietest in the world, and this, allied with an excellent take-off and landing performance, has meant that it is the only jet airliner to be able to operate into many airports close to city centres, including London City and Florence.

The differences between the RJ series and the original 146s include Category III automatic landing equipment and improved 31.1kN Allied Signal LF507 turbofans. The RJ70 first flew in 1992 and can accommodate 70 passengers five abreast or 82 six abreast, while the RJ85 takes 85 or 100, and the RJ100 takes 100 or 112. The RJ115 is a higher capacity variant of the RJ100, with mid-cabin emergency exits, high density seating allowing up to 128 passengers to be carried, and increased take-off weights and fuel capacity. The 146 and RJ series aircraft are somewhat slower than most modern jet airliners, with a maximum cruise speed of 430 knots, and a maximum altitude of 33,000 feet, all of which means that they are at their best on shorter flights. Although originally intended to appeal to smaller airlines buying relatively small numbers of aircraft, several larger airlines have ordered these aircraft, including Air UK (qv) and Crossair (qv).

A variant of the 146 is the QT, or Quiet Trader, freighter, developed for TNT (qv) and operated on TNT's behalf by a number of airlines, including Air Foyle (qv) in the UK. QTs can generally be converted to daytime passenger use, operating freight by night.

AIRBUS

The newest of the major airframe manufacturers, Airbus Industrie is in fact a consortium, or 'Groupement d'Iteret Economique', based in France. Preparations for the creation of the Airbus consortium were made during the mid-1960s, at a time when none of the major European manufacturers was able to initiate a project capable of competing against American dominance of the world market for large airliners. Indeed, after World War Two only the British had manufactured long-range airliners, such as the Bristol Britannia, de Havilland Comet, and Vickers VC10, while the sole significant French contribution had been the Sud Aviation Caravelle. The founding partners were Sud Aviation of France and a consortium, now Deutsche Airbus, of German manufacturers, with Britain's Hawker Siddeley Aviation as a subcontractor. Later

It is not difficult to see the difference in fuselage length between this Airbus A319 and . . .

the United Kingdom became a partner, and shareholding in Airbus today consists of Aérospatiale of France 37.9 per cent; Deutsche Airbus 37.9 per cent; British Aerospace (qv) 20 per cent; and CASA of Spain 4.2 per cent.

The first Airbus project was the A300, the world's first wide-bodied twin-engined aircraft, which first flew in 1972. Since that time a family of short, medium, and long-haul aircraft has been created.

Moves are in hand to convert Airbus into a conventional company, partly to establish a normal annual financial statement to allay suspicions of government subsidies.

The Aircraft

A300: First flown in 1972, the A300 entered airline service in 1974. The first production variant was the B2, followed by the B4, while the A300-600 – which entered service in 1984 – incorporated a two-crew EFIS flight deck and the rear fuselage and tail of

the A310, increasing passenger and cargo capacity slightly. A variant is the A300-600F freighter, mainly in service with FedEx (qv). So far more than 480 aircraft have been delivered. Typical powerplants are either 262kN GE CF6-80C2A1 or 249kN Pratt & Whitney PW4156 turbofans, with up to 361 seats at 81cm pitch and nine-abreast seating (although many airlines opt for eight abreast) in a single-class layout. Increased pitch or fewer seats abreast, and two- or three-class layouts reduce the maximum considerably, to around 250–280. Typical ranges are 5,000-6,000km (3,125–3,750 miles).

A310: The second Airbus, the A310 was a shorter fuselage and re-winged derivative of the A300, instantly recognisable by the wing-tip winglets. It entered service with Lufthansa (qv) and Swissair (qv) in 1983. Many A310s have been optimised for long-haul operation, although there are proposals for a lighter-weight, short-haul variant. The aircraft is available as A310-

. . . the stretched Airbus A321, as Airbus tries to establish a range of aircraft to meet all the needs of the major airlines.

The differences between the narrow-bodied A319/320/321 and the original wide-bodied range such as the A300/310 can also be seen clearly, while the A310 shown has a different wing from the A300.

200 standard version or -300 higher maximum take-off weight variant, better suited for long-haul operations. Some 260 aircraft have been delivered and demand remains steady. Typical powerplants are either 231kN Pratt & Whitney PW4152 or 237 GE CF6-80 2A2 turbofans on the -200, giving a maximum capacity of 280 seats at 76cm nine abreast, although most airlines use eight abreast. Two or three-class layouts are common, especially on long-haul scheduled services, and seating capacities of 180-220 are not uncommon. Typical ranges are 5,058km for the -200 to 8,975km for the -300 (3,160–5,800 miles).

A319/320/321: Airbus met the demand for a smaller single aisle aircraft with the A320, which entered service with Air France (qv) in 1988. The aircraft was the first subsonic commercial airliner to have a fly-by-wire flight control system and a 'side stick' instead of the conventional control column. The original aircraft was the A320-100, but only a few of these were built and the main production version is the A320-200. In contrast to Boeing practice of retaining the same designation for different variants of the same aircraft, Airbus designated the stretched version A321 and a shortened version A319. Seating capacities vary according to pitch and class-mix, but essentially the A320 is a 150-seat aircraft, the A321 a 185-seat aircraft, and the A319 a 124-seat aircraft, usually six abreast. A choice of powerplant is available, and on the A320-200 this is either a 118kN CFM International CF56 5A/5B or a 118kN IAE V2500 A1/A5 turbofan, giving a range of between 2,940 and 4,020km (1,850–2,500 miles) depending on whether a standard version or higher MTOW variant is specified. The aircraft set a record for orders before its first flight, and currently more than 800 A319/320/321s are in service, with another 500 or so on order.

A330: A high capacity twin suitable for high density short and medium-haul routes (A330-300) or long-haul routes (A330-200), the A330 was developed in conjunction with the four-engined A340. It has the same control system as the A320 series. The A330 entered service with Air Inter – now Air France Europe (qv) – in 1994. At 81cm pitch and eight abreast, maximum seating capacities are 253 for the A330-200 and 295 for the A330-300, in three-class layout. There is a choice of three engines, and for the A330-300 this consists of the 332kN Rolls-Royce Trent 700, 308kN Pratt & Whitney PW4000 or 317kN GE CF6-80E turbofan. The maximum range for the A330-300 is 6,900km (4,310 miles), and up to 12,000km (7,500 miles) for the A330-200.

A340: The first four-engined Airbus, the A340 was intended to rival the McDonnell Douglas MD-11 and provide an alternative for airlines with 'long thin' routes. It was developed in conjunction with the twin-engined A330. Two versions were provided, with the A340-200 seating 263 passengers in eight-abreast three-class layout, and the -300 seating 295 passengers in a similar configuration. Both types entered service in 1993, with Lufthansa (qv) operating the -200 and Air France (qv) the -300, while a high gross weight version of the -300 with longer range entered service with Singapore Airlines (qv) in 1996. More than 150 aircraft have been delivered so far, with another 50 or so on order. There is a choice of engines inasmuch as up to three different power ratings are offered on each version, but the engines on current production models are all variants of the CFM International CFM-56-5C turbofan, and on a standard -200 power ratings vary between 141kN and 154kN. Maximum range varies between 10,180km and 11,800km (6,750–7,375 miles).

Stretched variants are under development using Rolls-Royce Trent engines, which will be able to compete with the Boeing 747 range.

ANTONOV

Today, the Ukraine-based Antonov Design Bureau (qv) is probably most famous for its An-124 Ruslan, the largest aircraft in commercial service, but the organisation first came into prominence in 1947 with its small An-2, code-named 'Colt' by NATO. This 14-seat biplane seems to have been difficult to replace and many remain in service, even though – as with the DC-3/C-47 Dakota – there have been many attempts at finding a successor. Antonov had also built an earlier 'world's largest aircraft', the An-22 'Cock' turboprop having enjoyed this distinction for many years after it had first appeared in 1967. The unique capabilities of the An-124 have moved Antonov into joint ventures with air cargo specialists, such as Air Foyle (qv) and Volga-Dnepr (qv), but more recently the organisation has been operating aircraft on its own account. A larger development of the An-124 – the An-225 – has flown, but development has been suspended due to a shortage of funds, and the sole example is not believed to be operational.

Antonov is a fertile source of ideas for new aircraft projects, but difficulties over funding have also made these difficult to put into production. Coming soon are commercial examples of the An-70T military transport, the first aircraft to fly using prop-fan power, but development of the An-180, a 150–175 seat medium-range airliner, and the An-218, similar to the Airbus A330 but slightly smaller, has been delayed.

The Aircraft
An-24: Known to NATO as 'Coke', the An-

24 is a high-wing turboprop bearing some resemblance to the Fokker F-27 Friendship and Handley Page Herald, and like them it can carry up to 50 passengers. Twin Ivchenko AI-24 2,250shp turboprops give a maximum speed of up to 580kmh (360mph), and a range of up to 2,900km (1,800 miles). The number in service today is around 870.

An-26/32: Known to NATO as 'Curl' and 'Cline' respectively, the An-26 and An-32 are high-wing twin-turboprop transports. The An-26 has around 38 seats, and the An-32 development has up to 50, but is also a development of the An-26 offering improved take-off performance in hot and high conditions, including more powerful engines and high lift devices. The An-26 uses two 2,075kW ZMKB Progress A1-24VTs, giving a maximum cruising speed of 235 knots and a range of up to 5,500km (3,450 miles), while the An-32 has far more powerful 3,760kW ZMKB Progress AI-20Ds, giving a maximum cruising speed of 286 knots and a range of up to 6,700km (4,200 miles).

An-38: First flown in 1994, the twin-turboprop An-38 carries up to 27 passengers three abreast, and is intended for regional air services. Lack of funding is affecting production. In an attempt to improve the poor reliability and low utilisation of aircraft from the former Eastern Bloc, twin 1,100kW Garrett TPE331-14GR turboprops are used, giving a maximum cruising speed of up to 220knots and a range of up to 2,500km (1,560 miles).

An-124 Ruslan: First flown in late-1982, the giant An-124 Ruslan freighter entered service early in 1986. Originally intended as an outsize military airlifter, severe budgetary constraints have meant that the aircraft has found its market with specialised heavy lift air cargo operators, especially airlines such as Air Foyle (qv) and HeavyLift (qv) in the west, although Volga-Dnepr (qv) is another major user, and Antonov itself is now moving into operations using this aircraft. Four 229kN ZMKB Progress D-18T turbofans enable it to carry loads of around 150 tonnes over distances of 4,500km (2,770 miles). Around 50 aircraft have been delivered so

Antonov's range includes a number of fairly ordinary aircraft such as the An-24, but the design bureau has sprung into prominence with its An-124 Ruslan. Here the aircraft is seen with a variety of large or heavy loads. In the case of the motor yacht size, rather than weight, was the problem.

far. Hush-kits for the aircraft were certificated in mid-1997, but re-engining also remains a possibility. The even larger six-engined An-225, capable of lifting 250 tonne loads, is believed to have been grounded due to shortage of funds, and work has stopped on a second prototype.

An-140: First flown in 1997, the An-140 uses two 1,840kW Klimov TV3-117 VMA turboprops (or Pratt & Whitney Canada PWC27As) to carry 46–52 passengers at a maximum cruising speed of 310 knots over ranges up to 2,650km (1,650 miles).

BAC/AEROSPATIALE

The first collaborative aircraft project was the Anglo-French Concorde supersonic airliner, now the only supersonic airliner in service following withdrawal of the short-lived and unsuccessful Tupolev Tu-144. Today, BAC's successor, British Aerospace (qv), has responsibility for support of the aircraft.

The Aircraft

Concorde: Originally two separate projects by BAC and Aérospatiale, the two companies pooled their resources for development of the Concorde supersonic airliner, which first flew in 1969 and entered service with both British Airways (qv) and Air France (qv) in January 1976. It was designed for unrefuelled Paris–New York range, using four 169kN Rolls-Royce/Snecma Olympus 593 engines with after-burning, used for acceleration to supersonic speeds only. Despite most of the world's major airlines having options to buy Concorde, the American decision to abandon the larger Boeing 2707, coupled with environmental concerns, led other airlines to abandon the project, leaving BA and Air France with seven aircraft each. Utilisation is low by modern standards, at around 1,000 hours per aircraft per year, compared with the 3,000 plus hours generally regarded as necessary for jet airliners to be profitable; but the aircraft are fully depreciated and both airlines claim operations are profitable – the low utilisation is partly due to a shortage of suitable routes and to the desire to keep the aircraft in service until well into the next century. They carry 96 passengers in four-abreast seating, originally described as being between 'first and tourist class in width and leg-room', but the emergence of business class means that the seating is really between tourist and intercontinental business-class in width and leg-room. Maximum speed is Mach 2 – around 1,350mph (2,170kmh) – and the range is

up to 5,600km (3,500 miles), depending on payload.

In addition to transatlantic operations, it has been used in the past by Air France on services to Rio de Janeiro and Bahrain, and by BA on special flights for enthusiasts and day trips to Egypt.

BOEING

For many years the world's largest commercial aircraft manufacturer, Boeing reinforced this position by the acquisition of rival McDonnell Douglas (qv) in 1997. This acquisition had as much to do with enabling Boeing to benefit from the latter's extensive combat aircraft production as from acquiring a rival airliner builder, since McDonnell Douglas has been trailing well behind Boeing and Airbus (qv) in recent years.

Boeing has not always been synonymous with airliner manufacture, having also built a successful line of army and carrier-borne naval fighters between the wars, while during World War Two and for some ten years or so afterwards it produced a number of successful heavy bombers, culminating in the B-52, many of which remain in service as cruise missile

launch aircraft. It was at one time involved in air transport with one of the predecessor companies of United Airlines (qv).

Early Boeing airliners included the Boeing 80, which followed the late-1920s fashion for trimotors and carried 15 passengers. The company soon started to take sizeable strides towards the creation of the modern airliner, first with the 247, a ten-seat twin-engined monoplane with a retractable undercarriage. Still more significant was the Boeing 307 Stratoliner, the world's first pressurised airliner, this four-engined aircraft entering service with both TWA (qv) and Pan American in 1940, when both airlines took five aircraft. The advent of World War Two meant that this aircraft never realised its full commercial potential. During the late-1930s the Boeing 324 flying-boat did much to develop transatlantic and transpacific airline operations.

Post-war, Boeing introduced the 377 Stratocruiser, which saw service with many of the world's major airlines, including both Pan American and BOAC. Experience with jet bomber development led directly to the C-135 military transport and its tanker derivative, the KC-135, which in turn led to the Boeing 707 long-haul jet airliner, the second jet airliner in

Boeing was the first manufacturer to recognise the importance of producing a family of aircraft, and of developing existing designs rather than creating new ones. Perhaps the most popular member of the 737 family is the -300, shown here in Pakistani and Kenyan service.

A stretch of the 737-300 is the -400, until now the largest member of the 737 family, though the new -800 is larger.

service on the North Atlantic and the most successful of first generation jet airliners. A development of the 707 was the shorter-range 720, while a hybrid was the 707-120, which gave Qantas (qv) a smaller long-range jet airliner. Using its success with the 707, Boeing then embarked upon creating a family of aircraft using as much of the 707 design as possible, setting an example which other manufacturers failed to follow. The medium-range 727 tri-jet and early versions of the short-range Boeing 737 twin-jet also went one step further, using the same engines so that development and production costs were reduced and, far more important, airline spares holdings and engineer training costs were also cut.

A policy of continuous development has led to the 737 becoming by far the most successful jet airliner yet. Believing that the future for longer-range operations lay with supersonic transports, as an interim step Boeing scaled up the 707 to produce the 747, the world's first wide-bodied airliner, which for many years has effectively enjoyed a monopoly of the large long-haul airliner market, with the rival tri-jet Lockheed L-1011 TriStar and McDonnell Douglas DC-10/MD-11 being somewhat smaller. The 747 itself went into continuous development after Boeing had to abandon its 2707 supersonic transport. The 2707 is widely believed to have failed because it sought to use new technology, including what would have been, even today, the world's largest variable geometry (or swing) wing. By contrast, Concorde used up-to-date proven technology.

Boeing moved into the wide-body market for short and medium-range aircraft with the 767, a successful gamble given that it has an unusual seating arrangement, while at the same time replacing the

727 with the 757. The most recent innovation and the first completely new Boeing aircraft since the 767 has been the 777 wide-bodied twin for long-haul operations, a competitor to the Airbus A330.

The Aircraft

707: Approximately 130 Boeing 707s remain in commercial service, apart from many more with CFM engines in military service. Most of those surviving are 707-320s, and some have been converted to freight, although the aircraft has always been less popular as a freighter than the 727 and Douglas DC-8. The 707 was first flown in 1957 and entered service with Pan American in 1958 on the North Atlantic routes. The 320 uses four 18,000lb thrust Pratt & Whitney JT3D-3B turbofans and carries around 150 passengers, usually six abreast, depending on seat pitch and class mix. Maximum range is around 6,400km (4,000 miles) although modified

versions have operated over longer distances.

717: First flown as the MD-90 in 1993, the MD-90 entered service with Delta Air Lines in 1995. A variant, the MD-95, is the sole member of the McDonnell Douglas commercial airliner product range to remain in production following the acquisition of the company by Boeing, and has been redesignated the Boeing 717, giving Boeing a 100-seat airliner which fits neatly in below the smallest variant of the 737 family, the 737-600. Depending on seat pitch, the 717 can carry between 106 and 130 passengers. There is just a single version at present, designated the 717-200. The aircraft uses two 97.9kn (22,000lb thrust) BMW Rolls-Royce BR715-58 turbofans. There is speculation that Boeing might introduce a shortened version, both as smaller airliner and as a long-range corporate jet.

727: Deliveries of the Boeing 727 started in late-1963, with the 727-100 using three 14,000lb thrust Pratt & Whitney JT9D-1 turbofans mounted in the tail-plane. A stretch of this aircraft, the 727-200, with up-rated engines, proved to be even more popular and the 727 was the first jet airliner to pass the 1,000 production figure. A number of 707 components were used, including much of the fuselage and the nose, although a 'T' tail was used. Six-abreast seating allowed the -100 to accommodate 130 passengers and the -200 up to 190. More than 400 727-100s remain in service, and more than 900 727-200s, many of them converted for freight use. A number of 727s have been converted to Rolls-Royce Tay power by Dee Howard in the United States, including 44 aircraft belonging to UPS (qv), improving performance and reducing noise levels.

Next step up in size is the Boeing 757, originally designed as a 727 successor. It has also followed the 727 in being a popular charter aircraft with airlines such as Condor.

The Boeing 767 was Boeing's second wide-body, but with an unusual 2:3:2 seating layout. This is a 767-200ER (extended range) operated by Malév.

737: The most numerous jet airliner to-date, the Boeing 737 first flew in 1967 and deliveries of the first 737-100s were made to Lufthansa (qv) by the end of that year. The early aircraft used the same 14,000lb thrust Pratt & Whitney engines as the 727-100. Just 30 -100s were built before the aircraft was superseded by the larger 737-200, which remained in production until 1988. A modest stretch provided the 737-300, but more importantly this aircraft introduced the high by-pass ratio CFM International CFM56 3B turbofan to the 737, increasing range and reducing noise levels, while the aircraft also had an improved wing and digital avionics, in effect making it a second generation 737. A further stretch of 3 metres led to the 737-400, while the 737-500 reverted to the -200 fuselage, but with the other improvements of the -300. All three aircraft have been in production together, offering airlines between 102 and 168 seats, depending on pitch, variant, and class-mix. Boeing is now attempting to repeat the success of the first two generations with a third generation 737, starting with the -700, which entered service in October 1997. A new, larger wing and higher cruising speeds, as well as longer range, distinguish the performance of the new aircraft from earlier models. The -700 replaces the -300, using the same fuselage, the -600 replaces the -500, again using the -500 fuselage, and the -800 replaces the -400, but with a 2.79 metre fuselage stretch, allowing the aircraft to take up to 160 passengers in two-class configuration, or 189 in high density seating.

Boeing delivered 1,144 first generation 737s and more than 1,800 of the second generation, with a number still on order. More than 600 third generation aircraft

have been ordered so far, which augurs well for its success. The aircraft has proven to be a workhorse, popular with scheduled and charter airlines alike, not least because of its flexibility, which means that a range of 3,200km (2,000 miles) or more can be obtained.

747: The world's first wide-bodied airliner, the Boeing 747 introduced the term 'jumbo jet' to the English language. The first flight was in 1969, and the aircraft entered service with Pan American Airways the following year on the New York–London transatlantic service. The initial version was the 747-100, powered by four Pratt & Whitney JT9Ds, but a heavier and longer-range version, the 747-200, was introduced in 1971, and was available with a choice of JT9D, General

Aeroméxico is another 767 operator.

Electric CF6-50, or Rolls-Royce RB-211-524 engines, usually of around 194kN. Although initially the large hold capacity of the 747 worked against all-cargo aircraft, eventually, as traffic grew, many -200s were delivered as freighters or as passenger/freight Combis.

Two variations were the short-bodied 747SP, used by Pan American, United Airlines (qv), and South African Airways (qv) amongst others, of which just 45 were built, and the short-range high density seating versions built for domestic services within Japan. A development of the -200 was the -300, with an extended upper deck, known to Singapore Airlines (qv) as the 'Big Top'. This first entered service with Swissair (qv) in 1983.

Seating capacity of the 747 depended on layout and pitch, and while it usually had a ten-abreast seating layout, some airlines have considered raising the number of seats between the two aisles from four to five! Early models often had a reduced capacity, with the upper deck behind the flight deck being used as a first class lounge. Maximum capacity on the -100 and -200 with high density seating is 550, and 660 on the -300, but a more usual figure in three-class configuration would be around 370–380 passengers. One freight airline, Seaboard World, experimented for a while with carrying passengers on the upper deck.

The 747-400 retained the fuselage of the -300, but with a two-crew EFIS flight-deck, improved aerodynamics, including a 4.9m increase in wingspan, distinctive winglets (except for short-haul 747-400Ds for internal routes within Japan), and upgraded engines. Greater use of composites has also reduced weight, so that Boeing claims fuel consumption to be up to 13 per cent less per seat-kilometre than on the -300, and as much as 17 per cent less than on the -200. Range varies and depends on payload, and can be extended with additional internal fuel tanks, but can be as much as 13,190km (8,240 miles). The 747-400 entered service with Northwest Airlines (qv) in 1989, and so far Boeing has delivered more than 400, with another 140 or so on order, in addition to deliveries of 724 of the earlier versions, now known as 'classic' 747s. Many of the older aircraft are being converted to freighter use, and some are receiving new EFIS flight-decks.

Plans for stretched 747-500/600 variants have been shelved because Boeing believes the market for these aircraft would be too small.

757: The narrow-bodied successor to the 727, the Boeing 757-200 first flew in 1982, and entered service with Eastern Airlines the following year. Most 757s have Rolls-Royce RB.211-535E4 engines of 178kN, but there is also the choice of 170kN Pratt & Whitney PW2040s. Up to 239 seats can be fitted at 74cm, six abreast, but the aircraft is more usually operated with around 180 passengers in two or three-class layout, and British Airways (qv) operates 195-seat single-class versions on its domestic trunk shuttle routes from London to Edinburgh, Glasgow, Belfast, and Manchester. Range is up to 6,150km (3,850 miles), and the aircraft has been popular with transatlantic charter operators. Almost 800 aircraft have been delivered, with another 100 or so on order.

A stretched version, the 757-300, is 7.1m longer and has been ordered by Condor (qv) for 1999 delivery.

767: First flown in 1981, the Boeing 767 entered service in 1982 with United Airlines (qv). Originally Boeing considered building this twin turbofan aircraft as a tri-jet. Unusually it has a 2:3:2 seating arrangement, although some operators, especially inclusive tour charters, have switched to eight-abreast seating. The initial model was the 767-200, but extended range (ER) variants of this and the stretched 767-300 are also available. Up to 285 passengers can be carried in the -200

The appearance of an airliner can be changed dramatically depending on the colour scheme. Contrast the ornate Air India paintwork with the much more conservative Swissair, or even JAL's 'Super Resort Express' with the same airline's standard scheme.

and up to 328 in the -300, but a more typical capacity would be 261 passengers in a -300, with a range of up to 7,678km (4,798 miles), and 210 passengers in a 767-300ER, with a range of up to 11,562km (7,226 miles). A choice of 264kN Rolls-Royce RB.211-524G, 251kN GE CF6 80C, or 268kN Pratt & Whitney PW4060 turbofans is available on the 300ER and 300F. The aircraft has been designed so that crews can be dual-rated for the 757 and 767. So far some 700 767s have been delivered, with another 80 or so on order.

A development with a further stretch, the 767-400, is expected to make its first flight in 1999.

777: Boeing's latest aircraft, the large twin turbofan 777 first flew in 1994 and entered service with United Airlines (qv) in 1995. Designed from the outset to compete with the Airbus A330/340 range, and to provide airlines with ETOPS (extended-range twin-engined operations), the 777-200 is the basic model, capable of taking up to 440 passengers ten abreast with a 76cm seat pitch, while the stretched 777-300 – which has the distinction of being the world's longest aircraft – is able to accommodate up to 550 passengers. A more typical two-class seating arrangement would see 375 passengers in the 777-200, allowing a range of up to 8,917km (5,600 miles), or a three-class arrangement for 368 passengers in the 777-300, with maximum range of up to 10,545km (6,590 miles). The aircraft has been designed to allow maximum flexibility, and airlines can specify different interior layouts, including different toilet and galley positions, as they wish.

A choice of engines from the three main manufacturers is offered, and on the 777-200 these would be 342kN Rolls-Royce Trent 877s, 423kN GE90 95Bs, or 342kN Pratt & Whitney PW4077s.

More than a hundred aircraft have been delivered so far, out of an order book for over 300.

717-200: Adopted by Boeing after the 1997 acquisition of McDonnell Douglas, the Boeing 717-200 is the former MD-95, an airliner in the 100–120 seat category, and gives Boeing stronger presence at the lower end of the regional airliner market for aircraft smaller than the Boeing 737 series. Its first flight was in mid-1998. It uses two tail-mounted 82.3kN BMW Rolls-Royce BR715 turbofans, giving a maximum range of more than 1,500 miles.

BOMBARDIER

One of the more successful regional air-craft manufacturers in the traditional air-craft manufacturing nations, Bombardier owns Canadair (qv), de Havilland (qv), and Short Brothers (qv), and their aircraft are shown under these names.

BRITISH AEROSPACE (BAe)

A partner in the Airbus (qv) consortium, British Aerospace is the leading British airframe manufacturer. Now privatised, it was formed on the nationalisation of Hawker Siddeley Aviation and the British Aircraft Corporation during the 1970s. Both the constituent companies were themselves the results of government-inspired aircraft industry mergers during the early-1960s, which saw many famous companies disappear. In terms of airliner manufacture. Hawker Siddeley absorbed de Havilland – manufacturers of the world's first jet airliner, the Comet – and Avro, while itself completing development of the Trident, the first airliner to make fully automatic landings. BAC absorbed Bristol, manufacturers of the Freighter and Britannia, and Vickers, at the time completing development of the VC10 airliner, but more famous for the Viscount, the world's first successful turboprop airliner. Out of the clutch of aircraft inherited during the mergers, the BAC One-Eleven jet airliner and the HS 748 turboprop regional and feeder airliner were the most successful. However, BAC's principal claim to fame was the Concorde supersonic air transport developed jointly with Aérospatiale of France. BAe itself later acquired the production rights for the Handley Page Jetstream feeder airliner when that company went into liquidation.

The Aircraft

One-Eleven: Sometimes incorrectly referred to as the 1-11, the BAC (later BAe) One-Eleven originated from a Hunting Percival design, which BAC enlarged during development. It was the first jet airliner specifically designed for short routes, and the first British jet airliner to be ordered by American airlines, who at one time had more examples in service than their European counterparts. The first flight was in 1963, and deliveries to airlines of the first production version, the One-Eleven 200, started early in 1965. This was followed by slightly larger series 300 and 400 aircraft, and then the more extensively stretched 500, which, though originally designed to meet a BEA (British European Airways) requirement, was adopted by many other airlines as well. There was also the short-field series 475.

Two 11,400lb thrust Rolls-Royce Spey Mk.511 rear-mounted turbofans gave the 400 a cruising speed of 480 knots and a range of up to 1,970km (1,240 miles), although corporate versions had transatlantic capability. The original 200 could seat 69 passengers, but the 400 usually had around 80 seats. The series 500 had 99 seats in scheduled airliner form, and 119 in high density charter configuration. Before production in the UK ended, 232 aircraft were delivered, of which about

British Aerospace's 146 series was supposed to be a successor to the One-Eleven, but markets change and in many ways it has been the successor to turboprop aircraft. This is a stretched 146-300, now replaced on the production line by the RJ100.

half remain in service. A strong aircraft, there were plans to re-engine with the Rolls-Royce Tay turbofan, but the recession of the early-1990s stopped this. Production was continued by Rombac in Romania for some years.

146: Taken with the RJ development, this has been the most successful British jet airliner ever. The 146 started as a design concept by Hawker Siddeley, before the creation of British Aerospace, to produce a quiet jet airliner with good take-off and landing performance. More than 200 were built before the even more capable Avro (qv) RJ (for Regional Jet) series was introduced, and then marketing passed to Aero International (Regional) (qv), under which heading more details are provided.

748: Sometimes referred to as the Avro 748 or Hawker Siddeley HS 748, this twin turboprop first flew in 1960 and deliveries started in 1962. Two 2,105shp Rolls-Royce Dart engines gave a maximum speed of 240 knots and a range of 1,115km (700 miles). Up to 56 passengers or five tonnes of freight could be carried, although most airlines operated the aircraft with 46 seats. A stretched development, the Andover, with rear clamshell doors and a kneeling undercarriage, was built for the RAF, and the unsuccessful ATP used this fuselage stretch. Almost 280 aircraft remain in service of the 380 built, including those constructed under licence by Hindustan Aircraft in India.

ATP: Originally projected as a development of the 748, the Advanced Turboprop used the stretched fuselage of the Andover, and possibly lost many customers due to the absence of a smaller version in the 40–50 passenger range. Claimed to be the first turboprop to be able to use 'jet ports' at airports, its relatively long undercarriage earned this aircraft the nickname of 'Lada' amongst enthusiasts since it had the appearance of some Russian designs! Twin 1,975kW Pratt & Whitney Canada PW126A turboprops gave a maximum cruising speed of 265 knots, and a range of up to 1,115km (700 miles), while 72 passengers could be carried, although most airlines opted for 64–68-seats. A development was the Jetstream 61, with uprated 2,050kW engines, but production ended before this aircraft entered service. Just 55 ATPs were built.

Jetstream 41: Developed from the highly successful 19-seat Jetstream 31, itself an updated Handley Page Jetstream, the 29-seat Jetstream 41 had a modified wing position sitting underneath the fuselage and a larger tail-plane. Three-abreast seat-

ing was usually fitted, although the option of two abreast was available. Twin 1,240kW Garrett TPE331-14HR turboprops gave a maximum cruising speed of 295 knots and a range of up to 1,289km (805 miles). At one time it took some 60 per cent of all orders for aircraft in its class, but intense competition and the supply of second-hand aircraft as airlines traded up to larger types meant that losses were incurred on every one sold, and production ended in 1997.

CANADAIR

At one time a subsidiary of the American company General Dynamics, Canadair was mainly known for its work on military aircraft. Initially it generated few original civil designs of its own, but produced licence-built versions of the Douglas DC-4 (as the DC-4M with Rolls-Royce Merlin engines) and the Bristol Britannia (with Rolls-Royce Tyne turboprops and a fuselage stretch). One of its most notable products was the CL-215 amphibian, in widespread use as a water-bomber for fighting forest fires, and its 415 turboprop development.

Under Bombardier ownership Canadair has developed the Canadair Regional Jet, or CRJ, bringing jet standards of comfort and speed on routes hitherto the preserve of turboprop aircraft, or making direct routes viable between destinations which would otherwise have had to rely on passengers changing aircraft at hubs.

The Aircraft

CRJ: First flown in 1991, the Canadair Regional Jet started airline operations in 1992. The initial aircraft was the CRJ-100, but this has now been joined by longer-range versions, the CRJ-100ER and -100LR, and the -200 with uprated engines. Powered by two GE CF34-3A turbofans of 40kN each (CRJ-100) or CF34-3B of 41kN (CRJ-200), it has seats for 50 passengers four abreast with a seat pitch of 79cm. Range is around 1,800km (1,125 miles). More than 260 have been ordered, with almost 200 delivered.

A development is the stretched 70-seat CRJ-700, scheduled to enter airline service in 2000.

CASA

The Spanish manufacturer CASA, formed in 1923, has built a number of light transport aircraft, in addition to being a partner in Airbus (qv). Its most successful product so far has been the C-212.

The Aircraft

C-212: The original C-212-100 first flew in 1971 as a light utility transport and competed with the Shorts (qv) Skyvan and de Havilland (qv) Twin Otter, with 18 seats in three-abreast layout, and with a retractable undercarriage. The current production model, the C-212-300, seats between 23 and 26 passengers, and is also produced by IPTN in Indonesia as the 212-200. Two 670kW Allied Signal TPE331 10R turboprops provide a maximum cruising speed of 190 knots and a range of up to 660km (412 miles). Some 430 aircraft have been produced.

DE HAVILLAND

Originally a subsidiary of the British manufacturer of the same name, this company was founded in 1947 out of a wartime aircraft assembly plant as de Havilland Canada. Its initial product was a small basic trainer, the Chipmunk. While this was a great success, the company soon established a strong reputation as a manufacturer of short take-off and landing (STOL) aircraft, including the Beaver, Otter, and Twin Otter, as well as the larger Caribou and Buffalo military transports. The most successful of these designs, the 18-seat Twin Otter, sold more than 800 aircraft. The company moved into the airliner market during the mid-1970s with the four-engined 50-seat de Havilland Dash 7, following this with its most successful design so far, the twin-engined Dash 8.

There have been a number of changes of ownership over the years, and the company was at one time owned by Boeing, and known as Boeing de Havilland. It is now part of the Bombardier (qv) group.

The Aircraft

Dash 7: First flown in 1977, this four-engined, high-wing 50-seat four-abreast aircraft was designed to provide good STOL performance, yet operate quietly and provide passengers with greater comfort than earlier STOL aircraft. It was ideal for services from London City Airport, and from other difficult airports such as Plymouth in the south-west of England. Four 835kW Pratt & Whitney Canada PT6A 50 turboprops provided a maximum cruising speed of 230 knots and a range of up to 1,985km (1,245 miles). Perhaps surprisingly, just 113 were sold.

Dash 8: A family of aircraft, the original Dash 8-100 first flew in 1983 and entered airline service the following year. The original -100 was soon joined by the higher gross weight -200, with both air-

The de Havilland Dash 7 brought a significant improvement in comfort in aircraft with a good short field performance. Arkia is amongst the largest operators of the type.

craft able to take 36 or 39 passengers four abreast depending on seat pitch. A twin-engined high-wing aircraft, the Dash 8-200 used two 1,605kW Pratt & Whitney Canada PW121 turboprops for a maximum cruising speed of 295 knots and a range of up to 987km (615 miles). Later developments have been the 8-300, stretched fore and aft of the wing to accommodate 50–60 passengers, and the -400, which will enter service in early 1999 and be able to accommodate up to 70 passengers. Some of the more recent aircraft have a 'Q' suffix to indicate that they have been fitted with a cabin noise suppression system. Almost 500 aircraft have been delivered with about another 50 on order.

EMBRAER

Originally founded in 1969 as a joint state and private enterprise venture, Embraer enjoyed considerable success with its first commercial design, the 19-seat EMB-110 Bandeirante turboprop, of which 500 were delivered to airlines throughout the world. Embraer was able to build upon this success with its next aircraft, the pressurised EMB-120 Brasilia, and now hopes to follow this with the EMB-145 regional jet. Although there has been mention of a wider fuselage aircraft, provisionally known as the EMB-170, the development costs have caused some reluctance to proceed. A shorter variant of the EMB-145 with around 37 seats is more likely, which could be in service in 1999 or 2000.

The Aircraft

EMB-120: The first EMB-120 Brasilias were delivered in 1985 to Atlantic Southeast Airlines (qv). A 30-seat aircraft with passengers seated three abreast, two 1,340kW Pratt & Whitney Canada PW118 turboprops gave a maximum cruising speed of 300 knots and a range of up to 926km (578 miles), although this was increased when the -120ER was introduced in 1992, and the current production version is the -120ER Advanced with a range of 1,482km (926 miles). Cargo and Combi versions of the aircraft are also available. Almost 350 have been delivered, although orders are slowing down as airlines consider trading up to regional jets.

EMB-145: This regional jet entered airline service in 1997, with the order book boosted by the endorsement of Continental Express (qv) and AMR Eagle (qv), two of the major regional carriers. It is based on a stretch of the EMB-120 fuselage, albeit with a new tail and wing. It has 50 seats, and is powered by two tail-mounted 33kN Allison AE3007A turbofans, which provide a maximum cruising speed of 425 knots and a range of up to 2,500km (1,562 miles). More than 130 have been ordered, although Continental Express and AMR Eagle have orders and options for almost 300 aircraft, suggesting considerable potential for the future. About 60 are in service.

FAIRCHILD DORNIER

Dornier moved into commercial aircraft production for the first time post-war in 1981 with the small Dornier 228 light transport, the series 100 having 15 seats and the -200 having 19. More recently the company has moved into the market for aircraft with 30 seats or more with the 328, and is developing a jet version of this aircraft. In 1996 Dornier was acquired by Fairchild Aircraft, the US-based manufacturer.

The Aircraft

328: First flown in 1991, the 33-seat 328-100 high speed turboprop entered airline service in 1993. A 48-seat stretch had been planned by Dornier before being acquired by Fairchild, and the latter is now developing a jet version, the 328JET, for airline service in 1999, which may be stretched into a 50-seat aircraft. Two 1,625kW Pratt & Whitney Canada PW119B turboprops give the 328 a maximum cruising speed of 335 knots. Seating is three abreast. Almost a hundred aircraft have been delivered.

FOKKER

One of the most famous names in commercial aircraft manufacture, Fokker was declared bankrupt in March, 1996 and finally ceased production during 1997.

It had originally established its reputation with the single-engined F.VII in the mid-1920s. This was developed into the even more successful trimotor version, the F.VII/3M, which was followed by a number of other airliners before the outbreak of World War Two bought production to a halt. Post-war, the company manufactured military aircraft until returning to civil aviation during the late-1950s with the Fokker F-27 Friendship twin-turboprop, which was an immediate success and was also built under licence in the United States by Fairchild as the FH-227. A jet airliner, the F-28 Fellowship, followed.

An attempt at a cross-border merger with VFW of Germany in 1971 proved unsuccessful, and Fokker soon regained its independence, although the two companies also became subcontractors for Airbus, perhaps their only success since the VFW-614 regional jet was unconventional and too far ahead of its time, restricting its market acceptability.

In recent years Fokker had up-dated its range, replacing the F-27 with the Fokker 50 turboprop, and the F-28 with the 100, a stretched version, and also with the smaller 70. Nevertheless, confronted with intense competition and high costs the company was unable to survive. It may also be that the product range, despite updating, was beginning to appear less excit-

Fokker will long be remembered for its short-haul airliners, of which this Malév Fokker 70 is a fine example.

ing compared with completely new designs. When the company and its product line were offered for sale no purchaser could be found, despite initial interest from the Far East.

The Aircraft

F-27: First flown in 1955, the twin Rolls-Royce Dart-powered F-27 Friendship was intended to slip into a niche in the market beneath the Vickers Viscount, and proved successful at this, remaining in production until 1985. A large number of F-27s remain in service, with about 290 of the 787 aircraft built still in commercial service, many of them converted for freight use. Typical performance from the two 2,255shp Darts would be a maximum cruising speed of 260 knots and a range of up to 1,920km (1,200 miles). Up to 52 passengers could be carried.

F-28: Initially planned as an F-27 replacement, the F-28 Fellowship was produced alongside the smaller aircraft but did not enjoy the same degree of success. First flown in 1967, deliveries started in 1968, and almost immediately plans to build the aircraft under licence in the United States had to be abandoned because of the lack of an adequate market. Two Rolls-Royce Spey 555-15 turbofans provided a maximum cruising speed of 449 knots and a

range of up to 2,000km (1,250 miles), while up to 85 passengers could be carried in the F-28-4000 variant, seated five abreast. Many of the 172 aircraft surviving out of the 241 delivered may be eligible for conversion using Rolls-Royce Tay turbofans.

50: Successor to the F-27, the Fokker 50 first flew in 1985, and the first deliveries began in 1987. Amongst the changes to the earlier aircraft were an EFIS flight-deck, new nose-wheel unit, and six-bladed Dowty propellers, as well as new 1,865kW Pratt & Whitney Canada PW1258 turboprops. Up to 58 passengers could be carried at 76cm pitch. High-performance and utility versions were also offered. At the time production ceased, 212 aircraft had been delivered.

70/100: A stretched and re-engined development of the F-28, the Fokker 100 also incorporated many technological advances when it made its first flight in 1986. It entered service with Swissair (qv) in 1988. Seating up to 109 passengers at 81cm pitch, it is powered by two 67kN Rolls-Royce Tay 650 turbofans, giving a maximum cruising speed of 462 knots and a range of up to 2,870km (1,800 miles). The Fokker 70 is a shortened version, 4.6 metres shorter, with up to 79 seats, and was first flown by Sempati (qv) of

Indonesia in 1995. At the time production ceased, 180 100s and 46 70s had been delivered. The ending of production has placed some airlines in a difficult position with planned fleet expansion or replacement disrupted.

ILYUSHIN

Russia's Ilyushin Design Bureau came into prominence as a source of commercial aircraft after World War Two. The bureau's founder, Sergei Ilyushin, had originally entered aviation as a mechanic's helper in the Imperial Russian Air Service during World War One. During World War Two the bureau designed some effective combat aircraft.

Its first commercial project was the Il-12 transport, code-named 'Coach' by NATO, which first flew in 1944. Intended as a replacement for the Douglas C-47 and its licence-built Soviet counterpart, the Lisunov Li-2, it did not impress. An improved version was the Il-14, known to NATO as 'Crate'. A more modern aircraft was the Ilyushin Il-18, with four turboprop engines.

In more recent years Ilyushin has supplied Russian and other CIS airlines with a variety of aircraft, including the Il-62, a long-range jet airliner bearing a marked resemblance to the Vickers VC10; the Il-76 freighter; and Russia's first wide-bodied aircraft, the Il-86, with its Il-96 and Il-98 variants which could, if funds were made available, become a family of aircraft similar to that offered by Airbus (qv).

The Aircraft

Il-18: A large four-engined turboprop similar in concept to the Lockheed Electra, the Il-18 uses four 4,250shp Ivchenko AI-20M turboprops for a maximum cruising speed of 344 knots and a range of around 3,680km (2,300 miles) with a full payload of up to 122 passengers. Almost 500 remain in service.

Il-62: First introduced in 1963, the Il-62 with four tail-mounted engines bears an uncanny resemblance to the Vickers VC10, even to the extent of being the same size as the Super VC10 before this was reduced to meet a BOAC requirement. The original aircraft was superseded by the Il-62M, whose four 108kN Aviadvigatel/Perm D30KU turbofans provide a maximum cruising speed of 486 knots and a range of 7,800km (4,875 miles). Up to 212 passengers can be carried, although 174 at a generous 86cm pitch tends to be more usual.

Il-76: Originally specified as a high-wing heavy transport for the Soviet armed forces, the Il-76 was also prepared to meet an Aeroflot (qv) requirement, and a number are in service with other operators throughout the former Soviet Bloc. Built in Uzbekistan and first flown in 1971, it entered airline service in 1974. Four Soloviev D-30KP engines powered early versions, but the current production model is the Il-76MF, with a 6.6 metre stretch, which is claimed to carry an extra 1.5 tonne payload for a 12 per cent cut in fuel consumption. The four 157kN Aviadvigatel/Perm PS90AN turbofans provide a 459 knot maximum cruising speed and a range of up to 5,200km (3,250 miles), while the maximum payload is around 52,000kg. CFM International has been considering a programme to re-engine the Il-76, of which almost a thousand have been built, mainly for the military.

Il-86/96/98: Russia's first wide-bodied airliner, the four-engined Il-86 first flew in 1976 and entered service with Aeroflot in 1980, although only 104 had been delivered by the time production ceased in 1994. The four 127kN Kuznetsov NK 86 turbofans give the aircraft a maximum cruising speed of 486 knots and a range of 3,600km (2,250 miles), with up to 350 passengers being carried, seated nine abreast.

The first major development of the Il-86 was the Il-96-300, with a shortened fuselage, new wing, EFIS flight deck, and four 157kN Aviadvigatel/Perm PS90A turbofans. Maximum cruising speed for the Il-96 is 480 knots, but the range has been increased to 7,170km (4,480 miles), and passenger capacity reduced to 300 at 87cm pitch. The Il-98 is a project for a twin-engined variant of the Il-96, using western turbofans in the Rolls-Royce Trent power range.

LOCKHEED

Today, Lockheed's involvement in commercial aircraft production is limited to the commercial versions of its highly successful Hercules military transport, but for many years Lockheed was one of the leading airliner manufacturers. Its first foray into commercial aircraft was the Vega of 1927, a single-engined high-wing monoplane which could carry mail or up to six passengers, and a development of this aircraft, the Air Express, established a number of trans-USA speed records. The company's first twin-engined airliner was the Electra of 1930, and throughout the decade a succession of sleek airliners followed, including the Lockheeds 10, 12, and 14, and the Lodestar.

While Lockheed produced military aircraft during World War Two, including the P-38 Lightning long-range fighter, the Constellation transport was also produced and developed into a post-war airliner for longer-range operations. A development, the Super Constellation, followed, and played a part in the development of intercontinental air services. In common with most American manufacturers, who either ignored the first generation of turboprop airliners or were late into the field, Lockheed did not produce a turboprop until 1956, when the first flight of the L-188 Electra II took place, which entered service in 1959. This aircraft was less successful than the company deserved, with just 165 being built for airlines such as KLM (qv) and Tasman Empire Airways, the predecessor of Air New Zealand (qv). Nevertheless, almost 60 are still in service today as freighters. The loss of the civil market was probably academic by this time, since the company had a major success with the C-130 Hercules military transport, and the maritime-reconnaissance development of the Electra, the Orion, is the best selling western aircraft of its type.

Lockheed did not get involved with the first generation of jet airliners, but moved straight to the second generation with the L-1011 TriStar, its last purpose-designed commercial aircraft.

The Aircraft

L-100 Hercules: First flown in 1954, with deliveries starting in 1956, the Lockheed C-130 Hercules is the best-selling peacetime military transport to-date. The high-wing and rear ramp make it ideal for commercial operations in areas with poor infrastructure and without sophisticated cargo handling equipment. In certain circumstances up to 97 passengers can be carried, but the aircraft is primarily a freighter. Four Allison 501.D22A turboprops provide a maximum cruising speed of 315 knots and a maximum range of 3,182km (1,988 miles), while around 15,000kg of cargo can be carried. There have been 115 Hercules delivered to commercial airlines.

A commercial version of the new generation C-130J Hercules, the L-100J, is also available, offering a 61 per cent payload-range improvement, 15 per cent increase in cruising speed, and 21 per cent decrease in fuel costs.

L-1011 TriStar: First flown in 1970, the TriStar entered airline service in 1972. Development had been plagued by the collapse of Rolls-Royce, the sole engine supplier, which encountered heavy costs and teething problems with new technology on what eventually became the successful RB.211 series of engines. The aircraft was available with two fuselage lengths, with the longer fuselages on the TriStar 1, 100 and 200, and the shorter on the long-range 500. In some ways the aircraft helped cement the merger of BEA and BOAC into British Airways (qv), since the TriStar family was needed on the routes of both airlines, with the TriStar 500 being especially important to the hot and high airports on BA's African network. It also had better economics on long and thin routes than the larger 747. Four 222.5kN Rolls-Royce RB.211-254B.02 turbofans provided the -200 with a maximum cruising speed of 512 knots and a range of 7,890km (4,931 miles), although on the TriStar 500 this increased to 8,480km (5,300 miles). The longer fuselage aircraft could seat up to 400 passengers at 76 cm pitch and ten abreast, and the 500 333 passengers in a similar configuration, but in practice seating accommodation would be nearer 280 for the 200, and 224 on the 500.

Production ceased in 1983, by which time 249 aircraft had been sold, of which 185 remain in service.

MCDONNELL DOUGLAS

After 65 years of intense competition for the commercial airliner market between Boeing (qv) and McDonnell Douglas (or its predecessor Douglas), the two companies merged in 1997. Strictly speaking the products are now Boeing McDonnell Douglas, but since the current product range is entirely McDonnell Douglas derived a separate entry still seems appropriate.

Although both Boeing and Douglas dated from the period immediately after World War One, it was not until 1932 and the first flight of the Douglas DC-1 that Douglas established a strong presence in the commercial airliner market. The DC-1 marked the commencement of the 'Douglas Commercial' series which lasted up to the DC-10. The DC-2 which followed saw service with airlines in many parts of the world, but paled into insignificance compared to the tremendous success of the ensuing DC-3, known to the military as the C-47 or Dakota, in which form more than 10,000 were built during World War Two. The DC-3 was also joined in the war effort by the DC-4 and it military variant, the C-54, and these two aircraft types helped to found or rebuild many post-war airlines. The one exception to this success story was the DC-5, a high-winged twin-engined aircraft of which few were built.

The company's first pressurised aircraft was the DC-6 Cloudmaster, and the DC-6B development was amongst the first commercial aircraft to be radar equipped, and amongst other achievements helped to pioneer trans-polar flights. Non-stop transatlantic flight became possible with the DC-7C, the last Douglas piston-engined airliner, and the fastest piston-engined airliner ever.

Douglas was amongst the manufacturers involved in producing the first generation of long-range jets, with the DC-8, which first flew in 1959. This aircraft never enjoyed the same success as the Boeing 707, but had its adherents in airlines such as KLM(qv) and SAS (qv), and was available in a number of different fuselage stretches which eventually proved especially popular with cargo operators. The successful DC-9 series of short-haul jets first flew in 1965.

The position of being second to, and persistently challenging, the largest manufacturer in a small field can be costly, and by the mid-1960s Douglas was suffering from cashflow problems which were worsened by the high cost of developing its first wide-bodied aircraft, the DC-10. Rescue came in 1967 when McDonnell took over the company, in what was almost a portent of events 30 years later. McDonnell had enjoyed a period of considerable prosperity during the Vietnam War, when its F-4 Phantom II had proved to be one of the world's classic combat aircraft, and, with abundant funds, it was attracted to Douglas, appreciating that the market for military aircraft could change once the conflict ended.

The DC-10 tri-jet entered service in 1972, although it was never as successful as the Boeing 747. In recent years the DC-9 has been developed into the MD-80/90 series, and the DC-10 into the MD-11. McDonnell Douglas has been to the fore in negotiating production of some of its aircraft in China, but this has been beset with difficulties.

The Aircraft

DC-8: First flown in 1958, the Douglas DC-8 entered service in 1959, and almost from the start there were a number of variations. The DC-8-10 and DC-8-20 were intended for domestic service within the United States, while the DC-8-30 and Rolls-Royce-powered DC-8-40 were intended for transatlantic operations, as was the more powerful DC-8-50. The installed power on these aircraft varied

McDonnell Douglas entered the wide-body market with the DC-10, many of which remain in service with cargo operators or inclusive tour charter airlines.

considerably, with the -10 using four 13,500lb thrust Pratt & Whitney JT3C-6s; the -20 and -30 using 15,800lb thrust JT4A-3s; the -40 17,500lb thrust Rolls-Royce Conway 509s; and the -50, 18,000lb thrust JT3D-3s. The -50 was available as a convertible passenger-freight aircraft, the 'Jet Trader'. Up to 190 passengers could be carried on these aircraft.

The first of the stretched series, the DC-8-60, sometimes known as the 'Super Sixty', flew in 1966, and all of these aircraft used a variation of the engines used on the -50. The -61 had an 11 metre (36 foot) fuselage extension, so that up to 250 passengers could be carried, while the -62 had a smaller fuselage stretch but extended wing-tips and extended range. The -63

had the fuselage of the -61 with the range and wings of the -62, and a range of up to 12,800km (8,000 miles). The longevity of the aircraft has been such that a large number have been re-engined with 98kN CFM56 2-C5 turbofans, at one and the same time reducing noise levels, maintenance costs, and fuel consumption, while increasing payload, albeit at a slight drop in maximum cruising speed from 515 knots to 480 knots. Out of 556 aircraft built 263 remain in service, of which 110 have been re-engined.

DC-9: The DC-9 first flew in early 1965 and entered airline service at the end of the year. Five different models were produced, the DC-9-10, -20, -30, -40, and -50,

Successor to the DC-10 was the MD-11, which Japan Airlines has decided to call the 'J Bird'.

McDonnell Douglas had more success with its DC-9 and MD-80/90 series, of which these are examples from the Finnair and Aeroméxico fleets, but, faced with intense competition from Boeing and the narrow-bodied Airbuses, it seems unlikely that much money was made.

with four different fuselage lengths. The -10 and -20 used the same fuselage, while the -30 had a stretch and high-lift devices on the wings, and the -40 and -50 both showed further stretches. The -30 uses two 62kN Pratt & Whitney JT8D turbofans, giving room for up to 115 passengers seated five abreast, and a maximum cruising speed of 500 knots with a range of up to 2,630km (1,643 miles). Out of 976 aircraft built more than 700 remain in service, with more than 460 of these being the DC-9-30 series. Most of the surviving aircraft have been hush-kitted, but plans to re-engine them have been abandoned.

DC-10: McDonnell Douglas's offering in the first generation wide-bodied aircraft category, the three-engined DC-10-10 for short and medium-range routes first flew in 1970, and entered service with American Airlines (qv) the following year. The longer-range versions, the DC-10-30 and -40, first flew in 1971, and were introduced to service in 1972 by Swissair (qv) and Northwest Airlines (qv) respectively. Up to 380 passengers could be carried, ten abreast at 81cm pitch, but a more usual three-class arrangement – as used, for example, by British Airways (qv) – would be 229 passengers. Powerplants varied, with the -10 using three 178kN GE CF6 6D turbofans; the -30 an up-rated 233kN variant of the CF6; and the -40 a Pratt & Whitney JT9D. A 'hot and high' variant of the DC-10-10, the 10-15, was developed for Aeroméxico (qv) and Mexicana (qv) and entered service in 1981.

During the DC-10's early days in production consideration was given to building twin and four-engined variants, extending the market, but these ideas were abandoned.

While not as successful as the Boeing 747, the DC-10 – which, in common with the Lockheed TriStar, was sometimes referred to at first as an 'airbus' – outsold the TriStar. Of 446 built, including 60 for the USAF, 339 remain in service, many of them converted to freighter use. The largest commercial operator today is Federal Express (qv), which has 36, with flight decks modernised and converted from three to two-crew operation. Strengthened main decks mean that many of the freighters have had their cargo capacity increased.

MD-80: Originally conceived as the Douglas DC-9-80, the MD-80 series actually entered service with Swissair (qv) in 1980 as the DC-9-81, but has since been redesignated MD-81. The MD-81 could accommodate up to 155 passengers in one-class high density seating, although 135 seats in two classes was more common on European routes. Two 85.6kN Pratt & Whitney JT8D 209 turbofans provided a maximum cruising speed of 499 knots and a range of up to 2,879km (1,800 miles). The MD-82 had high-lift devices fitted, while the MD-83 offered extended range. The MD-87 had a shortened fuselage, cutting maximum capacity to 130 seats, or 114 seats in two classes. The MD-88 reverted to the original fuselage length, but with an updated flight deck, and first saw service with Delta Air Lines (qv) in 1988.

The MD-82 and MD-83 were also assembled at Shanghai, with 35 aircraft of both types completed from kits supplied by McDonnell Douglas.

Almost 1,200 aircraft have been delivered so far, but since it competes with the Boeing 737 series production has been run down during 1998.

MD-90/95: The MD-90 first flew in 1993 and entered service with Delta Air Lines in 1995. It is a stretched MD-81, with two 125kN IAE V2528 D5 turbofans and up to 172 seats in 78cm high density configuration. Maximum cruising speed is around 499 knots, with maximum range of 3,860km (2,412 miles). Orders at present stand at 145 aircraft, of which about half

have been delivered. A variant, the MD-95, has been ordered by Valujet (qv), but following this airline's merger with Air Trans (qv), the future of the order is uncertain. Nevertheless, while MD-90 production has also been run down during 1998, the MD-95 survives as the Boeing 717-200.

MD-11: The stretched and re-engined development of the DC-10 series, the MD-11 also incorporates distinctive winglets which immediately distinguish it from the earlier aircraft. First flown in early-1990, by the end of the year Finnair (qv) had launched the type into scheduled service. MD-11 sales have been far slower than for the DC-10, especially in recent years, although the aircraft has been popular with air freight operators, albeit in competition with conversions of older aircraft. A choice of engines is available, and on the MD-11 this includes 267kN Pratt & Whitney PW4460 or 251kN GE CF6 80C2 turbofans, giving a maximum cruising speed of 480 knots and a range of up to 11,100km (6,937 miles), although extended range versions are available. Up to 410 passengers can be carried ten abreast at 81cm pitch, but 295 seats are more usual. So far 183 aircraft have been ordered, and most of these have been delivered.

In common with the MD-95, the MD-11 is remaining in production, although marketing will emphasise the freight version of this aircraft and as yet a Boeing type designation has not been adopted.

SAAB

Dating from 1937, Saab (the name originally stood for Svenska Aeroplane AB) soon established a reputation as a builder of military training and attack aircraft, and only within the last 20 years has the company been associated with commercial aircraft. Despite the success of the Saab 340, intense competition within the market, limited potential for the new Saab 2000, competition from new regional jets, and high Swedish labour costs, have combined to make Saab decide to abandon commercial aircraft manufacture in 1997.

The Aircraft

340: The Saab 340A first flew in 1983 and entered airline service the following year as a fast turboprop, providing improved comfort on feeder and regional services. Designed to carry 33 passengers, it could carry as many as 37 three abreast at 76cm pitch. In 1989 an improved version with uprated engines, the 340B, entered service, and a further improvement came in 1994 in the form of the 340B Plus, with two 1,395kW GE CT7 9B turboprops giving a maximum cruising speed of 285 knots and a range of up to 1,210km (755 miles). Before production ceased 436 aircraft were built.

2000: Essentially a stretch of the 340 series, the Saab 2000 first flew in 1992, and entered service with Crossair (qv) in

Saab's move into commercial aircraft production was a bold attempt to provide a balance to its military projects, and at first was very successful, as with this Saab 340B. Sadly, Saab's concept was high speed turboprops, leaving it vulnerable as regional jets became smaller.

1995. It is meant to be a high speed turboprop capable of competing with the new regional jets, but there have been problems in meeting cabin noise guarantees. Two 3.095kW Allison AE2100A turboprops provide a maximum cruising speed of 370 knots and a range of up to 2,075km (1,300 miles), while the aircraft can seat 50 passengers three abreast at a pitch of 81cm. A head-up guidance system has been approved, enabling landings to be made in poor visibility – a significant advance for aircraft of this size and type. Just 58 aircraft were delivered before production ended.

SHORT

Sometimes referred to as 'Shorts', Short Brothers is now a part of Bombardier (qv), before which it was largely owned by the British Government. It works as a subcontractor on several of the parent company's other projects. Until recently it also built the wings for the Fokker (qv) F-28 and then for its successors, the Fokker 70 and 100. The company also has a successful surface-to-air guided missile business, and produces structures and assemblies, including engine nacelles, for a number of customers.

Short Brothers were amongst the first British aircraft manufacturers, having acquired a licence from the Wright brothers. It established a reputation in commercial aircraft with its flying-boats during the 1930s, especially the Short Empire flying-boats produced for Imperial Airways and Qantas (qv). Post-war there were relatively few Short aircraft, although the guided missile business proved extremely successful. However, it did conduct research into military VTOL, as well as building Bristol Britannia airliners for the RAF and developing and building a Britannia-derivative, the Short Belfast transport.

The company re-established its reputation in aircraft design and production with the Short Skyvan, which first flew in 1963 and was meant as a very basic turboprop utility aircraft, capable of seating up to 18 passengers. This enjoyed some success and encouraged the company to build an enlarged version for 30 passengers, known initially as the SH-3D, which entered production as the Short, or Shorts, 330, and first flew in 1974. A development of the 330 is the 36–39 passenger 360. Production of both aircraft has now ceased, but ex-airline 360s are being bought by the company and converted to Short Sherpa standard for the United States Army.

The Aircraft

330: First flown in 1974, the Short 330 is powered by two 820kW Pratt & Whitney Canada PT6A-45s and could seat 30 passengers, three abreast, in the unpressurised fuselage. During production 139 aircraft were delivered, of which 42 remain in service.

360: Introduced in 1982 as a stretched development of the 330, with a single tailplane in place of the twin-fin of its predecessor, the Short 360 could seat 36–39 passengers. Although still unpressurised, it had improved passenger comfort, including lower cabin noise levels. Two 1,060kW Pratt & Whitney Canada PT6A-67R turboprops powered the final production version, the 360-300. Production ended in 1991, by which time 165 had been delivered, of which 118 remain in airline service. A number of aircraft have been bought by Shorts for conversion to Sherpa standard for the United States Army.

TUPOLEV

Probably the main Soviet manufacturer of commercial airliners, the Tupolev Design Bureau bears the name of its founder, Andre Tupolev, who persuaded Lenin to establish a research institute shortly after the Russian Revolution. Tupolev himself had a chequered career, with many of his designs produced whilst imprisoned by Stalin. During its early years most of the bureau's output consisted of bomber aircraft, but it came into prominence in 1955 with the first flight of Russia's first jet transport, the Tupolev Tu-104, known to NATO as the 'Camel'. The Tu-114 turboprop followed, based on the Tu-20 bomber, and then the Tu-124 derivative of the Tu-104.

In recent years the mainstay of Tupolev output has been Tu-134 and Tu-154 airliners, approximating to the Douglas DC-9 and Boeing 727 respectively in general appearance. The Tu-144 was Russia's attempt to rival the Anglo-French Concorde supersonic airliner, and seems to have been based on the Concorde design, albeit with certain changes. The aircraft was a failure, having problems with cabin noise, resulting from the engines being located under the cabin floor, and range, in consequence of using turbofans instead of turbojets, which required reheat throughout the flight rather than simply for acceleration to supersonic speed. A serious accident finally grounded it, although it now appears that at least one example will be restored to operational standard for US-Russian research into supersonic commercial flight.

The Tupolev Tu-204, a rival to the Boeing 757, holds the most promise for the future, especially in Tu-204-120 form with Rolls-Royce RB.211 engines. The replacement market for Tu-154s which this aircraft could satisfy is huge, but it is doubtful whether many airlines will have the funds for it in the short-term, though a major Egyptian-backed leasing company has placed a substantial order.

For the future, Tupolev has plans for a Tu-334 and Tu-354 as a Tu-134 replacement, before which a new freight aircraft, the Tu-330, should be in production. The

Until more Tu-204s appear the most common Tupolev will remain the Tu-154, but airlines which can afford to do so are retiring these aircraft on to second line duties, as with this Tu-154M, which Malév has relegated to charter work.

Tu-334 may be built in Iran, using local funding. If funding permits, a new long-range wide-bodied twinjet will be launched, designated Tu-304, as rival to the Boeing 777 and Airbus A330.

The Aircraft

Tu-134: Russia's answer to the DC-9 and One-Eleven, the Tu-134 used much of the aerodynamic surfaces and fuselage of the Tu-104, albeit with a 'T' tail-plane and the engines moved to the tail. First flown in 1964, two 15,000lb thrust Soloviev D-30 turbofans provided a maximum cruising speed of 497 knots and a range of up to 2,400km (1,500 miles), while around 80 passengers could be carried. More than 400 remain in service.

Tu-154: First flown in 1968, the Tu-154 is of similar appearance to the Boeing 727-200 and Hawker Siddeley Trident 3. Early versions – the Tu-154, 154A, and 154B – used Kuznetsov NK-8 engines, but the Tu-154M, introduced to Aeroflot (qv) service in 1984, uses three Perm Aviadvigatel D-30KU 154-11 turbofans for increased performance and a higher take-off weight. In high density configuration up to 180 passengers can be carried, six abreast, at 76cm pitch. The aircraft has a maximum cruising speed of 514 knots and a range of up to 3,740km (2,337 miles). More than 1,000 have been built, of which over 700 remain in service. Faced with the likelihood of the aircraft having to remain in service for some years, projects are in hand to reduce both noise and engine emissions.

Tu-204/214: This rival to the Boeing 757 was first flown in 1989 and entered service with Aeroflot (qv) in 1995. The original version, 204-100, is powered by two 157kN Aviadvigatel/Perm PS 90A turbofans, which provide a maximum cruising speed of 458 knots and a range of up to 2,500km (1,560 miles), while 240 passengers can be carried, six abreast, at 81cm pitch. In an attempt to enhance reliability and reduce fuel consumption a westernised version has been developed, the Tu-204-120, using 191kN Rolls-Royce RB.211 535E4B turbofans, which provide an extra 1,000km (625 miles) range. The -120 first flew in 1992, and is being offered to airlines by a new leasing organisation, Sirocco Aerospace, formed by Egyptian company Kato Aromatic.

A higher-weight version, the Tu-204-200, or Tu-214, flew in 1996, while a Rolls-Royce powered version of this would become the Tu-224. A short fuselage variant of the Tu-204 is the Tu-234, which accommodates 166 passengers. So far 20 aircraft have been delivered.

XI'AN

The main Chinese manufacturer of transport aircraft, Xi'an has one model in production at the moment, the Y-7 turboprop.

The Aircraft

Y-7: A Chinese development of the Antonov (qv) An-24 twin-turboprop, the Y-7 entered service with CAAC, then the only Chinese airline, in 1984. It has a slightly wider fuselage and larger wing than the An-24, and there are plans for stretched versions using Pratt & Whitney Canada turboprops, while the structure would also be modernised with help from HAECO of Hong Kong. The current model uses two 2,080kW Harbin Dongan WJ5A1 turboprops for a maximum cruising speed of 263 knots and a range of up to 1,220km (760 miles), while up to 56 passengers can be carried in four-abreast seating at 75cm pitch. About 75 aircraft have been delivered.

YAKOVLEV

The smallest of the Soviet airliner manufacturers, Yakovlev was the first to certify an airliner to western standards with its Yak-40 in 1971. Its larger Yak-42 is sometimes seen as a successor to the Tupolev Tu-134.

The Aircraft

Yak-40: First flown in 1966, and available in the west since 1971, the Yak-40 uses three tail-mounted Ivchenko AI-25 turbofans of 3,300lb thrust each to carry up to 27 passengers in a three-abreast configuration. It has a maximum cruising speed of 417 knots and a range of around 800km (500 miles). out of 1,200 built, almost 800 remain in service.

Yak-42: A 120-seat tri-jet, the Yak-42 first flew in 1975 and entered service with Aeroflot (qv) in 1980. Three 63.7kN Progress D-36 turbofans provide a maximum cruising speed of 400 knots and a maximum range of 1,480km (925 miles). Up to 120 passengers can be carried, seated six-abreast, at a high density pitch of 76cm. Around 150 aircraft are in service.

Index of Airlines

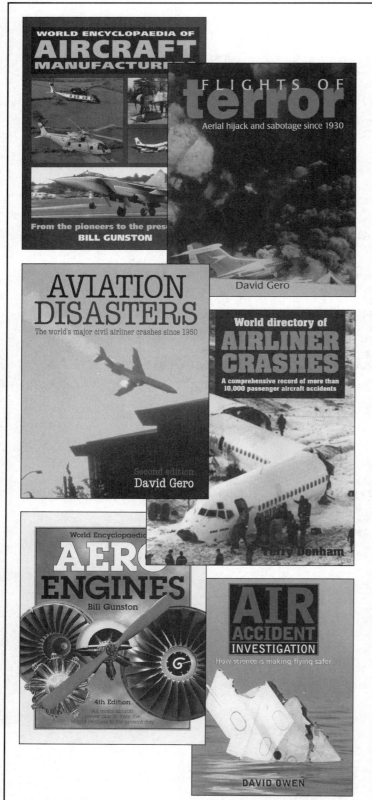